S0-AXV-619

LIWARCKTV

The Soviet Economy: Toward the Year 2000

HC
336.25
.S6834
1983

BCL3
B1P99

The Soviet Economy:
Toward the Year 2000

Edited by
ABRAM BERGSON

and

HERBERT S. LEVINE

London
GEORGE ALLEN & UNWIN
Boston   Sydney

GOSHEN COLLEGE LIBRARY
GOSHEN, INDIANA

© Abram Bergson and Herbert S. Levine, 1983

This book is copyright under the Berne Convention. No reproduction without permission. All rights reserved.

George Allen & Unwin (Publishers) Ltd,
40 Museum Street, London WC1A 1LU, UK

George Allen & Unwin (Publishers) Ltd,
Park Lane, Hemel Hempstead, Herts HP2 4TE, UK

Allen & Unwin, Inc.,
9 Winchester Terrace, Winchester, Mass. 01890, USA

George Allen & Unwin Australia Pty Ltd,
8 Napier Street, North Sydney, NSW 2060, Australia

First published in 1983
Reprinted 1984

British Library Cataloguing in Publication Data

Soviet economy.
1. Interindustry economics   2. Russia—
Economic conditions—1976–
I. Bergson, Abram   II. Levine, Herbert S.
339.2'3'0947   HC336.25
ISBN 0–04–335045–3

Library of Congress Cataloging in Publication Data
Main entry under title:
The Soviet economy.
1. Soviet Union—Economic conditions—1976–
—Addresses, essays, lectures. 2. Economic forecasting
—Soviet Union—Addresses, essays, lectures.
I. Bergson, Abram, 1914–   II. Levine, Herbert
Samuel, 1928–
HC336.25.S6834   1982   338.5'443'0947   82–15611
ISBN 0–04–335045–3

Set in 10 on 11 point Times by Computape (Pickering) Ltd, Pickering,
North Yorkshire and printed in Great Britain
by Mackays of Chatham

Contents

		page	ix
List of Tables		*page*	ix
List of Contributors			xiii
Preface			xv
1	An Overview *by Daniel L. Bond and Herbert S. Levine*		1
2	Technological Progress *by Abram Bergson*		34
3	Population and Labor Force *by Murray Feshbach*		79
4	Agricultural Organization and Management *by D. Gale Johnson*		112
5	Agricultural Production *by Douglas B. Diamond, Lee W. Bettis and Robert E. Ramsson*		143
6	Industrial Production by *Martin L. Weitzman*		178
7	Energy *by Robert W. Campbell*		191
8	Regional Economic Development *by Leslie Dienes*		218
9	Foreign Economic Relations *by Ed. A. Hewett*		269
10	Consumption *by Gertrude E. Schroeder*		311
11	Planning and Management *by Joseph S. Berliner*		350
12	Politics and Priorities *by Seweryn Bialer*		391
Appraisals			424
Index			447

Tables

Table 1.1   Baseline Projection, 1980–2000
Table 1.2   Soviet Supply and Utilization of Grain: Historic Data and Projected Values
Table 1.3   Alternative Scenarios, 1980–2000
Table 1.4   Average and Incremental Burden of Defense
Table 1.5   Key Soviet Foreign Trade Price Indices: Historic Data and Baseline Projection Assumptions
Table 1.6   Baseline Projection: Summary
Table 1.7   Baseline Projection: Industry
Table 1.8   Baseline Projection: Agriculture
Table 1.9   Baseline Projection: Energy and Fuel Balances
Table 2.1   Average Annual Rates of Increase of Output, Factor Inputs, and Factor Productivity, USSR, 1950–75
Table 2.2   Alternative Computations of Average Annual Percentage Rate of Growth, Factor Productivity, USSR 1950–70, for Alternative Elasticities of Substitution (σ) and Rates of Return on Capital (ρ)
Table 2.3   Average Annual Rate of Growth of Factor Productivity, USSR, Selected Periods
Table 2.4   Factor Productivity Growth
Table 2.5   Measured Factor–Productivity Growth and Technological Progress, USSR, 1950–75
Table 2.6   Average Income per Worker, 1970
Table 2.7   Farm and Nonfarm Employment, USSR, 1970–5
Table 2.8   Annual Growth Rates, Material Sector
Table 2.9   Comparative Indicators of Technological Change, USSR and Western Countries, 1960–73
Table 2.10   Comparative Timing of Introduction and Diffusion of New Technology, USSR and West
Table 2.11   Expenditures on R and D, Selected Countries
Table 2.12   Scientists and Engineers Employed in R and D, USSR and USA
Table 2.13   Factor-Share Weights, 1970
Table 3.1   Estimated and Projected Total Population, Percent Distribution, and Average Annual Rates of Growth, USSR and by Republic, 1970–2000
Table 3.2   Number of Population and Average Annual Rate of Growth, USSR, and by Republic: 1959, 1970, and 1979
Table 3.3   Age-Specific and Total Fertility Rates, USSR, RSFSR, Uzbekistan and Estonia: 1965/6, 1971/2 and 1975/6 to 1977/8
Table 3.4   Estimated and Projected Vital Rates, USSR and by Republic: 1950–2000

Table 3.5   Age Distribution of the Population of the USSR and of Selected Republics: 1950–2000

Table 3.6   Percent Male Among Total, Urban and Rural Population, USSR, and by Republic: January 1959, 1970 and 1979.

Table 3.7   Age-Specific Death Rates, by Sex, USSR: 1963/64 and 1973/74

Table 3.8   Estimates and Projections of the Population of Able-Bodied Ages (Males 16 to 59 Years, Females 16 to 54 Years), USSR and Selected Republics and Regions: 1970–2000

Table 3.9   Estimates and Projections of the Labor Force: 1959–2000

Table 3.10   Share of Urban Population, USSR and by Republic, 1913–79

Table 3.11   Changes in Number, Entrants to and Departures from Population of Able-Bodied Ages, USSR: 1970–2000

Table 3.12   Changes in Number, Entrants to and Departures from Population of Able-Bodied Ages, RSFSR: 1970–2000

Table 3.13   Changes in Number, Entrants to and Departures from Population of Able-Bodied Ages, Central Asia and Kazakhstan: 1970–2000

Table 5.1   USSR: Growth of Net Agricultural Output

Table 5.2   USSR: Value of Net Agricultural Output

Table 5.3   USSR: Output, Inputs and Factor Productivity in Agriculture, 1951–79

Table 5.4   USSR: Changes in Farm Product Supply for Domestic Use Attributable to Various Sources

Table 5.5   USSR: Projections of Growth in Net Agricultural, Livestock, and Meat Production Required to Meet Alternative Levels of Per Capita Consumption, 1978–2000

Table 5.6   USSR: Average Annual Rates of Growth of Output, 1961–70 and 1971–8

Table 5.7   USSR: Implied Change in the Gap between Meat Production and Demand, 1978–2000

Table 5.8   USSR: Feed Conversion Ratios, 1976–8

Table 5.9   USSR: Regional Shares of Fertilizer Applications to Grain, 1978, and Additions 1979–2000

Table 5.10   USSR: Projected Grain Production, Reference Case

Table 5.11   Reference Case: Projected Grain and Roughages Balance

Table 5.12   USSR: Projected Impacts on the Soviet Feed-Livestock Sector under Alternative Assumptions

Table 5.13   USSR: Current Feed Conversion Ratios for "Complexes" and "Traditional Farms"

Table 6.1   Soviet Industrial Output (OER)

Table 6.2   Industrial Output (Official Soviet GVO)

Table 6.3   Industrial Workers and Personnel

Table 6.4   Industrial Manhours
Table 6.5   Midyear Industrial Capital Stock
Table 6.6   Growth of Labor and Capital Productivity
Table 6.7   Growth Rate of the Residual with Labor–Capital Shares of 3:1
Table 6.8   Imputed Labor and Capital Shares from a CES Regression
Table 7.1   Rates of Growth of GNP and Energy Consumption
Table 7.2   USSR Fuel and Energy Balance, 1980
Table 7.3   Possible Energy Consumption in the Year 2000
Table 7.4   Energy Consumption in 2000 by Primary Source and Energy Form
Table 7.5   Possible Energy-Supply Structure in 2000
Table 7.6   The East–West Split in Soviet Energy Production in 2000
Table 7.7   Energy Conservation from Improved Utilization
Table 8.1   Growth and Per Capita Indices of Industrial Output in Soviet Regions and Republics
Table 8.2   Selected Economic Data on Soviet Regions and Republics (Industry, Transport Access and Export)
Table 8.3   Industrial Fixed Capital per Employee and Output–Capital Ratios
Table 8.4   Regional Distribution and Per Capita Levels of Investment 1959–78
Table 8.5   Distribution of Capital Investment in Regions of the Soviet North
Table 8.6   Industrial Structure of Soviet Regions in 1972
Table 8.7   Dispersion of Settlements and Density of Transport Infrastructure by Regions, 1970
Table 9.1   Quantity Indices for Soviet Foreign Trade, National Income, and Gross National Product: 1960–78
Table 9.2   Per Annum Growth Rates of Real Soviet Exports, Total, and by Area, 1960–78
Table 9.3   The Geographic Composition of Soviet Foreign Trade Measured in 1970 Prices and in Current Prices: 1960–78
Table 9.4   Commodity Structure of Soviet Foreign Trade in Current Prices: 1960–78
Table 9.5   Unit Value Indices for Soviet Foreign Trade: 1960–78
Table 9.6   Soviet Convertible-Currency Balance of Payments: 1960–79
Table 9.7   Soviet Convertible-Currency Trade: Quantity Indices, Unit-Value Indices, and Net Barter Terms of Trade, 1971–7
Table 9.8   Convertible-Currency Debt of the USSR: 1970–9
Table 9.9   Western Estimates of Soviet Gold Sales, Production, and Stocks: 1970–9
Table 9.10   Windfall Gains to the Soviet Economy Through Convertible-Currency Trade: 1970–9

Table 10.1   Average Annual Rates of Growth of Per Capita Consumption by Major Category, USSR, 1950–79

Table 10.2   Average Annual Rates of Growth in Real Consumption Per Capita, Selected Countries, 1951–78

Table 10.3   Comparison of Soviet and US Consumption Per Capita in 1976, Modified ICP Classification

Table 10.4   Relative Levels of Consumption Per Capita by ICP Category, Dollar Comparisons

Table 10.5   Structure of Consumption, USSR, Selected Years 1950–79

Table 10.6   Comparison of the Structure of Consumption in Selected Countries

Table 10.7   Shares of Food, Beverages, and Tobacco in Total Household Consumption, Selected Countries

Table 10.8   Consumption Elasticities for Selected Commodity Categories, USSR, 1950–60, 1960–70 and 1970–9

Table 10.9   Relative Levels of Earnings of Selected Occupational Groups, USSR, 1950–60, 1970, 1979

Table 10.10 Comparison of Nonagricultural and Agricultural Incomes, USSR, 1950, 1960, 1970 and 1976

List of Contributors

ABRAHAM S. BECKER: Senior Economist, Rand Corporation.

ABRAM BERGSON: George F. Baker Professor of Economics, Harvard University.

JOSEPH S. BERLINER: Professor of Economics, Brandeis University; Associate, Russian Research Center, Harvard University.

LEE W. BETTIS: Economist, Office of Soviet Analysis, CIA.

SEWERYN BIALER: Director, Research Institute on International Change and Ruggles Professor of Political Science, Columbia University.

DANIEL L. BOND: Director, Centrally Planned Economies Project, Wharton Econometric Forecasting Associates, Inc.

ROBERT W. CAMPBELL: Professor of Economics, Indiana University.

JANET C. CHAPMAN: Professor and Chair, Economics, and Director, Russian and East European Studies, University of Pittsburgh.

ELIZABETH M. CLAYTON: Professor of Economics, University of Missouri.

STANLEY COHN: Professor of Economics, State University of New York.

DOUGLAS B. DIAMOND: Deputy Director, Office of Soviet Analysis, CIA.

LESLIE DIENES: Professor of Geography, University of Kansas.

EVSEY D. DOMAR: Ford Professor of Economics, Massachusetts Institute of Technology.

ALEXANDER ERLICH: Professor of Economics, Emeritus, Columbia University.

MURRAY FESHBACH: Senior Research Scholar, Center for Population Research, Kennedy Institute of Ethics, Georgetown University.

MARSHALL I. GOLDMAN: Professor of Economics, Wellesley College; Associate Director, Russian Research Center, Harvard University.

ALICE C. GORLIN: Associate Professor of Economics, Oakland University.

DAVID GRANICK: Professor of Economics, University of Wisconsin.

DONALD W. GREEN: Vice President, Chase Manhattan Bank.

PAUL R. GREGORY: Professor of Economics, University of Houston.

GREGORY GROSSMAN: Professor of Economics, University of California.

JOHN P. HARDT: Associate Director for Senior Specialists, Congressional Research Service, Library of Congress; Adjunct Professor, George Washington University.

CHAUNCY D. HARRIS: Samuel N. Harper Distinguished Service Professor of Geography and Director, Center of International Studies, The University of Chicago.

ED. A. HEWETT: Senior Fellow, The Brookings Institution.

FRANKLYN D. HOLZMAN: Professor of Economics, Tufts University; Research Fellow, Russian Research Center, Harvard University.

HOLLAND HUNTER: Professor of Economics, Haverford College.

D. GALE JOHNSON: Eliakim Hastings Moore Distinguished Service Professor of Economics, The University of Chicago.

ARCADIUS KAHAN: Professor of Economics, The University of Chicago.

ARON J. KATSENELINBOIGEN: Professor of Social Systems Sciences, University of Pennsylvania.

ROBERT LEGVOLD: Senior Fellow and Director of the Soviet Project, Council on Foreign Relations, and Adjunct Professor, Columbia University.

HERBERT S. LEVINE: Professor of Economics, University of Pennsylvania.

MOSHE LEWIN: Professor of History, University of Pennsylvania.

MICHAEL MANOVE: Professor of Economics, Boston University.

PAUL MARER: Professor of International Business, School of Business, Indiana University.

JAMES R. MILLAR: Professor of Economics, University of Illinois.

GUR OFER: Professor of Economics, The Hebrew University.

ROBERT E. RAMSSON: Economist, Office of Soviet Analysis, CIA.

BARNEY K. SCHWALBERG: Associate Professor of Economics, Brandeis University.

GERTRUDE E. SCHROEDER: Professor of Economics, University of Virginia.

JUDITH A. THORNTON: Professor of Economics, University of Washington.

VLADIMIR G. TREML: Professor of Economics, Duke University.

MARTIN L. WEITZMAN: Professor of Economics, Massachusetts Institute of Technology.

Preface

This volume presents in revised form the proceedings of a conference held at Airlie House, Airlie, Virginia, October 23–25, 1980. The conference, which was sponsored and supported by grants from the National Council for Soviet and East European Research and the National Science Foundation, had as its theme the long-term prospective growth of the Soviet economy.

It is now more than 60 years since the Bolshevik Revolution, and over 50 years since the initiation of Soviet Russia's First Five Year Plan. On the eve of that plan, the Soviet economy had more or less completed its recovery from the losses inflicted by World War I, two revolutions and a civil war. Under the plan and its early successors, the Soviet government proceeded to transform the USSR from a relatively backward and still overwhelmingly agricultural country into one in which industry would be predominant. Despite World War II, that effort was already far advanced by the mid-fifties when, for example, over half of the Soviet labor force was employed outside agriculture.

More recently, as further plans have unfolded, the economy of the USSR has continued to advance, but growth has slowed, and signs abound that the forces making for retardation are potent. Such a slowdown in an economy advancing toward a late stage of industrial development, though hardly unknown, has perhaps not been as characteristic in the West as often supposed. At all events, this seemed to be an opportune time to inquire into the nature of the conditioning factors that lately have been shaping economic growth in the Soviet case, and to try to gauge to what extent, if at all, they will continue in future to be weighted in the direction of growth retardation.

In appraising prospects, participants were asked to take as a horizon the year 2000. No literal depiction of the state of the Soviet economy in that year was expected, and none has been provided. The concern rather was simply to assure a common focus on a lengthy interval such as the turn of the century demarcates.

In pursuing our theme, participants were asked wherever feasible to base their projections on a review of past trends. In view of inevitable uncertainties about the future, it was felt that the participants might often be able to contribute to the appraisal of prospects chiefly by systematically elaborating previous developments. There seemed generally to be little to be gained at this point, however, from pushing such investigations back more than two or three decades.

An inquiry such as was envisaged would, it was hoped, also contribute by shedding further light on the Soviet growth process at an advanced stage. Concerning that process there is now a sizable literature, but almost unavoidably it has often become increasingly dated, as the Soviet economy has become ever more extensively industrialized.

How the Soviet economy will evolve in the period ahead will depend on diverse circumstances, including not least the possible involvement of the USSR in a major war. What might happen to the Soviet economy should the USSR in fact be involved in such a conflict is an interesting question, but to explore it seemed to be a task properly left to another occasion. Granting that, however, the question remained open as to how Soviet defense outlays in future might compare with those of the recent past. While participants were expressly left to decide for themselves what assumptions might be appropriate in that regard, it was hoped that the implications drawn would contribute to evaluation of how plausible the assumptions had been to begin with. Such defense policies necessarily became a prime concern in one particular essay, that on politics and priorities. Participants were also left to determine appropriate assumptions on other matters. They were asked, though, to explore variants where that might be illuminating.

To our great regret, space did not permit inclusion in full, in this volume, of formal comments on main papers that were submitted at the conference. Thanks largely to the efforts of Holland Hunter, however, a summary of such comments has been prepared which appears here as a supplement to the main papers. This summary also covers some of the informal exchanges that took place at the conference, but in the space available it can not really do justice to that most stimulating discussion. The omission of the bulk of such exchanges is the more regrettable since several of the participants, attending the conference as general discussants, could not be otherwise represented in this volume. We refer particularly to Morris Bornstein, Keith Bush, Walter Connor, Evsey Domar, and Erich Klinkmüller. Holland Hunter also participated as a general discussant. Leslie Dienes, in revising his paper for publication, fully incorporated the comments of Vladimir Treml on the version that was presented at Airlie House.

Editing proceedings of a conference for style is apt to be a notably difficult task. If, nevertheless, this volume should prove unusually free of stylistic lapses, that is very largely due to the exemplary skill and devotion manifest by Truus Koopmans in editing the entire manuscript for the press. Warmest thanks are also due to Elizabeth Goldstein who did much to lighten our task in organizing the conference.

Cambridge, Massachusetts
and
Philadelphia, Pennsylvania
November 1981

Abram Bergson
Herbert S. Levine

1

An Overview

DANIEL L. BOND and HERBERT S. LEVINE

Time present and time past
Are both perhaps present in time future,
And time future contained in time past.
T. S. Eliot "Burnt Norton"

Introduction

While our paper begins this volume, it could just as well have been the volume's summary paper. For, indeed, the paper is more in the nature of a summary than it is a forecast. In it, we use the framework of our Soviet Econometric Model (SOVMOD) to draw implications for the economy as a whole from individual sector and other partial projections set forth in later chapters.

Since the model embodies a set of accounts and relationships embracing the entire economy, it serves to enforce consistency among the independent sectoral projections presented in individual papers, and to help bring out their implications.[1] A prime illustration of this is the calculation in SOVMOD, through its energy demand component, of the energy-consumption and foreign-trade consequences of the model's projections of domestic growth, and the energy- and fuel-production forecasts made by experts on Soviet energy. These consequences are perhaps surprising, or at least rarely noted in the literature on the future of the Soviet economy. They illustrate the important principle that projected difficulties affecting an economy are not necessarily additive. In fact, it often happens that one set of problems alleviates another set of problems.

The approach we take in this paper, which is more in the nature of what could be called prospective analysis than forecasting, is necessitated by the long time period over which the analysis is being conducted.[2] In any projection or forecast the attempt is made to distinguish relationships and trends that are more or less invariant over the relevant time period from those that can be affected by uncertain events and by policy decisions of central leaders. In short-term forecasting, the uncertainties are usually sufficiently limited so that the projections produced by a model like SOVMOD can be viewed with some confidence. But as the time period lengthens, the uncertainties increase, and the sensible use of a macromodel shifts from forecasting to prospective analysis. In this mode, the total-system-consistency property of the macromodel is used to produce a "reasonable" projection of the economy (a baseline), and then alternative assumptions about the course of uncertain events and policies are used to construct alternative projections (scenarios) that can then be compared with the baseline projection for analysis of differences or similarities.

This shift in role has required a number of revisions in the structure of SOVMOD from earlier versions that were designed primarily for medium-term studies. In essence, SOVMOD has been sufficiently altered so that it can be used more in a simulation mode than in the forecasting mode, which has marked its previous use. In making these alterations, less attention was given to the depiction of short-term response patterns which play an important role in other versions of SOVMOD, and greater emphasis was placed on introducing the detail and structural specifications necessary for ensuring consistency among forecast values over the long term. By consistency we mean that through the model we attempt to explicitly define the supply of factors and goods, the demand for these factors and goods, and the process by which the two are brought into balance. These issues are discussed in detail in the next section of the paper.

In the third section of the paper, the baseline projection is described. Sources and assumptions used in setting the values for key exogenous variables are discussed. This is followed, in the fourth section, by the construction and discussion of several alternative scenarios. The paper ends with a brief set of conclusions.

In developing the baseline projection we have attempted to use, as much as possible, the information and opinions on the likely future of the Soviet economy provided in the other papers, while, at the same time, providing a depiction of Soviet prospects that is neither overly optimistic nor pessimistic. This is important in that, when alternative projections are prepared and compared with the baseline case, we want to be able to discuss cases that suggest possible sources of better performance for the economy, as well as cases that assume more stringent limitations on future growth.

1.1   Structure of the Model

As stated in the introduction, the economic issues examined in this paper have been explored through an econometric model of the Soviet Union (SOVMOD), created at the University of Pennsylvania by a joint effort of Stanford Research Institute (SRI) International and Wharton Econometric Forecasting Associates, Inc..[3] The version of the model used for this study (SOVMOD IV), is a modified form of the original family of models and has been created especially for use in long-range forecasting. The main features of this model are briefly described below.

Before moving on to that description, however, it should be noted that the model itself is only one ingredient in the process of economic analysis and forecasting. The elaboration of a model projection is an interactive process between the model and the analyst. Frequently, the skill and judgment of the analyst are the most important factors in obtaining a valid projection. The model serves as a framework for superimposing regularities observed in the past upon the future while preserving a certain degree of consistency. The analyst must judge when and make explicit why past regularities should be relaxed and/or additional consistency should be imposed upon the model solution. For this study the authors have attempted to draw from the work of the other contributors to this volume, and wherever possible to use their expertise in setting projected values for exogenous variables and adjusting the baseline forecast when appropriate to fit their analyses.

There are advantages and weaknesses in using an econometric model like SOVMOD for analyzing Soviet economic trends. The major advantage: the results reflect a comprehensive, integrated, internally consistent model of the Soviet economy rather than an analysis of a single sector or several sectors loosely related in aggregative terms. In addition, since the model is an interdependent system of technical and behavioral relations, the analysis is able to encompass, in quantitative terms, the indirect as well as the direct effects — the total system impact — of the various assumptions under consideration in the alternative scenario projections.

At the same time, the limitations of the model should be recognized. Excessive precision should not be attributed to the results of the projections. Any projection reflects, to a great extent, the judgment and insight of the analysts and not merely the mechanical number-processing power and precision of the computer. It must also be added that, since the model has been specified to reflect past behavior or trends in the Soviet economy, if the basic structure of that system changes radically it is unlikely that the model will provide much guidance in projecting the future states of that system.

A. *Factor Allocation*

Theoretical analysis of the Soviet centrally planned economy considers the supply (production) side as dominant in contrast with the emphasis on demand factors in the analysis of Western market economies. Thus, broadly speaking, the direction of major causality in the model runs from fully employed inputs (labor and capital) through the production process to final uses.

Two very important variables in the model are total population and available labor force. Population is an exogenous variable and we have used the projections presented in Murray Feshbach's paper. For the baseline forecast we have also used Feshbach's assumption of a constant labor-participation rate of 88% (of the able-bodied population) in order to obtain values for the total labor force.

The first step in the simulation process is to allocate the total labor force among the various sectors and branches of industry used in the model. Six main sectors are identified, which are:

Agriculture
Industry
Construction
Transportation and Communications
Trade and Distribution
Government, Housing, and Other Services

Industry is divided into the following twelve branches:

Electric Power
Petroleum Products
Coal and Coal Products
Ferrous Metals
Nonferrous Metals
Chemicals
Machine Building and Metal Working
Forest Products
Paper and Pulp
Construction Materials
Textiles and Apparel
Food Products

In the model, the share of labor going into each sector or branch is determined as a function of a log time trend, with parameters estimated by using data for the last ten years. This specification has the convenient property of insuring consistency throughout the forecast period between total labor supply and the sum of sectoral employment levels. Of course there is little in terms of explanatory or predictive content to such equations, except that the inertia in the system of labor allocation is very strong — as is reflected by the close fits observed in such equations over the historic period of the last decade. To allow for simulations where the allocation of labor is set differently from that predicted solely on the basis of trends, adjustment terms are included in each equation that allow the model user to adjust the pattern of labor distribution but still retain the necessary consistency between the aggregate and sectoral allocations. For the baseline projection, however, no adjustments were made, and it, therefore, reflects continuation of current trends in labor allocation.

A similar approach is used in allocating total investment among sectors. However, in the baseline projection the adjustment options were used to direct greater investment into the fuel and transport sectors to correspond to the forecast presented by Robert Campbell in this volume that investment in these sectors would rise to levels observed in the "pre-oil" period of Soviet development.

The final step in the factor-allocation process is the conversion of the flow of investment into capital stock. This process is modeled using econometrically estimated functions relating net capital formation to current and past levels of investment in the sector, with allowance made for depreciation of existing stocks.

B. *Agriculture*

The agricultural component of SOVMOD is described in detail in Green (1979). Crop and livestock production are treated separately, with further disaggregation provided for forecasting the volume of grain and meat output.

"Normal" output of total crops and total grain (for which historic time-series values are obtained by interpolating between levels of output in years of moderate harvests) is determined using production functions in which the independent variables are land, labor, capital and current purchases (primarily fertilizer). The deviation of actual output from these "normal" output levels is then explained by three weather variables — spring and summer precipitation, winter temperature, and winter precipitation (snow cover).

The outputs of total animal products and meat are determined by the size of the herd and the amount of feed available for livestock. The ratio of feed supply to herd size varies with the state of the harvest. A key policy variable in this area is the rate of growth of the livestock herd. For the baseline projection an average annual rate of growth of 1.5% was used. This is a rather modest rate of growth, and would reflect a retreat by the Soviet leadership from their earlier, rather ambitious plans to increase domestic meat production.

Total agricultural production is the aggregate value of crops and of animal products with feed, home-produced or imported, subtracted.

A rather difficult problem facing the modeler of Soviet agriculture is the prediction of future weather conditions. One frequent approach is to assume average weather conditions for each year in the projection period. But this removes a major structural relationship from the analysis of Soviet agriculture, i.e. the impact of variable weather on the grain-harvest–feed–livestock–meat nexus. We have "solved" this problem by introducing variable weather in our projections through the use of historic weather conditions for the forecast period. The actual weather pattern from the period 1958 to 1978 was used to set values for 1980 to 2000 (with the sequence of yearly observations disturbed only where it was necessary in order that each five-year benchmark reported in our tables would be a year of fairly normal weather).

The agriculture component in SOVMOD has been expanded by the addition of a set of grain-balance equations that were designed to help project the level of Soviet grain imports. Using the USDA grain-balance estimates as a data base, the following equations were estimated:

(1) Grain used for seed as a function of area sown, a time trend, and winter temperature.
(2) Grain used for food as a function of population and a time trend.
(3) Grain used for industrial purposes as a function of time.
(4) Grain used for livestock feed linked to the endogenously deter-mined total feed variable referred to above.
(5) Grain wastage as a function of the size of the harvest and the summer-precipitation variable.
(6) Net change in grain reserves as a function of harvest conditions and the ratio of normal harvest to total grain reserves in the previous year.

The sum of the above uses of grain is then subtracted from the projected level of grain output to obtain an estimate of the volume of net grain imports.

C. *Nonagricultural Production*

Production functions have been used in SOVMOD to link levels of output in each of the nonagricultural sectors and branches of industry to available capital stock and labor. Electric power, petroleum products, and the physical output of coal are exceptions. In the case of the electric-power industry, output in physical terms is determined by the level of demand, and the value of output then linked to this variable. The production of oil and gas, in physical terms, is set exogenously, by assumption; and the value of output in the petroleum-products industry is then calculated as a function of these physical outputs. As for coal output in physical terms, we have altered the coefficient linking GNP originating in the coal industry and the physical output of coal in order to be in line with Campbell's projections of an increasing proportion of low-quality coal in the total coal output.[4]

An attempt has been made to specify and estimate the non-agricultural, non-oil, gas, and electricity production functions in the model in a way that is consistent with the analysis presented in the papers by Abram Bergson and Martin Weitzman. Thus, Cobb-Douglas production functions — with constant returns to scale, assigned factor-input coefficients, and a neutral technological-progress specification — were used. These functions are specified in the model in a rate-of-growth form, and for the baseline projection values for the rate of growth of the "residual" were set equal to the average calculated from data for the period 1968–78.[5] In this way it was possible to conform to the Bergson and Weitzman view that future rates of factor-productivity growth are not likely to be very different from those observed over the past decade. If we had been able to include the poor (negative) productivity-growth years of 1979 and 1980, our projection of productivity growth would have been somewhat lower.

D. *The Defense Sector*

The role of defense expenditures in the Soviet economy is depicted in two ways in the model. First, at the macro level, total defense expenditures are one claimant on final demand, and thus enter into an equation where GNP and the sum of all end-uses of GNP are balanced.[6] Second, at the sectoral level, military procurement enters into an equation where total production of machinery and equipment (M&E) is balanced against the sum of intermediate and final uses of M&E. The general specification of these balances is as follows:

(1) Macrobalance equation

$$C = GNP - D - I - G - (E - M)$$

where:

C = Total personal consumption
GNP = Gross national product
D = Total defense expenditures
I = Total (nondefense) investment and change in inventories
G = Total (nondefense) social consumption
E = Total exports
M = Total imports

(2) M&E balance equation

$$I_{m\&e} = GVO_{m\&e} - IP_{m\&e} - C_{m\&e} - D_{m\&e} - (E_{m\&e} - M_{m\&e})$$

where:

$I_{m\&e}$ = Total M&E used for civilian investment
$GVO_{m\&e}$ = Gross value of output of M&E
$IP_{m\&e}$ = Intermediate purchases of M&E by other sectors of production
$C_{m\&e}$ = Final demand for consumer durables
$D_{m\&e}$ = Military procurement
$E_{m\&e}$ = Exports of machinery
$M_{m\&e}$ = Imports of machinery

Thus, military expenditures, which are exogenous in the model and therefore require that their values be set by assumption in the projection process, have a direct impact on the levels of consumption and investment, and affect indirectly — via the investment/capital–stock–formation process — the level of GNP.

E. *Other Components of Final Demand*

As described above, the machinery component of investment is obtained in SOVMOD as the residual category in a balance equation for the machinery and equipment sector. In order to obtain an estimate of total investment, the structures component of investment, capital repairs, and changes in inventories are calculated and added to machinery investment. The structures component of investment is linked to the level of output of the construction sector, capital repair to the volume of capital stock, and changes in inventories to output in consumer-products industries.

Total consumption is also calculated as a residual, in this case the macrobalance described above, under D. Components of consumption — food, durables, nondurables and services — are determined simply by using share equations regressed on a time trend.

Finally, there is a sequence of equations linking wages – which are a function of labor productivity — to personal income, various categories of tax revenues, other government-budget revenues and the value of public-consumption expenditures.

F. *Energy and Fuel Demand*

The energy- and fuel-demand component of SOVMOD is described in detail in Bond (1978). The relationship of energy to the rest of the economy depicted in this model is one in which the direction of causality is strictly from levels of economic activity to levels of energy required to support those activities. A consequence of this approach is that a shortage in energy supply will not have the effect of slowing the rate of growth of the economy. It will, rather, show up in the need for net imports of fuels. This type of relationship is consistent with that presented by Campbell in his paper on the energy sector in this volume.

The determination of fuel demands is made in two steps. First, energy demands are forecast on the basis of production and population levels generated in SOVMOD. Three major classes of energy demand are identified: (1) electrical power, (2) thermal energy, and (3) direct motor power. Not only are these energy forms distinguishable by the nature of their use, but each can be associated with particular types of equipment needed for their generation. The technical characteristics of this equipment determine both the type of fuels required to generate this energy, and the degree of fuel substitutability that is possible.

There are also possibilities for substitution to occur among the various energy types. Electric motors can replace gasoline-driven motors, and electric heat can replace boiler and furnace heat in industrial processes and home heating. No attempt, however, is made to explicitly model such substitutions. These changes normally occur very gradually, and any major shifts that are already underway are probably captured in our equations since included in most of them is either a time-trend variable or some other variable that changes monotonically with time. Furthermore, it is also felt that most Soviet efforts aimed at changing fuel-use patterns will be focused on interfuel substitution within each form of energy production, and not at major changes in the forms of energy use themselves.

In the second step referred to above, the issue of fuel substitution is addressed. The major places where substitution among fuels of any significant degree can occur are in the electric-power plants and in boiler and furnace use. Over the past 15–20 years, there have been significant shifts in the fuel mix at these points, and together these uses make up over 70% of domestic fuel consumption. It is assumed that direct motor power will continue to be based on the use of light petroleum products.

In modeling interfuel substitution, the so-called "putty-clay" model of input requirements has been adopted. That is, we assume that fuel-input requirements of capital stock already in use will not change significantly, and that the fuel mix observed in any given year (which, when expressed in terms of shares of total fuel use, are referred to as "average" fuel-mix coefficients) is a weighted average of the fuel-input requirements of the various vintages of capital stock still in use (where the weights are the shares of each vintage in total capital stock). Faced with changing scarcities of fuels it is expected that there will be an attempt to replace the scarcer fuels with the less scarce. But this can be accomplished only by the introduction of new equipment designed for this purpose, the "vintage" coefficients of which reflect a mix of fuels more economical in terms of the changing conditions of fuel supply. We have not attempted to endogenously determine fuel-mix characteristics of new capital stock — this information is introduced by means of assumptions when making projections.

The measures of fuel use considered in the model are calculated in terms of standard fuel-equivalency units, and, in most cases, on the basis of data for actual use — that is, excluding losses and internal consumption. Therefore, a set of identities is provided to convert these values into their respective gross natural-unit values (million metric tons (mmt) for oil and coal, and billion cubic meters for gas).[7]

Once the physical quantities of oil, gas and coal needed to supply the Soviet domestic demands have been established, these amounts are subtracted from exogenously set levels of production in order to obtain estimates of "exportable surplus" of each fuel. The regional distribution of fuel exports is set by exogenous forecasts of export levels to Eastern Europe, with exports to the rest of the world determined as the residual.

G.   *Foreign Trade and Debt*

The foreign-trade sector of SOVMOD is disaggregated along both regional and commodity lines. Trading relations with the socialist countries are distinguished from trade with the rest of the world (the Developed West and the LDCs).

In the version of SOVMOD being used for this paper, the foreign-trade equations have been greatly simplified, with most of the relative-price-response specifications of earlier versions of SOVMOD eliminated. These have been replaced by equations linking trade in particular categories of goods to growth in related branches of the economy (in the case of exports), or simply by use of extrapolated trade shares to determine the composition of trade (in the case of most imports). However, for two of the most important components of Soviet trade — exports of fuels and imports of grain — the forecast values are obtained on the basis of explicit balances as described above.

Regional exports, to other CMEA countries and the Developed West, are derived from the sum of the projected exports in fuels, other raw materials, machinery, and nondurable consumer products to each region. The rate of growth of total imports from CMEA is tied directly to the rate of growth of total exports to CMEA. The link between imports and exports in trade with the West is less direct, taking into consideration the use of Western credits to finance imports. Here the ratio of imports to exports is modeled as a function of the debt-service ratio (the ratio of debt servicing — which includes payments of both interest and principal — to the sum of merchandise exports to the West plus the value of gold sales). Using data for the last few years, the following parameter estimates were calculated:

$$MTDW / ETDW = 3.00867 - 7.77234 * FDSRGOLD$$

where:

MTDW   = Value of imports from the Developed West
ETDW   = Value of exports to the Developed West
FDSRGOLD = Value of the debt-service ratio

This equation has the property of adjusting the level of imports each year in such a way as to maintain the debt-service ratio near the level of 0.25 — a reasonable level from both the perspective of the willingness of Western creditors to extend loans, and also from the perspective of the Soviet leaders' willingness to finance imports from the West on the basis of credit.

The level of net indebtedness to the West is calculated in the model by subtracting from the previous year's net debt the current-account balance, which in the model consists of the net balance of hard-currency merchandise trade plus gold sales, arms sales, and transfer payments (these three being exogenous variables) minus interest payments on the previous year's debt. The ratios of interest to debt, and of repayments on debt are econometrically estimated, and in the forecast period amount to approximately 8.5% and 16.5% respectively.

The linkage between the foreign-trade sector and the domestic economy is achieved at several points in the model. Linkage in one direction results from the determination of fuel exports from the oil, gas, and coal balances in the model. Feedback into the domestic economy occurs at three points. First, there is a "passive" relationship that is based on the assumption that any domestic shortfalls in the availability of grain will be met by increased imports. More "active" feedback is achieved by the inclusion of aggregate net exports in the GNP macrobalance, and of net machinery imports in the balance of the machinery-and-equipment sector. Total world exports and imports must remain in relatively close balance over time, so that the impact of foreign trade on the macrobalance is quantitatively not very significant. However, the volume of machinery imports over exports has increased steadily, and this trend continues in the baseline projection. This is a result of the difference in commodity structure of Soviet exports and imports. According to the estimates in our baseline projection, in the next two decades approximately half of the value of Soviet exports will be the result of fuel trade, while from one-half to two-thirds of the value of imports will be for purchases of machinery and equipment.

1.2 The Baseline Projection

Several of the assumptions that were used in developing the baseline projection have already been mentioned in the section describing the model. There are a number of additional assumptions that must be explained before we examine the baseline results.

For the defense sector, we have assumed that total military expenditures will grow at a constant rate of 4.5% over the projection period. This is consistent with CIA statements about their outlook for the 1980s.

As indicated above, the output levels of fuels are set exogenously (see Table 1.9). In the baseline projection, we have used Campbell's projections in this volume of gas and coal output, and his projections of the hydro and atomic parts of electric-power production. In regard to coal production, it is expected that the energy content of coal will diminish as more Siberian coal is used. This decline in quality is taken into account in the conversion between physical units and standard fuel-equivalency units. In the baseline simulation we have used the forecast provided in the Campbell paper to set the appropriate values for the decrease in the energy content of coal. In regard to the contentious issue of the prospects for Soviet oil production, we decided not to follow Campbell completely. Campbell uses a forecast of oil output that drops to a level of 400 million metric tons (mmt) in 1990, and then rises to 441 mmt in 2000, which is in line with the spirit of the CIA "worst-case" forecast. We have chosen not to use such a severe decrease in the baseline projection (although it is used in one of the alternative projections discussed in the next section of this paper). Instead we decided to have the oil output hold at 600 mmt through 1985, fall to 550 mmt by 1990, and then hold at that level to the year 2000. Many analysts feel that 550 mmt will be the lowest level that Soviet oil will reach, especially if strong actions are taken by the Soviet leadership to prevent further declines; as the baseline-projection results indicate, there will be substantial economic pressures to take such actions. In our baseline case, we have assumed additional actions on the part of Soviet economic management in response to decreased oil output. Most importantly, we have assumed that beginning in the early 1980s all newly installed thermoelectric power and boiler capacity will be gas- and/or coal-fueled. This assumption is not made on the basis of any specific knowledge of the technological possibilities of such a change, but has been used only to examine the implications of such a policy.

We have assumed that there will be no significant Soviet grain exports in the future, so that the net import figures obtained from the grain-balance equations are taken to be equal to total grain imports. In addition to assuming that livestock-herd growth will be limited to 1.5% per year, we have also projected a continued growth of the acreage sown to grain but a decrease in this growth to a rate of less than 0.5% a year.

In forecasting foreign-trade flows, the assumptions as to future foreign-trade prices play a critical role. Here we have drawn on a number of sources in an attempt to prepare a reasonable set of prices for the baseline case.[8] The key indices used are presented in Table 1.5. In order to simplify the interpretation of these indices in terms of relative price changes, we have chosen to use an average rate of total trade price inflation of 5% per year over the entire projection period.

Gold sales to the rest of the world, in physical terms, have been limited to a rate of growth slightly less than that of the assumed rate of growth in gold production (2.7%).

Detailed results of the baseline projection are provided in Tables 1.6 through 1.9. The growth of key macroaggregates over the entire period 1980–2000 are given in Table 1.1. These figures can be interpreted as characterizing an economy with moderate output growth, low productivity increases,[9] and moderate rate of improvement in consumption. This is quite in line with the general perspective found in the papers of the other contributors to this volume.

Looking below the aggregates, we find the following. First, at the sectoral and industrial branch levels, it is seen that given the allocation of labor and capital generated by the model, certain sectors — particularly chemicals and machine building — maintain their position as growth leaders. The petroleum products industry drops sharply in

Table 1.1   *Baseline Projection, 1980–2000 (average annual rates of growth, in percent)*

GNP	3.15
GNP by Sector of Origin	
Agriculture	2.54
Industry	3.69
Other	2.65
GNP by End Use	
Consumption	2.78
Consumption per capita	2.03
Investment	2.67
Defense	4.50
Labor Force	
Total	0.50
Agriculture	− 1.75
Industry	0.56
Other	1.37
Capital Stock	
Total	5.16
Agriculture	6.39
Industry	5.16
Other	4.83
Total Factor Productivity	
GNP	1.07
Nonagriculture	0.83

relative rate of growth. But this is due primarily to the assumed path of oil output. Electric power growth remains strong due to demand. The consumer goods branches and nonferrous metals hold their growth positions steady, while the ferrous-metals, construction-materials, and forest-product branches lose ground. This results from trends in factor allocation and productivity growth.

Strong growth in the machine building industry is essential for the expansion of the equipment component of investment, which in the baseline model grows at 5.3%. Since construction-sector growth slows to 2.7%, the structures component of investment grows at only 2.8%, and its share in total investment drops from 63% in 1980 to 50% by the end of the period. This corresponds to the avowed policy of Soviet planners to increase the rate of plant reequipping as opposed to new plant construction.

Overall, since investment grows slightly slower than GNP, its share of GNP slips from 32% to 30% per year in twenty years. The same is true of consumption, its share of GNP dropping from 56% to 52% annually. The share of defense expenditures grows from 13% to 17% per year over the projection period (all in 1970 prices).

Agricultural growth remains respectable by historical standards in the baseline projection, largely by continued high capital-stock growth, which is necessary to compensate for a declining labor force. The baseline results for the Soviet grain balance are summarized in Table 1.2. With the variable weather pattern that we have used, and by assuming that livestock herds grow at 1.5% per year, net grain imports fluctuate, with a maximum of about 33 mmt and an average of 20 mmt over the 1980–2000 period. Most of the growth in domestic-grain use is for livestock. Meat production increases at an average of 2.8% per year, which would allow an increase in per capita meat consumption of about 2% per year if this were all to be domestically consumed.

In our projective analysis, a key outcome of the use of SOVMOD, with its rather detailed portrayal of energy and fuel demand, is the projection obtained for total energy demand, with the corresponding requirements for oil, gas and coal. In the aggregate, growth in energy use over the twenty-year period is 2.3%, which can be contrasted to growth in GNP of 3.2% — implying an aggregate energy-to-GNP elasticity of 0.72. While this is lower than that suggested by Campbell in his paper, the fact that it is obtained by use of a model that relates energy use to activity levels at a fairly disaggregated level should give it some credence. For example, four of the most-energy-consuming sectors of the economy — construction, construction materials, ferrous metals and paper products — grow at relatively low rates over the projection period, thus contributing to a decreased energy-to-GNP ratio.

A detailed portrayal of the baseline fuel balance is provided in Table 1.9. With the volume of oil production that we have assumed, the "exportable surplus" of oil falls from 160 million metric tons in 1980, to 140 mmt in 1985, 100 mmt in 1990, and a little less than 75 mmt in 2000. But if we use Campbell's forecasts of gas and coal output the "exportable surpluses" of gas and coal rise substantially. There are many ways in which the Soviet Union could divide its energy exports between Eastern Europe and the rest of the world, under the competing objectives of supporting the economies of its East European allies and the earning of hard currency to finance the purchase of machinery and advanced technology from the West. We have not tried to explore this important issue in any depth, but one plausible strategy might be the following. The Soviet Union could maintain its oil exports to Eastern Europe at the current level of 80 mmt through 1985 (as apparently it has informed East European countries it will do); then drop these exports to 60 mmt by 1990, and maintain them at that level through the 1990s, while balancing the drop in oil exports with increases in gas and coal exports. This would allow its total energy exports to Eastern Europe to grow at an annual rate of about 2.5% over the period 1980–2000, which, though down substantially from the approximately 10% per year rate of increase of the 1970s, would be of some help to the East European countries of CMEA. At the same

Table 1.2   Soviet Supply and Utilization of Grain: Historic Data and Projected Values (annual average, million metric tons)

Period	Production	Utilization					Stock Change	Net Imports
		Seed	Feed	Industrial	Food	Wastage		
1971–5	181.6	27.2	98.4	3.0	45.0	19.6	–1.2	10.7
1976–80	203.8	28.9	120.9	3.7	45.4	22.6	1.9	19.9
1981–5	214.7	30.7	135.4	3.8	46.4	15.6	2.0	19.4
1986–90	245.7	32.4	156.0	4.1	47.2	22.7	3.2	19.8
1991–5	287.4	34.5	178.6	4.3	47.7	33.6	4.7	16.1
1996–2000	298.5	35.8	245.9	4.5	48.2	31.9	1.3	24.2

time, Soviet exports of oil to the rest of the world would drop steadily from their level of approximately 80 mmt in 1980, but would remain positive for the entire period, reaching a level a bit below 15 mmt in the year 2000.

Fuel-export volumes and prices play a key role in determining the volume of potential Soviet trade with the Developed West. In the baseline projection the value of such exports rise from about $18 billion in 1980 to $150 billion in the year 2000. This is an 11.2% average annual increase, which after correcting for the assumed rate of inflation gives a 5.9% per year increase in real terms. Growth is slightly stronger in the 1990s than in the 1980s, due to the assumed pattern of oil-output decline in the earlier decade.

On the import side of the trade balance with the West, grain imports are the single most significant item. However, since the value of grain imports ($4.7 billion in 1980, and $11.7 billion in 2000), grows more slowly than total imports from the West, its share of total imports declines from 20% to 7%.

The regional distribution of Soviet foreign trade shifts somewhat in the baseline projection. The share of trade with the West drops, from 34% of total trade turnover in 1980 to 29% in 2000. The largest gains are made in Soviet trade with its East European neighbors. The share of this trade increases from 50% in 1980 to 64% in 2000.

With the growth of trade between the Soviet Union and the Developed West dropping to only 10% per year in the projection period (as contrasted to 25% during the past decade), and with the model maintaining a debt-service ratio within the range of 25% to 30%, Soviet imports from the West are constrained to an increase of 10% annually (which means about 5% in real terms). If past trends continue, the largest share of these imports will be for machinery (35–45%). Machinery imports will also account for the largest portion of Soviet imports from Eastern Europe (about 50%). Together these purchases will play an important role in maintaining Soviet capacity for growth in the machinery component of investment.

1.3   Alternate Scenarios

Once a baseline projection has been prepared using a model such as SOVMOD, the model user can examine many interesting questions of the type: "What if the level of variable W is allowed to grow faster or slower — what then will be the implications for variables X, Y, Z?" We have carried out a number of such experiments, including those with assumption of lower productivity growth, lower oil output, higher growth of defense expenditures, and no growth of defense expenditures. These scenarios and some of their results will be briefly discussed below.

A. *Scenario A: Low Productivity Growth*

In the baseline case, it should be recalled, the rate of future total factor-productivity growth in the nonagriculture and non-oil, gas, and electricity sectors is controlled by the form of the production functions used (Cobb-Douglas), by exogenously set factor–output elasticities, and by use of disembodied productivity-growth rates set at 1968–78 levels consistent with Bergson's aggregate production function. But due to the fact that productivity in agriculture, oil, gas, and electricity was not constrained in this manner, our baseline GNP total-factor-productivity projection is different from (higher than) Bergson's all-sectors figure for the period 1968–78 (see his Table 2.3). Moreover, in the conclusion to his paper, Bergson suggests that the 1968–78 rate of productivity growth may not be maintainable in the future. Thus in Scenario A, we have reduced the rate of productivity growth in each of the nonagricultural sectors and all branches of industry except petroleum products and electric power by one percentage point starting in 1980. In the petroleum industry we have, at first, retained the baseline assumptions as to the path of output. Electric power, however, since it is demand-determined, grows more slowly than in the baseline case because of the general slowing of the economy.

Some of the results of these changes (as well as the other scenarios) are compared with the baseline projection in Table 1.3.

In Scenario A, total factor productivity related to GNP grows at the low rate of 0.3%, while nonagricultural productivity growth is slightly negative, at −0.1%. Overall GNP growth is down to 2.3% from the baseline level of 3.2%.

Perhaps most significant of all, especially since this low-productivity scenario is thought by many to be quite likely, is the very low projected growth of per capita consumption. If, as both Seweryn Bialer and Gertrude Schroeder suggest in their papers in this volume, an annual increase of at least 1% in per capita consumption will probably be necessary to maintain political calm, then this scenario could be considered a "crisis scenario" for the domestic economy.

With the lower growth of output in the economy, given that in the model energy use is linked to activity levels, there is a significant reduction in the level of domestic energy use. This leads, in Scenario A, to substantially larger exports of fuels than in the baseline case, thus reducing the energy-export problems that the Soviet Union will face, as discussed above. To explore the dimensions of an augmented crisis scenario, we ran a variation of Scenario A, with the Campbell oil forecast, i.e. with oil output falling to 500 mmt in 1985, 400 mmt in 1990, and then rising to 441 mmt in 2000. While this had hardly any effect on the growth of GNP (reduced from 2.3% to 2.2%), it did greatly decrease the exportable surplus of oil. This would fall rapidly, reaching a level below 70 mmt by 1985 (which would most likely mean no oil exports outside of CMEA), and turning slightly negative at its low point in 1990, then rising to a level of about 20 mmt in 2000. There would be surpluses of gas and coal to counterbalance these deficiencies in oil exports (in terms of standard fuel equivalent), but it is doubtful whether there would be sufficient transportation capacity to move these surpluses to border export points. In any event, this variant of Scenario A does exhibit sharp decreases in Soviet trade with the West. Soviet imports from the West, for example, would be about 35% lower over the 20-year period than they are in Scenario A itself. This, in turn, would contribute to a decreased rate of growth of investment, which is 1.8% in the low oil-output variant, compared to 2.1% in the low-productivity scenario.

B.   *Scenario B: Baseline, with High Defense Growth.*
Scenario C: Baseline, with No Defense Growth

To throw some light on the oft discussed issue of Soviet defense expenditures in an era of constrained economic growth, we ran two variations of our baseline projection with rates of growth of defense expenditures different from the rate of 4.5% per year assumed in the baseline case: one with a rate of growth of defense expenditures of 7.5% per year, and the other with no growth in defense expenditures.

The summary results are shown in columns 3 and 4 of Table 1.3. They indicate that the changes in the growth of defense expenditures have little impact on the growth of output — GNP, industry, and

Table 1.3   *Alternative Scenarios, 1980–2000 (average annual rates of growth, in percent)*

	1.	2.	3.	4.
			Scenario B:	Scenario C:
			Baseline Case	Baseline Case
		Scenario A:	with High	with No
	Baseline	Low producti-	Defense	Defense
	Projection	vity Growth	Growth	Growth
GNP	3.15	2.26	3.08	3.27
Industry	3.69	2.64	3.62	3.80
Agriculture	2.54	2.66	2.52	2.56
Consumption	2.78	1.43	1.58	3.44
Consumption Per Capita	2.03	0.69	0.83	2.68
Investment	2.67	2.07	2.08	3.48
Defense	4.50	4.50	7.50	0.00
Labor Force	0.50	0.50	0.50	0.50
Capital Stock	5.16	4.74	4.89	5.65
Total Factor Productivity GNP	1.07	0.33	1.09	1.03
Non-agriculture	0.83	−0.06	0.85	0.82

agriculture — over the projection period even though the impact on the growth of investment is not insignificant.[10] This result arises primarily because the change in the amount of annual investment that is caused by a change in defense expenditures (particularly procurement) is small relative to the size of the capital stock in the economy; and also because of the rather low output elasticity of capital in the production functions of the model. In this regard, note that there is less difference between the rates of growth of capital stock in Scenarios B and C than there is between the rates of growth of investment.

Compared to the impact on the growth of national product, there is more of an effect of variations in defense expenditures on the uses of national product. Comment has already been made about the effect on investment growth. In addition, the impact on consumption growth is worthy of attention. The 7.5% growth of defense expenditures in Scenario B results in a fall of the rate of growth of per capita consumption below the critical 1% level. The zero growth of defense expenditures in Scenario C leads to a rise of per capita consumption growth to 2.7%, compared to a rate of 2.0% in the baseline case.

Though the summary data may portray a picture of limited effect of variations in defense expenditure, the impact on Soviet policy makers might be quite different, because policy makers are more concerned with the allocation of increments of output among competing claimants than with the distribution of the flow of total outputs, the past amounts of which tend to be difficult to reallocate. The shares of incremental output going to defense, shown in Table 1.4, may thus be a better illustration of what the burden of defense, over the five-year-plan periods to the end of the century, will be in the view of Soviet policy makers.

First, the data in Table 1.4 show an increasing impact over time of defense expenditures, in all categories. Second, the incremental impact is substantially greater than the average impact. In the baseline case with defense expenditures growing 4.5% per year, which is higher than the projected rate of growth of GNP, the share of defense expenditures in GNP (the "average burden of defense") increases from a level of 13% in 1980 (not in the table) to 17% in 2000. But the share of the increment to defense expenditures in the increment to overall GNP rises from 16% in the period 1980–5 to 25% in 1995–2000. And what is probably most relevant to the issue of the effect of the growth in defense expenditures on Soviet policy makers, the increment in the procurement of defense equipment grows from a share of 35% of the increment in machine-building-and-metal-working output, in 1980–5 (which is about the same as its incremental share in the 1970s) to a share of 90% in 1995–2000. That is, even in our baseline projection, defense-expenditures growth of 4.5% compared to GNP growth of 3.2% builds up so that by the period of the 12th Five-Year Plan (1985–90), the increase in defense procurement will be taking more than half of the increment in MBMW, and by the period of the 14th

Table 1.4   *Average and Incremental Burden of Defense (in percent)*

	1.	2.	3.
			Share of Defense-Procurement
		Share of Defense	*Increment in*
	Share of Defense	*Increment in*	*MBMW*
	in GNP	*GNP Increment*	*Increment*[a]
Baseline Case			
1980–5	14	16	35
1985–90	15	21	54
1990–5	16	24	75
1995–2000	17	25	90
Scenario B:			
High Defense			
1980–5	16	29	45
1985–90	20	44	78
1990–5	25	58	120
1995–2000	31	70	163
Scenario A:			
Low Productivity			
1980–5	14	23	47
1985–90	16	32	82
1990–5	18	38	122
1995–2000	20	40	150

[a] The MBMW Increment is the increment to that part of machine-building and metal-working output going to final demand.

FYP, the share will be 90%. This will represent a tremendous problem for Soviet decision makers, who will have a severely constrained residual with which to augment the flow of investment equipment to all the sectors and branches of industry of the economy. It indicates the likelihood of significant pressure, at the top Soviet policy-making levels, to reduce the rate of growth of defense expenditures toward the level of GNP growth, especially in the 1990s.

Third, the data in Table 1.4 for Scenario B's 7.5% growth of defense expenditures indicate that, by the 1990s, the burden of defense looms very large across the board. The magnitudes greater than 100% in column 3 signify that in the 13th and 14th FYPs, the flow of investment equipment to the economy will be falling. Only in the direst of circumstances could such a policy be maintained.

Finally, it is worth noting the similarity between the burdens of defense in the low-productivity and high-defense scenarios, especially in regard to the defense share of incremental MBMW. In the low-productivity Scenario A, because of the slowdown in the growth of output, in particular industrial output, and the assumed steady 4.5% growth of defense expenditures, the incremental burden of defense takes on substantial proportions.

1.4 Conclusions

The major conclusions of our paper could be said to be the following. First, our baseline projection depicts a Soviet economy, in the last two decades of the twentieth century, that is growing at a lower rate than in previous decades, but still a rate that would be considered moderate by world standards.

Second, in the methodology used for our projection, the factors contributing to slower growth are primarily low growth in total factor productivity and the demographically induced low growth of the labor force. The assumed pattern of decreased oil output and the projection of energy output in general do not show up as constraints on output growth.

Third, given the way that the relationship between energy and economic production is modeled, the role of energy-demand factors is highlighted. In the baseline projection, with GNP growth at 3.2% per year, and oil output falling from 603 mmt in 1980 and 600 mmt in 1985 to 550 mmt in 1990 and holding at that level to the year 2000, the Soviet Union is able to meet its internal energy requirements, and maintain oil exports to Eastern Europe at their 1980 level until 1985, which then drop to 75% of their 1980 level by 1990 and remain there through the 1990s. Soviet oil exports to the West and other non-East European countries fall 50% from 1980 to 1990, and then another 65% from 1990 to 2000, ending at a fairly negligible 14 mmt per year. These shortfalls, however, can be made up by increased exports of gas and coal, if adequate transportation and pipeline capacity become available. In the low productivity growth scenario, with fuel output as in the baseline projection, the rate of growth of GNP falls to 2.3% per year, and the Soviets are able to meet domestic energy needs, maintain the 1980 level of oil exports to Eastern Europe, and though oil exports to the rest of the world fall somewhat, they end up at 60% of their 1980 level in the year 2000. This illuminates the importance of the effect that decreased economic growth has on the domestic demand for energy.

Fourth, though the baseline projection does not portray a Soviet economy verging on collapse, the low productivity scenario does have the growth of per capita consumption falling below 1%. This represents a potential source of trouble for the Soviet regime, giving the low productivity projection the air of a "crisis scenario."

Fifth, the high growth and no growth defense scenarios that we have run have not shown much effect on output growth from variations in growth of defense expenditures. They have, however, shown more effect on the uses of output. The growth of per capita consumption falls below 1% when defense expenditures grow at 7.5%, and rises to 2.7% when defense expenditures stop growing (i.e. remain constant). Also of significance is the incremental burden of defense that builds up especially in the 1990s. Since Soviet planners and policy makers are concerned primarily with the allocation of increments to output among competing claimants, the increasing share of these increments taken by defense-expenditure increments, not only in the high-defense scenario, but also in the low-productivity scenario, and in the baseline projection, point to a potential source of pressure to reduce the growth of Soviet defense expenditures below the assumed 4.5% per year rate of growth. Such a pressure was not indicated by other measures of defense impact on Soviet economic performance.

Sixth, a final word of caution. In addition to all the reservations that the reader may have in regard to the analysis we have presented, there is an additional one that we would like to put forth. In the alternative scenarios, the analysis is focused primarily on the results arising from alternative uses of resources. Although the model allows us to make calculations that are numerically consistent, primarily through the use of various balance equations, there is one dimension of the analysis that is quite weak. We assume in these alternative simulations that each of the factors of production is homogeneous in nature. Thus, imported machinery is treated as being no more productive than domestically produced machinery of the same value; labor and capital goods going into or out of the defense sector are no more or no less productive than labor and capital goods normally used for civilian purposes; etc. Obviously, this is not a very good depiction of reality. We have not attempted to treat factors with explicit regard to their qualitative nature primarily because of the difficulties in quantifying these differences. But in interpreting the results of these scenarios it is essential to consider the degree to which the results are biased in one direction or another by the lack of treatment of the qualitative differences in factors.

Table 1.5 Key Soviet Foreign Trade Price Indices: Historic Data and Baseline Projection Assumptions (average annual rate of increase)

	1970–5	1975–80	1980–5	1985–90	1990–5	1995–2000
Aggregate Price Index for:						
Soviet Exports	7.5	6.3	5.5	5.5	5.5	5.5
Soviet Imports	7.2	6.6	5.2	5.0	5.0	5.0
Export Price for:[a]						
Oil	32.0	22.0	8.0	8.0	8.0	8.0
Gas	11.5	22.0	10.0	10.0	10.0	10.0
Coal	28.9	17.0	6.0	6.0	6.0	6.0
Import Price for:						
Grain	22.3	2.3	5.0	5.0	5.0	5.0
Gold Price	32.5	28.4	1.6	5.0	5.0	5.0
Dollar/Ruble Exchange Rate	1970 1.11 1975 1.39		1980 1.55 1985 1.71	1990 1.86	1995 2.02	2000 2.19

[a] These rates of price increases are for fuel trade with the West. In the forecast period prices for Soviet exports of fuels to Eastern Europe are set using three-year moving averages of these prices.

Table 1.6 *Baseline Projection: Summary (all growth figures are average annual rates of growth over preceding five years)*

	1970	1975	1980	1985	1990	1995	2000
GNP, billion 1970 rubles	380.710	458.755	527.000	632.273	733.111	844.225	980.128
Growth (%)		3.80	2.81	3.71	3.00	2.86	3.03
GNP by Sector of Origin:							
Agriculture	70.484	68.722	72.000	89.846	101.449	111.392	118.832
Growth (%)		-0.51	0.94	4.53	2.46	1.89	1.30
Industry	157.119	210.539	249.819	305.618	362.642	428.879	515.163
Growth (%)		6.03	3.48	4.11	3.48	3.41	3.73
Construction	25.379	33.373	37.913	43.838	49.746	56.059	64.154
Growth (%)		5.63	2.58	2.95	2.56	2.42	2.73
Transport and Communications	31.581	43.666	53.559	70.869	92.002	116.801	146.468
Growth (%)		6.69	4.17	5.76	5.36	4.89	4.63
Trade and Distribution	16.665	20.848	24.176	27.807	31.257	34.716	38.931
Growth (%)		4.58	3.01	2.84	2.37	2.12	2.32
Services	40.606	48.037	55.587	60.157	62.965	64.565	66.335
Growth (%)		3.42	2.96	1.59	0.92	0.50	0.54
GNP by Sector of End Use:							
Consumption	219.645	268.928	296.373	341.789	380.317	438.309	513.058
Growth (%)		4.13	1.96	2.89	2.16	2.88	3.20
Investment	113.878	147.189	174.729	208.493	235.694	226.719	295.843
Growth (%)		5.27	3.49	3.60	2.48	2.50	2.09
Defense	45.000	56.000	70.000	87.233	108.708	135.470	168.820
Growth (%)		4.47	4.56	4.50	4.50	4.50	4.50
Consumption Per Capita, 1970 r.	900.552	1052.555	1107.686	1219.760	1306.509	1458.536	1655.366
Growth (%)		3.17	1.03	1.95	1.38	2.23	2.56

Total Population, millions	243.900	255.500	267.560	280.210	291.094	300.513	309.936
Growth (%)		0.93	0.93	0.93	0.77	0.64	0.62
Labor Force in millions:							
Total	118.559	127.976	136.809	139.586	141.773	144.512	151.261
Growth (%)		1.54	1.34	0.40	0.31	0.38	0.92
Agricultural	37.553	36.337	34.630	31.273	28.384	25.909	24.331
Growth (%)		−0.66	−0.96	−2.02	−1.92	−1.81	−1.25
Industrial	31.593	34.054	36.899	37.949	38.667	39.461	41.291
Growth (%)		1.51	1.62	0.56	0.38	0.41	0.91
Capital Stock, billion 1955 rubles:							
Total	702.333	1029.950	1442.195	1944.759	2530.523	3193.035	3947.342
Growth (%)		7.96	6.96	6.16	5.41	4.76	4.33
Agricultural	73.400	125.200	192.004	280.229	387.384	513.264	662.113
Growth (%)		11.27	8.93	7.86	6.69	5.79	5.22
Industrial	208.000	313.300	449.182	606.782	789.925	994.886	1227.803
Growth (%)		8.54	7.47	6.20	5.42	4.72	4.30
Total Factor Productivity Growth (%)							
GNP		0.12	−0.40	1.35	0.97	0.99	0.95
Nonagriculture		0.48	−0.55	0.81	0.85	0.87	0.95
Foreign Trade, million $ US:							
Total Exports	12659	33441	76511	141589	223596	380299	602384
Total Imports	11735	37164	68514	132846	210400	372326	575656
Exports to Developed West	2461	8534	24440	41314	66153	117827	175655
Imports from Developed West	2780	13489	24224	42488	65828	127091	171068
Net Hard-Currency Debt	1001	7847	22160	46628	74415	135623	196679
Debt Service Ratio	0.158	0.188	0.282	0.276	0.283	0.266	0.278

Table 1.7 Baseline Projection: Industry (all growth figures are average annual rates of growth over preceding five years)

	1970	1975	1980	1985	1990	1995	2000
Industry, 1970=100:							
Total	100.000	134.000	159.000	194.514	230.807	272.964	327.881
Growth (%)		6.03	3.48	4.11	3.48	3.41	3.73
Industrial Branch Growth Rates (%)							
Electroenergy		7.05	5.62	6.19	4.74	4.10	3.64
Coal Products		2.08	-0.38	0.62	4.57	3.66	2.88
Petroleum Products		6.49	6.76	3.16	0.98	1.64	1.32
Ferrous Metallurgy		3.76	2.17	1.71	1.07	0.72	0.90
Nonferrous Metallurgy		5.92	2.69	3.54	2.95	2.65	2.88
Construction Materials		5.13	2.32	2.15	1.52	1.17	1.31
Chemicals and Petrochemicals		8.58	6.05	5.73	4.80	4.29	4.47
Machine Building and Metal Working		8.07	6.29	5.67	5.07	4.84	5.14
Forest Products		2.51	0.84	0.87	0.60	0.55	0.97
Paper and Pulp		4.71	0.54	2.49	1.92	1.65	1.86
Textiles and Apparel		2.60	3.09	2.35	2.15	2.17	2.67
Processed Foods		4.15	1.69	2.26	2.01	1.97	2.42
Shares of branches in industrial output:							
Electroenergy	0.046	0.049	0.054	0.059	0.063	0.065	0.065
Coal Products	0.031	0.026	0.022	0.018	0.019	0.019	0.019
Petroleum Products	0.059	0.061	0.071	0.068	0.060	0.055	0.049
Ferrous Metallurgy	0.053	0.047	0.044	0.040	0.035	0.031	0.027
Nonferrous Metallurgy	0.031	0.031	0.029	0.029	0.028	0.027	0.026
Construction Materials	0.044	0.042	0.039	0.036	0.033	0.029	0.026
Chemicals and Petrochemicals	0.052	0.058	0.066	0.071	0.076	0.079	0.082
Machine Building and Metal Working	0.259	0.284	0.325	0.350	0.378	0.405	0.433
Forest Products	0.045	0.038	0.034	0.029	0.025	0.022	0.019

Paper and Pulp	0.008	0.007	0.006	0.006	0.005	0.005	0.004
Textiles and Apparel	0.165	0.140	0.138	0.126	0.118	0.111	0.106
Processed Foods	0.166	0.152	0.139	0.127	0.118	0.110	0.103

Shares of Branches in Industrial Investment:

Electroenergy	0.106	0.092	0.083	0.070	0.059	0.054	0.049
Coal Products	0.053	0.043	0.039	0.040	0.040	0.036	0.033
Petroleum Products	0.122	0.139	0.164	0.234	0.302	0.317	0.331
Ferrous Metallurgy	0.071	0.071	0.065	0.056	0.048	0.044	0.041
Nonferrous Metallurgy	0.106	0.097	0.089	0.078	0.069	0.065	0.061
Chemicals and Petrochemicals	0.082	0.094	0.104	0.010	0.094	0.097	0.010
Machine Building and Metal Working	0.209	0.238	0.250	0.247	0.239	0.248	0.256
Forest Products	0.046	0.044	0.042	0.038	0.034	0.032	0.031
Paper and Pulp	0.024	0.021	0.019	0.016	0.014	0.013	0.012
Construction Materials	0.058	0.047	0.041	0.033	0.026	0.022	0.019
Textiles and Apparel	0.043	0.040	0.038	0.034	0.030	0.028	0.027
Processed Foods	0.080	0.074	0.064	0.055	0.047	0.043	0.039

Table 1.8   Baseline Projection: Agriculture (all growth figures are average annual rates of growth over preceding five years)

	1970	1975	1980	1985	1990	1995	2000
Agriculture, billion 1970 rubles	70.484	68.722	72.000	89.846	101.449	111.392	118.832
Growth (%)		-0.51	0.94	4.53	2.46	1.89	1.30
Composition of Agricultural Output							
Crop Production, b. 1970 r.	37.596	34.121	46.110	49.726	57.525	61.509	67.197
Growth (%)		-1.92	6.21	1.52	2.96	1.35	1.78
Grain Production, mmt.	186.795	140.118	189.000	230.912	252.518	303.407	312.572
Growth (%)		-5.59	6.17	4.09	1.81	3.74	0.60
Animal Production, b. 1970 r.	55.653	59.700	70.936	81.693	93.643	108.285	120.206
Growth (%)		1.41	3.51	2.86	2.77	2.95	2.11
Meat Production, b. 1970 r.	28.798	35.243	41.568	48.159	54.990	63.372	72.225
Growth (%)		4.12	3.36	2.99	2.69	2.88	2.65
Inputs to Agricultural Production							
Value of Livestock, Dec. 31, b. 1970 r.	56.784	66.331	70.846	76.321	82.219	88.574	95.419
Growth (%)		3.16	1.33	1.50	1.50	1.50	1.50
Feed Fed to Livestock, b. 1970 r.	10.169	12.937	15.318	17.782	20.776	23.856	27.044
Growth (%)		4.93	3.44	3.03	3.16	2.80	2.54
Fixed Capital, July 1, b. 1970 r.	73.400	125.200	192.004	280.229	387.384	513.264	662.113
Growth (%)		11.27	8.93	7.86	6.69	5.79	5.22
Area Sown to Grain, m. hectares	144.671	151.613	158.500	161.548	165.210	168.960	172.794
Growth (%)		0.94	0.89	0.38	0.45	0.45	0.45
Total Employment, millions	37.553	36.337	34.630	31.273	28.384	25.909	24.331
Growth (%)		-0.66	-0.96	-2.02	-1.92	-1.81	-1.25

Grain Balance, mmt. (Average Over Preceding Five Years)

Grain Production	181.6	203.8	214.7	245.7	287.4	298.5
Grain Net Imports	10.7	19.9	19.4	19.8	16.1	24.2
Grain Utilization:						
Seed	27.2	28.9	30.7	32.4	34.5	35.8
Industrial	3.0	3.7	3.8	4.1	4.3	4.5
Food	45.0	45.4	46.4	47.2	47.7	48.2
Waste	19.6	22.6	15.6	22.7	33.6	31.9
Feed	98.4	120.9	135.4	156.0	178.6	245.9
Stock Change	-1.2	1.9	2.0	3.2	4.7	1.3

Table 1.9 Baseline Projection: Energy and Fuel Balances (all growth figures are average annual rates of growth over preceding five years)

	1970	1975	1980	1985	1990	1995	2000
Total Energy Production (million barrels per day, oil equivalent)	16.147	20.925	25.560	29.158	32.220	36.279	40.032
Growth (%)		5.32	4.08	2.67	2.02	2.40	1.99
Total Energy Use (mbd, oe)	14.944	19.252	21.152	23.855	26.608	29.696	33.192
Growth (%)		5.20	1.90	2.43	2.21	2.22	2.25
Fuel Balances							
Oil: Production (mil. tons)	353.039	490.801	603.000	600.000	550.000	550.000	550.000
Domestic Use	260.739	363.753	442.792	459.691	450.205	458.130	475.895
Difference	92.300	127.048	160.208	140.309	99.795	91.870	74.105
Gas: Production (bil. cu.m)	197.945	286.268	435.200	600.000	700.000	800.000	887.000
Domestic Use	196.849	279.180	366.329	452.952	529.461	593.773	658.006
Difference	1.096	7.088	68.871	147.048	170.539	206.227	228.994
Coal: Production (mil. tons)	624.114	701.280	715.000	770.000	970.000	1170.000	1359.000
Domestic Use	603.262	681.602	685.882	741.001	861.748	998.963	1164.463
Difference	20.852	19.678	29.118	28.999	108.252	171.037	194.537
Electric Power: Production: (billion KWH)							
Thermal	613.049	892.620	1042.100	1374.362	1633.613	1922.088	2242.282
Hydro	124.377	125.987	181.300	214.377	253.701	293.025	332.349
Atomic	3.500	20.000	72.000	250.178	427.581	611.359	801.513
Total	740.926	1038.607	1295.400	1838.917	2314.895	2826.471	3376.145

1: Notes

1 On this basic role of a model, see the remarks in Houthakker and Kennedy (1978), pp. 2–3.
2 See OECD (1979), pp. 3–6. We are also indebted to this source for the T. S. Eliot quotation appended to the beginning of the paper.
3 The background of the SOVMOD project and a description of the original version of the model are provided in Green and Higgins (1977).
4 This coefficient rises from zero in 1980 to 24% of output in the year 2000.
5 The capital coefficient for each branch and sector for which we employ production functions was calculated with the following equation:

$$B_i = D \times k_i / Y_i$$

where B_i is the capital coefficient for sector i, D is the marginal productivity of capital (which is assumed for this analysis to be constant across sectors), and K_i and Y_i are the value of capital stock and of GNP originating in sector i in 1970. The value of D is obtained using Bergson's assumption that $B = 0.34$ for the economy as a whole. Taking the 1970 value of Soviet GNP (380.71) and of capital stock, this gives:

$$D = 0.34 \times 380.71 / 677.5 = 0.191$$

The calculated capital coefficient and average value of the residual over the period 1968–78 for each sector is given below:

	Capital Coefficient B_i	*1968–78 Residual*
Branches of industry:		
Coal and Coal Products	0.45	0.28
Ferrous Metals	0.49	−0.32
Nonferrous Metals	0.43	1.67
Chemicals	0.43	1.83
Machine Building and Metal Working	0.19	3.15
Forest Products	0.20	0.85
Paper and Pulp	0.50	0.11
Construction Materials	0.39	0.22
Textiles and Apparel	0.07	2.06
Food Products	0.13	1.88
Construction	0.13	0.73
Transportation and Communications	0.57	0.67
Trade and Distribution	0.30	0.22
Nonproduction Services	0.42	−1.85

6 In order to incorporate this balance into the model, it was necessary to develop historic time series for Soviet GNP end-use categories that would be consistent with estimated total GNP. For both total GNP and consumption, we used estimates that are published by the Office of Economic Research, CIA. For total defense expenditures, we constructed a time series that would be consistent with CIA's estimate of the level of these expenditures in 1970 (as presented in CIA, 1978, p. 8), which had a rate of growth during the 1970s of 4.5% per year, consistent with CIA's estimate of growth in Soviet defense expenditures in rubles at constant 1970 prices.

Using domestic ruble to foreign-trade–ruble conversion coefficients provided by Vladimir Treml, we were also able to develop a time series for net exports in domestic prices. The 1970 value of net exports estimated in this way is also consistent with the 1970 GNP account prepared by the Office of Economic Research: CIA, Office of Economic Research (1978).

Starting with the time series for total GNP, and subtracting the estimates for consumption, defense, and net exports we arrived at a residual that should correspond to the remaining end use categories aggregate investment (that is investment in fixed and working capital and changes in inventories) and other government expenditures (a relatively minor category). Initially, there was some difficulty in reconciling our time series for investment with this residual. After some exploratory calculations, however, it was found that if the value of total investment (from Soviet statistical sources) was deflated by 1.5% per year, the sum of all components would be very close to total estimated GNP. This solution to the problem was deemed acceptable, though we realize is highly debatable. The issue of the degree of hidden inflation in the official Soviet investment series is a thorny one. Without going into any detail here, it should be noted that the question is not simply the application of the widely accepted downward bias in the official MBMW price index to the investment series, since the investment series is in a different set of prices, the so-called "comparable estimate prices." On this, see the recent discussion in Nove and Cohn (1981).

This solution does pose one problem for our presentation that should be pointed out. In examining our tables, the reader should be aware that we are using two measures of investment. In the GNP accounts we have used the above-described "double-deflated" figures for aggregate investment. But in the Shares-of-Industrial-Investment section of Table 1.7 we make use of the official Soviet investment data.

7 This note provides some additional information on the energy demand component of the model.

Demand equations for electric power are provided in the model for each of the major sectors of the economy — industry, agriculture, transportation, construction and urban municipal and household use. Transmission losses are also included. The explanatory variables chosen for the productive sectors represent measures of output, capital intensity of the sector, and an electric-power-supply constraint. As was expected, electric-power use per unit of output (or per capita) is directly related to the degree of mechanization of the sector, as represented by capital-stock to output ratios. Although time-series data on electric-power use by branch of industry are not available, it was still possible to capture, in the specification for total industry, the impact of differing requirements across individual branches by weighting branch output by 1970 ratios of electric-power use to value of output, which are available in Soviet sources.

Electric-power supply is determined separately for electric-power-generating capacity of thermal-, hydro-, and atomic-powered stations. Output of thermal stations is found as a residual after the output of hydro- and atomic-power stations is subtracted from total electric-power demand.

Total hydrocarbon-fuel requirements (in standard fuel-equivalency units) for electric-power production in thermal-electric plants is then determined on a per unit output basis. Because efficiency in generation has changed over time, a log time trend is used to estimate the rate of technological improvement. Another factor that has contributed to increasing fuel efficiency has been the shift from coal to oil and gas. The use of standard fuel-equivalency units, as defined in Soviet sources, leads to error since the conversion rate used for coal is too high. In order to correct for both real-efficiency differences between coal and other fuels and the statistical bias of Soviet figures, a correction term was added to the fuel-requirement equation.

In determining the fuel mix used in electric power plants we have followed the procedure outlined above, i.e. fuel mix is determined by the requirements of the various vintages of capital stock in use at a given time.

Two classes of thermal-energy use are distinguished in Soviet statistics and have been used in the energy component: boiler heat and furnace heat. Demand for boiler heat is forecast on the ratios of thermal energy use to industrial output and urban population, and of transmission loss to total output, which are fitted to log time trends. Furnace-heat use is forecast by using fixed 1970 ratios of thermal-power use to output of the ferrous-metals and construction-materials sectors.

The two primary sources of low- and medium-temperature thermal energy are from co-generation with electrical power in the so-called TETs (*teploelektrotsentral*) electric power plants and from industrial and municipal boilers. There is also some secondary heat recovery that should be included as a source. In the model, production of thermal power in the TETs is calculated as a function of their generating capacity, and secondary recovery is an exogenous variable. Output of boilers is then determined as a residual supply.

Since fuel requirements for the TETs are already included in the electric power equations, it is necessary only to calculate the needs for boilers and furnaces. Fuel mix equations for boiler and furnace use are specified in the same manner as for electric power plants.

Four categories of motor fuel use are identified in the model: (1) automobile use, (2) other transportation sector use of light petroleum products, (3) transportation sector use of coal, and (4) non-transportation sector use of light petroleum products. The specifications employed are very simple since the data available are limited.

The primary non-fuel uses of hydrocarbons are for coke required in the metallurgy industry, and oil and gas feedstocks in the chemical industry. These non-fuel uses were related to output measures of the corresponding sectors. The breakdown of total petrochemical feedstocks into its gas, light and heavy petroleum components is determined exogenously, with the aggregate value to be used as a control total.

8 The assumption that the price of gas would increase more rapidly than the price of oil, and the latter more rapidly than the price of coal, is consistent with the forecasts presented in Leontief (1977) and Houthakker and Kennedy (1978). Other sources consulted informally in setting the price forecasts were the WEFA US Annual and Industry Model and World Model forecasts to the year 2000 and a World Bank study of commodity price trends.

9 Growth in total factor productivity is calculated as follows:

$$(1+g_y)/[(1+g_l)^{0.66}(1+g_k)^{0.34}]$$

where:

g_y = rate of growth of GNP
g_l = rate of growth of labor force
g_k = rate of growth of capital stock

The total factor productivity growth of 1.07% related to overall GNP is somewhat high because of the quite low level of agricultural production in 1980. The non-agricultural productivity growth figure of 0.83% is more indicative of the level of productivity growth in the baseline projection.

10 The output growth impact would be greater over the long run if more of the additional investment were channeled into the creation of additional capacity in the machine building and metal working sector, rather than letting it be distributed across all sectors in the same proportions as in the baseline projection.

1: References

Bond, Daniel L., "Modeling the Energy and Fuel Sectors in SOVMOD." SRI International Technical Note SSC–TN–5943–5, 1978.

Bond, Daniel L., and Levine, Herbert S., "Energy and Grain in Soviet Hard Currency Trade." In *Soviet Economy....*, Vol. 2, 1979.

CIA, "USSR: Toward a Reconciliation of Marxist and Western Measures of National Income." ER 78–10505. Washington, DC, 1978.

Cohn, Stanley, "Estimation of Military Durables Procurement Expenditures from Machinery Production and Sales Data." SRI International Informal Note SSC–IN–78–13, 1978.

Cohn, Stanley, "A Comment on Alec Nove, 'A Note on Growth' ", *Soviet Studies*, 33, 2: 296–9, April 1981.

Green, Donald W., and Higgins, Christopher I., *SOVMOD: A Macroeconomic Model of the Soviet Union*. New York: Crane-Russak, 1977.

Green, Donald W., "Soviet Agriculture: An Econometric Analysis of Technology and Behavior." In *Soviet Economy....*, Vol. 2, 1979.

Houthakker, Hendrik S., and Kennedy, Michael, "Long-Run Energy Prospects." *J. of Energy and Developm.* 4, 1: 1–28, 1978.

Leggett, Robert E., and Rabin, Sheldon, "A Note on the Meaning of the Soviet Defense Budget." *Soviet Studies* 30, 4: 557–66, Oct. 1978.

Leontief, Wassily, et al., *The Future of the World Economy*. New York: Oxford Univ. Press, 1977.

Nove, Alec, "A Note on Growth, Investment, and Price Indices." *Soviet Studies* 33, 1: 142–5, Jan. 1981.

OECD, *Interfutures. Facing the Future: Mastering the Probable and Managing the Unpredictable*. OECD, Aug. 1979.

Soviet Economy in a Time of Change. Papers, Joint Econ. Comm., US Congress. Washington, DC: Govt. Printing Off., 1979.

2

Technological Progress

ABRAM BERGSON

Introduction

The aim of this volume is to appraise the future course of the Soviet economy. The aspect on which I focus, technological progress, is both central, and, by its very nature, particularly conjectural.[1] Perhaps I can narrow the range of uncertainty by inquiring summarily into past trends and the forces that have shaped them. Inquiry into these matters hopefully will provide a basis for speculation in the concluding section, about future prospects of Soviet technological advance.

Technological progress has been understood variously. Traditionally reference has been to the introduction and spread of new production methods that enable the community to increase output at a given resource cost. The new production methods often involve use of new sorts of capital goods or physical processes; but other changes in production modes, such as extension of intrafactory specialization, are also envisaged. Whatever their nature, the new methods enlarge the technological "opportunity set" of a production unit, thus generating a larger output at the same resource cost.

Output may expand at given resource cost, however, not only through such variations in production methods but also in other ways; for example, through a reform in labor incentives. Lately technological progress has often been understood to embrace such an institutional change as well. Indeed, technological progress has come to refer to output expansion at given resource cost on any and all accounts.

As between these concepts of technological progress, the last one perhaps has an advantage, for — and this has not always been considered — it is sometimes difficult, even in principle, to draw the line between the introduction and spread of new technologies and other causes of output expansion at given resource cost. Depending on the development stage, for example, amelioration of a historically distorted resource allocation in the process of industrialization may be a significant source of increase in output at the same resource cost. Such a gain is very often treated as technological progress apart from introduction and spread of new technologies. But a transfer of, say, labor from agriculture to industry serves in effect to extend the scope of advanced production methods. From that standpoint, it might be viewed more as a form of technological diffusion, albeit of a rather indirect sort. True, the advanced technologies applied may not be especially novel in any period considered, but that may also be true of technologies whose application is being extended more directly elsewhere in the economy.

I propose nevertheless to focus primarily on technological progress in its traditional and more limited sense. In fact, where a choice is open, I interpret the traditional concept as being less, rather than more, inclusive. A principal concern, however, is to assess quantitatively the pace of technological advance. In attempting that, it is difficult to do otherwise than view such progress, at least in the first instance, in a more inclusive way. That should be to the good, though, for technological progress in the inclusive sense that has come lately into use is also of interest. Thus where the concept in question needs to be distinctly stated I refer to technological progress in the less inclusive sense, relating to new production methods only, as technological progress proper (TPP), and in the more inclusive sense, which embraces also other causes of output expansion at given resource cost, as technological progress extended (TPE).

In either usage, the touchstone of advance is the increase in output at given resource cost. That, strictly speaking, still leaves open the question which treatment is to be accorded to introduction of novel products for household and other final consumption, and the resulting gains in final user values at given resource cost. Although such gains are obviously to be included in any complete accounting for technological progress, the advance realized exclusive of such gains has an interest of its own. Western quantitative research on technological progress has properly often focused on the more limited concept. As rarely noted, it is rather problematic how completely the statistical measures that are compiled do in fact exclude consumers' gains from new final products. But that is an intricate matter that cannot be disposed of in this essay. I compile measures for the USSR, however, that are of a sort usually compiled for Western countries. As will appear, there are reasons to at least be alert to the question regarding the coverage of consumer gains as posed above.

2.1 Productivity Growth

Technological progress, by its very nature, is manifest in productivity growth. An attempt to appraise the tempo of such progress, therefore, properly turns to that aspect. Measurement of productivity growth in a way that is indicative of technological progress has generally proven to be a difficult task, and the USSR is no exception to that rule. But the increase of productivity can still serve as an illuminating benchmark. Of particular interest are trends in factor productivity as indicated by the comparative growth of output and factor inputs. Such calculations have by now often been made for the USSR, but it is best to approach the matter afresh here.

I have compiled data on Soviet factor-productivity growth both for the whole economy and for a somewhat less comprehensive sphere. To refer first to the measures for the whole economy, as indicated in Table 2.1, these relate the growth of GNP to the growth of three major factor inputs, labor, capital and agricultural land. The calculations are made for most part in a usual way. Among other things, they entail the imposition of a Cobb-Douglas production function with assigned factor-input coefficients and neutral technological progress on underlying data on factor inputs and output.[2] The calculations also yield more or less usual results for the period studied: factor-productivity growth, not especially rapid to begin with, slows in successive intervals — and indeed is negligible in the final period considered.

This is not the place to reopen the perennial issue concerning the reliability of Western measures of real national output in the USSR, but it should be observed that the Greenslade (1976) measures that I use are compiled in terms of ruble weights (depending on the level of aggregation, prices or factor costs) which generally relate to 1970 or a nearby year. That is an appropriate weight year for our present purpose of calculating output growth for the latter part of the interval studied, but there might be much to be said for referring instead to a weight year more nearly contemporary to earlier intervals when their output growth is calculated. For well-known reasons, such a computation should yield higher growth rates than Greenslade's for those earlier intervals. For years since 1950, index-number relativity in measurement of aggregative Soviet output appears to be quite modest, indeed so much so that it is hardly perceptible in some relevant data.[3] But the Greenslade series probably does understate the retardation in output growth since the fifties. There must also be a corresponding understatement of retardation in productivity growth as calculated from those data.

Inquiries into the sources of Soviet post-war growth very often proceed without reference to penal labor. That is understandable in view of the uncertain nature of both the numbers and quality of such workers. But, by all accounts, there was a substantial reduction in the penal labor force in the early post-Stalin years. Even though I must resort to rather arbitrary figures, it seems appropriate now to explore the impact on my computations of an allowance of penal labor varying in this way: 1950, 3.5 millions; 1960, 1.5 millions; and 1970 and 1975, 1.0 million. In Table 2.1 the parenthetic figures for employment are obtained after addition of a penal labor force of these magnitudes.

I also show parenthetically the impact on variations in working hours of an allowance for changes in their quality. Although it is of a rule-of-thumb sort, the allowance probably does not differ very much from that indicated by Denison's (1967) well-known, more careful procedures. Also shown parenthetically is the joint effect of the

Table 2.1 Average Annual Rates of Increase of Output, Factor Inputs, and Factor Productivity, USSR, 1950–75* (percent)

	All Sectors			Material Sectors		
	1950–60	1960–70	1970–5	1950–60	1960–70	1970–5
Gross Product	5.89	5.26	3.83	7.55	5.53	3.92
Factor Inputs, Total	3.95 (3.92)	3.69 (3.75)	3.72 (3.66)	3.78 (3.72)	3.63 (3.71)	3.65 (3.56)
Labor	1.16 (1.11)	1.74 (1.84)	1.79 (1.70)	.98 (.90)	1.28 (1.41)	1.37 (1.25)
Employment	1.55 (1.30)	2.08 (2.01)	1.63 (1.60)	1.43 (1.12)	1.67 (1.60)	1.17 (1.15)
Hours	−.38 (−.19)	−.33 (−.17)	.16 (.10)	−.44 (−.22)	−.38 (−.19)	.20 (.10)
Capital	9.49	8.00	7.86	9.47	9.06	8.73
Farm Land	3.33	.18	1.04	3.33	.18	1.04
Factor Productivity	1.87 (1.90)	1.51 (1.46)	.11 (.16)	3.63 (3.69)	1.83 (1.75)	.26 (.35)

* Output for all sectors is the gross national product, and for material sectors, the gross national product less the gross product (i.e. net product plus depreciation) of housing and diverse services, chiefly health care, education, science, and repairs and personal care. Factor inputs are also calculated separately for the whole economy and for the material sectors as defined above.

Fixed capital is taken to represent capital generally, and the sown area to represent farm land. On the parenthetic figures on employment and hours, and the corresponding data on factor inputs and productivity, see the text and the Appendix. Factor inputs are aggregated by use of a Cobb–Douglas formula with the following "earnings share" weights: for all sectors, labor .62, capital .33, and for farm land .05; for material sectors, labor .62, capital .32, and farm land .06.

For further sources and methods, see the Appendix.

allowances for penal labor and changes in quality of hours on the rates of growth of labor and factor inputs and factor productivity.

Turning to factor-productivity growth of the "material" sectors, I refer in Table 2.1 to the whole economy less housing and diverse services. Productivity of the "material" sector varies broadly, as it does for the whole economy, but the initial rate of growth in the 1950–60 period is there much higher, so that its overall deceleration is more marked than for the economy as a whole.

I use essentially the same procedures for the material sectors as for the whole economy, and also the same sorts of data. That means that for output I again rely on Greenslade's (1976) calculations in 1970 rubles, so that the slowdown in factor-productivity growth relative to earlier periods should again be somewhat understated. The allowance for penal labor that was made previously is now assigned entirely to the material sectors. Hence, it has a more pronounced effect in these sectors than in the whole economy.

2.2   Some Methodological Issues

I have been referring to calculations where a Cobb-Douglas production function with assigned factor-input coefficients is imposed on factor inputs and output. Given that production function, the elasticity of substitution ( ) between factor inputs is unity. In post-World War II years there have been a number of econometric inquiries concerning the production function of the USSR. These different inquiries do not seem to converge to any clear and reliable consensus on either the general form of the production function or the magnitudes of parameters that are presupposed (see Bergson, 1979). The econometric studies do alert us, however, to diverse possibilities.

It is of interest, therefore, that if, in place of the Cobb-Douglas

Table 2.2   *Alternative Computations of Average Annual Percentage Rate of Growth, Factor Productivity, USSR 1950–70, for Alternative Elasticities of Substitution (σ) and Rates of Return on Capital (ρ)*

| Period | Percentage Rate of Growth of Factor Productivity | | | |
	$\sigma = 1.0$ $\rho = .12$	$\sigma = 0.5$ $\rho = .12$	$\sigma = 1.0$ $\rho = .06$	$\sigma = 0.5$ $\dot\rho = 6.0$
		All Sectors		
1950–60	1.87	.01	2.66	.87
1960–70	1.51	1.12	2.14	1.73
1970–5	.11	.32	.70	.81
		Material Sectors		
1950–60	3.63	1.40	4.47	2.38
1960–70	1.83	1.14	2.59	2.00
1970–5	.26	.50	.94	1.11

formula, we impose a CES production function with σ equal to, say, 0.5, the trends in factor productivity for the whole economy are somewhat changed. The rate of growth remains modest, indeed for years prior to 1960 it is distinctly lower than before (see Table 2.2, columns for which $\rho = .12$). As a result the sixties now bring some acceleration, but the rate of growth again slows in the seventies. For material sectors, with the shift to $\sigma = .5$, the earliest rate of growth is likewise much reduced, but remains relatively high, so that growth decelerates over the whole period as before.[4]

To judge from the econometric inquiries, $\sigma = 0.5$ is within the realm of possibilities. An even lower elasticity has sometimes been observed. As it turns out, however, even $\sigma = 0.5$ implies a notably high factor share and rate of return for capital in the early years. If only on that account, results of the econometric inquiries may perhaps be properly discounted at this point.[5]

Factor-input coefficients in the Cobb-Douglas formula are supposedly given by income shares that are imputable to the factors when earnings rates correspond to relative marginal productivities. In the CES formula, a similar correspondence is supposed to prevail between factor-input coefficients that appear there and such imputable income shares in the base year. In applying both formulas here, I obtain the needed coefficients from income shares indicated when the rate of return on capital is 12%. That was in a 1969 Soviet official methodological release the lower limit allowed for "normative coefficients" for appraisal of investment projects (Gosplan SSSR . . . , 1969).[6] How closely actual returns might have approximated that limit, however, is an interesting question.

Here, too, therefore, experimentation with alternative assumptions is in order. For this purpose, I consider a possible reduction in the postulated rate of return on capital to 6%. With that, as was to be expected, factor productivity grows somewhat more rapidly, but the variation in growth rate over time is essentially as before (in Table 2.2, compare columns for $\rho = .12$ and .06). These results hold for both the whole economy and for the material sectors by themselves.

Farm land in the USSR is publicly owned but made available without charge to those who till it.[7] Here too the earnings share is imputed rather arbitrarily, but I take as a benchmark Western, especially US, experience. Unless the resulting share (5% of the GNP and 6% of gross material product) is implausibly wide of the mark, any error at this point could only affect our results very marginally.

Factor productivity growth during 1970–5 is found to be especially slow. That is true regardless of the computation, although with σ as low as .5 the all-sector rate of growth during 1950–60 is even lower than that for 1970–5. For present purposes, the most recent Soviet performance is of particular interest, but the interval 1970–5 is a very brief and somewhat dated one from which to gauge any enduring trends. The terminal year of that interval was marked by a harvest failure that was severe even by Soviet standards. For that reason, too,

Table 2.3   *Average Annual Rate of Growth of Factor Productivity, USSR, Selected Periods* (percent)*

Period	All Sectors	Material Sectors
1950–60	1.87	3.63
1960–70	1.51	1.83
1965–75	.94	1.32
1966–76	.86	1.22
1967–77	.76	1.12
1968–78	.57	.91

* The calculations proceed essentially as in Table 2.1. Additional data for 1965–8, for output and employment, from sources of corresponding data in Table 2.1, armed forces being taken as constant at the 1965 level. For capital stock and farm land, see TSU (1968, p. 61; 1969, p. 334; 1970, p. 45). For 1976–8, for often rough extrapolations from 1975, I rely mainly on data in CIA (Aug. 1979, pp. 64–5); Feshbach (1978); TSU (1978, pp. 40–41, 224).

the 1970–5 growth rate is difficult to interpret. It should be observed, therefore, that the recent growth of factor productivity continues to be depressed, though not as much as in Table 2.2 if we refer to ten-year periods terminating in very recent years (Table 2.3). However, a tendency towards further retardation in growth is also evident as the interval considered advances in time.

In trying to gain perspective on future prospects of technological progress in the USSR, one might wish to know about trends in factor productivity not only in post-World War II years but in earlier times. Of particular interest is the pre-World War II peacetime interval that commenced with the initiation of the First Five-Year Plan in 1928. Unfortunately, the violent shifts in economic structure that this plan initiated had a statistical consequence that bedevils any attempt at incisive appraisal of these trends. I refer, of course, to the extreme dependency of aggregative measures of performance on the valuation year considered. There are nevertheless reasons to discount the high rates of growth of factor productivity obtained when valuation is in "early" ruble prices. In that case the 1928–40 performance may not have been much superior to that of the fifties, and possibly even inferior (see Bergson, 1978(c), pp. 117ff; p. 168, n. 21).

To return to the post-World War II years, I more or less implied that productivity growth in the USSR has been undistinguished by Western standards. Although the concern of this essay is with Soviet technological progress, comparison with Western experience can put Soviet trends in perspective. Hence, it should be observed that in respect of productivity growth such a comparison is in fact unfavorable to the USSR. The Soviet performance falls within the range of Western experience, but in the West the rate of productivity growth since World War II has tended to vary inversely with the stage of economic development as manifest by one or another conventional indicator (the level of output per worker, GNP per capita, and the like). For well-known reasons relating to "advantages of backwardness," such an inverse relation is not at all surprising.

If, as thus seems proper, we allow for the Soviet development stage, we find the Soviet performance in regard to productivity growth sub-standard. Over protracted post-World War II periods, the Soviet growth tempo surpasses those of the United States and United Kingdom, two relatively advanced countries, but falls short of those of Italy and Japan. The latter countries were both, midway through the interval we consider here, at development stages more or less comparable to that of the USSR. The USSR also underperforms in comparison with two more advanced countries, Western Germany and France. Here are data on the annual percentage growth of output per unit of inputs during 1955–70 that are broadly comparable to those for the whole economy in Table 2.1: USSR, 2.4; USA, 1.6; France, 3.9; Germany, 3.4; United Kingdom, 1.8; Italy, 4.4; Japan, 5.9 (Bergson, 1978(c), chaps. 9–11; also Bergson, 1968; Cohn, March 1976). These results rest on use of the Cobb-Douglas formula with a 12% return imputed to Soviet capital, but the Soviet performance is still undistinguished when alternative methodologies are employed (Bergson, 1979).

I have been considering productivity growth in the USSR both for the economy as a whole and for the material sectors. Western productivity research has very often focused on the first of these two spheres, but, for familiar reasons revolving around the conventional practice of measuring service output by inputs, the second is decidedly of more interest for us. To sum up to this point, then, in respect of Soviet productivity increase in material sectors, the rate of growth has declined in post-World War II years to a quite modest level. That is indicated by my initial calculations (Table 2.1). I shall rely primarily on these results in this essay, but deceleration is also evident, though in somewhat different degrees, in the alternative computations that we have considered. How the Soviet performance during post-World War II years compares with that under the pre-World War II five-year plans is uncertain; but it does not seem to compare well with contemporary Western achievements.

2.3 Productivity Growth and Technological Progress 1950–75

I have been referring to factor-productivity growth. Our more ultimate concern is with technological progress. In so far as technological progress is manifest in a divergence between the increase of output and factor inputs, the resultant "residual" is properly taken (as it often is) as an indicator of such progress. As usually calculated, however, the residual also reflects other forces.

Labor Quality

To begin with, the period we consider witnessed a marked advance in

Table 2.4   *Factor Productivity Growth (annual percentages)*

	Without Adjustment of Employment for Educational Attainment	With Adjustment of Employment for Educational Attainment
1950–60	3.63	3.26
1960–70	1.83	1.29
1970–80	.26	– .21

the educational attainment of the Soviet labor force. If we now adjust the growth in employment for the resultant increase in labor quality in the well-known way pioneered by Denison, we still observe the previous downward trend in the rate of growth of factor productivity. The growth tempos throughout, moreover, are appreciably reduced. And during 1970–75, there is now an absolute decline instead of a very modest annual percentage increase in factor productivity.[8]

In proceeding here in a Denison-like way, I also apply to the USSR indexes of the value of different levels of educational attainment that Denison derived for the United States. The results would be little affected, however, if instead reference were made to indexes reflecting Northwest European experience. Denison's educational-value indexes are, as is well known, rather arbitrary even in respect of the countries he was concerned with; their application to the USSR has to be read in that light.[9]

Labor quality can vary also as a result of shifts in the sex composition of the labor force. Trial calculations similar to those made for education suggest that such shifts were not a consequential element in the variation in Soviet factor productivity over the period in question.[10]

The omission of labor-quality improvement due to advances in educational attainment means that, as originally computed, factor productivity growth was overstated. This is so, rather, in so far as such growth is taken as an indicator of technological progress.

Farm land and Natural Resources

From the same standpoint, another source of bias in our computations, though with opposite effects, is the failure to allow in the case of farm land for the undoubted deterioration that occurred as the cultivated area was expanded. If only climatically, the deterioration must have been particularly marked under Khrushchev's famous New Lands Program, with its attendant great increase in the cultivated area in Kazakhstan and Siberia. However, in view of the limited share of farm land in total output the resultant distortion in our data must be slight.[11]

By similar reasoning we may also discount, I think, a comparable distortion due to the failure to account for deterioration of inputs of mineral resources. The distortion is comparable to the one in the case of farm land, for there must also often have been a qualitative deterioration. That would occur simply as resort is had to less rich deposits, but economically the result is the same when extraction must proceed to increased depths or to deposits that are less favorably located geographically. In common parlance, all these circumstances alike give rise to "diminishing returns." Although that is not the preferred analytic usage, the effect is nevertheless a tendency towards higher costs and lower productivity of labor and capital as output expands.

One need not subscribe fully to the more pessimistic Western appraisals of Soviet oil resources that lately have been published to conclude that such diminishing returns have indeed come to prevail, at least lately, in oil extraction (see CIA, June 1977; NATO, 1974). In the USSR diminishing returns have also been encountered in respect of numerous minerals other than oil.

For the magnitude of the resultant distortion of factor productivity, we may obtain some indication if we consider that in the USSR, on the average over the years studied, the ratio of mineral-resource inputs to GNP, exclusive of selected services, should not have been far from 9.3%, that being approximately the magnitude of the ratio in 1966. The real cost per unit of mineral output increased perhaps about 1.5% yearly, or by 45% overall, during the period 1950–75.[12] What this may have meant for factor productivity can most readily be seen by reference to an ingenious model that Solow (1979) has used in a similar context. Imagine that over the period studied the USSR produced no mineral resources but had to import all of them. The rising real cost of such production accordingly translates itself into a corresponding increase in real import prices. Then, Soviet final output net of resource costs would have grown by 0.14 of a percentage point (i.e. .015 × .093) less than if the real price of resources had been constant throughout. The USSR, of course, does not import, but produces domestically, the great bulk of its mineral resources, but the Solow (1979) model may still be applied on the understanding that reference is to the real price of mineral resources in terms of final product that must be foregone in order to free factors for their production.

The foregoing do not comprise all the forces other than techno-logical progress that might have contributed to the productivity residual that we computed, but we may conclude, I think, that technological progress probably was somewhat less rapid than indi-cated by the residual. The pace of technological advance also declined more or less as the residual does.

In the previous section I compared post-World War II productivity growth in the USSR with that in pre-World War II years. In view of the uncertainties regarding that comparison, it would be foolish to try to extend it now to allow for aspects of the sort just considered. I also concluded that Soviet post-World War II productivity growth has been undistinguished by Western standards. The comparative Soviet per-formance becomes even less impressive (cp. Cohn, 1976a) when factor productivity is adjusted to allow for improvement of labor quality. Because of their greater participation in world trade, Western countries until recently have probably been less affected than the USSR by diminishing returns in extractive industries. Thus, calculated productivity growth may understate Western less than Soviet technological advance on that account. All things considered, Soviet technological progress should compare only a little, if at all, more favorably with the West than our calculated productivity residual might seem to indicate.

2.4 Technological Progress Proper

I referred at the outset to two sorts of technological advance: technological progress proper (TPP) and technological progress extended (TPE). TPP occurs through introduction and spread of new production methods that enlarge the technological opportunity sets of production units. On that basis, a larger output is produced at a given resource cost. TPE embraces output expansion at given resource cost that is achieved not only through use of such new technologies, but also through other causes. The data on factor-productivity growth that we have considered thus far should reflect output expansion at given resource cost due to any cause, and thus bear more immediately on TPE than on TPP. Allowance for resource-cost variation due to causes discussed in the previous section should make calculated productivity growth the more congruent with TPE. Results of my calculations, summarized in Table 2.5, are hopefully more or less indicative of what such allowance might come to. Our primary concern, however, is TPP. How might the pace of TPP have compared with that of TPE?

Farm–Industry Labor Transfer

As we saw, the two sorts of technological progress are not easily delineated one from another even in principle, but on the narrow construction of TPP that is favored here, a principal cause of its divergence from TPE in the West has often been the transfer of "surplus", that is, relatively unproductive farm workers, to more productive uses in industry, which occurs as industrialization proceeds. As a result, output produced in the two sectors together at given resource cost increases. While contributing in this way to TPE, these transfers do not affect TPP.

Transfers of farm labor to industry have been occurring in the USSR in the years studied, and very likely have involved shifts from less productive to more productive uses. Allowing for possible differences in skill levels, average farm earnings perhaps have not been inordinately low compared with those in industry. That seems so even if an adjustment, such as described above, is made for the difference in sex

Table 2.5 Measured Factor-Productivity Growth and Technological Progress, USSR, 1950–75

| Average Annual Growth, Factor Productivity, Material Sectors as in Table 2.1, percent | Adjustment to Obtain TPE, percentage points, to Account for: | | | Adjustment to Obtain TPP, percentage points, to Account for: | | |
	Labor Quality Improvement due to Educational Advance	Natural Resource Exhaustion	Farm–Industry Labor Transfers	Economies of Scale	Weather	Planning Reforms; Other Changes in Working Arrangements
1950–60 3.63 (3.69)	−.37		−.39	−.13	...[a]	...
1960–70 1.83 (1.75)	−.54	} +.14	−.33	−.12	...	...
1970–75 .26 (.35)	−.47		−.30	−.12	+.65	...

[a] Assumed negligible

GOSHEN COLLEGE LIBRARY
GOSHEN, INDIANA

Table 2.6   *Average Income per Worker, 1970 (rubles)*

	Without Adjustment for Sex	With Adjustment for Sex
Farm	1473	1787
Nonfarm	1761	2073

structure of the farm and nonfarm labor force.[13] Farm–city price differences favor the farmer in the USSR as they do in the West, though probably to a lesser degree.

But Russia began industrialization with a vast agricultural labor force, and in 1950 farmers still constituted nearly three-fifths of all workers. In such circumstances in the West, the productivity of marginal farm workers has often been low relatively to that of marginal industrial workers, whatever the comparative levels of average earnings. Despite its nonmarket economy, the USSR should not be an exception to that rule.

Soviet industrialization has been notable, however, for the relatively limited contraction occurring in the farm labor force. Although the farm labor force was accordingly still large in 1950, transfers of farm labor to industry have still been comparatively restricted more recently (Table 2.7). The resulting gains in output relative to resource cost should have been reduced on that account.

We must try, though, to assess the gains qualitatively. To do so, I apply separately to farm and nonfarm sectors Cobb-Douglas production functions corresponding to the one already employed for the two sectors together. On this basis I compare the actual growth of factor productivity for the two sectors together with what it would have been if in each interval considered inputs in each sector were constant at their initial levels. Thus, there are no transfers of either labor or capital and, indeed, no changes in the proportions in which the two factors are allocated between sectors. Calculated in this way, factor productivity growth in the two sectors together is simply an average, with initial-year weights, of the tempos of growth achieved in the two sectors separately.

The indicated reduction in the rate of growth of factor productivity

Table 2.7   *Farm and Nonfarm Employment, USSR, 1970–5* (millions)*

	1950	1960	1970	1975
Farm	41.4	38.4	36.4	34.8
Nonfarm	29.4	43.2	60.1	67.5
All	70.8	81.6	96.5	102.3

* The data relate to material sectors, and exclude services. They are essentially from sources of employment data in the Appendix.

compared with the rate of growth originally computed (Table 2.5) is much less than the related magnitude — 1.04 percentage points — obtained by Denison (1967, pp. 202ff, 300ff) in analyzing productivity growth in Italy during 1950–62. That reflects to some extent the relatively more limited farm—industry labor transfers in the USSR, but, more importantly, in my calculation the marginal productivity of farm labor is in effect well below, but still a sizable fraction (in 1970, 46%) of, that of nonfarm labor. Denison assumes the marginal productivity of farm labor in Italy to be zero. Curiously, my adjustment at this point turns out to be of a similar order to Denison's related imputation for Northwest Europe during 1950–62, .46 of a percentage point.[14]

In the West, depending on the stage of development, labor may be in "surplus" not only in agriculture but elsewhere. Accordingly, transfers of such labor too can be a source of growth of output at given factor cost. In so far as they are, they contribute to TPE but might properly be excluded, along with farm—industry transfers, from TPP. A major instance in the West, however, has been transfer of labor from family enterprises in trade, crafts and the like. In the USSR, such enterprises were already largely eliminated under the early plans. Resultant gains in output, therefore, should have been realized before the years on which we focus.

Economies of Scale

In economics texts, exploitation of economies of scale is usually assumed to be quite another thing from application of a novel technology that enlarges the opportunity set of a production unit. The distinction is not always easy to make in practice. However, scale economies are considered here as falling outside of TPP and are thus a further source of divergence of TPP from TPE. With a GNP of $330 billion 1978 dollars, the Soviet economy of 1950 was already rather big by any standard. Reflecting the Stalinian proclivity for giantism in earlier years, the typical industrial firm was also already large compared with those in the West. As early as the fifties, plant size often approached or exceeded least-cost levels as determined by Bain (1962).[15] Scale economies, then, should not have been very consequential in the period studied. Econometric inquiries, such as those of Weitzman (1970) and Desai (1976), seem to point in the same direction, for scale economies are found to have little, if any, explanatory power regarding the growth of post-World War II Soviet industrial production.

Soviet plant scale, however, has continued to increase in size, and so too has the Soviet economy. According to serial data available for diverse industries, the increase in plant size since the fifties might have accounted for a major fraction of the growth of output in industry.[16] Gains from scale economies, therefore, should not be ruled out altogether. I assume that one-half of the growth in factor inputs of material sectors as a whole has been of a sort generating such economies, and that a scale coefficient such as the one inferred for Norway by Griliches and Ringstad (1971, p. 63) from Norwegian data applies here as well. The resultant adjustment (see Table 2.5) is small, and should, if anything overstate economies of scale. Because of the relatively modest size of Norwegian enterprises, such gains should have been more consequential there than in the USSR.[17]

Weather

The weather affects TPE but is clearly outside the range of TPP. I impute the difference between productivity growth during 1970–5 and 1968–78 entirely to subnormal weather during the former interval (see Table 2.5). Weather during 1950–60 and 1960–70 is taken to be normal. According to the CIA (Oct. 1976), though, weather in the USSR tended to be relatively favorable to agriculture during much of the sixties. In Table 2.5, perhaps some downward correction of TPE would be in order for the period 1960–70.

Productivity performance during 1968–78 no doubt differed from that of 1970–5 to some extent because of factors other than the weather, but by adjusting for the entire difference between the two intervals in respect of productivity growth we should obtain a closer approach to more persistent aspects. For our purposes, that should be to the good.

Working Arrangements; Planning Reforms

The period studied witnessed a host of changes in Soviet economic institutions and policies or "working arrangements." Many of these shifts were intended to stimulate the introduction and spread of new production technologies. So far as they had such an effect, they would have contributed to both TPP and TPE. Discussion of these particular shifts is postponed to Section 2.6.

Many changes in working arrangements, however, could have affected output relatively to resource cost quite apart from their impact on the introduction and spread of new technologies. In so far as they did, these shifts are properly considered as affecting TPE alone, and would be still another cause of divergence of TPP from TPE. I refer to the almost innumerable shifts that have occurred in arrangements bearing on labor and managerial incentives, organizational structure, coordinating procedures and the like.[18]

Most, if not all, of the changes were initiated, at least in part, out of a concern to remedy acknowledged deficiencies in existing working arrangements. In the process, the system's directors (to refer in a convenient way used elsewhere to those with ultimate economic responsibilities) clearly sought to increase output relatively to resource cost. It would be surprising if in the upshot there had not been a gain in that respect, yet the Soviet economy has become ever more complex in terms of the numbers of production units and varieties of products to be coordinated, and technological specifications to be met. Were it not for the shifts in working arrangements, performance measured by output relative to resource cost could even have retrogressed. We must, I think, consider seriously this possibility in any event at least in some sectors. Diminishing returns in petroleum extraction for example, must have been compounded by the particular policies pursued in oil development and extraction (see CIA, June 1977, July 1977).

Where in reforming working arrangements aims other than economy of resource cost have been pursued, they must sometimes have conflicted with the latter: a concern for equity, for example, could have been counter-productive in respect of output at given resource cost. At any rate, the period studied was marked by successive wage reforms resulting in a distinct compression of wage differentials that must have affected labor incentives adversely. One reform in working arrangements has sometimes only cancelled another out. The reorganizations of industry by Khrushchev and his successors are the outstanding but not the only case in point. Proverbial aberrations and oddities in planning and management continue to be a subject of complaint in the USSR long after the initiation of measures designed to remedy them.

In order to round out my calculations, I assume that shifts in working arrangements, on the one hand, and offsetting tendencies in complexity and the like, on the other, more or less balanced each other, and together have had no impact to speak of on output at given resource cost (Table 2.5). Should there have been a positive effect, I suspect it would have been modest. Possibly, as suggested, there could have been some retrogression. But any evaluation of the complex matter at issue must be speculative, and mine is clearly no exception. That should be borne in mind.

That completes my accounting for possible sources of divergence, first between TPE and factor productivity as initially calculated, and, now, between TPP and TPE. Table 2.8 gives the results, in terms of annual percentage growth rates.

The adjustments that have now been made to my initial calculations of factor productivity and TPE are glaringly crude, but even so a sharp deceleration in growth of TPP is clear. The presumption is that growth of TPP, along with that of TPE and productivity, has slowed in the course of time to quite a low level.[19]

Table 2.8 *Annual Growth Rates, Material Sector (percentage)*

	Factor Productivity	TPE	TPP
1950–60	3.63	3.40	2.88
1960–70	1.83	1.43	.98
1970–5	.26	−.07	.16

Table 2.9 Comparative Indicators of Technological Change, USSR and Western Countries, 1960–73

Item	1960[a]					1973/1960[b]				
	USSR	USA	UK	FRG	Japan	USSR	USA	UK	FRG	Japan
1 Electricity Consumed per Person Employed in Industry and Construction, thous. kwh	7.80	20.33	5.66	5.96	5.94	1.7	1.6	1.7	1.9	2.5
2 AC Transmission Lines of 300 kv and Above, Share of Total, percent	5.3	2.4	...[c]	2.1	n.a.[d]	2.0	n.a.	n.a.	2.7	n.a.
3 Nuclear Power, Share of Total Electricity Output, percent	.31	.32	8.32	.07	.02	4.1	13.4	1.2	56.1	136.0
4 O_2 Steel, Share of Total Steel Output, percent	3.8	3.4	1.7	2.7	11.9	5.6	16.3	27.8	25.1	6.8
5 Continuously Cast Steel, Share of Total Output, percent	1.3	0.8	1.4	2.1	1.0	4.1	n.a.	2.1	7.8	20.7
6 Metal-forming Machine Tools, Share of Total Stock in Machinery and Metal-working, percent	16.2	23.9	16.1	n.a.	n.a.	1.1	n.a.	.9	n.a.	n.a.
7 NC Machines, Share of Total Metal-cutting Machine-tool Output, percent	.03	1.14	0.11	0.36	.04	59.0	.8	5.7	2.4	32.5
8 Plastics and Synthetic Resins, Per Capita Output, kg.	1.46	15.77	11.20	17.39	7.91	6.4	3.0	3.2	5.9	n.a.

9 Chemical fiber, All, Per Capita Output, kg.	.98	4.28	5.12	5.07	5.92	3.4	3.9	2.6	3.2	2.9
10 Synthetic (noncellulose) Fibers, Per Capita Output, kg.	.07	1.70	1.16	.94	1.26	16.4	8.0	7.0	13.9	9.6
11 Synthetic Rubber, Per Capita Output, kg.	2.1	8.1	1.8	1.5	0.2	1.7	1.3	3.1	4.3	33.5
12 Telephones per Thous. of Population	20	411	156	108	59	2.7	1.5	2.0	2.5	5.4

Source: Amann, Cooper and Davies (1977, pp. 67ff.).

[a] For nuclear power, O_2 steel, and NC machines, 1965; for metal-forming machine tools, 1962.

[b] For electricity consumed and AC transmission lines, 1972/1960; for nuclear power and NC machines, 1973/1965; for metal-forming machine tools, 1973/1962.

[c] . . . = negligible.

[d] n.a. = not available.

Previously I compared Soviet performance with that of the West. In respect of TPP, that is especially difficult to judge. Suppose, as I have reasoned, that the Soviet performance in respect to TPE has been substandard. We must still consider that TPE may sometimes have been buoyed up in the West more than in the USSR by forces other than those contributing to TPP. With due regard for the development stage, for example, that may have been so regarding farm–industry labor transfers (see above, p. 44).

Concerning comparative Soviet and Western TPP, however, we have some further evidence. Taking Boretsky (1966) as a point of departure, Amann, Cooper and Davies (1977) (hereafter A–C–D) have compiled post-World War II data for the USSR and several Western countries on a number of technological indicators that are deemed especially significant. The import of each measure as a barometer of technological progress could be the subject of quite a discourse by itself; as might be expected, the comparative Soviet performance varies with the measure. But the Soviet rate of advance (Table 2.9) seems generally no more impressive than my comparative factor productivity would suggest. Relative to the USA and the UK, the USSR does less well than might have been expected.

The data in Table 2.9 refer to the period 1960–73. A–C–D have also compiled figures for some indicators for 1955–60 and for subintervals of the period 1960–73. These depict a fluctuating Soviet performance rather than any clear trend.

A–C–D have also compiled comparative data for the USSR and the West on the dates of first prototype or commercial production or first industrial installation for some novel technologies and products. They have determined for each country the length of time taken for the new technology of the product in question to represent a given share or output. The resulting indications of leads and lags for one country relatively to another bear immediately on relative technological levels. What counts for comparative TPP is the degree to which such relative levels are changing over time; a systematic difference in level would be consistent with a persistent corresponding difference in TPP. From that standpoint the A–C–D data in question (Table 2.10) seem broadly in accord with the technological indicators in Table 2.9, though perhaps somewhat more favorable to the USSR. In their inquiry A–C–D focus mainly on industry, and in that sector on a limited sample of technologies in basic branches. As they observe, the technologies covered are ones "in which the USSR is normally believed to be in a strong position." Their findings must be read accordingly.

In respect of TPP, I conclude provisionally that the USSR has tended to underperform relatively to the West at a similar development stage. The pace of TPP in the USSR probably has tended also to slow in the course of time. Why has the tempo of TPP in the USSR been modest by Western standards and why has it slowed? I turn now to these questions.

Table 2.10 *Comparative Timing of Introduction and Diffusion of New Technology, USSR and West*

Item	USSR	USA	UK	FRG	Japan
1 Oxygen Steel Making					
First industrial installation	1956	1954	1960	1955	1957
Years to 20% of steel output	16	12	5	11	5
2 Continuous Casting of Steel					
First industrial installation	1955	1962	1958	1954	1960
Years to 5% of steel output	17	7	16	14	10
3 Synthetic Fibers					
First commercial production	1948	1938	1941	1941	1942
Years to 33% of chemical fiber output	25	21	23	23	21
4 Polyolefins					
First commercial production	1953[a]	1941	1937	1944	1954
Years to 15% of plastics output	17	15	18	21	9
5 HVAC (300 kv and over) transmission lines					
First line	1956	1954	1962	1955	n.a.[b]
Years to 10% of lines over 100 kv	14	16	7	18+	n.a.
6 Nuclear Power					
First commercial station	1954	1957	1956	1961	n.a.
Years to 2.0% of electric power	21	14	6	9	n.a.
7 NC Machine Tools					
First prototype	1958	1952	1956	1958	1958
Years to 1.0% of machine-tool output	13	13	12	15+	15

Source: Amann, Cooper and Davies (1977, pp. 55ff.).

[a] Estimate.

[b] n.a. – not available.

2.5 Conditioning Factors: R and D versus Technological Borrowing

In order to advance technologically a country need not always be inventive. It may instead be able to import new technologies from abroad. Yet importing technologies takes time. Some domestic R and D effort can scarcely be avoided, if only to adapt imported technologies to local circumstances. The nature of the adaptation often determines the resultant economic benefit. Although imported technologies tend to be of a dramatic sort, technological advance must also turn on more pedestrian innovation, which may not be made at all unless prompted by domestic R and D.

Granting all this, a country at an early stage of development may

Table 2.11   *Expenditures on R and D, Selected Countries^a (percent of GNP)*

Country	All Outlays		All Outlays Excluding Those for Defense and Space	
	ca. 1967^b	*1975*	*ca. 1967^b*	*1975*
United States	2.9	2.2	1.2	1.4
France	2.2	1.5	1.5	1.1
West Germany	1.8	2.2	1.6	2.1
United Kingdom	2.7	2.1^c	1.9	1.6^c
Japan	1.8	2.0^d	1.8	2.0^d
Italy	0.6	.9–1.0^c	n.a.^{e}	n.a.
USSR	2.9	3.7	1.4	n.a.

^{a} For Western countries, see National Science Board (1977, pp. 184–7; for the United Kingdom and Italy, OECD (1967, p. 15) and OECD (1979, p. 42). For USSR, R and D from TSU (1976, p. 744); for defense and space R and D, mid-point of range of percentage shares in Nimitz (1974, p. vii). Soviet GNP from National Science Board (1977, p. 185).
^{b} Reference is to these years: USA 1966–7; France, 1967; West Germany, 1966; United Kingdom, 1966–7; Japan, 1969–70; Italy, 1963; USSR, 1965.
^{c} R and D as share of GDP.
^{d} 1974.
^{e} n.a.: not available.

find it economical to limit domestic R and D and to rely for technological advance primarily on imports of technology from abroad. As economic development proceeds, however, an inadequate or ineffective domestic R and D effort can become costly. How different countries compare in respect of technological progress, therefore, could turn in part on the relative magnitudes and effectiveness of their domestic R and D efforts. Differences in these respects should affect not only technological progress generally but TPP.

In trying to understand the substandard Soviet performance regarding TPP, then, it should be observed that the Soviet R and D effort, rather than being deficient in magnitude, appears to have been notably large. Available data on Soviet and Western R and D outlays are not fully comparable in scope, but in relation to GNP the Soviet expenditures have clearly matched or surpassed those of even many advanced Western countries (Table 2.11). Lately, as manifest in related manpower data (Table 2.12) the Soviet effort probably has even surpassed that of the United States.[20]

Our concern, however, is with TPP, and not all R and D outlays contribute to that process. Indeed, productivity measurements, as they have been considered in this essay for the USSR and Western countries, are often understood to exclude a major result of R and D: creation of new products yielding increased final-user values at given resource cost. To what extent that is so is a matter that perhaps merits more attention than it has received; but one need not probe too deeply to conclude that the productivity measures are at best apt to embrace only very partially final-user gains, which are especially relevant in the case of one sort of consumer: defense.

In pondering the import for TPP of comparative Soviet and Western R and D outlays, therefore, we must consider how much of the funds going to R and D in the USSR is assigned to defense. That is a matter on which the Soviet government is highly secretive, but, according to a careful inquiry of Nimitz (1974), defense, together with space, absorbed as much as one-half of all Soviet R and D outlay in the sixties. That is the same share of R and D as has gone to defense and space in the United States, but the Soviet defense and space component has been inordinately large compared with that in Western countries other than the United States.[21] The margin of superiority that the USSR enjoys over Western countries as to the share of R and D in the GNP is largely, if not entirely, obliterated when reference is made to civilian R and D alone (Table 2.11).

The Soviet margin of superiority is reduced the more if allowance is made for the familiar fact that a ruble is not always a ruble. Especially in the case of military expenditures it is often more than a ruble. In respect of both manpower and supplies, priorities for the military sector of one sort or another mean that the effective share of defense in R and D outlays in the USSR is greater than data on R and D outlays in rubles might indicate (Ofer, 1975).

In seeking to understand the sluggish technological progress in the USSR, then, Western analysts have rightly stressed the Soviet preoccupation with R and D for defense. R and D is devoted, however, to creation not only of new weapons but also of new products for household consumption. Here available productivity measures perhaps are not as incomplete as often assumed in their coverage, but

Table 2.12 *Scientists and Engineers Employed in R and D, USSR and USA**

Year	Thousands		Per 10,000 Workers in Whole Economy	
	USSR	USA	USSR	USA
1950	125.2	158.7	14.7	26.2
1955	172.6	254.3	18.5	39.0
1960	273.0	380.9	27.5	55.8
1965	474.5	494.5	42.6	67.0
1970	661.9	546.5	54.2	66.8
1975	873.5	534.8	66.0	61.5

*Scientists and engineers in United States excluding humanities specialists in all sectors and social scientists and psychologists in industry; and in the USSR, excluding humanity specialists. See Nolting and Feshbach (1979, p. 746). On employment in the whole economy in USSR, see Appendix; in USA, *Economic Report of the President* (1978, pp. 288, 290).

no doubt they are incomplete. Moreover, there is something of a counterpart in the West to the inordinately large Soviet allocation of R and D to defense. Of the continuing vast flow of new models of consumers' goods that is a proverbial feature of a Western mixed economy, a good part requires no R and D to speak of to produce them but a still significant fraction of R and D must often go to the generation of new goods for households (see National Science Board, 1977, pp. 29, 251–3; Denison, 1962, pp. 241–4). As for the USSR, varieties of consumers' goods are often observed to be still relatively limited, and so, too, is the frequency of introduction of style and model changes, and in fact of new products generally. Marginal changes are often reported, but many of these apparently are a means to evade price controls and entail hardly any R and D.

Available data on R and D outlays for both the USSR and Western countries can at most reflect only very fractionally the activities of independent inventors. Although not as important as they once were, independent inventors continue to play a significant part in the creation of new technologies in the West: in a limited sample of inventions made during 1953–73 and deemed "important", independent inventors accounted wholly or in part for 17% in the United States, 16% in France, 34% in West Germany, 2% in the United Kingdom and 7% in Japan (Gellman Research Associates, 1976, pp. 69–72; see also Jewkes et al., 1959, pp. 91 ff). Independent inventors are also active in the USSR, but at most their contribution probably only rivals that in those Western countries where independent inventors are relatively inactive. Reportedly they account for no more than 7% of all inventions that are awarded a certificate in the USSR, the Soviet counterpart of the Western patent (see Martens and Young, 1979, p. 477; Berliner, 1976, pp. 108–11).

To conclude, the precise magnitudes of Soviet and Western R and D efforts that might contribute to TPP is uncertain. The USSR, however, does not enjoy an advantage over the West such as their notably large outlays for R and D of all sorts might suggest.[22]

So much for magnitudes. In respect to R and D, effectiveness also matters, and a substandard performance in that regard must be a source of Soviet sluggishness in respect of TPP. So at any rate we are led to conclude by a number of Western studies of Soviet R and D administration. Apparently costly shortcomings, parallel to those in Soviet planning generally, have abounded. The system's directors have been by no means oblivious of or indifferent to such features. Over the period studied they have sought to counter them, but dubious practices somehow persist and R and D administration continues to be a subject of complaint.[23]

The deficiencies are by now fairly familiar. The following seem to be among the more noteworthy: imperfect, though as a result of successive reorganizations probably improving, integration of R and D with production, with a resultant tendency of R and D proposals to be of doubtful practicality; a tendency towards dubious incentive arrangements for R and D (especially in earlier years these seemingly provided R and D personnel with little, if any, inducement to be concerned with ultimately successful application, a paper "for the shelf" being a not unusual end result); a further tendency, related to the foregoing features, towards underemphasis on development work, particularly preparation of prototypes; the lack of competition in R and D work; overspecialization of R and D personnel and agencies; and bureaucratic obstacles to collaboration among agencies in different ministries.

This comment by *Pravda* (Oct. 19, 1973; quoted in Parrott, 1980, p. 86) indicates some of the more persistent deficiencies:

> The essential criteria for evaluating the activity of institutes and design offices must be the newness, promise and significance of their inventions and discoveries, the economic effect of their application and the number of licenses sold . . . The various possibilities for this have yet to be fully exploited. Some institutes remain for years outside of public and administrative influence and criticism. The lack of differentiation in terms of material incentives still persists. At times . . . those who provide our science and technology with original achievements and those who only repeat what is already known receive equal compensation. Bonuses are usually given out for all machinery and equipment that is developed or put into production, even if it is really not at all new. As a result, sizable funds are wasted as rewards for the redevelopment of equipment and technology from the past.

Sales of licenses referred to must be those made to foreign concerns; in the USSR inventions are made available domestically without charge.

A comparative study of Soviet and Western R and D administration has yet to be made. R and D administration in the West doubtless has its limitations, but whether overall those limitations can compare with those of R and D administration in the USSR is doubtful.

All of this, of course, is not to say that the USSR has suffered any corresponding lack of new technologies. A shortfall in the output of domestic R and D can in a degree be compensated for by borrowing technology from abroad. As explained, however, inordinate reliance on technological borrowing could be a source of sluggishness in TPP. Where — as in the USSR — considerable funds are actually expended on TPP and relevant R and D, inordinate borrowing from abroad must also put the effectiveness of the R and D administration in doubt. For the USSR that would tend to compound already existing misgivings.

Of interest, therefore, is a massive inquiry by Sutton into the origins of Soviet technology. Sutton (1973, p. 370) summarizes his findings on the sources of technologies employed in some seventy-six activities in a wide range of industries as follows:

> In the period 1917 to 1930 no major applied technologies originated in the USSR. In the period 1930 to 1945 only two such processes originated in the USSR, but in another five areas the Soviets developed and applied

some major technology and we find both Soviet and Western processes used. In the period 1945 to 1965 three processes were of Soviet origin and again five technical areas used both Soviet and Western processes.

If the USSR borrowed foreign technologies extensively during the period in question, it was not alone in doing so. Since World War II the USA by all accounts has been by far the chief contributor to the world's technological pool. Not only the USSR but most Western countries have borrowed foreign technology extensively, with the USA as a principal source. It seems doubtful, however, that the borrowing by Western countries could have matched that by the USSR, as depicted by Sutton. In any comparison between the USSR and the West, due regard must be paid to the still not very advanced Soviet stage of development. Reliance on borrowing might be expected to be greater the less advanced the country. But also to be considered is the large size of the Soviet economy, as indicated by a GDP in 1960 of over half that of the United States and several times that of such countries as France, Western Germany, the UK, Italy and Japan. Other things equal, comparative contributions of domestic inventive activity and technological borrowing from abroad should vary with size.

Sutton's findings are sometimes questioned, but, after a careful review of Soviet chemical technology, A–C–D (1977) conclude only that Sutton may overstate the degree to which the USSR has imported equipment embodying Western technology. As they acknowledge (pp. 43, 275–6), "the Soviet Union alone in this entire group of countries [the USSR, USA, FRG, UK, France, Italy and Japan] has never been the original innovator of a major plastic material or chemical fiber . . . . " A–C–D findings as to the first introduction of new technologies (Table 2.7) also seem consistent with Sutton's findings on the origins of Soviet technologies.

I conclude that limitations in the effectiveness, though not the volume, of Soviet R and D probably contributed to the relatively sluggish pace of TPP in the USSR. We would also wish to know to what extent, if at all, the decline in the growth rate of Soviet TPP since the fifties may have originated in the same factors. The known facts are readily stated. As a share of GNP, Soviet R and D outlays rose sharply over the period in question (Tables 2.11, 2.12; Greenslade, 1976, pp. 273, 297). The share of such outlays devoted to defense must also have risen. But it is difficult to discover at this point any reason for the slowdown in TPP. Similarly, in R and D, as in planning generally, reform in the USSR has again and again only been a prelude to more reform, while familiar complaints about underperformance have continued. The effectiveness of R and D, however, should not have deteriorated; there might well have been some improvement. Here, therefore, no explanation can be found for the slowdown in TPP.

I turn next to the Soviet innovation process. Perhaps we can gain some insight there into the slowdown as well as further understanding of the relatively slow pace of Soviet TPP.

2.6 Conditioning Factors: The Innovation Process

Innovation, which embraces not only the first introduction but also the later spread of new technologies, is generally agreed to be a flawed process in the West. Most importantly, patents may be used to prevent dissemination of new technologies. Even if that is not done and licensing is allowed, the fees charged must be viewed as an economic disadvantage (for, as the primers teach, new technological knowledge is, from a social standpoint, ideally distributed as a free good). In the absence of patents, moreover, commercial secrecy can still constitute an effective barrier to the spread of new technologies.

In the USSR, restrictive patents are practically unknown[24] and commercial secrecy, too, although sometimes reported, can be of only relatively limited significance. The Soviet innovation process, however, has limitations of its own, and these could easily be an important cause of the relatively modest pace of TPP in the USSR.

The limitations relate in part to the behavior of the individual enterprise (*predpriiatie*). The enterprise under Soviet centralist planning, of course, has only restricted autonomy, but, with responsibilities typically limited to a single production unit, its management possesses detailed knowledge of technologies in use. How vigorously potential innovations are pursued and what is achieved by their introduction necessarily depends on the management's interest in engaging in such activities. That interest is very often weak at best. Evidence of this began to surface long ago, but owing chiefly to Amann, Berry and Davies (n.d.) and Berliner (1976) we now grasp more clearly than we could before the main underlying causes: proverbial bureaucratic hurdles attendant on obtaining clearances and interdepartmental cooperation for a new technology, with its associated variations in inputs and outputs; uncertainty as to results, an inevitable feature anywhere, that seems often compounded under centralist planning, particularly if novel kinds of equipment or supplies are required; relatively modest material rewards compared with those obtainable if the risky innovation is not undertaken.

Here as elsewhere the system's directors have been aware of and have struggled to alleviate deficiencies, but apparently with only limited success. Writing in 1977, for example, the distinguished Soviet economist, Academician A. G. Aganbegian, had this to say on the Soviet innovation process:

> ... The introduction of many experimental systems is being held up by the excessive complexity of the instructions concerning the rights and possibilities of enterprises in this regard. Every change, even an insignificant one (in table of organization, pay, personnel assignments), requires paperwork of such proportions as to make even the most optimistic executives lose their taste for change.

Here is how Z. Sirotkin, Chief Design Engineer of the Belorussian Motor Vehicle Plant and USSR State Prize Laureate, viewed matters regarding incentives as recently as 1974 (quoted in Berliner, 1976, p. 490):

> Unfortunately the "mechanism" of the Economic Reform has proved insufficiently effective when applied to the question of putting new equipment into production. After all, for production workers, the manufacture of a new machine means, first of all, new concerns and difficulties. The work rhythm is disrupted, and many new problems appear. Under the existing situation, this causes the performance indicators to decline and the enterprise incentive funds to grow smaller. It is for this reason that some plant executives brush aside innovations proposed by science.
>
> ... This is especially true if the plant has achieved a stable work rhythm and high-quality output and has all the benefits the Economic Reform provides; as for material incentives to induce changes, there are none.
>
> In a time of general well-being the plant manager would have to be a very farseeing person indeed to feel any concern or anxiety and to undertake the preparatory work for producing a new model of the machine. For in the next few years that promises many difficulties.

As is often the case with Soviet "self-criticism," Sirotkin exaggerates the inadequacy of incentives for innovation. But, having probed carefully the intricate arrangements that prevail, Berliner (1976) concludes, perhaps too cautiously (p. 490):

> Our guess is that the differential reward for innovation, relative to the reward for competent but non-innovative management is too small to induce a high rate innovation, and that the small differential is a major obstacle to innovation.

Berliner focuses on managerial-bonus arrangements. Soviet policy and practice regarding promotion, demotion and dismissal of managerial personnel have yet to be explored in any depth, but an adverse impact on career prospects must be among the possible penalties for failure that are of concern to enterprise management when pondering potential innovations. The adverse impact must be the greater in an economy where ultimately there is only one employer. On an abstract plane, Bergson (1978c) has shown that, for risk-averse personnel, even modest career penalties might discourage risk taking unless success were rewarded not only with corresponding career gains but with bonuses possibly much exceeding the basic wage. Existing rewards for successful innovation in the USSR are the less effective when seen in that light.

In the West an enterprise is penalized when an innovation turns out awry, but it may also be penalized for not innovating, for a more venturesome competitor may encroach on the market of a less venturesome one. The competitive threat that is thus posed must be a major spur to innovation generally. And so far as there are laggards, and the threatened encroachment on their markets by innovative firms materializes, that in itself represents a way in which new technologies may spread. The fact that this spread is only indirect, via the supplanting of lagging by innovative firms, makes it not less effective, and must be a significant source of TPP in the West.

To what extent similar forces are operative under Soviet centralist planning is yet another relatively unexplored aspect of that system, but the counterpart to the Western competitive process must be slender at best. The consequences for TPP must have been and are correspondingly adverse. True, determination of technologies of *new* firms is essentially the province of superior authorities rather than of managers of existing enterprises, and superior authorities have not been lacking in initiative in that sphere. The systematic introduction of advanced technologies in new enterprises became a hallmark of Soviet development under the earliest five-year plans and has remained so ever since.

That is an important fact in itself. But for it Soviet TPP would have been even more sluggish than it has been. The resultant threat to and encroachment on the "markets" of older enterprises, however, must have been comparatively limited in an economy where superior authorities themselves are continually pressed to achieve intensive utilization of capacity in the interests of fulfilling taxing output goals. No doubt partly for this reason, enterprise liquidation is, clearly, an extraordinary rarity. Because of a concern to limit involuntary unemployment, staff curtailment which might free labor in older firms for employment in newer ones also encounters legal and administrative obstacles: even the venturesome firm might find it difficult effectively to exploit an innovation.[25]

So much for the domestic counterpart in the USSR, such as it is, of the competitive process that is so important to innovation in the West. In the West that process also embraces active foreign competition. With imports as a spur and direct investment from abroad as a carrier, innovation proceeds all the more expeditiously. Not the least of the reasons for a sluggish TPP in the USSR, therefore, must be the state trading monopoly, which carefully controls and mediates foreign access to Soviet markets and excludes altogether direct investment from abroad.

I have been discussing working arrangements regarding innovation in the USSR. In gauging Soviet performance in this sphere, reference should again be made to the comparative data of A–C–D that I discussed earlier (Tables 2.9, 2.10). Some of these data bear particularly on innovation, though, as noted, they relate more to relative technological levels than to changes in those relative levels over time. The latter are more immediately indicative of comparative TPP.

Also illuminating, though with the same caveat, are comparative data compiled by Martens and Young (1979) on "lead" times between application for a patent (in the USSR, certificate) and recorded first introduction of an invention. The data for different countries are admittedly not fully commensurate, but it is still of interest that among samples considered for different countries the Soviet lead time tended to be relatively long: at the end of two years, only 23% of Soviet inventions had been implemented. The corresponding figure for the United States was 66%, and Western Germany, 64%.

Results of a survey of the experience of British exporters of machine tools and chemical technology to the USSR (Hanson and Hill, 1979) bear immediately on technology transfer but are also indicative of the functioning of the Soviet innovation process more generally. In both industries, the time elapsing between receipt of an inquiry and final commissioning was found typically to be distinctly longer than for comparable transfers to Western countries: in machine tools, "an estimate of two and three times" that required for a comparable transfer to a Western country "would not appear to be too inaccurate"; in chemicals, lead-times averaged 6 years and 10 months, or "3½ to 4 years longer than a characteristic West European lead time." For machine tools, Soviet performance is compared with that of "advanced" Western countries. The particular West European countries considered in the case of chemicals are not indicated. In both cases, an explicit comparison with less advanced Western countries would also be of interest.

I have been focusing on aspects of the Soviet innovation process that prevailed more or less generally during the period studied. Like the facts set forth previously on R and D, those that have been considered regarding innovation appear to fit in with our prior finding on the likely substandard Soviet performance regarding TPP. We also inferred previously, however, that the pace of TPP in the USSR has slowed. We discovered no explanation for this slowdown in the sphere of R and D. I turn therefore for an alternative explanation to aspects of the innovation process that might have caused its performance to vary over time. These admittedly do not act in only one direction, but on balance they could have produced a slowdown in TPP.

One feature affecting the Soviet innovation process over time has already been alluded to: reforms in working arrangements bearing on coordination and managerial incentives. These apparently have not been especially effective, but should at least have been more a source of acceleration than of retardation of TPP. The reforms in managerial compensation, for example, should have been to the good, though incentives for risk-taking must still be weak.

The impact on the Soviet economy of technology transfers to the USSR that have been occurring under detente since around the mid-sixties has become a somewhat controversial issue. It is also a matter not to be settled here, but our concern in any event is with the long-term variation in Soviet performance regarding innovation. From that standpoint, it should be observed that Soviet technological borrowing is not exactly novel. It is true that transfers lately have, more often than previously, been of a turnkey or otherwise negotiated sort, but Soviet borrowing of technology in one form or another has been occurring on a wholesale scale ever since the earliest five-year plans.

Moreover, whatever the impact of detente, technology transfers if anything should have been more consequential in earlier post-World War II years. If so, the down-trend in transfers could have been a source of slowdown in TPP.

I refer particularly to the impetus to Soviet technology borrowing provided by the backlog of new Western technologies that must have been available to the USSR for exploitation immediately after World War II. Gains from "catching up" in that sphere would have been compounded by the possibility of applying advanced technologies in the restoration and reconstruction of partially destroyed industrial works. Although the USSR in 1950 had already exceeded its pre-war output (GNP in 1950 was 124% of 1940; Bergson, 1961, p. 210), much of the vast war-time destruction remained to be made good.[26]

Even according to an optimistic view the impact of technology transfers under detente appears to be rather modest overall, though significant in some industries. Thus, a hypothetical reduction of imports of Western machinery over the years 1968–73 that cumulatively came to some 16% of the entire stock of such machinery on hand in the USSR in 1973 would have meant a reduction of but 0.1 of a percentage point in the yearly rate of growth of the GNP during 1968–73 (Green and Levine, 1977). Reference, however, is only to technology transfers associated with imports of machinery. Although "indirect effects" through diffusion are supposedly also represented, the underlying statistical analysis can hardly have captured these fully. The above calculation is, moreover, not intended to and could not represent gains to the USSR from any and all technological borrowing, whether occurring through machinery imports or otherwise. But, to repeat, the gains from such borrowing in pre-detente years could well have been even greater. In this view, detente may only have arrested a downtrend that was already in process as post-World War II "catch-up" opportunities became progressively exhausted.[27]

In the course of time, opportunities for borrowing technologies from abroad should have declined in any event, but they should have diminished also as a result of the slowing of technological progress in the West. In the United States, the chief contributor to the world's technological pool, the slowdown has been marked. It seems to have occurred, however, primarily since 1973 (Denison, 1979, p. 105). Soviet TPP would have been affected, but only in the most recent years.

To the extent that new technologies are embodied in and require introduction of new sorts of capital goods, the innovation process is in part but an aspect of capital-replacement policy. We must record as one more source of sluggishness in Soviet TPP, therefore, the tendency in the USSR to discount obsolescence as a factor warranting capital replacement, and to seek rather to prolong service lives through continuing maintenance and repairs. As a result, service lives probably have often been unduly lengthy by Western standards (Cohn, 1976b; 1979). Obsolescence, however, while neglected in earlier years, has been accorded increasing attention in the course of time, and service lives have been correspondingly reduced. That by itself should have tended to accelerate TPP. But a related offsetting factor has been the progressive slowdown in the growth of gross investment in fixed capital, from 12.6% annually in the fifties to a planned increase of only 3.6% annually in the late seventies (Bergson, 1978a, p. 232). The resultant retardation in TPP, however, was probably well below .4 of a percentage point annually.[28]

The sharp decline in the rate of growth of investment volume since the fifties is part of a larger process that has been unfolding since Stalin and that has embraced also persistently rapid growth of consumption (Bergson 1978a). Although defense outlays have also tended to expand more or less in step with the growth of GNP, expansion of industries primarily serving the investment and defense sectors has come to be much more nearly in balance with expansion of those primarily serving consumption. I offer it as a hypothesis which I cannot try to verify here that in the USSR TPP has traditionally been more rapid in the former than in the latter industries. If so, the structural change that has occurred could be one more reason for a slowdown in TPP in the economy generally.

2.7 Conclusions

I have distinguished between two concepts of technological progress: technological progress proper (TPP), representing in a restricted way the introduction and spread of new technologies enabling the community to increase output at a given resource cost, and technological progress extended (TPE). The latter embraces not only the foregoing causes of an increase in output at given resource cost but also others, such as incentive reforms, amelioration of a historically distorted resource allocation, weather fluctuations, and so on.

In this essay I have focused primarily on TPP, but technological progress of either sort should be manifest in corresponding variations in output per unit of factor inputs, or factor productivity, as such a coefficient has come to be called. For purposes of quantitative appraisal, therefore, I first compiled data of a conventional sort on the growth of factor productivity. After allowing for changes in factor inputs not initially accounted for, I obtained measures of TPE. By adjusting additionally for the impact of causal aspects other than the introduction and spread of new technologies, I also derived measures of TPP.

The initial computation of factor productivity is flawed by limitations in both underlying data and methodology, while further adjustments to derive TPE and then TPP are often conjectural at best. In the upshot, however, TPP is found to have generated these annual percentage increases in output per unit of factor inputs in material sectors of the Soviet economy: 1950–60, 2.88; 1960–70; .98; 1970–5,

.16. Granting all the limitations of the computations, TPP probably has slowed to quite a low tempo over the period studied.

In respect of TPP, the Soviet performance appears to have been within the range of Western experience, but inferior to that expected of a Western country at a comparable stage of development.

The ultimate concern of this essay is with prospects for the future. Turning finally to that aspect, on such a complex matter the inclination must be simply to opt for the "naive" hypothesis that past trends will continue. On reflection, some such outcome does seem likely, but perhaps we can gauge prospects more clearly and with a better grasp of probabilities if we consider that a substandard Soviet performance hitherto could be a ground for optimism. There is clearly room for improvement.

And, while reforms in relevant working arrangements do not appear to have been especially effective thus far, numerous revisions were initiated only in the latter part of the period studied. They may require more time fully to bear fruit. It would be surprising if the years ahead are not also marked by still other reforms that have yet to be initiated or even conceived.

Yet, among all the sources of difficulty that the Russians have experienced in respect of TPP, three or four appear to stand out as relatively decisive: bureaucratic obstacles attendant on multiple clearances and organization of interdepartmental cooperation for a new technology; the weakness of domestic and foreign competition, that might spur innovation; impediments to labor transfers from lagging to more technologically advanced enterprises, and inadequate incentives.

While subject to amelioration, the first two aspects are more or less integral to the system of centralist planning that in essentials has now been in effect in the USSR for over six decades. There is no indication now of its prospective demise. Impediments to labor transfers originate chiefly in a commitment, apparently deemed fitting in a socialist society, to minimize involuntary unemployment. As for incentives, the system directors hitherto have proceeded with distinct caution in this regard. The USSR today is not notable for egalitarianism, but large and conspicuous managerial bonuses, such as might be needed to induce more adequate interest in innovation, probably are felt to be politically, if not ideologically dubious.

The slowdown in TPP is not due to any deterioration in working arrangements — as indicated, these should have improved. Rather, the reduced pace of TPP probably reflects the unfolding of other forces, principally the progressive exploitation of "catch-up" opportunities present after the war and the shift in the course of time towards a structurally more nearly balanced growth. By now these forces have practically run their course and should not be a further source of slowdown of TPP in future.

Encouragement afforded to technology transfers from the West by detente must have served to dampen somewhat the slowdown in TPP, but, as Afghanistan reminds us, such transfers can be discouraged as well as encouraged. Soviet technological borrowing from the West must suffer in any event should the recent slowdown in Western technological advance persist.

We can only speculate as to the sum of the diverse forces determining the future pace of Soviet TPP. A distinct acceleration is not precluded, but more likely advance will continue at a slow pace more or less comparable to that which has prevailed lately. A negative rate of TPP, although imaginable, is presumably not among the contingencies to be seriously reckoned with.

Although TPE was derived primarily as an element in the computation of TPP, it has an interest of its own. Given prospective TPP, the corresponding TPE now follows from a reversal of adjustments such as I made previously to derive TPP for the past years. In calculating TPP for 1970–5, however, one of the adjustments made to TPE was an addition to allow for abnormal weather (Table 2.4). In reversing the previous computation, no corresponding deduction from prospective TPP is to be made as we are now concerned with TPE in the long run.

With that understanding, TPE might, by projection of past experience, be expected to exceed TPP by from .4 to .5 of a percentage point. A larger differential than that is possible in the future, but does not seem very likely when it is considered that a deduction made previously from TPE for economies of scale probably overstated gains from that source. Reversal of the previous deduction now should be even more of an overstatement, for gains from scale economies are usually supposed to diminish as scale increases.

Still another deduction from TPE was made previously for output gains from farm to industry labor transfers. By Western standards such transfers have been inordinately low, and the farm labor force of the USSR has come to be notably large for a country at the Soviet stage of development (as measured, of course, by indicators other than that of the share of agriculture in the total labor force; say, by GNP per capita). There is thus a potential for increased output gains from this source. But additional costs for urban housing and infrastructure needed to accommodate transferees probably have caused the government to limit its exploitation previously. They should continue to do so in future. In deriving TPP from TPE I made no allowance one way or the other for the impact of changes in economic working arrangements apart from those bearing on R and D and innovation. Any gains in respect of output at given resource cost, in other words, were supposed to be offset by planning difficulties associated with increasing economic complexity and the like. If that supposition should be projected to the future, it must be understood that at this point an error is possible in either direction.

Note that TPE was obtained in turn by deducting from factor productivity as initially computed, an allowance for labor quality improvement due to educational advance. I also added to factor productivity as initially calculated an allowance for natural-resource exhaustion. Since the former adjustment exceeded the latter, factor productivity as initially computed exceeded TPE: by .2 to .4 of a percentage point. In the future, the educational quality of the labor force can change only slowly, but if the CIA is at all reliable on oil extraction, natural-resource exhaustion should be decidedly more costly to the USSR in the years ahead than it has been hitherto. The margin between these two aspects, therefore, should dwindle if it does not vanish altogether.[29]

In considering the sources of past productivity growth I made no allowance for labor-quality variation that may have occurred on account of the rapid increase experienced in consumption standards. Standards tended to increase practically throughout the period studied, but the gains over the low levels that prevailed under Stalin could have been particularly favorable to worker morale and productivity in the earlier post-Stalin years. If they were, that would have been a further source of divergence of factor productivity as initially computed, from TPE. In any event, in appraising prospects we must consider that any marked deceleration in consumption standards might have an adverse impact on productivity growth in the future. Hence, calculated productivity would then be further depressed relatively to TPE. Such a deceleration of growth in consumption standards seems a distinct possibility (Bergson, 1978a).[30]

In sum, if my projection of TPP is not too far from the mark, the USSR should find it difficult in the future to raise the rate of growth of calculated factor productivity much above the very modest tempo that has prevailed lately: .91% yearly.[31] More likely there will be further decline from this tempo.

I have been referring to productivity in material sectors. It should be recalled, therefore, that for the entire GNP productivity growth has been distinctly slower than for material sectors alone: during 1968–78, .57 compared with .91% annually. Productivity growth for the entire GNP has for some time been drifting downward relatively to that for material sectors (see Table 2.3). There is no basis to think that this trend will be reversed in the future.

I have now ventured well beyond TPP, the primary concern of this essay, and often into areas that are being explored in other contributions to this volume. Even a very provisional appraisal, however, may facilitate juxtaposition of my results with related findings of others.

To return to TPP, I tacitly omitted the possibility that in order to accelerate TPP, the government might increase the relative volume of resources devoted to civilian R and D. Although such outlays are already sizable, they could still be increased. Without a radical improvement in working arrangements for R and D and innovation, the resultant gains in TPP would likely be modest, but doubtless there would be gains. The gains would be more substantial if the increase in civilian R and D were at the expense of military R and D, for, as indicated, ruble-for-ruble the resources devoted to military R and D must be higher-powered than those devoted to civilian R and D. On any scale, however, a shift from military to civilian R and D is apt to occur only as part of a larger reallocation of resources from defense to civilian uses generally. That contingency and also the further possibility of a shift in resources from consumption to growth, including capital investment and civilian R and D, I must leave for a separate inquiry.

Civilian R and D might also be increased at the expense of investment. To what extent that might be appropriate must depend on the comparative returns to the two sorts of outlays. That is a matter on which Soviet authorities themselves are probably not too clear. Expenditures on all R and D, military as well as civilian, on the one hand, and investment, on the other, have varied closely together in the course of time.[32] Perhaps that reflects a policy decision that will not be abandoned easily.

In discussing prospective TPP and TPE, I assumed that in the future Soviet planning will continue to be of the centralist sort. Should that system of planning finally be abandoned, the alternative presumably would be some form of market socialism that would allow relatively great autonomy to the enterprise and involve extensive use of markets as a coordinating device. With such a change in working arrangements, the presumption must be that both TPP and TPE could be affected favorably. That eventuality must also be left for another inquiry.[33]

The subject of this essay, Soviet technological progress, is a familiar one. To my profit, I have been able to draw here on much previous research by Western scholars. It is striking, however, how much remains unsettled. That is inherently so regarding prospects for the future, but uncertainties also abound regarding past trends. To resolve such doubts I have often been able to offer conjectures. Hazardous as such a procedure must be, it may serve at least to underline the need for still more research on an important theme.

2   Appendix: Sources and Methods for Table 2.1

1.   Gross product

On the growth of the GNP, see Greenslade, 1976, p. 273. For material sectors, gross product is obtained by deducting from GNP the output of services, as given in Greenslade, p. 271. His index numbers for GNP and sectoral outputs are converted to ruble figures; see Greenslade, p. 284.

2.   Labor

(a) *Employment.* For all sectors, this is civilian employment plus the armed forces, as given in Feshbach and Rapawy (1976, pp. 132, 135) and Feshbach (1978). For material sectors, I deduct the armed forces, and also employment in services, as given in Feshbach and Rapawy (p. 135), but then restore employment in trade, public dining, and material technical supply, sales and procurement, as in Rapawy (1976, pp. 28–29).

In the foregoing, I refer to data outside parentheses. As to parenthetic figures, reference is to totals inclusive of an allowance for penal labor amounting in 1950 to 3.5 millions, in 1960 to 1.5 millions, and in 1970 and 1975 to 1.0 million. On these magnitudes, see Bergson (1961, pp. 443ff).

(b) *Hours*. For material sectors average annual hours per worker are obtained from civilian employment as above in 2(a) and corresponding data on such employment in man-hours in Feshbach and Rapawy (1976, p. 138), for all sectors. I also allow for hours of military personnel averaging 1780 a year, or the same as that indicated for civilian workers in 1970. For both all sectors and material sectors, I assume that hours in 1975 averaged the same as in 1974. For all sectors, I also adjust the resulting variation to allow for the fact that in the case of services changes in hours tend to have no effect on calculated output.

Data in parentheses are intended to allow for changes in the quality of hours associated with a change in their length. For the decade in question, I assume that with 1970 as base the variation in hours, after allowance for such qualitative changes, is simply one-half that without such allowance. For the decade 1950–60, when hours changed most, the result seems to come to much the same thing as might be indicated by more elaborate computations such as Denison's.

3. *Capital*

For all sectors, reference is to fixed capital as represented by Soviet official end-of-the year data on *osnovnye fondy* in TSU, 1961, p. 85; 1971, p. 60; 1973, p. 60; 1978, p.41. The Soviet data refer to fixed capital gross of depreciation and cover, among other things, draft and productive livestock. For material sectors, reference is to fixed capital as represented by corresponding official data for "productive" sectors.

4. *Farm land*

This is sown area as given in TSU, 1961, p. 387; 1966, p. 284; 1978, p. 224.

5. *Factor-share weights*

The underlying absolute data, which are intended to refer to 1970, are in Table 2.13. For all sectors, the labor share is obtained as the income of households, currently earned, less imputed net rents, plus social-security charges, as given in CIA (Nov. 1975, pp. 3, 10). For capital, I allow a 12% return on net fixed capital, as given in CIA, (Nov. 1975, p. 80). I allow only 6%, however, on the net fixed capital in housing, and no return on net fixed capital in services. The data on fixed capital in the cited source are in 1955 rubles. In the light of conflicting official and Western (e.g. Becker, 1974) data, I rather arbitrarily allow for a 15% increase in prices of capital goods from 1955 to 1970.

Table 2.13   *Factor-Share Weights, 1970 (billions of rubles)*

	All Sectors	*Material Sectors*
Labor	202.1	161.2
Capital	105.2	84.1
Farm Land	16.1	16.1

Interest at 12% on inventories is given in CIA, (Nov. 1975, p. 80). I also allow this rate on livestock for fattening and young livestock, as given there, too, pp. 59, 80, 81, 83.

The factor share for capital is intended to be gross of depreciation. On the basis of Moorsteen and Powell (1966, pp. 11–12), I allow for depreciation at the rate of 3.5% on the gross stock of fixed capital. The latter is given in CIA (Nov. 1975, p. 80), though again an upward revaluation of 15% seems indicated.

As for farm land, with US experience as a benchmark, I take agricultural rent to be 30% of farm-labor earnings as indicated in CIA (Nov. 1975, pp. 3, 10).

For material sectors, for labor I deduct from labor's share for all sectors, military pay and subsistence, social security on such earnings, and service-wages and other service earnings and corresponding social security as given in CIA (Nov. 1975, pp. 3, 10, 76).

I allow for a 12% return on the net fixed capital stock and inventories in all sectors, less the corresponding amounts in housing and services as indicated in CIA (Nov. 1975, pp. 80, 83). In the case of fixed capital I revalue capital as was done above. Depreciation is again taken to be 3.5% of the gross fixed stock. The latter is calculated in the same way as the net stock from data in CIA (Nov. 1975, p. 80).

2: Notes

1 To my profit Simon Kuznets kindly read and commented on an earlier version.
2 I thus apply the familiar formula:

$$Y = Ae^{\rho t} \; E^{\alpha} K^{\beta} L^{1-\alpha-\beta} , \quad .$$

where E, K and L are inputs of labor, capital and land; α, β and $1 - \alpha - \beta$ are corresponding factor-input coefficients; ρ is the rate of technological advance, and Y is output.

3 On the comparative growth of Soviet GNP since 1950 in terms of alternative valuation years, reference may be made to these alternative measures of annual percentage rates of growth: for 1950–55, in Bergson (1961) in 1937 prices, 7.6, and in 1950 prices, 7.6; in Cohn (1970), as revised in Bergson (1974), in 1959 prices, 6.3, and in Greenslade (1976), 6.0; for 1950–60, in Cohn (1970) as revised in Bergson (1974), 6.3; and in Greenslade (1976), 5.9; and for 1960–70, in Cohn (1970), as revised in Bergson (1974), 5.5, and in Greenslade (1976), 5.3. Unfortunately, differences in results from different sources are difficult to interpret because the calculations differ not only in valuation years but in other ways. Moreover, valuations are sometimes only partially made in the year to which they supposedly refer.

  Actually, according to further computations, the observed divergence for 1950–60, between Cohn (1970), Bergson (1974) and Greenslade (1976) could be due practically in its entirety to the difference in the nature of the weight imputed to "services," particularly the reduced interest allowed on housing and the exclusion altogether of interest on other fixed capital in the former computation. For purposes of compiling data that are comparable to those available for Western countries, however, there is, I think, much to say for the Cohn (1970), Bergson (1974) procedure, and the Greenslade tempo of growth for 1950–60 might be considered as somewhat understated at least on that account.

4 For both the whole economy and industry, use of $\sigma = .5$ instead of 1.0 evidently reduces the rate of annual growth for pre-1970 and raises it for post-1970 years. Recall that 1970 is our base year. As explained elsewhere (Bergson, 1979, p. 124), with factor inputs growing at different rates, a reduction in σ must have such contrary effects on factor productivity in pre- *and* post-base years.

5 Whether $\sigma = 1.0$ or .5, the earnings share imputed to capital in the base year is, for the whole economy, .52 of that for labor, and, for the material sectors, .54 of that for labor. With $\sigma = 1.0$, of course, the same shares obtain for 1950. With $\sigma = .5$, however, the corresponding ratios in 1950 are 2.1 and 2.4. On the rates of return on capital that such earnings shares might imply, see Bergson (1979).

6 In order to determine the earnings share of capital, therefore, it seemed appropriate to apply this assumed rate to the capital stock in prevailing rubles. In the USSR, however, ruble prices cover not only labor costs but a variety of additional and often more or less arbitrary charges, principally turnover taxes, subsidies and profits. At the same time, no systematic charge is made for interest and rent. If for comparison with rates of return familiar in the West we revalue capital to exclude Soviet nonlabor charges and to include interest and rent the assumed 12% return would rise to 13.6%. With the total of interest and rental charges taken to be the same as initially allowed, the revaluation assumes that the price of capital goods changes in proportion to the price level generally. Similarly a 6% return on capital in prevailing rubles translates into an 8.2% return on capital when that is revalued to conform to Western pricing.

7 More precisely, without explicit charge. Under the government's complex arrangements for procuring farm products, Soviet farmers, of course, have by no means been allowed to retain for themselves the entire proceeds of their labor.

8 Here and below, unless otherwise stated, factor-productivity data cited relate to material sectors.

9 To be more precise, I apply educational-value indexes which are adapted from those Denison derived for the United States and represent slight revisions of those in Bergson (1964, p. 371). I assume that the educational attainment of workers in material sectors in 1950 is the same as that of employment in all sectors and in later years the same as that of the entire labor force. Data that are needed on the distribution of employment and the labor force by educational attainment are from DeWitt (1962, p. 136) and CIA (June 1979, pp. 10, 14). On the comparative impact of use of United States and Northwest European educational-value indexes, see the CIA publication above.

10 I assume one female worker to be equal to .7 of a male worker. Earnings of female workers appear to have averaged about that amount relatively to those of male workers in the USSR. See Riurikov (1977, pp. 118–19). Taken together with available Western and official data on the branch and sex structure of the labor force, the indicated discount means that with adjustment for changes in sex composition employment growth would on the average be compounded by .05 of a percentage point yearly over the period 1950–75.

11 A discount for quality of one-half applied to the increase in cultivated area in the fifties, when the New Lands Program was in full swing, would raise factor-productivity growth during that decade by one-tenth of one percent.

12 The volume of mineral-resource inputs relatively to GNP in 1966 is inferred chiefly from data in Treml et al. (1973, pp. 46, 116) indicating that the gross output, less net exports, of minerals in 1966 amounted to 15.4 billion rubles at producers' prices. This represents, I believe, a nearly comprehensive total, but, improperly for our purposes, includes some processing and also limited inputs of minerals into the mineral-extraction branches themselves. In the light of Becker (1969, pp. 477–8), I raise the indicated total to 18.9 billion rubles in order to allow for subsidies. This is 9.3% of the Soviet 1966 GNP (exclusive of services) which, taken from data in diverse sources, amounted to 204 billion rubles at factor cost.

As for the real cost of mineral extraction, for purposes of the Solow Model (see below) reference is made appropriately to the trend over time in the comparative real cost of mineral extraction, on the one hand, and of final output in the economy generally, on the other. The cited average annual increase of 1.5% is intended to represent the trend in mineral-extraction costs in that comparative sense, and results from a somewhat impressionistic summarization of official price-index numbers in different extractive branches, as given in TSU (1971, p. 175; 1978, p. 142), and comparative trends in average money wages and output per worker in material sectors as a whole. On money wages, see TSU (1978, p. 385); output per worker in material sectors is calculated from data compiled in this essay. I use the implied measures of wage cost per unit of output to deflate nominal price changes in extractive branches, and so to obtain an indication of changes in real costs in the desired sense. The official prices considered are net of turnover taxes, but are still distorted by subsidies; how these may have varied over the period studied is conjectural.

Regarding the underlying calculation of the impact of the increase in the real cost of minerals, let Y be net output of the final good, Then

$$Y = Q - PR,$$

where Q is the corresponding gross output, R is resource imports and P the price of such imports in terms of the final good. We also have

$$Q = F(L, K, R),$$

where L is the labor and K the capital employed in producing Q. Finally,

$$\dot{Y} = (Q/Y) \dot{Q} - (PR/Y) \dot{R} - (PR/Y) \dot{P},$$

where $\dot{Y}$, $\dot{Q}$, $\dot{R}$ and $\dot{P}$ are the relative rates of growth.

13 Aggregate farm and nonfarm household earnings from CIA (Nov. 1975); corresponding employment data from Table 2.7. On the adjustment for sex, see note 10.

14 To be more specific, I assume Cobb-Douglas functions for the farm and nonfarm sectors whose coefficients for capital and labor are proportional to those in the Cobb-Douglas function that I applied to the two sectors together. With farm-land rent amounting as before to 16.1 billion rubles, or 23% of farm output in 1970, the resulting labor and capital earnings shares are for agriculture 51% and 26%, and for industry 66% and 34%. On labor inputs, see Table 2.7. On corresponding capital inputs, see sources and methods cited in the Appendix for such inputs in the two sectors together. On farm and nonfarm outputs, see Greenslade (1976).

With inputs and outputs as thus determined, I find that the marginal productivity of labor in 1970 is 960 rubles per worker in agriculture and 2110 rubles in nonfarm sectors. Note that the computation also implies a higher marginal productivity of capital in agriculture than in nonfarm sectors in 1970, but the difference is slight: 16.7 compared with 14.9%.

15 I am indebted to Leon Smolinski for allowing me to see results of his unpublished study of the size of the firm in the USSR.

16 For the industries in question, the rate of growth of plant size seems to average out at about 5% annually over the years 1956–65. Among industries for which Smolinski could compile serial data on plant size (I rely again on his unpublished study) I refer to 28 nonmachinery branches. Regrettably, among the machinery branches, only two industries—motor vehicles and tractors, with rates of growth of plant size of (-) 2.1 and 7.4% respectively — are covered. During 1956–65, industrial output grew by 7.7% yearly.

17 Of 20,944 mining and manufacturing establishments counted in the Norwegian census of 1963 (Griliches and Ringstad obtain their basic data from this source), only 73 had 500 or more employees. In the USSR in 1970, the *average* enterprise employed 644 workers.

18 Among the more noteworthy: the progressive transformation of agriculture through the liquidation of the Machine Tractor Station; the increasing stress on the state-farm compared with the collective-farm form of organization; introduction of wage-like payments in the collective farm itself and the sharp post-Stalinian increases in procurement prices; successive reorganizations of industry, with the traditional preeminent industrial ministry being superseded by regional councils under Khrushchev and then reestablished as the preeminent entity by his successors; the fluctuating responsibilities of the industrial enterprise (*predpriiatie*) under the 1965 planning reform and its evolving implementation; since 1973, the progressive shift to the association (*ob'edinenie*) as the basic operating agency in industry; the successive revisions of incentives for industrial management under and after the 1965 planning reform; the reforms in the industrial wage system and structure in the late fifties

and more recently; the successive reforms of industrial wholesale prices; and last but no doubt not least the progressively increased application of mathematical techniques and computers to planning.

19 The shifts in working arrangements were rather spread out over time, but I suspect any favorable impact on productivity would have been more pronounced in later than in earlier years. With allowance for such gains, therefore, TPP might, if anything, decline more sharply than I calculate. On the other hand, allowance for possible biases referred to below, n. 26 and p. 67, would have a contrary effect. In the summary tabulation in the text, I assume that the adjustment rate for natural-resource exhaustion that was derived for 1970–5 applies to each subinterval considered.

20 A chief source of incomparability in the R and D expenditure data is the exclusion of outlays for new investment from US totals. Depreciation, however, is apparently included in R and D outlays of the US business-enterprise sector. With the exclusion of investment in construction, the Soviet R and D ratio for 1965 falls to 2.4% and for 1975 to 3.2%. The Soviet totals also include social-science R and D in higher education. Such outlays are omitted from data for the United States and some other Western countries. On the other hand, the Soviet data are probably less inclusive than most Western data in respect of outlays for the development of prototypes. On the comparative scope of Soviet and Western R and D data, see Nimitz (1974); Nolting (1973); OECD (1967; 1979); Campbell (1978).

21 For Western countries, reference is to defense and space R and D that is government funded and supposedly represents activities that are "directly related to military purposes." Just what this means is not entirely clear. One wonders whether, in addition to work on new weapons, some funds do not go to activities of sorts that might raise the output of old weapons, and so clearly contribute to TPP. In compiling data on Soviet defense and space R and D, however, Nimitz has sought to achieve comparability with Western data. The result should be broadly indicative of the size of Soviet allocations to defense and space relatively to those in the West.

22 To return to the issue regarding the inclusion, in the productivity measures above, of increased values relative to resource cost that final users obtain from new products, note that such values would indeed be completely omitted if new products were included in underlying data on aggregate output at their long-run resource cost. Furthermore, such a valuation of new products is clearly the desideratum where the output data are taken, as is often the case, as observations on the community's "theoretic" production possibilities. Should the new products be valued at prices that include above-normal profits, however, the resulting productivity measures are apt to reflect to a degree additional final-user values at given resource cost. That could be so whether reference is to market prices or factor cost, for the latter as well as the former might include above-normal profits.

To what extent do underlying output data reflect additional user values as described above? This is a complicated question. I can only record here that, regarding output data for Western countries, it would be surprising if above-normal profits generated by new final products did not often have an imprint on calculated output. As for output data for the USSR, I have used those of Greenslade where valuation is supposedly at an imputed factor cost that is exclusive of any and all profits. In fact, Greenslade's valuation procedure (1976, p. 284) is decidedly more complex than that, and one wonders whether enhanced user values from new products may not sometimes have an impact even here.

Although I have focused on new products, all that has been said applies as well to quality changes. Indeed, it is difficult to know where one leaves off and the other begins. Note, though, that the question at issue here concerns the degree to which output measures reflect additional user values relative to resource cost. In discussion of quality changes, reference is simply to the degree to which output measures reflect such variations. The question whether there are additional values surpassing additional resource cost may often not be addressed.

On previous discussion of final user values and productivity measures, see Denison (1962, pp. 156–7; 1967, pp. 27–9; 1979, p. 124).

23 See particularly Amann, Berry and Davies (n.d.), Nolting (1973, 1976, 1978), Nimitz

(1974), Campbell (1978), Parrott (1980). Also informative on the Soviet R and D process generally is Germashev (1962).

24 I refer to patents issued to Soviet citizens. Although such patents are legally obtainable, and theoretically confer a restrictive entitlement on the recipient, Soviet inventors practically always find it expedient to apply rather for a "certificate of authorship." The invention is then available without cost for general use, though the persons responsible for it are suitably rewarded.

25 A principal obstacle to staff curtailment is the need to find alternative employment for released workers. See McAuley (1969, pp. 121ff), Berliner (1976, pp. 158ff), Granick (1979), also Manevich (1971, pp. 17, 20), Mikul'skii (1979, pp. 116, 249). I am indebted to Dr Tibor Vais for the last two references.

26 The catch-up process also must often have involved restoration to full operation, with relatively limited commitment of new-capital, of plant and equipment that had been largely or entirely written off. That, however, would only nominally boost TPP, for there would then be one more reason, additional to those considered in Section 2.3, why calculated productivity growth would have failed to allow accurately for the actual growth of inputs.

27 It remains to say that Soviet imports of Western machinery have been relatively very small through much of the period studied, though there has been some increase since 1955. Here are some benchmark estimates by Hanson (1976, p. 796) of the percentage relation between imports of Western machinery and domestic machinery investment: 1955, 1.0–2.0; 1960, 1.7–3.4; 1965, 1.1–2.2; 1970, 1.7–3.4; 1975, 2.4–4.8.

   Note that Green and Levine (1977) refer to imports of Western machinery, exclusive of transport equipment. On the impact of technology transfers under detente, see in addition to the essays of Green and Levine, Hanson (1976), Weitzman (1979), Green (1979), and Toda (1979).

28 An upper limit of .4 of a percentage point follows from an assumption that the capital stock consists of a single kind of asset with a service life of 25 years. I also assume that as of 1950 the capital stock had an average age such as would have materialized if *prior* to that year gross investment had grown steadily for at least 25 years at a rate of 12.6% annually, and that as of 1980 the capital stock had an average age such as would have materialized if *prior* to that year gross investment had grown steadily for 25 years at a rate of 3.6% annually. The resultant average ages are 6.18 and 10.57 years. Hence, over the 30-year interval 1950–80 the average age of capital stock increases by 4.39 years, or by .146 of a year per calendar year. A decline of .4 of a percentage point in TPP is indicated by that degree of aging if we suppose that the entire increase in TPP during 1950–60, 2.9% annually, was of an embodied sort that occurs simply with the introduction of successive new vintages (i.e. .4 = .146 × 2.9).

29 As readily seen, it would vanish if the growth of employment due to educational advance should continue at the 1960–75 rate, and, should the Solow (1978) model of the cost of mineral-resource exhaustion apply, with mineral output rising from 9.3 to 15% of the GNP. Also the real cost of mineral extraction, which I assumed previously to increase by 1.5% yearly, is now supposed to increase by 3.0% yearly.

   I have been referring to factor productivity as initially computed for material sectors. For comparative data on such productivity for the whole economy, see Table 2.1.

30 Consumption standards depend in part on government policy on resource allocation, particularly the division of national income between consumption, investment and defense. In a sense, then, the variation in these consumption standards might be viewed as one more aspect of the changing working arrangements that I discussed above. That might be the more so since the government's policy on consumption did in fact undergo a significant change in the period studied (Bergson, 1978a). But consumption trends are evidently determined by much more than policy, so that their classification with changing working arrangements could be confusing.

31 I refer to material sectors and, to allow for weather fluctuations, again cite the 1968–78 rate of growth.

32 Here are the annual percentage rates of growth of "science" and new fixed investment respectively: 1950–60, 10.5 and 11.5; 1960–70, 7.7 and 6.5; and 1970–5, 6.1 and 4.8. See Greenslade, 1976, pp. 275, 297.

33 Among existing socialist economies, only one, that of Yugoslavia, can be taken to exemplify market socialism, but the Yugoslav performance in respect of TPP and TPE has yet to be systematically studied. The Yugoslav experience is in any event made rather special by the prevalent system of "labor self-management."

Of more interest as a possible prototype for a reformed Soviet planning system is the New Economic Mechanism that the Hungarians have been operating since 1968. Although legacies of the previous system of centralist planning seem too numerous for the NEM to qualify fully as a form of market socialism, the Hungarian system represents a substantial shift in that direction. Here too the impact on TPP and TPE remains to be studied, but Hungarian economists themselves do not appear to claim any major gains in respect to such macroeconomics aspects. Rather the contention is that there have been improvements in quality, assortment and availability. For a survey of the Hungarian experience with NEM, see Portes (1977).

2: References

Aganbegian, A. G., "How to Outwit the Idler." *Current Digest Soviet Press*, June 8, 1977.

Amann, Ronald, Berry, M. J., and Davies, R. W., *Science and Industry in the USSR*. Part 5, no place, no date.

Amann, Ronald, Cooper, Julian, and Davies, R. W., eds., *The Technological Level of Soviet Industry*. New Haven, Conn.: Yale Univ. Press, 1977.

Bain, Joe S., *Barriers to New Competition*. Cambridge, Mass.: Harvard Univ. Press, 1962.

Becker, Abraham S., *Soviet National Income, 1958–64*. Berkeley: Univ. of California Press, 1969.

Becker, Abraham S., "The Price Level of Soviet Machinery in the 1960s." *Soviet Studies* **26**, 3: 363–79, July 1974.

Bergson, Abram, *The Real National Income of Soviet Russia Since 1928*. Cambridge, Mass.: Harvard Univ. Press, 1961.

Bergson, Abram, *The Economics of Soviet Planning*. New Haven, Conn.: Yale Univ. Press, 1964.

Bergson, Abram, *Planning and Productivity under Soviet Socialism*. New York: Columbia Univ. Press, 1968.

Bergson, Abram, *Soviet Post-War Economic Development*. Stockholm: Almquist & Wicksell, 1974.

Bergson, Abram, "Conclusions," in *The Soviet Economy in the Eighties*. Brussels: NATO, 1978a.

Bergson, Abram, "Managerial Risks and Rewards in Public Enterprise." *J. Comp. Econ.* **2**, 3: 211–25, Sept. 1978b.

Bergson, Abram, *Productivity and the Social System — The USSR and the West*. Cambridge, Mass: Harvard Univ. Press, 1978c.

Bergson, Abram, "Notes on the Production Function in Soviet Postwar Growth." *J. Comp. Econ.* **3**, 2: 116–26, June 1979.

Berliner, Joseph S., *The Innovation Decision in Soviet Industry*. Cambridge, Mass.: M.I.T. Press, 1976.

Boretsky, Michael, "Comparative Progress in Technology, Productivity and Economic Efficiency: U.S.S.R. versus U.S.A.." In *New Directions in the Soviet Economy*, IIA. Papers, Joint Econ. Comm., US Congress. Washington, DC: Govt. Printing Off., 1966.

Campbell, Robert W., "Reference Source on Soviet R & D Statistics 1950–1978." Mimeo. Washington, DC: National Science Foundation, 1978.

CIA, "USSR. Gross National Product Accounts, 1970." A(ER) 75–76. Washington, DC: Nov. 1975.

CIA, "USSR. The Impact of Recent Climate Change on Grain Production." ER 76–10577U. Washington, DC: Oct. 1976.

CIA, "A Discussion Paper on Soviet Petroleum Production." Washington, DC: June 1977.

CIA, "Soviet Economic Problems and Prospects." ER 77–10436U. Washington, DC: July 1977.

CIA, "USSR. Trends and Prospects in Educational Attainment, 1959–85." ER 79–10344. Washington, DC: June 1979.

CIA, "Handbook of Economic Statistics 1979." ER 79–10274. Washington, DC: Aug. 1979.

Cohn, Stanley H., "General Growth Performance of the Soviet Economy", in *Economic Performance and the Military Burden in the Soviet Union*. Papers, Joint Econ. Comm., U.S. Congress. Washington, DC: Govt. Printing Off., 1970.

Cohn, Stanley H., "The Soviet Path to Growth: A Comparative Analysis." *Rev. Inc. & Wealth* **22**, 1: 49–60, March 1976a.

Cohn, Stanley H., "Deficiencies in Soviet Investment Policies and the Technological Imperative," in *Soviet Economy in a New Perspective*, 1976b.

Cohn, Stanley H., "Soviet Replacement Investment," in *Soviet Economy in a Time of Change*, Vol. 1, 1979.

Denison, Edward F., *The Sources of Economic Growth in the United States*. New York: Comm. Econ. Developm., 1962.

Denison, Edward F., *Why Growth Rates Differ*. Washington, DC: Brookings, 1967.

Denison, Edward F. *Accounting for Slower Economic Growth*. Washington, DC: Brookings, 1979.

Desai, Padma, "The Production Function and Technical Change in Postwar Soviet Industry." *Amer. Econ. Rev.* **66**, 3: 372–81, June 1976.

DeWitt, Nicholas, "Costs and Returns in Education in the USSR." Unpubl. Ph.D. Thesis, Harvard University, March 1962.

Economic Report of the President 1978. Washington, DC: Govt. Printing Off., 1978.

Feshbach, Murray, and Rapawy, Stephen, "Soviet Population and Manpower, Trends and Policies," in *Soviet Economy in a New Perspective*, 1976.

Feshbach, Murray, "Employment Trends and Policies in the USSR." Mimeo, Aug. 1978.

Gellman Research Associates, "Indicators of International Trends in Technological Innovation." PB–263738. Washington, DC: US Dept. of Commerce, Nat. Techn. Information Service, April 1976.

Germashev, A. F., ed., *Izobretatel'stvo i ratsionalizatsiia*. Moscow, 1962.

Gosplan SSSR, Gosstroi SSSR and Akademiia nauk SSSR, *Tipovaia metodika opredeleniia ekonomicheskoi effektivnosti kapital'nykh vlozhenii*. Moscow, 1969.

Granick, David, "Labor Markets in the USSR", 78. Mimeo. Washington, DC: Kennan Institute, 1979.

Green, Donald W., and Levine, Herbert S., "Macroeconomic Evidence on the Value of Machinery Imports to the Soviet Union," in John R. Thomas and V. M. Kruse-Vaucienne, eds., *Soviet Science and Technology: Domestic and Foreign Perspectives*. Washington DC: George Washington University Press, 1977.

Green, Donald W., "Technology Transfer to the USSR: A Reply." *J. Comp. Econ.* **3**, 2: 179–80, June 1979.

Greenslade, Rush V., "The Real Gross National Product of the USSR," in *Soviet Economy in a New Perspective*, 1976.

Griliches, Zvi, and Ringstad, V., *Economies of Scale and the Form of the Production Function*. Amsterdam: North Holland, 1971.

Hanson, Philip, "International Technology Transfer from the West to the USSR," in *Soviet Economy in a New Perspective*, 1976.

Hanson, Philip, and Hill, Malcolm R., "Soviet Assimilation of Western Technology," in *Soviet Economy in a Time of Change*, v.2, 1979.

Jewkes, John, Sawers, David, and Stillerman, Richard, *The Sources of Invention*. New York: St Martin's Press, 1959.

McAuley, Mary, *Labour Disputes in Soviet Russia, 1957–1965*. Oxford: Clarendon, 1969.

Manevich, E. L., "Vosproizvodstvo rabochei sily i puti uluchsheniia ispol" zovaniia trudovykh resursov v SSSR," in E. L. Manevich, ed., *Osnovnye problemy ratsional'noga ispol'zovaniia trudovykh resursov v SSSR*. Moscow, 1971.

Martens, John A., and Young, John P., "Soviet Implementation of Domestic Inventions," in *Soviet Economy in a New Perspective*, 1979.

Mikul'skii, K. I., ed., *Effektivnost' sotsialisticheskogo proizvodstva i khoziaistvennyi mekhanizm*. Moscow, 1979.

Moorsteen, Richard, and Powell, Raymond P., *The Soviet Capital Stock, 1928–1962*. Homewood, Ill.: Irwin, 1966.

National Science Board, National Science Foundation, *Science Indicators 1976*. Washington, DC: Govt. Printing Off., 1977.

NATO, Directorate of Economic Affairs, *Exploitation of Siberia's Natural Resources*. Brussels: NATO, 1974.

NATO, *The USSR in the Eighties*. Brussels; NATO, 1978.

Nimitz, Nancy, "The Structure of Soviet Outlays on R & D in 1960 and 1968." R–1207–DDRE. Santa Monica, Calif.: RAND, 1974.

Nolting, Louvan E., "Sources of Financing the Stages of the Research, Development and Innovation Cycle in the U.S.S.R." FER—3. Washington, DC: US Department of Commerce, Bur. Econ. Analysis, Sept. 1973.

Nolting, Louvan E., "The 1968 Reform of Scientific Research, Development and Innovation in the U.S.S.R." Fer—11. Washington, DC: US Dep. of Commerce, Bur. Econ. Analysis, Sept. 1976.

Nolting, Louvan E., "The Planning of Research, Development and Innovation in the U.S.S.R." FER—14. Washington, DC: US Dep. of Commerce, Bur. Econ. Analysis, July 1978.

Nolting, Louvan E., and Feshbach, Murray, "R & D Employment in the USSR," in *Soviet Economy in a Time of Change*, vol. 1, 1979.

Organization for Economic Cooperation and Development (OECD), *The Overall Level and Structure of R and D Efforts in OECD Member Countries*. Paris, 1967.

OECD, *International Statistical Year 1975*. Paris, March 1979.

Ofer, Gur, "The Opportunity Cost of the Non-Monetary Advantages of the Soviet Military R & D Effort." R–1741 DDRE. Santa Monica, Calif.: RAND, 1975.

Parrott, Bruce, "Organizational Environment of Applied Research." In Linda L. Lubrano and S. G. Solomon, eds., *The Social Context of Soviet Science*. Boulder, Co.: Westview Press, 1980.

Portes, Richard, "Hungary: Economic Performance, Policy and Prospects." In *East-European Economies Post-Helsinki*. Papers. Joint Econ. Comm., US Congress. Washington, DC: Govt. Printing Office, 1977.

Rapawy, Stephen, "Estimates and Projections of the Labor Force and Civilian Employment in the U.S.S.R. 1950 to 1990." FER–10. Washington, DC: US Dep. of Commerce, Bur. Econ. Analysis, Sept. 1976.

Riurikov, Iu. B., "Deti i obshchestvo." *Voprosy filosofii*: pp. 111–21, no. 4, 1977.

Solow, Robert M., "Resources and Economic Growth." *Amer. Economist* 22, 2: 5–11, Fall 1978.

Soviet Economy in a New Perspective. Papers, Joint Econ. Comm., US Congress. Washington, DC: Govt. Printing Office, 1976.

Soviet Economy in a Time of Change. Papers, Joint Econ. Comm., US Congress. Washington, DC: Govt. Printing Off., 1979.

Sutton, Antony C. *Western Technology and Soviet Economic Development 1945 to 1965*, vol. 3, Stanford, Calif.: Hoover, 1973.

Toda, Yasushi, "Technology Transfer to the USSR." *J. Comp. Econ.* 3, 2: 181–194, June 1979.

Treml, Vladimir G., Kostynsky, B. L., Kruger, K. W., and Gallik, D. M., "Conversion of Soviet Input–Output Tables to Producers' Prices: The 1966 Reconstructed Table." FER–1. Washington, DC: US Dep. of Commerce, Bur. Econ. Analysis, July 1973.

TSU (Tsentral'noe statisticheskoe upravlenie), *Narodnoe khoziaistvo SSSR* (v 1960 g.–1977 g.). Moscow, various years, 1961–78.

TSU. *Narodnoe khoziaistvo SSSR za 60 let*. Moscow, 1977.

Weitzman, Martin L., "Soviet Postwar Economic Growth and Capital–Labor Substitution." *Amer. Econ. Rev.* **60**, 4: 676–92, Sept. 1970.

Weitzman, Martin L., "Technology Transfer to the USSR." *J. Comp. Econ.* **3**, 2: 167–77, June 1979.

3

Population and Labor Force

MURRAY FESHBACH

Introduction

On any basis, short-term or long-term, the prospects for the development of Soviet population and manpower resources until the end of the century are quite dismal. From the reduction in the country's birth rate to the incredible increase in the death rates beyond all reasonable past projections; from the decrease in the supply of new entrants to the labor force, compounded by its unequal regional distribution, to the relative aging of the population, not much glimmer of hope lies before the Soviet Government in these trends. It is true that a new sense of urgency has highlighted the period since the XXVth Party Congress of February–March 1976, but the question remains whether this recent concern is too little and too late, and whether the negative population trends are beyond State control. Moreover, since the initial entry age into the labor force has been defined as age 16, almost the entire labor force for the rest of the century has already been born (except for those expected during the next four years, when significant shifts in demographic trends cannot be anticipated in the very short-run period that four years represent).

At the 1976 Party Congress, Brezhnev called for an "effective demographic policy," without defining what that might be. Undoubtedly he had in mind the current and future trends in population growth — nationally and regionally; in fertility patterns; and in mortality, because these factors must be disturbing to the central authorities. The population as a whole can be expected to grow from the current (1980) level of approximately 265 million to somewhat more than 300 million at the turn of the century. The latter figure is constantly being revised downward as fertility continues its general decline, and as mortality — in all its aspects — climbs. By the last decade of the century the rate of growth of the population will drop to 0.6% per year, about one-third the 1951–5 rate. The projected total for the year 2000 of 308 million (let alone a lower figure), which is based on US computations, represents a sharp reduction from the Soviet expectations of 340 to 350 million persons, which TSU estimated not too long ago.

3.1   Population Growth, Overall and Regional

Despite its overall growth, the Russian population's share in the total population of the USSR is expected to decline from 52.0% of the national total in 1980 to only 48.0% by the year 2000 (see Table 3.1). This reflects an expected absolute increase of only 10 million Russians. These projections also assume a zero net migration between all republics. Actually, there *has* been a recent tendency towards net migration, albeit small, into the RSFSR for the first time in a quarter of a century.[1] This new pattern is undoubtedly due to the movement of labor from the Southern republics, apparently largely ethnic Russians, to such priority projects as the Baikal Amur Mainline (BAM), Sayansk, Ust-Ilimsk, the Non-Black Earth Zone, and so forth — all of which are located in the RSFSR. Given the forthcoming steeper decline in the growth of the Russian Republic's population of able-bodied ages, which will ensue from past fertility trends, the demand for labor to move from other areas into the RSFSR will undoubtedly continue for the rest of the century. (If past fertility trends persist in the republics of Central Asia and Kazakhstan, their population will increase by about 50% in the last two decades of the century, from 42 to 64 million, or at a level of increase roughly twice that of the Russian republic.)

These distributional changes are the logical consequence of differentials in republic rates of growth. Despite the slowdown of growth in all republics between 1970 and 1979, compared to 1959 and 1970 (Table 3.2), the annual average rate of growth in the Central Asian republics exceeds that of the RSFSR and the Ukraine by more than three times. (Compare Kirgiziia's 2.07, the lowest Central Asian rate, with 0.62 and 0.61 for the RSFSR and the Ukraine, respectively.) In the future, such regional differentials are likely to expand markedly, although not by as much as we believed several years ago.

Age-specific fertility rates measure the number of children born per 1,000 women in a given age group. Women's reproductive behavior is more accurately measured by this than by crude birth rates, which use the total (male plus female) population of all ages as the denominator. (Nonetheless, we will return to crude birth rates below.) As can be seen by the reported figures given in Table 3.3 for the USSR and three selected republics (the RSFSR, Uzbekistan and Estonia), fertility has declined universally since 1975/76 in all age groups within the 20–49 bracket (except amongst Estonian females ages 45–49), and has fallen especially in the prime childbearing ages of 20–29. Fertility has declined because of urbanization, higher female labor-force-participation rates, education, housing inadequacies, and other reasons. Reflecting a recent trend towards earlier age at marriage, there has been a perceptible increase in the age-specific fertility rates of 15- to 19-year-old women, except in Uzbekistan. (Again, we need to recall that these are republic-wide and not nationality-specific figures; nonetheless, the fertility rates for women in Uzbekistan — while

Table 3.1 Estimated and Projected Total Population, Percent Distribution, and Average Annual Rates of Growth, USSR and by Republic: 1970–2000 (in thousands, and in percentages; figures may not add to totals due to rounding)

USSR and Republics	1970	Percent of Total	1980	Percent of Total	Average Annual Rate of Growth (1970–1980)	1990	Percent of Total	Average Annual Rate of Growth (1980–1990)	2000	Percent of Total	Average Annual Rate of Growth (1990–2000)
USSR	241,640	100.0	265,049	100.0	0.93	289,206	100.0	0.88	308,050	100.0	0.63
RSFSR	130,036	53.8	137,946	52.0	0.59	144,830	50.1	0.49	147,834	48.0	0.21
Ukraine	47,111	19.5	50,058	18.9	0.61	52,118	18.0	0.40	53,248	17.3	0.21
Belorussia	8,999	3.7	9,667	3.6	0.72	10,463	3.6	0.79	11,010	3.6	0.51
Moldavia	3,568	1.5	4,033	1.5	1.23	4,470	1.5	1.03	4,777	1.5	0.67
Estonia	1,356	0.6	1,455	0.5	0.71	1,485	0.5	0.20	1,507	0.5	0.67
Latvia	2,363	1.0	2,512	0.9	0.61	2,537	0.9	0.10	2,549	0.8	0.05
Lithuania	3,127	1.3	3,397	1.3	0.83	3,618	1.3	0.63	3,804	1.2	0.50
Armenia	2,491	1.0	3,045	1.1	2.03	3,632	1.3	1.78	4,101	1.3	1.22
Azerbaidzhan	5,115	2.1	6,148	2.3	1.86	7,612	2.6	2.16	9,014	2.9	1.70
Georgia	4,685	1.9	5,112	2.0	0.88	5,745	2.0	1.17	6,202	2.0	0.77
Kazakhstan	13,004	5.4	15,367	5.8	1.68	18,157	6.3	1.68	20,507	6.7	1.22
Kirgiziia	2,932	1.2	3,693	1.4	2.33	4,644	1.6	2.32	5,614	1.8	1.91
Tadzhikistan	2,899	1.2	3,921	1.5	3.07	5,209	1.8	2.35	6,590	2.1	2.38
Turkmenistan	2,158	0.9	2,877	1.1	2.92	3,766	1.3	2.73	4,722	1.5	2.29
Uzbekistan	11,796	4.9	15,759	5.9	2.94	20,919	7.2	2.87	26,572	8.6	2.42

Source: Baldwin, 1979, pp. 8–11, 25–57.

Table 3.2 Number of Population and Average Annual Rate of Growth, USSR and by Republic: 1959, 1970, and 1979

USSR and Republics	Number of Population (in thousands)		Average Annual Rate of Growth (1970/1959)	Number of Population (in thousands)		Average Annual Rate of Growth (1979/1970)	Relative Growth (1979/1970) (1970/1959)
	1959	1970		1970	1979		
USSR	208,827	241,720	1.34	241,720	262,442	0.92	.687
RSFSR	117,534	130,079	0.93	130,079	137,552	0.62	.667
Ukraine	41,869	47,126	1.08	47,126	49,757	0.61	.565
Belorussia	8,056	9,002	1.01	9,002	9,559	0.67	.663
Moldavia	2,884	3,569	1.96	3,569	3,948	1.13	.577
Estonia	1,197	1,356	1.14	1,356	1,466	0.87	.763
Latvia	2,093	2,364	1.11	2,364	2,521	0.72	.649
Lithuania	2,711	3,128	1.31	3,128	3,399	0.93	.710
Armenia	1,763	2,492	3.20	2,492	3,031	2.20	.688
Azerbaidzhan	3,698	5,117	3.00	5,117	6,028	1.84	.613
Georgia	4,044	4,686	1.35	4,686	5,016	0.76	.563
Kazakhstan	9,295	13,009	3.10	13,009	14,685	1.36	.439
Kirgiziia	2,006	2,934	3.24	2,934	3,529	2.07	.639
Tadzhikistan	1,981	2,900	3.53	2,900	3,801	3.05	.864
Turkmenistan	1,516	2,159	3.27	2,159	2,759	2.76	.844
Uzbekistan	8,119	11,799	3.46	11,799	15,391	3.00	.867

Source: Based on official census results for each date.

remaining high — undoubtedly have declined somewhat in recent years.) In general, though, total fertility rates remain very far apart, with the Uzbek figures between 2.7 and 2.9 times greater than the totals for the RSFSR. Given the future decline in the share of 20- to 29-year-old women in the Russian Republic and a concurrent increase in their share in Uzbekistan,[2] we can expect that the divergences in total fertility rates between the two republics will increase — barring, of course, an extremely sharp drop in fertility in Uzbekistan.

Before data on fertility in the prime childbearing ages became available for 1976/77 and 1977/78, projections of crude birth rates were made (based on varying fertility assumptions). According to the medium series used for Table 3.4, the crude birth rate for the country as a whole was projected as a diminished 16.1 live births per 1,000 population by the year 2000. However, we now know that the March 1977 projection of 19.2 for 1980 was too high, since the rates reported for 1978 and 1979 remained in the range of 18.2–18.3 births per 1,000 population.[3] In reducing our projection of the overall crude birth rate for the year 2000 to perhaps 15.5 or so for the country as a whole, we can still anticipate a slight increase in the rate shown for the RSFSR and a slight reduction in the rates shown for the Central Asian republics.

Crude birth rates, of course, are only one-half of the equation for natural increase, the net growth measure. In addition, we need to examine the mortality trends. As indicated in the introductory statement, the Soviet mortality situation has deteriorated beyond any reasonable expectations. The three major components underlying the increases are the aging of the population, infant mortality, and death rates for males aged 20–44. Thus, by 1979 the crude death rate was officially reported to have jumped to 10.1 per 1,000,[4] an increase of 0.4 over 1978's figure, and 0.3 greater than the level projected in (March) 1977 for 1980 (see Table 3.4). This 1979 rise is only partially explainable by age standardization, which accounts for the relative increase in the older population. As can be seen from the estimates and projections of age distribution given in Table 3.5, we can anticipate a marked increase in the share of the Soviet pension-age population (60 years of age and older for males, 55 years of age and older for females): between 1950 and 2000, the relative size of the pension-age population will have almost doubled. The share of this population group is expected to be higher in the RSFSR than in the USSR as a whole (21.8 and 19.1% respectively, by 2000), and much lower in Central Asia and Kazakhstan 9.9%). Indeed, the latter share actually will represent a decline from the 1970 pension-age percentage figure, which was 10.3 for Central Asia and Kazakhstan. This drop will be due to high regional birth rates, and will contribute to the projected *decrease* in crude death rates in the four core Central Asian republics.

But it is not only the aging of the population that haš sparked the increase in the mortality rates. As I have described elsewhere (in particular with Christopher Davis,[5] the mortality rate among infants

Table 3.3 Age-Specific and Total Fertility Rates, USSR, RSFSR, Uzbekistan and Estonia: 1965/66, 1971/72 and 1975/76 to 1977/78 (per 1,000 women in each age group)

Age group	USSR					RSFSR				
	1965/66	1971/72	1975/76	1976/77	1977/78	1965/66	1971/72	1975/76	1976/77	1977/78
15–49	70.8	67.2	68.5	68.7	68.8	59.0	55.2	57.1	57.7	58.1
15–19	25.5	32.4	35.0	35.7	36.7	24.7	30.9	34.5	35.6	37.0
20–24	159.6	173.9	176.7	175.4	172.8	150.3	156.1	158.8	158.6	156.2
25–29	136.0	137.1	131.5	130.9	128.7	120.1	116.3	108.0	107.8	106.5
30–34	97.0	84.3	78.0	78.8	76.9	77.7	65.6	58.2	60.0	59.2
35–39	50.6	49.4	40.2	36.7	34.0	38.1	33.0	26.5	23.7	21.6
40–44	19.1	14.6	14.6	14.2	13.2	12.6	7.9	7.3	7.1	6.7
45–49	4.4	2.0	1.8	1.7	1.6	1.4	0.7	0.5	0.5	0.4
Total fertility rate[1]	2,461	2,468	2,389	2,367	2,320	2,124	2,052	1,970	1,966	1,938

	Uzbekistan					Estonia				
	1965/66	1971/72	1975/76	1976/77	1977/78	1965/66	1971/72	1975/76	1976/77	1977/78
15–49	165.3	163.0	157.1	154.0	150.6	55.3	59.8	58.5	59.2	59.2
15–19	30.2	45.4	39.1	37.8	37.2	22.7	31.5	34.6	35.9	37.2
20–24	252.8	275.0	297.0	290.6	282.4	131.5	165.9	165.4	166.4	164.8
25–29	270.2	284.6	301.3	293.6	286.3	119.4	130.7	122.1	122.6	121.4
30–34	238.1	247.7	225.2	224.1	216.9	69.4	70.3	60.9	62.6	60.9
35–39	181.3	198.5	170.6	157.5	141.3	30.7	31.9	26.1	25.4	24.6
40–44	99.2	93.7	82.0	78.0	71.9	9.5	6.5	6.2	5.9	5.7
45–49	41.0	23.3	16.8	14.9	13.4	0.7	0.5	0.3	0.2	0.3
Total fertility rate[1]	5,564	5,841	5,660	5,482	5,247	1,920	2,188	2,078	2,095	2,074

[1]Determined as the sum of the individual age-specific rates multiplied by 5.

Source:
1965/66, 1971/72 and 1975/76: Urlanis, Ed., 1978, pp. 75–6.
1976/77: Vestnik statistiki, no. 11, November 1978, p. 82.
1977/78: Vestnik statistiki, no. 11, November 1979, p. 66.

Table 3.4 Estimated and Projected Vital Rates, USSR and by Republic: 1950–2000 (rates per 1,000 population)

USSR and Republics	Crude Birth Rate						Crude Death Rate						Natural Increase					
	1950	1960	1970	1980	1990	2000	1950	1960	1970	1980	1990	2000	1950	1960	1970	1980	1990	2000
USSR	26.7	24.9	17.4	19.2	17.3	16.1	9.7	7.1	8.2	9.8	10.2	10.6	17.0	17.8	9.2	9.4	7.1	5.5
RSFSR	26.9	23.2	14.6	16.6	14.1	13.8	10.1	7.4	8.7	10.5	11.4	12.3	16.8	15.8	5.9	6.1	2.7	1.5
Ukraine	22.8	20.5	15.2	15.6	14.0	13.6	8.5	6.9	8.9	10.6	11.5	12.1	14.3	13.9	6.3	4.9	2.6	1.5
Belorussia	25.5	24.4	16.2	17.3	15.4	13.7	8.0	6.6	7.6	8.9	9.2	9.9	17.5	17.8	8.6	8.4	6.3	3.8
Moldavia	38.9	29.3	19.4	21.3	17.9	16.0	11.2	6.4	7.4	9.6	10.0	10.5	27.7	22.9	12.0	11.7	7.9	5.4
Estonia	18.4	16.6	15.8	14.6	13.7	13.7	14.4	10.5	11.1	11.9	12.2	12.7	4.0	6.1	4.7	2.6	1.4	0.9
Latvia	17.0	16.7	14.5	13.9	13.3	13.3	12.4	10.0	11.2	12.5	12.8	13.4	4.6	6.7	3.3	1.4	0.5	-0.1
Lithuania	23.6	22.5	17.6	16.1	15.5	14.0	12.0	7.8	8.9	9.8	9.7	10.3	11.6	14.7	8.7	6.3	5.8	3.7
Armenia	32.1	40.1	22.1	24.4	19.9	16.3	8.5	6.8	5.1	5.6	5.5	6.2	23.6	33.3	17.0	18.8	14.3	10.2
Azerbaidzhan	31.2	42.6	29.2	27.6	26.6	19.8	9.6	6.7	6.7	6.9	6.6	6.5	21.6	35.9	22.5	20.6	20.0	13.3
Georgia	23.5	24.7	19.2	19.2	17.3	15.3	7.6	6.5	7.3	8.2	8.4	8.9	15.9	18.2	11.9	11.0	8.9	6.3
Kazakhstan	37.6	37.2	23.4	24.8	21.5	17.6	11.7	6.6	6.0	7.2	7.3	7.6	25.9	30.6	17.4	17.6	14.2	10.0
Kirgiziia	32.4	36.9	30.5	31.5	28.1	23.2	8.5	6.1	7.4	7.8	7.1	6.9	23.9	30.8	23.1	23.6	21.0	16.3
Tadzhikistan	30.4	33.5	34.8	36.9	33.1	26.6	8.2	5.1	6.4	7.7	6.9	6.4	22.2	28.4	28.4	29.2	26.2	20.2
Turkmenistan	38.2	42.4	35.2	35.0	32.1	26.2	10.2	6.5	6.6	7.6	7.0	6.5	28.0	35.9	28.6	27.3	25.1	19.6
Uzbekistan	30.8	39.8	33.6	35.6	32.2	26.6	8.7	6.0	5.5	6.9	5.9	5.4	22.1	33.8	28.1	28.7	26.3	21.1

Source: Baldwin, 1979, pp. 13–14, 25–57.

Table 3.5   Age Distribution of the Population of the USSR and of Selected Republics: 1950–2000 (Numbers are in thousands as of January 1)

USSR and Selected Republics	1950	1960	1970	1980	1990	2000	Percent of USSR						Percent of Own Geographic Unit	
							1950	1960	1970	1980	1990	2000	1970	2000
USSR	178,547	212,372	241,640	265,049	289,206	308,050	100.0	100.0	100.0	100.0	100.0	100.0	100.0	100.0
0–15	57,386	66,647	74,769	69,304	77,955	78,144	32.1	31.4	30.9	26.1	27.0	25.4	30.9	25.4
16–59/54	102,656	119,467	130,589	154,806	160,796	170,968	57.5	56.3	54.0	58.4	55.6	55.5	54.0	55.5
60/55 and over	18,505	26,258	36,282	40,939	50,455	58,938	10.4	12.4	15.0	15.4	17.4	19.1	15.0	19.1
RSFSR	101,438	119,046	130,036	137,946	144,830	147,834	56.8	56.1	53.8	52.0	50.1	48.0	100.0	100.0
0–15	(NA)	(NA)	37,107	31,399	34,211	32,166	(NA)	(NA)	49.6	45.3	43.9	41.2	28.5	21.8
16–59/54	(NA)	(NA)	73,032	83,791	82,462	83,449	(NA)	(NA)	55.9	54.1	51.3	48.8	56.2	56.4
60/55 and over	(NA)	(NA)	19,897	22,756	28,157	32,219	(NA)	(NA)	54.8	55.6	55.8	54.7	15.3	21.8
Central Asia; Kazakhstan	17,208	23,890	32,789	41,617	52,695	64,005	9.6	11.2	13.6	15.7	18.2	20.8	100.0	100.0
0–15	(NA)	(NA)	14,433	16,522	20,772	23,208	(NA)	(NA)	19.3	23.8	26.6	29.7	44.0	36.3
16–59/54	(NA)	(NA)	14,978	21,347	27,025	34,436	(NA)	(NA)	11.5	13.8	16.8	20.1	45.7	53.8
60/55 and over	(NA)	(NA)	3,378	3,748	4,896	6,359	(NA)	(NA)	9.3	9.2	9.7	10.8	10.3	9.9
Kazakhstan	6,522	9,610	13,004	15,367	18,157	20,507	3.7	4.5*	5.4	5.8	6.3	6.7	100.0	100.0
0–15	(NA)	(NA)	5,158	5,133	5,960	6,034	(NA)	(NA)	6.9	7.4	7.6	7.7	39.7	29.4
16–59/54	(NA)	(NA)	6,491	8,664	10,106	11,671	(NA)	(NA)	5.0	5.6	6.3	6.8	49.9	56.9
60/55 and over	(NA)	(NA)	1,355	1,570	2,091	2,802	(NA)	(NA)	3.7	3.8	4.1	4.8	10.4	13.7
Kirgiziia	1,716	2,131	2,932	3,693	4,644	5,614	1.0	1.0	1.2	1.4	1.6	1.8	100.0	100.0
0–15	(NA)	(NA)	1,286	1,471	1,827	2,029	(NA)	(NA)	1.7	2.1	2.3	2.6	43.9	35.1
16–59/54	(NA)	(NA)	1,325	1,876	2,363	3,030	(NA)	(NA)	1.0	1.2	1.5	1.8	45.2	54.0
60/55 and over	(NA)	(NA)	321	345	454	555	(NA)	(NA)	0.9	0.8	0.9	0.9	10.9	9.9

Table 3.5 *continued*

USSR and Selected Republics	1950	1960	1970	1980	1990	2000	Percent of USSR						Percent of Own Geographic Unit	
							1950	1960	1970	1980	1990	2000	1970	2000
Selected Republics														
Tadzhikistan	1,509	2,045	2,899	3,921	5,209	6,590	0.8	1.0	1.2	1.5	1.8	2.1	100.0	100.0
0–15	(NA)	(NA)	1,411	1,789	2,306	2,658	(NA)	(NA)	1.9	2.6	3.0	3.4	48.7	45.6
16–59/54	(NA)	(NA)	1,225	1,842	2,513	3,434	(NA)	(NA)	0.9	1.2	1.6	2.0	42.3	47.0
60/55 and over	(NA)	(NA)	263	290	389	497	(NA)	(NA)	0.7	0.7	0.8	0.8	9.1	7.4
Turkmenistan	1,197	1,564	2,158	2,877	3,766	4,722	0.7	0.7	0.9	1.1	1.3	1.5	100.0	100.0
0–15	(NA)	(NA)	1,013	1,254	1,608	1,867	(NA)	(NA)	1.4	1.8	2.1	2.4	46.9	39.5
16–59/54	(NA)	(NA)	948	1,394	1,860	2,479	(NA)	(NA)	0.7	0.9	1.2	1.4	43.9	52.5
60/55 and over	(NA)	(NA)	197	230	299	375	(NA)	(NA)	0.5	0.6	0.6	0.6	9.1	7.9
Uzbekistan	6,264	8,540	11,796	15,759	20,919	26,572	3.5	4.0	4.9	5.9	7.2	8.6	100.0	100.0
0–15	(NA)	(NA)	5,565	6,875	9,071	10,620	(NA)	(NA)	7.4	9.9	11.6	13.6	47.2	40.0
16–59/54	(NA)	(NA)	4,989	7,571	10,183	13,822	(NA)	(NA)	3.8	4.9	6.3	17.7	42.3	52.0
60/55 and over	(NA)	(NA)	1,242	1,313	1,665	2,130	(NA)	(NA)	3.4	3.2	3.3	3.6	10.5	8.0
Transcaucasus	7,700	9,774	12,291	14,362	16,989	19,317	4.3	4.6	5.1	5.4	5.9	6.3	100.0	100.0
0–15	(NA)	(NA)	4,921	4,721	5,452	5,749	(NA)	(NA)	6.6	6.8	7.0	7.4	40.0	29.8
16–59/54	(NA)	(NA)	5,922	8,078	9,397	10,774	(NA)	(NA)	4.5	5.2	5.8	6.3	48.2	55.8
60/55 and over	(NA)	(NA)	1,448	1,563	2,140	2,792	(NA)	(NA)	4.0	3.8	4.2	4.7	11.8	14.5
Armenia	1,347	1,829	2,491	3,045	3,632	4,101	0.8	0.9	1.0	1.1	1.3	1.3	100.0	100.0
0–15	(NA)	(NA)	1,034	989	1,155	1,136	(NA)	(NA)	0.8	1.4	1.5	1.5	41.5	27.7
16–59/54	(NA)	(NA)	1,206	1,776	2,053	2,374	(NA)	(NA)	0.9	1.1	1.3	1.4	48.4	57.9
60/55 and over	(NA)	(NA)	251	280	424	590	(NA)	(NA)	0.7	0.7	0.8	1.0	10.1	14.4

Azerbaidzhan	2,859	3,816	5,115	6,148	7,612	9,014	1.6	1.8	2.1	2.3	2.6	2.9	100.0 100.0
0–15	(NA)	(NA)	2,364	2,315	2,739	3,052	(NA)	(NA)	3.2	3.3	3.5	3.9	46.2 33.9
16–59/54	(NA)	(NA)	2,244	3,305	4,145	4,977	(NA)	(NA)	1.7	2.1	2.6	2.9	43.9 55.2
60/55 and over	(NA)	(NA)	507	528	728	985	(NA)	(NA)	1.4	1.3	1.4	1.7	9.9 10.9
Georgia	3,494	4,129	4,685	5,169	5,745	6,202	2.0	1.9	1.9	2.0	2.0	2.0	100.0 100.0
0–15	(NA)	(NA)	1,523	1,417	1,558	1,561	(NA)	(NA)	2.0	2.0	2.0	2.0	32.5 25.2
16–59/54	(NA)	(NA)	2,472	2,997	3,199	3,423	(NA)	(NA)	1.9	1.9	2.0	2.0	52.8 55.2
60/55 and over	(NA)	(NA)	690	755	988	1,217	(NA)	(NA)	1.9	1.8	2.0	2.1	14.7 19.6

NA Not available.

Source:

1950: Vestnik statistiki, no. 4, April 1964, pp. 85–8.
1960: Vestnik statistiki, no. 2, February 1971, pp. 85–6.
1970–2000: Unpublished estimates and projections prepared by the Foreign Demographic Analysis Division, Bureau of the Census, US Department of Commerce in March 1977. Medium series.

0–1 year of age has systematically and dramatically increased in this past decade to a point where, on a comparable basis, it might now be over three times that of the United States (i.e. 39–40 compared to 12.9 deaths per 1,000 live births in 1979). If this trend — which has an obvious impact on overall mortality rates — continues into the future, the projections of the crude death rates in Table 3.4 may be too low, both for the USSR and all individual republics, inasmuch as the infant mortality rise is not a localized phenomenon but has been recorded throughout the country.

Higher death rates no longer characterize the very young population alone. The increase in male age-specific death rates within the ages of 20–44, during the decade 1963/64–1973/74 also was remarkable and probably underlies the decline in the intercensal rates of growth of the male population's proportionate size. Between January 1959 and January 1970, the percentage of males increased by 1.1 percentage points from 45.0 to 46.1% (see Table 3.6), or 0.1% per year. However, between 1970 and 1979 the share of males increased by only 0.6 percentage points or 0.067 per year, i.e. at a rate one-third lower than that of the previous intercensal period.

In making regional comparisons, it is clear that the Slavic republics manifest a lower share of males; this is partly — or even largely — due to wartime losses. Yet, the recent reduction in the rate of the male population's increase suggests a further debilitating phenomenon, and may well be due to the increasing death rates at the prime working ages of 20–44. The following data, comparing the male and female death rates (per 1,000 population in the given age groups), show a pronounced rise in mortality among all male age groups during 1963/64–1973/74, which must have predetermined the minimal 1970–9 changes in the "percent male" statistic (see Table 3.7). In general, the death rate for men aged 20–44 increased during this period to a level which is from 2.3 to 3.1 times that for women. The rates for males increased particularly among those aged 40–44. The increase in alcohol consumption may account for much of the increase in death rates for males in ages 20–44 during this period. Coronary death rates also have increased lately partly due to increases in ischemic heart disease which is thought to be related to alcohol consumption. Scattered reports indicate that at least half of the deaths due to accidents and traumas are alcohol-related. It is also hard to escape the conclusion that the increase in alcohol consumption is tied to the general attitude of Soviet workers towards conditions of Soviet society.

As a consequence of all the foregoing mortality trends, life expectancy at age 0 has dropped markedly for males, and may level off for females. Thus, between 1966/67 and 1971/72 — the last year for which such data have been published — male life expectancy *dropped* from 66 to 64 years at birth. In view of subsequently revealed trends, life expectancy must have dropped to 63 without a question, and perhaps to only 62 years. Given that this is an average, the prospects do not

Table 3.6 Percent Male Among Total, Urban and Rural Population, USSR and by Republic: January 1959, 1970 and 1979

USSR and Republics	Total			Urban			Rural		
	1959	1970	1979	1959	1970	1979	1959	1970	1979
USSR	45.0	46.1	46.6	45.2	46.3	46.7	44.9	45.8	46.6
RSFSR	44.6	45.6	46.0[a]	44.9	45.9	(NA)	44.3	45.2	(NA)
Ukraine	44.4	45.2	45.8	45.2	46.3	46.5	43.6	44.0	44.6
Belorussia	44.5	46.0	46.5	44.6	47.0	47.1	44.4	45.2	45.8
Moldavia	46.2	46.6	47.1[a]	45.7	46.8	(NA)	46.4	46.5	(NA)
Estonia	43.9	45.7	46.2	43.8	45.6	45.9	44.0	45.9	46.9
Latvia	43.9	45.7	46.1	43.3	45.7	(NA)	44.6	45.7	(NA)
Lithuania	45.9	46.9	47.2	45.2	47.2	(NA)	46.3	46.7	(NA)
Armenia	47.8	48.8	48.7	47.9	48.9	48.5	47.7	48.7	49.1
Azerbaidzhan	47.5	48.5	48.8	47.3	48.9	49.5	47.7	48.1	47.9
Georgia	46.1	47.0	47.1	45.5	46.7	46.7	46.6	47.2	47.5
Kazakhstan	47.5	48.1	48.3	47.3	48.2	47.7	47.7	48.1	49.0
Kirgiziia	47.2	47.8	48	46.9	47.0	48	47.3	48.3	49
Tadzhikistan	48.7	49.2	49.4[a]	47.7	49.0	(NA)	49.2	49.3	(NA)
Turkmenistan	48.2	49.2	49	48.1	49.6	50	48.4	48.9	49
Uzbekistan	48.0	47.7	49.1	47.1	48.3	49.0	48.5	49.8	49.2

NA Not available.
[a] 1978.

Note: Data are shown as reported.

Source: Official Soviet census volumes, newspaper reports on preliminary census totals by republic for the January 1979 census, and current statistical yearbooks for the RSFSR, Moldavia, and Tadzhikistan for the 1978 current estimate in each republic for the total percent male.

bode well for Soviet males, whose life expectancy may now be 10 or more years less than female life expectancy.

Combining all of these fertility and mortality phenomena, a set of projected natural-increase rates were derived; essentially, they were based on the republic-specific fertility and mortality assumptions, which in turn underlie the projected crude birth and death rates (see Table 3.4). In examining the data, we see that by the year 2000 there will be a 14-fold gap between the net rates of natural increase in Uzbekistan and the RSFSR. Even after rough adjustment for some decrease in fertility and an increase in mortality in Uzbekistan, on the one hand, and increases in both fertility and mortality in the RSFSR, on the other, the natural increase disparity still may well exceed 10 times. In absolute terms, using the original projected increase (see Table 3.4) in the rates to 21.1 per thousand population for Uzbekistan and 1.5 for the RSFSR by the century's end, and of their respective populations of the year 2000, Uzbekistan will grow by 560,000 persons per year and the RSFSR by 220,000, or only four-tenths of the Uzbekistan increase. (The base population difference, nonetheless, will remain enormous.)

3.2 Manpower Issues

Because of all of the above factors, the demographic aspects of manpower will undergo radical quantitative, qualitative and geographical shifts throughout the remainder of the century. The transition from a situation of excess labor supplies, comprising the non-working members of households, collective farmers, and under- and over-age population groups, to one of relative labor scarcity in number and place, impels the leadership to take full cognizance of the manpower issue. Although part of the solution to the problem may lie in eliminating poorly utilized labor, increasing mechani-

Table 3.7 *Age-Specific Death Rates, by Sex, USSR: 1963/64 and 1973/74 (per 1,000 population)*

Age	Males		Females		Male/female ratios (in percent)	
	1963/64	*1973/74*	*1963/64*	*1973/74*	*1963/64*	*1973/74*
20–24	2.2	2.5	1.0	0.8	220	312
25–29	2.8	3.1	1.2	0.9	233	344
30–34	3.7	4.4	1.5	1.4	247	314
35–39	4.5	5.4	1.9	1.8	237	300
40–44	5.4	7.4	2.5	2.6	216	285

Source:
1963/64 TSU 1964, pp. 36–37.
1973/74: Vestnik statistiki, no. 12, December 1975, p. 84.

zation, and exerting controls over the labor market, most of the effort appears to be devoted toward increasing labor productivity. This direction is nowhere more clearly seen than in Brezhnev's statement at the XXVth Party Congress, held in early 1976 at the beginning of the 10th Five-Year-Plan period:[6]

> Comrades! In order to successfully resolve the multiple economic and social tasks facing the country there is no other way other than the *fast growth of labor productivity, and a sharp increase in the effectiveness of all social production.* [Emphasis as in text.] The stress upon effectiveness, and about this it is necessary to speak again and again, is the most important component of our economic strategy.
>
> In the 1980s the resolution of this task will become especially imperative. This is linked first of all to the exacerbation of the problem of labor resources. We will need to depend entirely on raising labor productivity and not on mobilizing additional labor force. A sharp reduction in the share of manual labor, as well as complex mechanization and automation of production will be indispensable conditions for economic growth.

Later in the year a major institutional reorganization was implemented, when both the State Committee on Labor and Wage Problems and the 15 republic state committees on labor-resources utilization were abolished. In their stead, the government created a new consolidated union–republic State Committee on Labor and Social Questions (*Goskomtrud*), which now possesses enhanced influence in the social-security area (primarily related to the employment of pensioners), and commands increased control over the movement of labor between jobs. During the discussion of the 1977 Constitution, Brezhnev elaborated on the constitutional provision related to the "right to work," and noted that this right is "supplemented by the right to choose a profession, the type of occupation and work in accordance with the desires, abilities, professional training and education of the citizen, but also — and this is no less important — with consideration of society's needs."[7] This last underscored qualification provided the Soviet authorities with the license to change the rules of the game from a relatively free factor market to one of control, given the imperatives of the demographic and manpower trends.

Soon thereafter, in April 1978, the largest and most important conference on labor resources to be convened in the post-war period was held in Moscow. More than 1,000 persons attended the conference, which was jointly sponsored by Gosplan, Goskomtrud, TsSU, the USSR Academy of Sciences, the All-Union Central Council of Trade Unions, and the Ministry of Higher and Specialized Secondary Education of the USSR.[8] Many of their discussions and recommendations have been elaborated or implemented in the period following the conference. Thus, the July 1979 decree on improvement of the economic mechanism foreshadowed a series of implementing

Table 3.8 Estimates and Projections of the Population of Able-Bodied Ages (Males 16 to 59 Years, Females 16 to 54 Years), USSR and Selected Republics and Regions: 1970–2000 (in thousands, as of January 1)

USSR, Republic and Region	1970	1975	1980	1985	1990	1995	2000
USSR	130,58[c]	143,018	154,806	158,455	160,796	163,728	170,968
Net increment	(~)	12,429	11,788	3,649	2,341	2,932	7,240
Index[a]	(X)	100.0	94.8	29.4	18.8	23.6	58.3
RSFSR	73,032	78,835	83,791	83,543	82,462	81,817	83,449
Net increment	(X)	5,803	4,956	−248	−1,081	−645	1,632
Index[a]	(X)	100.0	85.4	(X)	(X)	(X)	28.1
Ukraine	26,214	27,896	29,289	29,250	29,237	28,975	29,159
Net increment	(X)	1,682	1,933	−39	−13	−262	184
Index[a]	(X)	100.0	114.9	(X)	(X)	(X)	10.9
Belorussia	4,766	5,276	5,727	5,861	5,886	5,908	6,132
Net increment	(X)	510	451	134	25	22	224
Index[a]	(X)	100.0	88.4	26.3	4.9	4.3	43.9
Moldavia	1,902	2,130	2,323	2,410	2,493	2,593	2,740
Net increment	(X)	228	193	87	83	100	147
Index[a]	(X)	100.0	84.6	38.2	36.4	43.9	64.5
Baltic republics	3,772	4,563	4,781	4,805	4,805	4,766	4,777
Net increment	(X)	791	218	25	−1	−39	11
Index[a]	(X)	100.0	27.6	3.2	(X)	(X)	1.4
Central Asia	8,487	10,392	12,683	14,789	16,919	19,488	22,766
Net increment	(X)	1,905	2,291	2,106	2,130	2,569	3,278
Index[a]	(X)	100.0	120.3	110.6	111.8	134.9	172.1

Kazakhstan	6,491	7,516	8,664	9,436	10,106	10,780	11,671
Net increment	(X)	1,025	1,148	772	670	674	891
Index[a]	(X)	100.0	123.0	75.3	65.4	65.8	86.9
Transcaucasus	5,919	6,917	8,079	8,879	9,398	9,900	10,775
Net increment	(X)	998	1,162	800	519	502	875
Index[a]	(X)	100.0	116.4	80.2	52.0	50.3	87.7

X Not applicable.

[a] Increment from January 1, 1970, to January 1, 1975 = 100.0.

Source: Based on Baldwin, 1979, pp. 91–92, 103, 107, 112, 116, 122–3, and 128.

Figure 3.2   *Entrants to and Departures from Population of Able-Bodied Ages, RSFSR: 1970 to 2000*

directives on manpower ceilings for enterprises and on reductions in manual labor, and, in December 1979, on tightening of the labor market through improved labor discipline and restrictions on movement.

Underlying these manpower concerns and deliberations are the actual data on the number and regional distribution of the net additions to the population of able-bodied ages that will arise during the remainder of the century. Because of past differentials in birth rates, and to some degree in migration patterns, there will be highly volatile decreases and increases in the national labor supply. For example, between January 1980 and January 1990, projections indicate that the net increase in the labor force will reach only 5,990,000 persons, whereas during the preceding ten years the estimated increase in the labor force was 24,217,000, or four times greater (see Table 3.8).

Regional comparisons evince a future pattern of differentials wherein the labor-force increments in the RSFSR and the Ukraine will become negative during the entire 15-year period from 1980 to 1995; the Belorussian labor-force increments between 1985 and 1995 will be down to less than 5% of the increment between 1970 and 1975; only in Central Asia will there be an increment in each period greater than that in the base period of 1970–5. The impact of the changes on a year-to-year basis in the USSR, the RSFSR and the Central Asian region are graphically presented in Figures 3.1 to 3.3. The gap between new 16-year-old entrants to the labor force, on the one hand, and departures of newly pension-aged males and females — coupled with deaths of persons within the "able-bodied" spectrum — on the other hand, reduces the final increment in the entire country to less than 300,000 in the mid-1980s. By contrast, the differential between entrants and departures peaked at over 2,700,000 in the 1970s, and should rebound to 1,900,000 by the year 2000. (See Appendix Table 3.11.)

The regional RSFSR and Central Asian trends may likewise be observed by reference to Figures 3.2 and 3.3, which are based on Appendix Tables 3.12 and 3.13. The RSFSR picture shows the depth of the drop in new entrants, from 2,653,000 at its peak in 1976 to 1,770,000 in 1985 — a figure which falls below the departure line. The Central Asia and Kazakhstan graph is one of continual net increases: annual increments hovered around 500,000–600,000 in the 1970s and will climb to more than 900,000 by the year 2000.

Estimates of labor-force participation indicate that about 88% of the population of able-bodied ages was actively in the labor force in 1970 and 1979 (excluding private subsidiary agriculture), based on the censuses of those years. Using a constant labor-force-participation rate (LFPR) of 88% for the years 1990 and 2000, we may obtain further projections that suggest a major reduction in the increments to the labor force and in its rate of growth (see Table 3.9). The underlying assumptions for retaining a constant LFPR include the knowledge of

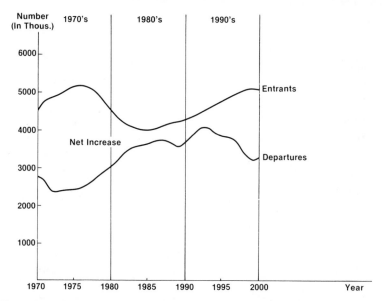

Figure 3.1 *Entrants to and Departures from Population of Able-Bodied Ages,*
USSR: 1970 to 2000

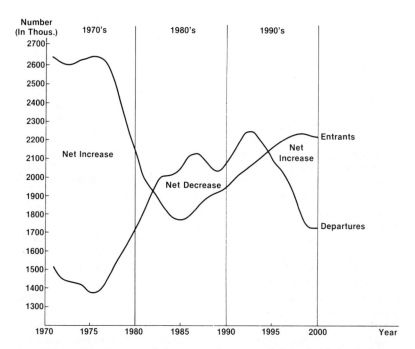

Figure 3.2 *Entrants to and departures from population of able-bodied, ages,*
RSFSR: 1970–2000

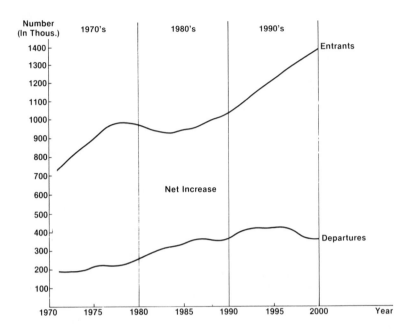

Figure 3.3   *Entrants to and Departures from Population of Able-Bodied Ages, Central Asia and Kazakhstan: 1970 to 2000*

an already extremely high LFPR for males, and an almost too high rate among women in the non-Muslim republics; efforts to increase population growth may lead working women to withdraw from the labor force to have children; in the Muslim republics, though, an increase in female LFPR can be anticipated, since increasing educational attainment, social pressure, slight declines in fertility and the continuing urbanization process (except in Tadzhikistan) encourage and facilitate female employment (see Table 3.10).

If the estimates and projections in Table 3.9 are reasonably accurate, the rate of growth of the labor force in the 1980s will be only about one-quarter of the previous decade's growth. Inasmuch as Table 3.9 holds the overall LFPR virtually constant from 1970 to 2000, it is clear that the declining growth reflects a numerical downswing in the population of able-bodied ages.

While Voronin, the Deputy Chief of Gosplan's Labor Department, could state in 1976 that "almost 100 percent" of the new increments to the labor force in the 10th Five-Year Plan period would come from young persons entering the able-bodied ages,[9] continuous attempts

Table 3.9 *Estimates and Projections of the Labor Force: 1959–2000**

Year	Population of Able-Bodied Ages (in thousands) (1)	Labor Force (in thousands) (2)	Labor Force Participation Rate (3)	Annual Average Rate of Growth (percent per year) (4)	Relative Increase in Labor Force (in percent) (5)	Absolute Increase in Labor Force (in thousands) (6)
1959 (January 15)	119,590	99,130	82.9	(X)	(X)	(X)
1970 (January 15)	130,589	115,204	88.2	1.38	16.3	16,173
1979 (January 15)	153,078	134,860	88.1	1.77	17.1	19,676
1990 (January 1)	160,798	141,500	88.0	0.44	4.9	6,640
2000 (January 1)	170,955	150,400	88.0	0.61	6.3	8,900

X Not applicable.
*Excluding private subsidiary agriculture.

Source:
Column 1: Unpublished estimates and projections of the population prepared by the Foreign Demographic Analysis Division, Bureau of the Census, US Department of Commerce in March 1977. Medium series.
Column 2:
1959, 1970, and 1979: Official census results.
1990 and 2000: Column 3 multiplied by column 1.
Column 3:
1969, 1970, and 1979: Column 2 divided by column 1.
1990 and 2000: Assumed to be the same as 1979, rounded.
Columns 4, 5, and 6: Based on column 2.

Table 3.10 *Share of Urban Population, USSR and by Republic: 1913–1979 (in percent)*

USSR and Republic	1913	1926	1939	1959	1970	1979
USSR	18	18	32	48	56	62
RSFSR	17	18	33	52	62	70
Ukraine	19	19	34	46	55	61
Belorussia	14	17	21	31	43	55
Moldavia	13	13	13	22	32	39
Estonia	19	(NA)	34	56	65	70
Latvia	38	(NA)	35	56	62	68
Lithuania	13	(NA)	23	38	50	61
Armenia	10	19	29	50	59	66
Azerbaidzhan	24	28	36	48	50	53
Georgia	26	22	30	42	48	52
Kazakhstan	10	9	28	44	51	54
Kirgiziia	12	12	19	34	37	39
Tadzhikistan	9	10	17	33	37	35
Turkmenistan	11	14	33	46	48	48
Uzbekistan	24	22	23	33	36	41

NA Not available.
Source: Based on official statistical yearbooks and census results.

have been made to expand the labor force by emphasizing employ-ment among the pension-age population. Furthermore, authorities have sought to broaden the labor participation of women, to rational-ize the workplace by introducing labor-saving devices, and to conserve potential labor resources through a wide variety of techniques. However, I do not believe they will be successful in obtaining much more labor through these efforts. First, since 1966, through changes in pension laws which enable pensioners to retain part or all of their pensions as well as salaries, the Soviets to date have been rather successful in convincing many older individuals, who have reached pension eligibility, to continue in their jobs; secondly, many of those in full retirement have already been enticed into resuming employment. At this writing, five million or more "pensioners" — i.e. some 25% of the old-age-pension population — are on a payroll. However, on a full-time basis this is equal to only about one million workers; and the head of the Labor Resources Sector of Gosplan's Scientific-Research Economics Institute, V. G. Kostakov, does not foresee a major increase in the scale of pensioner employment. More importantly, Kostakov is not particularly impressed with the overall quality of work that these laborers offer.[10]

In the 1960s, major gains were also scored in the sphere of female employment: approximately 10 million women found or were assigned to jobs during 1961–5, and another 3.7 million joined the labor force during 1966–70. Once these achievements had been secured, though, only another one million more were expected during 1971–5 to undertake employment in the next plan period.[11] On a nationwide basis, few additional increments to the female labor force appear forthcoming, although small and medium-sized cities of the RSFSR may tap some remaining female labor reserves. The latter scenario may arise as the government diverts capital resources into small-town development, thereby creating job opportunities for women — especially in heavy-industry localities that previously offered limited employment openings for women.

As mentioned above, the State hopes for a greater propensity toward female labor-force participation in Central Asia, as educational levels rise and start to delay, if not reduce, fertility. Given the limited increases in the urbanized population of Central Asia, and the generally lower levels of urbanization that obtain there, the educational factor may be unable to make a significantly large impact on labor participation in the near future. By the year 2000, however, more labor-force gains among the younger women of Muslim origin can be reasonably expected.

3.3 Other Sources of Labor Supply

Other sources of manpower supply can be viewed as relatively marginal, at least for the short term. The Shchekino experiment, intended to reduce the number of redundant workers, still remains very limited in application, despite its decade-long duration and despite enthusiasm on the part of some central authorities. Only major changes in the strength of applicable legislation will ensure more rational labor utilization, and will encourage the release of redundant manpower. Industrial managers, of course, are often reluctant to forgo maintaining labor surpluses at their enterprises, since surplus workers function as a cushion against unexpected demands on output levels, against labor turnover, against the call to release workers for the harvest, and against a system that still rewards bigger rather than smaller enterprises in regard to the wage category of plants.

Efforts to increase the mechanization of work, which reduces the demand for labor in a given production unit and concomitantly releases workers for employment in labor-deficit industries or regions, may be frustrated by the shortage of new capital investment. If the growth of State capital investments in 1979, compared to 1978, was only 1% (a historically unprecedented low rate of growth),[12] how much funding was available for labor-saving developments, after top-priority investments had been allocated to the food and energy sectors? I would anticipate, therefore, that the large-scale transfer of manpower from lesser productive jobs to more effective posts will be frustrated, especially in the European USSR.

The growth in employment during the 10th Five-Year Plan has begun to respond to the labor-force constraints described above. According to the latest report on employment, at the time of writing,[13] the annual average number of workers and employees was 110,580,000 of which one-third — or 36,450,000 — were classified as employed in industry. The rate of growth of all workers and employees continues to be much higher than the 1976–80 plan anticipated. In the first four years of the plan period, 1976–9 inclusive, growth was 2.0, 2.1, 2.1, and 1.8% per year, respectively — more than twice as high as the planned figure of 0.9% per year.[14] Some increments came from the collective farms, some from among the pensioners, and some from households.

Industrial employment has increased in all years of the five-year plan period, but the rate of growth has dropped off sharply, especially in 1979 as compared to 1978.[15] I believe we are seeing the beginning of the decline, albeit delayed, that Voronin predicted in the following direct comment:[16]

> In the current five-year plan, the balance of labor resources until now is more or less satisfactory. However, this relates only to the first two years when the growth in the able-bodied population remains at about the level of the Ninth Five-Year Plan. But in the third year it will decrease by about one-fifth, and in the fifth year, by almost two times.

Regardless of any reduction in the rate of growth of industrial employment overall, employment in machine-building and metal-working continues to grow, as does its share in the industrial workforce. The machine-building-and-metalworking contingents represented 40.1% of all industrial–production personnel in 1978 — up from only 31.9% in 1960, almost two decades earlier.[17]

Despite the USSR's dire need to improve food supplies for urban industry and services, Soviet labor experts continue to decry the high share of agricultural employment in the Soviet economy. At the 1978 All-Union Labor Conference, scholars and officials condemned the agricultural-employment situation on two scores. First, they lamented that the relative size of the Soviet agricultural labor force was "higher than in any developed country"; secondly, they criticized the quality of agricultural cadres by observing that "the labor-force problem in agriculture is acute, especially [because of the shortage of] machine operators."[18] Thus, in 1977 the share of agricultural employment in annual average or man-year terms in the national labor structure was 27.3%, or 21.1% if we exclude private agricultural activities.[19]

However, the problem is not only numbers, but labor-force composition and location as well. Shortages of machinery operators — due primarily to the outmigration of young trained personnel from rural areas to the cities — are especially debilitating, for example, in the RSFSR's Non-Black Earth Zone agricultural project. On the topic of composition, we can refer only to the 1970 census situation as compared to the 1959, since age data from the 1979 census are lacking at this point in time. For earlier periods, the age-composition data on the rural population of the RSFSR showed that in 1970 rural areas held only 51% of the number of the 20- to 24-year-olds they had claimed in 1959; 45% of that of the 25- to 29-year-olds; and 79% of that of the 30- to 34-year-olds. In·contrast to rural Russia's losses, rural Turkmeni-stan (the most positive case) in 1970 had 92% of the number of the 20- to 24-year-olds it had held in 1959; 80% of that of the 25- to 29-year-olds and 110% of that of the 30- to 34-year-olds.[20]

Brezhnev bemoaned the Soviets' agricultural-manpower problems at the spring 1978 Komsomol congress, where he particularly focused on this outmigration of youths from the village. During the conference he stated that raising the efficiency of agriculture "will be difficult to accomplish without the active participation of young people. . . . They personify the future and in many ways determine the present of the countryside. . . ." But, he continued, "needless to say, people cannot be ordered to stay in the countryside. . . ."[21] Despite his last statement, I expect that the demographic and manpower constraints will lead the Soviet authorities to place limits on freedom of movement. Some of the regional-deficit problems could be resolved if the surplus of native rural young people from the Central Asian region were in fact enticed into moving to the northern agricultural projects. However, the prospects for that to occur in large numbers and in the near future are limited indeed.[22] As we have seen earlier, there has been relatively little change in the urban (obversely, therefore, the rural) shares of the population in the Muslim regions. Outmigration of the local-nationality populations to their own cities — let alone to northern climes — is extremely unlikely in the near future unless "administra-tive measures" are adopted. While I consider that such measures, including forced migration specifically, are unlikely to be enacted and/or implemented, there is no doubt in my mind that the central authorities are contemplating and even initiating greater control over the labor market.

An early signal that this control is being, and will be, expanded is the current emphasis on assigning graduates of various Central Asian educational institutions to places of work in areas of the country other than Central Asia. Apparently, the labor officials hope that such job-entry assignments will thereby become permanent places of residence. Such external assignments are designed to establish a better equilibrium between regional supplies and requirements but — equally important to these authorities — also to foster a blending of the various peoples into a Soviet *narod* (people) and consequently to hasten the disappearance of traditional differences. Speculation about the probable success of the latter policy is beyond the scope of this paper; I would merely indicate the improbability of its success in the near future. Thus, the structural and compositional aspects of population and manpower trends do not bode well for the regime in the next two decades.

Table 3.11   Changes in Number, Entrants to and Departures from Population of Able-Bodied Ages, USSR: 1970–2000 (in thousands, as of July 1)

Year	Population of able-bodied ages[a]	Entrants (16-year-olds)	Departures, total	Of which, Deaths	Of which, New Pension-age population[b]	Annual net increments	Index (1980=100.0)
1970	131,685	4,500	2,772	587	2,185	1,728	113.5
1971	134,015	4,795	2,645	667	1,978	2,150	141.2
1972	136,491	4,853	2,377	488	1,889	2,476	162.6
1973	139,021	4,917	2,387	519	1,868	2,530	166.1
1974	141,663	5,047	2,405	527	1,878	2,642	173.5
1975	144,382	5,139	2,420	562	1,858	2,719	178.5
1976	147,122	5,218	2,478	612	1,866	2,740	179.9
1977	149,746	5,199	2,575	628	1,947	2,624	172.3
1978	152,036	5,011	2,721	643	2,078	2,290	150.3
1979	153,942	4,796	2,890	658	2,232	1,906	125.1
1980	155,465	4,553	3,030	671	2,359	1,523	100.0
1981	156,568	4,287	3,184	685	2,499	1,103	72.4
1982	157,307	4,159	3,420	696	2,724	739	48.5
1983	157,822	4,076	3,561	704	2,857	515	33.8
1984	158,248	3,996	3,570	712	2,858	426	27.9
1985	158,621	3,989	3,616	716	2,900	373	24.5
1986	158,906	4,025	3,740	720	3,020	285	18.7
1987	159,274	4,135	3,767	720	3,047	368	24.2
1988	159,853	4,218	3,639	717	2,922	579	38.0
1989	160,490	4,222	3,585	712	2,873	637	41.8

1990	161,106	4,288	3,672	709	2,963	616	40.4
1991	161,641	4,391	3,856	706	3,150	535	35.1
1992	162,075	4,470	4,036	701	3,335	434	28.5
1993	162,588	4,570	4,057	697	3,360	513	33.7
1994	163,310	4,671	3,949	697	3,252	722	47.4
1995	164,218	4,773	3,865	697	3,168	908	59.6
1996	165,250	4,870	3,838	698	3,140	1,032	67.8
1997	166,523	4,955	3,682	695	2,987	1,273	83.6
1998	168,165	5,024	3,382	689	2,693	1,642	107.8
1999	170,021	5,071	3,215	685	2,530	1,856	121.9
2000	171,888	5,091	3,224	681	2,543	1,867	122.6

[a] Males, 16 to 59 years of age, inclusive. Females, 16 to 59 years of age, inclusive.
[b] Males, 60 years of age and over. Females, 55 years of age and over.

Source: Unpublished estimates and projections prepared by the Foreign Demographic Analysis Division, Bureau of the Census in March 1977. Medium series.

Table 3.12 Changes in Number, Entrants to and Departures from Population of Able-Bodied Ages, RSFSR: 1970–2000 (in thousands, as of July 1)

Year	Population of able-bodied ages	Entrants (16-year olds)	Departures, total	Of which,		New Pension-age population	Annual net increments	Index (1980=100.0)
				Deaths				
1970	73,565	2,508	(NA)	(NA)		1,231	(NA)	(NA)
1971	74,694	2,640	1,511	377		1,134	1,129	272.7
1972	75,859	2,612	1,447	367		1,080	1,165	281.4
1973	77,023	2,596	1,432	366		1,066	1,164	281.2
1974	78,226	2,630	1,427	356		1,071	1,203	290.6
1975	79,487	2,634	1,373	324		1,049	1,261	304.6
1976	80,760	2,653	1,380	339		1,041	1,273	307.5
1977	81,914	2,617	1,463	378		1,085	1,154	278.7
1978	82,841	2,471	1,544	387		1,157	927	223.9
1979	83,514	2,309	1,636	394		1,242	673	162.6
1980	83,928	2,135	1,721	402		1,319	414	100.0
1981	84,102	1,985	1,811	409		1,402	174	42.0
1982	84,079	1,919	1,942	416		1,526	–23	(X)
1983	83,911	1,848	2,016	419		1,597	–168	(X)
1984	83,672	1,776	2,015	424		1,591	–239	(X)
1985	83,398	1,770	2,044	425		1,619	–274	(X)
1986	83,076	1,798	2,120	427		1,693	–322	(X)
1987	82,792	1,849	2,133	425		1,708	–284	(X)
1988	82,637	1,904	2,059	421		1,638	–155	(X)
1989	82,526	1,915	2,026	417		1,609	–111	(X)

1990	82,418	1,948	2,056	412	1,644	−108	(X)
1991	82,278	2,001	2,141	410	1,731	−140	(X)
1992	82,071	2,031	2,238	406	1,832	−207	(X)
1993	81,896	2,072	2,247	402	1,845	−175	(X)
1994	81,825	2,115	2,186	401	1,785	−71	(X)
1995	81,882	2,155	2,098	400	1,698	57	13.8
1996	82,029	2,189	2,042	398	1,644	147	35.5
1997	82,276	2,215	1,968	396	1,572	247	59.7
1998	82,688	2,230	1,818	392	1,426	412	99.5
1999	83,192	2,232	1,728	388	1,340	504	121.7
2000	83,681	2,219	1,730	384	1,346	489	118.1

NA Not available.   X Not applicable.
Notes and source: See Table 3.11.

Table 3.13 Changes in Number, Entrants to and Departures from Population of Able-Bodied Ages, Central Asia and Kazakhstan: 1970–2000 (in thousands, as of July 1)

Year	Population of Able-Bodied Ages	Entrants (16-year olds)	Departures, Total	Of which, Deaths	New Pension-age Population	Annual Net Increments	Index (1980=100.0)
1970	15,214	657	(NA)	(NA)	198	(NA)	(NA)
1971	15,733	730	198	18	180	522	79.7
1972	16,315	785	193	22	171	582	88.9
1973	16,926	820	194	24	170	611	93.3
1974	17,575	860	197	26	171	649	99.1
1975	18,224	895	219	48	171	649	99.1
1976	18,899	941	224	50	174	675	103.1
1977	19,619	977	212	31	181	720	109.9
1978	20,326	979	225	32	193	707	107.9
1979	21,010	973	240	32	208	684	104.4
1980	21,665	964	259	33	226	655	100.0
1981	22,272	939	281	34	247	607	92.7
1982	22,837	922	303	36	267	565	86.3
1983	23,383	920	319	36	283	546	83.4
1984	23,940	933	319	37	282	557	85.0
1985	24,490	945	338	38	300	550	84.0
1986	25,012	944	363	38	325	522	79.7
1987	25,557	971	367	39	328	545	83.2
1988	26,133	990	353	39	314	576	87.9
1989	26,724	1,000	348	39	309	591	90.2

Year						
1990	27,330	1,037	368	39	329	606	92.5
1991	27,937	1,072	401	40	361	607	92.7
1992	28,558	1,107	422	40	382	621	94.8
1993	29,212	1,144	425	40	385	654	99.8
1994	29,908	1,176	413	41	372	696	106.3
1995	30,632	1,211	419	43	376	724	110.5
1996	31,378	1,247	430	41	389	746	113.9
1997	32,178	1,282	411	42	369	800	122.1
1998	33,049	1,316	373	41	332	871	133.0
1999	33,968	1,347	353	41	312	919	140.3
2000	34,905	1,375	364	42	322	937	143.1

NA Not available.
Notes and source: See Table 3.11.

3: Notes

1 See Feshbach, 1979 (a), Vol. 1, p. 672.
2 Baldwin, 1979, pp. 92 and 117.
3 TSU SSSR, 1980, p. 36.
4 See note 3.
5 Davis and Feshbach, 1980.
6 Brezhnev, L. I., speech of February 24, 1976. In KPSS, *Materialy XXV s"ezd KPSS*, p. 43. Moscow: Politizdat, 1976.
7 Brezhnev, L. I., *O konstitutsii SSSR*, pp. 16–17. Moscow: Politizdat 1977.
8 For some details of the conference, see *Sotsialisticheskii trud* no. 9, Sept. 1978, pp. 7–95, especially the speech by L. A. Kostin, the First Deputy Chief of Goskomtrud.
9 Voronin, E., "Employment of the Population is Being Planned." *Leningradskaia Pravda*, August 17, 1976, p. 2. Cited in Feshbach, 1979 (b), p. 4.
10 See especially his article in *Sovetskaia kul'tura*, July 21, 1978, p. 6, and Kostakov, 1980, pp. 20–1.
11 Lebedinskii, 1969, p. 28.
12 *Pravda*, Jan. 26, 1980, p. 1.
13 TSU SSSR, 1980, p. 168.
14 In addition to the figure from TSU SSSR, 1980, p. 168, also see Rapawy's (1980) unpublished paper, p. 2, and Karpukhin, 1977, p. 18.
15 The rates are as follows: 1976 — 2.2%; 1977 — 1.7%; 1978 — 1.7%; and 1979 — 1.2%. Sources as in footnote 14.
16 Voronin, E., "Plan and Labor Savings." *Sotsialisticheskaia industriia*, Jan. 28, 1977, p. 2.
17 Based on Rapawy, 1980, p. 12.
18 Kostin, ed., 1979, p. 156.
19 Based on Rapawy, 1980, p. 8.
20 TSU SSSR, 1972, pp. 18–19 and 68–9.
21 Speech by Comrade L. I. Brezhnev," *Pravda*, April 26, 1978, p. 1.
22 Feshbach, 1979 (a), passim.

3: References

Baldwin, Godfrey S., *Population Projections by Age and Sex: For the Republics and Major Economic Regions of the U.S.S.R., 1970 to 2000*. International Population Reports, Series P–91, No. 26. Washington, DC: Bureau of the Census, Sept. 1979.

Brezhnev, L. I., *O konstitutsii SSSR*, Moscow, Politizdat 1977.

Davis, Christopher, and Feshbach, Murray. *Rising Infant Mortality in the U.S.S.R. in the 1970s*. Series P–95, No. 74. Washington, DC: Bureau of the Census, June 1980.

Feshbach, Murray, "Prospects for Migration from Central Asia and Kazakhstan in the Next Decade." In *Soviet Economy in a Time of Change*. Papers, Joint Econ. Comm., US Congress. Washington, DC: Govt. Printing Office, 1979a.

Feshbach, Murray, "The Structure and Composition of the Industrial Labor Force." In Arcadius Kahan and B. A. Ruble, eds., *Industrial Labor in the U.S.S.R.*, Kennan Institute Study No. 1. New York: Pergamon, 1979b.

Karpukhin, D., "Labor and Material Well-Being". *Sotsialisticheskii trud* no. 12, Dec. 1977.

Kostakov, V. G., *Prognoz zaniatosti naseleniia*. Moscow: Ekonomika, 1980.

Kostin L. A., ed., *Trudovye resursy SSSR*. Moscow: Ekonomika, 1979. *Materialy XXV s"ezd KPSS*. Moscow, Politizdat 1976.

Lebedinskii, N. G., "Basic Questions of Improving the Planning of National Economic Proportions." *Planovoe khoziaistvo*, no. 10, Oct. 1969.

Rapawy, Stephen, "Civilian Employment in the U.S.S.R.: 1950 to 1978." Foreign Demographic Analysis Division, Bureau of the Census, Feb. 1980.

TSU SSSR, Itogi Vsesoiuznoi perepisi nasaleniia 1970 g. Moscow: Statistika, 1972.

TSU SSSR, *Nar. khoz.* v 1964 g. Moscow, 1965.

TSU, *SSSR v tsifrakh v 1979 g.* Moscow, 1980.

Urlanis, B. Ts., Ed., *Narodonaseleniie stran mira, spravochnik*, second revised and enlarged edition. Moscow: Statistika, 1978.

Vestnik statistiki, various years.

4

Agricultural Organization and Management

D. GALE JOHNSON

Introduction

My task has been made immeasurably simpler by an excellent article by David M. Schoonover (1979), "Soviet Agricultural Policies" in the 1979 Joint Economic Committee volume on the Soviet Union.[1] Schoonover provides a competent and balanced review of Soviet agricultural policies, with emphasis on the period since Stalin's death. He traces the major changes in agricultural price policies, the important organizational and administrative changes, the continuing program to increase the scale of farms, the emphasis upon specialization in agricultural production, and upon interfarm cooperation and agroindustrial enterprises. Throughout the period surveyed runs a thread of vacillation with respect to decentralization of planning and management, with little real change evident as a result of numerous reorganizations of the bureaucracy and even more numerous pronouncements by the highest officials. Similarly Schoonover traces some of the twists and turns of official policy with respect to the private plots on collective and state farms.

Overriding and dominating almost all aspects of changes in agricultural organization and management have been the following:

1 Increased size of farm enterprises;
2 Emphasis upon specialization in agricultural enterprises;
3 Abolition of the Machine Tractor Stations;
4 Gradual reduction of the differences between state and collective farms;
5 Changes in agricultural-output price and procurement policies which, however, except for the increase in the average level of output prices, showed no systematic development over time;
6 Radical departure from the Stalinist exploitation of agriculture in favor of increased material incentives resulting in both higher and more secure incomes for farm people; and
7 Striking increases in the availability of nonfarm-produced inputs

for agriculture after 1965 and unprecedented rates of investment in buildings, capital equipment and machinery.

But with all of these changes, and others that might have been noted, much remains essentially unchanged from the 1930s. The fundamental features of Soviet agricultural organization and management have changed little during the past four decades. Equally important, as I shall argue, the fundamental nature of the interrelationships between agriculture and the rest of the economy has remained largely unchanged. True, the MTS are gone and compulsory deliveries at nominal prices have been abandoned. But farms still have too little involvement in the decisions with respect to the kinds, types and qualities of machines available to them; farm output is still procured according to purchase plans established by outside agencies. Decisions with respect to both inputs and outputs and production plans are still heavily circumscribed by decision rules that are inconsistent with the maximization of its own objectives or goals by each production unit.

After a relatively brief discussion of the ways in which Soviet agricultural performance might be described as disappointing, and some of the sources of those shortcomings, I present a simplified model of a collective farm and work out some of the implications of that model. The model is used to throw some light upon whether the collective-farm structure would necessarily result in inefficient allocation of resources.

The third part of the paper considers some of the ways in which the actual collective-farm structure deviates from the model and the effects of some of the policies adopted by Soviet officials to offset the sources of inefficiency and inequities in the distribution of income in the rural sector. The final part of the paper emphasizes the limited role for further changes in agricultural management and organization unless there are substantial modifications in the manner in which agriculture interacts with and is affected by the rest of the economy. Barring major improvements in pricing, marketing, input supply and bureaucratic intervention (planning) I see little scope for improving the functioning of agriculture through changes in the management and organization of agriculture.

4.1 Disappointing Performance

A full development of why the performance of Soviet agriculture since World War II can be described as disappointing is unnecessary. However, a few noteworthy points may be made in partial support of the description. A slow rate of output growth is not the primary basis for calling the performance disappointing. Since the death of Stalin the annual growth rate of agricultural output has been approximately 3.4%. Compared to the agricultures of Western Europe, North

America and Australia this is a very satisfactory growth rate. For the same period of time annual output growth in the United States has been less than 2%. However, along with the shortcomings noted immediately below, it appears that the rate of agricultural-output growth was significantly lower during the 1970s than in the 1960s. The annual rate of output growth from 1961–5 to 1970–2 was 3.3%; from 1970–2 to 1977–9, 2.3% (USDA, 1980b).

The basic shortcoming with respect to output growth has been that it has not kept pace with the growth of demand at the prices to consumers, especially of meat and milk, that have been considered consistent with political stability. These consumer prices have remained essentially unchanged since 1963. In 1980 the per capita consumption of food products with relatively high income elasticities — meat and fruits — was much lower in the Soviet Union than in other countries with comparable real per capita incomes.

Three major indicators of the disappointing performance of Soviet agriculture are the very high fraction of national investment devoted to agriculture, the high cost of farm products, and the instability of output. During the Ninth and Tenth Plans, approximately 26 and 27%, respectively, of total investment in the economy were devoted to productive activities on farms. A comparable figure for the United States for the same period would be about 5% of gross national investment, excluding investment in residential construction. In addition to the high rate of farm investment, very substantial investments were made in the farm input industries.

The high cost of Soviet farm output is reflected in the prices paid to the farms, especially for meat and milk. Even though consumers are using upwards of 40% of their income to purchase food (USDA, 1980c) subsidies to farms for meat and milk purchases have been at least 35 billion rubles in recent years.

The third shortcoming of Soviet agriculture is the wide variability in crop output, especially grain, feed and vegetable-oil output, from year to year. The economic costs are substantial, whether met by investment in storage, importation of grain and other feed materials, or through accepting the consequences of significant variations in meat and milk output. The primary means of coping with the variability of output of grains and other feeding materials during the 1970s has been through grain imports, including years of imports of more than 25 million tons. The political costs, represented by dependency upon external sources for fulfillment of plans and expectations, are also high. The Soviet Union is no longer in danger of famine, even if it imported no grain or other food following a very poor crop. But the leadership has for too long raised expectations to such a level that the capacity to prevent severe shortages of calories is not enough. Thus production variability carries with it the necessity of depending on the outside world and this means, to a very large extent, the United States.

The high average prices and costs of livestock products appear to reflect abnormally large feed and labor input per unit of output. Even though there have been heavy investments in livestock building and equipment during the last decade, there is no evidence that feed use per unit of output has declined, though there has been some reduction in labor input (Johnson, 1974). However, even with absolute levels of investment five to seven times that of US agriculture during the 1970s, labor input in Soviet agriculture declined at a slower rate than in the US (Diamond and Davis, 1979, pp. 38 and 41).

Many explanations have been given for the various shortcomings of Soviet agriculture. These have included the large scale of the socialized farms, on the one hand, and the tiny scale of private agriculture that still utilizes a major fraction of the total labor input, on the other hand: the low level of incomes received by workers; inadequate transportation; poor quality of farm inputs; the quality of land and climatic limitations; ineffectiveness of the marketing and storage systems; and the socialized forms of agricultural farms. I shall first consider one of these possible sources of an inefficient agriculture — the collective farm.

Many observers of Soviet agriculture have long held that a significant part of its poor performance could be explained by the collective-farm system and certain inherent features of that system. I am now not so certain of that view, and most of the remainder of this paper deals with a model or models of a collective or cooperative farm. It is possible to support the view that while one can find some reasons — actually two reasons — why a collective farm might not be as efficient as private agriculture, I conclude that adequate explanations of the poor economic performance of Soviet agriculture must be found elsewhere.

I recognize that over time the relative importance of collective farms has declined and that the changes envisaged for the future will result in an even smaller role for the collective farms. Collective farms now account for 58% of the employment and approximately half of the output of socialized agriculture. For the period since World War II the relative importance of the collective sector was greater, much greater, during the first half of the period. But I believe that the arguments that I make about the effect of the collective-farm system upon Soviet agricultural performance applies with nearly the same force to state farms. I shall return to this point briefly at the end.

4.2 A Model of a Collective Farm

An analytical model must start with certain key assumptions. I have not found any official Soviet analytical conception of the collective farm, but this is hardly surprising since the establishment of collective farms appears to have had four primary objectives that largely outweighed any niceties of organizational forms. These objectives were the liquidation of the kulaks, the achievement of effective political control over the countryside, to increase the percentage of farm output that was marketed, and the creation of large-scale production units as a means of achieving greater output than was possible on millions of small-scale farm units. The emphasis could as easily have been given to state farms, and has been to an increasing degree in recent years. The choice of the collective form of organization may well have been dictated by considerations of peasant resistance to completely giving up the land promised them by the revolution, to the inability to fully bring the rural sector into the monetary economy, and to greater capacity of the collective rather than of the state farm as a mechanism for the exploitation of the peasants.

Based on the collective-farm statute and other information, one can state three assumptions that may serve as the basis for an analytical model of collective farms:

1 The collective farms should be large-scale units.
2 Land was to be assigned to farms, rent free and in perpetuity, on the basis of the existing populations of the villages. Land cannot be bought or sold or transferred in any way.
3 The farms were to be organized as cooperatives, with management controlled by a meeting of the members and with all major decisions, such as work rules, membership and distribution of income, to be approved by the members.

Anyone who knows anything about Soviet collective farms will immediately say that the third assumption is largely, if not wholly, incorrect, and that it was always assumed that the state had the right to extract differential rent associated with advantages of fertility of the soil and location. But for the moment I shall accept these three assumptions and determine the possibilities of achieving an efficient allocation of resources within such a system.

If there were no additional economic restraints on the behavior of the cooperative, and if there were not significant economies or diseconomies of scale over the range of farm sizes, the cooperative form of organization would not result in economic inefficiency unless in the same circumstances privately organized firms would also be inefficient. In other words, if one assumes a competitive situation, a cooperative need be neither more nor less efficient than a private firm. This will be true even with the restraints on land assumed in the analytical model. The restraint on the amount of land available to a farm could be fully offset by varying the amount of other resources. This would be true even if there were only one other input, namely labor, so long as that other input can be freely bought and sold. The return to land would be maximized by employing labor until the value of the marginal product of labor used within the cooperative equals the value of its use in the best alternative outside the cooperative. It is clearly in the interest of the members of the cooperative to employ additional labor, paying it the value of its marginal product, if without the added labor the value of the marginal product were greater than the wage that had to be paid to the workers. Similarly, if the value of the marginal product of the labor of the members of the cooperative were less than alternative earnings outside the cooperative, it would be in the interest of the members to encourage some individuals to seek employment outside the cooperative while retaining their rights in the rent from the land and the return on other capital assets. These conclusions can be derived from several articles (Helmberger, 1964; Ward, 1958; Domar, 1966; Oi and Clayton, 1968; and Meade, 1979) that have presented economic models of cooperatives.

However, if restraints are imposed upon the model to prevent the cooperatives with a relatively high value of marginal product of labor from employing hired labor, then an industry consisting of cooperative firms cannot be efficient. If the primary means that a cooperative has to bring the value of the marginal product of labor down to the value in alternative uses is to admit new members, with a claim to a share of the rent on land and capital earnings, there is no incentive to expand the labor input. In this situation, resources will not be efficiently allocated among firms.

If labor were paid on the basis of its average product and allocated on the basis of maximizing the average product, the allocation of labor and complementary inputs among farm products would not result in the maximum possible value of output. It would do so only in the unlikely circumstance that land and labor were used in the same fixed proportions for all farm products or the average product of land were the same for all farm products. The natural tendency of the collective farms to allocate their labor to products with a high average product of labor rather than to products where the marginal products of labor is high and uniform can be partially offset by imposing procurement and production plans upon the farms. This approach is used, of course, though it is not clear if the reason given is the one used to rationalize the agricultural planning process.

A critical question is whether a system of farm cooperatives operating subject to the added restraints would move toward a more efficient allocation of resources than imposed by the original assignment of land. As long as land is an important factor of production, adding inputs other than labor does not modify the result significantly. Figure 4.1 depicts the situation of two different cooperatives. Each farm has, at the time of organization or some subsequent time (the labor–land ratio was changed significantly by World War II) a given amount of land and a given membership with a specified number of able-bodied workers. It is further assumed that the elasticity of supply of work from the members is zero. Cooperative "A" had a relatively favorable man-land ratio, while "B" had a less favorable one. It is assumed that there are no other factors that affect labor or land productivity; thus for the same labor–land ratio the average revenue product and the value of the marginal product of labor would be the same on the two cooperatives. Relaxing this assumption, as noted later, is not likely to improve the situation.

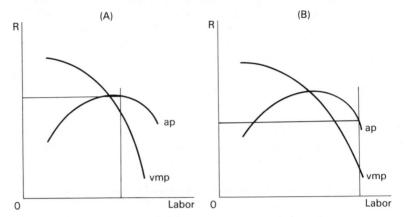

Figure 4.1 *Employment Determination in a Producers' Cooperative.*

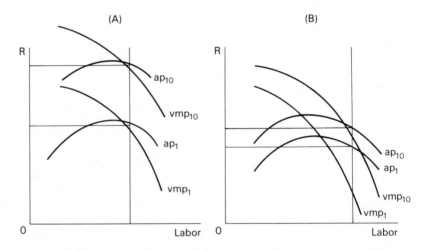

Figure 4.2 *Employment Determination in a Producers' Cooperative with Capital Investment.*

Cooperative "A" members would have significantly higher incomes and higher value of labor marginal product than Cooperative "B" members. Agricultural output of the two farms together could be increased if the members of "B" were admitted to "A" until the values of the marginal product of labor were equalized. But there is absolutely no incentive for "A" to permit this readjustment. The consequence would be a loss of income to the existing members of "A" and the loss could be substantial. This result is an empirically realistic one. Even though there are and have been substantial income differences among collective farms in the same community, there have been almost no additions to the membership of high-income collectives by transfers from other collectives.[2]

In Fig 4.1 it was assumed that the collectives had the same production function and that members received a payment equal to the average product of their labor. Even assuming that the product curves are net of all exactions made by the state in the form of taxes or required support for various public services, the actual payments to the members are less than those indicated. Collective savings, whether forced or voluntary, must come out of the average product and are not available for distribution. But the fact that collective savings on Cooperative "A" will be significantly larger than on "B" would almost certainly lead to an increase in the income disparity over time.

If the income differences between the two cooperatives were of the magnitude indicated, it is unlikely that the similarity in the average and marginal product functions would hold for long.[3] The high-income collective could make investments in its land that would increase the marginal product of land, for a given current labor input, to a much greater extent than the low income collective. This is depicted in Fig 4.2 by the disparate upward shifts over time in the product curves for labor on the two collectives.

Of course, if there were an efficient capital market, the low income collective could keep pace with the high-income one. But it could only keep pace; the income differential that existed at the beginning could only be narrowed by reducing the number of members in the low-income collective. Further, over time the high-income collective probably would improve the relative quality of its labor force, both as workers and managers, and thus further increase the income disparity. The improvement in labor-force quality would occur in two ways: more schooling for the younger people and higher retention rates of members with greater human capital. Soviet agriculture appears to lose through migration a very high percentage of its young people and, in particular, young people with marketable skills. High-income cooperatives would be in a better position to retain more of those with such skills. It appears that there is no substantial basis for expecting that income differences among the cooperatives would be reduced, given the assumptions about labor mobility.

Two caveats are required for the statement that the cooperative form of organization could be as efficient as a private firm in a competitive situation. First, if the members of the cooperative firm cannot sell the value of their rights in the cooperative, investment will not be optimal. There will be no way that existing members can assure themselves of receiving the full benefits of an investment. This feature of cooperatives, which seems to be nearly universal, would primarily affect long-term investments. If the full fruits of an investment could be realized within a fairly brief period — say two to five years — the impact would be much smaller than if a significant part of the investment could be realized only after a decade or more. This feature of collective farms may partially explain why soil erosion is such a major problem, or why land-reclamation projects such as drainage seldom achieve their goals, or why such a significant percentage of irrigated land is abandoned each year.[4]

Second, a farming cooperative may quite freely choose a method of distributing its net income that leads to some inefficiency in the use of resources within the farm. The net income of a cooperative is generally distributed according to the amount of a particular input contributed by the members. In the case of an agricultural cooperative the input used to allocate income is generally labor. This means that labor will be paid on the basis of its average product. If it is true that labor is both paid on the basis of its average product and allocated to maximize the average product of labor, the allocation of labor and complementary inputs among farm products (crops and animal products) would not result in a maximum value of output. It would do so only in the unlikely circumstance that land and labor were used in the same fixed proportions for all farm products or that the average product of land (and all other inputs beside labor) were the same for all farm products. As said above, the natural tendency of the collective farms to allocate their labor to products with a high average product of labor rather than on the basis of marginal labor product can be partially offset by imposing procurement and production plans upon the farms.

Let us turn now to the question of whether a system of farm cooperatives subject to the added restraints would over time move toward a more efficient allocation of resources than imposed by the original assignment of land. The added restraints are those related to the employment of hired labor and the prohibition on the sale of membership rights. As long as land is an important factor of production, the existence of inputs (machinery, fertilizer and energy) in addition to labor does not modify the result significantly.

One of the assumptions of the model of the cooperative farm was that land was originally assigned to farms on the basis of the prevailing distribution of village populations and the supply of land farmed by the members of the villages. For a variety of historical and economic reasons there were substantial variations in the amount of land per worker, a circumstance not unique to Russian agriculture. As the previous discussion has indicated, the particular' restraints that prevent cooperatives from adding new members without loss to existing members has prevented some adjustments that could reduce income inequalities among the collective farms within a region or between regions. As noted earlier, if hired labor were an acceptable practice, high-income collective farms could hire workers from low-income collective farms. This would not decrease the incomes of the members of the high-income collective farms; in fact, it would increase their incomes while also increasing the incomes of members of the low-income collectives. But this is not a solution that has been adopted to any significant degree.[5] Much of the hiring of labor for the traditional farm tasks has been of nonfarm people who, willingly or otherwise, make themselves available during periods of peak labor demand.

The substantial differences in rural income, both within regions and between regions, induced the government to devise programs specifically designed to reduce income inequality. There are some approaches to reducing such income inequalities that could result in a more efficient use of resources. Permitting the employment of hired labor, as noted above, is one approach to reducing income inequality while improving efficiency of resource use. Two other approaches that would have desirable impacts upon both the distribution of income and resource efficiency are noted — labor mobility from agriculture to urban areas and charging rent for land. But for a number of reasons, primary emphasis has been given to other approaches for reducing income inequalities. And as will be noted these approaches impose substantial costs in terms of inefficient use of resources.

A solution that would be consistent with the basic theory of collective agriculture (with legal or self-imposed restraints on hiring labor) and that would improve resource efficiency would be through differential mobility of farm people to urban communities. To the extent that regional and personal inequality of income has been reduced in agriculture in private market economies, differential mobility has been much more important than any farm policy. Differential mobility has functioned through both actual migration and by the increase in off-farm work in private-market economies. In recent years, the Stalinist policy of restricting the nonagricultural employment of collective-farm members has changed to one of encouraging collective farms through the development of "agrarian-industrial complexes" and by some other means. However, as my colleague, Arcadius Kahan (1976), has shown, the amount of employment, and especially off-season employment, provided to farm workers has so far been very small.

Another approach to offset some of the effects of the unequal labor–land ratios when mobility is limited is to charge or collect rent on land. Two main approaches for collecting differential rent have been considered since the abolition of the Machine Tractor Stations. One is through the price system and the other is by a direct rental charge.

A specific rental charge on land, if a part of an appropriate set of output and input prices, would go some distance toward reducing income inequality in agriculture without adverse effects upon resource allocation. If the rental charge were related to the value of the marginal product of land, a part of the source of the higher incomes of farms with relatively low man–land ratios would be captured by the state. However, a rental charge cannot fully offset the effects of labor immobility. Assuming that the quality of labor were everywhere the same, the amount of rent per unit of land collected on farms with a relatively high man–land ratio would be greater than on farms with a relatively low man–land ratio for land of equal productivity.[6]

It is not surprising, of course, that charging rent would not remove all or even most of the income inequality when land cannot be rented in or out, and labor cannot move freely among farms. The high man–land ratio farms, even though paying higher rent per unit of land, would not be able to acquire more land by renting (or buying). Thus the Soviet economists who favor charging rent probably would be disappointed in the resulting effects upon income distribution. If the rent charged per unit of standard land were set equal to the rent on farms with the lowest man–land ratios, some improvement in income equality would be achieved. My impression is that this is what at least some Soviet economists have in mind. This practice would then leave some of the rent for distribution as labor payments on farms with high man–land ratios. However, even this may be disappointing starting from the current situation, since the marginal productivity of land on the current high-income-per-worker farms may well be substantially higher than on the low-income-per-worker farms due to the long-term effects of higher-quality management, greater human capital and larger investments in land improvements on the higher-income farms.

The approach taken since the abolition of the Machine Tractor Stations has been to capture rent through the use of differential prices. The general practice has been to differentiate prices regionally, though there are some cases where regional prices have been differentiated according to productivity or incomes of groups of farms within a price region. I shall consider only the regional differentiation of prices. It should be added that price differentiation has been accompanied by minimum and guaranteed payments to workers per day of work. These minimum payments are relatively uniform both within and among regions, at least this is the impression one gets from the limited amount of data that has been published.[7]

Once minimum wages have been established by regions, output prices must be established that cover production costs on most farms. The criterion for establishing zonal prices was to cover average production costs plus some unspecified percentage of net income or profit. Land costs are not included in production costs. It is possible that regional or zonal price differentials and the minimum wages have reduced regional income differences. However, the reduction in income inequality has certainly been at the cost of efficiency. If land and labor were the only inputs used in agriculture, the added inefficiency other than that due to labor immobility would be small. However, purchased inputs have come to play an important role in

Soviet agriculture. Regions with high output prices would tend to increase their use of purchased inputs, such as fertilizer, relative to regions with low output prices. Thus the real value of the marginal product of fertilizer would be significantly lower in high-price than in low-price regions. I am assuming, to some degree inaccurately, that the decisions on the amounts of inputs to use are made by the farms. If this is not the case, then the inefficiency from regional price differentials would be relatively small.

It is uncertain how seriously the objective of reducing regional income differentials is actually taken. Most farm products now carry substantial premia for above-procurement-plan deliveries. These differentials, which are of the order of 50% for many products, have resulted in substantial income inequality due to inequities in establishing the delivery quotas, either regionally or among farms in the same region. The objective of the price premia is to increase output and marketing, and it is possible that this objective receives more weight than reducing income inequality.[8]

If the price system described above is not complex enough, in some republics experiments have been made to differentiate prices within a regional price zone (Kalnyn'sh, 1972). This was done by dividing farms into four groups according to their costs of production and differentiating prices so that higher prices were paid to relatively high-cost farms and lower prices to relatively low-cost farms. This is a witch's brew that could hardly be more effective in discouraging efforts to reduce production costs. If farms are reclassified among groups, as it appears they are, cost reductions will sooner or later be followed by price reductions. In fact, during some period of time it would be profitable to expand output through high-cost means in order to obtain a higher price in the future. Gray (1979, p. 553) was told that the extent of price differentiation by zone and "even by groups or noncontiguous farms" had increased during the 1970s.

It is possible that zonal price differentials and minimum wages were adopted for a primary reason other than reducing income differentials within agriculture. The highest zonal prices are in regions that have many disadvantages for farming. Without the minimum wages and higher prices, agriculture might well have disappeared in some areas. With the current emphasis on expanded food production, policy makers may well have felt that they simply could not accept a decline in food output in any part of the Soviet Union.

Private Plots and Ownership

I have so far ignored the existence of private plots farmed by collective-farm workers. In a competitive situation with market prices equating supply and demand for both outputs and inputs, private plots would present no problem in the organization of a collective or cooperative agriculture. Private plots present difficulties only because prices paid to the collectives are below market levels or because of significant inefficiencies in the functioning of the cooperative enterprises.

If the output of both the private plots and collective farms were priced at equilibrium market levels (at both producer and consumer levels) there would not be a significant encouragement to withhold labor from the cooperative enterprise during critical periods — if the labor on the cooperative received the value of its marginal product.

The continued importance of private plots in marketable output and in the incomes of collective-farm members in the Soviet Union is a clear indication that the cooperative sector is inefficient in the use of resources. Data for 1970 indicate that on collective farms only 47% of income was derived from the collective; the remainder came from private plots and other receipts. In the source the importance of private plots alone was given only for the Georgian Republic. In this republic "more than 50% of the family budget" came from private plots, and only 22% from the collective farm (Teriaeva, 1972, p. 51).[9]

But the inefficiency of the cooperative sector is due primarily to the policy setting within which it must function. Inappropriate prices, as well as other policy defects, limit the efficiency of the cooperative sector. The fact that the private plots provide higher returns for most resources — certainly for labor and land — than the cooperative sector is not proof that the private plots are efficiently operated and the cooperative sector is inefficiently operated. While the private plots operate under severe restraints with respect to site and the availability of many resources, the plot operators have the very real advantage of significantly high output prices and of being able to allocate whatever resources they may have without the benefit of Moscow planners.

As noted earlier, one limitation of the cooperative form of organization in Soviet agriculture is that investment may be inhibited by the inability of a member of the cooperative to realize any return from his investment if he should leave the farm. This problem is not unique to the Soviet collective farm but is true of cooperatives generally. Since cooperatives appear to operate with reasonable efficiency in a number of economies without well-defined ownership of their assets, it seems reasonable to conclude that the ownership structure of Soviet collective farms is not a significant source of inefficiency. This is not to say that the inability of a member of a collective to realize any benefit from past contributions to the assets of the collective or from the land owned by the collective has no effect on efficiency of resource use. One effect, in addition to the effects on long-term investments, is that farm labor may be retained in agriculture that would leave if the individuals would not lose the income from the assets that he "owns" as a member of the cooperative or collective.[10]

As might be inferred from the above, I do not believe that socialized ownership of agricultural land is, by itself, a significant source of inefficiency. As long as the system defines with some clarity who has the rights to the income from land, the land will be used with a reasonable degree of efficiency. The model of the cooperative farm as I have described it provides for such clarity. There is nothing in the collective-farm charter that is inconsistent with the members of a collective farm feeling secure in their control of the land assigned to the farm. Unfortunately for the members of the collective farms, actual practice of agricultural officials has resulted in numerous violations of the "inviolability" of the rights of the collective farms to the land that was assigned to them. These violations have included the amalgamation of collective farms or the transfer of collective farms to the state-farm sector by merging one or more collective farms with a state farm.

Scale of Collective Farms

Up to this point I have argued that the cooperative form of enterprise need not introduce significant inefficiencies. The only important negative factor is the area of long-term investment. In arriving at this conclusion, I have implicitly assumed that workers receive the value of their marginal product as payment for their labor though I recognize that such is not the case in Soviet agriculture. I shall now comment briefly on the possible inefficiencies that may have resulted from the Soviet penchant for large units.

The average size of a collective farm in the late 1970s was a sown area of approximately 3,000 hectares, something over 400 households and approximately 540 workers.[11] These are large farms, but are they so large that with appropriate forms of internal management they should be inefficient?

Whatever handicaps scale may bring to agriculture could be largely offset if there were willingness to delegate responsibilities within the farms. To a greater extent than many manufacturing activities, farming offers the opportunity to separate production activities into discrete functions or spaces with little or no interference with the rest of the functions and processes. Grain production can be largely separated from livestock production, if desired, and in the United States this has occurred to a considerable degree. Even within grain or other crop production, decentralization and separation of activities can be readily accomplished.

Given the nature of farming, there are very real problems of relating reward to performance when the units are large and decentralization has not been permitted. The magnitude of this problem is undoubtedly exaggerated by the assumption that where there are "n" workers, each worker views the reward from added effort in terms of 1/n share of the results of that added effort. But there is almost certainly some validity to this definition of the effort or work problem that seems to plague collective farms in the Soviet Union.

One can easily imagine, at least if one is not a Soviet ideologue, a number of approaches to decentralizing activities within a collective farm that would be consistent with the concept of a collective farm, and that would bring a much closer correspondence between reward and effort than now exists. The collective farm could remain as the primary unit for marketing output and purchasing inputs and for making a variety of decisions where externalities and economies of scale exist. Examples of such externalities and scale economies are irrigation, drainage, erosion control, roads, electricity, processing of certain products, maintenance of spare-parts inventory, repair services and provision of credit. If the collective farm were permitted to charge rent to each of the smaller divisions or units, there would be adequate resources for the provision of a wide range of social services and for technical assistance to each of the operating units.

State Farms

Over the past two decades there has been a major emphasis on the expansion of the state-farm sector. During the 1950s the importance of state farms grew due to their importance in the New Lands Program. But since 1960 the increased importance of the state-farm sector has occurred at the expense of the collective-farm sector — because collective farms were amalgamated with existing state farms. One might call the transforming of thousands of collective farms into state farms and the enlargement of the remaining collective farms through amalgamation the most significant administrative and organizational changes in agriculture during the past two decades. Yet, as with a myriad of other changes, these seems to have been no readily identifiable positive effect upon farm output or a reduction in the costs of producing that output as a result of the transfer of such a large percentage of the collective farms to the state-farm sector. In 1950 state farms accounted for 11% of the total crop area and three decades later for approximately half.

It may also be noted that over time the differences between collective and state farms have been reduced. The periodic payments to collective-farm members for their labor at an established minimum level has made them almost, if not quite, wage workers similar to those on the state farms. Collective farms have grown in scale and while still smaller than state farms, the collective farms of today are larger than state farms were a decade or so ago. Now, as in the past, state farms have been favored in terms of material resources and investment, but this is the result of a policy decision and has nothing to do with the form of organization.

The reader may well wonder why I have given almost all of the emphasis to the cooperative or collective form of farm organization even though this form is now no more important than the state farm sector. My reasons are mainly historical. I excuse my emphasis by noting that the state and collective farms suffer or benefit from approximately the same features and principles. The state farm sector has an important advantage over the collective — it can adjust its labor force more directly than can the collective. But other than this much of what I have said, or will say, applies to approximately the same degree to both collective and state farms.

4.3 Collective Farms and the Soviet Planned Economy

While I believe that there could be improvements in the performance of Soviet collective farms if the farms were smaller or if the internal organization were changed along the lines suggested above. I am not convinced that the poor performance of Soviet agriculture is primarily due either to its being a socialized agriculture or to the large scale of the units within that structure.

On the basis of the simple model developed earlier, and accepting the objective of Soviet planners to reduce income inequalities in agriculture, I put forward the following considerations that, I believe, largely explain the poor performance of Soviet agriculture:

(a) The output-price system provides farms with inappropriate signals and incentives for an efficient use of agricultural resources.
(b) The unwillingness of Soviet officials and planners to permit the collective farms reasonable scope of decision making clearly inhibits efficient resource use.
(c) The production, marketing, and transportation systems for agricultural inputs do not provide appropriate farm inputs in adequate quantities and qualities and in a timely manner to the farms.
(d) Rules and practices that prevent or inhibit labor migration within agriculture reduce significantly the efficient use of resources, and have resulted in inappropriate measures being taken to eliminate income disparities within agriculture.
(e) The pattern of time preference, as evidenced by a variety of decisions, implies an exceedingly high rate of discount of the future. The very great emphasis on a high level of output and marketing in the current year results in decisions that increase output variability through reducing summer fallow to a wholly inadequate level, and apparently minimizes carryovers of grain and feed, thus making livestock production a vulnerable sector.

While none of these points are new, some documentation or comment is in order on each.

(a) *Output Prices*

Prior to Stalin's death the price system was not a major element in the decision process either for planning officials or the farms, except for the producers of the technical crops. However, after Stalin the Soviet planners have used output prices to encourage output expansion, if not to significantly influence the allocation of resources among farm products. But policies have vacillated. Khrushchev significantly increased the level of output prices, but retained a two-price system for most farm products until 1958 when the Machine Tractor Stations and the stipulated delivery of part of the output to them were abolished. At that time a single-price system was introduced with great fanfare as the most appropriate approach (Nimitz, 1959, pp. 267–76). But under Brezhnev the multiple-price system was reintroduced, with premia of 50 to 100% for above-plan deliveries of crops. In 1970 a complicated set of prices were introduced for livestock products, calling for premia for above-plan deliveries and additional premia for achieving certain weights for cattle when sold for slaughter. Alongside these complex price systems were the regional price differentials, which were designed to reflect differences in costs of production. In effect, the regional price differentials appear to be a not very well disguised means of collecting land rent from the areas with good land, such as the Northern Caucasus and the Ukraine.

The radical revisions of procurement prices made by Krushchev were designed to cover average production costs and to permit some additional savings (Nimitz, 1959, p. 268). Average-cost calculations, as is well known, exclude any return to land and capital. Thus if there are to be funds left over for net accumulation or savings by enterprises, procurement prices must exceed the average production costs. But to provide incentives for expanding production of particular products it would not be enough to maintain the same differential of prices over production costs. Land and capital inputs vary among farm products; thus if the price system is to have an important role in influencing production decisions, output prices must reflect the contributions of land and capital in the production of various commodities. Generally speaking, the profitability levels are higher for crops than for livestock products. This reflects, at least to some degree, the greater importance of the land input in the production of crops than in the production of milk, pork, poultry and eggs. The negative profitability of milk, mutton, wool and potatoes led officials to increase procurement prices substantially in 1979 (Grushetskii, 1979).

But rising levels of costs, which presumably should not occur in an economy with a stable price level, may have already largely offset the 1979 price increase of 15% for milk. Assuming that the 1979 price increases were based on 1977 production costs, cost increases for 1978 through 1980 approach the magnitude of the milk price increase.

Except for the price increases made during 1979, average procurement prices did not increase significantly during the 1970s. Average annual production costs increased in the collective- and state-farm sector by 1 to 4%; perhaps the rough average was 2% or about 22% for the decade. Profitability of production clearly declined during the decade.

As viewed by state-farm workers or collective-farm members the increase in average production costs were not all bad. A significant part of the increase in production costs reflected increased payments to workers. From 1966 through the late 1970s man-day earnings on collective farms increased by 4.6% per year; on state farms by 5.2% (Schoonover, 1979, p. 96). Gross labor productivity increased at a slower rate — about 3.5% annually (Diamond and Davis, 1979, p. 38). Net labor productivity, after one accounts for the increase in capital stock and purchased inputs per man-day of labor, increased significantly less than gross labor productivity.[12]

Soviet planners have no easy answer to the need to offset rising production costs in order to maintain profitability and incentives to expand production, especially for meat and milk. The planners are caught between their unwillingness or inability to increase consumer prices and the resulting impact of rising procurement prices upon the magnitude of the subsidy required to make up the difference between purchase and selling prices for meat and milk. In announcing the 1979 procurement-price increases, the Soviet government simultaneously stated that retail prices would not be increased even though the procurement-price increases would cost the budget 3.2 billion rubles.

Premia for above-plan deliveries are supposed to encourage output expansion by providing a much higher marginal price than would be possible with a single output price. But there are two very real problems with such premia. One is to determine the size of the required or plan deliveries; there is no magic formula for an equitable or efficient distribution of such plans among farms. As one Soviet author, V. Iur'ev (1979, p. 83), states: "A considerable percentage of the markups is received by enterprises that strive for nonintensive plans they can easily surpass." It is not stated how a farm "strives for nonintensive plans" but some of the ways are not too difficult to imagine, if one puts one's mind to it.

The other difficulty is that in an agricultural economy that is subject to substantial year-to-year production variability, the payment of the premia increases income instability. This is not a new problem. Nimitz (1959, pp. 264–5) notes the income effects of the premia for above-plan deliveries, where the above-plan deliveries were paid for at a rate of three times the rate for the compulsory deliveries and resulted in a much higher average price in a region with a good crop than in one with a poor crop. She also presents data on three groups of farms in Stalingrad Oblast, where the required deliveries were the same per hectare for every farm regardless of yield. A rather small difference in yield — apparently not more than a fifth — resulted in a realized price difference of more than 100% in 1956.

Current studies show the same consequence of the premia — if a farm has a very good crop yield, its income increases both because of the higher output and because of a higher price. And when the crop yield is low, income declines accordingly. Iur'ev (1979, p. 86) presents data for a group of collective farms in Rostov Oblast. In 1973 when the value of gross agricultural output (in constant prices) was 672 million rubles, receipts for above-plan deliveries was 55.6 million rubles. In 1972 when gross agricultural output was only 287 million, income from above-plan deliveries was only 0.5 million rubles. The contribution of the premia to income instability is substantial.

(b)   *Planning from the Center*

What more can be said about the problems created by efforts to closely control from Moscow the agriculture of such an enormous range of soil and climatic conditions as exists in the Soviet Union? In spite of several reorganizations designed to reduce the scope of central planning, it is not obvious that anything has been accomplished in the past three decades. How little such efforts have accomplished was indicated, in a rather small matter, by a change for 1976–80 that farms would no longer be given two procurement plans — one for the base or plan deliveries and one for above-plan deliveries (Schoonover, 1979, p. 109). During the 10th Plan, farms would be given only the base procurement plan. However, the procurement agencies would be given both plans and it does not take a very great stretch of the imagination to conclude that the directors of collective and state farms will not see much difference in their relationships with the procurement agencies.

The Soviet planners do face difficult problems. Given the inappropriateness of both output and input prices, the output that would be called forth by the current price system operating without procurement and other forms of planned intervention would differ significantly from the desired output distribution. Without incentives for the management for plan fulfillment on collective and state farms, it is doubtful if livestock output could have achieved the level of recent years, since such output was unprofitable for most farms. Some of the incentives have been positive, such as bonuses; others have clearly been negative such as the pressure of the procurement agencies and local planning and party officials who have much to gain if all or most components of the plan are fulfilled.

But it is the planners who are involved in establishing the prices. One might argue that in a communist system prices are inappropriate so that planners and political officials will have a reason for maintaining their authority over the most minuscule detail of economic activity! But the problem may have even more sinister roots. Planners and officials apparently neither understand nor trust farm people. I have no reason to modify what I wrote almost a decade ago after a brief visit to the Soviet Union (Johnson, 1971, pp. 263–4):

> Despite frequent references to the role of incentives in economic activity, including agriculture, the real operating principle that seems to guide agricultural planners and officials is that farms cannot be trusted to make appropriate decisions. While there is a great deal of objective evidence to support this conclusion, the basic idea was well put in a speech at Minsk by A. M. Rumyantsev: "Every collective farm cannot take into account society's real needs in agricultural products. This can be done only by socialist society as a whole. The latter makes the necessary information

available to all collective farms in a centralized way, by drawing up its firm plan of purchasing farm products, by placing orders with these farms and thus ensuring the stability of their production."

(c) *Supply of Inputs*

An important reason for the differences in the resource costs of agricultural products in the Soviet Union and the United States is to be found in input and knowledge sectors that serve agriculture in the two countries. Also of significance is the very different functioning of the marketing and transportation sectors that process, move, and deliver the output of agriculture to the final consumer.

The mechanization of Soviet agriculture has long been plagued by machines of relatively poor quality and short working lives. To some degree a short machine life may be due to poor maintenance, but poor quality and lack of an adequate supply of spare parts must have an important role (Johnson, 1979, p. 9). The mania for large machines has also taken its toll; it has only been in recent years that relatively small-wheeled tractors have been available in reasonable numbers. The emphasis upon the large track-laying tractors has meant an enormous investment in a machine with known high-maintenance costs. It is not only that the original cost of the track-laying tractors is higher than for rubber-tired-wheel tractors of equivalent power, but maintenance costs are much higher as well. And for the vast majority of farm operations, the track-laying tractors have no advantage over the wheeled tractors. In a system that has great difficulty in providing both spare parts and adequate repair services, the track-laying tractor represents an enormous inefficiency.

In the 1950s a cotton picker that would not pick cotton satisfactorily continued to be produced even though thousands of them were left idle on the collective farms. In a market economy production would have been stopped because of lack of sales, but in the Soviet Union the planning system resulted in the continuing production and delivery of a useless product for several years. I do not intend to imply that there are no mistakes in a private-market economy in the design of machines, but such mistakes are relatively quickly detected and a correction occurs, either through foresight or the absence of sales.

Modern agriculture is dependent upon purchased inputs — fuel, fertilizer, insecticides, herbicides, machinery, spare parts, seeds, electricity and tools. It is also dependent upon a number of services, such as machinery repair, maintenance of electric transmission lines and telephones. In many cases, what appear to be minor delays in receiving a product or a service can result in very substantial economic losses. The seasons dictate the most appropriate times to apply fertilizer, insecticides and herbicides; if these products are not available at the appropriate time their values are substantially diminished. A delay in planting or seeding of a week can reduce output by a few percent. Note that in the Soviet Union each one percent loss of grain output is approximately two million tons. If a combine is waiting for repair at the beginning of the harvest and if a month is required to complete the repair, in most cases the investment in the combine has been wasted for the entire year.

(d)   *Labor Immobility*

Undue emphasis should not be given to labor mobility within agriculture as a possible corrective for inequality of the income distribution and for improving resource allocation in agriculture. Based on experiences in high-income countries, labor mobility reduces regional and personal income inequalities in agriculture through the transfer of labor from agriculture to the rest of the economy. Through differential regional rates of migration, migration reduces income differences both within and among rural areas and between rural and urban areas.

The reduction of income inequalities through mobility is a process that requires a considerable amount of time. In the United States net outmigration from farms started about 1880; the size of the farm population continued to increase absolutely until about 1915, and by 1950 the farm population had declined by 30%. The changes in the farm population in this period of more than a third of a century were not sufficient to significantly reduce the regional income differentials within US agriculture. But the next twenty years witnessed remarkable changes — by 1960 the farm population had declined 52% from its peak level and by 1970 the decline had reached 70%.

It was not only that the US farm population declined by more in terms of both percentage and absolute amount from 1950 to 1970 than between 1915 and 1950, but the population that continued to reside upon farms earned an increasing percentage of its income from nonfarm sources. In 1950, about 30% of the income of the farm population came from nonfarm sources; by 1970 the percentage had increased to 53 (USDA, 1979). During this twenty-year period there was a remarkable reduction in the income inequality among farm families that was formerly associated with region and farm size or the amount of farm resources owned.

The increase in the importance of nonfarm income and the sharp reduction in the farm population since 1950 can be attributed primarily to improved communication, a sharp reduction in the cost of personal transportation, increased education levels, and the growth of real incomes in the United States.

The long-run solution to the regional income inequalities (as well as many of the intraregional ones) in the Soviet Union is either to encourage migration away from the farms or to bring a wide range of nonfarm jobs within easy reach of farm people. Immeasurable harm was done to rural people by the Stalinist policy of preventing collective farms from establishing nonfarm-employment opportunities and by the destruction of the handicraft and other cottage industries that were so important to Russian rural people. The reversal of these policies during the past two decades will work to reduce income differentials, but it will take years before the effects of the Stalinist policies are overcome.

A further inhibition to a significant reduction in income inequalities by labor mobility is the high cost of personal transportation in rural areas. This high cost is due to the abysmal state of the rural-road network and the limited availability of personal vehicles. In addition, the limited development of the rural trade network and small-scale industrial enterprises means that there are relatively few nonfarm jobs available in most rural communities.

Regional or zonal price differentials have apparently become a permanent feature of Soviet agricultural-price policy. As noted above, regional price differences that do not reflect differences in transportation and marketing costs are a source of inefficiency in the use of resources. It is not obvious how important such inefficiency may be since resource allocation in the Soviet Union responds to many variables other than the prices of inputs and outputs. In fact, one of the important reasons for procurement contracts and for the direct allocation of certain inputs is to induce farms to behave in a way other than that which would be the most profitable given the prices that they face.

(e) *Time Preference*

Soviet agriculture is continually being pressed by the central authorities to maximize output *now*. With few exceptions, output plans are too ambitious and can be achieved only with good luck and good weather. Given the incentive structure that exists throughout the system, such plans put enormous pressure on all parts of the agricultural system to achieve a high level of output now — this year — even if the impact on future output is substantial. The discount rate is very high, apparently far higher than that used by farmers in market economies.

Let me give one illustration. Agronomists and other agricultural scientists have long recognized that the crop rotations used in most of the low-rainfall areas of the Soviet Union result in highly unstable yields and rather modest increases in output over a period of years (Johnson, 1977, pp. 15–19). The amount of grain sown on summer fallow is far smaller than in similar areas of North America, where as much as 50% of the crop rotation consists of summer fallow.[13] While the long-run impact of increasing summer fallow to the amount that would minimize the cost of producing the grain would result in a rather modest reduction in grain output, there would be a larger short-run loss of output during the transition period. A much greater use of summer fallow would significantly reduce production variability, which would have favorable cost effects upon marketing, storage, and livestock production.

There is little doubt that, given the existing variability of grain production, stocks of grain are too small in the Soviet Union. One reason for the small size of stocks is that the price system provides no incentive for farms to hold stocks from one season to another. There are no seasonal price differentials, and procurement prices are set for the indefinite future and are independent of annual-output variations. In fact, the premia for exceeding planned-procurement deliveries provide a negative incentive for holding stocks. If a farm has a good crop and can deliver more than the procurement plan, its marginal return for such deliveries is 50% above the regular procurement price. If it stored the grain instead of delivering it, it would run the substantial risk that in some subsequent year it would have to deliver the grain at the regular procurement price. Thus its "reward" for the storage costs and waiting might well be negative. Further, the farm manager may assume that he can acquire grain from the mixed-feed industry at a stable price during the years of low-grain yield. If this is possible, it is an added reason for not storing at the farm level.

Equally important, the price and reward system provides insufficient incentives to procurement agencies to hold stocks in adequate amounts. Given the internal stability of prices, holding grain from one year to the next adds only costs and no income to the procurement agency. And it appears that the costs of unusual imports, since such imports involve foreign exchange, are not reflected in the accounts of the procurement agencies.

Interrelationships

There are interrelationships among these sources of inefficiency and high cost in Soviet agriculture. All of the sources, I assert, start with the inappropriateness of the price system for agricultural outputs and inputs. By inappropriateness of prices I mean that the prices do not reflect the underlying supply (or cost) and demand conditions. The prices of some farm products require that numerous farms produce such products at less than the cost of current inputs while the prices of other farm products are such as to provide not only for recovery of current input expenditures but also a substantial return for capital and land. Under these circumstances criteria other than profitability, as viewed by the farms, must be used to influence output decisions. Similar comments apply to the prices for farm inputs; these prices fail to equate supply and demand in most cases and thus various forms of rationing and allocation must be imposed.

Consequently efforts to change agricultural management and organization to provide for greater initiative and decision-making authority at the farm or even the rayon or regional level cannot be carried through given the current price structure. Or at least to do so would carry the substantial risk that output of some important crop, such as potatoes, would drastically decline or that most of the fertilizer would be used very near where it was produced in order to minimize transport costs.

It seems clear that no one managerial or organizational change or a group of such changes will significantly improve the efficiency of Soviet agriculture until there is a radical reform of the Soviet price system and a major improvement in the performance and responsiveness of the farm-input-supply and marketing sectors of the Soviet economy.

Soviet agriculture has already undergone major administrative and organizational changes during the past quarter century. Among the very important changes was the abolition of the Machine Tractor Stations (MTS). Partial analysis clearly supported the decision taken by the Soviet planners. With the existence of the MTS there was a division of authority over the production of agricultural crops — the management of the farms, on the one hand, and the director of the MTS on the other. Appropriate incentives did not exist, in many cases, for the MTS workers to do work of high quality. In addition, with the complicated interrelationships between the MTS and the farms they served, it was difficult if not impossible to devise any form of accounting system that could reflect the underlying cost conditions. Yet actual experience following the abolition of the MTS indicated that nothing really changed. I am confident that if we had access to the required data we would find that there were many instances in which the MTS were well managed, that there were good relations between the MTS and the collective farms, and that farm output declined and costs increased after the abolition of the MTS. This is not to say that the MTS should have been continued, but only to indicate that where there are numerous sources of inefficiency, removal of one of the sources may not improve anything, since the new approach to performing the same tasks may be no more effective.

I know of no better way of illustrating what I have just written than a quite lengthy quotation from an article entitled "Improving the Management of Agriculture" by I. Buzdalov (1980). This quotation follows a discussion of higher output prices and increased enterprise costs of production of all major farm products between 1970 and 1977. After noting that procurement-price increases "cannot go on indefinitely" because such increases affect "basic questions of socio-economic development, including problems of retail prices, the national economic profitability of agriculture, etc.," Buzdalov (pp. 26–7) wrote:

> In this regard the question arises as to how to curb these trends and to turn them around. . . . Practically speaking, the problem is to develop and apply economic and organizational forms of relationships that ensure a close link between physical indicators of the plan and indicators of effectiveness, the quality of work, and material incentives.
>
> . . . The existing system of material incentives is expressed in a set of primarily quantitative indicators that frequently duplicate one another and therefore [it] does not sufficiently promote the development of true cost accounting and the creative initiative of enterprise collectives and

personnel in the rational distribution and utilization of resources and in increasing effectiveness. Economists have recently proposed using physical and conditional planning indicators (norm-days, norm-rubles, etc.). In so doing they usually advance a single argument: value indicators, especially profitability, are incomparable since prices are imperfect, and hence the fulfillment of the plan's volume indicators may be attained to the detriment of the necessary product mix, at the expense of costly types of products, by-products, etc. However, the proposed arbitrary indicators are divorced from the real forms of social accounting of the expenditures and results of labor, from the actual economic principles of the planned management mechanism and especially on the improvement of pricing. No manner of accounting price or other arbitrary indicator can provide the enterprise with normal conditions of economic activity if the actual price for a given type of product does not ensure the necessary profitability. Nor does the non-cost accounting redistribution of net income between profitable and unprofitable production facilities produce the proper effect. Of course, arbitrary calculated normative criteria on evaluations in planned management are admissible, but only if they play an auxiliary role and do not supplant the actual conditions and proportions of production.

To support his position, Buzdalov calls to the reader's attention a statement made by L. I. Brezhnev at the March (1965) Plenum of the Central Committee (p. 28): "The level of profitability is what must form the basis of evaluation of the economic activity of collective and state farms." He also, following common practice, noted that V. Lenin viewed self-recoupment as a "very important principle in the organization and evaluation of all economic planning work under cost-accounting conditions" (p. 29). And finally he noted that two CMEA countries — the German Democratic Republic and Hungary — have made effective use of economic levers and incentives in the planned agricultural-management mechanism and that doing that was "producing positive results" (p. 28). After noting a number of the features of the economic levers and incentives provided in these countries he noted that these measures "directly influence the improvement of production proportions and provide economic motivation for the rational use of internal reserves. The strengthening of the economic basis of planning on an objective basis, without excessive guardianship, compels producers to improve final quantitative and qualitative indicators" (p. 28).

I have not quoted Buzdalov at such length on the grounds that I expect his article (and probably others like it) to lead to a reform of the price system in the years ahead. I have called attention to this forthright expression of views for the quite obvious reason that it so fully supports what I have argued for a long time.

Two final conclusions can be stated. One is that while Soviet agriculture may well increase its output at a reasonable rate in the future, it will continue to be a high-cost agriculture and thus a source of difficulty to Soviet planners. Nevertheless, I do not anticipate that the required overhaul of the price and incentive systems will be made in the reasonably near future. The second conclusion is that I am now quite fully convinced that the socialized nature of agriculture is not the primary or even an important source of the inefficiency and high cost so prevalent in the Soviet Union.

4.4 The Tenth Plan and Implications for the Future

My paper presents a rather gloomy picture of the future of Soviet agriculture. My conclusion is that the important deficiencies of Soviet agriculture — high cost, output instability, the large demands on investment resources, and the slower growth of output than of demand for commodities with high income elasticities — are such that managerial and administrative changes will be insufficient to contribute significantly to their solution. Nothing short of a major overhaul of prices, greatly increased responsiveness of input suppliers and marketing agencies, and significant relaxation of central control can provide solutions for high costs and low returns on investment and make some contribution toward reducing production instability. As long as livestock production remains significantly less profitable than that of other major farm products, its output growth will lag behind demand. The commitment to fixed retail prices for meat and milk is imposing major costs on the economy, operating as this commitment does through the budget to restrain policy makers from providing appropriate incentives for meat producers.

In terms of the agricultural sector, performance during the Tenth Plan can only be described as a significant disappointment (USDA, 1980a). Output has generally lagged behind what were quite reasonable goals; only the goals for cotton and egg production seem likely to be met. There will be significant shortfalls for sunflower seeds (output will be lower during the Tenth than the Ninth Plan) and the same will be true for potatoes. Both meat and milk will fall short of the lower end of the very modest minimum goal of a 7% increase for the plan period.

It appears that grain used for feed will increase by about 23% during the Tenth Plan while meat and milk output will increase approximately 6% (USDA, 1980a, pp. 22 and 28). This may well be the most disconcerting aspect of the agricultural performance during the Tenth Plan for the top Soviet officials. An increase in grain use of more than 20 million tons produced less than a million tons of meat, 5 million tons of milk, and 0.5 million tons more eggs.

A rough calculation indicates that the annual increase in meat, milk and egg output between the two plans had a total value less than the increase in grain used as feed. The estimates of the value of output were generous — eggs at the current US retail value, milk at the high US price for manufactured milk and meat at $1,500 per ton, carcass weight. In recent months imported boneless beef was priced at the US border at about $1,300 per ton. It was assumed that the grain at the Russian border has a value of $180 per ton — a price at US Gulf Ports of $140 per ton plus transport and associated costs of $40 per ton. The increased value of meat, milk and egg output was estimated to be $3.05 billion annually; the value of the grain was estimated at $3.6 billion.[14] The cost of all feed, not just the grain, should not be more than 60 or 70% of the value of meat, milk and eggs produced.

Large specialized livestock enterprises were supposed to be the answer to high feed requirements. These enterprises are said to be more productive in the use of feed than the ordinary collective and state farms, though at enormously high investment per animal. But it remains to be the case that, as the importance of these specialized feeding operations has increased, feed requirements per unit of output for agriculture as a whole appear to have increased.

If resource productivity in the livestock sector continues to decline in the years ahead, as it has during the 1970s, Soviet officials will be faced with some very painful issues. Among them are the rapid growth in the subsidies for meat and milk or the even more painful possibilities of substantially higher consumer prices for meat and milk. Another of the painful issues would be the continuing growth of grain imports. With annual grain imports during the Tenth Plan at approximately 20 million tons (USDA, 1980a, p. 22), one could speculate that even modest   g als for meat and milk production during the Eleventh Plan could call for grain imports averaging 35 to 40 million tons. I am not projecting such a level of grain imports, but only trying to indicate some of the difficulties confronting Soviet officials.

Will these and other problems result in a dramatic reappraisal of agricultural policy in the Soviet Union? I believe the type of policy changes that would make a difference to agricultural productivity and output are not likely to occur during the 1980s. The Soviet Union now has high enough per capita income that it can, like Western Europe, sustain a very-high-cost agriculture for an indefinite period. In a real sense the planners' problems would be simplified if the primary sources of high cost and low productivity were the socialized nature of its agriculture, or the large scale of the farms or even the regional price differentials. Changing some of these aspects of policy would be painful, but one could imagine that such changes could be carried out. One might even imagine that farms could be given greater autonomy to make their decisions. But if my analysis is at all near the mark, these policy changes would have very modest effects upon the performance of agriculture. What is required is much more fundamental and, importantly, much more difficult to achieve.

Given the recent experience the Soviet Union has had with efforts to restrict their access to grain supplies, it is possible that an upper limit will be placed on the magnitude of grain imports. The fear that access to grain supplies may be restricted should put added pressure upon Soviet officials to consider a wider range of alternatives for improving agricultural productivity than it has been their wont to do so. Yet even in this setting and the difficulties that it presents, I do not see significant changes in Soviet agricultural policy during the Eleventh Plan Period.

True, there may be minor changes such as higher prices for livestock products, and a requirement that procurement agencies handle all output offered to them, or another reorganization of the Ministry of Agriculture. These changes, and others like them, will not be enough to permit a significant growth of livestock and poultry output without much greater dependence upon imported grains and other feeds.

4.5 Some Concluding Remarks

I hope it is clear to the reader that the socialized farm system as I have described it is a far cry from the actual Soviet socialized farm system. I have engaged in imagining what a reasonably efficient socialized agricultural system might look like in order to shed light on the reasons for some of the important shortcomings of Soviet agriculture. I happen to believe that the elimination of some of the shortcomings of Soviet agriculture, especially its instability of output and its increasing demands upon the world grain markets, would be of potential benefit to the rest of mankind. However, there is little likelihood that the Soviet Union would freely abandon the collective- and state-farm system. I am convinced that if the present agricultural system is retained without modification, Soviet agriculture will continue to exhibit major and increasing shortcomings. Thus it seemed reasonable to ask whether there is a socialized and cooperative agriculture that can function with a high degree of efficiency capable of production in competition with the agricultures of North America or Australia. I believe it is possible to devise such a system within the framework of Soviet law and the Model Collective Farm Statute. There is no feature of a collective or cooperative farm as suggested by me that could not be instituted in the framework of a socialized agriculture.

But I do not project or predict that the Soviet agricultural system will change in the direction outlined in this paper. While I argue that a socialized agriculture can be efficient, making that system efficient requires a reasonable approximation to a functioning price system. A price system that provides appropriate price signals for decisions made by farms, by the input-supply sectors and the marketing agencies requires major changes in the role and nature of central planning.

As noted above, per capita incomes in the Soviet Union are high enough so the economy can afford an inefficient, high-cost agriculture. The institution of an effective price system for agriculture and food is likely to occur, if at all, for reasons that are largely external to agriculture.

4: Notes

1 My paper is based, in part, on research support provided by the National Council for Soviet and East European Research. The views expressed are my own and should not be attributed to the National Council or the University of Chicago. Anything I

write about Soviet agriculture owes a great debt to my years as a colleague of Arcadius Kahan. The present paper is no exception.

2 In recent years some high-income collective farms have "voluntarily" combined with low-income farms.

3 The underlying production functions could still be the same on the two cooperatives. Investments made in the land, such as drainage, clearing, leveling, or irrigation, can be viewed as increasing the amount of land. But land in the two figures is measured by area and not productivity; differences in productivity that emerge over time are reflected in the shifting of the labor-productivity curves. Changes in the quality of labor are also likely to occur over time as noted later in the text.

4 It may also help to explain why such a large share of investments made on collective farms comes from the state rather than directly from the resources of the collectives.

5 Diamond and Krueger (1973, p. 330) estimated that in 1966 only about 2% of total labor payments by collective farms went to hired workers.

6 This assumes that products with the same labor intensity were produced when man–land ratios differ. Such is not likely to be the case. However, it is highly unlikely that shifting toward labor-intensive products on the farms with high man–land ratios could result in rent per unit of land and marginal products of labor to be equal to those of the low man–land ratio farms if the farms are in the same climatic and soil area.

Some authors (Ward, Domar, and Oi and Clayton) have argued that if rent were set at high-enough level, the reduction in income on a cooperative would be sufficient to induce the cooperative to increase the number of members. However, the assumptions under which such an effect would occur are very different from those I have made and are assumptions that do not reflect the alternatives facing collective farms in the Soviet Union or Eastern Europe.

7 The minimum wages on collective farms were to be set equal to wages on state farms in the same region. Variations in state-farm wages, based on republic averages, ranged from 81 to 128% of the union average in 1970 (Teriaeva, 1972, pp. 52–3).

8 In the late 1970s the percentage of the output that could be sold as "above plan" for bonus payments was smaller than during the early 1970s. In 1976 the base prices were increased for several important farm products. These two related changes contributed to a reduction in farm-income inequality.

9 Shmelev (1979, p. 87) indicated that 26% of the income of collective-farm members came from private plots in 1976 in the USSR. For the entire Soviet Union in 1970 private subsidiary activity provided 38% of all earned income, according to McAuley 1979, p. 132). Earnings, presumably from wages in the socialist sector, accounted for 10% of earned income. Transfer payments accounted for 10% of money income; earned income was 90% of money income. Thus, income from the collective farm was about 43% of total money income.

10 But this may not be a real problem with respect to outmigration. The organization to which a farm worker goes may also own assets from which he will benefit. While owning a house on a collective represents a considerable private investment, the migrant from a collective or state farm eventually obtains housing space in cities at significantly less than its cost.

11 In 1974 the 360,000 largest farms in the United States had an average of 192 hectares of cropland; the annual average employment on these farms would have been approximately six workers including the operator and family members.

12 Diamond and Davis (1979, p. 51) give data that permit estimates of capital stock per unit of labor. In 1965 the capital stock per man-day of labor was 4.7 rubles; in 1977, 16.8 rubles or an increase of 3.5 times. They also estimate that current input purchases per man-day (in 1976 prices) were 0.55 rubles in 1965 and 1.32 rubles in 1977.

13 Summer fallow is the practice of leaving land idle for a year while cultivating it in a way that controls weeds and conserves moisture. The serious weed problem confronting much of Soviet agriculture could be reduced by increasing the amount of summer fallow.

14 This review of livestock output during the Tenth Plan and the estimates of grain used for feed raise the disquieting prospect that grain-output data may have an increasing

degree of exaggeration over time. The other possibility is that meat- and milk-output data were overestimated in the past and some part of the overestimation is now being corrected. If the grain and livestock data are reasonably comparable over time, the high-cost nature of the Soviet livestock sector is quite fully revealed.

4: References

Buzdalov, I., "Improving the Management of Agriculture." *Probl. of Econ.* **22**, 11: 20–33, March 1980.

Diamond, Douglas B., and Krueger, Constance B., "Recent Developments in Output and Productivity in Soviet Agriculture." In *Soviet Economic Prospects for the Seventies*, pp. 316–90. Papers, Joint Econ. Comm., U.S. Congress. Washington: Govt. Printing Off., 1973.

Diamond, Douglas B., and Davis, W. Lee, "Comparative Growth in Output and Productivity in U.S. and U.S.S.R. Agriculture." In *Soviet Economy in a Time of Change*, pp. 19–59, 1979.

Domar, Evsey D., "The Soviet Collective Farm as a Producer Cooperative." *Amer. Econ. Rev.* **56**: 734–57, Sept. 1966.

Gray, Kenneth R., "Soviet Agricultural Specialization and Efficiency." *Soviet Studies* **31**, 4: 542–58, Oct. 1979.

Grushetskii, L. "The Stimulating Function of Purchase Prices." *Probl. of Econ.* **22**, 7: Nov. 1979.

Helmberger, Peter G., "Cooperative Enterprise as a Structural Dimension of Farm Markets." *J. Farm Econ.* **46**: 603–17, Aug. 1964.

Iur'ev, V. "Stimulating the Growth of Procurement of Agricultural Products." *Probl. of Econ.* **22**, 7: 80–95, Nov. 1979.

Johnson, D. Gale, "Soviet Agriculture Revisited." *Amer. J. Agric. Econ.* **53**, 2: 57–264, May 1971.

Johnson, D. Gale, "The Soviet Livestock Sector: Problems and Prospects." *ACES Bull.* **16**, 2: 41–62, Fall 1974.

Johnson, D. Gale, "Theory and Practice of Soviet Collective Agriculture." Office of Agric. Econ. Research, The University of Chicago, Paper No. 75: 28, Dec. 15, 1975

Johnson, D. Gale, *The Soviet Impact on World Grain Trade*. Washington, D.C.: British–North America Committee, 1977.

Johnson, D. Gale, "Soviet Agriculture in the Late 1970s." Office of Agric. Econ. Research, The University of Chicago, Paper No. 79: 4, Jan. 1979.

Kahan, Arcadius, "The Problems of the Agrarian-Industrial Complexes in the Soviet Union." In Zbigniew M. Fallenbuchl, ed., *Economic Development in the Soviet Union and Eastern Europe*, vol II. New York; Praeger, 1976.

Kalnyn'sh, A., "Concerning an Economic Experiment in Latvian Agriculture." *Probl. of Econ.* **15**, 8: 61–77, Aug. 1972

McAuley, Alastair, *Economic Welfare in the Soviet Union*. Madison, Wisconsin: University of Wisconsin Press, 1979

Meade, James E., "The Adjustment Process of Labour Cooperatives with Constant Returns to Scale and Perfect Competition." *Econ. J.* **89**: 781–8, Dec. 1979.

Nimitz, Nancy, "Soviet Agricultural Prices and Costs." In *Comparisons of the United States and Soviet Economies*, Pt. I, pp. 239–84. Papers, Joint Econ. Comm., U.S. Congress. Washington, DC: Govt. Printing Office, 1959.

Oi, Walter Y., and Clayton, Elizabeth M., "A Peasant's View of a Soviet Collective Farm." *Amer. Econ. Rev.* **58**: 37–59, March 1968.

RSEEA. Newsletter for Research on Soviet and East European Agriculture. Dep. of Econ., North Texas State University, Denton, Texas. **1**, 4, Dec. 1979.

Schoonover, David M., "Soviet Agricultural Policies." In *Soviet Economy in a Time of Change*, pp. 87–115. 1979.

Shmelev, G., "The Private Household Plot in CMEA Countries." *Probl. of Econ.* **22**, 1: 79–100, May 1979.

Soviet Economy in a Time of Change. Papers, Joint Econ. Comm., U.S. Congress. Washington, DC: Govt. Printing Office, 1979.

Teriaeva, A. "Necessary Labor and its Remuneration in Agriculture." *Probl. of Econ.* **15**, 7: 42–64, July 1972.

U.S. Department of Agriculture (USDA), Farm Income Statistics. *Stat. Bul.* No. 627, Oct. 1979.

USDA, "Agricultural Situation: Review of 1979 and Outlook for 1980: USSR." Suppl. 1 to WAS-21. Washington, DC, April 1980 (a).

USDA, "Indices of Agricultural and Food Production for Europe and the U.S.S.R., Average 1961–66 and Annual 1970 through 1979." *Stat. Bul.* No. 635, June 1980 (b).

USDA, "World Agriculture Situation". WAS-22, June 1980 (c).

Ward, Benjamin, "The Firm in Illyria: Market Syndicalism." *Amer. Econ. Rev.* **48**: 566–89, Sept. 1958.

5

Agricultural Production

DOUGLAS B. DIAMOND,
LEE W. BETTIS and ROBERT E. RAMSSON

Introduction

Low labor productivity and high costs of production characterize the performance of agriculture, the most serious, abiding, and intractable problem area of the Soviet economy. Moreover, despite an average annual rate of growth in total agricultural output that has exceeded that of both the United States and the rest of the world, the USSR has not managed to produce the required quantity and quality of farm products to meet domestic demand. As a result, the Soviet Union has become one of the world's major importers of farm products.

The steady growth in the Soviet population, the continued rise in per capita income, and the rapidly rising expectations of the populace have combined to generate high demands on agriculture. A large part of this demand is directed to the reduction in the proportion of starchy staples — grain products and potatoes — in the diet and to a concomitant rise in the proportion of quality foods, especially meat. Thus, the Soviet leadership must respond to domestic pressures for a better — and more costly—product mix, as well as attempt to free itself from major dependence on Western sources of food.

Central to this quest for both self-sufficiency and a rapid improvement in the quality of the diet is the future of the livestock sector and the supporting feed base. Even with the surge in the 1970s in the importation of grain for feeding, the annual rate of increase in output of meat and other livestock products has slowed markedly. If the forward momentum achieved earlier in upgrading the diet is to be reattained, the output of livestock products must accelerate. This will require a sharp expansion of domestically produced grain and nongrain feedstuffs, under present levels of efficiency in converting feed to livestock products.

A primary purpose of this paper is to explore the prospects in the 1980s and 1990s for the feed and livestock sectors under alternative assumptions concerning (a) the future demand for livestock products, (b) the domestic supply of grain and nongrain feedstuffs, and (c) the functional relationships between feed inputs and livestock-product output. This analysis will provide insight into the future Soviet import demand for grain and other feedstuffs.

We do not attempt to derive single-value forecasts in projecting future Soviet import demand for grain and other feedstuffs to the years 1990 and 2000. Rather, emphasis is on obtaining a notion of the degree of uncertainty by testing alternatives and identifying possible problems. As the recently released "Global 2000 Report" states, "highly aggregated food projections with so distant a time horizon are not forecasts of what will happen but rather educated guesses of what could happen" (Barney, Dir., 1980, p. 73).

Before exploring the future for the feed-livestock economy, we review in Section 5.1 trends in farm output and productivity for the period 1950–79. Section 5.2 looks beyond the broad measures of overall output, inputs, and productivity and considers underlying factors associated with increased availability of farm products in the past.

The outlook for the future of the feed-livestock economy and the implications for international trade of grains and grain supplements is assessed in Sections 5.3 and 5.4. Section 5.3 projects alternative demand patterns of future food consumption and their implications for both farm output and its livestock component. Section 5.4 focuses on the prospects for grain and nongrain feed production in support of the livestock program and explores the impact on the results of alternative paths of change in the several important sources of growth. Section 5.5 briefly places in perspective the implications of the baseline (reference) case established in Section 5.4 and productivity in the period 1980–2000.

5.1   Trends in Agricultural Output and Productivity

A.   *Output*

By 1979, Soviet farm output had reached 2½ times the 1950 level. Although progress has been uneven, the average annual rate of increase has been 3½% per year, nearly double that of the United States and more than the 2% average growth in farm output for the rest of the world. The major part of this growth took place in the 1950s, when production expanded at an average of nearly 5% per year (Table 5.1).

A comparison of the average annual *values*[1] of net farm output during the three successive 10-year periods affords a broader view of relative changes over the past 30 years (Table 5.2). Annual net production in the 1960s averaged more than 40% above the average annual level in 1950–59, highlighted by a boost of nearly 45% in the value of livestock output. This was followed in the 1970s by a further gain of roughly 30% in both overall and livestock production. The rise in domestic output, coupled with a higher level of net imports of farm products, has permitted a marked improvement in the quality of the Soviet diet since the early 1950s. Per capita consumption of animal products has doubled since that time.[2] Conversely, the share of calories supplied by starchy staples dropped from roughly 70% in 1950 to 54% in 1965 and to 46% in 1979. As suggested by the slowing of the decline in the starchy-staple ratio, the rate of improvement in the quality of the diet parallels the growth record in farm output, which showed a marked slowdown in the 1970s.

B. *Inputs and Productivity*

For the period 1950–79 as a whole, the flow of land, labor, capital, and other conventional inputs to Soviet agriculture has increased by roughly 75% compared with a 150% increase in output.[3] Assuming that errors of measurement of the type frequently cited do not radically affect the overall productivity measure, the difference between the average annual rate of increase in agricultural production of about 3½% and of additions to inputs of 2% was due to an average annual increase in productivity of 1½%.[4] But the average for the 30-year period obscures important differences in trends in inputs and productivity for the several subperiods (see Table 5.3). Most of the gain in productivity occurred before 1970; in the 1971–9 period, nearly all of the increase in output was attributable to additional inputs. More importantly, the continuous decline of Soviet productivity growth since the 1950s has been the strongest factor influencing the slowdown

Table 5.1 *USSR: Growth of Net Agricultural Output* (percent)*

	Average Annual Rate of Growth
1951–60	4.8
1961–70	3.0
1971–9	1.8

* See Note 1. The base year for the calculations shown in this table and other tables in this paper is the year before the stated initial year of the period. Because of the wide annual fluctuations in Soviet agricultural production, a three-year moving average is used.

Table 5.2 *USSR: Value of Net Agricultural Output* (billions of rubles)*

	Average Annual Output		
	1951–60	*1961–70*	*1971–79*
Total	48.2	68.7	87.8
Crops	23.0	32.3	40.2
Livestock	25.2	36.4	47.6

* See Note 1. Prices used to aggregate agricultural output are the average prices realized by all producers for products sold in 1970.

Table 5.3   *USSR: Output, Inputs, and Factor Productivity in Agriculture, 1951–79 (percent)*

| | *Average Annual Rate of Growth* | | | |
	1951–60	*1961–70*	*1971–9*	*1951–79*
Output[a]	4.8	3.0	1.8	3.4
Inputs	2.7	2.1	1.6	2.1
Factor Productivity	2.1	1.0	0.2	1.2

[a] Because of the wide annual fluctuations in Soviet agricultural production, a three-year moving average is used.

in the rate of growth of farm output. Of the fall-off of 3 percentage points in the average annual rate of increase in Soviet farm output between the 1950s and the 1970s, approximately three-fifths can be attributed to a reduction in productivity growth and only two-fifths to a slowing of input flows.

Although the average annual growth of total inputs to agriculture slowed during the 1970s, the annual increases in flow of industrial goods to farms was up slightly. Compared with the last half of the 1960s, the annual level of deliveries of machinery, equipment, and industrial materials (e.g. fertilizer, fuels) was 50% higher in 1970–9.[5]

5.2   Factors Associated with Increased Agricultural Output

In the foregoing, we distinguished two sources of growth of Soviet farm output: the increase in factor inputs and the increase in productivity. As background for inquiry into the future of Soviet agricultural production, with special reference to the livestock-feed linkage, it is also useful to explore sources of increased output, as delineated in another way. We refer to these sources:

(a) change in sown acreage;
(b) change in yield per hectare;
(c) change in the efficiency of converting feed into livestock products;
(d) change in feed available for output of livestock products due to reduction in use of draft animals, and other workstock.

For convenience, by referring also to net foreign trade in agricultural products, we extend the analysis to sources of domestic supply, as distinct from output.

We consider for successive time intervals the impact of the foregoing factors on observed changes in agricultural supply. In each case, the effect of a change in acreage is calculated on the assumption that yields are unchanged at the *ex ante* level. The impact of the change of yields is then computed on the assumption that the acreage is unchanged at the *ex ante* level.

Table 5.4   *USSR: Changes in Farm Product Supply for Domestic Use Attributable to Various Sources[a] (millions of rubles and percent)*

Sources of Change	Average Annual Change			
	1960–9 from 1949–53		1970–79 from 1960–9	
	Value	Share	Value	Share
Sown Acreage[b]	6,306	30.1	427	2.5
Crop Yields per Hectare[c]	9,946	47.4	9,083	53.9
Feeding Efficiency[d]	2,896	13.8[h]	2,579[i]	15.3
Diversion of Feedstuffs from Animal Draft Power[e]	2,055	9.8	977	5.8
Net Imports[f]	−238	−1.1	3,780	22.5
Total[g]	20,965	100.0	16,846	100.0

[a] Farm-gate price weights for 1970 were used in aggregating the various indicators expressed in physical terms. In most cases, these are average realized prices received by all producers.

[b] If crops grown exclusively for feed (e.g. hay) were *excluded*, the change in the acreage factor for 1960–9 compared with 1949–53 would be 4,500 million rubles; and for 1970–9, compared with 1960–9, 400 million rubles.

[c] If crops grown exclusively for feed were *excluded*, the change in the yield factor for 1960–9 compared with 1949–53 would be 9,000 million rubles; and for 1970–9 compared with 1960–9, 9,900 million rubles.

[d] Changes in efficiency in converting feed to livestock products expressed in terms of value of livestock output per feed energy unit. The figures include shifts in the product mix to livestock of a higher or lower efficiency in converting feeds.

[e] Horses only. In terms of price weighted feedstuffs saved by a reduction in horse numbers.

[f] Net trade of each agricultural commodity weighted by 1970 ruble price weights. The USSR was, on the average, a net importer in all three periods when trade values are expressed in 1970 domestic prices received by producers:

Period	Average Annual Exports	Average Annual Imports	Balance
	(million 1970 rubles)		
1949–53	736	−1,001	−265
1960–9	2,120	−2,147	−27
1970–9	1,927	−5,734	−3,807

[g] A summation of these five sources of additional domestic supply. The ruble values associated with the five factors—separately and together—are not to be confused with the changes in net agricultural output shown in Table 5.2. The values shown here provide a basis for comparing the *relative* importance of the major sources of additional domestic supply but do not take into account all sources (e.g. increase in livestock numbers).

[h] 1963–9.

[i] 1970–78.

As for the successive intervals, we relate the average annual levels attained in the 1960s to the average level for the base period 1949–53; and the average annual levels attained in the 1970s, to that for the 1960s. The years 1949–53 marked the last five-year period of the Stalin era, which was followed by major changes in agricultural policy instituted by the post-Stalin leadership.

The span of years embraced by the periods under review provide a broad enough view to dampen possible effects on agricultural output from climate fluctuations.[6] The results are summarized in Table 5.4.

A. *Increase in Sown Acreage*

Dramatic changes in the use of crop land occurred after Stalin's demise, and the expansion of acreage associated with these changes contributed substantially to the growth of total output. Between the 1949–53 base period and 1960–9, 30% of the change in the aggregate ruble value of the five sources of product growth considered in Table 5.4 was attributable to expansion in acreage. Total sown acreage in 1960–9 averaged 209 million hectares, or 39% above the average for the 1949–53 period. In a series of programs inaugurated between 1954 and 1962, Khrushchev directed an expansion of more than 60 million hectares in sown acreage and a radical restructuring of crop patterns. The "new lands" campaign, initiated in 1954, was quickly followed by an even more ambitious "corn program" in 1955. The former program resulted in the plowing up of some 42 million hectares of virgin and long-fallowed lands, mostly in Kazakhstan and Siberia. The "corn program" expanded the acreage of corn for grain, silage, and green feed from 4½ million hectares in 1952 to a peak 37 million hectares in 1962.

When the effects of these two programs on output began to taper off, Khrushchev initiated yet another program, the "plow up" campaign in 1962. This campaign was designed to shift the cropping pattern radically, principally through a drastic reduction in the area sown to perennial grasses and a restriction of the practice of clean fallowing. The newly released acreage from the reduced area under fallow was to be cultivated in crops (Diamond, 1966, p. 366).

Overall sown acreage peaked in 1963 at 218.5 million hectares, 68 million hectares above the 1949–53 average; 25 million hectares of the increase is attributable to an expansion in grain acreage. Increasing indications that the new-lands program had extended grain sowings into marginal and submarginal soils, coupled with several poor harvests, persuaded the post-Khrushchev leadership to reduce acreage (Laird, 1976, p. 2). It was not until the latter half of the 1970s that sown acreage reattained the level of the early 1960s. In addition to changes in overall acreage, the ruble value of sown acreage shown in Table 5.4 reflects changes over time in the relative importance of high-value- and low-value-per-hectare crops.

B. *Crop Yields*

As indicated in Table 5.4, increases in crop yields per hectare have been the primary source of increase in farm output. Crop yields in 1960–9 and 1970–9 averaged about 45 and 70%, respectively above the early 1949–53 base period.[7] Grain yields led the way with an average annual rate of increase of 2.7% between 1950 and 1978, the year yields peaked. The rate of increase in grain yields would have been greater if it had not been for the moderately depressing effect of locational shifts between the early 1950s and the early 1960s. The new-lands program was centered in the relatively low-yielding areas of the Volga Valley, Kazakhstan, and West Siberia. As a result, average grain yields in 1962–4 were 8% lower than if shifts among regions had not occurred. Since the early 1960s there has been no further net change in grain yields attributable to such shifts.[8]

C. *Increased Feeding Efficiency*

Livestock output relative to total feed has increased when various kinds of feeds are aggregated in terms of nutritive values.[9] Between the base period in the early 1950s and the 1960s, the ruble value of output per feed unit increased on the average by 12%, although in the 1970s feeding efficiency stagnated.[10] Improved overall efficiency in converting feed to individual livestock products seems to explain the differences among the periods. Indeed, a correction for the shift in composition of output from products requiring divergent-from-average amounts of feed per ruble of output led to virtual offsets in both periods.

The improvement in efficiency is consistent with trends in productivity per animal. For example, the rising productivity of cows when expressed in kilograms of milk per cow annually argues in favor of a rise in the efficiency and some apparent improvement in the overall quality of the feed ration.[11] Although the deficit in the protein content of the feed ration apparently remains as large as before, a much higher proportion of grain, especially in the form of processed (mixed) feeds, as well as the substitution of corn silage and legume hays for wild hay and other poor quality roughages, have provided some improvement in livestock diets and, hence, in efficiency in converting feed into meat, milk, and other products.[12]

D. *Diversion of Feedstuffs previously used for Draft Animals*

The substitution of mechanical for animal power has meant a substantial release of pasture and cropland previously used to feed draft animals. The share of total feed (expressed in feed units measured in equivalent oats) required for horses fell from approximately one-fifth in 1949–53 to an average of 5% in 1970–9. The average annual saving of 20 million tons in feed units between the base period and the 1970s was enough to produce roughly 2 million tons of pork (carcass weight), equivalent to 17% of average annual meat output in 1970–9; or nearly 14 million tons of milk, equivalent to 16% of milk output in 1970–9.

In value terms, replacing workstock with tractors and other mechanized sources of power (thereby providing more feed for other livestock) made possible roughly one-fifth of the total increase of net livestock output from 1949–53 and 1970–9. This source of increased output has now been largely exhausted.[13]

E.   *Net Trade of Agricultural Products*

The net imports shown in Table 5.4 reflect the balance of exports and imports when they are valued in domestic average realized prices received by producers in 1970. In the period of the three decades under review, the USSR was a net exporter of farm products in only six years. Exports exceeded 3 billion rubles annually in three of those years (1967–9). Since 1972, when the Soviets adopted a policy of relying on grain imports to raise meat production (Johnson, 1977, p. 20), gross imports (in constant prices) have ranged between 4 billion (1972) and 9 billion rubles (1979), while exports reached 2 billion rubles in only 2 years (1974, 1977). As a result of this surge in imports, the net supply of agricultural products from domestic production was enhanced by roughly 7½% in the period 1977–9. In effect, a sharply higher average annual rate of increase of *domestically* produced farm products (0.9 percentage point above the 2.3% average annual rate achieved between the 1967–9 and 1977–9 periods) would have been required to balance the value of imports and exports and to maintain the same level of domestic use of farm products.

Despite the importance attached to the highly publicized grain purchases in the expansion of the USSR's net imports over the past decade, imports of other selected farm products have also risen dramatically over the past decade. Grains can explain less than two-fifths of the increase in net agricultural imports between 1967–9 and 1977–9, when trade flows are expressed in domestic prices. Major boosts in net imports of meat, butter, and sugar accounted for two-fifths of the swing in agricultural trade from net exports to net imports. The only major increase in net exports came in cotton, up 0.7 billion rubles between 1967–9 and 1977–9.

F.   *Summary of the "Sources of Change"*

Among the five sources of change in the domestic supply of farm products considered in Table 5.4 three findings can be highlighted:

(i) Enhanced crop yields have been the primary source of expanded output. If net imports are excluded from consideration, 70% of the average annual increase in supply from 1960–9 to 1970–9 is attributable to greater output per hectare of sown acreage.

(ii) Expanded acreage, the second most important source in 1960–9 when compared with 1949–53, dwindled in importance in the 1970s.

(iii) Net imports of farm products in the 1970s replaced sown acreage as the second most important source of increased supply.

These past trends are useful to keep in the forefront, as we look at the future. We argue in Section 5.4 that the recent trend towards ever increasing reliance on larger crop yields per hectare is a harbinger of likely developments. To the extent that, together with boosts in other less important sources of domestic supply, crop productivity per hectare cannot accelerate rapidly enough to keep the gap between domestically produced supplies and requirements from widening, the outlook is for even larger net imports.

5.3 A Look to the Future — Demand Considerations

In Sections 5.1 and 5.2 we (a) briefly reviewed the USSR's agricultural production and productivity record since the end of the Stalin era and (b) estimated quantitatively the contribution of the major sources of change in the domestic supply of agricultural products. In this and the following section we focus on prospects for the next two decades.

The current indications of official intentions for agriculture are limited to a few targets for 1985. After a spate of press references during 1976–8 to the pending promulgation of a Fifteen-year-plan — spanning the period 1976–90 — discussion in the media has been muted. The lack of official guidelines beyond 1985 requires the use of scenario analysis for projecting both future supply and demand.

In this section we consider alternative projections of demand based on official Soviet nutritional standards and currently achieved levels in Poland and the US. The required rates of progress in both overall domestic agricultural production and livestock output to support alternative consumption patterns are developed.

A. *Implications for Production*

As measured by past rates of growth, Soviet farm production performance has been impressive. This has been reflected in considerable progress in improving nutritional levels since the end of the Stalin era. To feed the growing Soviet population at current nutritional levels, farm output must increase 10% by 1990 and another 5% between 1990 and 2000. But just to maintain the status quo is incompatible with the Soviet leadership's commitment to improve the quality of the diet. The recent record high levels of imports of grain and other feedstuffs to maintain the meat program — the centerpiece of Soviet consumer welfare policy — is adequate testimony to this commitment for a better and more varied diet.[14] Soviet per capita meat consumption in 1978 was nearly 50% below the average per capita consumption of the five East European satellites and at the level attained by Poland in 1965. The proportion of calories derived from starchy staples (46%) in the average Soviet diet in 1978 was 4 percentage points above the US level of 1909–13.

How much of an increase in agricultural output is needed in the future will be largely determined by requirements for food, especially livestock products. In value terms, roughly 90% of output underlying the CIA's Office of Economic Research's index of Soviet net agricultural production has consistently been attributable to output of food-related products.[15] In considering likely future targets for total agricultural output and the associated goals for the grain and livestock sectors, we have chosen three alternative food-consumption standards:

(a) the Polish diet in 1978;
(b) the Soviet planners optimal or "scientific norm" diet; and
(c) the US diet in 1978.

Using these as consumption standards for the projected Soviet population in 1990 and 2000, we develop five series of projections to obtain the rate of growth in net agricultural production required to support these alternative levels of consumption (without a rise in imports). Four of these projections use the Polish 1978 and Soviet "optimal" diets as benchmark goals to be met, on the one hand, by 1990 and, on the other hand, by the year 2000; the fifth projection is based on the attainment of the US 1978 diet by the year 2000 (see Table 5.5).

From the rates of required growth shown in the table the five sets of projections can be roughly divided into two groups.

(i) Average annual growth of Soviet output required to achieve the *Polish 1978 and Soviet "Optimal" Diets by 1990* and the *US 1978 Diet by 2000*:
     — total, 2½ to 3%,
     — livestock, 3 to 3½%,
     — meat, 3½ to 4%.
(ii) Average annual growth of Soviet output required to achieve the *Polish 1978 and Soviet "Optimal" Diets by 2000*:
     — total, 1½ to 2%,
     — livestock, 2%,
     — meat, 2 to 2½%.

The group of higher rates of growth ((i), above) would be roughly in keeping with Soviet performance in the 1960s; the second group of lower rates ((ii), above) (with the important exception of meat output) are consistent with those in the 1970s as shown in Table 5.6.

Table 5.5   *USSR: Projections of Growth in Net Agricultural, Livestock, and Meat Production required to meet Alternative Levels of Per Capita Consumption, 1978 to the Year 2000*[a] *(percent)*

| | Average Annual Rate of Increase | | | | |
| | Polish 1978 Diet | | Soviet "Scientific Norm" Diet | | US 1978 Diet |
	By 1990	By 2000	By 1990	By 2000	By 2000
Net Agricultural Output	2.5	1.7	3.1	1.9	2.5
Livestock Output	3.4	1.9	3.3	2.0	3.0
Meat Output	3.5	2.1	3.8	2.3	3.9

[a] Soviet levels of consumption of the various types of food products including livestock products in 1978 were used to derive the base year in the above calculations.

Table 5.6   USSR: *Average Annual Rates of Growth of Output, 1961–70 and 1971–8 (percent)*

	1961–70	1971–8
Total Output[a]	3.0	1.8
Livestock Output	3.7	1.8
Meat Output	3.5	3.0

[a] Three-year moving average.

The slowing of agricultural production in the 1970s has been accompanied by:

(a) A slowing in the annual rate of improvement in the diet.
(b) Continued high rates of growth in demand for meat and other quality foods engendered by large annual boosts in per capita disposable money income coupled with a firm official policy of maintaining stable prices in state retail outlets.
(c) Record high levels of food imports.
(d) Signs of increasing excess demand for quality foods (as a result of (a) and (b) and despite (c)) as reflected in acceleration in the rise of collective-farm-market prices and in reports of unusual shortages of meat and other quality foods in state stores.

In considering likely targets for the 1980s and 1990s, official concern with mitigating consumer discontent over the loss in forward momentum in improvement of the diet must be considered. From this standpoint, the Polish consumption pattern in 1978 perhaps represents a particularly plausible Soviet target for 1990.[16] Achievement of this goal would still put the average Soviet consumer more than a decade behind his Polish counterpart in terms of the quality of his diet. Indeed, the attainment of the 1978 Polish dietary level by 1990 would be consistent with maintaining the Soviet-Polish "time-gap" of more than a decade, since the Soviet dietary levels in 1978 were at roughly the Polish level of 1965. A related goal for 2000 was set by extrapolation of the required average growth rate in the 1980s through the following decade.

B.   *Consistency of Meat Consumption Targets with Growth in Real Income*

In choosing consumption goals, however, Soviet planners must also consider the consistency of their targets with planned growth in real incomes and the policy of maintaining state retail prices at relatively low levels. Given an income elasticity of demand, and assuming a continuation of the firm commitment since 1965 not to raise state retail prices on food, we can derive the implied change in the gap between meat availability and demand where availability is given by the alternate consumption goals that have been delineated and demand is determined by income growth.[17]

We have estimated an income elasticity of demand for meat by applying a double-logarithmic regression model, with meat consumption per capita regressed on real income per capita for the years 1963–78. Because of the evidence that excess demand for food was greater at the end of the 15-year period than at the beginning, we added as an explanatory variable a collective-farm-market (CFM) price index (reflecting prices that are free to respond to supply and demand). This regression yields an estimated income elasticity of 0.91.[18]

Using this income elasticity, we have calculated the difference between the meat consumption goals and demand where demand is computed under two assumptions about growth in per capita income. Results of these calculations are shown in Table 5.7.

The achieved average growth of real per capita income was about 3% annually in the 1970s. Assuming a 3% annual growth in the period 1978–2000 and no change in CFM prices, the Soviet Union would have to achieve the highest meat production target of those examined — the 1978 US diet by 2000 — in order to keep supply and demand roughly in balance. With this growth in per capita income, substantial disequilibrium would occur if only the lower targets were reached.

Given the outlook for continuation of the decline in Soviet GNP growth, we would expect a slowdown in the growth of real personal disposable income. This will tend to reduce growth in the demand for meat and other high-quality food products. Assuming growth of per capita income of 2% per year, achieving the Polish 1978 level of meat consumption by 1990 would result in a rough equilibrium in 1990 while maintaining CFM meat prices. Indeed, as indicated in Table 5.7 under the "Polish 1978 diet by 1990," after 1990 there would even be a tendency for these prices to fall since supply would actually increase more than demand.

Table 5.7 *USSR: Implied Change in the Gap between Meat Produc-tion and Demand, 1978–2000[a]*

	Change in "Meat Gap"[b] (million metric tons)	
A. *Assuming 3% Annual Growth in Real Per Capita Income*	*1990*	*2000*
Soviet "Scientific Norms" by 1990[c]	3.1	4.8
Soviet "Scientific Norms" by 2000[c]	5.4	10.5
Polish 1978 Diet by 1990	2.3	2.5
Polish 1978 Diet by 2000	5.0	9.7
US 1978 Diet by 2000	1.5	0.2
B. *Assuming 2% Annual Growth in Real Per Capita Income*		
Soviet "Scientific Norms" by 1990[c]	0.7	−0.9
Soviet "Scientific Norms" by 2000[c]	3.0	4.8
Polish 1978 Diet by 1990	−0.1	−3.2
Polish 1978 Diet by 2000	2.6	4.0
US 1978 Diet by 2000	−0.9	−5.5

[a] Demand is estimated using our empirical demand function, assuming no change in CFM meat prices. The results presented in the table are intended to be illustrative. In fact, existence of a positive gap will tend to increase CFM prices and bring demand more in line with supply.
[b] Change in size of the already existing gap in the base year 1978 assuming that relative prices for meat and other consumer goods and services remain constant. As indicated in the Table the gap widens if there is a delay until the year 2000 (compared to 1990) in achieving either the Soviet "scientific norm" or the Polish 1978 level of consumption (e.g. achieving the Polish 1978 level of meat consumption of 72 kg per capita), because the projections reflect constant growth rates.
[c] Also referred to as the Soviet "optimal" diet in the text.

In considering the future of Soviet agriculture, center stage is held by the livestock sector and the requisite feed base. The latter, in turn, depends in large part on the performance of grain production. The outlook for supply discussed in the following section focuses on the output of meat and other livestock products for human consumption.

5.4 Outlook for Growth of the Soviet Livestock and Feed Sectors

In examining the long-term prospects for the feed and livestock sectors, we try to identify problem areas and make reasonable guesses about possible changes in key variables rather than attempting to forecast performance. Our methodology is based on an economic model. In the following sub sections, the model is described, key assumptions are discussed, and a reference case is presented. The impact of changes in reference-case conditions are considered indi-vidually and as a whole.

A.   *Description of the Model*

There are, of course, numerous variables that influence the progress of the Soviet livestock sector. In considering the principal variables, we use a model with an accounting framework comprising roughly 100 relationships. The model contains a number of empirically estimated equations focused primarily in the area of grain yields and fertilizer response. A brief description of the model's principal components is given in the Appendix. For present purposes, we can capsulize its central elements as follows:

(a) The establishment of a set of hypothetical livestock-product targets for benchmark years in the simulation period 1980–2000.
(b) The derivation of a set of feed requirements to support the livestock-product goals. These are estimated on the basis of Soviet feed-input coefficients per unit of meat (including inventory change), milk, and eggs. The estimates take into account the maintenance requirements for cows and horses. These input/output coefficients (hereafter referred to as "feed-conversion ratios" — FCRs) are available for total feed and for concentrates.[19]
(c) The derivation of the non-feed-consumption components of the grain balance in 1990 and 2000. These consist of seed, food use, and industrial use of grain.
(d) The projection of future grain- and forage-crop output.
(e) The comparison of our point estimates of feed requirements and availability to obtain a net deficit or surplus of feed expressed in grain equivalents. A net deficit implies grain import requirements.

B.   *Key Assumptions in the Reference Case*

The reference case is defined by specific assumptions about livestock-product targets, feed-conversion efficiency, fertilizer use, weather patterns, sown area, and trends in yields.

As mentioned above, the reference-case production target is Soviet achievement of the 1978 Polish consumption pattern by 1990. The target for 2000 was set by extrapolating the required average growth rate in the 1980s.

Besides the growth of overall meat production, an important determinant of required feed is the mix of meat produced. For example, varying the proportions of beef and poultry in meat production affects both the level and composition of required feed. Poultry are more efficient converters of feed to animal proteins and consume essentially concentrates (largely grain) while cattle have a high proportion of roughages in their ration. Thus, relatively more beef production implies not only an increase in demand for total feed, but in particular greater need for forage crops (including pasture) compared to concentrates. We assume in our reference case that the future structure of meat production changes gradually towards the structure called for in the Soviet "scientific norm" diet. The shift toward relatively more poultry and less beef would be consistent with higher conversion efficiency:

	Share of Production in 1979 (percent)	Assumed Share of Production in 2000 (percent)
Beef	50	40
Pork	35	30
Poultry	10	20
Mutton	6	10

In our reference projection we have chosen to hold conversion efficiency — described by feed conversion ratios (FCRs) — constant; in a later analysis we look at the sensitivity of our basic results to hypothetical improvements in conversion ratios.[20] The FCRs used in the reference projection reflect recent Soviet practices and are given separately for both total feed and concentrates (see Table 5.8). Requirements for roughages are obtained as the difference between total feed requirements and that for concentrates. Requirements for grain are calculated as 86% of concentrates, equal to grain's current share.

The key variable affecting trends in grain yields is fertilizer applications. Despite the poor performance of the fertilizer industry in the last couple of years, we assume in the reference case that fertilizer production will grow at a rate of 7.5% per year through 1985, 5% in 1986–90, and about 2% in the 1990s. These figures are based in part on Soviet plans. Assuming that fertilizer applied to grain is a stable share of production — about 30% — projected applications on grain in 1990 are 14 million tons and in 2000 about 19 million tons.[21] Thus, with 1978 applications at 7 million tons, we are allowing fertilizer applied to grain to reach two and one-half times the 1978 level by 2000.

Aggregate fertilizer use is simply one side of the fertilizer issue. An equally important assumption concerns the distribution of fertilizer

Table 5.8   *USSR: Feed Conversion Ratios, 1976–8[a]*

	Feed Units[b] Per Unit of Output					
	Beef	Pork	Poultry	Eggs	Milk	Mutton
Total	12.8	8.53	6.23	2.07	1.45	10.32
of which: Concentrates	3.20	7.03	5.61	1.86	0.36	1.55
of which: Grain	2.75	6.05	4.82	1.60	0.31	1.33

[a] The FCRs for meat products are given in kilograms of "feed units" (equivalent oats) per kilogram of liveweight gain. The FCR for eggs is expressed in kilograms of feed units per 10 eggs; that for milk, per kilogram of milk.
[b] A feed unit is defined by total digestible nutrients contained in a unit of oats.

Table 5.9   *USSR: Regional Shares of Fertilizer Applications to Grain, 1978, and Additions 1979–2000* (percent)*

	1978 Share of Total	Assumed Share of Incremental Applications, 1979–2000
Ukraine	21	17
Kazakhstan	4	16
Drought Prone—RSFSR	25	23
Non-Black Soil—RSFSR	18	16
Other RSFSR	9	22
Other USSR (Including Baltic Republics)	24	7

*See Figure 5.1, p. 159.

use among grain producing regions. The RSFSR is broken down into three regions in the grain-output projections: the Non-Black Soil Zone (the Northwest, Central, and Volga–Vyatka economic regions); the Drought-Prone Region (the Central Chernozem, North Caucasus and Volga economic regions); and Other RSFSR (the Urals, West Siberia, East Siberia, and Far East economic regions). The other republics are treated as three additional regions: the Ukraine; Kazakhstan; and Other USSR (essentially Belorussia, Moldavia, and the Baltic, Central Asian, and Transcaucasian republics). Since regions such as the Baltic republics presently use much more fertilizer per hectare than Kazakhstan, it is unrealistic to apply constant shares of a growing fertilizer base to all producing regions. Consequently, we developed a hypothetical future pattern of fertilizer application that allows larger shares of incremental fertilizer applications to go to regions that are relatively deficient in fertilizer use when compared with analogous regions in the West (Table 5.9).[22]

Two final important assumptions underlie our projections of grain production. Since our analysis is obviously concerned with long-term trends, we assume average weather conditions over the simulation period, with average weather defined by mean temperature and precipitation data for the Sixties and Seventies.[23] Secondly, given the severe constraints on further net expansion in arable land in the Soviet Union, we fix acreage to grain at the recent average of about 129 million hectares, the average acreage harvested during the period 1975–7.[24]

Projections of nongrain feeds are broken down into pasture and fodder crops. The average utilization of pasture during 1965–78 was about 0.3 feed units per hectare, and we assume no change in this use in the future. A Soviet source has indicated that land area in pasture by 2000 should reach 308 million hectares compared with about 285 million hectares currently, and we have used this area expansion figure in our reference case (Trifonova, 1980, p. 3).

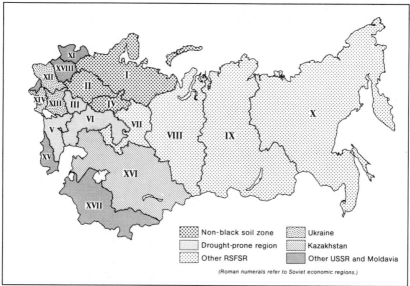

Figure 5.1 *Economic Regions used in the Model.*

Key: I Northwest, II Central, III Central-Chernozem, IV Volga-Vyatka, V North Caucasus, VI Volga, VII Ural, VIII West Siberia, IX East Siberia, X Far East, XI Baltic, XII Southwest, XIII Donets-Dnepr, XIV South, XV Transcaucasus, XVI Kazakhstan, XVII Central Asia, XVIII Belorussia.

Since 1965 the average yield per hectare for fodder crops has grown at a rate of roughly 1½% a year, reflecting primarily major increases in fertilizer applications. (Fodder crops include hay, corn silage, root crops, and green chop weighted by "feed unit" values.) The area in fodder crops has not increased substantially over the last 10–15 years and there is little room for future expansion without reducing other crops. We assume, therefore, no increase in acreage of fodder crops by 2000, but allow yields to continue to grow at the historical rate.

C. *Reference Projection Results*

Our reference projections of grain production by region and crop for 1980, 1990 and 2000 are shown in Table 5.10.[25] Despite widely varying trends in yields and fertilizer use, shares of individual crops in the total are relatively stable over the 20-year period at about 20% for winter wheat, 25% for spring wheat, 30% for spring barley, and 25% for other grains. Regional shares in overall grain production are also generally stable, although the relative contribution of Kazakhstan rises and that of the drought-prone area of the RSFSR falls.

To reach our projected total grain production of about 300 million tons in 2000 would require a one-third boost in the average annual rate of increase in grain yields compared to the recent past. Between 1965 and 1979 grain yields increased at an average annual rate of 1.4% per year. The assumed increase in fertilizer applications on grain is 12

Table 5.10 USSR: Projected Grain Production, Reference Case^a (million metric tons)

	Winter Wheat			Spring Wheat			Spring Barley			Other Grain			Total		
	1980^b	1990	2000	1980^b	1990	2000	1980^b	1990	2000	1980^b	1990	2000	1980^b	1990	2000
Total	48.2	56.8	63.8	53.9	68.0	76.4	65.1	76.4	85.4	57.2	66.1	73.3	224.4	267.5	299.0
Ukraine	23.7	27.4	30.0	—	—	—	12.8	14.9	16.4	12.8	15.6	18.3	49.3	57.1	64.7
Kazakhstan	1.3	1.7	2.0	19.4	26.5	30.0	7.5	11.5	14.7	2.6	4.3	5.6	30.8	44.0	52.3
Drought-Prone RSFSR	18.7	21.9	25.0	8.4	8.4	8.4	20.0	22.8	25.5	13.0	13.0	13.0	60.1	66.1	71.9
Non-Black-Soil RSFSR	2.2	2.4	2.6	1.4	1.8	2.2	7.8	9.3	10.7	7.4	7.4	7.4	18.8	20.9	22.9
Other RSFSR	—	—	—	24.7	31.3	35.8	9.9	11.2	11.6	10.2	12.9	14.8	44.8	55.4	62.2
Other republics	2.3	3.4	4.2	—	—	—	7.1	6.7	6.5	11.2	12.9	14.2	20.6	23.0	24.9

^a Grain statistics in this report reflect the Soviet concept of grain production. The USSR reports grain production on a "bunker-weight" basis, that is, as the grain comes from the combine before preliminary cleaning and drying is done and before handling and transportation losses occur. Because bunker-weight includes excess moisture, trash, dirt, weed seeds, and grain admixtures, all of which are reduced to acceptable standards in several stages from farm to user, gross production must be discounted. In order to obtain grain output data in standardized terms comparable to generally accepted world statistics, a discount should be applied. The Office of Economic Research, CIA, applies an average rate of 11% for waste and losses. This includes an estimated 3% loss during handling and an estimated 8% loss from the bunker-weight measurement. The 8% rate is an average of 10 years of estimated discounts based on officially reported data.
^b These are projected trend-line estimates not to be confused with *actual* output figures for 1980.

million tons. Soviet specialists expect that half of future growth in grain output will be due to increased fertilizer use. Using this projection as a rule of thumb, our results imply an average grain-response rate of 3.2 tons per ton of nutrients over the 1980–2000 period.[26] This is at least 30% below the average for the 1970s, but is consistent with the general diminishing returns one would expect as fertilizer use is expanded.

The projected grain and roughages balances that emerge from the reference-case assumptions are given in Table 5.11. Under our assumed targets for meat, eggs, and milk — consistent with the Soviet attainment of the 1978 Polish levels in 1990 — grain-feed requirements rise rapidly, almost doubling by 2000. Through 1990, incremental grain output almost keeps pace with increased demands so that the grain gap rises only slightly. During the Nineties, however, additional requirements substantially outstrip additional production, and the potential grain gap approaches 60 million tons (57 million tons in Table 5.11). The Soviets could make the necessary investment in facilities to handle imports of this magnitude, but whether the world market could provide grain in such volume or whether the leadership would be willing to rely on the West for roughly 20% of grain requirements is another matter. Moreover, the cost in hard currency would be substantial, about 7.5 billion dollars at the 1980 price of grain.

The outlook for the feed situation is much worse once the roughages balance is examined. In fact, it appears that problems on the nongrain feed side are the real constraint on future growth in the Soviet livestock sector.

Production of roughages consists of fodder crops and feed obtained from pastures. We project an increase in total roughages production of 33 million tons by 1990 and another 38 million tons (in oat-equivalent terms) in the 1990s, or an average annual growth of 1.2%. This compares with the historical growth since 1960 of around 1.4% per year. The share of pasture in roughages production has been falling historically, from about 35% in the late 1960s to 27% in 1978. Our projections show a continuation in this trend: by 2000 the share of pasture is just 17%.

Given our assumed goals for consumption of livestock products, growth in requirements for roughages is quite rapid and a very large gap (expressed in oat equivalents) emerges. Requirements increase by almost 50% by 1990 and almost double by 2000, with an average annual growth over the two decades of 3.0%. This trend is due essentially to the high targets for production of beef and milk, which together account for 80% of roughages consumption.

The total gap in feed supplies would approach 90 million tons (87 million tons in Table 5.11) by 1990 and 215 million tons by 2000 if the livestock-product component of the Soviet diet is to match recent Polish levels by 1990 and then continues to grow at the same rate to 2000. Clearly this gap cannot be closed by the conventional device of the 1970s — large grain imports from the West. Either livestock-production targets would have to be lowered — with the political

Table 5.11 *Reference Case: Projected Grain and Roughages Balance (million metric tons)*

	Grain			Roughages[a]			Total		
	1980	1990	2000	1980	1990	2000	1980	1990	2000
Net Domestic Supply	200	238	266	271	304	342	471	542	608
Production (bunker-weight)[b]	224	268	299	271	304	342	495	571	641
Waste and Losses in Production[b]	−24	−29	−33	—	—	—	—	—	—
Net Domestic Requirements	216	260	323	276	369	500	492	629	823
Feed (incl. Waste and Losses)[c]	136	182	247	276	369	500	412	551	747
Waste and Losses in Feed[d]	−20	−23	−25	—	—	—	—	—	—
Nonfeed use	100	101	102	—	—	—	—	—	—
Shortfall (Gap)	16	22	57	5	65	158	21	87	215

[a] We have not attempted to account for waste and losses in production and use of roughages. Roughages (expressed in "oat equivalent" feed units) include pasture and fodder crops. The latter include hay, silage, root crops, and green chop.

[b] See footnote a of Table 5.10.

[c] Grain used for feed derived from the official series on concentrates fed to livestock roughly equals grain feed when calculated from FCRs, meat production and herd inventory change. Since the official series on concentrates fed includes waste and losses, the FCRs used to project grain feed in the model also must reflect waste and losses.

[d] Waste and losses in grain feed are calculated as 80% of production wastes and losses. This share reflects higher-than-average storage losses for feed and yields a reasonable net-grain-feed and implied grain-stock-change series in reconstructed Soviet grain balances.

fallout that would entail — or the technology of producing feed and converting it into livestock products would have to improve faster than our reference case assumes. In the analyses below, we look at the options open to the Soviets for narrowing the feed gap and try to define an outlook for the feed and livestock sector that is reasonably consistent with our present understanding of Soviet capabilities.

D. *Projections Under Alternative Assumptions*

(1) *Lower Livestock-Product Targets.* Perhaps the most straightforward policy that could be adopted would be to accept lower targets for production of meat, eggs, and milk than we have assumed. This certainly holds political risks, in that consumer dissatisfaction with the availability of these products could increase, especially if real incomes were to continue to grow at a substantially faster rate than the supplies of such goods and thereby worsen the existing excess demand for them.

As an alternate set of livestock-product targets, we considered attaining by 2000 the "scientific nutrition norms" published by the Soviet Academy in 1970 (see Table 5.5, p. 153). Since these norms are a fair approximation to the 1978 Polish diet, reaching these targets by 2000 would put the Soviets a full 20 years behind the East European diet as far as livestock products are concerned. In terms of meat, targets based on the scientific norms would reduce the required annual rate of growth from about 3.5% (in our reference case) to a little more than 2%.

The result of this substantial reduction in livestock-product goals is, of course, much smaller projected feed shortfalls for 1990 and 2000. Grain-feed requirements would fall by 20 million tons in 1990 and 50 million tons in 2000, while the shortage of roughages would decline by 44 and 109 million tons respectively (Table 5.12). The remaining overall shortfall conceivably could be covered through substitution of grain imports. To cover this gap (in grain-equivalent terms) implied grain imports in 1990 would be around 25 million tons and in 2000 about 55 million tons. However, with the level of imports in 2000 approaching 20% of production, Soviet planners might find dependence on imports too risky, especially since a year of poor weather could easily increase import needs by 50% or more. Thus, even much less ambitious targets would result in an implied need for grain imports by 2000 that may well exceed what the Soviet Union would consider prudent.

(2) *Higher Fertilizer Use.* Another option open to Soviet planners would be to raise fertilizer applications on grain crops. Since area sown to grain is not likely to increase, greater fertilizer applications mean higher average intensities of use. Without breakthroughs in the development of new plant varieties, the impact of higher fertilizer intensity is limited by diminishing returns.

Table 5.12 USSR: Projected Impacts on the Soviet Feed-Livestock Sector under Alternative Assumptions (million metric tons)[a]

| | Reference Case Level[b] | Impact due to: | | | | | Partial Combination of the Individual Measures in Cols. 2 to 6[c] |
| | | Lower livestock product targets | Higher fertilizer use | Lower FCRs | Reduced beef share | Higher fodder yields | |
	(1)	(2)	(3)	(4)	(5)	(6)	(7)
A. Meat Output							
1990	22.1	−2.7	0	0	0	0	−1.1
2000	31.7	−7.0	0	0	0	0	−2.9
B. Grain Production							
1990	268	0	+13	0	0	0	+7
2000	299	0	+17	0	0	0	+9
C. Grain Use for Feed							
1990	182	−20	0	−8	0	0	−12
2000	247	−50	0	−30	+4	0	−39
D. Grain Shortfall[d]							
1990	22	−20	−13	−8	0	0	−19
2000	57	−50	−17	−30	+4	0	−48
E. Roughages Production							
1990	304	0	0	0	0	+40	+20
2000	342	0	0	0	0	+63	+31
F. Roughages Use							
1990	369	−44	0	−13	−20	0	−40
2000	500	−109	0	−34	−46	0	−98

G. Roughages Shortfall[e]

1990	65	−44	0	−13	−20	−40	−60
2000	158	−109	0	−34	−46	−63	−129

H. Total Shortfall (D plus G)

1990	87	−64	−13	−21	−20	−40	−79
2000	215	−159	−17	−64	−42	−63	−177

[a] Roughages are expressed in feed units of equivalent oats. Meat output is expressed in slaughter weight, bone-in-basis (see CIA, 1980, p. 198 for a more complete statement of coverage for Soviet meat statistics).

[b] See text for discussion of assumptions behind this case.

[c] See text. Impact of measures when combined at one-half of the scales assumed individually.

[d] Net effect of B, C and nonfeed grain use, where this use does not change from the figures in Table 5.11. A 13 million ton increase in grain output in 1990 as a result of higher fertilizer use shows as a 13 million ton reduction in the grain shortfall.

[e] Net effect of E and F. A 40 million ton (oats equivalent) increase in roughage production in 1990 shows as a 40 million ton reduction in the roughage shortfall.

To test the sensitivity of our earlier results to this factor, we arbitrarily assumed a 50% increase over the reference case in the *annual increment* of fertilizer applications on grain crops and developed a new set of projections of grain output. There are several potential sources of this extra fertilizer for grain, including higher overall production, reduced exports (or even net imports), or a shift in allocation away from nongrain crops. Whatever the source, the opportunity costs of such extra fertilizer applied to grain would be high. Under this assumption, fertilizer use on grain increases over the reference case in 1990 by 3.1 million tons of nutrients (22%) and in 2000 by 5.7 million tons (30%).

The resulting impacts on production are, however, not large in percentage terms — in 1990 grain production is up about 5% and in 2000 about 6%. These gains barely dent the reference-case feed shortfall. These small production increments reflect steep diminishing returns in our estimated fertilizer-response curve.[27] The implied average fertilizer response in this case is 4.2 tons of grain per ton of nutrients in 1990 but only 3 tons of grain per ton of nutrients in 2000, compared with recent historical rates that are around 5 tons of grain per ton of nutrients.

(3) *Lower Feed-Conversion Ratios*. The Soviet livestock sector has considerable potential to increase the efficiency of converting feed into livestock products. This potential reflects several factors:

- Because of a persistent shortage of protein supplements such as soybean meal, it takes about twice as long for cattle and hogs to reach slaughter weight in the Soviet Union as it does in the US and other Western countries; this roughly doubles the maintenance component of feed requirements.
- Only about 3–4% of the Soviet cattle herd is made up of animals especially bred for beef production. The remaining cattle are dual-purpose animals suited both for milk production and beef.
- Modern processing of feed promotes its digestibility and hence the efficiency of conversion into products. Currently only about a third of grain used for feed in the USSR is processed this way.
- Substantial losses occur in the quality of feed because modern harvesting and storage technologies are not utilized. Consequently, it takes more feed to meet the nutritive demands of livestock.

Not all livestock-raising enterprises in the Soviet Union are subject to these drawbacks. In fact, many modern facilities exist, especially for raising hogs and poultry, which also receive high priority in the distribution of quality feeds and supplements. Thus, these "complexes" show relatively high efficiency of feed use (low FCRs).

To examine the impacts that lower FCRs could have in reducing feed requirements, we used a method presented in a recent OECD study (OECD, 1979, p. 75). Accordingly, two sets of FCRs are used to

Table 5.13   *USSR: Current Feed Conversion Ratios for "Complexes"*
and "Traditional Farms"* (feed units per unit of output)

| | For "Complexes" | | | |
	Beef	Pork	Poultry	Milk
Total Feed	7.1	5.5	2.8	1.0
Concentrates	2.7	4.7	2.4	0.4
Grain	2.3	4.0	2.1	0.3
	For "Traditional" Farms			
	Beef	Pork	Poultry	Milk
Total Feed	13.2	9.0	9.5	1.5
Concentrates	3.2	7.4	8.7	0.4
Grain	2.8	6.4	7.5	0.3

*The Soviets view a "complex" as a mechanized and automated livestock-raising facility, which in addition is given priority in supplies of feed, other material inputs, and skilled labor. See Gray (1979) and Davis (1980). The FCRs for complexes are taken from Davis (1980). The current *average* FCRs (see Table 5.8) represent weighted averages of FCRs on complexes and on traditional farms. Thus, we are able to solve for the traditional farm FCRs, given the information we have on (a) current *average* FCRs, (b) FCRs for complexes, and (c) current shares of production on complexes.

represent production possibilities for each livestock product — one set for "complexes" and another for "traditional farms" (see Table 5.13). The average FCR for a particular product at any point in time is derived as the weighted average of the FCR for complexes and the traditional farm FCR, with the weights equal to the shares of production attributable to each farm category. The average FCR, therefore, declines as the share of production on complexes rises. Of course, any increase in the share of production on complexes implies not only more direct investment in farm equipment and structures but also corresponding increases in supplies of good-quality feed, feed supplements, skilled labor and management, and other inputs needed to achieve such low FCRs.[28]

In the reference case we assumed constant FCRs that imply no increases in the shares of production on complexes. For the purpose of this scenario, we started with the current shares of production of each type of product on complexes (see Davis, 1980) and then assumed the ambitious goals shown below:

	Share of Production on Complexes in 1979	Assumed Share in 2000
Beef	7	20
Pork	14	50
Poultry	49	100
Milk	3	10

All of the shares are increased by three times except the share for poultry, which doubles. Nevertheless, the shares for beef and milk remain relatively small. Most of the assumed expansion of advanced-farm technology is in hog and poultry enterprises, which follows the established pattern and reflects the smaller claims on feed and distribution resources of these enterprises compared to milk and cattle-raising operations.

Our projection results show, however, that the lower FCRs do not have a large enough impact to affect appreciably the feed shortfalls obtained in the reference case (see Table 5.12). Required grain for feed would fall by only 4% in 1990 and roughage requirements by even less in percentage terms. The basic reason for the small impact on the *total* shortfall of a dramatic expansion in production on complexes is that those products where the most expansion can be expected in applying advanced farm technology — pork and poultry — are also products that consume mostly grain, so that the fundamental problem of the roughages gap is not substantially affected.

(4) *Reduced Beef Share in Total Meat Production.* Beef is substantially more expensive in terms of feed than other livestock products. If the central objective is to obtain more meat per unit of feed, clearly one way to do this is by producing relatively less beef and more pork and poultry. This shift would also help reduce the heavy demand for nongrain feeds where, as we have seen, the supply outlook is even more pessimistic than for grain.

To test the sensitivity of our original projections to an alternate composition of meat in the target levels, we ran a projection assuming the same growth rates for meat, milk, and eggs as in the reference case but with changing shares: beef falling to 30%, pork rising to 35%, and poultry rising to 25% by 2000. As a result of greater poultry and pork production, where grain is the major component of the feed ration, grain requirements increase slightly by 2000. However, the savings in roughages and pasture feed requirements from lower beef production would easily offset the increase in grain needs (the saving in roughages is 5% of requirements in 1990 and approaches 10% in 2000). These are noticeable savings, but again they do not alter the basic imbalance between livestock-product targets and feed production in the reference case.

(5) *Higher Fodder Crop Yields.* The largest share of total feed units comes from fodder crops — hay, silage, root crops, and green chop. Expansion of land sown to these crops is limited by the total availability of arable land and could occur only at the cost of reducing area sown to other crops. However, the potential clearly exists for obtaining higher yields of fodder crops.

We looked at a case in which the yield of fodder crops grows at 2% a year over the simulation period — one-third faster than the historical growth rate assumed in the reference case. With higher yields, fodder production in 1990 is about 13% greater than in the reference case; in 2000, about 18% greater (Table 5.12). However, the total shortfalls in feed — about 50 million tons in 1990 and 150 million in 2000 — still imply an unmanageable level of grain imports. In order to reduce the shortfall to roughly manageable levels, growth in the yield of fodder crops would have to approach 4% a year — two and a half times the historical rate.

(6) *Combination of Measures.* Although the shifts we have considered have all been examined intentionally at very ambitious levels, the only one that independently succeeded in substantially narrowing the feed gap projected in the reference case was the case of lower livestock-product targets. To examine the possibility of a combination of improvements — although at less ambitious rates than assumed above — making feasible somewhat greater output targets, we allowed factor shifts at one-half the scale allowed above. For example, instead of assuming as above a 50% increase over the reference case in the yearly increment of fertilizer use on grain, we here assumed a 25% increase. After making comparable adjustments for the three other options we then lowered the livestock-product targets to obtain manageable implied grain imports, which we judged to be around 50 million tons in 2000.

We found that by reducing annual total meat growth to 3% and milk growth to 2% — from 3½% for meat in the reference case and 2.9% for milk — the resulting overall shortfalls in feed supplies could be met through grain imports of about 10 million tons in 1990 and 40 million tons in 2000 (see Table 5.12). More specifically, the reference-case total shortfalls of 87 and 215 million tons of "oat equivalent" feed units in 1990 and 2000 respectively (Col. 1), are reduced by 79 and 177 million tons (Col. 7) respectively, leaving an import requirement of 8 million tons in 1990 and 38 million tons in 2000. With growth of 3% per year in meat production, per capita consumption in the Soviet Union would not reach the 1978 Polish standard until 1992. This situation would still depend on substantial improvements in fertilizer use, feed conversion efficiency, fodder crops yields, and a lowered share of beef in meat production.

5.5 Impact on Resource Use for the Balance of the Century

As indicated above we adopted as the basic reference case for the USSR the attainment of the 1978 Polish dietary level by 1990. It was observed that to achieve this level of consumption, net agricultural output in the USSR would have to proceed at an average annual rate of increase of 2½% per year. The goal for 2000 was set by extrapolation of the required average growth rate in the 1980s through the following decade. This rate of increase in total output is roughly consistent with the average annual rate of growth observed for the period 1961–79 of

2.4%. The output performance since 1960 was associated with an average annual rate of increase of inputs of 1.8% and of productivity of 0.6% per year. Underlying the averages for the nearly two decades, however, is a marked slowing in rates of growth of inputs, output and productivity in the 1970s (see Table 5.3 above).

Hence, when viewed from this highly aggregated level of resource use and productivity the results roughly reinforce the findings of the previous section. In both cases there would have to be a marked acceleration in growth over the rates of progress observed in the 1970s. More specifically, from the perspective of the "disaggregated" view of Section 5.4, increases would have to be realized in yields per hectare of grains and fodder crops, in fertilizer applications, and in livestock-feeding efficiency. These and other types of indicators underly the aggregated measures.

5: Appendix: The Livestock Product and Feed Simulation Model

A. *Overview*

The projections of livestock products and feed balances presented in this paper were developed using a long-term simulation model of the Soviet livestock sector. The model integrates assumptions about livestock-product targets, feed-conversion efficiencies, and feed-production technologies into a consistent picture of future feed balances (see Fig. 5.2). The model can be used to test the feasibility of any given set of targets as well as to search for future policy options that might be open to the Soviet leadership to improve performance in the livestock sector.

B. *Key Inputs and Assumptions*

Model calculations are driven by selection of a specific set of *livestock-product targets* to be met by the year 2000 or earlier. These targets define both the level of total meat production to be attained and the shares of beef, pork, poultry, and mutton in this total. *Assumed feed-conversion ratios* (*FCRs*) serve to translate these targets into livestock feed requirements.[29]

Area harvested of grain and certain nongrain feed crops is specified outside the model. Area harvested of hay, root crops, and green feed is taken on a national basis. In the case of grain, area harvested is broken down both by region and crop. Grains considered are winter wheat, spring wheat, spring barley, and other grains. The RSFSR is broken down into three regions in the grain-output projections: the Non-Black Soil Zone (the Northwest, Central, and Volga-Vyatka economic regions); the Drought-Prone Region (the Central Black-Soil (Chernozem), North Caucasus, and Volga economic regions); and Other RSFSR (the Urals, West Siberia, East Siberia, and Far East economic regions). The other republics are treated as three additional regions: the Ukraine; Kazakhstan; and Other USSR (essentially Belorussia, Moldavia, and the Baltic, Central Asian, and Transcaucasian republics).

Production of feed crops depends upon assumptions about *fertilizer* and *technology trends*. Only grain production is explicitly affected by fertilizer availability in our calculations because there are no reliable Soviet data on the response of roughage yields to fertilizer. Fertilizer use is described by fertilizer

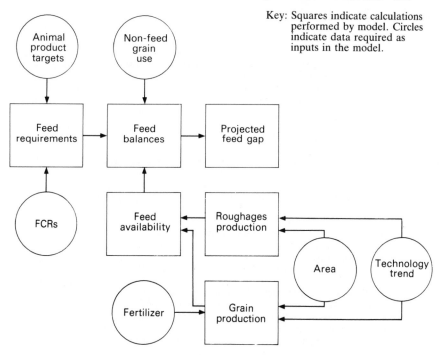

Key: Squares indicate calculations performed by model. Circles indicate data required as inputs in the model.

Figure 5.2   *Flow diagram of livestock product and feed simulation model*

output, the share applied to grain, and the allocation among regions.[30] Technology trends — reflecting such factors as mechanization and varietal improvements — are obtained from analysis of historical yield data.

Nonfeed grain use affects the grain balance by reducing the availability of grain for use in livestock feed. Besides livestock feed, grain is used in industrial applications, in food, and as seed. Nonfeed uses are relatively stable, so that most of any increment in grain output can be devoted to feed use.

Model Projections

The core of the model projections is a *feed balance* out of which emerges a *projected feed gap* that would be covered, hypothetically, by grain imports. Separate balances are computed for both the grain and roughages components of livestock feed. *Feed requirements* are calculated on the basis of total feed, concentrates, and grain. *Feed availability* depends upon both *roughages and grain production*, as well as on nonfeed uses of grain. On the grain side, projections of grain output are made for each of the four grain crops considered in each of the six regions analyzed.

5: Notes

1 The measure of agricultural production used in this paper is an approximation of the value of farm output available for sale and home consumption. It is based on the physical output of 41 crops and animal products weighted by average prices received by all producers (collective and state farms, other state agricultural enterprises, and individual producers) in 1970 for output sold through state procurement channels and the collective-farm-market and commission trade. This value of agricultural output is then adjusted for changes in inventories of four classes of livestock and d by all producers (collective and state farms, other state agricultural enterprises, and individual producers) in 1970 for output sold through state procurement channels and the collective-farm-market and commission trade. This value of agricultural output is then adjusted for changes in inventories of four classes of livestock and deductions are made to account for the intra-agricultural uses of farm products such as feed and seed; that is, deductions are made for the amounts of grain, potatoes, and milk fed to livestock, for the quantity of eggs used for hatching, and for the amounts of grain and potatoes used as seed. For more details concerning the construction of the index of farm output see Diamond and Krueger (1973).

2 Includes meat, fish, milk and milk products, and eggs.

3 The several inputs considered are aggregated into a geometric function of the Cobb-Douglas type as presented in Diamond, 1966, p. 376. Each input is weighted with its relative share or contribution to total output in the base period (1966). The concept of output considered is the value added by agriculture plus the agricultural sector's purchases from nonagriculture of materials for current use.

The five series of inputs are combined by use of 1966 weights that represent the monetary value of imputed costs attributed to each of the inputs. Data are available on actual expenditures for labor and for current purchases from other sectors of the economy, but not for the other inputs. This is because there is no explicit accounting in the USSR for returns to land, fixed capital, and productive livestock. To obtain an "expenditures" weight for fixed capital and productive livestock rather arbitrary assumptions were adopted. First, the income share or service flow for these two factors was derived by assuming an interest rate of 12% and depreciation allowances for capital (excluding draft animals) were then added in order to obtain a gross return on total capital stock.

The derivation of the expenditures weight for land in the production function is explained in Diamond and Krueger, 1973, p. 329.

4 Interpretation of the trends in output per unit of input of combined resources is subject to important limitations. In addition to capturing productivity increases related to changes in techniques used in production, the difference between total inputs (as conventionally measured) and output can be explained in part, by:

(a) inadequate allowances for quality change (especially in average quality of the labor force);
(b) difficulties in obtaining consistent estimates of a single measure of an input;
(c) the failure of factor prices, used to aggregate inputs, to adequately measure the relative contribution of individual inputs to the growth in output; and
(d) an assumption that no gain or loss in efficiency can be had from increasing the scale of operations of a farm.

For a fuller discussion of limitations of the meaning of the results in factor productivity, see Diamond, 1966, pp. 355–7 and Diamond and Davis, 1979, pp. 32–3.

5 During the period 1965–9, the annual level of delivery of industrial goods averaged 49% above the annual average for 1960–64. "Industrial goods" are defined to include the machinery and equipment component of investment and off-farm purchases of fuels and lubricants, current repairs, fertilizer, electric power, and industrially processed feedstuffs.

6 During the base period 1949–53, weather conditions were roughly balanced, with two years of slightly favorable growing conditions (1950 and 1952), a subnormal year (1951), and two normal years (1949 and 1953). The decade of the 1960s was marked by relatively dry, unstable conditions in the early years followed by unusually moist,

stable conditions in the latter part of the decade. Similarly, conditions in the 1970s have tended to "even out" — the moist, stable conditions that continued into the early 1970s were replaced by more normal dry, unstable conditions beginning in 1975. (CIA, Oct. 1976.)

7 A yield index holds the relative importance of the various crops in the base weighting period constant. Hence, it is a weighted average of yield relatives, involving use of constant weights per unit of yield. One centner yield of corn, for example, is given a value weight proportional to its relative importance in the value of crop production in the sample in the base period (see Diamond and Davis, 1979, p. 34, for details). Indexes of yield for the three primary categories of crops are as follows:

Years	Grains	Technical[a]	Forage[b]
1949–53	100	100	100
1960–9	132	132	157
1970–9	180	160	170

[a] Sugar beets, cotton, sunflower seeds, and flax.
[b] Perennial, annual, and wild hays, and potatoes. Potatoes were given a weight proportional to the quantity of potatoes fed in 1970. The other important forage crop in the 1960s and 1970s, corn silage, was not grown in the base period, 1949–53.

8 The overall reduction in yields, reflecting shifts *among areas of the USSR*, was due both to the contraction of grain production in high-yielding regions (e.g. Ukraine), and the expansion of grain production in low-yielding regions (e.g. Kazakhstan). Thus, although shifts *among kinds of grains* in the USSR since the early 1950s has resulted in an increase in overall average yields, the shifts in regional locations of production have offset some of this increase. The net effect of shifts both *among kinds of grain* and *among areas of the USSR* in 1975–7 was an unchanged overall yield.

9 The efficiency index and the total savings attributable to feeding efficiency shown in Table 5.4 are based on an intertemporal comparison of official data on feed use and product output in collective and state farms and estimates for the private sector. A recent (unpublished) paper by Barbara Severin (1980) indicates that the official series of feed usage understates the usage by the private sector.

Johnson (1974) used US–Soviet comparisons to point out the apparent inconsistency between Soviet claims of livestock-product output and feed usage. In short, Johnson argued that the measured higher dollar value of output per feed unit in the USSR in comparison to the US was inconsistent with a number of technical factors that would strongly point to the contrary. A more striking incongruity appears when USSR livestock output is distributed between (1) state and collective farms and (2) private enterprises. The dollar value of output per feed unit on state and collective farms drops below that of the US, while that of the private sector is nearly 50% greater.

Johnson presented four hypotheses for explaining this apparent contradiction, one of which was that the quantity of feed available in the USSR had been underestimated. The recent work by Severin (1980) supports this proposition. Although the full results of her findings cannot be reproduced here, she finds, in short that official data for product output and feed usage in state and collective farms are consistent with a number of independent checks including US–Soviet comparisons of relative feeding efficiency. On the other hand, the evidence clearly points to a major underestimation of feed usage in the private sector, which accounts for 29% of total livestock output. Indeed, as Severin argues, given the composition of feed available to the private sector, the feed-conversion ratios (FCRs) expressed in feed units per unit of private output are likely to be at least as high in the private sector as on state and collective farms in the same period. The gains from better-quality forage and more careful tending in the private sector are probably offset by the lack of mixed feed, protein supplements (except whole milk), other additives, and, to some extent, of grain and other concentrates. Moreover, the evidence supporting a rise in efficiency on state and collective farms (e.g. a better-balanced feed ration) is absent in the case of the private sector. Nevertheless, because any adjustment would be purely arbitrary, for these calculations we assume that FCRs for the nonstate, noncollective farm sectors are equal to those of state and collective farms.

10 Feed-conversion ratios expressed as feed units per unit of physical output of meat differ by type of livestock. The ratio, for example, for converting feed (aggregated into feed units of equivalent nutritive value) into one kilogram of beef is roughly three times the ratio for poultry. Hence, if poultry rises as a share of meat output and beef falls there will be an apparent gain in overall feed efficiency. Applying ruble-price weights to the final product leads to a ratio of feed units required per ruble of final output of beef and poultry but, because the relative meat prices are only narrowly different, the relative efficiencies expressed in feed units per ruble of output do not affect the results. The ruble valuations permit the aggregation of the various types of meat with other livestock products (e.g. milk). The gain in ruble value of savings attributable to feeding efficiency shown in Table 5.4 between 1963–9 and 1970–8 reflects the much higher level of output of livestock production and, accordingly, the higher *absolute* level of feed units fed in the latter period, compared with the 1949–53 base period or with 1960–9. In other words, only a minor proportion of the savings between 1963–9 and 1970–8 was attributable to a further rise in the feeding-efficiency index between the two periods.

11 A cow producing a higher quantity of milk requires less feed per unit of milk than a lower-yielding cow. Annual milk production per cow in the Soviet Union has increased from 1,370 kilograms in 1950 to 2,259 kilograms in 1978. On the other hand, the trend towards higher slaughter weights of beef cattle has tended to raise the required feed units per unit of output.

12 There is a well-documented literature concerning qualitative problems with Soviet livestock feed rations (Johnson, 1974; Schoonover, 1973; Kellner and Waedekin, 1976; Zahn, 1979 and 1980; OECD, 1979). It is difficult to measure accurately the nutritive value of feedstuffs, especially of hay and other roughages.

13 Horses also contribute to livestock-product output, mostly as meat and hides. In 1959, the last year for which figures are available, production of horsemeat was 195,000 tons, or less than 2.2% of total meat output. In addition to horses, other categories of workstock include oxen, donkeys, mules, and camels. Inventory numbers are available for camels, donkeys, and mules for selected years in the period 1950–71. On 1 January 1951, there were 1,036,000 head of donkeys, mules, and camels — a number equivalent to 7.5% of the horse numbers for that date; on 1 January 1971 the aggregate for the same three categories came to 850,000, 11.4% of the number of horses. Although no figures are available for oxen, they probably also declined proportionately less than horses. Hence, if the feed consumed by the four other categories of workstock was included as inputs and if their gross contribution (as well as that of horses) to livestock-product output (meat, milk, hides, and camel's hair) could be netted out, the figures on feedstuff savings between the base period (1949–53) and the two later periods probably would be slightly less than shown in Table 5.4. (*TSU*, 1960 and 1971.)

14 Recent statements concerning policies towards the consumer are in keeping with the regime's long-standing commitment to improve substantially the quality of the diet. In addition to further enhancing excess demand for quality foods by maintaining annual boosts in personal disposable income, Moscow has firmly restated its earlier policy not to raise retail prices on food. As a result of this policy, some excess demand finds expression in food buying at collective-farm markets (CFMs), where prices are relatively free to respond to supply and demand. In Moscow, CFM average meat prices rose by 40% in the 1975–9 period and are now about three times the state retail level. Because of the firm commitment not to raise retail prices on food, the Ministry of Finance is forced to shift a portion of rising costs of agricultural production to the state budget. The average retail price for all types of red meats is roughly one-half of the average cost to the meat industry (Emel'ianov, 1979). As a result, state subsidies on meat and milk products, during 1976–9 averaged more than 20 billion rubles annually to cover the difference between the state purchase prices for meat and milk and the retail prices fixed by the state. This is roughly equivalent to two-thirds of agricultural investment in 1979, or 30% of agriculture's current contribution to gross national product.

It is unlikely that Moscow could renege on its frequently reiterated promise to maintain meat prices in state retail outlets at current levels without running the risk of engendering widespread consumer discontent.

15 The index of agricultural output confined to products in support of food consumption (A) can be compared to CIAs overall index of net agricultural output (B):

	Average Annual Rate of Growth (percent)	
	A	B
1951–78	3.4	3.3
1951–60	4.3	4.2
1961–78	2.9	2.8

The nonfood-related components include cotton, flax, tobacco, and minor commodities.

16 In order to attain the 1978 Polish levels of per capita consumption by 1990, Soviet livestock-products output would have to increase annually between 1978 and 1990 on the average as follows: meat – 3½%; eggs – 1.2%; milk – 2.9%. The distribution of the overall 1978 Polish meat target for the USSR by type of meat (beef, pork, poultry, mutton) was based on the relative shares as formulated in the official Soviet "scientific norm" of consumption.

17 Long queues and other evidence indicate excess demand for meat exists currently in the USSR. We have not attempted to measure the existing gap, so the discussion in this section is restricted to examining changes in the gap. For a more detailed discussion of the evidence indicating the persistence of disequilibrium between supply and demand for meat in state retail outlets see CIA, Jan. 1979.

18 We use the data of the Office of Economic Research, CIA, on meat consumption per capita. The series on disposable income per capita comes from Denton (1979, p. 775). A discussion of the CFM price index used is presented in Severin (1979). Both the income and price series were deflated with the "alternative" retail price index (Denton). The range of our data sample is 1963 to 1978. We took 1963 as the initial year because the last major change in *official* consumer prices occurred in 1962. The income-elasticity estimate of 0.91 is highly significant. The estimated elasticity with respect to the CFM meat-price index is minus 0.45, also statistically significant.

19 Concentrate feedstuffs include grain, oilseed meals, milling byproducts, and alfalfa and grass meals. By Soviet definition, feeds of animal or synthetic origin are not included in concentrates. Nonconcentrate feeds include harvested forage crops ("coarse" and "succulent" in Soviet parlance) and pasture. Coarse feeds have a fiber content in excess of 19% and include hay, straw, and stover. Succulent feeds are those with water content in excess of 40%. They include silage, green chop, potatoes, sugar beets, feed roots, melons, wet beet pulp, and distillers mash.

20 For some products, there have been clear trends in these ratios. In beef production, for example, the trend has been towards higher FCRs—or lower efficiency—because of an increase over the last ten years in the average slaughter weight of cattle. Conversely, FCRs for hogs and poultry have tended to fall as "factory methods" have increasingly been applied in raising these livestock. Extrapolation of any of these trends into the future is, however, highly speculative: change in conversion efficiency depends upon a complex set of Soviet policy decisions.

21 Quantities of fertilizer in this paper are expressed in nutrient content.

22 Application rates in the year 2000 were projected using information on current recommended application rates and feasible application rates in 2000 for small grains (wheat, barley, etc.) in North American analogous regions, taking into account recent Soviet application rates per hectare treated. The current recommended rates and future feasible rates for North American analogous regions were provided by US and Canadian soil scientists. A methodological note titled "The Availability and Use of Fertilizer on Grain in Regions of the Soviet Union" is available to interested readers on request.

23 The results presented in this paper are shown generally only for 1990 and 2000. The introduction of a variable weather pattern over the projection period would not

appreciably alter these figures as long as average weather was assumed for the bench-mark years 1990 and 2000.

24 As indicated in Section 5.2, increase in sown acreage was a major contributor to the expansion of farm output between the early 1950s and the early 1960s, but its contribution since then has been nil. Since the mid-1960s the stock of arable land has remained stable (in the 225–6 million hectare range), with gross additions offset by the loss of farmland to the increasing sprawl of urban areas and industrial enterprises, construction of dams and reservoirs, and growth of open-pit mining. The evidence, presented in a typescript available from the authors, indicates, on balance, at best continued maintenance of the present stock of land.

25 Current and future trends in yields of major grains by region in the Soviet Union were estimated by fitting regression models with regional data for 1965–78. The explanatory variables were time — a proxy for technology and other time-related variables — and weather variables. The estimated regression trend lines were adjusted to account for future changes in the regional pattern and for growth of fertilizer use on grain. The adjusted trend equations were then used in the model to project grain yields to 2000. A methodological note titled "Trends in Grain Yields by Region in the Soviet Union" discusses the methods used for projecting grain yields, grain response to fertilizer, and the linkage between fertilizer use and grain yields in the future and is available on request.

26 If half of the increase in grain output reflects increased fertilizer use, then the rest of the grain increment must be explained by other factors. The prospects for Soviet progress in "nonfertilizer" technology — including mechanization and introduction of new grain varieties and tillage techniques — are discussed in CIA (1978). Also see CIA (1976) and CIA (1977) for other relevant discussions concerning the role of technology in expanding yields.

27 A logistic response function was fitted to 84 pooled observations on total grain yields and overall fertilizer-application rates for all 15 Soviet republics from 1974 to 1979. The estimated equation is:

$$Y = \frac{3.003 + 0.442 \ln F}{(14.24) \quad (5.37)} \quad R^2 = 0.50$$

where Y is total grain yield and F is the overall fertilizer-application rate for grain. Yields are measured in metric tons per hectare; application rates are measured in metric tons (nutrient units) per hectare.

28 Although growth in the number of complexes means improved rates of feed conversion, Davis (1980) finds that the use of resources required to support them may not be relatively efficient compared to alternative uses of the same resources.

29 The FCRs need not be held constant over time but can be made to vary during a projection to reflect such factors as increases in the share of meat produced in livestock complexes.

30 Historical data on fertilizer applications by crop were too sparse to allow a further breakdown in that dimension.

5: References

Barney, Gerald O., Study Director, *The Global 2000 Report to the President*. Washington, DC: Govt. Printing Office, 1980.

CIA, "USSR: The Impact of Recent Climate Change on Grain Production." ER 76–10677. Washington, DC: Oct. 1976.

CIA, "The Impact of Fertilizer on Soviet Grain Output, 1969–80." ER 77–10557. Washington, DC: Nov. 1977.

CIA, "Influence of Agrotechnology and Geoclimate on Grain Yield Potential in the USSR." SI 79–10058. Washington, DC: May 1978.

CIA, "USSR: Long Term Outlook for Grain Imports." ER 79–10057. Washington, DC, Jan. 1979.

CIA, "Handbook of Economic Statistics, 1980." ER 80–10452. Washington, DC: October 1980.

Davis, W. Lee, "Comparative Feeding Efficiencies in Soviet Livestock Complexes." Mimeo, 1980.

Denton, M. Elizabeth, "Soviet Consumer Policy: Trends and Prospects." In *Soviet Economy in a Time of Change*, Vol. 1, 1979.

Diamond, Douglas B., "Trends in Output, Inputs, and Factor Productivity in Soviet Agriculture." In *New Directions in the Soviet Economy*. Papers, Joint Econ. Comm., U.S. Congress. Washington, DC: Govt. Printing Office, 1966.

Diamond, Douglas B., and Krueger, Constance B., "Recent Developments in Output and Productivity in Soviet Agriculture." In *Soviet Economic Prospects for the Seventies*. Papers, Joint Econ. Comm., U.S. Congress. Washington, DC: Govt. Printing Office, 1973.

Diamond, Douglas B., and Davis, W. Lee, "Comparative Growth in Output and Productivity in U.S. and U.S.S.R. Agriculture." In *Soviet Economy in a Time of Change*, 1979.

Emel'ianov, A. M., "Problemy i perspektivy razvitiia sel'skogo khoziaistva SSSR v svete reshenii Iiul'skogo (1978 g.) Plenuma TsK KPSS." *Vestnik Moskovskogo Universiteta. Ekonomika*, No. 1, 1979.

Gray, Kenneth R., "Performance and Organizational Developments in Soviet Red Meat Production." *ACES Bull.* **21**, 3: 45–65, Fall–Winter 1979.

Johnson, D. Gale, "The Soviet Livestock Sector: Problems and Prospects." *ACES Bull.* **16**, 2: 41–61, Fall 1974.

Johnson, D. Gale, *The Soviet Impact on World Grain Trade*. The British–North American Committee, 1977.

Laird, Roy D., "The Widening Soviet Grain Gap and Prospects for 1990: Revised." Mimeo, 1976.

Kellner, Philip, and Waedekin, Karl-Eugen, "The Fodder and Grain Problem in the Soviet Livestock Industry." Cologne, *Berichte des Bundesinstituts fuer Ostwissens-chaftliche und Internationale Studien* 1976, no. 21: 1–34, Aug. 76 (in German). Transl. in *JPRS* 5058, CSP; 8120/0247.

OECD, *Prospects for Soviet Agricultural Production in 1980 and 1985*, Paris, 1979.

Schoonover, David M., "The Soviet Feed-Livestock Economy: Preliminary Findings on Performance and Trade Implications." In *Prospects for Agricultural Trade with the USSR*. Washington, DC: USDA, Econ. Res. Service, 1973.

Severin, Barbara S., "USSR: The All-Union and Moscow Collective Farm Market Price Indexes." *ACES Bull.* **21**, 1: 23–36, Spring 1979.

Severin, Barbara S., "Reconstruction of Soviet Feed Statistics." Mimeo, 1980.

Soviet Economy in a Time of Change. Papers, Joint Econ. Comm., U.S. Congress. Washington, DC: Govt. Printing Office, 1979.

Trifonova, E. V. "O metodakh vyiavleniia i obosnovaniia sel'skokhoziaistvennogo osvoeniia reservnykh zemel." *Vestnik sel'skokhoziaistvennoi nauki*, no.7, 1980.

TSU, *Sel'skoe khoziaistvo SSSR*. Moscow, 1960; 1971.

Zahn, Michael D., "Soviet Livestock Feed in Perspective." In *Soviet Economy in a Time of Change*, vol. 2., 1979.

Zahn, Michael D., "Issues for Soviet Agriculture in the 1980s." Mimeo. May 1980.

6

Industrial Production

MARTIN L. WEITZMAN

Industry has been the dominant economic sector in the Soviet Union and is likely to remain so for the rest of the century. In its current post-agriculture, pre-service stage of growth, industrial production would be a natural priority of Soviet planners even without Marxism. That economic philosophy, as is well known, has had the effect (at least in the past) of glorifying industrial production at the expense of other sectors, notably agriculture and housing construction.

To discuss Soviet industrial production in the second half of this century is a very general mandate. My treatment will naturally reflect my own preferences and prejudices as an economist. There will be a major theme and several minor ones. The major theme concerns how we are to understand the post-war record of Soviet industry. In more technical jargon, I want to inquire into the proper "model" of economic growth, to be in a better position to understand the past and to predict the future.

Now this set of issues might be construed as rather technical and narrow, but I don't see it that way. Without adequate understanding of the mechanics of economic growth, we are not in a position to say much of any real substance as economists; we are then left with rather impressionistic descriptions and it is difficult to say where Soviet industry is coming from and where it is going.

Although I will try not to make the present paper overly technical, behind it lies a fairly thorough econometric investigation of Soviet industry from 1950–78 that extends and updates earlier work, and in which many different specifications and regressions have been tried out with varying degrees of success.

Unfortunately, it is not as if production-function-type analysis provides unambiguous answers to the questions we are asking or should be asking. Indeed, one of the depressing things about the analytical approach is the wide scope of uncertainty about methods, specifications, and results. But the alternative approaches, as I see them, are practically nonexistent. If you are going to analyze economic growth, you must have some model, explicit or implicit.

In some ways, Soviet industry provides a relatively hospitable subject for applying analytic methods. The output-measurement problems for industry are far less severe than for such sectors as services or construction, where there are basic difficulties defining output and in practice one is frequently forced to fall back on measuring outputs by inputs. Compared to capitalist economies, Soviet industry is relatively free of fluctuations, which increases the possibility of identifying sources of growth. Although there are problems with official Soviet statistics, these can be circumvented to some extent, and we do have a capital-stock series. It is perhaps less wild to assume an aggregate constant-returns-to-scale production function for industry than for agriculture, services, or some other sectors.

Putting the matter somewhat more negatively, if we cannot use analytic methods to understand and project industrial output, there is little hope of doing it in other places.

What is the growth record of Soviet industry? In Table 6.1 are recorded output series from 1950 to 1978 reconstructed by the Office of Economic Research (OER) of the CIA.

This is a synthetic series made by aggregating with value-added weights individual component sub series, consisting largely of physical units, but with some ruble values.

A conceivable alternative might be Soviet gross-value-of-output (GVO) indices, preferably reaggregated by synthetic value-added sectoral weights. The official unadulterated Soviet GVO for all industry is displayed in Table 6.2, primarily for comparison purposes. The later years are from *Nar. khoz.* volumes and the earliest years have been chain-linked from *Promyshlyennost' SSSR* (1964). There are so many things wrong with this index as a conceptual measure and

Table 6.1 *Soviet Industrial Output (OER) (1970=100)*

Year	Output	Growth (%)	Year	Output	Growth (%)
1950	20.36		1965	73.65	7.0
1951	22.68	11.4	1966	77.98	5.9
1952	24.61	8.5	1967	83.82	7.5
1953	27.33	11.1	1968	89.59	6.9
1954	30.22	10.6	1969	94.03	5.0
1955	33.64	11.3	1970	100.0	6.4
1956	37.1	10.3	1971	106.87	6.9
1957	41.18	11.0	1972	112.03	4.8
1958	45.77	11.1	1973	119.02	6.2
1959	50.42	10.2	1974	126.46	6.3
1960	53.59	6.3	1975	133.49	5.6
1961	56.9	6.2	1976	138.45	3.7
1962	61.3	7.7	1977	144.12	4.1
1963	64.75	5.6	1978	149.46	3.7
1964	68.81	6.3			

Source: CIA (OER) *Handbook*, various years.

Table 6.2   *Industrial Output (Official Soviet GVO) (billion rubles)*

Year	Output	Growth (%)	Year	Output	Growth (%)
1950	52.00		1965	229.4	8.0
1951	60.53	16.4	1966	248.3	8.2
1952	67.55	11.6	1967	285.9	15.1
1953	75.55	11.8	1968	322.8	12.9
1954	85.55	13.2	1969	345.0	6.9
1955	96.17	12.4	1970	374.3	8.5
1956	106.4	10.6	1971	395.7	5.7
1957	117.0	10.0	1972	420.0	6.1
1958	129.0	10.3	1973	447.3	6.5
1959	143.8	11.5	1974	479.6	7.2
1960	157.4	9.5	1975	511.2	6.6
1961	172.6	9.7	1976	527.9	3.3
1962	188.4	9.2	1977	553.7	4.9
1963	201.0	6.7	1978	577.0	4.2
1964	212.4	5.7			

Source: Nar. khoz., various years; *Promyshlyennost' SSSR,* 1964 (later years in current rubles; earlier years in constant rubles chain-linked).

they are so well known that I will not spend time going over this issue here. Incidentally, the two series move together. Regressions I have run indicate that the official Soviet GVO series grows at about 1.6% faster per year than the OER reconstruction but with no systematic time trend in the difference.

Both series show a rather marked slowdown over nearly three decades. While the meaning and significance of this slowdown will be discussed presently, I just want to note for now that it is too pronounced in various aggregate and disaggregate series to be dismissed as a statistical artifact.

While we will be using the OER numbers of Table 6.1 because they are undoubtedly the most accurate complete series available for Soviet industrial production, they are not without their own points of controversy. If the OER and GVO indexes are disaggregated into subsectors, most of the difference in growth rates shows up in but two subsectors: machine building and metal working (MBMW), and chemicals. Now these happen to be precisely the two sectors with most extreme differentiation of commodities and proliferation of new products. The usual Western explanation for the relatively large gap between the growth of Soviet GVO and Western reconstructions based primarily on physical samples is the notorious Soviet practice of introducing new products at artificially inflated prices. This practice is too widely reported, both inside and outside the SU, to be of no significance. Still, I have a feeling the issue is overstressed. There is another side of the coin, which is rarely mentioned. It is exactly in such sectors as chemicals or MBMW, with their wide spectrum of heterogeneous and new products, that indexes based on a few standardized, old-fashioned models or types would be most likely to bias growth rates downward. This is a subject worthy of future study, for the issue has not yet been resolved, at least in my mind.

At any rate, the trends in Table 6.1 are clear enough, and if the growth rates should be slightly but unsystematically altered, that would most likely reflect itself only in different estimates of the rate of technical change.

Even considering the slowdown of later years, and without yet inquiring of the input side, the industrial-growth reward of Table 6.1 is more than respectable by world standards. Of course it does not match the magnificent Japanese industrial performance, but it does compare favorably with the other large industrialized economies in the postwar period.

Incidentally, one quick explanation for the very fast growth rate of Soviet industry in the fifties, which then slackens in the later periods, might be that the early years represent some form of postwar recovery. I don't find this explanation compelling because already by 1949 every subbranch of Soviet industry was producing at higher than prewar peak levels.

It is traditional to analyze economic growth in terms of its two major factor inputs, labor and capital. With this in mind, Table 6.3 presents the OER series on industrial workers and personnel (this is very close to the official Soviet numbers), whereas Table 6.4 presents Rapaway's (1976) estimates of worker-hours of industrial employment. The two series differ primarily by the average hours worked per person per year, which does not systematically change very much except in those years from 1956 to 1961 after a program was initiated by the Twentieth

Table 6.3 *Industrial Workers and Personnel (in millions)*

Year	Labor Force	Growth (%)	Year	Labor Force	Growth (%)
1950	15.324		1965	27.447	4.3
1951	16.241	6.0	1966	28.514	3.9
1952	16.889	4.0	1967	29.448	3.3
1953	17.641	4.5	1968	30.428	3.3
1954	18.535	5.1	1969	31.159	2.4
1955	18.922	2.1	1970	31.593	1.4
1956	19.641	3.8	1971	32.03	1.4
1957	20.312	3.4	1972	32.461	1.3
1958	20.988	3.3	1973	32.875	1.3
1959	21.67	3.2	1974	33.433	1.7
1960	22.62	4.4	1975	34.054	1.9
1961	23.82	5.3	1976	34.815	2.2
1962	24.677	3.6	1977	35.417	1.7
1963	25.442	3.1	1978	36.014	1.7
1964	26.313	3.4			

Source: Nar. khoz., various years.

Table 6.4   *Industrial Manhours (in billions)*

Year	Manhours	Growth (%)	Year	Manhours	Growth (%)
1950	33.054		1965	49.377	3.5
1951	34.927	5.7	1966	51.553	4.4
1952	36.209	3.7	1967	53.389	3.6
1953	37.736	4.2	1968	55.288	3.6
1954	39.569	4.9	1969	56.741	2.6
1955	40.531	2.4	1970	57.405	1.2
1956	41.02	1.2	1971	58.554	2.0
1957	41.386	.9	1972	59.217	1.1
1958	42.393	2.4	1973	59.557	.6
1959	42.56	.4	1974	60.725	2.0
1960	42.752	.5	1975	61.737	1.7
1961	43.061	.7	1976	63.12	2.2
1962	44.616	3.6	1977	64.069	1.5
1963	45.897	2.9	1978	65.149	1.7
1964	47.713	4.0			

Source: Rapawy, 1976; updated by personal communication.

Congress of the CPSU to gradually reduce the standard work week from 48 to 41 hours.

The weekly working hours in Soviet industry fell as much as 15% from 1955 to 1961. That is a sharp decline, and there might well have been some offsetting increase in the quality of a working hour. While the effects on quality must remain speculative, it seems to be the case that overall results or conclusions are not very sensitive to the differences in the two series.

For the purposes of this paper I have used labor hours of Table 6.4 as my primary labor-input series. In most cases I have verified that substituting "workers and personnel" from Table 6.3 would not reverse major conclusions.

The capital series is the least controversial, in part because we have little choice but to use the only official Soviet data available, the TSU series on "industrial productive basic funds." The capital stock of a given year listed in Table 6.5 refers to the (arithmetic) average of what is in place at the beginning and end of that year.

The growth of labor and capital productivity (Table 6.6) show some interesting trends. The growth of labor productivity is very high by world standards. Note the decline in the growth of capital productivity, reflecting an increase in the capital-output ratio. This effect would be more pronounced if we detrended technical change from output.

What I am going to do now is engage in some standard exercises in growth accounting and production-function analysis, applied to the context of Soviet industry, 1950–78.

The aggregate production function is an incomplete or even ambiguous concept, but it may be one of the few useful ways of piecing together an overall picture of economic growth. The standard

Table 6.5 *Midyear Industrial Capital Stock (billion rubles)*

Year	Capital Stock	Growth (%)	Year	Capital Stock	Growth (%)
1950	31.9		1965	160.65	9.7
1951	35.55	11.4	1966	175.45	9.2
1952	40.0	12.5	1967	190.1	8.4
1953	44.35	10.9	1968	205.75	8.2
1954	49.3	11.2	1969	223.7	8.7
1955	55.4	12.4	1970	244.1	9.1
1956	62.0	11.9	1971	266.3	9.1
1957	68.5	10.5	1972	288.75	8.4
1958	76.05	11.0	1973	313.2	8.5
1959	84.75	11.4	1974	340.8	8.8
1960	94.4	11.4	1975	370.05	8.6
1961	105.55	11.8	1976	400.5	8.2
1962	118.1	11.9	1977	431.5	7.7
1963	132.1	11.9	1978	463.95	7.5
1964	146.4	10.8			

Source: Nar. khoz., various years (1959–78 in 1973 prices, earlier years in chain-linked constant prices; midyear calculated as average of end years)

Table 6.6 *Growth of Labor and Capital Productivity*

Year	Growth of Labor Productivity (%)	Growth of Capital Productivity (%)	Year	Growth of Labor Productivity (%)	Growth of Capital Productivity (%)
1951	5.7	0.0	1965	3.5	−2.7
1952	4.8	−4.0	1966	1.5	−3.3
1953	6.9	0.2	1967	3.9	−0.9
1954	5.7	−0.6	1968	3.3	−1.3
1955	8.9	−1.1	1969	2.4	−3.7
1956	9.1	−1.6	1970	5.2	−2.7
1957	10.1	0.5	1971	4.9	−2.2
1958	8.7	0.1	1972	3.7	−3.6
1959	9.8	−1.2	1973	5.6	−2.3
1960	5.8	−5.1	1974	4.3	−2.5
1961	5.5	−5.6	1975	3.9	−3.0
1962	4.1	−4.2	1976	1.5	−4.5
1963	2.7	−6.3	1977	2.6	−3.6
1964	2.3	−4.5	1978	2.0	−3.8

Source: Tables 6.1, 6.4, 6.5.

exercises like looking at capital–output ratios or labor productivity are but special cases of this approach rather than genuine alternatives in any real sense.

The basic starting point is an explicit or implicit assumption about the form of the aggregate production function. Typically it is assumed that the expression

$$Y(t) = A(t) \, F(K(t), L(t)) \tag{1}$$

is a serviceable approximation relating aggregate output Y to aggregate capital K and labor L at time t.

Because there are inherent difficulties in disentangling economies of scale from technical change in any time series, and also because there do not seem to be any compelling reasons toward economies or diseconomies of scale in the aggregate industrial sector of a large, advanced economy, the production function $F(K,L)$ is typically assumed to be homogeneous to degree one, often Cobb-Douglas. Alternatively, this can be viewed more mechanically as simply a convenient way to combine factor inputs into one synthetic aggregate input. The Hicks–neutral technical-change term $A(t)$ is really a catch-all, since it is capturing any contribution to growth other than of capital and labor as conventionally measured and combined in a constant-returns-to-scale production function. For this reason I prefer the term "residual" or "total factor productivity" for $A(t)$, rather than "technical change", "technical progress", etc., which sound too purposeful about what is really a measure of our ignorance.

The most useful form into which Eq. (1) can be transformed is the so-called "growth equation"

$$g_y = g_a + \eta_l \, g_l + \eta_k \, g_k \tag{2}$$

where the symbol g stands for growth rates. Thus

$$g_y = \frac{\frac{dY}{dt}}{Y}, \tag{3}$$

$$g_a = \frac{\frac{dA}{dt}}{A}, \tag{4}$$

$$g_l = \frac{\frac{dL}{dt}}{L}, \tag{5}$$

$$g_k = \frac{\frac{dK}{dt}}{K}. \tag{6}$$

The symbol η_l and η_k stand for the imputed shares of labor and capital, respectively, under a marginal-productivity theory of distribution:

$$\eta_l = \frac{L\frac{\partial Y}{\partial L}}{Y}, \tag{7}$$

$$\eta_k = \frac{K\frac{\partial Y}{\partial L}}{Y}. \tag{8}$$

because Y is homogeneous of degree 1 in K and L,

$$\eta_l + \eta_k = 1 \tag{9}$$

Thus, under formulation (1) the rate of growth of output is a weighted average of the growth rates of capital and labor, plus the growth rate of the residual. In standard growth accounting, Eq. (2) is the starting point for analyzing the contribution of the three sources of growth: labor, capital, and the "residual".

Since the residual is the least understood component and cannot usually be independently quantified, g_a is typically calculated as a true residual

$$g_a = g_y - \eta_l\, g_l - \eta_k\, g_k \tag{10}$$

The growth rates g_y, g_l, and g_k are obtainable from Tables 6.1, 6.4, 6.5. Estimating η_l and η_k presents somewhat of a problem for Soviet industry. In competitive economies, we might use market shares, although personally an aggregate production function has always struck me as being a tenuous-enough idea even without assuming a marginal-productivity theory of distribution. At any rate this is not really a meaningful alternative for Soviet industry. Instead, what is typically done is to use empirical shares from the manufacturing sectors of advanced capitalist countries, usually about three-quarters for the share of labor and a quarter for the share of capital.

If this procedure is followed, something paradoxical and downright peculiar emerges. In Table 6.7 the growth of the residual, g_a, is calculated with $\eta_l = 3/4$, $\eta_k = 1/4$. If we are to believe this approach, the growth of the residual has declined rather dramatically from about 5 or 6% in the early fifties to about 1% in the late seventies.

Such a conclusion is a bit difficult to absorb in its entirety. Why should total factor productivity be increasing so much faster two decades ago than now? Certainly judging by the literature, far greater attention is paid to questions of economic efficiency in more recent years than in the past.

An alternative explanation goes something like this. In a generation of time from the early fifties to the late seventies, Soviet industry has

Table 6.7 *Growth Rate of the Residual with Labor – Capital Shares of 3:1*

Year	Residual Growth (%)	Year	Residual Growth (%)
1951	4.3	1965	2.0
1952	2.6	1966	0.3
1953	5.2	1967	2.7
1954	4.2	1968	2.1
1955	6.4	1969	0.8
1956	6.4	1970	3.2
1957	7.7	1971	3.1
1958	6.5	1972	1.8
1959	7.0	1973	3.6
1960	3.1	1974	2.6
1961	2.7	1975	2.2
1962	2.0	1976	−0.6
1963	0.5	1977	1.3
1964	0.6	1978	0.5

Source: Tables 6.1, 6.4, 6.5.

been transformed from a labor-surplus sector, where capital was the main constraint on output (as in the Harrod-Domar growth model), into a labor-scarce sector not unlike that of other modern industrial economies. Labor was essentially "free" in the old days because vast amounts of it were available to be siphoned out of low-priority, low-marginal-productivity agriculture. That is no longer the case, and the change has come about relatively swiftly because of the incredibly rapid accumulation of industrial capital and the unfavorable demographics of the work force.

In the jargon of economic theory, I am arguing that an alternative historical explanation to the Soviet industrial slowdown is not to make the residual take all the blame, but to allow a low elasticity of substitution between capital and labor to share some of it. The standard approach, which fixes η_k and η_l, in effect assumes a Cobb-Douglas or unit-elasticity-of-substitution production function.

The elasticity of substitution is a measure of the rate at which diminishing returns set in as capital is increased relative to labor. A lower-than-unity elasticity of substitution would have special relevance to understanding the slowdown in Soviet industry because the growth of capital and labor has been so disproportionate in the postwar period. What happens in such a situation is that the weight on capital in the growth equation, η_k, declines relative to the weight on labor, η_l. In Table 6.8 are displayed a time series of imputed shares of capital and labor derived from the econometric estimation of a constant-elasticity-of-substitution production function with constant growth of the residual. The estimated value of the elasticity of substitution is .5 (with a standard error of about .1) and that of technical change is .9%. I have verified that the trend behavior of imputed shares is roughly similar for "elasticities of substitution" and "distribution parameters" differing by one standard deviation in either direction.

Now the sad truth is that without further information we do not know how to decide on statistical grounds alone between the unit-elasticity (Cobb-Douglas) production function with declining growth of the residual (Table 6.7) and the constant growth of residual, less-than-unity elasticity-of-substitution specification that generates factor shares like those of Table 6.8. Both regressions yield about the same error sum of squared residuals. The real world might even be some mixture of the two scenarios. Fortunately the choice may not make that much difference for short-term forecasting at the current time.

Incidentally, the work of Desai (1973) seems to indicate that the results observed here are not merely coincidences of aggregation, but occur as well on the sectoral level for individual branches of industry.

The extended time period examined in this paper, from 1950 to 1978, allows us to inquire about a phenomenon that has struck some observers. Looking casually at the numbers, it appears that there might perhaps be a structural break in the data sometime in the early 1960s. Some people have felt that maybe the production function changed qualitatively at some break point in the early 1960s.

Dividing the period 1950–78 into the two equal subperiods 1950–63 and 1964–80, we have run a standard F-test for structural change between the two subperiods. In all the different cases of production-function forms (and the choice of workers or manhours) we are unable

Table 6.8   *Imputed Labor and Capital Shares from a CES Regression*

Year	Imputed Labor Share	Imputed Capital Share	Year	Imputed Labor Share	Imputed Capital Share
1950	.21	.79	1965	.52	.48
1951	.22	.78	1966	.54	.46
1952	.23	.77	1967	.55	.45
1953	.25	.75	1968	.56	.44
1954	.26	.74	1969	.58	.42
1955	.28	.72	1970	.60	.40
1956	.31	.69	1971	.62	.38
1957	.33	.67	1972	.64	.36
1958	.35	.65	1973	.66	.34
1959	.38	.62	1974	.68	.32
1960	.41	.59	1975	.69	.31
1961	.44	.56	1976	.71	.29
1962	.54	.46	1977	.72	.28
1963	.49	.51	1978	.73	.27
1964	.50	.50			

to reject the null hypothesis of no structural shift. For what it is worth, the statistics do not appear to support the idea of a structural break in the data.

So far as projections are concerned, without going into all the details, which are technical, the two approaches represented by Tables 6.7 and 6.8 do approximately converge, as luck would have it, to give about the same recommendations for predicting Soviet industrial growth in the near future (presumably mixed or intermediate approaches would also give similar answers).

The growth of Soviet industrial output should be a sum of about 75% of the growth of industrial labor plus 25% of the growth of industrial capital plus a bonus of about 1% representing growth of the residual (assuming it continues to grow at about that level).

My honest opinion is that this represents the current state of the art in forecasting the growth of Soviet industry. I have gone into some background details to emphasize controversial aspects of the Soviet growth story and to point out why there may be special dangers in making mechanical long-term projections on the basis of this or another model because we really don't know the long-term stability of basic parameters with a great deal of assurance.

After having made that long-winded caveat, let me proceed to the business of exploring future prospects.

If we accept the growth equation

$$g_y = \tfrac{3}{4}\, g_l + \tfrac{1}{4}\, g_k + 1\% \tag{11}$$

I feel we have some legitimate basis for projecting industrial growth for the next 5 or 10 years or so. Basically I am assuming: either a Cobb-Douglas specification with share weights of $\tfrac{1}{4}$, $\tfrac{3}{4}$ and a constant rate of technical change equal to what it has been recently, or a CES specification with constant rate of technical change where the share weights are not expected to change much because the rate of growth of capital has slowed down considerably or because the capital-scarcity period is over and the future elasticity of substitution is likely to be closer to 1 than to $\tfrac{1}{2}$. A low elasticity of substitution would put a lower weight than 1:3 on capital relative to labor in future years, but my hunch is this second-order effect will not be operative for another decade, and even then it should not change the conclusions much.

Even if we accept Eq. (11), we still have to plug in estimates of the growth of industrial capital and labor, difficult to do without a complete specification of planners' intentions. Since growth projections are not an exercise for the timid-hearted, my feeling is we may as well throw in some numbers without pretending to too much scientific basis. It is very difficult to predict the growth of industrial inputs of capital and labor because they depend on planners' preferences about relative commitments to industry, as well as absolute levels of investment and labor-force growth. Bearing these caveats in mind, for industrial inputs of the next decade perhaps $g_l = 1.5\%$ and $g_k = 7\%$ is an upper bound. As lower bounds I might pick $g_l = 1\%$, $g_k = 4\%$. This results in a range of industrial growth as measured by OER from about 3% to about 4%, which sounds approximately right to me. The reader who wants to can plug different numbers into the formula (11) but I think the analysis is suggesting to us that Soviet industry will be growing in the 3 to 4% range over the next several years, certainly not more.

Let me conclude this selective survey of Soviet industrial production by opinionating briefly on two related areas not treated so far: energy and technology transfer.

I do not believe the *direct* effects on Soviet *industry* of petroleum scarcity are going to be severe or profound. The Russians, even more than we, are wastefully burning large amounts of mazout, or what we call Bunker #6, in electricity and heat-generating plants. At about $4 a barrel, this heavy-grade residual could be upgraded to high-grade distillates. The Soviet Union has very significant reserves of natural gas, some of which are just starting to come on line. And the development of nuclear power, which is by far the cheapest form of electricity when correctly calculated, is not subject to the political constraints present in democratic countries. Indeed, the Soviet Union is proceeding with a very ambitious nuclear program. Soviet coal is abundant even if its quality and location sometimes represent problems and the Soviet transportation system already handles more coal than any other country. My feeling is that the "energy crisis" is perhaps not going to represent a significant drag on its industrial production, especially once the Soviet Union starts to get its act together about national priorities, and industry comes out near the top of the list as usual. A formal study of the possibilities of substitution between energy and other inputs would be useful, but is beyond the scope of the present paper.

The issue of technology transfer is potentially an important one for Soviet industry. Several case studies have been performed, but opinions differ on the overall impact of technology transfer on Soviet industry. I have undertaken a production-function study that in principle could estimate the marginal productivity of machinery imported from the West for Soviet industry, and for the subsectors of chemicals, petroleum, and machine building and metal working during the period 1960–75 (Weitzman, 1979).

The conclusion seems to be that the marginal productivity of imported Western capital is not significantly different from that of capital of non-Western origin. Without in any other way trying to prejudge the issue, I believe a fair summary statement is that we are unable to detect any influence of Western technology on the Soviet economy from the aggregate time-series data we currently have available. This is not to say that new information may not appear, but at the moment there seems to be no evidence on the aggregate level that technology transfer is a significant contributor to Soviet growth.

6: References

Bergson, Abram, "The Soviet Economy in the Eighties." In NATO, *The USSR in the Eighties*. Brussels: NATO, 1978.

Bergson, Abram, "Notes on the Production Function in Soviet Postwar Industrial Growth." *J. Comp. Econ.* **3**, 2: 116–26, June 1979.

CIA (OER), *Handbook of Economic Statistics*. Washington, DC, various years.

Desai, Padma, "Soviet Industrial Production: Estimates of Gross Outputs by Branches and Groups." *Oxford Bull. Econ. & Stat.* **35**, 2: 153–71, May 1973.

Desai, Padma, "The Production Function and Technical Change in Postwar Soviet Industry." *Amer. Econ. Rev.* **66**, 3: 372–81, June 1976.

Gomulka, Stanislaw, "Soviet Postwar Industrial Growth, Capital-Labor Substitution, and Technical Changes: A Reexamination." In Zbigniew M. Fallenbuchl, ed., *Economic Development in the Soviet Union and Eastern Europe*. New York: Praeger, 1976.

Gomulka, Stanislaw, "Slowdown in Soviet Industrial Growth Reconsidered." European Economic Review, **10**, 1: 37–49, October 1977.

Greenslade, Rush V., "Industrial Production Statistics in the USSR." In Treml and Hardt, eds, 1972.

Nar. khoz., see TSU.

Promyshlyennost' SSSR. Moscow, 1964.

Rapawy, Stephen, "Estimates and Projections of the Labor Force and Civilian Employment in the USSR 1950 to 1990." Foreign Econ. Report No. 10, US Department of Commerce, Bureau of Economic Analysis, Sept. 1976.

Rosefielde, Steven, and Lovell, C. A. Knox, "The Impact of Adjusted Factor Cost Valuation on the CES Interpretation of Postwar Soviet Economic Growth." *Economica* **44**, 176: 381–392, Nov. 1977.

Treml, Vladimir G., and Hardt, John P., eds, *Soviet Economic Statistics*. Durham, NC: Duke Univ. Press, 1972.

TSU, *Naradnoe khoziaistva*. Moscow, various years

Weitzman, Martin L., "Soviet Postwar Economic Growth and Capital–Labor Substitution." *Amer. Econ. Rev.* **60**, 4: 676–92, Sept. 1970

Weitzman, Martin L., "Technology Transfer to the USSR: An Econometric Analysis." *J. Comp. Econ.* **3**, 2: 167–77, June 1979.

7

Energy

ROBERT W. CAMPBELL

Introduction

The beginning of the eighties is an appropriate time to look forward to
ask how problems of energy supply will influence the growth of the
Soviet economy between now and the end of the century. The USSR is
currently at a turning point in energy policy, and at a turning point in
the way energy supply interacts with economic growth. The two
decades ahead are likely to provide a sharp contrast in this respect with
the two decades just finished. It is, therefore, useful to review briefly
the relationship between energy production and economic growth in
the recent period as a way of posing the problems of energy supply that
will emerge over the next two decades.

In the sixties and seventies output and energy consumption in the
Soviet economy grew at the rates indicated in Table 7.1.[1] The
estimates of GNP growth rates are those produced by the CIA. We
might argue with them for various reasons, but they are more useful as a
measure of growth than official Soviet data. They reflect the generally
accepted interpretation that Soviet growth has decelerated as the
economy has matured. If GNP grew in the immediate postwar period
at approximately 6% per year, in the sixties it grew at only 5% per year
and in the seventies at less than 4% per year. Growth at these rates has
required rapidly increasing supplies of energy, as shown by the rates of
growth of energy consumption in the second column of the table.
Taking the two decades as a whole, growth of GNP has been associated
with an equally rapid growth of energy consumption — indeed for the
two decades taken together the GNP elasticity of energy consumption
(the ratio of the percentage growth of energy consumption to the
percentage growth of GNP) has been somewhat over 1. Between 1965
and 1975 the elasticity fell appreciably below 1, probably because of
the sharp gains in energy efficiency associated with the shift away from
solid fuel to the more efficiently used hydrocarbons. (It is a little
puzzling that there was no similar gain in the first half of the sixties,
when the shift in energy composition was well underway.) The most
striking feature of Table 7.1 is that elasticity has again risen above 1 in

Table 7.1   *Rates of Growth of GNP and Energy Consumption*

Period	GNP	Gross Energy Consumption
1960/1950	5.8	6.4
1965/1960	4.9	5.9
1970/1965	5.3	4.9
1975/1970	4.1	4.0
1976/1975	4.3	NA
1977/1976	3.4	NA
1978/1977	3.2	NA
1979/1978	0.7	NA
1980/1979	3.0	NA
1980/1975	3.0	3.8

Sources: GNP growth rates are taken from CIA, *Handbook* 1979, p. 26, with the following exceptions: 1950–60 is from Greenslade, 1976, p. 271; 1979 and 1980 are from CIA, *The Soviet Economy in 1978–79, and Prospects for 1980*, pp. 19, 25. Data for growth of energy consumption are from Campbell, 1978, and for 1980/1975 from Table 7.2 below.

the second half of the seventies, at a time when the government has pursued a vigorous campaign to encourage energy saving and to reduce waste.

The task of providing the energy increments for growth in the sixties and the seventies was greatly simplified by the fact that output expansion was accompanied by a shift from solid fuel to hydrocarbons. At the end of the fifties, 65% of Soviet consumption of primary energy was covered by solid fuel — coal, shale, peat, and firewood. In the 20 years after 1959, however, during which consumption more than doubled, 80% of the incremental consumption has been met by expanding oil and gas production.[2] Output of solid fuels stagnated or grew very slightly. By the end of the seventies the share of solid fuel in total primary-energy consumption had fallen to 34%.

In retrospect, it seems quite clear that this shift to oil and gas greatly eased the cost of providing the energy required for growth. It permitted huge resource savings in production compared to providing the same amount of energy in the form of solid fuel. The hydrocarbons make it possible to save fuel itself, since they are utilized more efficiently than solid fuels. It takes many fewer calories to haul a ton of freight a mile in a train pulled by a diesel locomotive, for example, than in one pulled by a coal-burning steam locomotive. Hydrocarbon fuels also permit large savings of other resources at the consumption stage. A gas-fired power station, for example, can do away with the elaborate and costly facilities necessary to store and handle the fuel used in a coal-burning station and to prepare it for combustion.

Furthermore, these increments of oil and gas output were won cheaply enough to make these fuels attractive as exports as well as for domestic use and the Soviet Union used energy exports, especially oil, both to support the strategy of technology transfer, and to keep growth going in Eastern Europe in the face of that region's crucial deficit. Net energy exports grew during these two decades at almost 10% per year (compared to 4.4% for domestic energy consumption) and by 1980 accounted for about 42% of all export earnings and about half of hard-currency earnings from export.

It is probably a valid generalization to say that this growth of oil and gas output was obtained without imposing particularly rigorous technological demands on the economy. The hydrocarbons were found in relatively easily accessible formations, and the wells to find and produce them were drilled with a novel but relatively simple technology — the turbodrill. This technology was adequate to the geological situations the industry encountered and permitted a dramatic end-run around the low productivity the Soviet oil industry achieved in standard rotary-drilling technology, which the USSR had found very difficult to improve. Moreover, most of the oil was in the kind of reservoirs where it was possible to apply effectively the new science of reservoir engineering, an innovation that speeded up extraction and saved on investment and operating costs by combining sparse well-spacing patterns with pressure maintenance through water injection. The gas was brought to market relatively cheaply under conditions that were not especially demanding technologically — the Russians used large investments of metal in the form of very-large-diameter pipe to substitute for the more sophisticated technology and quality levels that are generally characteristic of pipelines in other countries. In addition, crucial elements of pipeline technology could be and were imported on a large scale. The technological and investment demands associated with processing hydrocarbon fuels were side-stepped — in the case of oil by refining it only lightly and using it to a very large extent in the form of residual fuel oil for boiler and furnace purposes, and in the case of gas, simply by doing minimal processing. Only a small fraction of the valuable liquid and liquifiable byproducts of gas production were extracted and devoted to their higher-value uses.

All in all, meeting the energy requirements of a growing economy during the sixties and seventies imposed a relatively modest burden on Soviet investment resources and on Soviet technological sophistication. Indeed, the fact that energy-supply expansion was so easy and thus permitted exports made the growth of energy output not so much a burden on growth as a special contributor to it through foreign-exchange earnings and the technology imports these earnings supported.

This impression of relative ease in energy expansion during the sixties and seventies is strengthened by extending our retrospective look to the late forties and the fifties. Energy supply grew rapidly in the first fifteen years after World War II, but these increments required very large investments in solid-fuel production and expensive experiments in fuel processing. Whereas in the sixties and early seventies the energy sector was taking only 28–9% of industrial investment, during the Fifth Five-Year-Plan (1951–5) the energy branches had absorbed 37.2% of all industrial investment to cope with the output expansion required. In the Sixth Five-Year-Plan (1956–60), when the transition to hydrocarbons had already started, the energy branches took 32.7%. (TSU, *Nar. Khoz. SSSR*, various years.)

As the Russians look ahead to the remaining two decades of the century, however, the hydrocarbon-energy bonanza shows signs of disappearing. It is predicted that the USSR will be lucky to keep oil output near its present level, let alone achieve its expansion. The CIA (July 1977) in fact, forecasts a large decline in petroleum output during the eighties, perhaps to as low as two-thirds of the 1980 output of 603 million tons, natural measures (MTnat). For gas, reserves are clearly adequate to support an expansion of output well above the 1980 level, but under adverse changes in location that will lead to very significant increases in the cost of producing and transporting it. The effects of a decline in hydrocarbon potential are exacerbated by the fact that coal, which has continued to supplement hydrocarbon supplies, will undergo very significant adverse changes in quality and location, as reserves give out and production costs rise in the European USSR.

7.1   Energy Supply and Economic Growth

One approach to exploring the impact these energy difficulties will have on Soviet economic growth would be via an econometric model. The CIA has used this approach in its short-term forecasts (CIA, "Simulations", March 1979). A formal model seems less appropriate to a long-range projection over two decades, however, and in any case, that is not my style. My analysis is much looser than that of a formal model, and instead of an explicit quantitative forecast, I offer consideration of possible alternatives and the structural changes that the makers of energy policy will need to deal with.

It will be useful to start by explaining how I envisage the relationship of the energy sector to economic growth over the next twenty years. From the demand side, I see growth of GNP, and an associated level of final demand of energy as essentially exogenous to energy policy. This aggregate energy demand also has a structure that includes a regional dimension, a type-of-use dimension (e.g. boiler and furnace use versus internal-combustion-engine use) and a sector-of-demand dimension. This structure, also, presents itself to energy planners as fairly autonomous. The major exceptions would be the extent to which energy-policy makers can influence the choice of technologies by final energy consumers to alter the type of energy demanded (e.g. direct-fuel furnaces versus electric furnaces) or to improve the efficiency of energy use (e.g. insulating buildings or raising the efficiency of internal-combustion engines).

On the supply side, the natural-resource base does not completely rule out choice, but still imposes serious constraints on planners' choice regarding both the kinds of energy sources to be used and their location. For example Soviet energy planners will probably find it impossible to meet motor-fuel demand within the European USSR from oil sources located within the region.

These respective structures on the demand and supply side are mediated by the various transport and transformation activities, and choices in this area constitute some of the major choice variables with which energy-policy makers will be concerned. To meet an electric-power need in the Ukraine, for example, the planners have, among other alternatives: Ekibastuz coal to mine-mouth generation to high-voltage transmission; Ekibastuz coal to slurry pipeline to Ukrainian generating plant; Ukrainian nuclear-power station. It is in the reconciliation of these two sides that most of the energy-policy issues will be found.

The reconciliation may be possible in part by influencing the demand and supply structures, but much of the decision making in these areas is outside the reach of the energy-policy makers. They can probably do very little to influence the regional distribution of demand. A lot of the production choices are made by the energy suppliers on the basis of internal considerations and other pressures — e.g. the respective role of breeders and standard fission reactors. The primary task of energy policy is to stand above all these actors to make certain that their actions get coordinated. The energy-policy makers have to make sure that if oil is going to cease to be allocated to the electric-power industry, that the power industry be given coal to make up for it, and that power-industry policies and plans get modified accordingly.

Finally, the most important reverse linkage in my view of energy–GNP interactions is the investment demands and cost levels that grow out of these constraints and choices, as they will divert investment funds and current inputs from the activities that would otherwise be generating energy demands. Some other modelers, particularly the CIA in its short-term modeling, treat potential shortfalls in energy supply as a direct constraint on output. That may happen — indeed it is very likely to within short periods. But in thinking about economic expansion over a relatively lengthy period it seems more appropriate to assume that short-term disproportions can be overcome, and that enough energy will be produced to meet demand.

My goal in this paper is not so much to make a concrete forecast of what the energy situation will be in the year 2000 as it is to examine how energy problems will affect growth in the intervening period. The best way to get at this, however, will be to project some current trends to the year 2000 and then examine the resulting scenario for contradictions and implications that may raise problems that will prevent the USSR's actually arriving there.

The next two sections describe the current energy-supply and

Table 7.2 USSR Fuel and Energy Balance, 1980

Primary Sources and Energy Products	Unit	Primary Energy Supply						Consumption Sectors						
		Output	Losses & Internal Consumption	Net Trade	Intrasector Transfers Inflow	Outflow	Available for Distribution	Non-fuel	Electric Power	Industry	Household & Municipal	Agriculture	Transportation	Construction
Hydropower	BKWH	181.3	—	—	—	—	—	—	—	—	—	—	—	—
	MTst	54.9	—	—	—	—	54.9	—	54.9	—	—	—	—	—
Nuclear Power	BKWH	72	—	—	—	—	—	—	—	—	—	—	—	—
	MTst	23.7	—	—	—	—	23.7	—	23.7	—	—	—	—	—
Natural Gas	Bm³	450.5	64.2	52.0	.5	5.4	329.4	23.5	104.2	149.6	45.1	2.6	1.4	3.0
	MTst	536.1	76.2	61.9	.4	6.5	391.9	28.0	124.0	178.1	53.4	3.1	1.7	3.6
Liquified Gases	MTst	—	—	.5	15.1	—	14.6	5.9	—	.9	7.7	—	.1	—
Manufactured Gas	MTst	—	.8	—	1.2	.4	—	—	—	—	—	—	—	—
Crude Petroleum	MTnat	603	31.9	110.0	—	461.1	—	—	—	—	—	—	—	—
	MTst	862.3	45.6	157.3	—	659.4	—	—	—	—	—	—	—	—
Petroleum Products	MTnat	—	29.5	40	461.1	6.0	385.6	26.6	101.0	88.0	9.9	53.9	88.2	18.0
	MTst	—	42.2	57.2	659.4	8.6	551.4	38.1	144.4	125.8	14.2	77.1	126.1	25.7
Coal	MTnat	716	88.4	9.2	—	1.0	617.4	—	339	211.3	30	7.7	11.5	17.9
	MTst	482	25.1	9.2	—	.7	447	—	222	172	23.7	6.1	9.1	14.1
Peat	MTst	16.8	1.6	—	—	—	15.2	—	13.6	.8	.8	—	—	—
Oil Shale	MTst	12	—	—	—	.5	11.5	1.2	7.4	2.9	—	—	—	—
Firewood	MTst	24	—	—	—	—	24	—	.5	12	9.5	1	1	—
"Decentralized" Fuel	MTst	20	—	—	—	—	20	—	—	—	20	—	—	—
Total Primary Output	MTst	2031.8	191.5	286.1	—	—	1554.2	73.2	590.5	492.5	129.3	87.3	138	43.4

This table was revised in February 1981, and absorbs information available to the author at that date. The methodology underlying the construction of this balance is explained in Campbell, 1978. A detailed explanation of the data sources and estimates of 1980 magnitudes is given in an appendix available on request to the author.

Secondary Allocations

BKWH	Electric Energy	212.4	—	12	1295	1071	—	690.8	177.3	76.4	100.0	26.5
MTst		26.1	—	1.5	159.1	131.5	—	84.8	21.7	9.4	12.3	3.3
MGK	Heat from TETsy	23.0	—	—	1150.0	1127	—	897.0	230.0	—	—	—
MTst	Other Sources	3.3	—	—	164.3	161	—	128.1	32.9	—	—	—
MTst	Total Secondary Allocations	10.0	—	—	50.4	40.4	—	253.3	54.6	9.4	12.3	3.3
MTst	Total Primary and Secondary Allocation					1296.6[a]	73.2	745.8	183.9	96.7	150.3	46.7

[a] Available primary less expenditures in power stations plus available secondary.

BKWH: billion kilowatt hours; MTst: million tons of standard fuel; MTnat: million tons, natural measure; MGK: million gigacalories; Bm³: billion cubic metres.

-demand situation, and develop a possible scenario for the year 2000. This will set the stage for a discussion in the last part of the paper of what problems must be solved to get from here to there.

7.2   Current Supply and Demand

The first step is to sketch the current demand–supply situation. In an earlier work, I have provided energy balances for 1950–75 (Campbell, 1978), but it would be preferable to describe the 1980 situation as the starting point. At this point actual 1980 data for many elements in the fuel and energy balance are still unavailable. Still, it is possible to produce for 1980 a simplified but reasonably accurate version of the fuel-balance table in the form published earlier and this is presented in Table 7.2.

I would like to draw attention to several distinctive features of the Soviet energy balance that are important to keep in mind in thinking about possible futures.

(a) Despite the talk about the tightening of energy supply, the Soviet Union was still exporting heavily in 1980. Indeed energy exports apparently grew faster than consumption in 1975–80 and increased their share in total production. A pronounced shift in export composition toward gas is taking place, and the domestic difficulties of the coal industry appear to be forcing a reduction in solid-fuel exports. This export surplus is an important cushion for meeting future domestic-demand growth, though giving up energy exports will impose its own constraints on growth.

(b) Electric-power stations account for a very large share of all primary-energy consumption — 590.5 million tons of standard fuel (MTst) out of the 1481 MTst available for domestic consumption in energy uses, or almost 40%. This is somewhat above the analogous share in the US and Western Europe.

(c) Industry is the dominant final consumer, accounting for 58% of net consumption, and indeed has continued to increase its share since 1975.

(d) The greatest novelty of Soviet energy policy compared to other countries' experience has been the employment of cogeneration on a large scale. In 1980 the Soviet electric-power industry captured and utilized more of the energy of the fuels it burned in the form of by-product heat than in the form of electric power, and was able largely by that means to achieve an efficiency in the conversion of fuel to electric power higher than the US power industry does.

(e) Gas, too, is used in a very different way in the USSR than in other countries, i.e. it is heavily dedicated to boiler use, including extensive use in power stations, rather than to the high-value uses such as household use that mark the pattern of other countries. In the US we use about 40% of gas in the residential and commercial markets and 18% in electric-power stations (DOE, *Energy Data*, 1978), whereas the corresponding figures for the USSR are 13% for the housing and municipal sector and 32% in power stations, i.e. the proportions are essentially reversed.[3]

(f) The Soviet economy faces a petroleum stringency only in a very special sense. The USSR produces a larger petroleum output than any other country in the world. But with total output of crude petroleum and condensate at 603 MTnat for 1980, domestic consumption of petroleum products was only about 386 MTnat, of which 166 MTnat was burned in boilers and furnaces. The requirements of the Soviet economy in 1980 for the high-value, nonsubstitutable uses of petroleum such as motor fuel, petrochemicals, and so on, was less than 200 MTnat, compared to the US consumption of over 700 MTnat. The Soviet Union has a large room for maneuver in dealing with a tightening oil-supply situation by improving the way it uses oil — getting a higher-quality mix out of its oil to cover motor fuel and petrochemical needs, and replacing residual fuel oil with other boiler and furnace fuels.

(g) The USSR has never gone as far as the US and Western Europe in pushing solid fuel out of the fuel balance. In the USSR at the end of the seventies, solid fuel covered about a third of primary-energy consumption, in the US less than 20%. At the same time the Soviet economic planners have kept its share this high only by forcing themselves to accept very low quality in solid fuel. The heat content of shale is only 32% of that of good hard coal, of peat only 34%. And the average heat value of Soviet coal itself is only about 67% of the kind of good hard coal that is usually taken as a standard.

As Soviet planners let coal gradually increase its share once again, or even maintain its present share, the two main sources they plan to use have quality characteristics that are drastically inferior to the current average. Ekibastuz coal has such a high ash and rock content that what is loaded and shipped to consumers is scarcely distinguishable from what is dumped on the spoil banks. When Kansk-Achinsk coal is shipped, half the mass transported is water and ash rather than anything combustible. The technological problems of processing this low-quality fuel are among the most pressing ones energy planners face, and the costs and energy losses associated with this beneficiation will be very great.

(h) The evidence is mounting that energy is used very wastefully in the USSR. As indicated earlier in Campbell (1978) energy consumption in industry and agriculture seem disproportionately large compared to US consumption, given the relative size of the two countries' output in these sectors. The divergence in the two countries' experience with GNP elasticity of energy demand since 1975 dramatizes the point still further. As shown in Table 7.1, for every percentage-point increase in Soviet GNP between 1975 and 1980, energy consumption has grown 1.26%. The corresponding elasticity for the US in the same period[4] was .6. The Russians are now busy searching for ways to cut energy consumption, and in the process are documenting the many alarming ways in which energy is wasted. They are still wasting enough oil-well gas (15.5 billion cubic metres (Bm^3) per year) to cover the total energy needs of a small country, e.g. Portugal or Greece. There are huge evaporative losses of liquid fuels in tank farms and transport. Tremendous amounts of coal are lost in transit, by wastage during storage and by use in unsuitable equipment. Gas, electricity, hot water and steam are often supplied to users without metering or control and are used very wastefully. There would thus seem to exist a considerable potential for conservation as an alternative to supply expansion, though conservation efforts would need to be directed at different targets than those we consider most important in the US. Whether Soviet energy-policy makers have the instruments to mobilize these potentials is a subject we will discuss more fully at the end of the paper.

7.3 A Possible Scenario for the Year 2000

It is probably unrealistic to try to develop an elaborate projection of energy supply and demand to the end of the century. There are simply too many uncertainties to allow one to have much faith in the results. But it will be instructive to try to sketch a basic quantitative framework that can be used to examine the major issues of energy policy over the next two decades.

(a) *Level and Structure of Aggregate Demand.*

The first step is to estimate a plausible level of aggregate demand for the year 2000. In doing so I will make heavy use of a fairly extensive Soviet literature directed toward the same goal. Two recent books (Makarov and Vigdorchik, 1979; Beschinskii and Kogan, 1976) provide rather comprehensive descriptions of the current status and trends in the Soviet fuel and energy balance, based, I believe, on the most extensive and authoritative work of this kind in the USSR. I have also been able to use three papers prepared by various combinations of these authors and other Soviet energy-forecasting specialists for a US-Soviet seminar on energy forecasting (Makarov and Melent'ev, 1979; Styrikovich and Cherniavskii, 1979; Beschinskii and Vigdorchik, 1979) and much of what follows is based on those papers. Those papers have been especially useful for my purposes since they are more specific than much of the other published output of these authors in giving data, and in their greater conscientiousness in covering all the important variables. The data in these sources are reasonably well echoed in a set of energy forecasts submitted by the USSR to the Economic Commission for Europe showing in rather aggregated form the energy-balances forecast for 1990 and 2000. It is thus probably fair to say that these projections constitute a semiofficial view of the Soviet energy future. One could not call them operational forecasts; they represent rather the views held by a kind of energy-forecasting "establishment" at the research level of energy-policy making. Melent'ev and Styrikovich are Academicians, the others appear to work in various R and D organizations in the Academy system or the energy sector.

Most Western observers expect the Soviet rate of GNP growth through the 1980s to remain at the relatively low levels experienced in the last several years. In the 'nineties the adverse labor-force prospects that are an important factor in that forecast will ease, but other adverse influences may well keep the growth rates from recovering even then. I consider that projection of growth at 2.5–3.0% per year for the 20-year period as a whole is moderately optimistic. I further believe that it will prove impossible for the Soviet system to bring the GNP elasticity of energy demand below 1 over the next two decades. There is certainly room for conservation, but the record so far has shown very little success in reducing the elasticity of demand below 1, even in the most recent five-year period when there has been a vigorous campaign to that end. The question of conservation is a complicated subject to which we will return in the concluding section, but for the moment I will operate on the assumption that the GNP elasticity of energy demand will be in the range of .9 to 1.

The effect of differing assumptions regarding growth rates and GNP elasticities is shown in the following tabulation (Table 7.3) of possible energy consumption in the year 2000, starting from the 1980 gross consumption figure of 1481 MTst, indicated in Table 7.2, i.e. 1554.2 MTst "available for distribution" less 73.2 MTst of non-fuel use.

It will be much easier to proceed with this exercise if we pick a single aggregate-demand figure — I suggest 2500 MTst as a plausible projection. For some perspective on the magnitude of this task, the absolute increment (1019 MTst) is somewhat larger than that experienced in the preceding two decades (907.2 MTst) but the rate of growth is much smaller.

Soviet forecasts generally envisage a demand larger than 2500 MTst,

Table 7.3 *Possible Energy Consumption in the Year 2000 (MTst)*

GNP Growth Rate (percent)	Elasticity of Energy Consumption	
	1	.9
2.5	2427	2311
3.0	2678	2523

based on a more rapid rate of growth of the total output of the economy than I would be willing to accept, somewhat offset by more optimistic expectations regarding energy conservation. Styrikovich and Cherniavskii (1979, p. 17) assume a 3.7% per year rate of growth for net material product (NMP) for 1975–2000 but an elasticity of .76 – .86, to give a figure for energy consumption in 2000 of 2615–2823 MTst. The forecast reported to the ECE shows consumption in the year 2000 as 2735–3285 MTst. If 2500 MTst seems too high or low, one can easily trace through the kind of alterations needed in the following analysis and will find that the changes don't much affect the nature of the problems, but only their acuity.

In thinking about the composition of this demand, let us first figure the demand for conversion to electric power. There is a great deal of contradictory evidence on the likely share of electric power in gross consumption of primary energy at the end of the century. Makarov and Vigdorchik (1979, p. 202) say that electric stations will in the future take 40% of the energy resources consumed in the country, and let us suppose that the year they have in mind is 2000. But only part of that consumption will be charged to electric power, since some will be captured as by-product heat. Styrikovich and Cherniavskii (1979, p. 19) forecast that the amount charged to power will be 30–3% of all primary consumption by 2000, while the forecast submitted to the UN suggests a share of only 27.4–29.6%. If we accept 40% as the share consumed in power stations, and 30% as the amount charged to power, the amount of primary energy consumed in power stations would be 1,000 MTst, the amount charged to power would be 750 MTst, and the amount captured as cogenerated heat 205 MTst, i.e. the remaining fuel corrected for boiler efficiency. The tables submitted to the ECE forecast a conversion efficiency of 41.7% in the year 2000, so that the amount of energy embodied in the electric power produced is 313 MTst. The resulting ratio of cogenerated heat captured or the energy in the form of power 205 MTst/313 MTst) is a smaller ratio than that at present, but that makes sense in the light of the fact that power generation is likely to undergo regional shifts that reduce the potential for cogeneration — i.e. to mine-mouth stations in the East. Since there are 8,140 KWH per tons of standard fuel, the electric power produced would be 2548 BKWH, and since 1980 output was 1295 BKWH, the annual average rate of growth would be 3.4%

There are several possible indications of the share that might be met by nuclear-power stations. Styrikovich and Cherniavskii (1979) say that by the end of the century nuclear power might account for 8–10% of total primary-energy supply (p. 20). The forecast submitted to the ECE shows 9.4% and using that figure implies a contribution of 235 MTst that would produce 798 BKWH at the conversion efficiency of .417 which I am assuming for fossil-fired plants.[5] On the reasonable assumption of 5,000 hours utilization, they would require 160 GW of nuclear capacity. Capacity at the end of 1980 is about 18 GW, so capacity would have to grow at 11.5% per year and annual average additions would be 7.1 GW per year. That seems at the outer limits of feasibility. The forecast given to the ECE shows the nuclear contribution in 2000 as 300–400 MTst, but that seems to me quite impossible to achieve. For present purposes, I will accept that the output of electric power from nuclear plants in 2000 could be 798 BKWH.

It is also intended to continue development of hydroelectric power. What might hydropower output be by 2000? According to Nekrasov and Pervukhin (1977, Chap 7) studies performed by Gidroproekt in recent years show that it would be possible to add capacity *in the European part* of the USSR totaling 11 million KW, with a long-term average output of 27 BKWH. Added to 1975 capacity and potential, that would bring the total to 31.5 MKW and 110 BKWH. It seems to me unlikely that all this capacity would be added by 1990, just because of the lead times involved, but I will assume that the 110 BKWH can be considered a target for 2000. The additionally developable potential *in the Asian part* of the USSR is much greater, and the authors say that completions in 1975–80, plus new projects to be started in the same period, will aggregate 39.0 million KW. Added to capacity in operation at the end of 1976, this would bring the total to 58.4 million KW, which at 3500 hours utilization would provide 204.4 BKWH. Let us suppose that by the end of the century, enough capacity will have been added to bring the Asiatic total to 200 BKWH. The total for the USSR in 2000 would thus be 310 BKWH. The forecast submitted to the ECE is 288–339 BKWH; so 310 BKWH is reasonably in line with Soviet expectations.

Any electric power provided by solar, tidal, and geothermal sources by 2000 would be very small; thus, approximately 1440 BKWH would be left to be covered by fossil-fired generation, requiring 424 MTst of fossil fuel.

Styrikovich and Cherniavskii (1979, p. 20) have a three-way breakdown in which energy is used as electric power, steam and hot water (*teploenergiia*), or directly in equipment such as engines and furnaces. I am not using their electric-power figure, but use their 30–40 split between *teploenergiia* and direct use. *Teploenergiia* would be 750 MTst, and direct use 1000 MTst. They further suggest that about 43% of direct fuel use will consist of liquid fuel (that would be 430 MTst). Some part of that will be residual fuel oil (*mazut*) or distillate fuel oils burned as furnace fuel, but by the end of the century most direct use of liquid fuel will surely be as motor fuel — let us say 80% — which would be 344 MTst, or about 241 MTnat of light fractions from petroleum refining suitable as fuel for internal-combustion engines. The other 86 MTst (60 MTnat) of liquid fuel will be essentially fuel-oil fractions burned in boilers and furnaces.

As for the primary-energy consumption devoted to producing steam and hot water (*teploenergiia*), which will amount to 750 MTst, a significant fraction will be supplied as cogenerated heat from electric-power stations that we figured above as 205 MTst. Remember that in figuring the fossil-fuel requirements to generate electric power we have allowed only for the fuel to be charged to power.[6] This would leave 545 MTst to be accounted for by steam and hot water produced in conventional boilers.

Adding the fossil-fuel consumption for power estimated above as 424 MTst, and that charged to heat in cogeneration plants (250 MTst) we get a total of 674 MTst of fossil fuel burned in power stations. What might be the composition of the fuel burned in power stations by 2000? Makarov and Melent'ev (1979, pp. 13–14) say that studies have shown that it is possible to replace one-half to three-fourths of the current uses of residual fuel oil (*mazut*) with coal and gas. Power stations, which we estimated earlier to be burning about 100 MTnat of liquid fuel in 1980, probably have even better replacement potential than other *mazut*-burning equipment, so let's say that power stations may still be burning maybe as much as 30 MTnat (43 MTst) of liquid fuel for power, or 6.4% of total fossil-fuel consumption in power stations. Subtracting 43 MTst of liquid fuel and about the same amount of minor solid fuels as in 1980 (25 MTst) leaves 600 MTst to be covered by coal and gas in the year 2000. In 1980 the coal/gas ratio in fossil fuel consumption in power stations was 1.7 to 1 but the report submitted to the UN forecasts a ratio of over 2.5 to 1 by 2000. That seems to me a bit overambitious and I will assume a coal/gas ratio in power stations of 2. On the basis of the foregoing calculations, the overall consumption balance is as shown in Table 7.4.

(b)   *Production Structure*

How might the total of 2500 MTst be supplied? Let us assume that non-fuel use and own consumption will be at least as large in relation to final energy consumption in 2000 as in 1980, i.e. 17.7%. That means

Table 7.4   *Energy Consumption in 2000 by Primary Source and Energy Form (MTst)*

Energy Form	Total	Primary Source			
		Liquid	Gas	Solid	Nuclear and Hydro
Power Generation	750				326
Cogenerated Heat (Steam and Hot Water)	250 (205)[a]	43	202	429[b]	—
Other Heat (Steam and Hot Water)	545	NA	NA	NA	—
Direct Use	1,000	NA	NA	NA	—
Total	2,500	NA	NA	NA	326

[a] 250 MTst is the fuel charged to cogenerated heat, but corrected for boiler efficiency the amount delivered is only 205 MTst.
[b] This figure consists of 404 MTst of coal and 25 MTst of minor solid fuel.

the energy sector would have to produce 2942 MTst to cover the final energy consumption we have analyzed. Styrikovich and Cherniavskii (1979, p. 19) forecast an energy-production structure for 2000 as shown in column 1 of Table 7.5 below. Column 2 shows the structure in the ECE forecast already mentioned. In the third column I have made adjustments to these forecasts that (*a*) make the total equal 100; (*b*) reflect my view that both these forecasts are over-optimistic on oil; (*c*) use the amounts for hydro and nuclear estimated earlier in the paper; and (*d*) accept what I take as more recent Soviet thinking underlying the forecast for the ECE that the role of gas will be greater and that of coal smaller than was earlier thought.

How plausible is it that these amounts can be produced? First consider *oil*. One view of Soviet oil prospects holds that considering the prospective area and the relatively light degree of exploration so far, output can be sustained at more or less the present level for many years to come. But the opposing view, even accepting the reality of this potential, holds that low exploration effectiveness, missing infrastructure and the lead times required for new technologies will make for slow realization of this potential. My own view is that the 441 MTnat of crude oil and condensate used in this paper is an optimistic forecast, as can be seen if we think about the amounts of oil that it implies must be found and explored to the production stage in the next two decades. I do not want to get involved in a discussion of reserve concepts and estimates, but consider the following simple analysis. If output falls steadily to about 400 MT in 1990, as the CIA (1977) suggests it may, but then rises smoothly after 1990 to 441 MT by 2000 as in Table 7.4, cumulative production 1981 through 2000 would be 9.1 billion tons. With falling production, the working inventory of reserves can be smaller in 2000 than in 1980, but the total discoveries would still have to be 7.5 billion tons.[7] The largest fields ever found in the USSR — Samotlor and Romashkino — are said to have contained about 2 billion tons of recoverable reserves each (Dienes, 1979, p. 58; CIA, July 1977, p. 3). Given that no giant field of this kind has been discovered in the last 15 years (since Samotlor in 1965) it is difficult to convince oneself that the problem will be easily solved by finding a few such fields in the next 15 years. Given the adverse trends in exploratory effectiveness experienced in recent years, discovering this much oil seems a formidable task.

If it can be achieved, however, an output of 441 MT of oil in the year 2000 certainly seems adequate to domestic needs. With 5% field losses, 4% refinery losses, and 10% of refinery runs in the form of nonfuel items — such as feedstocks for petrochemicals and asphalt — such an output would provide 382 MTnat of refinery products for energy use. That is more than adequate to meet the liquid fuel needs we have outlined — i.e. 241 MTnat of light fractions for motor-fuel use, 30 MTnat for electric power, and 60 MTnat for other furnace uses. It would involve a refinery mix significantly different from the present one, however — 241 MTnat of light fractions is about 73% of

Table 7.5 *Possible Energy-Supply Structure in 2000*

	Cherniavskii and Styrikovich (1) (percent)	Forecast for ECE (2) (percent)	(3) (percent)	Adjusted by Author (4) (MTst)[a]	(5) Natural Units
Oil	25–30	25–27	21	631	441 MTnat
Gas	25–30	33–36	35	1053	887 BM³
Coal	26–29	23–28	28	842	745 MTnat (K-A + E)[b]
					614 MTnat (Other)
Nuclear	8–10	9–10	9.4	235	—
Hydro	2–3	2–3	3.6	91	—
Other	2–3	2–3	3	90	—
Total	88–105	94–107	100	2942	—

[a] Neither of the Soviet forecasts makes any allowance for losses and own consumption within the energy industries or nonfuel use, which must be allowed for in my approach. Given the way hydro and nuclear energy are figured, they do not involve losses and own consumption, so I load the allowance for such losses and nonfuel use fully onto the other four sources.

[b] Based on assumptions that the heating value comes half from Kansk-Achinsk and Ekibastuz coal (with equal weights) whose heat contents are 3570 and 4340 gigacalories per ton (Gkal/T) respectively (Nekrasov et al., 1974, pp. 81–2) and half from other sources with heat value maintained at the 1978 average of 4,796 Gkal/T (Nar.khoz. 1978) and the fact that K–A output 1978 = 32 MTnat (Shabad 1980) and Ekibastuz output 1978 = 50.3 MTnat (*Elektricheskie stantsii*, p. 8, no. 10, 1979).

the listed total of uses, compared to a ratio of less than 50% today.

In translating the *coal* requirements into actual sources, I assume that by the year 2000, half of the heat value of coal output would come from the low-quality strip-mined coals of the East, with an average heating value of 3955 Gkal/T, and that the average heating value of coal from other sources will have been maintained at the 1979 level. To maintain that heating value, it will have to undergo more processing than at present, with large losses. The implication that coal output from the traditional basins can be kept as high as 614 MTnat, i.e. about the 1980 level, is probably overoptimistic. The figure of 745 MTnat for Ekibastuz and Kansk-Achinsk coal may thus be an underestimate of how much those basins would have to supply. But even at the forecast level the costs of developing the technology for, and financing the investments in, producing, processing, and transporting this coal or energy forms derived from it are going to be formidable. The technologies for using the Ekibastuz coal are reasonably well established, but for the Kansk-Achinsk coal there are three large steps — burning it in large power-generating units, processing it into some kind of transportable fuel, and shipping it by pipeline — the technologies for which are still quite undeveloped at the moment. When the power-transmission technology is added to this list, there can be no doubt that getting Eastern coal to make the contribution suggested is subject to terrible hazards. And it is clear that much of this coal will have to be processed by some technique less certain than combustion in power plants. Even the most ambitious projections discussed for the Ekibastuz and Kansk-Achinsk mine-mouth-power complexes imply that they would not consume more than 150 MTst of these coals,[8] and even allowing for considerable additional amounts to be consumed in the Ural, and at moderate distances from Kansk-Achinsk, the 421 MTst forecast for these basins implies huge amounts to be processed for long-distance shipment with very large energy losses in the process.

The estimated volumes of *gas* would come to a very large extent from Siberia, where reserves to support these output levels do exist. The question will be whether the capacity to transport it can be built — a point on which at least some commentators are pessimistic. If we assume that the average transmission distance does not rise above 2000 km, the transport work would be 2,106,000 Bm^3km (about 2.5 times the 1980 level), and would itself consume perhaps as much as 75 Bm^3 with total own use on pipelines as much as 100 Bm^3.[9]

One of the greatest uncertainties, and the most controversial issue in any forecast of the energy situation in the next two decades will be the competition between gas and coal, each with its distinctive potential bottle-neck. Soviet studies show that gas currently has a significant cost advantage over coal, even in such uses as raising steam in power stations. The advantage is said to be between 4 and 5 rubles per ton of standard fuel in most regions of the USSR (Il'ina and Utkina, 1978, pp. 138–9), and compared to the Soviet estimate of the marginal cost of coal (the so-called *zamykaiushchie zatraty*, which are discussed more fully below) of about 20–22 rubles per ton of standard fuel, that is a significant saving. My guess is that the discrepancy will increase significantly as coal quality and location deteriorate. But there is a big offsetting obstacle in the way of a victory for gas, i.e. the demands it puts on the steel industry. As Makarov and Vigdorchik (1979, p. 195) say one cannot assume that enough pipe can be gotten either by domestic production or by import to fully utilize the potential contribution of gas.

The amounts shown for *nuclear* and *hydro* power are, as already suggested, at the upper end of what might be considered feasible. The amount for "*other*" is probably attainable. Shale oil, peat, and firewood are unlikely to grow from their 1980 level of 73 MTst, and little can be expected from tidal, geothermal, and solar. The best bet is better utilization of secondary sources, poorly exploited at present. Combustible by-products (such as coke-oven gas) are already fairly heavily utilized, but it is estimated that large amounts of secondary heat resources go unutilized in the major energy-intensive branches. It was planned that total secondary energy resources in industry in 1980 would be about 83 MTst, of which a little over 20 MTst would be unutilized (Sushon et al., 1978, p. 265). With growth, and serious efforts to capture these resources, it would be possible to reach the 94 MTst shown in Table 7.4.

(c)   *The East-West Transport Problem*

Finally, what does all this mean about the European-Asiatic split? Styrikovich and Cherniavskii (1979, p. 11) predict that even by the end of the century, the share of the European part of the USSR in total energy demand will still be 65–70%. Taking the midpoint of this range implies 1,986 MTst to be made available in the European USSR. What levels might be expected for the output of coal, oil, and gas in the European USSR by the year 2000? I suggest the amounts shown in the first column in Table 7.6 as optimistic estimates, on the following arguments:

Table 7.6   *The East-West Split in Soviet Energy Production in 2000 (MTst)*

	Europe	Asia	Total
Hydro	32	59	91
Nuclear	235	negl.	235
Oil	286	345	631
Gas	119	904	1023
Coal	137	735	872
Other	60	30	90
Total	869	2073	2942

European output of coal in 1980 was about 330 MTnat, which

represented a decline from 1975. Many of the mines are being exhausted, and are being replaced only partially by new mines. When specialists look at individual basin and mine capacities they see European output as barely holding its own or falling further by 1985. The Russians will continue to develop some new capacity here, even at high cost, because they need the coking coal. But total output must continue to decline, just because the investment cost is so high that Soviet planners will prefer to replace exhausted capacity with new mines in the East, rather than here.

Petroleum output in the European SSSR has fallen by about 40 MTnat in the Tenth FYP. Its still substantial production of about 350 MTnat in 1980 will continue to fall sharply in the '80s as the big fields in major producing regions are exhausted. Development of new small fields in the traditional producing areas will continue, but the industry is already doing that on a large scale, without stopping the slide in output. On the other hand some of the best long-range prospects for additional oil production are in the European areas — at great depths in the Pri-Caspian depression, offshore in the Caspian, Baltic, and Black Seas, and in the far north. The postulated 200 MTnat allows for extensive new discoveries offshore and at deeper horizons.

Output of gas in the European SSSR has stayed about constant in the Tenth FYP, and stands in 1980 at slightly over 150 billion cubic meters. It has managed to keep this position only because development of new areas — especially the growth of output from the Orenburg field — offsets declines in older fields. To expect 100 Bm^3 in 2000 is optimistic, and assumes that a great deal more gas will be found as a concomitant of the intensive search for oil in the European areas.

The regional split on hydro power has already been indicated earlier. Nuclear will be almost exclusively in the West, as will most of "other."

The implication is that 1117 MTst will have to flow from the East to the West in the form of coal, oil, gas, and to some extent in the form of electric power generated in the East. This is somewhat overstated, since much of the own use within the energy sector that differentiates production and final consumption will occur in the East and along the transport routes. On the other hand, these are probably overoptimistic projections for what is feasible in the European areas. The nuclear contribution is estimated generously, and the European prospect for coal and oil are probably also on the high side. Overall, these calculations suggest a transport problem more serious than Makarov and Vigdorchik (1979, p. 201) are willing to admit — they see a 2.5 fold increase in the East–West flow between 1975 when it was 360 MTst, and the end of the century, which implies a movement in 2000 of about 900 MTst compared to the 1117 calculated above.

(d) *Conservation*

Before concluding, we should consider a bit more fully the possibilities of conservation. How strong a case could one make for a radically different vision in which growth was accommodated to a considerable extent by conservation rather than by supply increases? If elasticity could be cut fairly sharply, say from the assumed value of 1 to a value of .6, GNP growth at 2.5% per year would require an energy supply 432 MTst less in the year 2000 than I have projected. Looked at in another way, with elasticity at .6, and assuming that other constraints are not binding, the 2500 MTst of consumption I think could be produced in the year 2000 would be consistent with much more dynamic economic growth or with a significant growth of exports. Whether the GNP elasticity can indeed be brought down significantly is a very complicated question, and one that will merit continued assessment as the Soviet efforts along these lines unfold. Depending on how the system evolves, significant energy conservation might be possible, though I am dubious that the USSR can achieve a reduction in the elasticity of energy demand to anything like .6. It is worth spelling out the reasoning behind this position in more detail.

As indicated in the previous section, the peculiarities of the Soviet demand structure mean that potential energy savings are much more heavily concentrated in industry, agriculture, and other "productive" sectors than in the household and municipal sectors where conservation efforts are focussed in the US. The other side of this difference in demand structure is the relative unimportance of energy use in the household sector at the present time. These are uses with high personal income elasticity, and over a twenty year period of growth at 2.5–3%, if consumers are allowed to participate reasonably evenly in economic growth, we should expect sharply rising household demand.

In the production sectors, where conservation efforts must now focus, the problem in the Soviet institutional setting is to find policy instruments that will induce "rational" energy savings that do not reduce production. One possibility is price increases. Heretofore, as in the US, energy has seemed cheap and abundant to Soviet decision makers, partly because it has been priced well below its social cost. The evidence for this assertion is developed in another paper (Campbell, 1981) and only a sketch of the argument can be included here. Energy represents a unique case in Soviet price policy because an attempt has been made to evade the irrationalities of Soviet pricing and to develop measures of the real opportunity cost of energy in the form of *zamykaiushchie zatraty* or ZZ. These can be thought of as marginal cost-based prices, or as the shadow prices associated with an optimizing program for producing and allocating energy. They are mandated as the official indices of energy cost in project-making decisions about what energy source or what technologies to use. There are two difficulties, however: (a) for a large range of decisions about energy use (i.e. enterprise-level, current-operating decisions) it is transactions prices rather than the ZZ that control decisions, and transactions prices are well below the ZZ for most energy forms; (b) the ZZ themselves are probably well below the true opportunity costs.

New ZZs, higher than those used in the 'seventies, have now been promulgated (Makarov and Vigdorchik, 1979, p. 240) but they are still below real costs, especially since they do not reflect the opportunity cost of foregoing energy exports. New, higher transactions prices for energy are also to be introduced as part of a general price reform. The fact that the new prices will not be introduced until January 1, 1982, however, suggests something less than full appreciation of the urgency of the matter. And it seems that the new prices, on petroleum products at least, are to be kept well below marginal costs by squeezing out rent in the pricing of crude oil. The overall level of crude oil prices is to be raised by 2.3 times. But that will not be high enough to cover the marginal cost of oil from sources that will have to be used to meet the output goals of the eleventh Five-Year-Plan. For deciding on the extensive and intensive margin of extraction, there will also be introduced a notional price five times higher than the old level of oil prices. (*Ekonomika neftianoi promyshlennosti*: pp. 2–4, no. 8, 1980.)

A related question is how significant price rises will be in discouraging consumption in the Soviet institutional setting. Given the present incentive system controlling managerial behavior, I doubt the price increases will be very effective in inducing conservation, though we should not rule out the possibility that over the twenty-year period contemplated here there may be significant systemic changes that will increase sensitivity of decision makers to prices as signals of scarcity.

Soviet writers are fairly optimistic about conservation. According to Makarov and Vigdorchik (1979, p. 25) the coefficients for useful work in relation to energy consumed for various fuels and uses could change over the next two decades as shown in the first two columns of Table 7.7. If we apply these efficiency gains to the major end-use categories described in the 2000 scenario, the savings would be as shown in the last column of that table.

This is an extremely crude calculation, but the implication is that efficiency increases in end use could make a very significant contribution to solving the energy problem — 318 MTst is a good fraction of the 400 MTst saving mentioned above as associated with a drop in elasticity to .6. But here again how seriously one takes these possibilities depends on one's view of the ability of the Soviet system to innovate. These putative gains depend on an extraordinary variety of R and D efforts, commercialization, and diffusion of equipment innovations. Imagine, for example, the kind of redesign of equipment, changes in fuel quality, service, etc. that will be required to raise internal-combustion-engine efficiency from 31 to 47%! This kind of flexibility and innovational drive is conspicuous by its absence in the Soviet system, and I just don't see these kinds of changes taking place in two decades. There *is* one notable example of such a rapid change — the heat rate in power generation has been cut by almost one-third in the last two decades, from 468 grams of standard fuel per net KWH in 1960 to 330 grams in 1980. But I see this kind of achievement as

Table 7.7   *Energy Conservation from Improved Utilization*

	Efficiency in Energy Use (percent)		Consumption Forecast (MTst)	Corrected for Efficiency Gain (MTst)	Savings (MTst)
	1980	2000			
Steam and Hot Water (teplovaia energiia)	.825	.85	795	772	23
Furnaces[a]	.50	.62	400	323	77
Electricity	.39	.45	750	650	100
Engines	.31	.47	347	229	118
Other Fuels (Peat, Firewood, Shale)	Constant		—	—	—
Total					318

[a] Direct use other than internal-combustion engines was calculated as 653 MTst, but I believe that Makarov's efficiency gain for furnaces must refer to a much smaller universe than the 653 MTst.

dependent on a very special situation. It was made possible hitherto, by focussing innovational efforts on a few strategic variables in a small number of facilities. In other sectors a much broader, diffuse, heterogeneous set of changes is likely to be required, calling for much greater low-level initiative and co-ordination.

Over a third of primary-energy consumption takes place in electric-power stations, and we might well ask about possible additional improvements in efficiency for this large component of total demand. Fuel expenditure per unit of output was reduced here by heavy use of cogeneration and by a technological policy that has emphasized large units using steam at supercritical parameters. I doubt that much further improvement along these lines is possible in the future. Indeed, the heat rate may well rise, as the share of cogeneration falls. The major innovation that might help is the introduction of MHD (magnetohydrodynamic) generation but it is difficult to predict when MHD will become a working innovation; for any reasonable estimate of timing and magnitude, its impact on overall fuel expenditure per unit of output will not be great. Even if we suppose that MHD could account for 20% of fossil-fired generation by the year 2000, its differential efficiency of 50% versus the 41.7% we have been using for conventional power generation would raise average efficiency only to 43% and result in savings of 13 MTst of fossil fuel. Soviet energy planners themselves may be having doubts as to the feasibility of much improvement in the heat rate. In contrast to the .45 efficiency forecast by Styrikovich and Cherniavskii 1979, which we also used in Table 7.7, the forecast supplied to the ECE showed an efficiency rising to only 40.3% by 1990 and to 41.7% by 2000.

(e) *Conclusion*

I hope I have avoided the trap of leading readers to believe that the foregoing quantitative sketch is my considered conclusion as to what the Soviet energy future will look like in the year 2000. Each major building block in the argument really warrants an in-depth study in itself, and I have sacrificed detailed justification of individual elements to focus instead on the interrelations of major separate elements in the situation. Thus the most appropriate form for some concluding remarks is probably some questions about whether or not the overall view developed seems plausible, in terms of consistency both internally, and with some major aspects of the environment within which energy policy will develop. I would like to speak to that from three points of view.

(i) I believe the energy scenario described is feasible in terms of technical and energy-resource constraints. The coal and gas resources it requires have already been discovered. It may be perhaps a bit optimistic in relation to the amount of oil resources it requires the Soviet oil industry to discover over the period, but as suggested above, the economy could probably get by with somewhat less oil than forecast here. The USSR possesses a working nuclear-power technology, and has made a good start on commercializing the breeder technology that will overcome possible limitations in resources of fissionable material. In the major technological areas the issues are not so much whether a given job, such as gas transport, can be performed, but whether technological progress can proceed fast enough to avoid the crippling resource inputs that present technological levels imply. Even in cases where one could not say that a working technology has been mastered in the Soviet economy as in offshore work or in slurry transport, the technological problems have been solved abroad, and the technology can probably be imported.

(ii) The path outlined will be costly in terms of investment requirements. It would be an exceedingly ambitious and uncertain task to attempt to quantify those requirements in detail, but we can think about the problem in terms of the basic proportions of the Soviet economy in the recent period. With investment at 22% of GNP, industrial investment at 35% of all investment and investment in the fuels and power industries at about 28% of all industrial investment, energy investment takes about 2.2% of GNP (CIA, *Handbook*). As I understand the way the Soviet statistics work, that includes investment in energy transport insofar as oil and gas pipelines and power transmission are concerned, but not in other forms of energy transport. It does not seem unrealistic to suppose that the share of the fuels and power sector in all industrial investment should rise again to the 40% of all industrial investment it required in the pre-hydrocarbon period. If one assumed that the share of industrial investment in GNP could not be raised, that would be equivalent to diverting to the energy sector, to compensate for the rising capital intensity, 12% of the flow that normally goes into growth-inducing projects. Some of the sacrifice might be in nonindustrial investments; as an alternative measure of the pressure on the economy, in order to keep the fraction of GNP that goes to growth-inducing investments of all kinds from falling, almost one percent of GNP would have to be diverted from some other end use such as consumption or defense to compensate for the rising relative capital intensity of energy expansion. This is not a dramatic diversion, but is certainly large enough a change from recent experience that over an extended period it would have a palpable independent effect on growth. The energy-expansion path this paper has described seems feasible in part because of the relatively modest role of economic growth that we assumed, but the investment demands of that expansion path seem sufficiently heavy to validate the original pessimism about economic growth.

(iii) It will not have escaped notice that this sketch of a possible energy situation in 2000 envisages neither exports nor imports of energy. Is that plausible? The analysis suggests to me that it is realistic to expect that Soviet domestic energy demand at the end of the century can be met from domestic energy sources. It also seems quite clear to me that the USSR is going to be unable to export any significant amounts of energy to the non-socialist world (there may be small exceptions in the form of some gas and some coking coal, especially from Siberia). Without such exports, it seems obvious that it will not be possible to continue the present policy of large-scale importation of technology in the coming years, and I see that as another force that will keep Soviet economic growth down to 2.5–3% per year. What *is* implausible about the picture presented is the implication that the USSR will be able to get out from under the burden of energy exports to Eastern Europe, and I believe that all during the next two decades it will be exporting amounts to Eastern Europe that will rise from the present level to something of the order of a couple of hundred million tons of standard fuel in various forms. I believe the USSR could produce this much of an increase above the magnitudes already described, especially if it were in the form of gas. Nor does the addition of this extra demand seem incompatible with growth at the postulated rates, in part because the USSR would make sure that much of the associated investment burden is borne by the East European importers, rather than by itself.

This exercise should end with heavy emphasis on a reminder that this is a highly tentative and unfinished analysis. There are too many uncertainties at this point to be very dogmatic about how the problem of provisioning the economy with energy is going to interact with its overall growth over the two decades ahead. Each of the elements treated as feasible could run into insoluble problems — the nuclear contribution could be blocked by a serious nuclear accident, technologies for processing Kansk-Achinsk coal may be delayed for a decade or two. There may be breakthroughs on possibilities I have ruled out — the discovery of fabulous oil fields or significant success in conservation. But the author will consider this paper a success if it has succeeded in establishing a framework that will be productive in focussing attention and defining issues for continuing research on this important question.

7: Notes

1 Energy consumption can be conceptualized in numerous ways and at various levels of grossness. I find it most useful to operate with a concept of energy consumption that is essentially delivery of energy forms to final users. This is a concept difficult to follow consistently, and the departures from it forced by expediency will be clear from careful study of the energy balances cited later. For example, I treat expenditure of energy in pipeline transportation as own use, and hence not as energy consumption, but energy consumption in other forms of energy transport (e.g. railroad haulage of coal) is treated as final consumption and counted as final demand.

   Electric-power generation from fossil fuel can be considered either a form of final demand or as a transformation within the energy sector. In this paper I use "gross energy consumption," to refer to the former, "net energy consumption" to mean the latter. In the latter case, conversion losses in electric-power stations and losses in transmission and distribution are a form of own use within the energy sector. But even when I treat electric-power stations as part of the energy sector rather than as a demand sector, I am inconsistent in failing to treat consumption of electric power in other energy branches (say use of electric power on pipelines) as a form of own use within the energy sector.

   Much of Soviet energy analysis operates with a consumption concept based on "useful energy," i.e. the work produced by energy-using equipment and processes. The rationale is that this concept bears a more stable relationship to output than does my concept of energy supplied to energy-using equipment and processes. This is probably true, though I don't believe that "useful energy" is ever really measured, being rather derived by applying some estimate of utilization efficiency. But such Soviet data as there are on "useful energy" can usually be exploited for my estimates, since they can be reconciled with my concept through a coefficient of energy-use efficiency.

   Given the concept I am using, the measures of consumption in this paper must be adjusted upwards for nonfuel use and for own use to arrive at figures for apparent consumption, and then for net trade to arrive at production.

   There are data available based on other concepts of energy consumption, such as the series that appears in *Nar. khoz. SSSR* in the table on the "fuel and energy balance." This is the series Marshall Goldman has used in commenting on the measures of elasticity in this table. The *Nar. khoz. SSSR* series involves some conceptual peculiarities that make me prefer my own. For example, it includes hydropower at its theoretical energy content rather than at the amount of fossil fuel saved, includes a significant, unexplained "other" category, and does not mention nuclear power. And various anomalies in that series — such as no growth in consumption in 1971 — make me distrust it.

2 Oil and gas accounted for an even larger share of the increment in production — about 85%.

3 The contrast is not quite so strong as these figures suggest, since some of the gas burned in Soviet power stations produces cogenerated heat that is used for urban space heating. But allowance for this would shift no more than about 2 percentage points from power stations to households (Ryps, 1978, pp. 13–14; Campbell, 1979, pp. 26, 29).

4 DOE, *Monthly Energy Rev.*, June 1980, p. 12.
5 Throughout this analysis, I treat the contribution of nuclear and hydropower to primary production as the heat content of the fuel they replace at the contemporary heat rate in fossil-fired stations rather than the energy content of the nuclear and hydro-generated power itself.
6 The Soviet heat rate in power generation is figured by dividing fuel consumption, less the captured cogenerated heat (converted for boiler efficiency), by the power output. I have used a projection of the heat rate so conceptualized to translate electric-power output into fuel consumed for power. The current heat rate is about 340 grams of standard fuel per KWH, which implies a conversion efficiency of about .36, and I have assumed this would rise to .417 by 2000.
7 Assume that on the average the working inventory of recoverable contents in fields being produced is ten times the annual output. The suggested production profile could thus be compatible with a reserve drawdown of 1.6 billion tons.
8 The Ekibastuz complex is to consist of four stations of 4 GW each, and the Kansk-Achinsk complex is talked about in terms of 30, 50, or 70 GW (Shelest', 1975, pp. 226–9, 239–49). Assuming average utilization of 5,000 hours and a heat rate of 340 g/KWH, 34 GW would consume about 80 MTst per year; 74 GW would consume 146 MTst. They may well succeed in getting the stations above 5,000 hours — Shelest' implies an expectation of 6,250 hours.
9 In 1976, when gas pipelines did $405 \times 10^{12} m^3 km$ of transport work, they consumed about 15 billion cubic meters of gas themselves, and, in addition, had losses of about 5.5 billion cubic meters. In 1976 only 71% of the compressor capacity on gas pipelines used gas turbines as prime movers, and this share is likely to increase considerably over the next two decades. (Campbell, 1981; *Ekonomika gazovoi promyshlennosti*: p. 27, no. 11, 1977.)

7: References

Arkhipenko, A. S., and Nazarov, V. I., *Ekonomicheskaia effektivnost' geologorazvedochnykh rabot na neft' i gaz v zapadno-sibirskoi nizmennosti* (Economic Effectiveness of Geological Exploratory Work for Oil and Gas in the West Siberian Depression). Leningrad, 1973.
Beschinskii, A. A., and Kogan, Iu. M., *Ekonomicheskie problemy elektrifikatsii* (Economic Problems of Electrification). Moscow, 1976.
Beschinskii, A. A., and Vigdorchik, A. G., "Analiz sviazi mezhdu tempami prirosta natsional'nogo dohkoda i tempami potrebleniia energii" (Analysis of the Connection between the Rates of Growth of National Income and of Energy Consumption). Paper presented to joint US-Soviet seminar under energy agreement. Mimeo, 1979.
Campbell, Robert W. *Trends in the Soviet Oil and Gas Industry*. Baltimore: Johns Hopkins Press, 1976.
Campbell, Robert W., "Soviet Energy Balances." Santa Monica: RAND, R–2257–DOE, Dec. 1978.
Campbell, Robert W., "Basic Data on Soviet Energy Branches." Santa Monica: RAND, N–1332–DOE, Dec. 1979.
Campbell, Robert W., "Soviet Technology Imports: The Gas Pipeline Case." California Seminar on International Security and Foreign Policy, 1981.
CIA (Central Intelligence Agency), "Prospects for Soviet Oil Production: A Supplemental Analysis." ER 77–10425. Washington, DC, July 1977.
CIA, "Simulations of Soviet Growth Options to 1985." ER 79–10131. Washington, DC: March 1979.
CIA, *Handbook of Economic Statistics*. Washington, DC, 1979.
CIA, "The Soviet Economy in 1978–79 and Prospects for 1980." ER 80–10328. Washington, DC: June 1980.
Dienes, Leslie, and Shabad, Theodore *The Soviet Energy System*, New York: Halsted Press, Wiley, 1979.
DOE (Department of Energy). *Energy Data Reports, Natural Gas Production and Consumption*, various years.

ECE (Economic Commission for Europe), *Annual Bulletin of Gas Statistics for Europe*, various years.

Greenslade, Rush V. "The Real Gross National Product of the USSR." In *Soviet Economy in a New Perspective*. Papers, Joint Econ. Comm., US Congress. Washington, DC: Govt Printing Office, 1976.

Iakubovich, I. L., *Praktika primeneniia "Osnovnykh uslovii postavki uglia i slantsa" pri novoi sisteme upravleniia ugol'noi promyshlennosti* (Practical Application of the "Guidelines for Shipping Coal and Shale" under the New Management System in the Coal Industry). Moscow, 1979.

Il'ina, E. N., and Utkina, L. D., *Ekonomicheskaia effektivnost' ispol'zovaniia prirodnogo gaza* (Economic Effectiveness of Utilizing Natural Gas). Moscow, 1978.

Kalinin, I. A., and Karpov, P. N., *Metody razrabotki material'nykh balansov* (Methods of Working Out Material Balances). Moscow, 1977.

Makarov, A. A., and Vigdorchik, A. G., *Toplivno-energeticheskii kompleks* (The Fuel and Energy Complex). Moscow, 1979.

Makarov, A. A., and Melent'ev, L. A., Issledovaniia perspektivnoi struktury toplivno-energeticheskogo balansa SSSR i osnovnykh zon strany" (Research on the Prospective Structure of the Fuel and Energy Balance of the USSR and the Main Zones of the Country). Paper, presented to joint US-Soviet seminar under energy agreement. Mimeo, 1979.

Mytus, M., ed., *Problemy manevrennosti toplivosnabzhenia* (Problems of Flexibility in Fuel Supply). Tallin, 1978.

Nar. khoz. SSSR, see TSU.

Nekrasov, A. S., *et al.*, *Postroenie i analiz energeticheskogo balansa* (Construction and Analysis of the Energy Balance). Moscow, 1974.

Nekrasov, A. M., and Pervukhin, M. G., *Energetika SSSR v 1976–1980 godakh* (Electric Power in the USSR in 1976–1980). Moscow, 1977.

Ryps, G. S., *Ekonomicheskie problemy raspredeleniia gaza* (Economic Problems of Allocating Gas). Leningrad, 1978.

SEV (Sovet Ekonomicheskoi Vzaimopomoshchi or Comecon). *Statisticheskii Ezhegodnik* [Statistical Yearbook], various years.

Shabad, Theodore, "Geographical Distribution of Soviet Energy Production." *Soviet Geography*, April 1980.

Shelest', V. A., *Regional'nye energoekonomicheskie problemy SSSR* (Regional Energy Economics Problems of the USSR) Moscow, 1975.

Stern, J. P., *Soviet Natural Gas Development to 1990*. Lexington, Mass: Lexington Books, 1980.

Styrikovich, M. A., and Cherniavskii, S. Ia., Puti razvitiia i rol' iadernoi energetiki v perspektivnom energobalanse mira i ego osnovnykh regionov (Paths of Development and Role of Nuclear Power in the Prospective Energy Balance of the World and Its Main Regions). Paper presented to joint US–Soviet seminar under energy agreement. Mimeo, 1979.

Sushon, S. P., *et al.* Vtorichnye energeticheskie resursy promyshlennosti SSSR (Secondary Energy Resources in the Industry of the USSR). Moscow, 1978.

TSU SSSR, *Narodnoe Khoziaistvo SSSR* (The National Economy of the USSR). Moscow, various years.

Voprosy tsenoobrazovaniia (Questions of Price Formation), *Referativnyi sbornik*, vypusk II. Moscow, 1976.

Soviet Periodicals Used

Ekonomika gazovoi promyshlennosti [Economics of the Gas Industry].
Ekonomika neftianoi promyshiennosti [Economics of the Oil Industry].
Ekonomicheskaia Gazeta (The Economic Newspaper).
Elektricheskie stantsii (Electric Power Stations).
Khimiia i tekhnologiia topliv i masel (Chemistry and Technology of Fuels and Oils).
Neftianik (The Oil Worker).
Ugol' (Coal).

8

Regional Economic Development

LESLIE DIENES

Introduction

Geographic space is almost everywhere a cardinal factor in economics. The spatial dimension may be brought into economic research implicitly, by disaggregating national income and growth analysis and the models used therein to the regional level. Such subnational macroeconomics concentrates on interregional differences in economic structure, in standards of living, and in population characteristics; it also attempts to assay the efficiency and equity of interspatial movement of goods and production factors. Geographic space may much more explicitly form an integral part of economic analysis. A detailed areal distribution of current and potential resources and markets, and of environmental amenities and barriers form dynamic building blocks in the evolution of the spatial structure itself. And in the longer run, locational change itself becomes a central component of the space economy (Richardson, 1969, pp. 5–7). In addition, ideological and strategic concerns also have a manifest regional aspect.

While attempting to treat almost the entire geographic space of the Soviet economy, this paper is something of a hybrid, picking eclectically from both the regional-disaggregation and the areal-distribution approaches, though with somewhat greater stress on the latter. The paper also emphasizes industrialization, including the exploitation of minerals and their primary processing. The Soviet leadership has always viewed industrialization as the principal vector of economic growth and military strength. Even the modernization of agriculture, much emphasized over the last decade, and the development of some service activities, are thought to be achievable only through massive industrial inputs. In the end, it is the industrial sector (broadly interpreted), with its tangible material inputs and commodity flows, that most readily lends itself to the kind of locational inquiry undertaken in this paper.

8.1 The Regional Framework

The regional framework for this analysis had essentially been set by the close of the 1950s. By then, the impact of the massive Easterly displacement of Soviet industry produced by World War II had run its full course, and the worst dislocations of the Virgin Land Campaign were absorbed, while the prewar economic potential of the ravaged Western areas was fully restored and was even surpassed. At the same time, novel conditioning factors presented Soviet planners with locational choices and opportunities far more complex than those that confronted them in earlier decades. Among these factors were the lifting of wartime restrictions on labor movements, the beginning of a massive shift to more mobile and versatile hydrocarbon fuels and feedstocks, the appearance of new growth industries and the first tentative efforts to turn COMECON into a functioning organization.

At the end of the 1950s, the USSR contained all the regional types, with widely different resource endowments and problems, that regional policy planning has ever addressed in any country. One could readily recognize (1) older economic cores that were in need of modernization and/or diversification; (2) environmentally harsh pioneer regions that possessed vital industrial resources for future growth but were not yet fully integrated into the national economy; and (3) heavily rural, populous areas that were either left behind or never touched by the geographically selective march of industrialization (see Fig. 8.1). These last-mentioned underdeveloped rural regions readily fell into two groups (with some overlapping). This

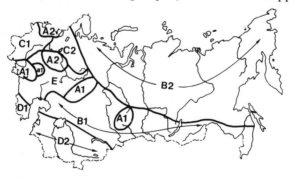

A	Developed industrial regions	C	Western rural periphery
A1	Heavy industrial center	C1	Non-Russian
A2	Diversified manufacturing –	C2	Russian
	high value added	D	Southern non-Slavic periphery
a1	Emerging iron and steel center	D1	Caucasus
B	Resource-rich pioneer regions	D2	Central Asia – Southern
B1	Zone of continuous settlement		Kazakhstan
B2	The North	E	Remaining European core
			(not discussed)

Figure 8.1 *Regions Discussed in the Text*

Table 8.1 Growth and Per Capita Indices of Industrial Output in Soviet Regions and Republics

Regions and Republics	Growth of Industrial Output in Soviet Regions and Republics by Five-Year Plans, 1960–1979					Indices of Per Capita Industrial Output for Economic Regions and Union Republics, 1960–1978			
	1 1960–65 1960=100	2 1965–70 1965=100	3 1970–75 1970=100	4 1975–79 1975=100	5 10th FYP Target for 1979 1975=100	6 1960	7 1970	8 1975	9 1978
USSR	151	150	148	123	125.7	100	100	100	100
RSFSR	145	149	142	122	125.7	116	117	118	118
North-West	137	142	136			146	131	124	
of which Leningrad	132	135	133						
Central	131	143	137			162	144	142	
of which Moscow & Moscow Oblast	125	138	138						
Volgo-Viatka	145	159	146			90	105	113	
Central-Chernozem	163	152	147			68	84	93	
Volga	161	159	152			96	110	118	
North Caucasus	154	148	135			88	85	80	
Urals	148	147	139			135	142	143	
West Siberia	150	151	151			95	104	112	
of which Altai Krai	157	148	142						
Kemerovo Ob.	142	138	132						
East Siberia	161	159	150			90	105	110	
Far East	159	149	140			107	108	99	

Region	1	2	3	4	5	6	7	8	9
Ukraine	153	150	141	121	124	92	97	97	98
Donets-Dnepr	148	142	136			137	132	128	
South-West	160	161	152			53	65	70	
South	160	160	137			85	89	84	
Moldavia	177	157	155	124	132	53	64	67	68
Belorussia	164	179	164	135	130.5	64	86	99	108
Baltic	163	161	142			103	122	120	
Estonia	160	151	141	119	119	124	135	133	130
Latvia	158	157	136	116	119.4	125	141	134	131
Lithuania	174	136	149	121	123	79	107	111	113
Transcaucasia	145	146	145						
Georgia	141	153	139	131.5	131.6[b]	67	65	64	67
Armenia	157	172	145	136.5	133	76	78	74	78
Azerbaidzhan	141	137	150	138.5	130[b]	76	56	57	60
Kazakhstan	164	156	142	119	127	66	65	62	60
Northern Kazakhstan[a]	190	160	157						
Rest of Kazakhstan	158	155	122						
Central Asia	151	146	150			58	46	43	
Uzbekistan	150	136	150	125	128	61	45	43	41
Kirghizia	167	184	152	122	127	44	50	50	49
Tadzhikistan	154	150	133	123	125	50	41	36	34
Turkmenistan	134	150	154	110	117.5	65	49	47	42

[a] Kokchetav, Kustanai, Pavlodar, Severo-Kazakhstanskaia, Turgai and Tselinograd Oblasts. Growth rates for the two Kazakh subregions computed from data in AN Kazakhskoi SSSR, 1976, p. 15.

[b] Estimated as proportionate 4th year expectation from Five-Year Plan target. Abramov, 1977, p. 222.

Sources: Columns 1–3: Standard statistical yearbooks of the USSR, RSFSR and the Ukraine. To compute growth rates for the respective regions, the Baltic, Transcaucasian and Central Asian republics are combined according to 1960 and 1970 weights. The 1960 industrial-output figures can be computed from regional labor-productivity ratios applied to the Soviet average. Data from AN SSSR, 1967, p. 226; *Nar. khoz. SSSR v 1960 g.*, pp. 164–5. The 1970 output is given in Divilov, 1976, p. 77. For 1972 output see Table 8.2, Columns 3–5; *Ekonomicheskaia gazeta* No. 5, Jan. 1980, p. 8; *Radio Liberty Research*, Jan. 26, 1979. Columns 6–8: Gillula, 1979, p. 658.

has proved crucial to the timing and course of their development and will continue to do so into the 1990s: on the one hand, there were those areas with a European population and rapidly declining birth rates; on the other those inhabited by peoples of non-European traditions experiencing a demographic explosion.

An examination of industrial and urban growth rates since the late 1950s confirms the well-documented deceleration of industrial expansion in the USSR. Within this general slowdown, however, significant regional variations appear (Table 8.1). An outstanding feature of this development has been the decreasing *relative* importance of the historic hearths of Soviet manufacturing: the Central (Moscow) and Leningrad regions, the Donets-Dnepr (all major centers even before the Bolshevik era), the central Urals and the Kuzbas. In the reannexed Baltic Republics, two of which were quite developed already as parts of Imperial Russia, growth remained above the average until the seventies, but has declined sharply since. Labor shortages, the increasing claim of service activities on the constricted labor pool, resource exhaustion, obsolescence and social-environmental costs in different combinations have taken their toll.[1]

In contrast with the industrial slowdown in these old established centers, one finds a continuation of above-average growth in resource-rich Siberia (outside the Kuzbas–Altai complex) and the adjoining parts of northern Kazakhstan. The relative decline of the Far East during the first half of the seventies most likely has been reversed because of the huge construction projects underway in the region. The novel feature of the past 20–25 years, however, has been the surge of industrialization in the formerly backward rural periphery of the European USSR occupied by non-Russian republics, a surge that recently has begun to spill over into Transcaucasia as well. By contrast, the Great Russian parts of the periphery, with minor exceptions, have continued to stagnate. Very adverse demographic developments combined with an unfavorable settlement structure most likely will prevent any turning of the tide there in this century.

The growth and economic fortunes of regions depend, to a large extent, on the mix of activities within their borders. In the USSR the impact of the "industry mix" is likely to be even more important than in market economies. The Soviet leadership, in Koropeckyj's words, attempts to maximize not total GNP, but GNP of a predetermined structure (Koropeckyj, 1970, p. 258). Profitability does not serve as an instrument of resource allocation among sectors. Indeed, products of high-priority branches, by receiving preferential allocation of capital and labor, have been historically underpriced and often subsidized. Regions dominated by such industries, consequently, tend to show low productivity of investment and generally also of labor. Yet, they may be growing at rates above the national average, especially if their natural resources are not yet fully tapped. The tangible and intangible advantages of location, accessibility, levels of infrastructure and labor skills, of course, should not be overlooked; these factors operate in the

USSR as strongly as elsewhere. But given the Soviet price structure and the dominance of material balances in an economy managed along branch lines, these factors are very difficult to assess for Soviet decision makers and still more for Western researchers.

An analysis of the performance and prospects of the regions, therefore, must place great stress on their place in the centrally planned economic structure. For each region, productivity indices ideally should be assessed and aggregated from branch data, but these are very scanty for republics and wholly unavailable for the diverse areal units of the vast RSFSR. Nor can production functions be derived on a regional basis even for total output. The average and incremental ratios of output to fixed capital (see Tables 8.2–8.3) are greatly influenced not only by the "industry mix" but, via that mix, also by the differential availability and quality of manpower and natural resources and their very uneven rates of change among Soviet regions. One would expect that lack of manpower or resource supplies and/or insufficient improvements or deterioration in their quality would affect the output-capital ratios adversely.

8.2 Developed Industrial Regions: Declining Productivity

Developed, traditional centers of industry have early Soviet, indeed, pre-Revolutionary foundations. They fall into two distinct groups: (1) citadels of heavy industry with a substantial, though diminishing resource base for such an economic profile; they are the Donets–Dnepr, Kuznets–Altai and Ural areas; and (2) diversified manufacturing regions with much more skill-demanding, higher-value-added specialization: the Central Region with part of the Volgo–Viatka, Leningrad, and the two Northern Baltic republics.

The three heavily industrial citadels of group 1 noted above still contained a quarter of all fixed assets of Soviet industry in 1972 but accounted for only 21% of its output, suggesting low returns to capital (see Table 8.2; Belorusov *et al.*, 1976, pp. 191–2). The stress on bulky goods with high resource but low skill content is shown by the high volume-to-value ratio of their metal-fabricating, engineering and chemical branches (Dienes, 1977 pp. 6–7; Belorusov *et al.*, 1976, pp. 191–2). In these regions, such volume-to-value ratios for engineering products ranged from 22% to more than 50% above the Soviet average during the 1960s (Evstigneev, 1972, pp. 93–4); I find no evidence of improvement since. As a consequence of such specialization, the Ural and Donets–Dnepr regions and the Southern zone of West Siberia handled almost half of all railway loading for the USSR in 1970, with the last two showing a huge and swiftly growing dominance of outgoing over incoming freight (*Transport i sviaz' SSSR*, 1972, pp. 68–9).

Exactly the opposite applies to the main historic centers of diversified manufacturing: much higher shares in output than fixed capital, a discrepancy especially pronounced in the Center and Latvia

Table 8.2 Selected Economic Data on Soviet Regions and Republics (Industry, Transport Access and Export)

Regions and Republics	Industrial Fixed Capital 1972 (billion rubles 1955 prices)	Industrial Fixed Capital 1972 (% of total)	Gross Output by Industry 1972 (billion rubles 1967 prices)	Average Output-Capital Ratios (column 3 ÷ by column 1)	Gross Output by Industry 1972 (% of total)	Estimated Net Output by Industry 100=126.3 billion 1968 rubles (% of total)	Least Transport Efforts to Reach All Regions ca. 1970 (1000 km.)	ca. 1970 (% of lowest-cost region)	Relative Importance of Export to National/Regional Income, 1972–1976 Average (Soviet mean=1.00)
	1	2	3	4	5	6	7	8	9
USSR	250.35	100.0	407.7	1.63	100.0	100.0	—	—	1.00
RSFSR	156.11	62.4	255.2	1.63	62.6	66.8	—	—	n.d.
Northwest	17.3	6.9	26.2	1.51	6.4	8.2	44.8	120.4	1.80
Central	26.5	10.6	66.3	2.50	16.3	19.5	37.2	100.0	0.99
Volgo–Viatka	6.96	2.8	14.8	2.13	3.6	5.0	39.3	105.7	0.75
Central–Chernozem	6.39	2.55	11.2	1.75	2.7	2.3	37.7	101.4	0.55
Volga	26.0	10.4	35.2	1.35	8.6	6.7	39.4	105.8	1.53
North Caucasus	11.1	4.4	19.8	1.78	4.9	4.3	42.1	113.2	1.10
Urals	24.5	9.8	36.0	1.47	8.8	8.9	46.1	123.9	1.10
West Siberia	15.2	6.1	21.5	1.41	5.3	5.8	61.3	164.7	0.59
East Siberia	12.6	5.0	13.7	1.09	3.4	3.1	72.7	195.5	1.19
Far East	9.56	3.8	10.5	1.10	2.6	3.1	148.0	397.8	0.81
Ukraine	47.55	19.0	76.0	1.41	18.6	18.6	n.d.	n.d.	1.15
Donets–Dnepr	30.8	12.3	43.5	1.41	10.7	10.2	38.3	102.9	n.d.
Southwest	11.4	4.55	23.2	2.04	5.7	6.25	44.8	120.4	n.d.
South	4.35	1.7	9.3	2.14	2.3	2.15	47.4	127.3	n.d.

	1	2	3	4	5	6	7	8	9
Moldavia	1.61	0.6	4.0	2.48	1.0	n.d.	49.8	134.0	0.08
Belorussia	6.63	2.6	13.9	2.10	3.4	3.3	42.5	114.1	1.03
Baltic	7.95	3.2	15.8	1.99	3.9	3.8	47.4	127.3	0.94
Estonia	2.21	0.9	3.1	1.40	0.8	0.9	n.d.	n.d.	n.d.
Latvia	2.64	1.05	6.9	2.61	1.7	1.4	n.d.	n.d.	n.d.
Lithuania	3.10	1.2	5.8	1.87	1.4	1.5	n.d.	n.d.	n.d.
Transcaucasia	9.77	3.9	12.7	1.30	3.1	2.5	61.0	163.9	0.42
Georgia	3.19	1.3	5.0	1.57	1.2	0.9	n.d.	n.d.	n.d.
Armenia	2.68	1.1	2.7	1.01	0.7	0.65	n.d.	n.d.	n.d.
Azerbaidzhan	4.51	1.8	5.0	1.11	1.2	0.9	n.d.	n.d.	n.d.
Kazakhstan	12.40	4.95	14.4	1.16	3.5	2.7	71.0	190.9	0.61
Central Asia	9.33	3.7	15.7	1.68	3.85	2.7	70.7	190.1	0.89
Uzbekistan	5.37	2.14	9.3	1.73	2.3	1.65	n.d.	n.d.	n.d.
Kirghizia	1.45	0.6	2.57	1.77	0.6	0.5	n.d.	n.d.	n.d.
Tadzhikistan	1.21	0.5	1.95	1.61	0.5	0.3	n.d.	n.d.	n.d.
Turkmenistan	1.30	0.5	1.85	1.42	0.45	0.25	n.d.	n.d.	n.d.

Sources to Table 8.2

Columns 1–5: Gillula, 1981, p. 18. Data apparently refer to mid-year estimates of capital stock. The aggregate figures for the Baltic, Transcaucasian and Central Asian regions are distributed among the respective republics according to end-year proportions, also referring perhaps to a slightly larger universe. Gillula, Table A.6–A.8.

Column 6: Telepko, 1971, p. 82. The aggregate figures for the Baltic, Transcaucasian and Central Asian regions distributed among the respective republics according to 1970 proportions are given in Zakumbaev, 1975, p. 65.

Columns 7–8: Evstigneev, 1972, pp. 84–5. Transport effort computed for machinery and fabricated metal products.

Column 9: Zaitsev, 1979, p. 200. A definition and independent check for export coefficients in 1970 provided in AN SSSR and Gosplan SSSR, SOPS, 1975, pp. 195–6. Except for Transcaucasia, the data seem fairly consistent with the earlier source.

Table 8.3   *Industrial Fixed Capital per Employee and Output–Capital Ratios*

Regions and Republics	Industrial Fixed Capital per Industrial Employee (1955 constant prices)			Growth of Output ÷ by Growth of Fixed Capital		
	1960	1968	1975	1960– 1968	1968– 75	1960– 75
USSR	3984	6280	10,084	1.24	1.03	1.28
RSFSR	3815	6116	10,129	1.16	0.99	1.15
Northwest	3870[a]	5800[a]		1.13		
Central	2560[a]	3890[a]		1.08		
Volgo–Viatka	2700[a]	3910[a]		1.35		
Central–Chernozem	3460[a]	5370[a]		1.37		
Volga	4550[a]	7220[a]		1.36		
North Caucasus	4710[a]	5750[a]		1.64		
Urals	4830[a]	6520[a]		1.41		
West Siberia	4110[a]	6140[a]		1.31		
East Siberia	4540[a]	9180[a]		1.06		
Far East	6260[a]	8670[a]		1.47		
Ukraine	4202	5860	9,122	1.41	1.06	1.48
Donets–Dnepr	5150[a]	7180[a]		1.32		
Southwest	2930[a]	4070[a]		1.55		
South	3910[a]	5000[a]		1.65		
Moldavia	3139	4614	7,368	1.63	1.13	1.84
Belorussia	2567	4223	7,743	1.61	1.11	1.60
Estonia	3652	6089	10,616	1.24	0.95	1.17
Latvia	2871	4562	7,553	1.33	0.96	1.28
Lithuania	3242	4632	8,209	1.71	1.05	1.78
Georgia	5159	6798	10,000	1.38	1.12	1.55
Armenia	4141	5477	8,550	1.62	1.17	1.90
Azerbaidzhan	11662	12742	16,137	1.55	1.35	2.10
Kazakhstan	5479	10704[b]	14,944	1.12[b]	1.02[c]	0.99
Uzbekistan	4010	6822	11,045	1.09	1.02	1.11
Kirghizia	3607	5482	9,816	1.64	1.05	1.72
Tadzhikistan	4161	6102	11,921	1.38	0.78	1.07
Turkmenistan	7230	13318[b]	20,235	0.94	1.01[c]	1.11

[a]These figures apparently are in current prices and not comparable to those in the rest of the table which are in 1955 constant prices. However, this discrepancy should not affect the comparability of the marginal-productivity ratios very significantly. Data for 1960 are given in AN SSSR, Inst. ekon., 1964, p. 8; for 1968 in Telepko, 1971, p. 81.
[b]Fixed capital for 1970. Marginal capital productivity for the 1960–1970 period.
[c]Marginal capital productivity for the 1970–75 period.
Sources: Except for those with [a], industrial fixed capital in 1955 prices taken from Gillula, 1981, pp. 22–30, Tables A.1–A.18. Industrial growth rates from *Nar. khoz. SSSR v 1968 g.*, p. 189, v 1970 g., p. 141 and v 1975 g., p. 203.

(see Table 8.2), low volume-to-value ratios, lower freight tonnage and dominance of incoming over outgoing freight. Nevertheless, these centers share with the first group a problem of increasing obsolescence in their industrial base, a sharply constrained labor supply, resulting in much commuting and heavy pressure on transport infrastructure, as well as growing environmental woes. To compound the manpower shortage, labor productivity has grown little faster than the Soviet average (*Nar. khoz. SSSR v 1975g., Nar. Khoz. RSFSR, v 1975*); data available for the sixties, though unfortunately not for later years, show surprisingly low ratios of the growth of output to that of fixed capital (see Table 8.3). Clearly, even though they have developed in a very different institutional milieu, these regions in the Soviet Union suffer from some of the structural ills that beset the manufacturing belt in the United States. The very large shares that these two groups of regions represent of the country's infrastructure, industrial capital and, especially in the second group, of the research and scientific base,[2] all require that solutions to their problems ultimately be found. Yet, given past investment and accumulated skills, the momentum built into their industries should be sufficient to carry these regions forward through the next decade without special attention. Their structural ills, in my judgment, do not rate the same priority as the securing of energy and raw materials from the resource-rich hinterland and the resolution of the geographic and ethnic maldistribution of the labor supply. These latter problems have already had an impact on the performance of the Soviet economy and will increasingly have that during the 1980s. Therefore, it is these two issues that, in their spatial dynamics, constitute *the core of* regional problem for the Soviet leadership in the forthcoming years. Soviet regional policy in the eighties must focus on these two sets of key issues: (1) the strategy, speed and cost of developing resource-rich Siberia–North-Kazakhstan and (2) the further industrialization of the rural periphery, which enjoys manpower reserves ranging from adequate to ample, but which differs greatly in demographic and cultural characteristics and geographic linkages. The rest of this paper focuses on these regions and issues.

8.3 Resource-Rich Pioneer Regions: Problems of Accessibility

These regions comprise the vast stretch of land between the Urals and the Pacific, North of the Aral Sea, Lake Balkhash and the Chinese-Mongolian border. (The Kuzbas-Altai area, which had been agriculturally settled since Imperial times and developed into one of the bastions of heavy industry of the Soviet state before World War II, is more akin to the Urals or even the Donets-Dnepr, although it shares many common problems with the rest of Siberia.) About three-fourths of this land is north of the zone of agriculture and its associated continuous permanent settlement. Together with the rather more developed European North, this raw pioneer zone comprises over two-thirds of the Soviet landmass but is the home of only 40 million people. Of these a mere 7 million live in the Northland and only half of them East of the Urals (*Nar. khoz. RSFSR v 1975 g.*, p. 28; Aparin and Krinitskaia, 1979, pp. 3 and 11).

Although Soviet economic performance in the eighties will be decisively linked with the fate of this resource-rich hinterland, the latter's critical role in the country's history is nothing new. Through Imperial and early Soviet times, "waves of resource exploitation have spread out from the European core area, channeled by transport routes" (North, 1977, p. 126). The sequence of resource development has been greatly influenced by the transportability and per-ton value of commodities needed. Thus, precious metals and tin have long been mined in Northeast Siberia for the European market, while rich coal reserves remained untouched and hydrocarbon potentials were barely scratched; but in the much better located European North and the less forbidding Southern belt of Siberia-North Kazakhstan coal is now extensively produced. By contrast, the feverish development of oil and gas in the uninhabited wilderness of Tiumen 'Oblast' (Northwest Siberia) proceeds overwhelmingly for the markets of the European regions and for exports beyond the Western frontiers. National needs, the relative transportability of hydrocarbons and distances manageable with current technology have all combined to accord this province the highest priority in Soviet resource exploitation today.

Spatial orientation and accessibility clearly mark off the eastern half of the Trans-Ural territories from their western half. The location of the Pacific and Trans-Baikal provinces prevents domestic and European demand from serving as the major stimulus for resource exploitation, except in the case of rare and precious metals. Strategic factors, especially along the Chinese border, and export opportunities to the Pacific Basin must provide the main incentives for development east of Lake Baikal. The peripheral position of the Far East is well illustrated by comparing the transport effort, i.e. the total length of railway hauls, required to reach *all* geographic markets (the metropolitan centers of every region) from each of the 18 economic planning areas. The 148,000 km of transport effort to do so from the geographic center of population of the Far East is double what would be needed to reach all major geographic markets by rail from East Siberia, Kazakhstan and Central Asia (Columns 7–8, Table 8.2). And it is 2.4 times greater from the Far East than from West Siberia or Transcaucasia.

The relatively high export (foreign-trade) index for East Siberia (Table 8.2) and much lower ones for West Siberia are at first surprising. However, they are explainable by the commodity structure of these regions' exports plus the time period they refer to. The high export index of East Siberia is due mostly to aluminum, a high value, relatively transportable metal serving as the vehicle of indirect resource export, in this case cheap hydroelectricity.[3] The hydrocarbon fuels of West Siberia barely began to enter international trade during the 1972–6 period, since depletion of the better located European deposits was not yet very severe. As for the Far East, potential export stimuli clearly had no time yet to be turned into reality. While the growth of export from the Trans-Baikal regions clearly will be tied to resource development, the creation of the Trans-Siberian Land Bridge may provide some additional stimulus to foreign trade. By the late 1970s, the Siberian overland route had captured a quarter of the Japan to Europe containerized trade and 15% of such trade between the entire Pacific basin and Europe. In 1975, the Land Bridge earned $140 million for the Soviet treasury (Miller, 1978, p. 224, and Mote, No. 6, 1978, pp. 13–14).

Even more than the heavy metallurgical, metal and machinery centers of the country (see above), the pioneer hinterland accounts for a share of the nation's industrial fixed assets that is disproportionally large relative to its industrial output on a value basis (Table 8.2). Of all major economic regions, Siberia, the Far East and Kazakhstan showed the highest ratios of fixed capital to output, though reference here to gross output and the relative undervaluation of resources in the Soviet price system bias their performance downward. If the Leningrad area could be separated from the Northwest, the latter would also show a high capital-output ratio.

Yet, because of mounting resource dependence on this hinterland, reinforced by perceptions of national security and Great Russian nationalism, the efforts to develop these provinces have not slackened. While Table 8.4 shows virtually constant shares of investment from 1965 to 1975 in Siberia and the Far East as a whole (as well as in Kazakhstan and the Northwest), the picture changes when the Northlands, which comprise some 86% of the Trans-Ural parts of the Russian Republic, are separated out. The quantity of investment in the Asiatic North quadrupled between 1965 and 1975 and its share in Soviet total investment grew from less than 2.6% to almost 4% (Table 8.5), with strong indications of a further relative increase since. Similarly, the aggregate for Kazakhstan conceals mounting investment in North Kazakhstan, which today is part of both the Russian economic and demographic realm and of the pioneer resource hinterland (AN Kazakhskoi SSR, 1976, pp. 15–17).

8.4 Development of the Rural Periphery

As the depletion of accessible natural resources, particularly of energy, has magnified the importance of Siberia for the Soviet economy, the exhaustion of manpower reserves and/or their insufficient mobility has enhanced the economic significance of the rural periphery. Already in the past two decades, a novel feature of development has been a surge of industrialization in a widening circle of these rural backwaters. All signs indicate that regional differ-

Table 8.4 Regional Distribution and Per Capita Levels of Investment 1959–78

Republics	In Percent of USSR[a]				Per Capita Level Relative to USSR			
	1959–1965	1966–1970	1971–1975	1976–1978	1960–1965	1966–1970	1971–1975	1976–1978
USSR	100.0	100.0	100.0	100.0	100	100	100	100
RSFSR	60.6 (60.3)[b]	59.0	60.4	61.7	109(114)[b]	109	113	117
North west	6.7[b]	6.1	6.2		114[b]	128	128	
Central	13.0[b]	11.1	11.2		111[b]	99	100	
Volgo–Viatka	2.5[b]	2.6	2.8		68[b]	74	84	
Central–Chernozem	2.3[b]	2.8	3.0		65[b]	83	95	
Volga	8.6[b]	9.0	9.1		112[b]	118	120	
North Caucasus	5.0[b]	5.5	5.4		87[b]	93	90	
Urals	7.7[b]	6.5	6.5		116[b]	102	106	
West Siberia	6.5[b]	6.2	7.1		122[b]	121	145	
East Siberia	5.5[b]	4.7	4.1		126[b]	152	147	
Far East	4.4[b]	4.3	4.1	15.1	187[b]	178	179	79
Ukraine	17.2	16.25	15.7	7.2	87	85	82	88
Donets–Dnepr	9.05	8.5	7.6	5.4	101	99	94	66
Southwest	5.35	5.4	5.5	2.5	57	64	66	91
South	2.8	2.8	2.5	1.2	106	110	96	80
Moldavia	1.0	1.05	1.2	3.3	69	76	81	92
Belorussia	2.5	2.9	3.3	2.95	59	83	90	102
Baltic	2.7	2.9	3.1	0.6	96	110	108	106
Estonia	0.7	0.65	0.65	1.0	123	128	115	103
Latvia	1.0	1.0	1.1	1.35	105	109	111	100
Lithuania	1.0	1.25	1.35		85	103	104	

Transcaucasia	3.6	3.55	3.45	3.45	79	76	66	65
Georgia	1.3	1.3	1.2	1.25	86	71	63	65
Armenia	0.8	0.9	0.9	0.8	94	101	82	71
Azerbaidzhan	1.5	1.35	1.35	1.4	78	69	60	61
Kazakhstan	6.95	6.2	6.2	6.2	140	124	113	106
Central Asia	5.4	5.95	6.4	6.2	81	82	74	46
Uzbekistan	3.05	3.6	3.75	3.8	74	82	71	67
Kirghizia	0.8	0.8	0.8	0.75	73	72	65	56
Tadzhikistan	0.8	0.75	0.8	0.75	77	69	60	53
Turkmenistan	0.8	0.8	1.05	0.9	107	112	108	89

[a]Because of rounding and small amounts of geographically undistributed funds, percentages may not add up.

[b]For these periods, the shares and per capita levels of investment in regions of the RSFSR could be computed only without outlays made by collective farms. Relative to corresponding figures to the right showing all investment, they are thus slightly underestimated for regions where agriculture is important (e.g. North Caucasus, Central-Chernozem) and overestimated for those where agriculture is much less significant (e.g. Center, Urals, East and West Siberia and the Far East).

Sources: Standard statistical yearbooks of the USSR, RSFSR and the Ukraine. Relative levels taken from Schroeder, 1978, p. 128. Levels computed according to mid year population data.

ences in the quantity and quality of labor will have an increasing influence on economic growth and industrial location in the labor-short eighties.

A. *The Western Periphery: Past Neglect and Recent Growth in Non-Russian Parts.*

This vast tract of land may be delimited as the arc around the western and northern flank of the developed industrial Moscow and Donets–Dnepr regions, *exclusive* of Leningrad, Estonia and Latvia (Fig. 8.1). This large territory was the cradle of the Eastern Slavs and is steeped in a memorable historic past. In the Soviet era, however, it has badly fallen behind economically. Poverty of resources for heavy industry and, for a long period after the Revolution, economic isolation from world trade, discouraged investment by the government, and that greatly contributed to its depressed condition. A large section of the region was lost to the USSR during the interwar years, while the Southwestern Ukraine (Galicia) had never been part of the Russian political realm before World War II. Thus, under other governments and regimes, the region was often neglected; moreover, it was also much affected by wartime devastation.

The area of the western periphery (the west and north of the European USSR within the continuous belt of agricultural settlement) is almost as large as that of the nine-member European Community. It had a population of 47–48 million in 1960, or 23% of the country's total population in 1960. Yet it could muster a mere 13–14% of the country's industry in terms of employment and output[4] and less by way of industrial fixed assets. Moreover, about a quarter of this employment and a third of output was concentrated in 6–8 large cities that almost completely monopolized the technologically more advanced growth industries, such as engineering.[5] The abysmally low per capita consumption of electricity was yet another indication of economic underdevelopment. Primarily, it reflected the low level of indus-

Table 8.5 *Distribution of Capital Investment in Regions of the Soviet North (in billion rubles)*

Regions	1960	1965	1970	1975 esti- mates
Whole North of which	1.5	2.6	4.6	7.3
European North	0.9	1.5	2.2	2.9
West Siberian North	0.1	0.2	0.9	2.2
East Siberian North	0.1	0.2	0.3	0.6
Far Eastern North	0.4	0.7	1.2	1.6

Source: Dogaev, 1975, p. 52.

trialization of these Western peripheries, but also, to a degree, the neglect of personal and farm demand as well.[6]

The rapid industrialization of the non-Russian parts of this European periphery since the late 1950s is certainly among the notable features of the recent spatial development of Soviet manufacturing. Between 1960 and the end of 1979, the combined industrial output of Belorussia, Lithuania, Moldavia, and the Southwest Economic Region of the Ukraine grew by 4.9 times, compared to much less than 4 times for Soviet industry as a whole (Table 8.1). The lag in per capita output has been either overcome or greatly reduced. This growth was accompanied by significant diversification and a move towards a more balanced and somewhat more modern industrial structure.[7] Parts of these regions also experienced noticeable improvement in their energy and power supply (Dienes, 1979, pp. 14–31; Dienes and Shabad, 1979, pp. 24 and 210).

Not surprisingly, the emphasis through most of this developing periphery is on labor-intensive light-engineering goods and consumer durables, demanding only moderate skills. While primary and semi-finished metals have to be brought in, the accessibility of this region to both historic and newly emerging steel centers of the European USSR, which are responsible for most of the growth in Soviet steel capacity, is excellent (Fig. 8.1). So is accessibility to the great bulk of the national and entire COMECON market (Columns 7–8 of Table 8.2; Harris, 1970, pp. 220–5). This allows even such a steel-short province as Belorussia, with heavy metal-consuming, though still labor-intensive, machinery industries, to enjoy a highly "competitive" location for a wide range of engineering branches (Evstigneev, 1976, passim).

(a) *The Impact of Foreign Trade.* The strengthening of economic ties with the rest of COMECON and the increasing participation in world trade have clearly provided added stimuli for the growth of this western zone. They should continue to do so in the future. They prompted the creation or expansion of production facilities at least partly for export and the strengthening of the transport infrastructure from and through these regions. Even though these western provinces are poor in minerals, resources and resource-processing industries are playing a major role in this export orientation. Proximity to Eastern Europe has proved enough of an advantage to counteract the disincentive of low quality and to entice COMECON credits and participation in the Soligorsk potassium and Kingisepp phosphate mining and enrichment projects.[8] Similarly, the construction of Western oil refineries, such as Mozyr, Novopolotsk and Mazeikiai, including some petrochemical units associated with them, were initiated both with the local and the East European markets in mind.[9] Despite the scarcity of local-fuel energy resources, the L'vov area and Moldavia are also heavily involved in electricity export, both transmitting some 30% of their mid-1970 output to Eastern Europe (Shabad, 1979b, p. 240 and North, 1980, p. 20). With more large projects com-

Table 8.6 Industrial Structure of Soviet Regions in 1972 (% of gross output; row totals=100)

Economic Regions	Fuel and Mineral Extraction	Fuel Processing (Refining) Metallurgy[a]	Metal Fabricating Electric Power, Chemicals	Machine Building	Forest Products Pulp and Paper	Building Materials Industry	Light and Food Industries[b]
Northwest	11.4	3.7	10.8	24.4	13.5	4.1	32.1
Central	2.1	7.4	12.5	25.9	3.3	3.3	45.5
Volgo–Viatka	3.9	4.8	16.0	34.9	8.7	2.6	29.1
Central–Chernozem	2.3	8.2	18.5	23.6	1.5	4.0	41.9
Baltic	5.6	1.1	11.9	16.2	6.7	4.1	54.4
Belorussia	2.8	4.1	12.8	24.1	4.6	3.9	47.7
Volga	9.3	11.2	18.7	27.0	2.7	3.8	27.3
North Caucasus	8.8	9.0	12.4	16.0	3.6	4.2	46.0
Donets–Dneper	13.1	25.5	12.7	21.2	1.0	3.4	23.1
Southwest	4.3	1.7	12.5	18.9	5.7	4.4	52.5
South	3.6	3.2	8.9	21.8	1.9	4.5	56.1
Transcaucasia	5.1	11.3	14.4	13.1	2.5	4.6	49.0
Urals	7.4	29.2	12.4	25.3	5.3	3.4	17.0
West Siberia	16.0	10.1	16.2	23.0	5.0	3.6	26.1
East Siberia	22.1	5.5	16.9	10.9	14.4	5.2	25.0
Far East	25.2	4.2	14.2	12.7	12.3	7.2	38.4
Kazakhstan	16.3	12.7	20.7	7.1	2.5	7.0	40.2
Central Asia	8.6	neglig.	13.5	1.3	1.7	6.0	58.3
USSR	8.5	10.2	13.5	21.4	4.9	4.1	37.4

[a]Calculated as a residue.   [b]Apparently includes fishing.

Source: Zakumbaev, 1977, p. 182.

pleted and agreed upon since then, such exports should continue to expand very significantly.[10] Without foreign trade and participation some of these projects would have been constructed on an appreciably smaller scale. And one big chemical work at least (Kalush in the Western Ukraine) would not have been built at all.[11]

The impact of foreign trade on the expansion of engineering and consumer industries across this Western periphery is much more difficult to separate from other, frequently more important, factors. Exports constitute only a few percent of the output of most factories that produce for trade; such sales bring no extra income to the plant above that from domestic sales. On the factory and local level, therefore, the incentive to trade is non-existent or slight, while on the national level the locational advantage of the western provinces may be entirely submerged by a host of other considerations. Be that as it may, export activities and COMECON ties can be identified as important factors in the rapid growth of manufacturing activities in a number of western cities, such as Minsk, L'vov and Novovolynsk (Borodinoi, 1978, p. 34; North, 1980, p. 40).

Finally, increased foreign trade, the bulk of which is through western border cities and ports, has generated a great deal of new construction (pipelines and port facilities) as well as improvements of the existing network and transshipment points. Between 1955 and 1976, the tonnage of foreign shipment by sea grew more than 11 times, by pipelines (oil and gas) over 10-fold and by rail 3.2 times. More than 90% of the rail movement and nearly 80% of the pipeline traffic is with Eastern Europe, all of it moving through this western periphery, which also forms much of the hinterland for several ports. In 1976, about 90 million tons of railway freight moved across the western frontier (Shabad, "News ... ", Jan. 1980, pp. 48–9), roughly 60% of that through the Polish and Hungarian borders (Ptashek, 1974, p. 134; Shanina, 1978, p. 62). Despite the extension of three broad-gauge lines beyond the frontiers into Eastern Europe, "much transshipment and gauge changing is still necessary—a boost to the economies of these border regions. . . . The heavy westward traffic has also forced the upgrading of Soviet railways and the construction of new lines" (North, 1980, p. 46).

Investment in these western border regions in the broad sense (*pogranichnye raiony* as opposed to the immediate border oblasts or *prigranichye raiony* where rapid development may not be the rule[12]) in the main shows a high return, though the relatively large share of food processing and consumer products in their industrial structure may be the principal cause. Yet, these areas evidence not only high output per unit of fixed capital but also very high ratios of growth of output to that of fixed capital. The latter are much more favorable than those found not only in most Trans-Ural provinces but also in Latvia, Estonia, the Central and Northwest regions, where the industry mix should similarly favor above average capital productivity. The tangible and intangible advantages of accessibility and of, by

Soviet standards, well-developed infrastructure, combined with reasonably skilled manpower reserves have also contributed to the development of this region.

The gradual weakening of the early dependence on the external economies of initial concentration and the accelerating centrifugal movement of industry from the US Manufacturing Belt have been well documented (in the last decade, even California experienced a negative *relative* shift in earnings and a negative industry-mix effect on manufacturing growth (Beyers, 1979, pp. 38–40; Rees, 1979, pp. 48–51. See also, among others, Sternlieb and Hughes, 1978; Weinstein and Firestine, 1978). This process appears to operate in the USSR as well.

(b) *Stagnation in Russian Parts.* The diffusion of economic growth, however, appears to miss most parts of the RSFSR belonging to the western-northwestern periphery. Here stagnation is the rule, with most oblasts experiencing below-average industrial expansion. Even those few cities (Novgorod, Pskov, Kaluga, Smolensk) that had seen an upsurge during the 1960s lost that new-found vitality in the following decade (*Nar. khoz. RSFSR v 1969g.*, pp. 39–41; . . . *v 1975 g.* p. 49). Since the agricultural resource base here is worse than in the non-Russian parts of the Western USSR and ethnic barriers to outmigration are absent, this non-black-earth belt of European Russia has been a classic zone of *Flucht* throughout the postwar years. Most provinces in that zone have been losing population or experiencing virtually no growth for two decades. The age and sex distributions have become so distorted that by the early seventies two oblasts and several raions were experiencing a *natural* decrease of population, with the number of deaths exceeding births (Rybakovskii, ed., 1976, pp. 132–3).

The unfavorable settlement structure impedes the modernization of this zone and limits amenities and their accessibility, especially to the rural population. Only 1.5% of rural settlements here contained more than 1000 persons (accounting for a mere 20% of the rural population) and 95% of them have less than 500 inhabitants. Average distance between villages of over 1000 persons and even between those of over 500 are much greater than elsewhere in the European USSR (Table 8.7).[13] If one considers only the provinces South of the 61° parallel and therefore within the agricultural belt, the mean distance between villages of 1000 population and over in this non-chernozem (non-black-earth) periphery of the RSFSR is almost 14 km. Even between villages of over 500 the mean distance reaches almost 8 km (calculated from *Vestnik statistiki*, No. 5, 1971, pp. 80–81).

There are no clear signs so far that a resurgent Great Russian nationalism or the specific Non-Black-Earth Program, which at least in part was a response to the former, have turned around the fortunes of this historic land, dear to Russian hearts but increasingly marginal to the economy. With the exception of Novgorod and Pskov oblasts, the

Table 8.7 Dispersion of Settlements and Density of Transport Infrastructure by Regions, 1970

	Average Distance between Cities[a] (km)	Average Distance between Rural Settlements (km)[a]			Length of Transport Routes per 1000 sq. km (in km). Early 1970s		
		under 500 Souls	over 500 Souls	over 1000 Souls	Rail-roads	Hard Surface Roads	Internal Waterways
	1	2	3	4	5	6	7
USSR	63	2.3	6.3	9.8	6.0	25.3	6.5
Northwest	70	2.1	12.1	21.3	7.3	17.9	12.1
Central	29	0.9	4.3	7.8	26.6	87.1	13.2
Volgo–Viatka	36	1.1	3.8	6.4	13.7	61.9	14.1
Central–Chernozem	39	1.3	2.5	4.0	27.4	49.7	6.6
Volga	48	2.0	3.8	6.4	13.5	45.6	10.9
North Caucasus	43	2.4	3.4	4.6	16.6	100.0	4.5
Urals	45	0.4	5.2	9.1	15.2	35.4	8.0
West Siberia	110	4.9	9.8	15.7	2.7	6.3	12.6
East Siberia	135	7.3	16.1	24.9	1.7	5.9	5.8
Far East	138	13.9	25.1	42.1	0.9	2.4	4.2
Donets–Dnepr	19	1.6	2.5	3.8	41.1	142.5	6.3
Southwest	24	2.1	1.7	2.4	37.5	199.2	9.3
South	28	2.1	2.7	3.8	25.6	148.2	8.2
Moldavia	25	2.7	1.7	2.0	32.5	225.5	20.8
Belorussia	32	0.9	3.2	6.4	26.0	139.2	18.4
Baltic	26	0.4	4.9	13.3	34.9	288.3	11.1
Transcaucasia	24	1.8	2.2	3.3	29.4	194.6	2.7
Kazakhstan	104	3.9	8.6	12.6	5.2	17.5	2.2
Central Asia	63	2.9	4.0	6.7	4.6	39.5	2.4

[a] Average distance computed as $\sqrt{\dfrac{\text{Area}}{\text{No. of Settlements}}}$

Sources: Column 1: Litovka, 1976, p. 23. Columns 2–3 computed from data in Vestnik statistiki, No. 5, 1971, pp. 80–95. Columns 4–6: Danilova et al., 1976, p. 246.

Figure 8.2 Regional Coefficients of Extra Construction Costs in the Siberian North

accessibility of the Russian parts of this Western periphery to Eastern Europe and the world at large is also signally worse than that of the Western border republics. Convenient location in an era of increased COMECON ties thus cannot be expected to help counterbalance the cumulative losses suffered since the early Five-Year Plans. During the rest of this century, at least, with many competing pressing problems facing the leadership, the long secular decline here is most unlikely to be reversed.[14]

B.   *The Southern Periphery*

South of the Slavic heartland of the European USSR and its eastward extension beyond the Urals lies a good portion of Western Asia. Its place in the Soviet regional system is mostly a result of Imperial colonial conquests and it remains an undigested and undigestibly separate realm of the USSR. Not only is this region overwhelmingly non-Slavic but, because of a much higher rate of native population growth, the share of the Slavic *colons* has decreased sharply since the late 1950s, with an especially rapid decline over the past decade. South of the Caucasus, Aral Sea and Lake Balkhash, Slavs today comprise only 14% of the population as against almost 20% in 1970 (Sheehy, March 27, 1980, p. 16 and April 8, 1980, p. 5; *TSU SSR, Itogi . . . 1970*, Vol. IV).

(a)   *Transcaucasia: Potential Workshop in a Stagnant Economy?* Although quite distinct from the Slavic world to the North, this Southern arc is internally even more diverse than the Western periphery. More specifically, Transcaucasia is in a more advanced stage of demographic transition and socio-economic development than Central Asia. It is geographically much more accessible to the European core area, to the national market as a whole (Table 8.2, Column 7–8) as well as to seaports. Its location has made it more of an extension of the European USSR through much of its economic history than a part of Soviet Asia. Male rates of higher education for the three main Caucasian nationalities in 1970 well exceeded those for Russians nationwide, though the figures may be somewhat inflated,[15] while east of the Caspian these rates, not to mention those for women, were much lower (Andrews, 1978, p. 455, based on data in the 1970 census). Throughout the Soviet period, Caucasians have been strongly represented in the Party and government, a position that has also brought the region unquestionable economic benefit.

Industrial growth rates in Armenia have long been exceeding the Soviet mean, but in the two other republics of Transcaucasia they have lagged behind until recently (Table 8.1; *Promyshlennost SSSR, 1964*, pp. 50–2). During the last decade, however, a turnabout has clearly taken place. Industrial development in Transcaucasia decelerated only slightly, compared to the precipitous decline nationwide, and in the 1975–9 period output in the region as a whole grew some 10%

faster than Soviet industry. At the same time the whole area, even Moslem Azerbaidzhan, has entered the last phase of the demographic revolution, with birth rates dropping rapidly almost to the USSR average today. The rates of improvement in labor productivity show a reversal relative to the national trend: lagging behind during the 1960s, but surging ahead of the Soviet average in the following decade (*Nar. khoz. SSSR v 1970 g.*, p. 163; *v 1978 g.*, p. 128).

This industrial turnabout is all the more interesting because Transcaucasia failed to receive any increase in its share of investment from the Soviet state. Instead, a more reasonably trained and ample labor force seems to have made good use of incremental capital (Table 8.3).[16] As in the Western periphery, the industrial structure of Transcaucasia has greatly broadened out from the preponderance of resource-based food processing, fuel and mineral production and smelting to embrace the whole range of manufacturing (Abramov, 1977, pp. 75–98). Today the relative importance of a fairly diversified engineering complex is not very much less than in the country as a whole and that of the chemical industries is significantly greater. At the same time, the region retains a comparative advantage in light industries, particular food-processing branches (Table 8.6; Kobakhidze, 1979, pp. 128–9; Adamesku *et al.*, 1973, pp. 58–82 and 116–35), hydroelectric power for peak demand (Shelest, 1975, p. 295; Ryl'skii *et al.*, 1974, pp. 161–9) and specialized recreations and health resorts of which a fifth of the nation's assets are concentrated in the Caucasus (Adamesku, 1973, p. 14, and 166–73).

Transcaucasia, where today 45% of a reasonably skilled population is in the 10–35 age group versus 40% in the RSFSR and 37% in the Ukraine (Baldwin, 1979, pp. 92, 103 and 112), will probably play a similar role in industrial development for most of the remainder of this century as was played by the Western periphery in the past two decades. The level of urbanization in Transcaucasia slightly exceeds the national mean, but industry is very heavily concentrated in the three republic capitals, with almost 63% of gross output and 59% of industrial employment (seven cities hold three-fourths of all industry, according to Adamesku, 1977, p. 158 and Silaev, 1967, pp. 230–1). That leaves a large underutilized labor pool in the rest of the ca. 140 cities, well over a third of which have over 15,000 inhabitants.[17] Although Transcaucasia still lags well behind the European USSR and the Soviet average in infrastructural development and government-supplied communal services,[18] (Abramov, 1977, pp. 99–114), there is, to counterbalance this lag, a widespread network of cooperative service and repair shops and an especially vigorous second economy. All in all, the region today is probably not worse off in amenities and activities that support a broadly-based industrial expansion of all-Union significance than was the Western periphery in the 1960s. While exports are as yet relatively low (Table 8.2)[19], the accessibility needed for a vigorous participation in foreign trade is also present.

In forecasting such a role for Transcaucasia in the forthcoming years, however, three caveats are in order. One of these relates to the relative importance and scope of the "second economy," which has always been exceptionally vigorous in these republics. Given the decreasing family size, illegal and semilegal activities may prove an even more attractive alternative to the official economy in the future, providing a still higher share of personal income. More resources could thus be siphoned away for a sector that benefits only the local population and is beyond the pale of national planning. This would most likely dampen official growth rates and lower economic indicators, though the region itself and certainly its population may well be better off.

Secondly, we cannot predict the impact of nationalism and rising anti-Russian sentiment on economic development either directly or indirectly through a possible backlash expressed as reduced investment allocation. It is significant that the Russian population in Georgia has been declining since 1959 at an accelerated rate, with the outflow linked by some emigré opinion to the inimical attitude of the Georgians. Over the last decade, Azerbaidzhan experienced an even larger outmigration, in this case more likely oil-workers shifted to Siberia. Transcaucasia as a whole lost 56,000 Russians (Sheehy, 1980, p. 16). If increased national restlessness produces a backlash of reduced capital investment, economic performance is certain to be affected. Finally, investment in the region may fail to rise or be even cut back simply because of the sheer shortage of funds. In 1979, for example, the commissioning of new capacity in the country remained essentially stagnant and total investment grew by only one percent (*Ekonomicheskaia gazeta*, No. 5, January 1980, p. 8). At a time of extreme capital stringency, investment in Transcaucasia may well be reduced absolutely to a significant degree, preventing the region from taking full advantage of its ample, reasonably skilled manpower and relative proximity to the European core areas.

(b)   *Central Asia (including Southern Kazakhstan): Uncertain Prospects.* While it is a part of the Southern periphery, Central Asia – Southern Kazakhstan presents much more intractable problems than the Caucasus. The overwhelmingly Moslem population has barely begun to limit its birthrate, which still exceeds 30 per thousand by a substantial margin[20] (*Nar. khoz. SSSR v 1978 g.*, pp. 26–7). Given the massive size of young cohorts in the under-20 age group, rapid population growth is destined to continue for the rest of this century. Central Asians so far have also been poorly represented at the highest levels of Party and government and even among the technical elite and industrial labor force within the region itself.[21]

The economy of Central Asia is in large measure still colonial. It has by far the least manufacturing per capita, with the relative level actually declining in every republic because of the burgeoning population and, recently, the sagging industrial growth rates (Table 8.1). At the same time, the region's resources of cotton, natural gas, and metals, especially gold, are shipped overwhelmingly to the European USSR and for export in virtually unprocessed form. With nine-tenths of the Soviet and about one-sixth of the world's cotton-fiber output in the mid 1970s, Central Asia produced a mere 5% of all cotton textiles and 4.4% of all sewn garments in the USSR, shares unchanged since 1960. These shares are far too small to satisfy even half the demand of the region itself, let alone allow for exports of such goods (Afanas'evskii, 1976, pp. 208, 211 and 226). Nor are these republics even self-sufficient in food products,[22] with the per capita output of the food industries being less than half the Soviet average and less than the mean for every major branch of these industries (Zakumbaev, 1977, p. 185). Similarly, for many years now, Central Asia has been piping to the RSFSR more than three-quarters of its natural gas production, with Turkmenia, the largest producer, exporting 97% (Mun'ko, 1977, p. 54; Dienes and Shabad, 1979, pp. 70–1 and 80–4). The contribution of machine building to the region's industrial structure is negligible, a mere 1.3%, by far the lowest among all economic areas of the USSR (Table 8.6).

The economic indicators of Central Asian industry seem less than satisfactory. While in recent years ratios of gross output to fixed capital and corresponding ratios of the growth of these variables approximated the Soviet mean[23] (Tables 8.2 and 8.3) this is explained by the high material-intensity and consequent doublecounting of output for branches with high resource content. The share of net output appears to be much smaller than that of gross production in all Central Asian republics (Table 8.2). Even in such technically simple and low-skill-demanding industries as textiles and apparel, output – capital ratios in Uzbekistan during the 1960–75 period reportedly reached only half of the Soviet average. Labor productivity in these branches is similarly lower by 17 to 30% throughout the four republics, despite the fact that the capital–labor ratio in them is high (Afanas'evskii, 1976, pp. 219–20). Nor did the region show any relative improvement: the productivity of industrial labor, in fact, has been rising less rapidly than the national average (*Nar. khoz. SSSR v 1970 g.*, p. 163 and *Nar. khoz. SSSR v 1978 g.*, p. 128). Although cost allowances for new construction in Uzbekistan are officially set 10–15% above those in other, better located regions[24] and cost of equipment 6% higher, a recent Uzbek study finds these coefficients too low. A shoe factory built in Fergana in 1969 cost a shocking 41% more than an analogous plant that went into production in Abakan, Krasnoiarsk Krai, East Siberia, a year earlier (Khikmatov *et al.*, 1978, pp. 111–12).

Central Asian development is also hindered by the increasing shortage and cost of water. The more easily accessible water resources have all been tapped, even if inefficiently with great losses,[25] and irrigation costs have been increasing rapidly in recent years. Mounting irrigation expenses must have been the chief cause of the much faster growth of costs relative to increments of *net* output in the agriculture of Uzbekistan during 1970–6 when compared to Soviet agriculture as a

whole for the same period.[26] At the same time, major water projects of
the 10th Five-Year Plan, such as the lengthening of the Kara–Kum
Canal and expansion of the Karshi Steppe, Golodnaia Steppe and
Fergana Valley systems demanded large new doses of investment. For
the longer term, water diversion from West Siberia is being most
seriously considered and evaluated (Micklin, 1978, pp. 15–22).

Given all these constraints to even maintaining previous economic-
growth rates, the problem of what to do with the burgeoning
population in these Moslem republics will loom increasingly large. The
probability of large-scale outmigration from Central Asia as well as the
alternative of using migrant workers from the region for specific
projects and durations have been thoroughly analyzed by Western
researchers. Lewis and his associates (1976, pp. 343–83) maintain that
"socioeconomic, demographic and ethnic processes in the Soviet
Union are fundamentally very similar to these same processes in all
multinational states". . . Neither birth control nor accelerated economic development is expected to relieve the mounting population
pressure in Central Asia. Universal experience thus suggests rather
considerable outmigration and redistribution of indigenous ethnic
groups into the labor-short Slavic republics, with attendant nationality
conflicts in the forthcoming decades. Other researchers, attributing
much greater role to inhibiting cultural, religious, linguistic and
climatic barriers for large-scale outmigration, question that hypothesis. Given substantial additional income from private plot, subsidiary
activities and transfer payments, plus lower living costs than in most
Slavic provinces, the "push factor" of declining living standard is held
to be insufficient to initiate such an exodus (Feshbach, 1979, pp.
656–709; Hodnett, 1974, pp. 65–88). Still others maintain that
selective relocation of Central Asians for fixed terms of service to
European rural areas, combined with somewhat greater efforts at
regional development, seems the most likely scenario (Wimbush and
Ponomareff, 1979).

The author agrees with those who believe significant outmigration to
be both unfeasible and highly improbable and thinks that even
Gastarbeiter-type movements will be practicable only on a very limited
scale. Yet he deems it unlikely that the Soviet leadership will have the
resources and the consensus of purpose to embark on a forceful,
comprehensive program for the region over the next decade, perhaps
even longer.

A developmental strategy suitable for Central Asia requires dispersed investment in large numbers of small- and medium-scale
plants, particularly in small towns and rural areas, both to soak up the
surplus labor and to provide continued upward mobility for the
native population (Burg, 1979, p. 76). Some effort is apparently being
made toward such dispersed industrialization, while the beginning
of commuting from rural villages to towns is also observable, a
practice particularly suited for the region "in view of the demonstrated reluctance of rural residents to shift to urban living con-

ditions." (Shabad, 1979a, pp. 121–2). Such dispersed industrialization, however, entails still higher capital costs than the construction of a few large plants of the same capacity. Yet, according to data for the footwear and silk industries, investment requirements per factory floor space in the region well exceeds those in West Siberia and is much above those in the European USSR on account of the low level of construction organization and supporting services (Afanas'evskii, 1976, pp. 118, 154–9).

Under these circumstances it is questionable whether current efforts will be anywhere near adequate to draw into production the accumulating labor surplus.[27] A recent Western study cogently argues that the structural, institutional and functional constraints in the Politburo, combined with a rising tide of Great Russian nationalism, will prevent the channeling of enough investment in a focused, coordinated fashion to provide for a sufficient rise of employment and standard of living in these republics. On the one hand, the power of those Politburo members "with territorial constituencies in the relatively underdeveloped and demographically growing republics" is still fairly weak (only the Kazakh first secretary is presently a full voting member) and is more than counterbalanced by "those members with constituencies in the more developed but demographically static territories of Leningrad, Moscow, Belorussia and the Ukraine." On the other hand, members with functional constituencies (major industries, transport, defense, etc.) also will probably resist accelerated investment in Central Asia. Instead, they are "highly likely to view the development of Siberian raw materials and energy resources as essential to the continued expansion of the bureaucratic domains" that compose their bailiwicks. (Burg, 1979, p. 77.)

In addition, "members with territorial and functional constituencies in the RSFSR undoubtedly view development of Siberia as essential for ... the Russian Republic [apart from the mystic importance and ethnic meaning the Siberian frontier may hold for Great Russians]. Consequently, substantial capital investment in Siberian development not only offers potentially greater economic benefits to the Russian members of the Politburo responsible for functional constituencies than investment on an equivalent scale in Central Asia ... [but also] promises them important ethno-national benefits. [It] allows them to accommodate Russian national sentiments in a way which is highly utilitarian and which does not increase disproportionately the power of any one of them." (Burg, 1979, p. 78).

The leadership's sensitivity to any potential threat to domestic stability, however, should moderate somewhat such a bias against the accelerated development of Central Asia. Led perhaps by the General Secretary and the member responsible for security (at present the Chairman of the KGB), a consensus may therefore emerge for limited development of the Central Asian economy. While possibly somewhat more vigorous than that of the recent past, such a strategy would not threaten the priority accorded to what Hooson (1972, p. 539) called "effective national territory", and within it Siberia in particular. But even so it cannot provide employment on a scale to "solve" the Central Asian problem. Yet it is the only strategy on which, barring radical changes in the composition and orientation of the Politbureau during the succession struggle, the Soviet leadership, in the absence of large external sources of capital, is likely to be able to agree (Burg, 1979, p. 80).

It may be that the above explanation is just too "pat," the pragmatism of a basically Anglo-Saxon discipline applied beyond its limits.[28] Yet the reasoning that, from its own resources, the Soviet leadership will be unable to channel enough funds into Central Asia to sharply boost its economy seems sound. Irrespective of the Byzantine intricacies of Soviet decision making, the quantities of available investment capital relative to needs will be severely limited. Mounting energy and raw-material requirements have pushed Siberian development irreversibly to the front for the 1980s. The capital demands and lengthening lead times of these projects, together with the need to keep the aging physical plant of the European USSR functioning on at least current technological levels, will put Central Asia on an economic backburner. Barring a major Moslem upheaval which, if it comes at all, is very unlikely before the end of the decade, the primary focus of Soviet regional policy for the next 10–15 years will be Siberia. Briefly considered in a previous section, Siberia must now be the subject of closer scrutiny.

8.5 Siberia (including the Far East and North Kazakhstan)

Besides sheer size, the most salient feature of Siberia is its environmental harshness, resulting in low population densities, lack of infrastructure and very high investment requirement for any strategy of development. Half of that vast territory (an area as large as the US west of the Mississippi) experiences more than 120 days with mean daily temperatures of below 5°F. Close to half of the remainder, with higher temperatures, must contend with a severe wind-chill factor and/or the quagmire of primeval swamps which make conditions only marginally better than in the first half of the region (Mote, 1978, especially pp. 19–36). Almost 70% of the area (four-fifths without North Kazakhstan) is underlain with permafrost, which extends all the way into Mongolia and China east of the Enisei. And because so much of this permafrost has formed on sedimentary strata, the presence of ice complicates construction still more than in corresponding areas of Canada.

Table 8.7 shows eloquently the sparseness of the settlement network and of transport routes. The relative supply of other types of infrastructure and services, such as housing, household services and nursery schools, also fall well below those in the European areas (Vitebskii, 1978, pp. 48–53; Mil'ner, 1979, p. 63).[29] This lag, however,

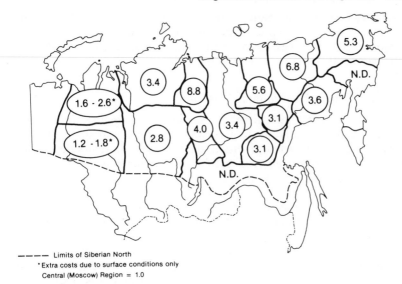

————— Limits of Siberian North
ᐟ Extra costs due to surface conditions only
Central (Moscow) Region = 1.0

Figure 8.2 *Regional Coefficients of Extra Construction Costs in the Siberian North*

simply cannot be remedied soon. Compared to the European Plain, primitive conditions and the natural environment boost construction costs in Southwest Siberia by perhaps one-third, in the Tiumen oil and gas province by some 100% and in the Northeast by three to nine times (see Fig 8.2).

Finally, the physical environment sets limits to the extent of agricultural land and is the chief factor in determining its value. Only 2.34% of Siberia is arable and no more than 5.1% is agriculturally utilizable in any way. With North Kazakhstan added, these shares rise to 4.9 and nearly 20% respectively, the big jump in the utilizable category resulting from the inclusion of vast expanses of poor pastureland in the Kazakh desert (*Nar. khoz. SSSR v 1975 g.*, pp. 20 and 344; *Nar. khoz. RSFSR v 1973 g.*, pp. 9–10 and . . . *v 1975 g.*, p. 162). East of the Enisei in particular, large stretches of arable land are found only in the Amur-Ussuri Valleys. Low fertility aggravates the shortage. In both Siberia and the Far East the average per hectare value of agricultural land falls below 60% of the Soviet mean and barely exceeds one-third of the mean in Kazakhstan (*Zemel'nyi kadastr SSSR, 1967*).[30] The poor land quality, combined with rural depopulation, reduces returns to land to levels lowest in the USSR outside the poorest oblasts of the European non-black-earth belt (Zamkov and Valeshko, 1975, pp. 41–61). Only the wooded steppe zone of West Siberia is endowed with land of roughly average fertility and is the only Siberian region with an agricultural surplus. Siberia, as a whole, cannot feed itself and the provisioning of new industrial nodes thus becomes a major added cost of development.[31] In recent years, the deficit has apparently worsened for animal products, most probably also for vegetables and has barely improved for food grain (Kopach and Novoselov, 1979, pp. 76–7).

A.   *Investment Growth and Productivity*

While Soviet pronouncements on regional issues have long shown a positive bias towards the vast Asian hinterland, the share of total investment channeled to Siberia until 1975 changed very slowly, with the only noticeable jump registered in Khrushchev's Seven-Year Plan. As shown earlier, however, allocations to the Trans-Ural Northlands quadrupled between 1965 and 1975, reaching 4% of the total (Table 8.5). Equally significant is the fact that in every five-year period between 1960 and January 1976 Siberia's share of capital investment consistently exceeded its share of new fixed assets commissioned. While the latter excludes dry holes in the oil and gas industry, imparting a small downward bias to Siberia's claim to the nation's fixed assets, it still appears that relatively more investment is squandered here or frozen in unfinished projects than elsewhere.[32]

Given the harsh environment and the grossly inadequate state of infrastructure and services, the continuing low priority accorded to so-called "nonproductive" (infrastructural and service) construction is a perpetual bane of Siberian development.The problem is reflected with monotonous regularity in Soviet literature. From 1960 through 1975, the percentage of "nonproductive" outlays in total investment was lower in Siberia than in the USSR as a whole (Aganbegian *et al.*, 1974, pp. 30–40 and 210). In the first half of the 1970s, *per worker* allocation for social infrastructure in the West Siberian oil-extraction industry actually suffered a drastic *absolute* decline—from almost 33 rubles to 12.5 rubles per year and only marginally exceeded the branch average for the USSR as a whole (Guzhnovskii, 1977, p. 42). A recent source claims further decrease since that time (*Pravda Ukrainy*, May 23, 1979, p. 2). And in the Tiumen' swamps, of course, a given ruble of such investment results in a far smaller total of housing space and fewer service facilities than in most other provinces of petroleum extraction.

The problem is clearly exacerbated by the well-known production bias of branch ministries. It is also aggravated by the lack of lateral cooperation in an economy organized and managed along vertical lines.[33] Not only do housing and service facilities bear the brunt of any shortfall from planned construction goals (being the first to be skimped on), but they are grossly underplanned to begin with. And the situation is getting worse. A recent scathing article, for example, reveals that in city-planning calculations for the new South Iakutian coal-mining complex the posited ratio between family housing and singles housing was 20 to 80% "in pursuit of an imaginary cheapness." In contrast to these wholly unrealistic assumptions, the actual ratio is turning out to be the exact reverse, with adverse consequences for the activities of the entire complex (*Sotsialisticheskaia industria*, Jan. 21, 1979, p. 2). As to departmentalism, it "has penetrated even deeper" in the zone of the Baikal–Amur Mainline Railway (BAM) than was the case so far in West Siberia.[34]

Given the harsh environment and the rudimentary infrastructure, the economic development of Siberia demands vast investment resources and a long pay-back period. Correspondingly, capital and labor productivity, on the average, is lower than in western regions or the RSFSR as a whole. The share of *zadely*, defined as all types of preliminary and preparatory work done for investment in *forthcoming* Five-Year Plans, reached over 17% of total outlays during the 1966–70 period rising to 18.5% in the first half in the 1970s.[35] Labor productivity, though growing somewhat faster than the Soviet average throughout the 1960–75 period, still was substantially below the Soviet mean in 1975 (*Nar. khoz. SSSR v 1975 g.*, p. 113; *Nar. khoz. RSFSR v 1969 g.*, pp. 50–3; *Nar. khoz. RSFSR v 1975 g.*, pp. 53–6; Legkostup *et al.*, 1979, p. 4). Capital productivity, on the other hand, improved more slowly than the Soviet average, at least during the second half of that decade, with Siberia thus dropping farther behind (Aganbegian, 1978, p. 129).

B. *The Problem of Industrial Structure*

In the economically more rational post-Stalin climate at least, theoretical work on regional growth by Soviet scholars also has focussed attention on the nature of principal, region-forming industries, associated supporting activities and activities that meet purely local needs. Region-forming industries "determine the place of a region in the national and international division of labor" and are said to be those "that make the most efficient use of natural and economic conditions for the production of a commodity (or commodities) for the national or international markets." (Nikol'skii, 1972, p. 17). Given the system of output targets for all major products and a traditional sellers market under taut planning, locational criteria for "most efficient use" imply not profitability, but an oversimplified yardstick of least production cost. (In addition, of course, "most efficient use" in the USSR has never been judged solely by economic criteria). With such an oversimplified locational yardstick, accessibility, demand linkages and the market factor in general are easily neglected in favor of volume and low production costs at mine and factory sites. In the process, rapid regional growth leads to severe imbalances in the economic structures of many areas: problems of employment are created and the transport network becomes overstrained.

This conclusion clearly applies to much of Siberian development to date. Thanks to the hydroelectric, fuel and mineral riches of the Trans-Ural area, an unsophisticated least-production-cost measure could frequently be used to reinforce the location principle "bringing industry closer to sources of raw materials." Large centers for extractive and other primary industries have been created, but processing activities and the industrial market in general remained concentrated in the European USSR. In addition, World War II and the resulting evacuation has left its legacy in a substantial heavy-machinery concentration, particularly in and around the Kuzbas. Such a onesided industrial structure depressed the output-capital ratio in the Siberian economy (Table 8.2) and contributed to the chronic transport bottlenecks east of the Urals. In the extreme case of electric power (with its exclusive dependence on a unique transport medium that can span only moderate distances) such a location bias had periodically led to large unused capacities, idling for want of consumers.

The heavy dominance of fuel and mineral extraction, power production, heavy chemicals, forest and wood-processing activities east of the Kuzbas is strikingly clear (Table 8.6). West Siberia is also strong in fuel processing, metallurgy, and machine building (almost all of it heavy-engineering and agricultural machinery), but even these branches are very poorly represented in the rest of the Trans-Ural RSFSR. The percentage of light industries and food industries falls well below the Soviet average except in the Far East, where fishing accounts for about a fifth of the region's total industrial output and over a third of the entire Soviet fish catch (Gladyshev *et al.*, 1974, p. 11; and Shabad, "News . . . ," June 1978, p. 426). Food industries, and also agriculture, however, are prominent in Northern Kazakhstan, which is part of the Siberian realm.

Also striking is the rather weak development even of the primary stages of manufacturing, such as refining and metallurgy, or of the chemical industry, especially east of the Enisei.[36] As highly energy-intensive branches, ferrous metallurgy and chemical synthesis have long been regarded by pro-Siberian officials as proper specializations for the Trans-Ural territories. Pro-Siberians have long argued that despite the existence of huge, high-grade iron-ore resources and of large refinery complexes West of the Urals, the development of metallurgy, petrochemicals and synthetic polymers should be acceler-ated in Southern Siberia and stopped in the European regions in order not to aggravate the energy problem.

Yet such a reorientation so far has not occurred and no evidence of it is discernible in the current Five-Year Plan. Energy, which itself is not a homogeneous category, is not the only, or even the distinctly preponderant, input in the industries in question, which also profit from agglomeration, locationally associated production linkages and access to markets. In addition (as a Soviet critic himself observed), while manpower inputs in metallurgical and heavy equipment produc-tion do not appear dominant *per unit value of output*, total labor requirement for most plants in these industries are still large because of the high economic threshold of modern integrated facilities. And given the conditions east of the Urals, it is the total labor and associated population requirement per optimum-sized plant, not the manpower input per unit value produced, which becomes the relevant criterion.[37]

Not surprisingly, the eastward movement of metallurgical and associated steel-consuming industries had petered out by the end of World War II and the relative contribution of the trans-Ural RSFSR to Soviet machinery production declined steadily through the 1950s and 1960s with no sign of a reversal in the past decade either (Aganbegian, 1978, p. 215; Nekrasov, 1979, p. 59; Shabad and Mote, 1977, p. 54, and Shabad, "News ...," April 1978, pp. 289–93).[38] Nor did Siberia succeed in accelerating the development of its chemical and petrochemical industries, and the province's contribution to the national output of these branches dwindled from almost 12% in 1965 to 8.4% ten years later (Gramoteeva, 1979, pp. 139–40).

Though no longer advocating complex full-scale development for the Asian RSFSR, pro-Siberian planners and officials continue to agitate for the expansion of a relatively broad range of industries in the Southern belt of the region. The recent sharp attacks leveled against Gosplan and the Ministries of Ferrous Metallurgy, Chemical Industries, and Agricultural Machinery, reflect, in part, local Siberian interests and, in part, a valid fear that the very unbalanced nature of industrialization east of the Urals endangers the success of the ambitious plans for rapid economic growth in these pioneer areas. Thus, in the words of the secretary of the Amur Oblast Party Committee, both Gosplan and the Ministry for Agricultural Machine Building have been avoiding the implementation of authoritative decisions obliging them to plan the construction and commissioning of an agricultural-machinery plant in the Amur Region (Mavrin, 1978, pp. 68–9). Similarly, the reconstruction of the old Kuznetsk Metallurgical Combine, "a keystone to the industrialization of Siberia," is obstructed by the Ministry of Ferrous Metallurgy, while the huge Tomsk petrochemical combine, badly behind schedule, "has become just another building site." The appropriate ministries lack interest in these projects and resist being "driven" to Siberia (Aganbegian ed., 1979, pp. 101–27; Nekrasov, 1979, pp. 54 and 58–9; *Pravda*, April 7, 1978).

The narrow and unbalanced economic structure of the Trans-Ural RSFSR has aggravated the problems of manpower and transport, both of which are critical bottlenecks in the development of Siberia. In specialized regions only specialized labor can find employment, and as a rule, such labor will be unstable. Similarly, specialized regions that depend heavily on resource extraction must cope with a heavy transport burden. In particular, pioneer provinces in continental interiors must send their freight to distant markets (or ports) overland through a sparse rail and road network.

C. *Recent Population Trends and Prospects*

The problems of population and labor force in the development of Siberia have been well documented and only the most recent trends are discussed here. The most obvious broad change of the last decade has been the reversal of the relative population loss (resulting from a turnabout in *net* outmigration) that characterized the Trans-Ural RSFSR during the 1960s.[39] Yet, a closer look reveals that the population upsurge was largely limited to the Far North and to the Baikal-Amur lands along the Mongolian–Chinese border, in both cases augmented by the high age-specific birth rates of sizable indigenous nationalities in certain provinces. The more populous forest–steppe zone eastward to Lake Baikal (and even Chita Oblast in Transbaikalia) increased its population at a slower rate than the country as a whole and much more slowly than during the previous decade. The West Siberian steppe, in particular, registered very sluggish growth, below the rate of natural increase for the province during 1970–75, pointing to continued outmigration (Bond and Lydolph, 1979, pp. 464–5 and 476–8).[40]

Nor does inmigration represent long-term or permanent settlement any more than it did during the 1960s, when population mobility exceeded that in the European USSR by two to four times and even more (Lydolph, 1979, pp. 151–3).[41] In fact, given the much increased role of the "tour-of-duty" and "expedition" methods of employment, every sign points to even greater labor turnover and instability. Such methods entail flying workers into northern, makeshift settlements from southern base cities (in the former case from within Siberia; in the latter, all the way from the European USSR) for a predetermined period and then returning them for rest and recreation before their next tour. By Soviet estimates, more than 210,000 persons are so employed today in geological work and in the oil, gas and forest industries, the overwhelming majority in the Trans-Ural RSFSR. In 1978, over 30% of all those working on pipeline construction in West Siberia were transients from other economic regions and their numbers alone were expected to swell to 70–80,000 in the future (Khaitun, 1979, p. 48). In the spring of 1980, Soviet planners announced a three-year plan for accelerated housing construction in Tiumen' Oblast, with a total of some 1.5 million sq. meters of new housing by 1983. Assuming 10 sq. meters per person, the plan would settle 150,000 persons, but its fulfillment, requiring a tripling of housing-construction capacity in Tiumen' Province in three years, is open to doubt (*Sotsialisticheskaia industriia*, April 17, 1980). Perevedentsev, the noted demographer and sociologist, declared forcefully (*Zhurnalist*, Aug. 1979, pp. 36–7).[42] in 1979 that the rate of population growth for the North, which "swallowed" 11% of the total increment, during the 1970s, is too rapid and cannot be maintained. (The rate of increase was four times the national average.) Compared to its output, the North is really overpopulated and major efforts are needed to reduce its requirement for additional labor resources.

D.   *The Transport Bottleneck and the Growing Transport Burden*

By all evidence, Soviet planners' traditional view of transport as a service, provided grudgingly and only when absolutely necessary, continues to hold today. The Baikal–Amur Mainline Railway may be the only partial exception, but in that case the strategic military role seems as strong as the economic one. In new regions of resource exploitation transport facilities are provided primarily and sometimes exclusively for the product, when exploitation is ready to begin or has been underway for a number of years. Roads and railways, even communication lines, remain primitive or entirely nonexistent throughout the preparation and developmental phase (Altunin, 1979, p. 22). Several recent sources support the frustrated judgment of F. G. Arzhanov (1979, pp. 26–7), chief of GLAVTIUMEN'NEFTEGAZ (the Tiumen' Oil and Gas Trust), that West Siberian oilmen habitually arrive to develop new deposits in the mud, swimming through marsh, only to leave the nearly worked-out fields gaily and with ease on freshly completed hard-surface roads. The Party Secretary of Tiumen' Province declares in equally strong language: "To build fast, one must be able to transport swiftly. But we must haul as if by oxen" (Altunin, 1979, p. 20).

(a)   *The Railroads and the Prospects of Siberian Development.* Since the days of the Ural-Kuznetsk Combine, the rail lines leading to the Urals from the East have been the most overworked in the country. From 1940 to 1970 they accounted for 16–17% of all Soviet freight turnover in peace time (and much more during World War II), as against some 10% in 1928 (North, 1979, p. 303). Since the late sixties, traffic over these lines appears to have grown at a rate well above the national average and especially so in recent years. According to the Minister himself, in 1977, for example, more than two-fifths of the total increase in the volume of work by Soviet railroads was accounted for by the Sverdlovsk, Southern Urals, Virgin Lands, West Siberian and East Siberian lines, which have the greatest difficulty in assimilating new freight traffic (*Pravda*, March 29, 1978, p. 2).

Even more than those in other regions, the above-mentioned railways are dominated by a few bulk commodities that move primarily westward, resulting in a severe imbalance of flow. The accelerated exploitation of resources East of the Urals will further choke these lines and accentuate the imbalance. During the second half of the 1960s, coal, coke and ores were responsible for 55% of all the loadings on the railroads of West Siberia and North Kazakhstan, the principal direction of their flow being westward. Adding petroleum products and grain, these few commodities made up at least two-thirds of all the loadings (North, 1979, pp. 286–7). The sharp growth in coal shipment on these railroads during the past decade is especially striking (Dubinskii, 1977, p. 48). Kuzbas and Ekibastuz coals, in fact, accounted for over nine-tenths of all the increase in the ton-kilometer freight turnover for coal from 1970 to the end of 1975 (Dienes, 1979, pp. 41–4). Earlier enthusiasm for massive coal hauls from Siberian and Kazakh fields, both through the existing railways and through a new "super-trunkline," has given way to much greater caution and fuller appreciation of the costs and problems involved.[43] Perhaps during the 1980s the Soviets will be able to handle some 50 million tons of extra freight, mostly coal, with the improvements under way.[44] However, when one adds all other commodities that must move to European Russia and beyond, it becomes clear that the speed and success of economic development will depend on a very substantial expansion of transport capacity.

Despite some piece-meal improvements, I seriously doubt that Soviet planners can open the severe railway bottleneck sufficiently to speed up development in the Ural-Baikal zone through the next decade. In contrast to the 1930s and 1950s, relatively cheap techno-logical innovations will not suffice and, at any rate, are not in sight. Large expansion in carrying capacity today can be achieved only by a major construction effort. At present, however, the Soviet economy is already struggling with two gigantic railway and several pipeline projects besides other prodigious tasks and is entering a period of sustained squeeze on its capital and labor resources. It cannot conceivably undertake another Ural-Baikal railway until, at best, the late 1980s, with little chance of completion before the following decade.

(b)   *The Pipeline Bottleneck.* Pipeline transport represents the most dramatic growth in Soviet freight movement in the past two decades. If natural gas piped through long-distance lines is counted at its calorific equivalent in standard tons of oil, the transport work by pipelines multiplied 20-fold in less than 20 years. It reached over 26% of all domestic freight turnover during 1977 as against less than 4% in 1960 (Furmann, 1978, p. 14, and *Nar. khoz. SSSR v 1977 g.*, p. 305). Pipelines, however, are far too specialized carriers to spur extensive development in pioneer areas. Once pipelines are in place, hydrocar-bons move with ease, at very low operating costs and, despite the high fixed investment for transport, at lower total costs than most other resources. This means that associated production complexes and consuming industries tend to agglomerate at great distances from the often isolated and harsh regions of hydrocarbon extraction. Since the entire increment of Soviet oil and gas today is coming from Northwest Siberia, the growth of pipelines in and from the province is critical to the nation's economy, but, except during the construction phase, will have little impact on Siberia itself.

The pipeline bottleneck applies mainly to natural gas. Crude oil today suffers from little transport difficulty although, especially in West Siberia, some temporary worsening of the situation is likely as average size of and accessibility to new fields decrease during the 1980s. The lack of oil-product pipelines will also continue to be a problem, adding to the burden of the overtaxed railways, especially East of the Urals. However, the major constraint is on natural gas whose transport overland is exclusively dependent on pipelines, many more of which are needed to move a same amount of calories in the form of gas than of oil.[45] Since the gas industry today depends on the huge fields of Northwest Siberia for its entire increase and increasingly also to compensate for declining output elsewhere, the rate of delivery of North-Tiumen' gas will have a crucial and *direct* impact on the economic performance of more than half a dozen Soviet regions, accounting for a full half of the country's industrial production.

The tremendous demand for rolled steel, nonferrous metals, compressors, cement, etc. that comes from the West Siberian gas industry is placing immense strain on the Soviet economy and represents severe constraints on continued rapid expansion. Planned increments of 100 billion cubic meters of gas from these fields every 2–3 years require 20–30% capacity expansion in some key supplying industries during the next decade (Dienes, 1977, pp. 48–9; Dienes and Shabad, 1979, p. 255). Recently one of the foremost Soviet experts on the gas industry stated that 30,000 kilometers and 20 million metric tons of top-grade large-diameter pipes, requiring 22–25 billion rubles of capital investment, would be needed to transport an additional 300 billion cu. meters of gas per year into the European USSR. The official admits that "it is virtually impossible for us to allocate such large amounts" to that branch (Bokserman, 1978, p. 19); in addition, pipeline quality and long delays in the installation of compressor stations remain chronic problems.[46] Despite the mortgaging of the entire 1976–80 gas export for pipes and compressors already received, the original 1980 pipeline target is only 55% fulfilled (*Ekonomicheskaia gazeta*, No. 6, February 1977, p. 2; Shabad, "News Notes," April 1981).

A deeper understanding of all these constraints is leading to greater caution among gas-industry officials and functionaries of Tiumen' Oblast', the linchpin in the Soviet gas drive. In an unusually frank interview, a former chief of the Tiumen' gas industry, now Secretary of the Province's Party Committee, reveals the spirited struggle waged against Gosplan's attempt to force the industry prematurely to fields yet farther north (150–300 miles beyond the Arctic Circle), because it is technologically unprepared for pipeline and field construction on the ice-saturated permafrost, far worse than experienced to date (Altunin, 1979, p. 22).

The pipeline bottleneck and constraints on field development in the North Tiumen' wilderness should prevent the gas industry fully to compensate for the serious shortfalls in coal and oil production and to satisfy, at the same time, the increase in fuel demand in the forthcoming decade. Together with the oil, the gas resources of Tiumen' Oblast' represent the centerpiece of the Soviet energy system during the 1980s. Their performance will have a decisive economic impact, both direct and indirect, on the prospects of the entire Soviet geographic space and most of its constituent regions.

8.6   Conclusion

Among a galaxy of economists, a geographer should not attempt to be one. This paper makes no pretense at systematic economic analysis; nor does it treat in a general way the process of development or the factors controlling it in the USSR. Rather, it is the diverse regional characters and profiles of economic-geographic space that formed the subject of this inquiry and provided the organizational framework for the study. Yet the system of regions examined is far more than a set of passive containers for the operation and growth of the economy. As the textbooks teach, the task of an "economy is to allocate scarce resources to given ends." That *is*, among other things, a spatial process.

The Soviet economy today is on the threshold of a new era. Despite all exhortations, it has not yet succeeded in moving from an extensive to an intensive pattern of growth. As a result, for the first time in years of peace, it is at the beginning of a concurrent sustained squeeze on all the factors of production, i.e. accessible natural resources, land, labor, and capital. The widely known slowdown is in a major way a function of that squeeze and will be still more clearly so in the forthcoming years.

Yet only in the context of geographic space does that constraint on production factors have real meaning. With one-sixth of the earth's surface and a late start in industrialization, the natural-resource base of the USSR as a whole is very far from exhausted or even fully catalogued. This is especially true of energy and industrial materials. While population growth has clearly slowed, the Soviet Union over the next decade is still expected to add some 7.7 million to the 15 to 39 age group, estimated to be 101 million in 1980 (Baldwin, 1979, p. 91). This represents an almost 8% increase in this youthful age category for the 10-year period, certainly adequate for a modern economy, especially if augmented by new labor-saving technology[47]. Finally, "the USSR has always overinvested, judged at least by Western standards ... Total investment and new fixed investment between 1950 and 1978 increased on the average by 7.7% per year ... and the share of investment (in the GNP) rose from 14.8 to 31% "(Block, 1979, p. 130). Despite the recent slowdown, new investment during 1976–9 still grew by an average rate of 4.1% (Bush, 1979, p. 3). The 1980 Plan calls for a further 5.4% increase,[48] to a grand total of 135 billion rubles (*Ekonomicheskaia gazeta*, No. 1, 1980, p. 2), which in real terms appreciably exceeds the amount the US invests today in its much larger economy.

Yet when we consider the concrete world of sheer distances, physical environment, resource distribution and resource quality variations, that squeeze on production factors becomes very real indeed. As this paper made clear, through the vast Soviet territory, resources (in their broadest meaning) are distributed in an exceedingly lopsided, contradictory fashion. Varied and divergent regional endowment can, of course, promote regional specialization and trade, a multifaceted economy, and vigorous growth. But distances, physical geography, cultural and ethnic heterogeneity, especially when coupled with distinct geographic subunits within the confines of a single state, can also present obstacles to economic development and national cohesion. Economic growth in the USSR increasingly involves the successful linking of the European core with a vast raw hinterland plus a broad arc of non-European periphery. Each of these three worlds shows great diversity within itself. Yet broadly speaking the first possesses the established industrial capacity, infrastructure and skill and the location for foreign trade, the second the great bulk of natural resources, the third all future increments to the labor force for the next 10–15 years. Combining the increments in production factors from these incongruous worlds across the breadth of a land one-sixth of the earth surface would surely tax the ingenuity even of the most flexible and imaginative leadership.

During the next decade the most urgent task of the Soviet economy will be the procurement of natural resources, particularly energy and minerals, in order to keep its industry, plus a good part of industry in the rest of COMECON, running and to earn the amount of hard currency planners consider essential. This means that Soviet regional policy will accord priority to Siberia, but this priority will focus on the exploitation and transport of natural resources even more strongly than in the past. Because of the physical obstacles and inaccessibility, this policy requires an intensification of the investment bias in favor of that region. While observable since the beginning of the Five-Year Plans, that bias, with the exception of the creation of the Ural–Kuznetsk combine, had not been overpowering in the past. During the last few years, however, a number of signs point to an appreciable rise in Siberia's share in investment allocation, though apparently the Trans-Ural provinces of the Russian Republic also have not escaped the impact of slower investment growth in the Soviet economy as a whole.[49]

The pressing and inescapable dependence of the Soviet economy on Siberian resources through the next decade is indisputable. So is the urgency of the problem. Nor can it be denied that with current and foreseeable world prices for minerals, and especially for hydrocarbons, the enormous investment program in Siberian resources seems to be economically fully justified. Academician Aganbegian (1979, p. 844) pointed out in 1979 that the 1700 million tons of hydrocarbons (in oil equivalent) that West Siberia was expected to produce during the 1976–80 Plan was worth no less than 150 billion rubles to the national economy at 1979 world prices for oil and gas, valued at over 100 foreign-trade rubles per ton.[50] That may be compared with the roughly 25 billion domestic rubles funneled directly into the West Siberian oil and gas complex during that five-year period. The respected economist A. G. Granberg (1980, p. 102–3) calculates that because of the immense and increasing role of Siberia in the supply of crucial basic inputs Siberian development has an immediate and large multiplier effect on the entire Soviet economy. Because Siberia still accounts for less than one-tenth of Soviet GNP, such a multiplier effect leads Granberg to conclude that the optimum rate of expansion for the region, that which maximizes national growth, lies between 1.2 and 1.4 times the national rate. A deviation from that ratio upward would result in a minor negative impact; a deviation downward would retard national expansion to a very substantial degree.

On the other hand, even pro-Siberian scholars admit that this whole argument may be vitiated if the capital and labor costs of Siberian development are not kept within bounds. During the past 15 years, the capital intensity of Siberian industry rose by one-third, as against 24% for Soviet industry as a whole. Continued relative growth in this capital intensity and a substantial rise in Siberia's share in investment allocation could well lead to an absolute reduction in outlays for other regions, especially West of the Urals. This in turn would retard the country's expansion both directly and via its impact on Siberian development, since it is the European core that is the main provider of capital goods, scientific innovation, and skill for the rest of the USSR and not the least for the new energy-mineral complexes of Siberia (Granberg, 1980, pp. 97 and 101). In a similar vein, Perevedentsev (*Zhurnalist*, No. 8, Aug. 1979, p. 37) warns that the recent precipitous growth of population in the North-lands which since 1970 "swallowed up" 11% of all increments in the population as a whole and stood at four times the national rate, simply cannot be kept up and is becoming self-defeating. Major efforts must be made towards a relative reduction in the North's requirement for additional labor resources. "Opening of the North is a great achievement, but great achievements are possible and needed in established regions as well."

It is clear therefore that, despite the undeniable complementarity between the country's Eastern and Western parts, the competitive relationship between them is equally strong. The rival pressures for energy and materials, investment and human resources between these two halves of the Slavic realm (the "effective national territory" in Hooson's fitting phrase) continue to exert a strong influence on planning and may even be on the rise. Regional and institutional rivalries have long been manifest concerning the development priorities of Siberian resources, the degree of processing in and out of the region, the nature and location of supply bases and the choice of transport modes (North, 1979). In the most recent years, the growing strain on Soviet investment resources, combined with the drastic slowdown in the expansion of the labor force, has strengthened those forces that seek to subordinate the development of Siberia and the Far East to the needs of the European economic core. The advocates of this strategy press for priority for the exploitation of locationally mobile, transportable energy sources and materials that can be siphoned out of the East with little or no processing for the needs of the European USSR or for export. The clearest example of the dominance of this strategy since 1970 has been the crash development of the Tiumen' oil and gas fields (continuing today), and of the Ekibastuz and South Iakutian coal deposits versus the delays and very sluggish growth of the long-heralded energy complex in the Kansk–Achinsk Basin whose products are not transportable or can be moved only at very great expense.

The vexing issues of the Southern periphery, especially Central Asia, are willy-nilly on an economic backburner today. Judging from recent scholarly writings, Soviet scholars are aware of the sensitive and potentially explosive nature of the problems there. Concerted attention to Central Asia, however, would not yield the immediate economic benefit that crash development of transportable Siberian resources or modernization and reequipment in the European provinces are likely to do. Nor would it provide to a Russian-dominated leadership the ethno-cultural and emotional rewards that emphasis on the country's Slavic triangle can produce. Both the pro-European and the pro-Siberian lobbies in the planning hierarchy should find themselves in agreement on that point. Moreover, even the non-Russian nationalities West of the Urals, such as Ukrainians and Balts and even those of the Caucasus, are very unlikely to be supporters of a vigorous Central Asian economic strategy.

Only in case of a major Moslem upheaval, perhaps, would these perceptions change. But relative to the Slavic regions, income levels in Central Asia are not that much lower and population pressure on resources, while growing, is still some way from reaching the flash point. Nor has Moscow's control slipped enough, if at all, to make such an upheaval likely, certainly in the present decade. In a decade of increasing resource shortages and capital stringency, Soviet planners will likely follow a development strategy that concentrates on the crash development of energy and material supplies indispensable to the economic and military might of the Slavic core. This is all the more true since the primary resource of the Moslem periphery, namely labor, would be extremely difficult, costly, and even dangerous to marshal for projects that have priority for the leadership. Minor investment efforts, combined with control of any incipient discord (in which the leadership has practice, sophistication and reasonable confidence) will be in store for Central Asia for the next decade.

Geography is not destiny. I make no claim that with an imaginative leadership and radical economic reforms, especially if combined with foreign investment and some degree of participation in key projects, the powerful, stubborn constraints of the geographic dimension examined in this paper could not be loosened or even overcome. But aside from the fact that I perceive no such changes on the horizon, these issues are for others to analyze. I have taken the present structure and management of the Soviet economy as given. The performance, efficiency and prospects of that system I considered only insofar as these were inseparable from the spatial dimension. Assuming no fundamental changes in economic management and political relationship with the world at large over the next decade, I expect the contraints and forces of geographic space to channel development in the manner described and to act as a major brake on the rate of growth of the Soviet economy.

8: Notes

1 Industrial growth would have been slower still without the radical change in these regions' fuel supplies and chemical and synthetic raw-material base in the past two decades, particularly in the sixties. Efficient hydrocarbon fuels and feedstocks became available on a large scale, resulting in much modernization and improved labor productivity (Dienes, 1969). A general lack of hydrocarbons and, until recently, the total absence of natural gas from Kemerovo Oblast, were major factors in the particularly poor growth performance of industry in the Kuzbas.

2 Of the 700 large scientific institutes and universities, 140 or one-fifth are found in Moscow and Leningrad alone. These two cities, the Donets–Dnieper region and the Baltic republics concentrate over a third of the total. One-fourth of all Soviet scientific personnel and 35% of Doctors of Sciences work in the city of Moscow (Andrews, 1978, p. 446; Hoffman and Kamerling, 1979, pp. 436–9; Lappo *et al.*, 1976, p. 81).

3 Nevertheless, with questionable economic logic, some heavy-machinery exports also originated from East Siberia. Krasnoiarsk is claimed to be one of the main exporters of heavy cranes (North, 1980, p. 40).

4 Reliable output figures for major economic regions and republics for 1960 can be computed in 1955 prices from AN SSSR, 1967, p. 226. For some regions industrial-production personnel is from *Nar. khoz. SSSR v 1960 g.*, pp. 164–5 and 640–41. Breakdown in labor force, output and fixed capital for the Ukraine can be computed from 1962 ratios from Palamarchuk et al., 1966, p. 78. Percentage breakdown for most relevant oblasts of the RSFSR in the 1958–63 period is available from AN SSSR, Inst. geog., 1964, p. 166; Mints, 1960, p. 20; Khorev, 1964, p. 51; *Moskva. Razvitie khoziaistva . . .* , 1967, p. 47; *Moskva v tsifrakh . . .* , 1967, p. 57.

5 Outside these cities, the overwhelming share of industrial production was made up of the traditional and technologically "weak" group of food, textiles and wood processing (Bukhalo, ed., 1965, passim; AN URRS, 1970, pp. 18–21; Voloboi and Popovkin, 1972, pp. 226–7; Kazlouskaia, 1968, p. 48; *Stat. ezhegodnik Belorusskoi SSR*, 1973, pp. 47, 54–62; Granik, ed., 1967, pp. 39, 114, 198; Gorovoi and Privalovskaia, 1966, p. 64; Frolov, ed., 1972, p. 83).

6 Per capita electricity consumption in Belorussia and the Southwest Economic Region reached less than one-third of the Soviet average in 1960, while in Moldavia and a number of oblasts in the Western Ukraine it came to less than one-fifth. Such low consumption levels were unequaled even in Moslem Central Asia (Palamarchuk *et al.*, 1966, p. 78; Neporozhnii, ed., 1972).

7 The share of engineering products, durables, and chemicals greatly expanded and the preponderance of food and light industries lessened (see columns 3–4 and 7 in Table 8.6; Borodina et al, 1978, pp. 11–17; Kotyk and Bondarev, 1976, pp. 34–9). Such a change, however, is somewhat deceptive, since both the engineering and chemical industries represent very varied groups. Many of their branches established in these provinces represent traditional outdated manufacturing that have long ceased to be technologically advanced even in the Soviet Union.

8 Already by 1975, over 30% of the Soligorsk potassium output was exported, primarily to Poland and Hungary (Borodina *et al.*, 1978, p. 52; Shabad, 1979b, pp. 247–8); the volume of export has increased appreciably since. By 1980, Poland had planned to satisfy about two-thirds of its potassium consumption from Soviet imports, overwhelmingly from Soligorsk, Belorussia. Polish credit for the project totals 70 million rubles (Ptashek, 1974, pp. 130–31).

9 The Mazeikiai, Lithuania, refinery has been designed specifically for the East

European, particularly the Polish market, with Polish workers laying a pipeline from Novopolotsk to Mazeikiai (Shabad, 1979b, p. 235). At the Novopolotsk refinery an ethylene shop was set up with East German assistance under a compensatory agreement (North, 1979, p. 26).

10 Through the recently completed Vinnytsa-Albertirsa (Hungary) 750 kv high-tension line the Soviet Union guaranteed the delivery of an *additional* 1200 MW of power, half of that to Hungary. With the supplementary saving from peak exchange, this will enable Eastern Europe to forgo 1500 MW of new capacity. With 66.6% availability, the new 1200 MW delivery capacity is equivalent to an *incremental* 7 billion KWH. Soviet export of power in 1978 amounted to 12 billion KWH. (Szili, 1979, p. 396; *Vneshniaia torgovlia SSSR v 1979 g.*, pp. 61–2). The USSR also agreed to the construction of two new 4000 MW nuclear stations in the Western Ukraine jointly with East European states. The first to be started at Khmelnitskii, at an estimated cost of 1.5 billion transferable rubles, will be 50% financed by Poland, Czechoslovakia and Hungary (Bajbakov, 1978, p. 1197; DIW, *Wochenbericht* 35: 365, 1979).

11 Kalush, in the Western Ukraine, furnished almost half of all increment in vinyl-plastic output during the 9th Five-Year Plan (Shabad, "News Notes", March 1975, p. 198). Only very close cooperation, initiated by the Hungarians, with the large ethylene project at Leninváros made the location in that peripheral region of high energy costs viable (North, 1980, pp. 25–6). The cooperation involves an ethylene pipeline between the two centers and the exchange of intermediates and products.

12 According to North, this distinction is clearly made by Soviet writers. "Whereas extra growth of the *pogranichye* regional economies can readily be seen, the *prigranichnye raiony* often remain little more developed than they were when border locations were basically unattractive. In other words, relative location at this scale is not a major force. In addition, while individual republics can build up discretionary funds, on the oblast level such authority is entirely absent." (North, 1980, p. 51.)

13 The great number and frequency of *khutors* (individual farmsteads) in the Baltic republics distorts comparisons of this region with the rest of the USSR. In Latvia, where *khutors* are most numerous, 347,100 or almost nine-tenth of rural settlements had 10 or less inhabitants. However, the small size of the Baltic republics and their dense network of paved roads practically obviates the problem of inaccessibility for any segment of the population.

14 Though his brush may have been too broad, Hooson (1966, p. 247) seems to have been correct in writing about this Northwestern zone of the RSFSR some 15 years ago: "... it seems likely that its most distinctive function ... will be that of a partly fossilized shrine of Russia's heroic past."

15 The male rate of higher education for Georgians was 90% above that for Russians and 62% above that for Armenians in 1970, casting some doubt on the reliability of these figures. But it would be surprising if the flourishing "second economy," especially vigorous in the Caucasus, did not extend to the field of education. At any rate, according to émigré opinions, the purchasing of diplomas here is quite widespread.

16 The low average-output-to-fixed-capital ratios in two of the Transcaucasian republics in 1972 (Table 8.2) reflect the legacy of the historic dominance of petroleum production in Azerbaidzhan, now in sharp decline, and the unfortunate Sevan project built in the 1950s and early 1960s that saddled Armenia with a white elephant for many years to come. In 1972, the fuel industries still accounted for 45% of Azerbaidzhan's industrial fixed assets (Gillula, 1981, Tables B2–B3). In Armenia, the threatening drop in the level of Lake Sevan led to the complete revision of the project *after* the bulk of hydrocapacity was completed. "Electrical output ... was cut back sharply, as the flow through the dams was limited solely to irrigation needs" (Shabad, "News Notes", March 1977, p. 207).

17 In January 1974, 48 cities — excluding the three capitals — had over 15000 people. The 1970 census listed 131 cities, 39 of which — excluding the three capitals — were over 20,000 and 18 exceeded 10,000 in 1970 (*USSR. Administrativno-territorial'nye delenia* ..., 1974, pp. 636–50; *Itogi* ..., vol. 1, p. 112).

18 These are also badly concentrated geographically, especially in Azerbaidzhan. 86% of the sewage network in the latter republic is located in Baku, Kirovabad and Sumgait. Similarly, slightly over half of all everyday services and repair services (*bytovye uslugi*) is found on the Apsheron peninsula on which Baku is located (Abramov, 1977, pp. 135 and 186).

19 Another source, however, claims a much higher index for 1971 (Avdeichev *et al.*, 1976, p. 135).

20 Among the nationalities of this area the Kazakhs have gone farthest in limiting the size of their families. Yet birthrates in Kazakhstan actually rose from 23.4 per 1000 in 1970 to 24.4 per 1000 in 1978. In addition, the republic contains almost 6 million Russians of low fertility (41% of its total population), most of whom reside in the Northern half of the republic where the native population comprises only a rather small minority. Between 1970 and 1979, the Kazakh population increased by almost 24%, or 2.4% per annum. Assuming that the death rate among them is no higher today than among the population of Kazakhstan as a whole, birth rates must exceed 25 per 1000 even among the Kazakhs (*Nar. khoz. SSSR v 1978 g.*, p. 27; Sheehy, 1980 a, pp. 10 and 13).

21 In Uzbekistan, the most advanced and by far the most populous of all the Central Asian republics, less than one-third of the labor force in light industry consisted of indigenous ethnic groups during the mid 1970s. Yet the 1979 census lists the share of indigenous Moslem groups in the population as over 80%. Large textile *kombinaty* in Tashkent, Fergana, Askhabad and Dushanbe employed the local nationalities for only 9% to 16% of their total labor force. In more-skill-demanding occupations the participation of native groups must surely be lower still (Afanas'evskii, 1976, p. 216).

22 Products of the food industries comprised almost a fifth of all interregional imports into Central Asia in 1972, while this group represented only a negligible portion of exports (Popadiuk, 1979, p. 61).

23 In gross output, Uzbekistan accounted for 59% and Kirgizia for 16% of all Central Asian industry in the early 1970s (Table 8.2). Their respective shares in net output, i.e. value added, were estimated as 61 and 17% (Zakumbaev, 1975, p. 65).

24 Although the warm climate reduces construction costs slightly, this is more than counterbalanced by adverse factors such as seismic characteristics and the relatively underdeveloped state of construction organizations. For the 1972/73 revaluation of fixed capital *Gosstroi* (State Committee for Construction) used coefficients of 1.07–1.10 for Central Asia but apparently this applied to fixed capital already in place (Gillula, 1981, p. 19).

25 In the low-flow years of 1970–73, almost 79% of the surface flow to the Aral Sea was withdrawn, while only one-third of it was returned. The diminution of the basin discharge, therefore, ranged around 50%. By 1980, total withdrawals from the Amu and Syr Daria, the two rivers supplying nearly all the water to the Aral Sea, could reach 97% of their surface flow, of which consumptive use would be 64% (Micklin, 1978, p. 16). Some of the smaller rivers of Central Asia are even more heavily affected. In the region as a whole, three-fourths of all water consumed is for irrigation and, according to Soviet experts, "if more water is not available by the 1990s further development will cease." (Gustafson, 1980, p. 1343). Improper practices, exacerbating soil salinity, are a pervasive problem, resulting in land abandonment, which in some periods equalled the area of newly irrigated land (Micklin, 1978, p. 15).

26 Between 1960 and 1970 the growth rates of gross agricultural output in Uzbekistan exceeded that of net output by almost the same margin as in the USSR as a whole. After 1970 the difference between the two growth rates in Uzbekistan was much greater, indicating escalating costs (Popadiuk, 1979, pp. 48–9). And the 1970–76 period included two years of very poor harvests that depressed net output for the USSR much more than for Uzbekistan without affecting costs. During that period, the rate of increase in the delivery of fertilizers was much slower in Central Asia than in the USSR (or the RSFSR and the Ukraine), which therefore cannot be responsible for the more rapid rise in costs in Uzbekistan (*Nar. khoz. SSSR za 60 let*, 1978, p. 327).

27 A 1973 source claims that 5 million workers need to be drawn into production in Uzbekistan alone, "and therefore almost 10 million in Central Asia – Southern Kazakhstan as a whole," in order to maintain the (then prevailing) labor-force-participation rate of 44–5% (Feshbach, 1979, p. 666).

28 Burg's (1979, p. 82) conclusions that the Central Asian problems and the Soviet leadership's attempts to solve them present the political leadership of the West with a remarkable opportunity to influence the course of Soviet domestic and foreign policy, even to the extent of linking "the provision of Western capital with the reduction of military expenditure" certainly appear dubious.

29 Altogether per capita consumption allocation from the state budget is about 70% of the RSFSR average, although private consumption lags by only 5% (Legkostup *et al.*, 1979, p. 10).

30 Average land value by economic regions reproduced in Kovalenko, 1972, p. 32.

31 Even the Bratsk complex, located in the more favorable cis-Baikal zone on the same latitude as Gor'kii and Riga, has managed to achieve self-sufficiency solely in potatoes and that only in good years (Tarasov, 1979, p. 53). The problem is complicated by the large number of newborns on the big construction projects lacking any agricultural base, more than 30,000 infants on the BAM (Baikal-Amur Mainline) alone since the mid 1970s (Kopach and Novoselov, 1979, p. 76).

32 Regional figures for new fixed assets are available only without those put on line by collective farms, but these are of small importance in Siberia. Shares in capital investment, therefore, were also computed without the contributions by collective farms (*Nar. khoz. SSSR v 1970 g.*, pp. 471–8; *Nar. khoz. SSSR v 1975 g.*, pp. 495–502; *Nar. khoz. RSFSR v 1970 g.*, pp. 313–20; *Nar. khoz. RSFSR v 1975 g.*, pp. 318–29). Because of the exclusion of dry holes only about 81% of the oil and gas industries' fixed assets show up in the published statistics vs. 93% for industry as a whole.

33 Altogether more than 150 separate vertically managed organizations (branch ministries and departments) are today involved in the planning and management of the Soviet economy (Kazanskii, 1979, p. 11).

34 "Whereas in Surgut, for example, the 'underlings' of different ministries carefully kept apart from one another (geologists from petroleum engineers, they and others from power engineers, and so on), on the BAM this fragmentation can be observed on the industrial-association level, even among people subordinated to the same ministry. Take any of the settlements along the line and you will see 'subsettlement' within them: ... the construction and erection team, ... the engineering column, and over there somebody else again." (*Komsomolskaia pravda*, Jan. 18, 1977).

35 During the 9th Five-Year Plan, more than 5 billion rubles of capital investment and preparatory work was laid out in Siberia for basic construction that would begin only during the 10th Five-Year Plan (Aganbegian *et al.*, 1978, pp. 74 and 79).

36 Although in Table 8.6 the author was forced to lump chemicals with two unrelated industries, another source, dealing with only Siberia, indicates that chemicals and petrochemicals contribute only 6.7% to the region's industrial output or hardly more than in the country as a whole, and a mere 1.1% to that of the Far East (Aganbegian *et al.*, 1974, p. 38).

37 With a 10,000–15,000 labor force and 30,000–45,000 aggregate population requirement, large iron-and-steel and steel-intensive, heavy-equipment manufacturing plants would hardly find Siberia an attractive place (Evstigneev, 1976, pp. 318–19).

38 Even the limited blast-furnace capacity is partly fed by iron ore from outside Siberia, surely ironic for a region whose comparative advantage is in resources. Iron-ore pellets today are shipped to the Kuzbas from both Kazakhstan and the Kursk Magnetic Anomaly (KMA), south of Moscow. The KMA, in addition, already supplies more than a quarter of all ferrous-ore requirements of the Urals (*Sovietskaia Rossiia*, June 7, 1978; Shabad, "News ... ", April 1979, p. 270).

39 Between 1959 and 1970, population growth in Siberia remained well below the Soviet average, only marginally exceeding that for the RSFSR or the two other Slavic republics of the USSR. The small net migration gain of the Far East could not balance the heavy losses from East and, still more, from West Siberia (*Itogi ....*, 1970, vol. 1, pp. 10–21; Malinin and Ushakov, 1976, pp. 42–3). Since the 1970

census, population in the Trans-Ural RSFSR increased faster than the Soviet average and almost twice as fast as in the three Slavic republics. In the first three years of the 1970s the migration flow reversed itself, resulting in a substantial net migration gain for the Asiatic RSFSR during the rest of the decade (Shabad, "News . . .", Sept. 1979, pp. 441–2; Malinin and Ushakov, 1976, pp. 2–43).

40 A 1979 source clearly states that net outmigration from Altai Krai, Kemerovo and Chita Oblasts did not cease, while in Novosibirsk, Tomsk, Omsk and Sakhalin Oblasts and the Buriat ASSR the positive migration balance during the 1970s was insignificant (Mil'ner, 1979, p. 63).

41 According to a very recent source, for example, only 4000 of the 18,000 people at Novy Urengoi live in wooden buildings which are themselves poorly suited to the local climate. The rest stay in trailers and makeshift huts. Only one-third of the laundries and baths and only 13% of kindergarten accommodations required by the population is in existence (*Sotsialisticheskaia industriia*, Jan. 23, 1981, p. 2).

42 In the face of such expert opinion, extreme statements that eventually 2–3 million people will live and work in the North of Tiumen' Oblast' alone appear foolish (Fainburg, 1978, pp. 113–14).

43 A recent work, produced in Siberia, claims that a new 3,000–3,200 km.-long single-track railway could handle 80–85 million tons of extra coal if restricted entirely to solid fuels. It also admits that such heavy use would require the replacement of the rails in less than a decade (Popov, ed, 1978, pp. 206–07). All this coal would, of course, be equivalent to the calorific content of only 40 million tons of oil. A study by Gosplan arrives at the unequivocal conclusion that the long-distance rail shipment of Kansk-Achinsk and Ekibastuz coal is "irrational." Only Kuzbas coal should be considered transportable to the European USSR (Troitskii, 1979).

44 For railway improvements under way between the Urals and the Enisei, see CIA, March 1980, pp. 13–14.

45 In addition, gas pipelines are subject to more stringent quality requirements than oil pipelines, since they operate at increasingly high pressure.

46 Many breaks, noted in the Soviet press, occur at pressures as low as 20–50 atmospheres, while modern large-capacity lines operate at 75 atmospheres, and Soviet plans call for still higher pressures. The Tiumen' Oil and Gas Trust was, in fact, forced to establish an entire factory in the West Siberian Wilderness for the repair of defective pipes (Arzhanov, 1979, p. 30; *Oil and Gas Journal*, April 2, 1979, p. 42). Fewer than half of the compressor stations are generally installed at the time the gas pipelines are completed (*Gazovaia promyshlennost'*, No. 4, 1977, p. 5; *Oil and Gas Journal*, April 2, 1979, p. 42).

47 Still less can the already visible problems of labor supplies during the seventies be attributed to constriction on numbers. "Only since 1978/79 have the entry of 16-year-olds into the labor force and the annual net increment to the population of able-bodied ages begun to diminish. Moreover, per unit of GNP, the USSR uses from 1.3 times to 2.8 times as much labor as Italy, Japan, West Germany and the US." (Block, 1979, p. 131).

48 Planned growth rate refers to state investment which is to represent 88.2% of total investment (*Ekonomicheskaia gazeta*, No. 1, 1980, p. 2).

49 Table 8.4 shows that between 1966 and 1975 the investment share of Siberia and the Far East as a whole increased minimally, the very substantial rise for West Siberia being almost entirely counterbalanced by declines in the shares of East Siberia and the Far East. Since 1975, the Soviets have stopped to release investment data below the republic level, but figures show that allocations for the RSFSR have grown faster than for the USSR as a whole and still more than for the non-Russian republics combined (*Nar.khoz. SSSR v 1978 g.*, p. 338; *Nar. khoz. RSFSR v 1978 g.*, p. 183). Given the number of huge construction projects in the harsh environment of Siberia (10 of the 15 "territorial-production complexes" whose development is presently under way are in Siberia and the Far East), these Trans-Ural territories must be responsible for most of the above-average increase enjoyed by the RSFSR.

Still more indicative of the growing stress on Siberian resources in Soviet investment allocation is the crash program on fuel development approved by the

December 1977 CPS Plenum. In 1978, more than one-third of all increment in total investment went to the three primary-fuel industries, while the 1979 plan directs 85% of *all* new fixed investment in the Soviet economy to these same branches (CIA, Aug. 1979, p. 39). Given the geography of incremental fuel production in the USSR, the overwhelming share of that new capital is clearly funneled into the Trans-Ural territories, especially West Siberia.

50 For 1976, Treml (1980, p. 187) calculates the ratio of domestic to foreign-trade prices for Soviet commodity exports as 0.89, which—given the trend for the rest of the decade—corresponds closely to that implied by Aganbegian for 1979.

8: References

Abramov, M. A., *Proizvodstvo i sfera obsluzhivaniia*. Moscow: Mysl', 1977.

Adamesku, A. A., ed., *Zakavkazkii ekonomicheskii raion*. Moscow: Nauka, 1973.

Adamesku, A. A., and Belorusov, D. V., *Razvitie i razmeshchenie proizvoditel'nykh sil SSSR v Desiatoi Piatiletke*. Moscow: Mysl', 1977.

Afanas'evskii, E. A., *Legkaia promyshlennost': ekonomicheskie problemy razmeshcheniia*. Moscow: Mysl', 1976.

Aganbegian, A. G., ed., *Ekonomicheskie problemy razvitiia Sibiri*. Novosibirsk: Nauka, 1974.

Aganbegian, A. G., ed., *Razvitie narodnogo khoziaistva Sibiri*. Novosibirsk: Nauka, 1978.

Aganbegian, A. G., "Ekonomicheskie problemy razvitiia Sibiri." *Ekonomika i matematicheskie metody*, No. 5, 1979.

Altunin, E. G., "Strategiiu vybirat' segodnia." *Ekonomika i organizatsiia promyshlennogo proizvodstva*: 12–22, no. 2, 1979.

AN (Akademiia nauk) Kazakhskoi SSR, Institut ekonomiki, *Dolgosrochnoe prognozirovanie razvitiia otraslei narodnogo khoziaistva*. Alma-Ata: Nauka, 1976.

AN SSSR, Inst. ekon., *Promyshlennost v khoziaistvennom komplekse ekonomicheskikh raionov SSSR*. Moscow: Nauka, 1964.

AN SSSR, Institut geografii, *Severo-Zapad RSFSR*. Moscow: Mysl', 1964.

AN SSSR, Otdelenie ekonomiki, *Sovershenstvovanie planirovaniia i upravleniia narodnym khoziaistvom*. Moscow: Nauka, 1967.

AN SSSR and Gosplan SSSR, SOPS, *Regional'nye problemy ekonomicheskoi integratsii SSSR v systeme stran SEV*. Moscow: Nauka, 1975.

AN URSR, Rada po vyvchenniu produktivnikh sil Ukrains'koii RSR, *Rozmishchennia produktivnikh sil Ukrains'koii RSR*, Vipusk 9. Kiev: Naukova Dumka, 1970.

Andrews, Alice, "Spatial Patterns of Higher Education in the Soviet Union." *Soviet Geography: Rev. and Transl.*: 443–457, Sept. 1978.

Aparin, I. L., and Krinitskaia, M. E., *Industrial'naia baza stroitel'stva Severnoi zony*. Leningrad: Stroiizdat, 1979.

Arzhanov, F. G., "Vokrug burovoi." *Ekonomika i organizatsiia promyshlennogo proizvodstva*: 23–31, No. 2, 1979.

Avdeichev, L. A., ed., *Geografiia proizvoditel'nykh sil SSSR i mezhdunarodnoe ekonomicheskoe sotrudnichestvo*. Moscow: Mysl', 1976.

Baishev, S. B., ed., *Effektivnost' regional'noi ekonomiki Kazakhstana*. Alma-Ata: Nauka, 1977.

Bajbakov, N. K., "Hosszú távu célprogramok: új szakasz a KGST-országok szocialista gazdasági integrációjának fejlödésében." *Közgazdasági Szemle*: 1194–1200, no. 10, 1978.

Baldwin, Godfrey S., "Population Projections by Age and Sex: For the Republics and Major Economic Regions of the USSR, 1970–2000." Washington, DC: Bureau of the Census, Foreign Demographic Analysis Division, Series P–91, No. 26, 1979.

Belorusov, D. V., *et al.*, *Problemy razvitiia i razmeshcheniia proizvoditel'nykh sil Zapadnoi Sibiri*. Moscow: Mysl', 1976.

Beyers, B. Williams, "Contemporary Trends in the Regional Development of the United States," *Professional Geographer*: 34–44, no. 1, 1979.

Block, Herbert, "Soviet Economic Performance in a Global Context." In *Soviet Economy in a Time of Change*, Vol. 1, pp. 110–40; 1979.

Bokserman, Iu., "O novykh progressivnykh vidakh transporta." Planovoe khoziaistvo: p. 19, No. 11, 1978.

Bond, Andrew R., and Lydolph, E. Paul, "Soviet Population Change and City Growth, 1970–79: A Preliminary Report." *Soviet Geography: Rev. and Transl.*: 461–88, Oct. 1979.

Borodina, V. A., et al., eds., *Razvitie otraslei narodnogo khoziaistva Belorussii*. Minsk: Vysshaia Shkola, 1978.

Bukhalo, S. M., ed., *Ekonomichni raioni URSR*. Kiev: Naukova Dumka, 1965.

Burg, Steven L., "Soviet Policy and the Central Asian Problem." *Survey*: 61–82, Summer 1979.

Bush, Keith, "Soviet Economic Growth Slows." *Radio Liberty Research*: 1–11, Nov. 16, 1979.

CIA, *The World Oil Market in the Years Ahead*. ER 79–10327U, Aug. 1979.

CIA, *USSR: Coal Industry, Problems and Prospects*. ER 80–10154, March 1980.

Danilova, A. D., et al., eds., *Ekonomicheskaia geografiia SSSR*. Moscow: Vysshaia shkola, 1976

Dienes, Leslie, "Locational Factors and Locational Developments in the Soviet Chemical Industry." University of Chicago, Dep. of Geography, Research Paper No. 119, 1969.

Dienes, Leslie, "Investment Priorities in Soviet Regions." *Assn. of Amer. Geographers, Annals*: 437–54, Sept. 1972.

Dienes, Leslie, "Basic Industries and Regional Economic Growth: The Soviet South." *Tijdschrift voor Economische en Sociale Geografie*: 2–15, No. 1, 1977.

Dienes, Leslie, "The Regional Dimension of Soviet Energy Policy." Discussion Paper No. 13, Assn. of Amer. Geographers, Project on Natural Resources in the World Economy. Department of Geography, Syracuse University, August 1979.

Dienes, Leslie, and Shabad, Theodore, *The Soviet Energy System: Resource Use and Policies*. Washington, DC: Winston; distr. by Wiley, New York, 1979.

Divilov, S., *Chislennost i strucktura zaniatykh v narodnom khoziaistve*. Moscow: Ekonomika, 1976.

DIW (Deutsches Institut fuer Wirtschaftsforschung), *Wochenbericht* **35**, Aug. 30, 1979.

Dogaev, Iu. M., *Ekonomika nauchno-tekhnicheskogo progressa*. Moscow: Nauka, 1975.

Dubinskii, P. K., *Analiz raboty zheleznodorozhnogo transporta ugol'noi promyshlen-nosti v deviatoi piatiletke*. Moscow: Ministerstvo ugol'noi promyshlennosti SSSR, TsNEI ugol', 1977.

Edwards, Imogene, *et al.*, "US and USSR: Comparisons of GNP." In *Soviet Economy in a Time of Change*, pp. 369–401; 1979.

Evstigneev, Viktor P., *Effektivnost' razmeshcheniia mashinostroeniia v vostochnykh i zapadnykh raionakh SSSR*. Moscow: Nauka, 1972.

Evstigneev, Viktor P., "The Location of Metal-Intensive and Labor-Intensive Industries in the Eastern Regions." *Soviet Geography: Rev. and Transl.*: 314–24, May 1976.

Fainburg, Z. I., in Round Table Conference on comprehensive development of West Siberia. *Planovoe khoziaistvo*: 97–114, Nov. 9, 1978.

Feshbach, Murray, "Prospects for Outmigration from Central Asia and Kazakhstan in the Next Decade." In *Soviet Economy in a Time of Change*, Vol. 1, pp. 656–709; 1979.

Frolov, N. P., ed., *Razvitie i razmeshchenie proizvoditel'nykh sil Moldavskoi SSR*. Moscow: Nauka, 1972.

Furman, I. Ia., *Ekonomika magistral'nogo transporta gaza*. Moscow: Nedra, 1978.

Gillula, James W., "The Economic Interdependence of Soviet Republics." In *Soviet Economy in a Time of Change*, pp. 618–55; 1979.

Gillula, James W., "The Regional Distribution of Fixed Capital in the USSR." Foreign Econ. Report No. 17. Washington: US Bureau of the Census, Foreign Demographic Analysis Division, March 1981.

Gladyshev, A. N., et al., *Problemy razvitiia i razmeshcheniia proizvoditel'nykh sil Dal'nego Vostoka*. Moscow: Mysl', 1974.

Gorovoi, V. A., and Privalovskaia, G. A., *Geografiia lesnoi promyshlennosti SSSR*. Moscow: Nauka, 1966.

Gramoteeva, L. I., *Effektionost'territorial'noi organizatsii proizvodstva*. Moscow: Mysl', 1979.

Granberg, A. G., "Sibir' v narodnokhoziaistvennom komplekse." *Ekonomika i organizatsiia promyshlennogo proizvodstva*: 84–106, no. 4, 1980.

Granik, G. I., ed., *Severo-Zapadnyi ekonomicheskii raion*. Moscow: Nauka, 1967.

Gustafson, Thane, "Technology Assessment, Soviet Style." *Science*: 1343–1348, June 20, 1980.

Guzhnovskii, L. P., "Sibirskii vklad v neftianoe mogushchestvo strany." *Ekonomika i organizatsiia promyshlennogo proizvodstva*: 35–43, No. 6, 1977.

Harris, Chauncy D., *Cities of the Soviet Union: Studies in Their Functions, Size, Density and Growth*. Chicago: Rand McNally, 1970.

Hodnett, Grey, "Technology and Social Change in Soviet Central Asia: The Politics of Cotton Growing." In Henry W. Morton and R. L. Tökes, eds, *Soviet Politics and Society in the 1970's*. New York: Free Press, 1974.

Hoffman, Phillip, and Kamerling, David S., "Comparative Geography of Higher Education in the United States and the USSR: An Initial Investigation." *Soviet Geography: Rev. and Transl.*: 412–39, Sept. 1979.

Hooson, David J. M., *The Soviet Union: People and Regions*. Belmont, Calif.: Wadsworth, 1966.

Hooson, David, "The Outlook for Regional Development in the Soviet Union." *Slavic Rev.*: 535–54, Sept. 1972.

Itogi vsesoiuznoi perepisi naseleniia 1970 goda. Tsentral'noe statisticheskoe upravlenie SSR. Moscow: Statistika, 1972–4.

Ivanchenko, A. A., *Metodologicheskieosnovy sotsial'no-ekonomicheskogo razvitiia regionov SSR*. Moscow: Nauka, 1979.

Kazanskii, N. N., "Intensifikatsiia proizvodstva i problemy sovershenstvovaniia territorial' noi organizatsii proizvoditel'nykh sil." *Akademiia nauk SSSR, Izvestiia, Seriia geograficheskaia*, No. 2, 1979.

Kazlouskaia, L. V., " Za gady Savetskai ulady." *Vestsi Akademi navuk BSSR, Seriia gramadskikh navuk:* 43–51, No. 5, 1968.

Khaitun, A. D., "Mezhregional' noe ispol'zovanie turdovykh resursov," *Voprosy ekonomiki*: 48, no. 8, 1979.

Khikmatov, A. Kh., et al., *Problemy povysheniia effektivnosti kapital'nykh vlozhenii v Uzbekskoi SSR*. Tashkent: Fan, 1978.

Khorev, V. S., *Volgo-Viatskii raion*. Moscow: Prosveshchenie, 1964.

Kobakhidze, E. D., *Promyshlenno-territorial'nye sistemy soiuznykh respublik*. Tbilisi: Metsniereba, 1979.

Kopach, N., and Novoselov, Iu., "Razvitie sel'skogo khoziaistva Sibiri." *Voprosy ekonomiki*: 75–84, No. 8, 1979.

Koropeckyj, I. S., "Industrial Location Policy in the USSR During the Postwar Period." In *Economic Performance and the Military Burden in the Soviet Union*, pp. 232–95. Papers, Joint Econ. Comm., US Congress. Washington, DC: Govt. Printing Off., 1970.

Kotyk, E. N., and Bondarev, P. P., *Problemy sovershenstvovaniia territorial'noi organizatsii mashinostroeniia*. L'vov: Vyshcha Shkola, 1976.

Kovalenko, Iu. N., *Tekhniko-ekonomicheskie i sotsial'nye problemy razmeshcheniia promyshlennykh predpriiatii*. Kiev: Budivel'nyk, 1972.

Lappo, G., et al., *Moscow – Capital of the Soviet Union*. Moscow: Progress Publ., 1976.

Legkostup, L. I., et al., "Ispol'zovanie mezhotraslevykh balansov v analize vosproiz- vodstvennykh proportsii ekonomiki Sibiri." *Akademiia nauk, Sibirskoe otdelenie, Izvestiia*, Seriia Obshchestvennykh nauk: 3–11, No. 11, 1979.

Lewis, Robert A., Rowland, R. H., and Clem, R. S., *Nationality and Population Change in Russia and the USSR*. New York: Praeger, 1976.

Litovka, O. P., *Problemy prostranstvennogo razvitiia urbanizatsii*. Leningrad, Nauka, 1976.

Lydolph, Paul E., *Geography of the USSR. Topical Analysis*. Elkhart Lake, Wisconsin: Misty Valley Publ., 1979.

Malinin, E. D., and Ushakov, A. K., *Naselenie Sibiri*. Moscow: Statistika, 1976.

Mavrin, I. F., "Iz tsekha-v pole, s polia – v tsekh." *Ekonomika i organizatsiia promyshlennogo* proizvodstva: 65–74, No. 2, 1978.

Micklin, Philip P., "Irrigation Development in the USSR During the 10th Five Year Plan." *Soviet Geography: Rev. and Transl.*: 1–24, Jan. 1978.

Miller, Elisa B., "The Trans-Siberian Land Bridge, New Trade Route Between Japan and Europe." *Soviet Geography: Rev. and Transl.*: 223–43, April 1978.

Mil'ner, G., "Problemy obespechennosti resursami raionov Sibiri i Dal'nego Vostoka." *Ekonomicheskie nauki*: 61–8, No. 2, 1979.

Mints, A. A., "Nekotorye voprosy geografii promyshlennosti Moskovskoi oblasti." *Voprosy geografii*: 16–26, No. 49, 1960.

Moskva. *Razvitie khoziaistva.* Moscow: Statistika, 1967.

Moskva v tsifrakh za gody Sovetskoi vlasti. Statisticheskoe upravlenie goroda Moskvy. Moscow: Statistika, 1967.

Moskva v tsifrakh, 1978. Statisticheskoe upravlenie goroda Moskvy. Moscow: Statistika, 1978.

Mote, Victor, "Environmental Constraints to the Economic Development of Siberia." Vol. 1. Discussion Paper No. 6, Assn. of Amer. Geographers Project on Soviet Natural Resources in the World Economy. Syracuse University, 1978.

Mote, Victor, "The Baikal–Amur Mainline and Its Implication for the Pacific Basin." Discussion Paper No. 22, Assn. of Amer. Geographers Project on Soviet Natural Resources in the World Economy. Syracuse University, 1978.

Mun'ko, N. P., *Ekonomicheskaia effektivnost' vyravnivaniia energopotrebleniia v Srednei Azii.* Tashkent: Fan, 1977.

Nar. khoz., see TsSU.

Nekrasov, N. N., "General'naia skhema i zhizn'." *Ekonomika i organizatsiia promyshlennogo proizvodstva*: 42–63, No. 4, 1979.

Neporozhnyi, P. S., ed., *Razvitie elektroenergetiki soiuznykh respublik.* Moscow: Energiia, 1972.

Nikol'skii, "The Role of Economic Sectors in the Formation of Regional Production Complexes." *Soviet Geography: Rev. and Transl.*: 16–26, Jan. 1972.

North, Robert N., "The Development of Soviet Asia." *Current History*; 123–7 and 136–8, Oct. 1977.

North, Robert N., *Transport in Western Siberia: Tsarist and Soviet Development.* Vancouver: Univ. of British Columbia Press, and Center for Transportation Studies, 1979.

North, Robert N., "The Impact of Recent Trends in Soviet Foreign Trade on Regional Development in the USSR." Discussion Paper No. 21, Assn. of Amer. Geographers Project on Soviet Natural Resources in the World Economy. Syracuse University, 1980.

Palamarchuk, N. M., *et al.*, "Rivni ekonomichnogo rozvitku raioniv URSR i osnovni napriami ikh zblizhennia." In Akademiia nauk URSR, Sektor heografii and heohrafichne tovaristvo URSR, *Suchasni problemi heografichnoi nauki v URSR*, pp. 77–81. Kiev: Naukova Dumka, 1966.

Popadiuk, K., *Obshchestvennyi produkt i effektinost'ego proizvodstva v period razvitogo sotsializma.* Tashkent: "Uzbekistan," 1979.

Popov, V. E., ed., *Toplivno-energetichkii kompleks Sibiri.* Novosibirsk: Nauka, 1978.

Promyshlennost' SSSR. Tsentral'noe statisticheskoe upravlenie SSSR. Moscow: Statistika, 1964.

Ptashek, Ian, *Pol'sha – SSSR. Ekonomika Sotrudnichestvo.* Moscow: Progress, 1974.

Rees, John, "Technological Change and Regional Shifts in American Manufacturing." *The Professional Geographer*: 45–54, Feb. 1979.

Richardson, Harry W., *Regional Economics.* London: Weidenfeld & Nicolson, 1969.

Rybakovskii, L. L., *Territorial'nye osobennosti narodonaseleniia RSFSR.* Moscow: Statistika, 1976.

Ryl'skii, V. A., *et al.*, eds, *Elektroenergeticheskaia baza ekonomicheskikh raionov SSSR.* Moscow: Nauka, 1974.

Schroeder, Gertrude E., "Soviet Regional Development Policies in Perspective." In NATO, *The USSR in the 1980's*, pp. 25–40. Brussels: NATO Directorate for Econ. Affairs, 1978.

Shabad, Theodore, and Mote, Victor L., *Gateway to Siberian Resources (The BAM)*. Washington: Scripta Publ. Co; distr. by Wiley, New York, 1977.

Shabad, Theodore, "News Notes." *Soviet Geography: Rev. and Transl.*: Various Issues. Noted by month and year.

Shabad, Theodore, "Some Aspects of Central Asian Manpower and Urbanization." *Soviet Geography: Rev. and Transl.*: 113–23, Feb. 1979a.

Shabad, Theodore, "Soviet Regional Policy and CMEA Integration." *Soviet Geography: Rev. and Transl*: 230–54, April 1979b.

Shanina, V. A., *Transportno-ekonomicheskie sviazi stran-chlenov SEV*. Moscow: Nauka, 1978.

Sheehy, Ann, "Overall Industrial Plan Results for the Union Republics in 1978." *Radio Liberty Research*, Jan. 26, 1979.

Sheehy, Ann, "The National Composition of the Population of the USSR According to the Census of 1979." *Radio Liberty Research*, March 27, 1980 and April 8, 1980.

Shelest, V. A., *Regional'nye energo-ekonomicheskie problemy SSR*. Moscow: Nauka, 1975.

Silaev, E. D., "Problemy razmeshcheniia proizvodstva i ispol'zovaniia trudovykh resursov v Zakavkazskom ekonomicheskom raione." In Gosplan SSSR, *Razvitie i razmeshchenie proizvoditel'nykh sil ekonomicheskikh raionov SSSR, pp. 219–33*. Moscow: Nauka, 1967.

Soviet Economy in a Time of Change. Papers, Joint Econ. Comm., US Congress. Washington, DC: Govt. Printing Office, 1979.

Statisticheskii ezhegodnik Belorusskoi SSR. Minsk: Belarus', 1973.

Sternlieb, George, and Hughes, G. W., *Revitalizing the Northeast*. New Brunswick, N.J.: Rutgers Univ., Center for Urban Policy Research, 1978.

Szili Géza, "Villamosenergia-iparunk szovjet kapcsolatainak föbb eredményei." *Energia és Atomitechnika*: 395–8, No. 9, 1979.

Tarasov, V. A., "Bratsk, Stolitsa TPK." *Ekonomika i organizatsiia promyshlennogo proizvodstva: 48–58, No. 5, 1979.*

Telepko, L. N., *Urovni ekonomicheskogo razvitiia raionov SSSR*. Moscow: Ekonomika, 1971.

Transport i sviaz' SSSR. Tsentral'noe statisticheskoe upravlenie. Moscow: Statistika, 1972.

Treml, Vladimir G., "Foreign Trade and the Soviet Economy: Changing Parameters and Inter-relations." In Egon Neuberger and L. D. Tyson, eds, *The Impact of International Economic Disturbances on the Soviet Union and East Europe*, pp. 184–207. New York: Pergamon, 1980.

Troitskii, "Elektroenergetika: Problemy i perspektivy." *Planovoe khoziaistvo*: 13–25, No. 2, 1979.

TsSU-RSFSR (Tsentral'noe statisticheskoe upravlenie), *Narodnoe khoziaistvo RSFSR*. Moscow: Statistika. Annual.

TsSU-SSSR, *Narodnoe khoziaistvo SSSR*. Moscow: Statistika. Annual.

TsSU-USSR, *Narodnoe khoziaistvo Ukrainskoi SSR*. Kiev: Tekhnika. Annual.

Ukrainskaia SSR v tsifrakh v 1975 godu. Tsentral'noe statisticheskoe upravlenie Ukrainskoi SSR. Kiev: Tekhnika, 1976.

USSR. Administrativno — territorial'nye delenia. Moscow: Izvestiia sovetov deputatov trudiashchikhsia SSSR, 1974.

Valentei, D. I., ed., *Nechernozem'e: Demograficheskie protsessy*. Moscow: Statistika, 1977.

Vitebskii, R., "Regional'nye razlichiia v zatratakh na infrastrukturu." *Voprosy ekonomiki*: 44–53, No. 9, 1978.

Vneshniaia torgovlia SSSR v 19. . g. Ministerstvo vneshnei torgovli. Moscow: Statistika. Annual.

Voloboi, P. V., and Popovkin, V. A., *Problemi territorial'noi spetsializatsii i kompleksnogo rozvitku narodnogo gospodarstva Ukrains'koi RSR*. Kiev: Naukova Dumka, 1972.

Weinstein, Bernard L. and Firestine, Robert E., *Regional Growth and Decline in the United States*. New York: Praeger, 1978.

Wimbush, Enders S., and Ponomareff, Dmitry, "Alternatives for Mobilizing Soviet Central Asian Labor: Outmigration and Regional Development." Santa Monica: RAND R-2476-AF, 1979.

Zaitsev, I. F., "Regional'nye problemy razvitiia vheshneekonomicheskikh sviazei SSSR." In AN SSSR and Gosplan SSSR, SOPS, (Sovet po izucheniiu proizvoditel'nykh sil) *Metodologicheskie problemy sotsial'no-ekonomicheskogo razvitiia regionov SSSR*. Moscow: Nauka, 1979.

Zakumbaev, A. K., *Metody otsenki urovnia ekonomicheskogo razvitiia soiuznykh respublik i raionov*. Alma-Ata: Nauka, 1975.

Zakumbaev, A. K., *Ekonomicheskoe razvitie soiuznykh respublik i raionov*. Alma-Ata: Nauka, 1977.

Zamkov, O. K., and Valeshko, G. I., "Otsenka zemel'po osnovnym zemledel'cheskim zonam i raionam SSSR." In *Voprosy geografii, No. 99: Perspektivy sel'skokhoziaistvennogo ispolzovaniia zemel'nykh resursov*, pp. 41–63. Moscow: Mysl', 1975.

Zemel'nyi Kadastr SSSR, 1967.

9

Foreign Economic Relations

ED. A. HEWETT

Introduction: An Overview

This paper ventures an assessment of how the institutions that operate in the foreign sector of the Soviet economy will evolve over the next two decades; and how that evolution, combined with other important factors, will affect performance in that sector.[1] The uncertainties attendant on such an undertaking are enormous, and quite humbling. There are vast areas in which educated guessing is the only possible way to proceed. In such circumstances all one can do is state his assumptions alongside his predictions.

Any assessment of the future must be based primarily on the past, and Section 7 of this paper discusses the past of the Soviet foreign sector in some detail. The most important fact that emerges is that the performance of the Soviet foreign sector over the last two decades has been rather good overall. The share of national income devoted to foreign trade had risen considerably, and simultaneously the balances of trade and payments have been quite satisfactory. Consequently, while it is no doubt accurate for many Western economists (including myself) to characterize the institutions that manage Soviet foreign transactions as cumbersome, antiquated, and prone to discourage trade, it is equally true that, while the Soviet Union relied on those institutions over the last several decades, its foreign sector turned in a quite credible performance. Any conclusion that the 1980s might differ from the 1970s will have to show either that the institutions will prove to be more dysfunctional in the 1980s than ever before, or that other factors will serve to create less favorable circumstances for Soviet foreign trade in the 1980s.

The latter part of Section 1 addresses part of this issue by showing how a portion of the good performance of the Soviet foreign sector was a result of sheer luck as the world economic crises in the 1970s brought windfall gains for the Soviet economy. Relative prices increased for fuels and primary products, the traditional mainstays of Soviet convertible-currency exports. Gold-price increases revalued the Soviet gold stock. The enormous dollar flows into OPEC treasuries provided the Soviet Union with convertible-currency markets for military goods. Had the 1970s been like the 1960s, what would then have been the performance in the Soviet foreign sector? More important, if the 1980s are more like the 1960s than the 1970s, what will that mean for the Soviet economy, and its foreign sector?

If indeed the windfall gains to the Soviet economy in the 1970s do not repeat themselves in the 1980s, then the most feasible path towards sustaining high levels of export, hence import, growth will be through manufactured goods. And here the institutions that link the foreign and domestic sectors in the Soviet Union do play a crucial role. The institutions seem to be quite capable of handling the production and export of primary products, but they work very poorly for sophisticated manufactures. Section 2 discusses why this is the case, outlining what is known, or can be guessed, about how institutions operate in the Soviet foreign sector. While there have been no major changes of substance in these institutions in a very long time, there have been minor changes of form; and, more importantly, the pressures for rather fundamental changes seem to be growing. This section discusses those pressures, and how they relate to Soviet leaders' concerns about the Soviet foreign sector's performance.

The prospects for the Soviet foreign sector's economic performance over the next two decades are inextricably intertwined with the institutions in that sector and in the domestic economy, and with the performance of the economy. Section 3 explores these interconnections, and develops a scenario for the interaction of economic performance and the evolution of institutions in the Soviet foreign sector to the year 2000.

9.1 Economic Performance in the Soviet Foreign Sector: 1960–80

This section discusses the record of economic performance in the Soviet foreign sector since 1960. It begins with an overall view of trends in the quantities and prices of total trade, trade by major groups of trade partners, and trade by commodity group. Soviet foreign-trade statistics are the basic source here, those being generally recognized as the most comprehensive and reliable indicators of Soviet trade in civilian commodities (Gullo, 1979).

A second subsection discusses convertible-currency trade, balance of payments, and debt, focussing in particular on the major sources of convertible-currency earnings: primary products, military goods, services, and gold. Much of the data in this part comes from Western sources since the USSR does not publish information on total convertible-currency trade and debt.

A third subsection discusses the windfall gains that have accrued to the USSR in the 1970s as a result of substantial increases in gold prices, and improvements in its terms of trade.

Soviet Foreign Trade, and Terms of Trade, 1960–78

(a) *Real Trade Flows, Total, and by Country Groups.* The price changes in the world economy in the 1970s have had different effects on the valuation of Soviet trade flows with Western countries and trade flows with CMEA and other socialist countries. It is therefore important to work with quantity indices and price indices separately in order to ascertain which of the apparent changes in the geographic and commodity composition of trade are a consequence of price changes, and which represent changes in real trade flows.

Table 9.1 summarizes changes in the volume of Soviet exports to, and imports from, the world, all socialist countries, the subset of those which are members of CMEA, and the remaining countries, which are all called "capitalist" in Soviet terminology.[2] Soviet data on the value of exports and imports distinguish between developed and developing capitalist countries, but unfortunately there is only one quantity index published for all capitalist countries.

The "A" index for total trade, and the indices for trade with various country groups, are based on quantity indices published in the foreign-trade statistical yearbook, *Vneshniaia torgovlia: statisticheskii sbornik* (hereafter: VTSS, to distinguish it from the journal *Vneshniaia torgovlia*). The indices have different weights for different years; they have been linked together so that they approximate what would be obtained from pure Laspeyres quantity indices. Details are given in the Data Appendix.

In the 1970s the indices for total quantities appear to be inconsistent with the two underlying indices for trade with socialist and capitalist countries. This is most evident in 1971 where the "A" quantity index for total exports lies above the component indices for trade with socialist and capitalist countries, and the "A" index for total imports lies above the component indices. Neither of these can be a true average of the component index. For other years in the 1970s, no plausible socialist/capitalist weights would produce the index of total trade shown. As an alternative to the officially reported indices of total exports and imports, the "B" indices were computed, which represent a weighted average of the socialist and capitalist indices, and use 1970 trade values as the weights. These are almost identical to the "A" index in the 1960s, and the differences in the 1970s are relatively minor. There are a number of possible explanations for this apparent inconsistency among the quantity indices reported for Soviet trade, but these inconsistencies are minor enough that no attempt at reconciliation will be made here. Rather, the quantitative and unit-value trends will be discussed in terms of the "A" indices, and the "B" indices will only be mentioned when the results are significantly different.[3,4]

Table 9.1 also presents two measures of the growth rate of real national income, one the official Soviet index of real Marxian National Income (MNI), and the other the CIA index of real GNP. The real

Table 9.1 Quantity Indices for Soviet Foreign Trade, National Income, and Gross National Product: 1960–78 (1970 = 100)

Year	Exports					Imports					Marxian National Income	GNP
	Total		Soc. Ct.	CMEA	Cap. Ct.	Total		Soc. Ct.	CMEA	DCC's +LDC's		
	A	B				A	B					
1960	41	nd	nd	nd	nd	51	nd	nd	nd	nd	50	61
1961	44	nd	nd	nd	nd	52	nd	nd	nd	nd	54	64
1962	52	nd	nd	nd	nd	58	nd	nd	nd	nd	57	67
1963	54	54	54	54	53	64	67	71	67	52	59	67
1964	57	56	57	58	54	66	71	73	69	55	64	73
1965	62	62	61	62	64	70	69	77	73	59	69	77
1966	71	71	68	68	76	69	76	73	71	62	74	82
1967	77	78	74	73	84	75	85	83	81	64	81	86
1968	85	85	83	84	88	84	91	89	92	76	88	91
1969	94	94	89	90	104	90	94	92	94	89	92	93
1970	100	100	100	100	100	100	100	100	100	100	100	100
1971	106	103	104	104	101	104	106	106	105	106	106	104
1972	109	106	104	106	111	122	125	122	119	131	110	106
1973	124	121	112	114	138	140	143	130	127	168	120	114
1974	153	148	137	136	170	157	160	145	139	189	126	118
1975	157	154	139	151	181	186	190	159	163	246	132	120
1976	169	167	144	155	210	197	202	164	166	271	140	125
1977	185	183	156	167	233	201	206	179	182	254	146	130
1978	194	190	163	175	242	230	236	205	209	293	153	134

Sources: The quantity indices are close to Laspeyres, and discussed in the Data Appendix. The "A" variant of the indices for total imports and exports is taken directly from *Vneshniaia torgovlia*, (VTSS) as discussed in the appendix. As I discuss in the text, this index does not appear to be a true average of the socialist and capitalist indices. I have constructed the "B" variant as an alternative index. It is a weighted average of the socialist and capitalist indices, where the weights are the value of trade in 1970. The Marxian National Income series is from *Nar. khoz* (1978, p. 38), and the GNP series is from Block (1979, p. 135).

Definition of terms: "CMEA," or Council for Mutual Economic Assistance, includes Bulgaria, Czechoslovakia, East Germany, Hungary, Poland, Romania, Mongolia (since 1962), Cuba (since 1972), and Vietnam (since 1978). "Soc. Ct." includes the CMEA countries, and China, North Korea, North Vietnam (then Vietnam), and Laos (since 1978). "Cap. Ct." includes the remaining countries with which the USSR trades. "Nd" means no data are available.

Table 9.2 *Per Annum Growth Rates of Real Soviet Exports, Total, and by Area, 1960–78[a] (in percents)*

	1960–78[b]	1960–70[b]	1970–8
Exports			
Total			
"A" Variant	8.5	9.0	8.0
"B" Variant	8.3[d]	9.5[d]	8.0
Exports to Socialist Countries[c]	7.3	9.0	6.0
Exports to CMEA	7.7	8.9	6.9
Exports to Capitalist Countries[c]	9.9	10.5	11.1
Imports			
Total			
"A" Variant	8.3	6.4	9.6
"B" Variant	9.0[d]	6.3[d]	9.7
Imports from Socialist Countries[c]	7.0	4.9	7.7
Imports from CMEA	7.4	6.2	8.1
Imports from Capitalist Countries[c]	12.4	9.3	12.7
Marxian National Income	6.2	7.0	4.7
Gross National Product	4.4	5.0	3.3

Notes:
[a]These are growth rates given by the coefficient "b" in the regression Log $(X) = a + b$ (time) where:

X = quantity indices of exports and imports (see Table 1).

Time = 1 ... 19 for 1960–78, and so on.

It is possible that the 1960 (or 1963))–1978 growth rates will lie outside the intervals for the two sub-periods. For example the 1963–78 growth rate for exports to capitalist countries is lower than either of the two subperiods. This will occur if the growth rates at the boundary between the intervals differ markedly from the growth rates in each subperiod. For example in the case of exports to capitalist countries, the growth rates of exports are negative in 1970 and low in 1971, but high in the years before 1970 and after 1971. The 1963–70 subperiod regression tends to ignore the drop in 1970, emphasizing instead the high growth rates in all other years (the simple compound growth rate using only end points would be 9.5%, thus giving heavier weight to that last year). The 1970–8 regression picks up some of the effect of the very low starting point in 1970, giving a relatively high growth rate (the simple compound growth rate would have been even higher, 11.7%). The 1963–78 regression takes the 1970–71 slowdown into account, hence the lower growth rate.
[b]Beginning year is 1963 for the three country groups.
[c]For a list of countries in these categories, see "Definition of Terms" in Table 9.1.
[d]Beginning date is 1963.

GNP index grows more slowly due to different price weights and different coverage.

Table 9.2 summarizes these data in terms of growth rates obtained by regressing the log of the quantity indices on time. The growth rates are computed for the entire 1960 (or 1963)–1978 period, and for 1960 (or 1963) to 1970, and 1970 to 1978. Over the last two decades both exports and imports have grown much faster than either MNI or GNP. The per annum growth rate of exports is almost twice the per annum growth rate of GNP, and half again as large as the growth rate of MNI; the same is true for imports.

Throughout the 1960–78 period the growth rate of real trade with capitalist countries exceeded that of socialist countries, and even trade with CMEA. Unfortunately the Soviets only publish indices for trade with all capitalist countries, developed and developing, which intermingles different trends. For example, part of the rapid growth of exports to all capitalist countries comes from the dramatic increase in military-goods exports to LDCs in the 1970s; exports to developed capitalist countries have therefore surely grown somewhat slower than this total figure would suggest. Other potential data sources that treat developed countries or convertible-currency trade separately present too many difficulties to be used here.

The growth rates for the two subperiods show the dramatic differences lying behind the 1960 (1963)–1978 averages. During the 1960s the growth rate of imports was similar to the two national-income growth rates, although imports from capitalist countries were growing more rapidly at 9.3%. Exports during this period were growing at a respectable 9% per annum, while exports to capitalist countries were growing at an even more rapid pace of 10.5%.

During the 1970s the results of the Soviet leaders' decision to dramatically increase imports are easy to see. Import growth rates rise from all areas, while national-income growth rates fall. Imports from capitalist countries grew 12.7%, faster than the 11.1% growth rate of exports to those countries, reflecting a partial reliance on credits during the 1970s.

The resulting shift in the geographic composition of Soviet foreign trade is presented in Table 9.3 for selected years of the 1960–78 period. In current prices, the share of socialist countries in Soviet exports dropped about ten percentage points on the import side, and about fifteen percent on the export side. The constant price ratios are not dramatically different, since Soviet trade prices with CMEA have roughly followed world-price movements with a lag. Whichever way one looks at it, *the Soviet Union has realized a dramatic shift in the geographic direction of its trade away from socialist countries and toward capitalist countries.*

The data on total trade confirm the observations of Treml (1980) and Dohan (1979) about the rapid increase in the role of foreign trade in the Soviet economy. Treml estimates that in 1974–6 exports accounted for about 6.5% of MNI, up from 3.7% in 1960, and that imports were about 13% of MNI in 1974–6, up from 7% in 1960.

One must be very careful in utilizing the levels of these Soviet trade-participation ratios for comparisons with Western countries. Even after adjusting for the difference between MNI and GNP, two major problems remain. First, the fact that the ruble/dollar ratio on imports (about 2/1) exceeds that on exports (about 1/1) (Treml, 1980, Tables 1 and 27) may simply mean that the Soviet planners are using the exchange rate to collect a rather sizable tariff on all imports. This

Table 9.3　*The Geographic Composition of Soviet Foreign Trade Measured in 1970 Prices and in Current Prices: 1960–78*

	All Countries		All Socialist Countries		CMEA–7[a]		Capitalist Countries	
	curr. prices	1970 prices	curr. prices	1970 prices	curr. prices	1970 prices	curr. prices	1970 prices
			Imports					
1960	1.00	1.00	.71	nd	.51	nd	.29	nd
1965	1.00	1.00	.70	.72	.59	.60	.30	.28
1970	1.00	1.00	.65	.65	.57	.57	.35	.35
1975	1.00	1.00	.52	.56	.43	.50	.48	.44
1978	1.00	1.00	.60	.58	.55	.52	.40	.42
			Exports					
1960	1.00	1.00	.76	nd	.58	nd	.24	nd
1965	1.00	1.00	.68	.64	.57	.54	.32	.36
1970	1.00	1.00	.65	.65	.54	.54	.35	.35
1975	1.00	1.00	.61	.58	.51	.52	.39	.42
1978	1.00	1.00	.60	.55	.51	.49	.40	.45

Note:

[a]For purposes of comparison, this includes only Bulgaria, Czechoslovakia, East Germany, Hungary, Poland, Romania and Mongolia. Cuba and Vietnam, both of whom became members of CMEA in the 1970s, have been left out of CMEA, but are included in the "socialist" column.

Source: Data on the geographic composition of trade in current prices is from VTSS, various years. Data in 1970 prices were obtained by multiplying the 1970 values of trade with each area by the quantity index for exports to or imports from that area over the 1960–78 period. Those values, which represent trade in 1970 prices, were used to derive the constant-price proportions in the second, fourth, sixth, and eighth columns.

soaks up purchasing power and protects the domestic economy from foreign competition. The consequently high import/MNI ratio does not imply a high level of trade participation, but rather a high tax on imports.

The second problem is far more important, and involves MNI itself. In Western countries a trade/GNP ratio reflects the relative magnitudes of trade flows and value added, both valued in prices prevailing on international markets. In the Soviet case, because tradables sell domestically at relative prices substantially different from their international prices, domestic value-added (MNI) is potentially much different from value-added computed in international prices. Therefore the only way to obtain a trade-participation ratio for the Soviet Union comparable to a similar ratio for a Western country is to recompute Soviet value-added at international prices, and use that in the denominator. The numerator should be trade flows (possibly also recomputed for CMEA trade) converted at a proper exchange rate.[5] The resulting numbers could differ substantially from those obtained by Treml.

Whatever results one might obtain from recomputations along the lines discussed above, the fact remains that a growing proportion of Soviet national income is involved in international trade, and that there has been a substantial shift in the geographic composition of that trade towards capitalist countries.

(b) *Commodity Composition of Trade.* The Soviet foreign-trade yearbooks only report data on the current ruble value of trade in selected commodity groups, and then only for all countries and socialist countries. These data, which are presented in Table 9.4, are of only limited utility in attempting to assess how the commodity composition of Soviet trade has evolved over time; yet without major recomputations, which could not be done for this paper, this is the best available. There are two basic problems with the data as they are presented. The first, and most obvious, one is that the relative price of fuels has risen over time, and consequently the current-price data will overstate the change in the relative importance of those goods in Soviet exports.

Secondly, the prices at which the Soviets trade with CMEA, differ substantially from those at which they trade with the rest of the world.[6] Fuels, for example, are relatively cheaper in Soviet exports to CMEA than they are in Soviet exports to the rest of the world; and if, therefore, one were to recompute the share of fuels in Soviet exports to socialist countries using the prices the Soviets charge the rest of the world, the share would come out higher than the published number. Consequently one cannot directly compare the product shares in current rubles for Soviet trade with all countries, and for Soviet trade with socialist countries. Thus one must be careful in interpreting these numbers but nevertheless they do convey some useful information about the commodity composition of Soviet trade.

Throughout the 1960s and 1970s, the mainstay of Soviet exports to the world has been fuels, primary products, and some semifabricates. Those groups together (the second through the fifth rows of Table 9.4) accounted for 53% of the value of Soviet exports to the world in 1960, 57% of those exports in 1978, and 58% of the value of its exports to socialist countries in 1978. This dependence on primary products for export proceeds is strongest in exports to developed capitalist countries. In 1976 a little over 70% of all Soviet export proceeds to developed capitalist countries came from nine products: coal, petroleum and petroleum products, natural gas, iron ore, nonferrous metals, rolled ferrous metals, cotton, timber, and lumber (Hewett, 1979, pp. 8–10).

The share of machinery and equipment in Soviet imports has risen steadily over the last two decades, comprising in recent years 40% of the value of total imports, and almost one-half of the value of imports from socialist countries. Food accounts for approximately another 20% in total and socialist-country imports; and the remainder of

Table 9.4 Commodity Structure of Soviet Foreign Trade in Current Prices: 1960–78 (percent of trade)[c]

	Exports								Imports							
	1960		1970		1975		1978		1960		1970		1975		1978	
	Tot.[a]	S.C.[b]	Tot.	S.C.	Tot.	S.C.	Tot.	S.C.	Tot.	S.C.	Tot.	S.C.	Tot.	S.C.	Tot.	S.C.
Machinery and Equipment	.21	nd	.22	nd	.19	.23	.20	.26	.30	nd	.35	nd	.34	.39	.42	.47
Fuels and Electrical Energy	.16	nd	.16	nd	.31	.26	.36	.32	.04	nd	.02	nd	.04	.03	.04	.03
Ores, Concentrates, Metal Fabricates	.20	nd	.20	nd	.14	.20	.10	.15	.17	nd	.11	nd	.12	.07	.10	.05
Chemicals, Fertilizer, Rubber	.04	nd	.04	nd	.04	.04	.03	.04	.06	nd	.06	nd	.05	.04	.04	.03
Forestry, Cellulose, and Paper Products	.06	nd	.07	nd	.06	.05	.05	.04	.02	nd	.02	nd	.02	.01	.04	.03
Textile Raw Mats. and Semifabricates	.07	nd	.03	nd	.03	.03	.03	.03	.07	nd	.05	nd	.02	.00	.15	.06
Food and Materials for its Production	.14	nd	.09	nd	.05	.06	.02	.03	.12	nd	.15	nd	.23	.21	.02	.01
Manufactured Consumer Goods	.03	nd	.03	nd	.03	.03	.03	.03	.17	nd	.18	nd	.13	.19	.19	.18

Notes:
[a]"Tot." means total trade.
[b]"S.C." means trade with socialist countries.
[c]Data do not sum to 1.00 in the original source.

Sources: VTSS, various years.

imports are dispersed among various groups. Constant-price data would probably tell about the same story on the import side.

On both the export and import side, the major distinguishing feature of socialist trade in comparison to total trade is the relatively larger role for machinery and equipment. This is not by design. Soviet planners have consistently sought to increase the share of machinery and equipment in total trade, and especially in trade with capitalist countries, but to little effect. This will be an important point in the discussion of the planning and management of Soviet foreign trade.

(c) *Unit Values and the Terms of Trade.* Table 9.5 presents estimates of unit-value indices and the net barter terms of trade (hereafter simply "terms of trade") for Soviet foreign trade. These are derived by dividing the quantity indices of Table 9.1 into indices of changes in the total value of exports or imports. Because the quantity indices were close approximations of Laspeyres indices, these are close approximations of Paasche price indices. It is in this table that the problems with the "A" quantity indices of total exports and imports are most apparent, especially on the import side. Note, for example, that in 1971–3 and 1976–7 the total import unit-value index lies above both the capitalist and socialist indices, and therefore could not be an average of those two indices. The "B" unit-value indices are weighted averages because the "B" quantity indices are.

In 1978, Soviet terms of trade with the world were about where they had been in 1960. They had dropped in the mid-1960s mainly due to price changes in CMEA that favored manufactured-goods exporters over primary-product exporters. In the 1970s, total terms of trade increased, first because of a major increase in terms of trade with capitalist countries, followed by changes in terms of trade with socialist countries, and to a lesser extent, CMEA. Up to 1976, Soviet terms of trade with CMEA had increased at a very moderate pace compared to what the Soviets would have been allowed to do under CMEA pricing rules in light of changes in world-market prices (Hewett, 1980a). It would appear that Soviet restraint continued through 1978.

Trade and Payments in Convertible Currencies

Published Soviet foreign-trade statistics do not report any balance-of-payments data, nor do they report separately on trade in convertible currencies. Nevertheless the convertible-currency balances of trade and payments of the USSR are of considerable interest in the West. Those balances measure the ability of that system to manage trade and payments in very tough competitive markets. Furthermore, now that the USSR has significant net convertible-currency debts on Western markets, the interest of bankers and governments in Soviet convertible-currency trade and payments has grown. This section

Table 9.5 Unit Value Indices for Soviet Foreign Trade: 1960–78 (1970 = 100)

	Unit Value Indices										Terms of Trade				
	Exports					Imports					Total				
	Total		Soc.		Cap.	Total		Soc.		Cap.	Total		Soc.		Cap.
Year	A	B	Ct.	CMEA	Ct.	A	B	Ct.	CMEA	Ct.	A	B	Ct.	CMEA	Ct.
1960	106	nd	nd	nd	nd	94	nd	nd	nd	nd	113	nd	nd	nd	nd
1961	106	nd	nd	nd	nd	96	nd	nd	nd	nd	111	nd	nd	nd	nd
1962	106	nd	nd	nd	nd	95	nd	nd	nd	nd	111	nd	nd	nd	nd
1963	105	106	113	114	93	94	93	92	94	97	112	113	123	121	95
1964	105	107	113	115	95	100	99	96	98	106	105	109	118	117	90
1965	103	103	109	108	92	98	97	95	97	101	105	106	114	111	91
1966	97	98	103	103	88	98	97	94	95	104	100	100	109	108	84
1967	98	97	103	103	88	97	95	94	95	99	101	102	110	108	89
1968	98	98	103	100	90	95	95	94	93	98	102	103	110	108	92
1969	98	97	103	102	86	98	97	95	96	99	99	100	108	106	87
1970	100	100	100	100	100	100	100	100	100	100	100	100	100	100	100
1971	102	105	104	102	107	102	100	101	104	99	100	105	103	98	108
1972	101	104	106	104	100	103	101	102	103	99	98	103	104	101	101
1973	111	113	108	107	121	105	103	103	105	102	105	110	105	102	119
1974	118	121	108	107	142	114	111	103	105	122	104	109	104	102	116
1975	133	136	139	129	131	136	133	128	122	140	98	102	109	106	94
1976	144	146	154	141	138	138	135	134	129	136	104	108	113	109	102
1977	156	158	163	153	152	142	139	139	134	138	110	114	117	114	111
1978	160	163	173	161	149	142	139	147	142	128	112	117	118	113	117

Source: All indices were obtained by dividing indices of total value (using total values reported in various years of VTSS) by the quantity indices in Table 9.1. Definition of terms: see Table 9.1.

discusses what is known about Soviet convertible-currency trade. Virtually all of the data here have been developed in recent years by the CIA.

Table 9.6 presents CIA estimates of the Soviet covertible-currency balance of payments. This includes (in recent years) Soviet trade with all developed capitalist countries except Finland, the developing countries of Europe, and a considerable number of developing countries with which the Soviet Union settles its accounts in convertible currencies.[7]

Virtually all the items in this table are estimates, many of them based on guesses about such things as interest rates, the prices at which gold was sold, the proportion of dollar earnings in total transport earnings, and convertible-currency earnings from military sales. Therefore these estimates should be viewed as the middle of a rather broad range of possible balances, a point which the discussions of these estimates are careful to make (see Ericson and Miller, 1979). Nevertheless, these estimates are very carefully done, and they are probably the best we shall have unless the USSR decides to publish its own figures.

In the 1970s, with the exception of the years where major grain purchases were made, the Soviet current-account balance has been in surplus; and recently the surplus has become quite substantial, reaching \$4.1 billion in 1979. The balance on merchandise trade has traditionally been negative, running somewhere between −\$2.0 and −\$6.5 billion in the later half of the 1970s. Table 9.7 contains estimates of the increase in the volume of convertible-currency exports and imports, the changes in unit values, and the net barter terms of trade, all for the 1971–7 period. The terms of trade increased 50% over these years primarily because of rapid increases in the price of Soviet hydrocarbon exports. Yet even with those improved terms of trade, the quantity of imports increased so much more rapidly than the quantity of exports that the merchandise-trade balance remained negative.

Three current-account items have counterbalanced that deficit: gold sales, sales of military equipment, and net services. In recent years the latter surplus has dwindled as interest payments on the debt have increased dramatically.

The capital account shows the large debt accumulations that occurred in the mid-1970s, and abated by 1977–8. These were driven in part by large grain purchases, but also there was obviously an underlying flow of over \$1 billion per year in borrowing, presumably to finance new machinery and equipment. Soviet commercial assets were increasing simultaneously, and Table 9.8 shows, as a consequence, how net debt changed over time. Soviet net debt stagnated in 1976–9 at \$10 – \$11 billion. In part this may have been a result of improved financial management achieved by moving (in 1976) V. Alkhimov, a specialist on financial matters, from his position as Deputy Minister of Foreign Trade to the Directorship of Gosbank (Ericson and Miller, 1979, p. 231). Even without that change, the dramatic increases in gold

Table 9.6 Soviet Convertible-Currency Balance of Payments: 1960–79 (million US dollars)

	1960	1963	1966	1969	1970	1971	1972	1973	1974	1975	1976	1977	1978	1979
I. Current Account Bal.	-118	198	-311	-351	22	160	-587	1151	2014	-4714	-2931	751	1266	4111
A. Balance on Goods and Services	-92	232	-270	-302	77	217	-521	1234	2115	-4616	-2824	nd[a]	nd[a]	nd[a]
1. Balance on Mdse. Trade	-250	-275	-238	-311	-500	-313	-1356	-1757	-978	-6422	-5985	-3300	-3794	-2069
a. Exports, f.o.b.	768	1012	1517	2125	2201	2630	2801	4790	7470	7835	9721	11345	13157	19524
b. Imports, f.o.b.	-1018	-1287	-1755	-2436	-2701	-2943	-4157	-6547	-8448	-14257	-15316	-14645	-16951	-21593
2. Sales of Non-monetary Gold	200	550	—	—	—	79	380	900	1178	725	1369	1597	2673	2200
3. Military Sales	nd	nd	nd	nd	100	87	122	1345	1000	793	1108	1500[b]	1644[b]	nd
4. Net Income from Services	-42	-43	-32	9	477	364	333	746	915	288	294	309[b]	89[b]	nd
a. Tourism, net	25	31	38	56	43	45	53	116	117	136	150	175[b]	200[b]	nd
b. Transport, net	-65	-60	-50	10	517	367	340	710	900	720	860	980[b]	970[b]	nd
c. Interest, net	-2	-14	-20	-57	-83	-48	-60	-82	-102	-568	-716	-846[b]	-1081[b]	nd
II. Capital Account Bal.	88	10	126	369	266	227	-77	522	386	5694	2952	1917	173	-1127
A. Borrowing from Abroad	nd	nd	nd	nd	291	288	602	1340	1426	5402	4694	1777	1785	-27
B. Lending to Other Countries	nd	nd	nd	nd	-25	-55	-679	-809	-1029	295	-1711	140	-1612	-1100
III. Net Errors and Omissions[c]	30	-208	185	-9	-288	-387	664	-1673	-2400	-980	21	-2668	-1439	-2668

Sources: 1960–76, Farrell, 1973, p. 703; Ericson and Miller, 1979, p. 212. 1977–9, CIA, June 1980b, p. 17. The latter appears to include upward revisions of Ericson and Miller's estimates for 1977–8 of the current account balance.

Notes:

[a] CIA, June 1980b, does not report these figures.

[b] These are the Ericson and Miller figures, which may have been revised in making the estimates reported in CIA, June 1980b; that source does not say, and does not report these numbers.

[c] Negative of the sum of the Capital-Account- and Current-Account-Balance rows, those two having been estimated separately.

Table 9.7   *Soviet Convertible–Currency Trade: Quantity Indices, Unit-Value Indices, and Net Barter Terms of Trade, 1971–7*

	1971	1972	1973	1974	1975	1976	1977
Quantity Indices							
Exports	100	103	122	106	116	138	141
Imports	100	151	193	182	273	297	250
Unit-Value Indices							
Exports	100	103	149	268	257	268	306
Imports	100	94	115	158	178	175	199
Net Barter Terms							
of Trade	100	111	130	170	145	153	154

Source: The quantity indices are from Ericson and Miller (1979, p. 228). They do not discuss the weights in these indices. The unit-value indices are derived by dividing the quantity indices into indices of the total value of convertible-currency merchandise exports and imports (also from Ericson and Miller, p. 212). The net barter terms of trade are the export unit-value index divided by the import unit-value index.

prices and the terms of trade would have allowed Soviet financial authorities to cease net borrowing.

In international financial térms the Soviet Union was in very good shape by the end of 1979. Total net debt equalled about half of 1979 convertible-currency exports; the 1979 debt-service ratio was 18% (CIA, 1980a, p. 8). This, combined with the Soviet Union's very substantial gold reserves, provide a very considerable financial buffer against whatever shocks may hit the Soviet Union in the early 1980s (for example, oil-production problems or problems in Eastern Europe).

I turn now to a brief discussion of the four key sources of convertible-currency earnings for the USSR: primary products, gold, military sales, and services.

(a) *Primary Products*. In 1913, the five top foreign-currency earners in Soviet exports (most of which went to West European countries) were grain, sawn timber, eggs and egg products, cotton fibers, and logs (*VTSS 1918–1966*, p. 235). Three of those product groups remain among the top earners of convertible currency for the Soviet Union today — sawn timber, logs, and cotton. The other top exports are also primary products: petroleum and petroleum products, natural gas, coal, iron ore, rolled ferrous metals, and nonferrous metals. These products account for about three-fourths of Soviet merchandise exports to the West, which is not the same as exports for convertible currency, since in these data the "West" includes Finland (not a convertible-currency trade partner), and excludes all developing countries (many of which do settle their accounts with the USSR in convertible currency) (Hewett, 1979). Petroleum and petroleum-products exports are by far the most important source of convertible currency; in 1978 these alone accounted for about $5.3 billion of all

Table 9.8 Convertible-Currency Debt of the USSR: 1970–9 (millions of Dollars)

	1971	1972	1973	1974	1975	1976	1977	1978	1979
Gross Debt	1807	2409	3749	5176	10578	14853	15728	17227	17200
Commercial Debt	407	858	2041	2787	6947	9667	9858	10316	9500
Officially Guaranteed									
Export Credits	1400	1551	1708	2389	3631	5185	5870	6911	7700
Commercial Assets	1225	1854	2583	3522	3127	4738	4498	6010	7000
Net Debt	582	555	1166	1654	7451	10115	11230	11217	10200

Source: CIA, June 1980a, p. 15.

Soviet convertible-currency merchandise exports of $13.2, 40% of the total.[8]

This heavy reliance on a few primary products for the bulk of convertible-currency proceeds is not totally by design. Analyses by Soviet economists who work on foreign trade, and the statements of Soviet leaders, are replete with references to the desirability of increasing the share of manufactures in total exports, particularly in exports to developed Western countries.[9] But these efforts have in the main failed for well-known reasons best elucidated in Franklyn Holzman's writings on Soviet foreign trade (Holzman, 1974, 1979). The fundamental problems in Soviet manufactured-goods exports are exactly those which plague the domestic economy: producers working in sellers' markets simply have no incentive to produce and service the manufactured goods that customers want, whether they be foreign or domestic customers. The tremendous pressure from above for continuous increases in the quantity of output encourages producers to emphasize quantity over quality, and to favor known technology over new technology. While these factors discourage manufactured-goods exports, they favor the production and export of primary products. There is very little manufacturing and no after-sales service involved in primary-product extraction and sales; technological advances in production processes are possibly not as important as in manufacturing processes, and when they are, central planners can more easily introduce them from above; and the emphasis on quantity tends to generate large quantities of primary products, including an exportable surplus. This is why, even though Gosplan may not have planned it this way, the primary-products industry has become a major export industry in the USSR.

As for petroleum, far and away the most important of the primary products used to earn convertible currencies, there are very serious problems ahead. The facts are well known, and are discussed in the contributions to this volume by Professors Campbell and Dienes. The predicted problems in petroleum production are a direct outcome of years of emphasis on high quantities *now*, hence the drop in output that is pending could be precipitous. This will have very serious consequences either for Soviet merchandise exports for convertible currency, or for Soviet exports of energy to Eastern Europe, probably the former. It is very unlikely that primary products, particularly fuels, can play the role in the 1980s they played in the 1970s as a major source of convertible currency. Something else will have to replace them, and no one, including Soviet planners, can say now what that might be.

(b) *Gold.* Gold represents a potentially important source of convertible-currency earnings in the near future and could replace some, but hardly all, of the revenues lost due to a decline in petroleum production. As Table 9.6 shows, gold sales have been substantial for many years in comparison to the value of merchandise exports for convertible currency. Over the entire 1960–79 period gold sales have

Table 9.9 Western Estimates of Soviet Gold Sales, Production, and Stocks; 1970–9

	Gold Sales			Gold Production[a] (metric tons)			Gold Reserves (metric tons)	
	Quantity (metric tons)	Value (mln. Dol)	Dollars per Ton (mln. Dol)	CIA	Kaser	Schoppe	CIA	Schoppe
1970	0	0	—	200	347	193	1610	1730
1971	60	79	1.317	204	360	201	1717	1895
1972	200	380	1.900	219	379	254	1700	1950
1973	280	900	3.214	236	398	302	1620	1935
1974	230	1178	5.122	246	421	355	1675	2025
1975	140	725	5.179	251	408	404	1746	2230
1976	340	1369	4.026	257	444	451	1614	2330
1977	340	1597	4.697	265	444	500	1510	2465
1978	430	2673	6.216	270	453	nd	1366	nd
1979	225	2200	9.778	nd	nd	nd	nd	nd

Sources:
Col. 1. Gold Sales: 1970–78: Ericson and Miller, 1979, p. 239. 1979: Consolidated Gold Fields estimate in *Business Week*, February 11, 1979, p. 82.
Col. 2. Value of gold sales: Table 9.6.
Col. 3. Dollars per Ton: second column divided by first.
Col. 4. The CIA estimates are from CIA, 1979, pp. 69 and 167.
Col. 5. The Kaser estimates are from Kaser, 1979, p. 228.
Col. 6. The Schoppe estimates are from Schoppe, 1979, pp. 64–5.

Note:
[a] Kaser's data include production of gold as a main product, and as a by-product. The other two sources do not say whether by-products are included. Kaser shows by-products in recent years to be about 50 tons.

averaged 14% of the value of convertible currency exports; in 1978, gold sales were valued at $2.673 billion, which was almost exactly half the value of petroleum and petroleum-products sales that year.

The Soviet Union publishes no information on gold sales, production, or stocks; all such information must be estimated using data available in the West. All that is known with acceptable accuracy is sales tonnages; those are reported by Western gold traders. The prices at which the sales are made are not reported, and must be estimated, which is difficult for the very important period of the 1970s where gold prices were fluctuating so rapidly and by such large amounts. Soviet gold production and gold stocks have been estimated by the CIA (1979), Michael Kaser (1979, for Consolidated Gold Fields of London), and Siedfried Schoppe (1978, 1979). Table 9.9 summarizes all of these data.

Soviet gold sales have been substantial throughout the 1970s, reaching a peak of 430 tons in 1978. In 1978–9 gold sales on world markets averaged 1750 tons per annum, making the Soviet Union the second largest gold seller (behind South Africa, which supplied 700 tons in each of those years) (Frey, 1980, p. 43). Apparently the Soviet traders play an important stabilizing role on world gold markets. In recent years, they have tended to sell when prices are rising, and hold back supplies when prices are falling (Ericson and Miller, 1979, p. 230). In 1976 when the IMF began its substantial gold auctions, the predicted fall in gold prices did not transpire in part because the Soviet Union withdrew from the market as soon as the price began to fall (Schoppe, 1979, p. 80).

It is not at all clear how this has affected Soviet gold reserves because there is no agreement among available sources on either the level of Soviet gold production, or reserves. The CIA estimates production of 270 tons in recent years, which would imply that stocks have fallen somewhat, given sales of larger amounts.[10] Both Schoppe and Kaser estimate much higher production figures which, if they are correct, mean that gold reserves are rising. Other than much higher production estimates, one other possible explanation for Schoppe's high gold-reserve figures and the lower figures of the CIA is that Schoppe includes "Spanish gold" held by the Soviet Union, and the CIA may leave that out.[11] None of these sources are clear enough in how they arrived at their estimates to choose among them. In fact only Kaser notes the discrepancy, but makes no attempt to explore it (Kaser, 1979, p. 228). At the very least Soviet gold stocks in 1979 were at about 1375 tons (assuming the CIA data will show a slight increase over 1978), which at 1979 prices was worth $16.4 billion. The stocks could be as high as 2500 tons, worth $24.5 billion in 1979 prices. 1980 prices are, of course, much higher. A conservative value for 1980 would be $500 a troy ounce, or $16.35 million per ton, which puts the value of Soviet gold reserves at somewhere between $27.4 billion to $40.9 billion. It would obviously be beneficial for the authors of these estimates to somehow identify the reasons for the discrepancies in their figures. Whatever the true figures may be, it is clear that the Soviet Union possesses substantial gold stocks. In the future it can, as it has in the recent past, use those stocks to partially insulate the economy from the foreign-exchange consequences of problems in petroleum production, or further difficulties in grain production. For example, at a conservative sales level of 200 tons of gold a year, and at a conservative $500 an ounce, the Soviets could earn $3.27 billion a year, about 60% of their 1978 earnings from oil.

On the other hand, it is difficult to predict how the price of gold will change in the future. Soviet planners are given to conservatism in many things, and in this matter it seems likely that they will not plan for gold to replace export proceeds from commodities with more predictable prices. They will probably plan for their future convertible-currency proceeds to come from elsewhere, while quite naturally hoping that the gold boom will continue (and probably helping it to do so where possible).

(c) *Military Goods*. Sales of military goods have, since 1973, become an important source of convertible currency for the USSR. The Soviet Union has become part of the petrodollar-recycling process through its sales of modern military equipment for convertible currency. The magnitudes involved are difficult to estimate. The CIA estimates, given in Table 9.6, suggest that convertible-currency earnings from military sales were about $1.5 billion per year in 1976–8, which constituted about 11% of convertible-currency earnings from merchandise trade in those years.

The actual figures could be substantially different. The CIA data, which are the sole data available, are the result of a careful estimate for one year only (1977) of the proportion of military sales that were in convertible currencies, and then that proportion has been applied to total military sales in other years (CIA, Nov. 1978; Ericson and Miller, 1979, p. 214). There is no doubt, however, that Soviet sales of military equipment for convertible currency are large, and the prospects of the continuation of those sales are surely good, at least on the demand side. These sales represent one class of sophisticated manufactures in which the Soviet Union is competitive on convertible-currency markets.

There is still much more one needs to know about the production and sales of these commodities in order to say with any degree of certainty what role they might play in future convertible-currency sales. One wonders, for example, whether the supplies involved are putting significant pressure on Soviet arms manufacturers, hence on the domestic economy. Arms sold for convertible currency are presumably high-quality products in a high-priority industry, and significant increases in their production must have a telling effect on the remainder of the system. While the USSR is earning valuable hard currency for the sale of these products, it is using some very scarce inputs to produce them, in particular presumably scarce inputs of strategic metals and highly skilled labor. It is entirely possible that special export industries producing civilian goods, to be discussed below, would be a cheaper way to earn additional hard currency.

These are important issues about which nothing very substantive has been written; hopefully more work will be done on them. Whatever the answers to these questions, it is important to note that military weapons are not simply sold by the USSR because they need more convertible currency; there are obviously foreign-policy considerations involved. Nevertheless these weapons sales are a potentially important source of convertible currency. Combined with gold sales they represent a major counterweight to the deficits on merchandise trade. In the period of 1973–9 gold and military sales covered all, or virtually all, of the merchandise-trade deficit in five of those seven years (excluding the big-grain-purchase years of 1974–5).

(d) *Services*. Shipping and other transportation services are becoming another important source of net convertible-currency earnings, with net receipts approaching $1 billion in the late 1970s. The growth of the merchant marine, and the increasing role of the Soviet Union in world shipping, has been discussed elsewhere (Hardt, 1979; Carr, 1979). There seems to be every prospect that the Soviets will continue to successfully develop this as a major source of convertible currency.

In addition to shipping, the receipts from transport reflect the rapid growth of convertible-currency receipts from container shipments over land on the Siberian land bridge (Miller, 1978). The Soviets are pushing very hard to capture a significant portion of the traffic between Japan and Asia on the one end, and Europe on the other. They are offering shipments in both twenty- and forty-foot containers at significant discounts relative to sea routes, and they are apparently very successful.

Windfall Gains to the Soviet Economy Through Convertible-Currency Trade

In the 1970s several factors exogenous to the Soviet economy have provided it with large windfall gains through its convertible-currency trade. The tremendous increase in gold prices has provided the Soviet Union, as a major producer and seller of gold, with enormous increases in dollar revenues. These in turn have presented Soviet planners with the pleasant options of retiring debt without changing exports or imports, or reducing exports without reducing imports, or increasing imports without increasing exports. Similar windfalls have accrued through the improved terms of trade in convertible currencies. The 50% increase in the terms of trade between 1971 and 1977 provides to Soviet planners, again, the three choices mentioned above. Finally, the substantial redistribution of wealth towards OPEC countries has provided the Soviet Union with improved prospects for selling weapons to the "right" trade partners for convertible currency.

Table 9.10 Windfall Gains to the Soviet Economy Through Convertible-Currency Trade: 1970–9 (millions of US Dollars)

	Additional Imports Possible Due to Improved Terms of Trade	Additional Imports Possible Due to Higher Gold Prices	Merchandise Exports for Convertible Currency	Increase (+) or Decrease (−) in Net Convertible-Currency Debt
1971	0	0	2630	nd
1972	278	116	2801	−27
1973	1105	531	4790	611
1974	3076	875	7470	488
1975	2432	541	7835	5797
1976	3367	921	9721	2664
1977	3978	1140	11345	1115
1978	nd	2107	13157	−13
1979	nd	1904	19524	−1017
1971–7	14236	4124	46592	9618
1971–9	nd	8135	79723	10684

Sources: For first two columns, see Data Appendix. Merchandise exports are from Table 9.6. The debt figures are from Table 9.8.

The additional import possibilities from increased gold prices and improved terms of trade are windfall gains whose importance to the Soviet economy can be quantified. Table 9.10 does that by estimating, in current US dollars, the additional import capacity available to the Soviet Union as a result of these two factors.

The first column estimates the additional dollars available for imports due to improved terms of trade in convertible-currency trade alone. The data only go through 1977 because the CIA estimates of terms of trade in convertible currencies end there. This column is the difference between the nominal value of exports each year and that value deflated by the terms of trade that same year. That difference represents export proceeds in current dollars, net of the amount of additional proceeds needed to buy imports at their new, higher, prices.[12] The second column of Table 9.10 quantifies additional imports possible because gold prices have risen. It is the product of the quantity of gold actually sold each year and the difference between the price obtained that year, and the price obtained in 1971. The (admittedly simplifying) assumption here is that the Soviet Union is a price taker on this market, and that it would have marketed the quantities of gold it marketed in any event; the price differences therefore generate pure windfall gains.

The remaining two columns are placed in the table for reference, the third column giving total merchandise exports for convertible currency, and the fourth column giving the net increase or decrease in the convertible-currency debt over this period. All columns are summed for 1971–7, for which complete data are available, and for 1971–9, for which data are available for all save the gains from improved terms of trade.

The windfall gains to the Soviet Union were quite substantial by any measure. Of the increased import capacity available to the USSR in the 1970–77 period because of increased borrowing, improved terms of trade, and increased gold prices, combined, 50% of that amount was due to the terms-of-trade improvement, and 34% was due to increased borrowing. Put another way, had the terms of trade and gold prices not improved, the Soviet Union would have had to borrow almost $28 billion to finance the additional imports over and above what could be financed through exports at the 1971 terms of trade. If terms-of-trade data were available for the 1978–9 period, these figures would be even higher. Over that period the gains from higher gold prices alone comprised 80% of the value of net convertible-currency debt outstanding.

These windfall gains have made it possible for the Soviet Union to postpone changes in its planning and management of foreign trade (and for that matter, the economy) for some time. Its economic system is best at producing and marketing primary products, fuels and semimanufactures; the relative values of those products rose on the world economy in the 1970s, hence so did the Soviet terms of trade. The Soviets happen to have large gold reserves, and the world valuation of gold drastically changed in the 1970s. Without these changes the pressures for much greater economies in imports, or much increased exports, would have been felt throughout the 1970s, which surely would have hastened system change. The question now is whether pressures for change will grow in the 1980s. I suspect they will and that as a consequence the system will begin to change. The next section discusses these issues, beginning with a discussion of the planning and management system in foreign trade, and then a discussion of the pressures for change.

9.2 The Planning and Management of Foreign Economic Relations in the Soviet Union

In studying any system it is difficult to separate out the fundamental features, which are the true source of the important performance characteristics of that system, from the surface appearance of the system, which may change quite frequently. It is nevertheless imperative that such a separation be made, since only the fundamental features matter; changes in form are irrelevant, and sometimes meant as camouflage.

The fundamental features of the institutions that control Soviet foreign economic relations have not changed in half a century. The State's monopoly control over foreign trade, payments, and the resource allocation decisions that influence those, remains quite secure. The Soviet foreign sector today is, as it was in the 1930s, a highly centralized information and decision-making system.

This section is confined primarily to discussing those fundamental features, and the pressures to change them. The particular form that the monopoly of foreign trade takes today will be discussed only in a general way in order to elucidate what is fundamental about the system. Recent changes in the management of foreign-trade organizations (FTOs) will be discussed only to illustrate that the changes have no effect on the basic structure of the system.

Pressures to change this system are intertwined with pressures to reform the entire economy; poor performance in the foreign sector is in fact a manifestation of problems in the entire domestic economy. Such pressures for change have always existed. In the 1970s they did not grow worse in part because of the windfall gains discussed above. As the windfall gains disappear and the pressures begin to grow, then true reforms will grow more likely. The later portion of this section discusses the two major sources of pressure for change, and the last section ventures a guess at how this will affect institutions and economic performance in the next two decades.

(a)   *The Institutions That Control Soviet Foreign Economic Relations*

The term "foreign economic relations" is, in Soviet (and in fact Western) terminology a broader concept than "foreign trade." It includes trade, but also matters concerning currency, aid, and all foreign economic contacts, for example cooperation agreements between Soviet and foreign firms in the Soviet Union, or abroad.

As in all other matters in the Soviet economy, the ultimate authority over major policy issues concerning foreign economic relations resides in the party, effectively in the Party Central Committee, its Secretariat, and the Politbureau. But for other than the issues of paramount importance, presumably it is the various governmental institutions that effectively control the conduct of Soviet foreign economic relations. The USSR Council of Ministers has a complete monopoly over all aspects of foreign economic relations, and it uses various institutions to administer particular aspects of the monopoly.[13] Gosplan plays a crucial role through its authority over all major resource-allocation decisions. It is Gosplan that has final authority over all decisions concerning foreign trade, in particular the level of trade and its commodity composition.

Economic ministries and some enterprises are playing an increasingly important role in foreign economic relations as the government seeks to increase the role of cooperation agreements in foreign-trade flows with all countries. The domestic ministries, and not the Ministry of Foreign Trade, have full authority here to conclude cooperation agreements, and the responsibility to carry them out. The Ministry of Foreign Trade is only involved as a facilitator for the resulting trade flows. The increasing importance of cooperation agreements is a reflection of an attempt by Soviet planners to connect decisions on production and investment more directly to foreign economic considerations, a natural and inevitable development in an economy that wishes to increase its gains from specialization and trade. In effect, the Ministry of Foreign Trade is sharing control over many trade flows with ministries and large enterprises. And in fact, the portion of Soviet foreign economic relations exclusively controlled by the Ministry of Foreign Trade is openly regarded by Soviet planners as the least dynamic and promising part of their relations with other countries.

The Ministry of Foreign Trade regulates all pure commodity-trade transactions. Although the Planning–Economic Administration of the Ministry participates in the planning process, it does so apparently primarily as a source of information to aid Gosplan in constructing the foreign-trade plans; the Ministry itself is decidedly the junior participant here, its primary concern being the state of foreign-trade relations. The Ministry of Foreign Trade has in its central apparat the administrations or directorates (upravleniia) regulating trade with various geographic areas (Asian socialist countries, European socialist countries, Western Europe, North and South America, Southeast Asia and the Middle East, and Africa); regulating major functional areas of foreign trade (for example, planning and economic matters; treaties and legal matters; currency); and regulating trade by major product group and geographical areas (export of primary products; export of industrial equipment; export of transport, road construction, and agricultural machinery; export of ready-made products and consumer goods; import of industrial raw materials, food, and ready-made products; import of machinery and equipment from capitalist countries; and import of machinery and equipment from socialist countries) (Hewett, 1978, p. 30).

The administrations control approximately fifty foreign-trade organizations (FTOs), each of which controls trade in a carefully specified set of products, usually involving both export and import trade. It is the FTOs that conduct the bulk of Soviet merchandise trade on behalf of Soviet enterprises, and at the command of the Ministry of Foreign Trade, itself operating according to the annual plans set by Gosplan. Domestic enterprises ship goods for exports and obtain imported goods according to that same annual plan, receiving the domestic wholesale price (and possibly some special bonuses) for export production, and paying the domestic retail price for imports.

Trade in services is in part outside the control of the Ministry of Foreign Trade. For example, the State Committee for Foreign Economic Relations, which acts as general contractor on turn-key and other projects abroad involving Soviet equipment, Soviet construction agencies, and so on, has twelve of its own FTOs to manage those projects. The Ministry of the Maritime Fleet has three FTOs under its jurisdiction to handle all shipping. And, finally, the State Committee for Science and Technology has its own FTO to handle trade in disembodied technology (Bozek, 1979, pp. 514–16).

Matters relating to finance, for example management of Soviet convertible-currency reserves, management of the debt, sales of precious metals, and so on, are handled by Gosbank and the Ministry of Finance. Gosbank is directly subordinate to the USSR Council of Ministers.

As a group these institutions are the practical realization of what is meant by the state monopoly of foreign trade in the USSR. Their main function is to centralize in the hands of the Council of Ministers the control of all foreign economic relations. As a necessary by-product, the domestic economy is virtually cut off from the world economy. In a market economy world economic conditions exert their influence on the domestic economy automatically unless the state intervenes to alter those influences; in the Soviet economy it is only through state intervention that the enterprises and final users of their products feel any influences from the world economy.

Consequently the determinants of the structure of trade, and its level, lie in the planning process itself, in the information it gathers about opportunity costs and world economic demand and supply, and in the way that information is used. Our information on how foreign-trade planning operates in the Soviet Union is quite uneven, most of it relating to descriptions of how the bureaucracy is supposed to operate, and very little of it relating to how the system actually generates decisions. Formally, the entire process is integrated with the system of national balances, and is closely tied to an increasingly complex set of efficiency calculations that insure that trade, new investments, and cooperation agreements will only be undertaken when they represent net benefits to the economy.[14]

It is not at all clear, in fact, what role efficiency calculations play in this process. They are cumbersome and require a great deal of data at a very disaggregated level. That very complexity means that, not unlike cost-benefit ratios in project decisions in the US, they can be distorted to support decisions already reached for other reasons. Finally, they are necessary because the domestic price system is insulated from world prices, consequently they are at best a poor substitute for real opportunity-cost information. They may, as Gardner (1980) contends, have some influence on Soviet decisions concerning foreign economic relations. But one doubts whether that impact is either systematic or major.

The most important consequence of this system for Soviet economic performance is that it deprives enterprises of sufficient information to intelligently specialize and trade with the world economy, and, even more important, that it fails to give enterprises any significant incentives to participate in the world economy. The enterprise, which best knows its production possibilities, does not know what would sell in the world economy. Furthermore it has little reason to care. Its main concern is what its ministry expects of it, and that means gross output (or now, *maybe*, normative net output), and not exports. In fact, most Soviet enterprises are in such a frantic seller's market, with a virtual monopoly in their product, so that to be interested in exports practically amounts to an act of selfless sacrifice on the part of the manager and his staff. Export production is more expensive, more trouble, and less certain to be sold; and in the Soviet system very few managers would voluntarily choose to increase production of products with those characteristics. Likewise, on the import side there is almost no incentive to economize on imports. They cost the same as comparable domestic products, where those can be found, and otherwise are priced to reflect the cost of an imaginary Soviet counterpart. It would only be by accident, or bureaucratic communication from above, that the Soviet user of imports might get the notion that he is using an item with a very high opportunity cost to the Soviet economy.

This is why on the export side manufactured-goods exports are such a problem, and why (one supposes) Gosplan is most likely constantly faced with import demands from the ministries far in excess of what can be met. But it is also because Soviet central planning is so oriented towards quantity instead of quality that the USSR has managed to turn in a very satisfactory balance of payments performance in convertible currencies. The system is very good at finding large deposits of primary products and fuels, and supplying them to industry, or exporting them. As long as the primary-product deposits hold out, along with good luck on prices, economic indicators in the Soviet foreign sector will be satisfactory. Planners can suppress import demands, possibly at some cost, but not at such an enormous cost so as to cripple the economy. In a large, well-endowed economy such as the USSR, suppression of imports is probably of only moderate importance unless that is done without any concern for costs, and the Soviet case does not seem to fit that description.

Fundamental change in this system would mean giving enterprises the information and incentive to participate profitably in the international division of labor. The state could then still keep control over trade flows through tariff and exchange-rate policy, but enterprises would have to be exposed to world economic competition. Obviously this goes far beyond changing institutions in the foreign sector; it would mean a change in the entire planning process, and redistribution of power from Gosplan to the market. That sort of change would not be voluntarily introduced by the current Soviet leadership, or by any conceivable successor group. If and when such change comes to the USSR it will only be because it is unavoidable, because economic performance is so bad, and the sources of its problems are so obviously linked to the separation of the system from the world economy, that the bureaucratic inertia against change is shattered. The next section is a discussion of the pressures for change now evident in the Soviet economy, of the actual changes that have transpired to date, and of what is being discussed for the near future.

(b) *Pressures for Change in the Foreign Sector, and Changes Introduced to Date*

The Soviet leadership has exhibited a dissatisfaction with performance in the foreign sector in two interrelated areas. The first area — a matter of common knowledge — is machinery and equipment exports for convertible currency. Soviet planners have for several decades aspired to raise the share of machinery and equipment in their hard-currency exports, but to no avail. Attempts at special bonuses for export production (Treml, 1980, pp. 195–6) have — not surprisingly — had no perceptible effect on machinery and equipment exports for convertible currency. The source of this problem is correctly perceived to lie in the lack of effective incentives towards the production and marketing of high-quality manufactured-goods exportables, and the underdeveloped nature of the links between industry and the FTOs. In the last few years the problem of manufactured-goods exports seems to have taken on somewhat more urgency as the increasingly severe constraints and high costs associated with expanding exports of primary products and fuels become more generally known and discussed: the general problem has received attention for some years now.[15]

The second source of pressure for change in the organization and management of the Soviet foreign sector comes from, interestingly enough, trade and cooperation with CMEA. Unlike the USSR, most East European countries have, in varying degrees, streamlined their foreign-trade management system, decentralizing many decisions to enterprises more or less directly attached to international markets. While these measures were primarily taken in an attempt to improve performance on convertible-currency markets, they have also been having their effect on trade with the USSR; many East European enterprises are prepared to enter into complex, and potentially quite profitable, cooperation agreements with Soviet enterprises, but the inflexible Soviet system presents numerous impediments. It is, of course, official Soviet policy to push cooperation with CMEA; and that would appear to reflect an increasingly strong conviction among Soviet leaders that there are substantial benefits to be gained from cooperation with leading East European industrial sectors. Thus there is an increasing realization that the Soviet economic system is one contributor to problems in the further development of CMEA cooperation (Popov, 1976; Baibakov, 1979).

Medvedkov (1979) provides an excellent illustration of the difficulties here. He is reporting on experiences in Soviet-GDR cooperation agreements. Domestic ministries have the authority to negotiate and sign these agreements in the USSR, but all trade matters are to be handled through the Ministry of Foreign Trade. The difficulty here is that complicated cooperation agreements will involve numerous small transactions for which prices and quantities must be determined by the respective FTOs. Unfortunately, the FTOs are not interested in working quickly on the price and quantity negotiations for such small deals since the fixed costs of such negotiations are high; yet the enterprises can hardly sign final agreements until they know what the prices will be. This is particularly difficult in cooperation agreements involving advanced technology where many of the trade flows involve new, high-technology parts for which world-market prices are difficult to find. A further source of opposition from the FTOs is that trade flows under cooperation agreements can involve temporary deficits, making contemporary bilateral balancing impractical.

At present, problems such as these are being handled partly outside the system at high levels on a case-by-case basis. For example in the case of GDR–USSR trade, individual ministries are authorized to conduct trade up to a certain amount (presumably in preliminary prices) using a swing credit, and then the FTOs later negotiate the actual prices (Medvedkov, 1979, p. 36). The basic problem here is closely connected to problems concerning manufactured-goods exports. The Ministry of Foreign Trade, designed to centralize control over all trade flows in the hands of planners, is itself a formidable institutional impediment to the complex cooperation, specialization and trade characteristic of foreign economic relations in the post-war period. And now, because the Soviet Union has not matched the modest advances Eastern European countries have made in redefining the monopoly of foreign trade to allow somewhat more advanced forms of foreign economic relations to develop in their systems, genuine accomplishments in USSR–East European industrial cooperation are few in comparison to the possibilities. And that should continue to be the case until Soviet leaders are willing to go beyond minor changes and *ad hoc* solutions to changes in the fundamental structure of the system.

Actual changes to date have been extremely modest in scope and should have no appreciable effect on the problems discussed above. In 1978 and 1979 the Ministry of Foreign Trade's FTOs were reorganized and two changes were introduced in their operations.[16] First, a new governing body (*pravlenie*) was introduced for each FTO consisting of one-half representation from the domestic ministries producing goods that the FTO manages in trade, and one-half from the Ministry of Foreign Trade (presumably the product administrations). The *pravlenie* has limited authority, its main purposes being to figure out how the enterprises and FTOs together can act better to meet existing plans of increasing the production and sale of exportables. This measure is accompanied by new bonuses for export, differentiated by FTO; and the FTOs are authorized to set up new funds for material incentives, which will evidently be formed as a function of their performance. None of these changes alters the authority of the Ministry of Foreign Trade over the FTOs, or over foreign-trade relations. The Ministry still appoints the leading personnel in the FTO, and it still issues an obligatory plan to the FTO. The *pravlenie* in each FTO is an export-promotion committee that, it is hoped, will bridge the gap between FTOs and domestic enterprises. This is hardly a new idea. For some time the domestic ministries in the USSR have had several committees with the responsibility to improve export performance and coordinate the relations between their enterprises and the FTOs (Berman and Bustin, 1975, pp. 1007–9). All that is new is that these committees have been set up directly in the administrative apparatus of the FTOs.

The second major set of changes relate to the operation of the FTOs themselves. The old *kontory* that handled various product groups and functions within each FTO have been replaced by *firmy* that handle product groups supposedly defined to closely correspond to the domestic-sector nomenclature.[17] These *firmy* seem to have enhanced right of signature in foreign-trade contracts within parameters set by the director of the FTO; and this is a change compared to the powers of the *kontory*. A complete evaluation of the legal ramifications of these changes is beyond my expertise, and practical experience in the next few years will reveal whether there are any major effects on economic performance. It would appear that these changes are of a minor operational nature, and that they do not affect any of the fundamental arrangements in the system.

(c) *Possible Changes in the Near Future*

Further, more far-reaching, changes in the organization and management of the Soviet foreign sector are possible in the near future, although not likely. It would appear that in the late 1970s there was some discussion of a major reorganization of the foreign sector, along the lines of what has transpired in Eastern Europe, involving a considerable decentralization of decisions on foreign trade to the level of the enterprise or, more likely, the association. The Ministry of Foreign Trade was apparently, and predictably, opposed to such changes; and to date that opposition seems to have effectively stopped the discussion.[18] Still, Patolichev (1978b) notes that foreign economic relations are considered an increasingly important determinant of Soviet economic performance, and that, at least in the few years including and preceding 1978, they were discussed at virtually every Politbureau meeting. One doubts that matters have changed since then. The main issues discussed are improvement in foreign-trade effectiveness, increases in export potential, improvements in planning and management of foreign trade, and strengthening of the links between the sectoral ministries and the foreign sector.

There was an August 1976 decree on all aspects of foreign economic relations (which is still unpublished) that led to the 1978–9 changes discussed above (Patolichev, 1978b, p. 5). In addition, judging from published statements in the last five years, this decree — and the numerous Politbureau meetings — must have discussed increased concentration of the production of manufactured goods for export in a few firms, each of which would direct a high proportion of their output for exports. Kosygin raised the matter at the Twenty-Fifth Party Congress ("Osnovnye napravleniia ...", 1976, p. 2). Alkhimov (1976), then Deputy Minister of Foreign Trade, expanded on the notion of special export enterprises dedicated to producing products in demand on foreign markets. He states that matters are moving forward in concentrating existing export capacity in fewer firms. He also suggests it would be useful to build small enterprises, requiring little capital, that could quickly pay for themselves on export markets. In the longer term he anticipated expanding capacity to produce exportables in areas such as shipbuilding, computers, aircraft and automatic power-station equipment.

In fact, it would appear that almost nothing of substance has been done. There may be a few enterprises specialized in exports, but there is nothing like a move towards the creation of a *group* of export enterprises, that is, a special export sector.[19] And while pressures arising from difficulties in export performance may stimulate re-invigorated efforts in this direction, in the final analysis this is an attempt to avoid fundamental change, and will therefore have only a minor impact on export performance.

9.3   Prospects for the Next Two Decades

Concerning the foreign sector, the key question for the next two decades is whether, and when, the Soviet institutions that control foreign economic relations will change in any fundamental way. This is really a question of when the entire institutional system that governs the Soviet economy will be restructured. Soviet problems in producing manufactured goods, exportable for convertible currency, are the direct result of a planning system that consistently generates taut plans, which — in the context of a highly protected domestic market — perpetuates a sellers' market; a planning and management system that discourages the introduction of new technologies in production processes; and a price system that provides neither sufficient information nor incentives to economize on imports or to stimulate exports. While the foreign sector may be separate from the domestic economy in the minds of Soviet policy makers and many Soviet economists, and while the Soviet economic literature may focus solely on the foreign sector in discussing the problem of exports, that myopia cannot be allowed to obscure the fact that problems in the Soviet foreign sector originate in the domestic economy. Any attempt to improve export performance without addressing the ultimate source of the problem — the institutions that allocate resources in the domestic economy — is destined to produce at best very modest improvements in economic performance.

Soviet economic institutions, particularly those that have a major effect on foreign-trade performance, will not be changed unless such change is unavoidable. The entire governmental and Party hierarchy, and their authority over the economy, would have to undergo dramatic change in the event of truly meaningful reform in the system; and that is something that individuals in those hierarchies will accept only when failing to do it guarantees that they will lose their power. As Foreign Trade Minister Patolichev has made crystal clear, the monopoly of foreign trade means only one thing: that Gosplan, and through it the Ministry of Foreign Trade, retains absolute control over trade transactions. Any suggestions to the contrary are attacks at the foundations of socialism (Patolichev, 1978a). The vested interests in favor of retaining the essential elements of the current institutional structure are so firmly entrenched that the only way their opposition can be overcome is when economic performance is bad enough long enough to weaken their bargaining power.

In the 1970s the Soviet economy enjoyed windfall gains through its foreign sector, and because of that the pressures for institutional change were less than they otherwise would have been. Soviet capacity to produce and increase net exports of primary products for convertible currency rose in the 1960s and 1970s not because planners were sure that relative prices of those products would continue to rise, but because the system could not successfully develop other goods exportable for convertible currency, and therefore it had to push traditional exports. If in the 1970s the world price of oil, natural gas, other primary products and gold, had plummeted, the pressures for change in the Soviet economy would have multiplied rapidly in the face of increasing debts and a decreasing ability to import advanced machinery and equipment. In fact the opposite occurred; the changes in the net barter terms of trade provided Soviet planners with an unexpected, *ex post*, ratification in world-market prices for a decision made for reasons unrelated to those prices.

The probability is very low that the 1980s will be as favorable for the Soviet economy, and particularly for Soviet convertible-currency exports, as the 1970s. The Soviets will be lucky if they can increase net petroleum exports for convertible currency in the face of growing domestic demands, the growing needs of Eastern Europe, and a dramatic slow-down in growth rates for petroleum extraction; they could easily see their exports of petroleum dissipate by 1985, if the CIA is correct in their projections. Natural-gas exports can replace part, but hardly all, of hard currency lost from decreased petroleum exports. In addition, as petroleum products lose some of their importance in exports (or gain importance in gross imports), that will cause the (Paasche) terms of trade to deteriorate, thus reversing the windfall gains of the 1970s from that source. Therefore, without venturing a guess at the level of convertible-currency earnings possible from exportable primary products and fuels, it is highly probable that in the early 1980s convertible-currency export performance will deteriorate, and that the pressures for system change will increase.

At first these pressures may not be very strong. The Soviet Union enters the 1980s with substantial possibilities for borrowing on convertible-currency markets: their debt-service ratio is quite low by world standards, and their gold reserves are large. They could easily borrow dollars to cover several years of zero petroleum exports, assuming those would have equaled $5 billion or $6 billion a year. Furthermore, *if* (and this is not a prediction) gold prices sustain their present level, or continue their upward trend, then that $40 billion (or higher) gold stock is another buffer allowing the Soviet leaders to buy time in their search for a solution to stagnating or falling convertible-currency exports. It would not seem to be at all difficult for planners to do nothing new about system arrangements in 1981–5, and yet replace temporarily the convertible-currency proceeds lost as capacity in traditional exports sectors deteriorates.

One obvious solution to a deterioration in real export capacity is to cut back on hard-currency imports, but this is probably an option that Soviet planners will reject. There isn't a great deal of obvious "fat" in the Soviet hard-currency import bill. For example in 1976–8 34% of imports were machinery and equipment. These are really imports of embodied technology and it is likely that as the USSR continues to push for higher productivity-growth rates to sustain GNP growth rates, imported machinery (hence technology) will be more, rather than less, important to them. Another 20% of 1976–8 hard-currency imports were food, mostly grain; there is little prospect that the Soviet agricultural sector will soon improve its performance so dramatically as to reduce the need for hard-currency food imports. Another 14% of the imports were rolled ferrous metals, of which the most important component was pipe. Here, again, Soviet import demands are likely to increase as they push the development of their gas industry.[20] Therefore, while Soviet planners may consider reducing hard-currency imports when the growth of their hard-currency export capacity falls, they will probably conclude that they cannot afford significant cuts in hard-currency imports; on the contrary, the press-ures to increase those imports will grow.

As planners turn their attention from conserving imports to expanding exports, their first attempts will surely focus on efforts to develop special enterprises devoted primarily or totally to export for convertible currency. This will certainly appeal to Soviet planners, who see in it the possibility to retain control over the bulk of the domestic economy, while dedicating selected enterprises to earning convertible currency. In fact there is a precedent in the military sector, which, unlike the remainder of the Soviet economy, produces high-quality goods that are apparently quite acceptable to the Soviet military and to foreign customers alike.

It is unlikely that this approach will succeed, although it could be late in the 1980s before that is evident. The most obvious problem is that this would entail creating a second "defense" industry while attempt-ing to sustain, and probably increase, the output of the first, the true, defense industry. This new export sector would not be allowed to drain resources from defense, so it would have to draw on the remainder of the system, which means consumer goods, capital for consumer-goods industries, and so on. That could affect the supply of labor, or at least the supply of effort, and it would surely influence the already skeptical political opinions in the population at large concerning the justification for a special export sector that makes high-quality products for people in other countries, and low-quality products for Soviet citizens.

Also, there are social and economic problems attached to a special export sector. The export sector will somehow have to draw out of the labor force more, and higher quality, work than most Soviet enter-prises seem able to manage. This probably will require higher wages, and, in effect, partial wage payments in convertible currency. That means the creation of an elite among workers, hard to justify, particularly as the remainder of the population suffers cutbacks in the quality, and possibly the quantity, of consumables available for purchase.

Thirdly, there are a number of issues involved in establishing an export sector which — while they have always plagued the Soviet economy — would be particularly tricky in this case. Because prices for goods and labor in the USSR are misleading indicators of true costs (even true private costs, let alone true social costs), planners must ensure that the export sector does not become a funnel through which domestically cheap, but actually quite expensive and scarce, inputs are incorporated into manufactures and then sold too cheaply on world markets. This is, of course, a problem in any export of any economy like the USSR. But the existing Soviet resource-allocation system informally compensates for this in part because as highly valuable inputs (say highly skilled labor) grow scarce, and various users bid for those inputs, in the process the inputs may indeed end up going where they are most needed, where they are paid for with a low price, but with side-payments reflecting their actual value. A special export sector, if given first claim on all inputs, and an ultimatum to maximize dollar profits, could surely avoid the bargaining process, buying at cheap domestic prices, and then selling the resulting output at world-market prices.

To avoid the possibility of giving away national income in this way, planners would have to establish an iron-clad rule that export enterprises buy absolutely everything they use either from the world market, or from the domestic economy, but at world-market prices. This concerns not only the purchase of current inputs, but also buildings, machinery and equipment, and money itself.

Finally, all of these issues aside, probably the most formidable obstacle to the formation of a special export sector is the bureaucracy itself. The establishment of such a sector would attack the power base of several important lobbies in the economy. Gosplan and the ministries would lose control over what would surely be the best-run enterprises in the economy, and they would lose control over valuable material and human inputs. The Ministry of Foreign Trade would lose control over exports of manufactured goods for convertible currency, something it will fiercely oppose. Party officials would have to relinquish controls over operative decisions in these key enterprises. Consequently, important elements of the Soviet governmental and Party apparatus would oppose the creation of a pure export sector. If difficulties in convertible-currency exports are severe enough that some sort of special export sector is created, then the opponents will do all they can to dilute the actual implementation of the changes.

Despite all of these obstacles, something like a special export sector will probably emerge in the 1980s in the Soviet Union. Problems in export performance will force them to do something, and this is the one substantive avenue of change that seems destined to do the least harm to vested-interest groups. All of these changes will transpire simultaneously with the political succession, and that might smooth the way a little bit; but I suspect that the second tier of Party and government officials is as committed to the fundamental structure of the system as the old generation.

Major losses to the Soviet economy in the early 1980s (say because the most pessimistic of the CIA scenarios on petroleum transpires) could speed up this process; major new windfall gains could slow it down. But in the absence of anything terribly dramatic, in the late 1980s the Soviet economy should be well along the path of attempting to develop a special export sector. This will probably improve export performance somewhat, but not a great deal; and, for reasons discussed above, the cost to the domestic economy will be large.

In the 1990s, if hard-currency export performance has not improved considerably, or if — which seems more likely — it is generally considered by the leadership to be poor and unsustainable, then further changes will be forced through. The changes involved will probably go beyond the special export sector to a more decentralized system that finally makes major alterations in the substance of the monopoly of foreign trade. A likely outcome is a move towards what the Hungarians have been doing since 1968, namely a controlled partial decentralization of all decisions on production, sales, purchases, and therefore foreign trade. Planners in this system do not lose control, but rather shift to using more indirect instruments (prices, interest rates, taxes, and subsidies) and to less formal, but still quite effective, techniques that might be called "moral suasion." Planners would retain virtually total control over investment, thus over increments to productive capacity; they would control the income distribution at the enterprise level through taxes; and they would use tariffs and licensing to ensure that the foreign sector does not become a major source of disruption. Within these tight controls enterprises would be encouraged to maximize profits when faced with prices, interest rates and exchange rates that roughly reflect the true cost to the economy of the goods, capital, and foreign exchange involved.

This is the route the Hungarians have followed. They were forced into these changes by the problems they encountered in their convertible-currency exports, which in turn reflected problems in their economic institutions similar to those in the Soviet economy today. Of course the Soviet economy is a far larger, and consequently more complex, political-economic system, and it can hardly be expected to replicate the Hungarian experience. The Hungarian reformers faced what were surely less well entrenched bureaucrats than Soviet reformers would face, yet even so, the Hungarian reformers have experienced several setbacks as antireform groups managed to resist reform, or roll back new reform measures (Hewett, 1980b). But the most valuable lesson of the Hungarian experience does seem to be transferable to the Soviet situation: it is possible to decentralize in some areas, retain control in others, and considerably improve export performance.

Something like this option could not be introduced in the USSR much before 1990 and could not even receive serious consideration and debate until, and if, the succession reaches into key parts of the bureaucracy, including the major institutes dealing with economics. Even then, a long period of discussion and debate would have to ensue before the requisite support would come from the Party, the government, and in particular the economists. The redefinition of words such as "planning," the "monopoly of foreign trade," and "prices" will not come easily in Soviet society. Unlike Eastern Europe where reforms came only twenty years after the initial imposition of Stalinist central planning, in the Soviet Union virtually the entire Soviet population has known only one system. It will not be an easy or a quick matter to reverse years of propaganda surrounding that system and convince people that a new system will serve them better. This is particularly true because transition to a system such as the Hungarian system will mean increased uncertainty about prices (subsequent to some major price reforms), and increased pressure for productivity increases in the workplace, but with the reward of possibly considerable improvements in living standards.

Because of these impediments to major system change, it seems likely that the 1990s will be a period in which Soviet problems in convertible-currency exports persist, while simultaneously a transition begins to a system the Hungarians introduced in the late 1960s. As long as no major disasters befall the Soviet economy this is not an at all implausible scenario. Soviet leaders would like to avoid all change, but they cannot. Either they would have to starve the economy for imports, eventually sell their entire gold stock, or ask the international banking community for more than it is willing to lend. So they will begin to change, but as slowly as possible. The reserves they have (in money, and even in unrealized opportunities within the framework of the current system) are formidable enough that it is possible for them to go quite slowly. But if in 1990 they are beginning to talk about a Hungarian-type reform, and if by the year 2000 they are beginning to introduce such a reform, that will be a more rapid and fundamental change than they have undergone in the last twenty years; and it just may be enough change to allow the Party and the government to maintain — in an admittedly restructured way — their basic control over Soviet society.

9: Appendix

Quantity Indices in Table 9.10

Over the years 1960–78, which are the years covered in the tables, the USSR Ministry of Foreign Trade has published in its *Vneshniaia torgovlia: statisticheskii obzor (Foreign Trade: Statistical Compendium*, abbreviated here as VTSS) a quantity index for total exports and imports. Since 1963, indices have also been published for exports and imports to and from socialist countries, the CMEA countries, and other (that is, capitalist) countries. The weighting of the indices has changed over time, but since the indices are published for two years at a time, there is always a one year overlap, and it is possible to link the indices into one quantity index.

This procedure can lead to more than one index, depending on the decisions one makes along the way, and this for two reasons. First, there are, from time to time, unannounced revisions of the quantity indices. For example the 1972 and 1973 VTSSs both reported quantity indices weighted in 1970 prices, with 1960 = 100. Yet in almost every case the values of the quantity index for the year 1972 differ in the two sources. In all cases of this sort I have taken the later value in constructing the index.

The second problem relates to weights and samples, and it became extremely important beginning in the mid-1970s. The sample problem becomes obvious in comparing the data from VTSS 1974 and 1975 concerning the 1974 quantity index. VTSS 1974 reports the 1974 quantity indices weighted in 1970 prices with 1965 = 100; VTSS 1975 reports the 1974 quantity indices, weighted in the same prices (1970), but with 1970 = 100. Yet for total trade and for each country group, for exports and for imports, the indices for 1970 = 100 are lower (sometimes by more than 20%) than the indices where 1965 = 100, converted to 1970 = 100. The sample must have changed with the base year. I used the percentage changes inplied by the indices beginning in 1974, multiplied by the earlier value, so that the resulting quantity index is at the high end of the 1970 = 100 quantity indices one could obtain.

In data reported in VTSS 1976, the price basis is changed once again to 1975 prices; and then in VTSS 1977 onward, the indices are computed with what are called "comparable prices," which means prices of the previous year. This means that from 1975 onward these indices have almost become Paasche indices, which are probably below what Laspeyres quantity indices would record. Again, I simply used the percentage price changes given by these indices multiplied by the previous year, so that the quantity index obtained is the highest index suggested by the data.

An alternative, and lower, quantity index would be obtained for 1970, and 1974–8 by simply taking the reported quantity indices straight out of the VTSSs (instead of applying their implied percentage price change to the high 1974 value). What matters here, other than the record of the quantitative change in the level of foreign trade, is the implied unit-value indices and the terms of trade. Of course, the unit value indices are higher using the Paasche, 1970 = 100, quantity indices. *But the terms of trade come out almost the same.* The quantitative records concerning the changes in foreign-trade flows are not so far apart as to alter the fact that foreign trade has grown much faster than national income.[21]

The tables documenting these indices are extensive and are not reproduced here. A copy of them is available on request.

Estimates of Windfall Gains in Table 9.10

The first column of Table 9.10, "Additional Imports Possible Due to Improved Terms of Trade," is obtained by dividing nominal exports for convertible currency (from Table 9.6), by the terms of trade in convertible currency (Table 9.7) to obtain deflated exports. Those are then subtracted from nominal exports to obtain the first column. For example, nominal exports in 1974 were $7,470 million, and the terms of trade were 1.70 (1971 = 1.00). 7,470/1.70 = $4,394 million, which is deflated exports. That subtracted from $7,470 million yields the figure $3,076 million in Table 9.10.

The second column represents the quantity of gold sold (Table 9.9) multiplied by the difference between the price of gold in 1971 ($1.317 million per metric ton) and its price in every year since 1971. The prices are from Ericson and Miller (1979, p. 239) through 1978, and for 1979 a price of $9.778 million per metric ton was used, which is the unweighted average of monthly gold sales prices in Zurich in 1979 (reported in the *International Monetary Market 1978–79 Yearbook*).

9: Notes

1 I am grateful to Ms Mina Mohammadioun for her research assistance on this project and to the University Research Institute, University of Texas, for its financial support of the research. I also wish to thank Abram Bergson, Morris Bornstein, Franklyn Holzman, Herbert Levine, Paul Marer, and Jan Vaňous for their comments on an earlier draft of this paper.

2 The socialist countries include the CMEA countries (Bulgaria, Cuba (since 1972), Czechoslovakia, East Germany, Hungary, Mongolia (since 1962), Poland, Romania, and Vietnam (since 1978)), North Korea, China, and Laos (since 1978), and Cuba, Mongolia and Vietnam before they were CMEA members.

3 One possible explanation for the inconsistency is that the index for total trade is computed using a sample different from the indices for trade with capitalist and socialist countries. The former predates the latter and, given the way Soviet bureaucracy works, it is conceivable that separate samples have been developed. Another possibility is that the total indices are indeed an average of the capitalist and socialist indices, but the weights are some mixture of base and current-year weights. It is virtually impossible to choose intelligently among these and other possibilities because official Soviet sources provide almost no information on samples and computational procedures for these indices. For a discussion of what is known about the indices, see Hewett (1980a, Appendix B).

4 Recently the Economic Commission for Europe published estimates of price and quantity indices for trade of "Western" countries (West Europe, the US, Canada and Japan) with the Soviet Union and Eastern Europe covering the period 1965 to 1977 (UN Economic Commission for Europe, 1979). These could conceivably be used in combination with the Table 9.1 data to estimate Soviet trade with developing and developed capitalist countries separately, and I did experiments along that line. But the problem is that these are data from Western sources, and it is well documented that there is frequently strong disagreement with Eastern data on the same trade flows; the growing consensus is that the Eastern data are right (see Gullo, 1979). Furthermore the split between Laspeyres and Paasche unit-value indices on Western exports to the Soviet Union was enormous. The authors blame this on changing price weights, which is no doubt true, but one must wonder if the underlying sample included some incredibly high price changes reflecting changing composition in the product group (pp. 57–8). My experience with computing unit-value indices showed that it was quite possible for a commodity of no consequence to total trade to have such a large price change that it caused a significant split between Paasche and Laspeyres and either deflated or inflated both. The authors do not discuss how they watched for such commodities, if they did so at all; and until they clarify this, these indices should be used with great care, if at all.

   Finally, the study states that the quantity and price indices are both Paasche (pp. 124, 127, 166, and 169); but that is obviously not the case. The methodological discussion (p. 58) states that the volume indices are obtained by dividing indices of total value by Paasche price indices, which yields Laspeyres quantity indices; and indeed a check of their data indicates that is indeed what they have got. Even more puzzling is the fact that their Laspeyres indices for the one-digit SITC groups, used to derive trade by one-digit SITC level in 1965 dollars, are obviously inconsistent with the indices for total trade.

   The CIA (June 1980) has published some estimates of quantity and unit-value indices for Soviet convertible-currency trade. They are not useful here since the Soviets are clearing so much of their trade with developing countries in convertible currencies, but they will be discussed below in the section on convertible-currency trade.

5 Actually a "proper" exchange rate and a "proper" price system both of which accurately reflect the supply and demand conditions for currency and goods could well produce rather high trade–national income ratios since tradeables are probably undervalued in the Soviet economy.

6 This pricing problem extends to comparisons of the relative magnitude of Soviet

exports to CMEA countries and to other countries. The exchange rates the Soviets use to convert their trade flows with CMEA into rubles overstates the value of those trade flows relative to the ruble value of Soviet trade with other countries, and consequently it overstates the relative share of CMEA in total Soviet foreign trade. For a discussion of this and an attempt to adjust the data, see Vaňous (1980).

7 Ericson and Miller (1979, pp. 237–9) give a list of all the countries with which the Soviet Union reportedly settles its trade accounts in convertible currencies. The 1978 convertible-currency export figure reported by the CIA (given here in Table 9.6) is $13.157 billion. The Soviet data that year reported exports to developed capitalist countries less Finland of $7.695 billion, which *with* the exports to Finland equal $11.312 billion. Thus, estimated convertible-currency earnings in 1978 from partners other than developed countries was $1.845 billion. These estimates do not include CMEA hard-currency trade.

8 The petroleum and petroleum-products export data are taken from *VTSS* (1978), and are a total of the value of exports of those products to all countries that reportedly settle their accounts with the USSR in convertible currencies, multiplied by the dollar/ruble ratio in 1978 (1.47).

9 See, for example, the excerpts from Brezhnev's speech to the XXV Party Congress in *Vneshniaia torgovlia* No. 5 (1979), pp. i–iii, and in Klochek (1976, pp. 2–9).

10 There are some important ambiguities in the CIA numbers. It is not clear if their production figures include gold as a by-product in nonferrous metal production; the Kaser figures do include that information. Also note that stocks will fall even if gold sales on world markets equal production, due to internal use, which Schoppe estimates at 50 tons in recent years (Schoppe, 1979, pp. 64–5).

11 In 1936 about 500 tons of gold were sent to the Soviet Union from Spain for safe keeping. The Franco regime was unsuccessful in reclaiming it, and the Soviet Union now claims it as its own (Schoppe, 1978, p. 44).

12 For further details, see the Data Appendix.

13 For more detailed accounts of how institutions are set up in the Soviet foreign sector see "Institut Mirovoi Ekonomiki ..." (1977), Hewett (1978), Gruzinov (1975, 1979), Berman and Bustin (1975), and Quigley (1974).

14 Hewett (1974, Chap. 4) gives a general discussion of this planning process, which is updated in Hewett (1978). The efficiency of foreign trade, really the gains from trade, has been a concern of parts of the planning apparatus in the Soviet Union since the 1960s. In 1968 Gosplan published a "temporary" methodology for computing foreign-trade efficiency that was to be used in justifying all proposed exports and imports. In 1980 that methodology was formally adopted in an expanded form that relates also to agreements on specialization and cooperation, USSR participation in projects abroad, the expansion of productive capacity in the USSR as part of plans to expand trade, and Soviet participation in agreements on the purchase and sale of new technology ("Metodika opredeleniia ... ", 1980.

15 For a discussion of these issues see Kirillov (1978), Alkhimov (1976), "Osnovnykh napravlenii ... " (1976).

16 For further details see "Polozhenie o vsesoiuznom ... " (1978), "Vashnye zadachi ... " (1978), Smirnov (1978, 1980), Tret'iukhin (1979).

17 Smirnov (1978, 1980) gives the details. Bozek (1979, pp. 524–5) contains several good examples of how the changes were carried out for Stankoimport and Prodintorg.

18 I am guessing about this entire discussion, based on Patolichev (1978a, 1978b). In those two speeches Mr. Patolichev, the Minister of Foreign Trade, vigorously defends the monopoly of foreign trade against unnamed attackers who suggest that the planning and management of foreign trade should be decentralized. This involves notions

> ... of more open access to the markets of socialist countries, of the establishment of direct contacts between producers and users of products, of a closer connection between internal and world prices, and so on. One cannot help but see that all of this 'advice' is directed at weakening the monopoly of

foreign trade and undermining the planned basis of our economy. This requires of us great vigilance and a decisive rejection of any attempts by our non-friends (*nedrugy*) to seek out changes in the basic foundations of socialism. (Patolichev, 1978a, no page).

While the speech seems directed at outsiders trying to break the monopoly of foreign trade, one suspects that they have friends on the inside. In fact Patolichev (1978b) notes that opposition to the monopoly of foreign trade has, since its beginning under Lenin, come not only from capitalists, but also from rightist forces in the USSR.

19 The most convincing evidence of a lack of progress here is the absence of articles praising the positive effects of new export-oriented enterprises. Also, Savin (1979), in his discussion of the export potential of the central RSFSR, makes it abundantly clear that there are virtually no enterprises that devote a significant amount of their output to export, and it appears that there are no administrative moves underway to change that.

20 The numbers are computed from Ericson and Miller, 1979, Appendix G, p. 241.

21 On the total import side, the high quantity index shows imports in 1978 at 2.3 times their 1970 level; the low index shows the ratio to be 2.16. On the export side the numbers are 1.94 and 1.74, respectively.

9: References

Alkhimov, V., "Razvitie vneshneekonomicheskoi sviazei SSSR v svete reshenii XXV s"ezda KPSS" ("The Development of Foreign Economic Connections in View of the Decisions of the XXV Congress of the Communist Party of the Soviet Union"). *Vneshniaia torgovlia:* 2–9, July 1976.

Baibakov, N., "Sovershenstvovanie sotsialisticheskogo planirovaniia v stranakhchlenakh SEV" ("The Improvement of Socialist Planning in the Member Countries of CMEA"). *Planovoe khoziaistvo:* 9–18, June 1979.

Berman, Harold J., and Bustin, George L., "The Soviet System of Foreign Trade." *Law and Policy of Internat. Bus.* **7**: 987–1057, Fall 1975.

Bozek, Scott, "The U.S.S.R.: Intensifying the Development of Its Foreign Trade Structure." In *Soviet Economy . . . .*, Vol. 2, pp. 506–25, 1979.

Carr, William, "The Soviet Merchant Fleet: Its Economic Role and Its Impact on Western Shipowners." In *Soviet Economy . . . .*, Vol. 2, pp. 663–77, 1979.

CIA (Central Intelligence Agency), "Communist Aid to Less Developed Countries of the Free World." ER 78–10478U. Washington, DC: Nov. 1978.

CIA, *Handbook of Economic Statistics 1979.* ER 79–10274. Washington, DC, Aug. 1979.

CIA, "Estimating Soviet and East European Hard Currency Debt." ER 80–10327. Washington, DC, June 1980a.

CIA, "The Soviet Economy in 1978–79 and Prospects for 1980." ER 80–10328. Washington, DC, June 1980b.

Dohan, Michael R., "Export Specialization and Import Dependence in the Soviet Economy, 1970–77." In *Soviet Economy . . . .* Vol. 2, pp. 342–95, 1979.

Ericson, Paul G., and Miller, Ronald S., "Soviet Economic Behavior: A Balance of Payments Perspective." In *Soviet Economy . . .* Vol. 2. pp. 208–43, 1979.

Farrell, John T., "Soviet Payments Problems in Trade with the West." In *Soviet Economic Prospects for the Seventies*, pp. 690–718. Papers, Joint Econ. Comm., US Congress. Washington, DC: Govt. Printing Office, 1973.

Frey, Walter, The International Gold Market." *J. Soc. and Pol. Stud.* **5**, 1 & 2: 39–48, Spring/Summer 1980.

Gardner, H. Steven, "Recent Developments in Soviet Foreign Trade Planning." IREX Occasional Paper, June 1980.

Gruzinov, V. P., *The USSR's Management of Foreign Trade.* Translation, edited and with an introduction by E. A. Hewett, of *Upravlenie vneshnei torgovlei* (Moscow, 1975). White Plains: M. E. Sharpe, 1979.

Gullo, Damian T., "Reconciliation of Soviet and Western Trade Data: The United States as a Case Study. In *Soviet Economy*.... Vol. 2, pp. 526–50, 1979.

Hardt, John P., "Maritime Developments involving the Soviet Union, the United States, and the West." In *Issues in East-West Commercial Relations*, pp. 247–66. Papers, Joint Econ. Comm., U.S. Congress. Washington, DC: Govt. Printing Office, 1979.

Hewett, Ed. A., *Foreign Trade Prices in the Council for Mutual Economic Assistance.* Cambridge: Cambridge Univ. Press, 1974.

Hewett, Ed. A., "Most-Favored Nation Treatment in Trade Under Central Planning." *Slavic Rev.* 37, 1: 25–39, ·March 1978.

Hewett, Ed. A., "Soviet Primary Product Exports to CMEA and the West." Assn. of Amer. Geographers Project on Soviet Natural Resources in the World Economy, Discussion Paper, May 1979.

Hewett, Ed. A., "The Impact of the World Economic Crisis on Intra-CMEA Trade." In Neuberger and Tyson, eds, pp. 323–48, 1980a.

Hewett, Ed. A., "The Hungarian Economy: Lessons of the 1970s and Prospects for the 1980's." In *East European Assessment.* Papers, Joint Econ. Comm., US Congress. Washington, DC: Govt. Printing Office, 1980b.

Holzman, Franklyn D., "Foreign Trade Behavior of Centrally Planned Economies." In Franklyn D. Holzman, *Foreign Trade under Central Planning*, pp. 139–63. Cambridge, Mass.: Harvard Univ. Press, 1974.

Holzman, Franklyn D., "Some Theories of the Hard Currency Shortage of Centrally Planned Economies." In *Soviet Economy* ..., Vol. 2, pp. 297–316, 1979.

Institut Mirovoi Ekonomiki i Mezhdunarodnykh Otnoshenii (Institute of the World Economy and International Relations), "Organizatsiia vneshnekonomicheskikh sviazei v SSSR" ("The Organization of Foreign Economic Relations in the USSR"). Moscow; Mimeo, 1977.

International Monetary Fund Yearbook 1978–1979.

Kaser, Michael, "Soviet Gold Production." In *Soviet Economy* ... Vol. 2, pp. 290–6, 1979.

Klochek, V., "Vneshniaia torgovliia SSSR na rubezhe desiatoi piatiletki" ("The Foreign Trade of the U.S.S.R. on the Eve of the Tenth Five-Year Plan"). *Vneshniaia torgovliia:* 2–9, May 1976.

Medvedkov, Iu., "Programmu spetsializatsii i kooperirovaniia proizvodstva do 1990 goda i nekotorye voprosy organizatsii vneshnei torgovli sotsialisticheskikh stran" ("On the Program of Specialization and Cooperation of Production to 1990, and Several Questions on the Organization of Foreign Trade of the Socialist Countries"). *Vneshniaia torgovlia:* 31–6, Feb. 1979.

"Metodika opredeleniia ekonomicheskoi effektivnosti vneshneekonomicheskikh sviazei SSSR" ("The Method of Determining the Economic Effectiveness of Foreign Economic Connections of the USSR"). *Planovoe khoziaistvo:* 125–7, June 1980.

Miller, Elisa B., "The Trans-Siberian Landbridge, A New Trade Route Between Japan and Europe: Issues and Prospects." *Soviet Geography* 19, 4: 223–43, April 1978.

Nar. khoz., see TSU.

Neuberger, Egon, and Tyson, Laura D., eds, *Transmission and Response: The Impact of International Disturbances on the Soviet Union and Eastern Europe.* New York: Pergamon Press, 1980.

"Osnovnykh napravlenii razvitiia narodnogo khoziaistva SSSR na 1976–80 godu" ("Basic Directions of Development of the Economy of the USSR for 1976–1980"). *Vneshniaia torgovlia*, no pages, June 1976.

Patolichev, N. "K60-letiiu leninskogo dekreta o natsionalizatsii vneshnei torgovli" ("On the Sixtieth Anniversary of the Leninist Decree on the Nationalization of Foreign Trade"). Insert in *Vneshniaia torgovlia*, May 1978a.

Patolichev, N., "Leninskii dekret v deistvii' ("The Leninist Decree in Action"). *Vneshniaia torgovlia:* 2–6 May 1978b.

"Polozhenie o vsesoiuznom khozraschetnom vneshnetorgovom ob"edinenii, khodiashchem v sistemu ministerstva vneshnei torgovli" ("Statute on All-Union, Economically Accountable, Foreign Trade Associations, in the System of the Ministry of

Trade"). *Sobranie postanovlenii pravitel'stva Soiuza Sovetskikh sotsialisticheskikh Respublik*, No. 13, 1978.

Popov, K., "Po puti sotsialisticheskoi ekonomicheskoi integratsii" ("On the Road of Socialist Economic Integration"). *Vneshniaia torgovlia*, Feb. 1976.

Quigley, John, *The Soviet Foreign Trade Monopoly: Institutions and Laws*. Columbus: Ohio State Univ. Press, 1974.

Savin, V., "Eksportnyi potentsial tsentralnogo raiona SSSR" ("The Export Potential of the Central Region of the USSR"). *Vneshniaia torgovlia*: 20–23, Dec. 1979.

Schoppe, Siegfried G., "Myth and Reality of the Soviet Gold Policy." *Intereconomics*: 44–8, Jan.-Feb. 1978.

Schoppe, Siegfried G., Changes in the Function of Gold Within the Soviet Foreign Trade System Since 1945–46." *Soviet and Eastern Foreign Trade* 15, 3: 60–95, Fall 1979.

Smirnov, P., "Pravovoe polozhenie vneshnetorgovogo ob"edineniia" ("The Legal Position of the Foreign Trade Association"). *Vneshniaia torgovlia*: 34–41, Oct. 1978.

Smirnov, P., "Novye organizatsii v sfere vneshnei torgovli — firmy, vkhodiashchie v sostav vneshnetorgovykh ob"edinenii" ("New Organizations in the Sphere of Foreign Trade — Firms That Form the Components of the Foreign Trade Associations"). *Vneshniaia torgovlia*: 48–50, Jan. 1980.

Soviet Economy in a Time of Change. Papers, Joint Econ. Comm., US Congress. Washington, DC: Govt. Printing Office, 1979.

Treml, Vladimir, "Foreign Trade and the Soviet Economy: Changing Parameters and Interrelations." In Neuberger and Tyson, eds, pp. 184–207, 1980.

Tret'iukhin, N., "Uluchshenie planirovaniia vneshnei torgovli — postoiannoe vnimanie" ("The Improvement of the Planning of Foreign Trade — A Constant Concern"). *Vneshniaia torgovlia*: 2–5, Dec. 1979.

TSU SSSR, *Narodnoe khozaistvo SSSR: statisticheskii ezhegodnik* (The National Economy of the USSR: Statistical Annual). Published annually by the USSR Statistical Administration.

United Nations Economic Commission for Europe, *Economic Bulletin for Europe* 31, 1: 54–69 and 118–83, 1979.

Vaňous, Jan, "Soviet and Eastern European Foreign Trade in the 1970's: A Quantitative Assessment." Discussion Paper No. 80–11, Department of Economics, University of British Columbia, April 1980.

"Vashnye zadachi rabotnikov vneshnei torgovli" ("Important Tasks of the Workers in Foreign Trade"). *Vneshniaia torgovlia*: 2–4 Oct. 1978.

VTSS, *Vneshniaia torgovlia SSSR: Statisticheskii obzor* (Foreign Trade of the USSR: Statistical Compendium). Published annually by the USSR Ministry of Foreign Trade.

10

Consumption

GERTRUDE E. SCHROEDER

Introduction

Raising the material welfare of the Soviet people has been an avowed aim of Soviet socialism from the outset. The present leadership has declared it to be the "main goal" of recent plans, and future leaderships no doubt will emphasize that theme. Over the more than six decades of socialist central planning, actual accomplishments — especially those related to consumer welfare — have often diverged greatly from stated goals, and the specific content of the concepts underlying the goals has been modified at times. Nonetheless, all observers probably would agree that much has been achieved albeit often with considerable delay. But much also remains to be done, if Soviet consumers are to enjoy levels of living in terms of material goods and services that have long been available to consumers in the industrialized, market-oriented countries in the West.

This paper focusses on the material welfare of the Soviet population, that is, provision of goods and services as measured in statistics of real per capita consumption. Income distribution, a related concern, is properly the subject of a separate inquiry. A summary discussion of it in an addendum suggests that there has been a sizable reduction in differentials among groups of workers in the post-World War II period, but that elite groups continue to enjoy significant nonpecuniary privileges.

10.1 Trends of Soviet Consumption

Consumers fared poorly under Stalin. In 1950, real household consumption per capita, after large declines during the early 1930s and during the war, had reached a level only about one-tenth above that in 1928 (Chapman, 1963). The Soviet people were ill-clothed, ill-housed, and ill-fed by any modern standard. Compared with 1928, the quality of the diet had deteriorated, consisting as it did of relatively larger shares of bread and potatoes and smaller shares of meat and dairy

Table 10.1   *Average Annual Rates of Growth of Per Capita Consumption by Major Category, USSR, 1950–79*

Category	1951–79	1951–60	1961–70	1971–9
Total Consumption	3.5 (3.0)	4.3 (3.5)	3.8 (3.2)	2.5 (2.2)
Goods	3.6 (3.0)	4.6 (3.9)	3.7 (3.0)	2.5 (2.2)
Food	2.6 (2.2)	3.4 (3.0)	3.0 (2.4)	1.4 (1.3)
Soft Goods	4.8	6.9	4.4	2.9
Durables	9.6	14.2	6.8	7.6
Household Services	4.3 (3.1)	3.9 (2.9)	5.0 (3.6)	3.8 (2.8)
Housing	2.0	2.1	2.3	1.6
Utilities	5.3	4.4	6.8	4.6
Transportation	7.5	9.5	8.2	4.5
Communications	6.0	5.7	6.6	5.6
Repair and Personal Care	3.7	0.7	5.1	5.5
Recreation	2.5	5.0	1.9	0.3
Communal Services	2.5	2.4	3.5	1.5
Education	2.4	1.5	4.1	1.5
Health	2.7	3.9	2.6	1.5

Sources: Rates of growth were calculated from indexes of per capita consumption given in *Gross National Product of the USSR, 1950–1980*. Figures outside parentheses are those obtained when component indexes are aggregated with weights in established prices. Figures inside parentheses are those obtained when component indexes are aggregated with factor-cost weights.

products. Urban housing space per capita also was well below the 1928 level, ands consumer durables and personal services were almost nonexistent. In sharp contrast, education and health services, mostly provided by the state without direct charge, had grown rapidly, as the government sought to provide a healthy and skilled labor force to man the industrialization drive. By 1950, illiteracy among the younger generation had been largely eliminated, and death and infant-mortality rates had fallen to near-modern levels. Combined household and communal consumption per capita increased at an average annual rate of 1.1% during 1928–50.

Since 1950, the growth of per capita consumption has been substantially faster, reaching an average annual rate of 3.5% (Table 10.1). In contrast to the earlier period, household consumption rose far more rapidly than communal consumption, the result of higher investment priority accorded to the long-neglected agricultural and consumer-goods sectors and also to personal services. Although overall gains have been continuous, rates of growth have fluctuated considerably, influenced, in particular, by the harvest.

The trend in these growth rates has been strongly downward — from an annual average of 4.3% in the 1950s to 2.5% in the 1970s. The gains in per capita consumption were widely shared, occurring in rural as well as urban areas and in all of the USSR's constituent republics, but evidently at widely differing rates (Schroeder, 1981).

The growth rates cited above and hereafter in the text are those obtained by using weights valued in established (prevailing) prices. Because of well-known deviations of these prices from theoretically appropriate standards, growth rates based on weights valued at factor cost also are of interest. Such rates are shown in parentheses in Table 10.1. With factor-cost weights the growth rate of consumption as a whole is slower in each period. Growth rates for services are most affected, mainly because of the much larger weight given to the slow-growing housing component. The large rise in consumption in the postwar years reflects a willingness of the post-Stalin leadership to give the goal of raising living standards a higher priority by allocating to consumption a nearly constant share of increments in the national product. As a result, the share of consumption in real GNP has changed relatively little since 1955.[1]

Growth rates among major categories of consumption vary considerably. The fastest gains were made in household services, especially public transportation and communications. The slowest progress was made in housing with rural residents scoring somewhat better than urban residents. Although urban housing (living) space per capita increased from 4.7 m^2 in 1950 to 8.6 m^2 in 1979, it is still below the norm for "minimum health and decency" — 9 m^2 per capita — set by the government in 1928; moreover, over one quarter of all urban families still must share kitchens and baths with others. Aside from housing, growth has been slowest in recreation services, reflecting reduced attendance lately at movies, theaters and the like, a consequence, not at all unique to the USSR, of the advent of television. In the 1960s, the government began a program to build up the supply of state-provided services for repairs and personal care, a long neglected area. Although the supply of such services, by the state and private, has increased quite rapidly, they are still only available in quantities, minuscule by Western standards, and their quality is poor, by all accounts.

Next to household services as a group, the most rapidly growing major category has been the supply of goods, particularly durables. In 1950, both capacity for manufacturing consumer durables and household stocks of them were exceedingly small. But by 1979 over four-fifths of all families had television sets and refrigerators, and seven-tenths had a washing machine. However, there was only one privately owned car for every 25 persons. Relatively fast growth in consumption of soft goods has meant more and better clothing and footwear and the supply of many new sundries. For food, the slowest growing of the three goods categories, the gains have, nevertheless, brought substantial quantitative and qualitative improvement in the people's diet. Per capita consumption of food, including beverages and tobacco, doubled over the period. Among foods, per capita consumption of meat, fish and eggs, measured in physical units, more than doubled, whereas per capita consumption of potatoes and grain products has fallen by more than half. Little qualitative improvement of this kind has been made since 1975, however, and in the 1970s gains in food consumption generally were at less than half the rates of the previous two decades.

As noted, gains in communal services — education and health — were much smaller than for household consumption. This result stems partly from the strong emphasis given them in prewar years, but also reflects a reorientation of consumption priorities by planners and a marked slowing of population growth, especially in the 1970s. Nonetheless, provision of these services doubled per capita over the period, as the government continued to invest in human capital on a large scale. Average educational attainment of the population age 16 and over rose from 5 years in 1950 to an estimated 9.1 years in 1980.[2] Educational progress has been widely shared among groups in the population. One of the most rapidly growing segments of education has been in nursery and kindergarten schooling, thus providing child-care facilities to enable more women to remain in the labor force. In health services, the gains have entailed a more than doubling of the number of both doctors and hospital beds per 10,000 persons. Even though the quality of health services may be poor by Western standards, they have been made universally available at a minimum level without direct charge. The cost has been kept low by fixing the wages in the health services relatively low (wages in "health, physical culture and social security" rank the lowest of all major branches except for "culture"). Universal availability, of course, does not mean equally available. By all accounts, both quantity and quality of services are much poorer in rural areas than in cities, and in Central Asia than in the RSFSR and the Baltic republics. Moreover, the best of the services are reserved for elite groups (Matthews, 1978).

Comparative Levels

While Russian consumers have made substantial gains in the postwar period relative to previous decades, rates of growth are within bounds of gains achieved in other countries with which the USSR may be appropriately compared. Table 10.2 shows comparative growth rates during 1950–78 in per capita consumption for the USSR, six Western countries and four socialist countries of Eastern Europe. Growth of household consumption per capita in the Soviet Union was faster than in the USA and the UK, but was exceeded by Japan, West Germany, France and Italy. Except for East Germany, Soviet growth rates considerably exceeded those in the socialist countries compared. Since 1960, consumers in the European market economies and in Japan experienced more rapid improvement in levels of living than did Soviet consumers; and in growth rate of consumption the margin of the USSR over that of the United States was greatly reduced. In the 1970s, only Italy, the UK, and Czechoslovakia had smaller rates of growth of consumption than the USSR. This comparison could be extended to other countries, with similar results. Thus, for the period 1960–77, the Soviet record was equalled or exceeded by Belgium, Netherlands,

Table 10.2 *Average Annual Rates of Growth in Real Consumption Per Capita, Selected Countries, 1951–78*[a]

	1951–78	1961–78	1971–8
USSR	3.7 (3.6)	3.3 (3.2)	2.6 (2.5)
United States	2.3	2.9 (2.9)	3.0 (3.0)
Japan	6.5[b]	7.1	4.3
France	3.9	4.2	3.2
West Germany	4.8	3.6	3.0
Italy	3.8[c]	3.9	1.8 (1.9)
United Kingdom	2.1[c]	1.8 (2.0)	1.7 (1.9)
Czechoslovakia	1.6	1.9	2.1 (1.9)
East Germany	4.6	2.6	3.7 (3.4)
Hungary	2.6	2.8	2.7 (2.6)
Poland	2.9	3.2	4.0 (3.7)

[a]Figures outside parentheses refer to private consumption expenditures; figures inside parentheses refer to private consumption expenditures plus government current expenditures on health and education services. Rates for the latter in Western countries are estimates based on data through 1976–7.
[b]1953–78.
[c]1952–78.

Sources: USSR: growth rates are based on the indexes in 1970 prices underlying Table 10.1. *Western countries*: growth rates are based on values in constant prices given in OECD, *Nat. Accounts, 1950–1978*. Data for the most part are in 1975 prices. *Eastern countries*: growth rates are based on data in studies published by the Research Project on National Income in East Central Europe (see References). Data for East European countries are in 1968 prices. Growth rates for the 1950s are calculated from Ernst, 1966, pp. 880, 886.

Austria, Finland, Greece, Norway, Portugal and Yugoslavia; Soviet growth of consumption was higher than in Denmark, Switzerland and Sweden. Although these comparisons pertain to household consumption, the picture changes little when government outlays on education and health are added. Such services have a small weight, except in the UK. The incomplete evidence indicates that in the West real public outlays on such services have increased more rapidly than private outlays on goods and services, the reverse of the pattern for the USSR.

Even in the 1930s, Soviet spokesmen asserted that the USSR would "soon" catch up and surpass its capitalist rivals in levels of living. In 1961, Khrushchev declared: '... strictly scientific calculations ... show that in 20 years we will have built, in the main, a Communist society", when the Soviet Union "will have the highest living standard in the world".[3] It is of considerable interest to assess the USSR's progress toward that goal. To that end, we refer to a new study of comparative international per capita consumption for the Soviet Union and the United States for 1976, based on purchasing power parities (see Schroeder and Edwards, 1981). This study has been extended to several other countries, using the recently published results of the United Nations International Comparison Project (ICP) (see Kravis and Associates, 1978). Although the extension of the

Table 10.3 Comparison of Soviet and US Consumption Per Capita in 1976, Modified ICP Classification

	Per Capita Expenditures		Purchasing Power Parities (Ruble-Dollar)		Quantity Per Capita, US=100		
	USSR (Rubles)	US (Dollars)	US Weights	USSR Weights	Dollar Comparison	Ruble Comparison	Geometric Mean
Total consumption	**1,152.61**	**5,583.30**	**0.748**	**0.483**	**42.8**	**27.6**	**34.4**
Food, Beverages, Tobacco	546.09	1,130.45	0.985	0.831	58.2	49.0	53.4
Food	382.29	868.46	1.036	0.789	55.8	42.5	48.7
Breads and Cereals	59.55	110.33	0.612	0.519	103.9	88.2	95.7
Meat	101.43	281.56	1.040	1.063	33.9	34.6	34.3
Fish	16.57	48.40	0.886	0.293	116.7	38.6	67.2
Milk, Eggs, Cheese	63.20	116.09	1.012	0.850	64.0	53.8	58.7
Oils and Fats	26.22	38.33	1.203	0.938	72.9	56.9	64.4
Vegetables	18.25	110.52	0.858	0.853	19.4	19.2	19.3
Potatoes	16.39	13.50	1.342	1.342	90.4	90.4	90.4
Fruit	20.03	60.73	1.618	1.730	19.1	20.4	19.7
Sugar and Confectioneries	47.08	50.38	1.622	0.893	104.7	57.6	77.6
Other Foods	13.56	38.62	1.025	0.774	45.4	34.2	39.4
Beverages	148.98	186.66	0.710	0.933	85.6	112.4	98.0
Alcoholic	138.27	133.03	0.767	0.933	104.7	135.5	119.1
Nonalcoholic	10.71	53.63	0.570	0.524	38.1	35.0	36.5
Tobacco	14.83	75.33	1.090	1.087	18.1	18.1	18.1
Clothing and Footwear	199.03	358.05	1.426	0.994	55.9	39.0	46.7
Clothing	158.61	304.43	1.530	1.104	47.2	34.0	40.1
Footwear	40.42	53.62	0.834	0.715	105.4	90.4	97.6
Gross Rent and Fuel	62.33	997.94	0.380	0.355	17.6	16.4	17.0
Gross Rent	43.30	787.73	0.361	0.361	15.2	15.2	15.2
Fuel and Power	19.03	210.21	0.451	0.344	26.3	20.1	23.0

	61.55	372.54	1.202	0.557	29.7	13.8	20.2
House Furnishings and Operations							
Furniture and Appliances	39.56	219.35	1.391	0.654	27.6	13.0	18.9
Supplies and Operations	21.99	153.19	0.931	0.439	32.7	15.4	22.4
Medical Care	45.47	646.63	0.400	0.117	60.1	17.6	32.5
Transport and Communications	64.99	813.25	1.065	0.412	19.4	7.5	12.1
Transport	58.78	710.16	1.170	0.421	19.7	7.1	11.8
Private	27.34	665.16	1.231	0.890	4.6	3.3	3.9
Public	31.44	45.00	0.266	0.289	241.9	262.7	252.0
Communications	6.21	103.09	0.346	0.344	17.5	17.4	17.5
Recreation and Education	131.78	889.17	0.438	0.211	70.3	33.8	48.8
Recreation	61.94	417.04	0.680	0.368	40.4	21.8	29.7
Education	69.84	472.13	0.225	0.153	96.7	65.7	79.7
Other Expenditures	40.13	375.27	0.553	0.547	19.6	19.3	19.4
Personal care	37.63	131.99	1.016	0.567	50.3	28.1	37.6
Miscellaneous Services	2.50	243.28	0.302	0.361	2.8	3.4	3.1

Source: Schroeder and Edwards, 1981.

comparison to other countries was necessarily indirect because specific ruble/domestic-currency parities could not be calculated, the results are probably not seriously misleading.

With Soviet expenditures measured and grouped in the ICP format, Soviet per capita consumption in 1976 is shown to be a little over one third (34.4%) of that of the United States, the result given by the geometric-mean comparison; the ruble and dollar comparisons are, respectively, 27.6% and 42.5% (Table 10.3). Extrapolation on the basis of real growth in both countries yields a relative level of 28% in 1955 by the geometric-mean comparison, fairly close to results obtained in current prices and ruble/dollar parities by earlier investigators (CIA, 1964; Bornstein, 1959; Bergson, 1972). By any standards, the Russian progress toward catching up with the United States has been modest; the gap is still enormous and has widened in the 1970s. In respect to major categories of consumption, and using the geometric-mean comparisons, the Russians led the USA only in consumption of alcoholic beverages and public transport. Expenditures on education were four-fifths of the level in the USA. Expenditures on food and on clothing and footwear were close to half, and those on medical care about one-third. Moreover, expenditures on housing services and related goods and on communications were in the neighborhood of one-fifth the level in the USA, and outlays on private transportation were only one-twenty-fifth. Soviet consumers have made the largest relative gains since 1955 in consumption of goods and some personal services, but their relative position in respect to housing, health and education has been seriously eroded, the consequence of greatly stepped-up priority for these services in the United States in recent years.

When other countries are brought into the comparison, we observe that Soviet per capita consumption in 1976 (geometric-mean value) was perhaps half that in France and West Germany, somewhat more in the case of the UK, about two-thirds of that in Japan and about three-quarters of that in Italy. By this measure, Hungary exceeded the Soviet level by nearly one-fifth. (I emphasize that these relative figures are obtained indirectly via a comparison carried out directly in purchasing-power parities relative to the United States in 1973 and extrapolated to 1976 with real-product indexes for the respective countries.)

Using dollar comparisons for the USA and the USSR in 1976 and for the USA and six other countries in 1973 (taken from the ICP study), we can assess roughly how the Soviet Union compares with other countries in per capita consumption of major types of goods and services (Table 10.4). By this comparison, the Soviet Union falls below all of the others in per capita expenditures on food, beverages and tobacco; gross rent and fuel; household furnishings and operations; and medical care. The USSR leads all others except the USA in provision of education. For the other categories, the Soviet Union tends to rank low, but not lowest. While comparisons such as these are

Table 10.4 *Relative Levels of Consumption Per Capita by ICP Category, Dollar Comparisons (United States=100)*

	USSR 1976	Hungary 1973	Italy 1973	Japan 1973	West Germany 1973	United Kingdom 1973	France 1973
Total Consumption	42.8	49.5	54.0	56.8	68.1	68.6	73.7
Food, Beverages, Tobacco	58.2	75.2	72.1	65.9	77.4	81.1	113.2
Clothing and Footwear	55.9	41.2	50.8	55.2	71.7	66.3	55.3
Gross Rent and Fuel	17.6	27.7	40.2	36.6	59.3	56.2	65.4
Household Furnishings and Operations	29.7	33.8	33.7	52.8	94.6	51.3	63.2
Medical Care	60.1	79.7	92.3	119.6	104.5	82.4	111.1
Transport and Communications	19.4	17.9	32.5	18.4	38.4	50.4	40.8
Recreation	40.4	76.5	44.5	31.2	76.9	97.7	83.3
Education	96.7	66.9	63.0	67.6	64.6	83.7	58.7

Source: USSR—Table 10.3.
Other countries—ICP, Phase II (see Kravis and assocs. 1978).
In all cases, the percentages reflect comparisons carried out in dollars. The ICP classification has been modified to allocate expenditures in restaurants and cafes to Food, Beverages and Tobacco, and expenditures on hotels and lodging to Recreation. The transferred categories were estimated on the assumption that their respective shares of miscellaneous services were the same as in 1970. They were converted to dollars using the applicable purchasing-power parities for miscellaneous services.

Table 10.5   *Structure of Consumption, USSR, Selected Years 1950–79*

	Constant Prices				Current Prices	
	1950	*1960*	*1970*	*1979*	*1955*	*1976*
Total Consumption	100.0	100.0	100.0	100.0	100.0	100.0
Goods, Total	77.2	79.8	78.9	78.5	78.8	79.6
Food	59.8	54.9	51.1	46.4	53.0	48.9
Soft Goods	15.4	19.8	21.0	21.6	21.0	21.5
Durables	2.0	5.1	6.8	10.5	4.8	9.2
Services, Total	22.8	20.2	21.1	21.5	21.2	20.4
Housing and Utilities	3.5	3.1	3.2	3.3	4.0	3.2
Transportation	1.0	1.7	2.6	3.0	1.7	2.8
Communication	0.4	0.4	0.6	0.7	0.5	0.6
Repair and Personal Care	3.2	2.3	2.6	3.6	3.2	2.8
Recreation	1.4	1.5	1.2	1.0	1.9	1.0
Communal Services	13.3	11.2	10.9	9.9	9.9	10.0
Education	8.6	6.6	6.8	6.2	6.4	6.3
Health	4.7	4.6	4.1	3.7	3.5	3.7

Sources: Shares in constant 1970 prices were calculated from ruble values underlying the growth rates shown in Table 10.1. Shares in current established prices for 1955 and 1976 are from Schroeder and Edwards (1981).

imprecise, they probably are reasonable "ballpark" values, some of which can be roughly supported by comparisons measured in physical units (e.g. consumption of meat in kg., housing space in m^2). The author believes that the overall results shown here would be generally confirmed, if careful binary comparisons of Soviet expenditures with those in European countries and in Japan could be carried out. Regrettably, the Soviet government, unlike most of its East European partners, has declined to join in the UN's cooperative International Comparisons Project.

10.2   Structure of Consumption

Our measures of Soviet consumption by detailed category in the postwar years permit us to examine in a comparative framework the pattern of consumption and the pace and direction of change. Table 10.5 presents the relevant data for various years, with the underlying values measured in constant as well as in current prices. In both sets of prices, the share of goods rises somewhat, with a concomitant drop in the share of services, a result contrary to what one might expect. Among the three classes of goods, expenditures for food, beverages and tobacco drop as a share of total consumption expenditures, as one would expect from Engel's law. The fall is shown to be greater in constant than in current prices, as is the corresponding rise in the share of soft goods and durables. The almost unchanged share of communal services, measured in current prices, as contrasted with its sizable

Table 10.6 Comparison of the Structure of Consumption in Selected Countries[a]

	USSR 1976	Hungary 1973	Italy 1973	Japan 1973	United Kingdom 1973	West Germany 1973	France 1973	United States 1973	United States 1976
Total Consumption	100.0	100.0	100.0	100.0	100.0	100.0	100.0	100.0	100.0
Food, Beverages and Tobacco	47.4	43.3	40.3	36.9	29.8	25.7	32.3	20.8	20.3
Clothing and Footwear	17.3	11.0	8.5	9.5	7.7	9.7	7.8	7.1	6.4
Gross Rent and Fuel	5.4	7.4	12.7	14.6	17.1	14.0	13.2	17.4	17.9
House Furnishings and Operations	5.3	8.6	5.6	8.7	6.7	11.6	8.0	7.4	6.7
Medical Care	3.9	5.9	7.3	8.0	6.0	10.0	10.5	10.4	11.6
Transport and Communications	5.6	7.0	10.3	4.5	12.3	10.8	10.3	14.6	14.6
Recreation	5.4	6.2	7.4	5.6	8.9	8.7	9.2	7.7	7.5
Education	6.1	5.8	6.1	7.8	7.4	6.2	6.1	8.2	8.5
Other Expenditures	3.5	4.8	1.7	4.8	4.2	2.4	2.7	6.3	6.7

[a]Consumption is the sum of private consumption expenditures and government current outlays on education, health, recreation and rent subsidies. The underlying values are in current prices paid by consumers; government expenditures are actual current outlays on the indicated services.

Source: USSR—Table 10.3. U.S., 1976—Table 10.3. U.S., 1973 and other countries, 1973—calculated from data for 1970 and 1973 given in ICP Phase II (see Kravis, 1978).

The ICP classification has been modified to allocate expenditures in restaurants and cafes to Food, beverage and tobacco and expenditures on hotels and lodgings to Recreation. Their respective shares in the ICP category Miscellaneous Services given for 1970 were assumed to be the same in 1973.

decline as a share in real terms, reflects mainly rising wage rates in education and health services.

International comparisons

For an international perspective, we refer to the comparisons in the ICP system of classification, in which goods and services are combined within major categories (Table 10.6). As one would expect from relative levels of per capita national products, the consumption pattern in the Soviet Union differs markedly from that in the United States and the more advanced countries of Western Europe. There, the shares of food and clothing in total expenditures lie in the range of 27 to 40%, compared with 65% in the Soviet Union. The shares of housing and related goods and services range from 21 to 25%; the share is 9% in the Soviet Union. The shares of medical care, transport and communications, and recreation are also relatively much larger in the Western countries. The Soviet consumption pattern most closely resembles that of Hungary and Italy. Within the category "food, beverages and tobacco", the share of alcoholic beverages in the Soviet pattern (25%, over two-thirds spirits) is uniquely large, but the share of tobacco (3%) is small relative to the other countries. Only in the United Kingdom was the share of alcoholic beverages even close to the Soviet level, but even there spirits comprised only 28% of its total.

Considering that the share of food and related products in total household consumption tends to decrease as incomes rise (Kuznets, 1966), it is of interest to compare the pace of change in the Soviet Union with countries elsewhere. Unfortunately, the data available for such a comparison are not as one would desire. Nonetheless, a tentative assessment can be made on the basis of comparative data relating to the share of food, beverages and tobacco in total private expenditures on consumption in 1960, 1970 and 1976 (Table 10.7). Again, the Soviet Union stands out, with shares that resemble those in countries at much lower levels of development; in each year, for example, the Soviet share is higher than in Greece. Also notable is the small decline in the share in the 16-year period — only 3 percentage points. Considerably faster decreases were registered elsewhere.

Changes in consumption patterns may also be assessed by calculating consumption elasticities for the various major categories. These elasticities measure the percentage change in real outlays on a particular category relative to the percentage change in real outlays on all private consumption. Bergson (1978) has made such calculations for the USSR and several Western countries over the period 1955–70. He found that the Soviet pattern tended to resemble that in the West, more or less, with elasticities for food less than 1 and falling, those for clothing around 1 and fairly stable, those for durables much above 1 with no clear trend, and those for housing mixed, but declining somewhat. The similarity of the Soviet elasticities to those in the West suggest a broad similarity in tastes. An effort is clearly made by the planners to gratify these tastes. (Planners' decisions are required to alter the production mix; planners' supply decisions are primarily responsible for the intertemporal swings in the consumption elasticities.)

Table 10.8 presents consumption elasticities for the USSR for several periods during 1950–79, based on revised indexes of consump-

Table 10.7 *Shares of Food, Beverages, and Tobacco in Total Household Consumption, Selected Countries (percent)*

	1960	1970	1976 A	1976 B
Per Capita GNP More than $7,000				
Belgium	34.9	31.4	27.0	31.2
Canada	25.5	25.5	21.0	27.5
Denmark	32.6[a]	30.0	27.1	31.3
France		27.1	23.3	29.8
West Germany	36.8	30.0	27.2	
Norway	32.0[b]	31.4	27.9	31.5
Sweden	30.7[c]	28.4	27.0	30.3
Switzerland	34.7	31.4	28.5	
United States	21.9	18.7	16.9	22.5
Per Capita GNP $5,001 to 7,000				
Australia	34.0	28.3	25.4	
Austria	38.8[d]	34.5	28.0	39.0
Finland	44.2	39.5	37.4	40.5
Japan		30.0	28.5	
Per Capita GNP $4,001 to 5,000				
Italy		40.7	36.6	42.4
USSR	49.4	48.9	46.4	54.4
United Kingdom	37.5	33.2	31.6	36.1
Per Capita GNP $1,570 to 3,189				
Ireland		46.5	44.8	46.2
Greece	48.7	42.6	43.1	47.9
Spain		37.4	35.3[e]	41.9[e]
Portugal	57.1	54.2	50.1	

[a]1966.
[b]1967.
[c]1963.
[d]1964.
[e]1974.

Source: Calculated from OECD, *National Accounts, 1960–1977* using data in current prices. Percentages for the USSR are based on calculations of consumption in current prices and data on restaurant sales given in *Nar.khoz* 1978, p. 433. Countries are grouped by per capita GNP in 1978 as given in Block, 1979, pp. 27–8, 33.

Note: For 1976, Column A excludes restaurant purchases, Column B includes them. The data for 1960 and 1970 exclude restaurant purchases: comparable data on restaurant purchases are not available for most countries in those years.

Table 10.8   *Consumption Elasticities for Selected Commodity Categories, USSR, 1950–60, 1960–70 and 1970–79*[a]

	1950–60	1960–70	1970–79
Food, Beverages and Tobacco	.83	.86	.66
Soft Goods	1.18	1.11	1.07
Durables	2.13	1.52	2.28
Housing	.63	.71	.71

[a]For each category in each period, the consumption elasticity is calculated as the ratio of the percentage increase in real expenditures on that category over the period to the percentage increase in real expenditures on all private consumption during the period. In each case, the base of the percentage is the arithmetic average of the initial and final real expenditures. The underlying values are taken from *Indexes of Gross National Product in the USSR, 1950–1980*, 1981.

tion. The large reduction in the consumption elasticity for food, beverages and tobacco in the 1970s, for example, reflects in part a planners' decision to curtail the growth of alcoholic-beverage production, part of a many-faceted program to combat rising alcoholism. In respect to durables, the 1950s witnessed a swift increase in capacities to produce household durables; the jump in the elasticity in the 1970s reflects the impact of the decision to mass-produce automobiles for sale to the population.

10.3   Qualitative Aspects of Consumption

Thus far, we have focussed on the quantitative aspects of consumption. To the extent possible, of course, the measures of real per capita consumption as well as the international comparisons have taken relevant quality changes and differences into account where quality was a feature of particular goods and services being assessed. Further consideration needs to be given to the quality problem per se, however, including matters of assortment and mix. Moreover, other aspects of the consumption environment that are important in consumer utility cannot be captured in the quantitative measurements. We refer here to the narrow assortment and range of choice, to the pervasive imbalances in supply and demand for individual goods and services, and to the backward and inefficient distribution and service facilities. The inability to take these important aspects of consumer utility into account biased the international comparisons of the previous two sections in the USSR's favor, both in respect to relative levels and to rates of growth.

That the quality, i.e. durability, style and appearance, of most Soviet-made consumer goods is poor by comparison with the West (or even much of the East) can hardly be disputed. The situation is demonstrated by the fact that few Soviet consumer goods are saleable in Western markets; that even East Europeans complain about the quality of Soviet-made goods; by the observations of visitors to the Soviet Union; but above all by an endless stream of anecdotal testimony in the Soviet press. The author has surveyed this evidence over the years (Schroeder, 1973 and 1975; Schroeder and Severin, 1976). Thus, a sample of recent evidence will suffice to bring the picture up to date; I detect no essential change in the volume or character of such reporting. Unsaleable goods accumulate in inventories; in 1978, they amounted to some 4.6 billion rubles.[4] Each spring, such goods are offered for sale at discounts averaging 60% or more, and even then fail to sell. The state budget allocates about a billion rubles each year to cover losses on such goods. Moreover, matters do not seem to be improving: "Year after year the proportion of goods rejected or lowered in grade when they are received by trade organizations has been increasing";[5] "Trade refuses to accept one out of every 10 garments, one out of every 8 pairs of shoes, and one of every 10 meters of fabric".[6] Numerous complaints are made about the quality of consumer durables, a large share of which require repair within the guarantee period; in 1978, for example, on 227,000 refrigerators from enterprises of one ministry alone and on more than 1.5 million television sets produced by another ministry.[7] As a consequence of poor quality and style, consumer-service enterprises, where productivity is relatively low, often have to correct the defects, e.g. stitch shoes that come unglued or modify clothing to make it more stylish.[8]

The range of choice (mix and assortment of products) available to Soviet consumers is extremely limited in comparison with the West. In the case of women's shoes, for example, the ratio may be perhaps one to ten. The restricted range of choice is partly a consequence of the government's reluctance to import finished consumer goods in large quantities. Most of all, however, few styles and models reflect even planners' preferences, which reveals the predilection of Soviet industry for turning out a small number of simple, standardized models and the reluctance of enterprise managers to change the product mix.

Pervasive imbalances in demand and supply for individual goods and services are a persistent feature of the quasi-market for consumer goods in the Soviet Union. This malaise manifests itself in periodic inventory build-ups for one or another type of good[9] and seemingly random shortages of others — meat grinders today, pots and pans tomorrow, meat the next day, and so on. In a speech in November 1979, Brezhnev himself mentioned shortages of "medicine, soap, detergents, toothbrushes and toothpaste, needles, thread, diapers and others goods produced in light industry."[10] If anything, failure to meet consumer demand has become a more frequent theme in the press. Annual plan-fulfillment reports regularly provide a list of goods for which demand was not satisfied. In a major article written in 1979, an official of Gosplan referred to unsatisfied demand for meats and dairy products, fruits and vegetables, cotton textiles, furniture, wood products, motorcycles, cars and "many other products."[11] Another source declares that the list of so-called "trifles" (sundries) in short supply continues to grow.[12] The hoary theme of shortages of children's clothing is reiterated, despite numerous measures that were supposed to correct the problem.[13] Shortages and poor quality of many consumer services are also perennial themes.

The costs to consumers and to society of such persistent malfunctions in the consumer sector are diverse and high. First, there is simple dissatisfaction, with its negative impact on morale and labor productivity, at being unable to spend earned income on desired goods and services. Secondly, a large cost is incurred in time spent in queuing and going from store to store in search of a wanted item. Surveys reveal that the average family spends 1.9 hours each day in shopping.[14] The burden is borne mainly by women, who do four-fifths of the shopping, either alone or with their husbands.[15] Women also do most of the cooking and general housework, only about 15% of which is mechanized.[16] Thirdly, unsatisfied demand results in forced savings or spills over into illegal markets, both undesirable consequences from the point of view of the government. Finally, the manifest difficulty of satisfying consumer demand is hardly flattering for a system of centrally planned socialism, that claims to be able to outperform alternative systems in almost all ways.

Another factor affecting the utilities derived from consumption is the relatively primitive and inefficient system for distributing goods and services. Housing is rationed, crowded and scarce, providing a fertile soil for the growth of bribery and corruption. Medical care and education, while supplied without direct charge, are also rationed, in effect; both quantities and qualities in many cases are not provided in accord with people's desires. Queues are long for some services, and quality is poor for most others, with the predictable result of spawning networks of special privilege and corruption. Retail-trade facilities are woefully backward by international standards. In 1972, the United States, with a population one-fifth less than the USSR, had nearly 2 million establishments in retail trade and some 675,000 in personal and automotive services. In 1978, the USSR had 528,000 retail establishments and 265,700 "everyday" service establishments. Stores are small (an average of 82.5m^2 in 1978), poorly laid out and badly lighted. According to a Soviet source, there was only 154 m^2 of retail floor space per 1,000 urban residents, below that of the GDR, Czechoslovakia, Poland and the developed capitalist countries.[17] The cumbersome, three-queue system is still a prevalent form of retail service, although so-called "self-service" arrangements are becoming more common. According to a Soviet source, as of the beginning of 1977 over half the stores, accounting for 54.5% of total sales, were of that type,[18] but only one quarter of the cashier stations were provided with a cash register. Usually, checkout by department rather than by store prevails, and often "the counters have been taken away, but in their place immediately appear rope barriers, barricades made of boxes and other improvised means. . . . " Frequently, the buyer is subjected to a dual control at payment points, where he is required to open his own bag (to check for theft).[19] Also, packaging of foods and other products is in an embryonic state. In 1976, only 25.5% of the food products were supplied to the trade network in packaged form,[20] fruits and vegetables were not packaged at all, and the quality and design of packaging is poor; in 1977, the RSFSR Ministry of the Food Industry supplied in packaged form only about 20% of its confectioneries, macaroni products and vegetable oil, and only 6% of the sugar; the Ministry of Procurement supplied only 12.5% of the flour in packages.[21]

10.4 Roots of the Problems in the Consumer Sector

The causes of the perennial malaise in the consumer sector are numerous, complex and interconnected. Many aspects have been treated in detail elsewhere (Goldman, 1963; Ofer, 1973; Hanson, 1968; Schroeder and Severin, 1976). We can provide only a sketch here, primarily by updating the setting. First, part of the explanation for the backwardness of the consumer sector lies in the investment priorities adhered to by successive Soviet leaderships. Priorities have always been heavily oriented toward investment and defense goods. Stalin's neglect of the consumer sector, including agriculture, is notorious. In the post-Stalin years, investment has been pushed from time to time in one or another consumer-oriented activity — housing in the late 1950s, retail trade and personal-service facilities in the 1960s, and agriculture in the 1970s. Nonetheless, the food and light industries have persistently been allocated only 10 to 12% of total industrial investment. This share has been declining lately, despite a boost in agriculture's share; this may help to explain the evidence of large waste of food products in these industries following the harvest. Housing has typically claimed 15 to 17% of total investment, but its share, too, has dropped — to 13.3% in 1979. Investment in the so-called "Group B" industries has averaged a mere 4 to 5% of total investment over the years. The long relative neglect of the consumer sector means that huge backlogs of needs have accumulated and that a major restructuring of investment would be required to effect more than marginal progress in modernizing the consumer-related capital stock.

As a consequence of the investment priorities, the average technological level of consumer-goods industries lags that in the West by decades, a situation that contributes to poor quality and design of products. Although most processed food products and soft goods are produced in specialized plants under the aegis of two ministries, consumer durables and a host of "trifles" are manufactured as side-lines in plants of heavy industry under a large number of ministries. A 1979 press report states that refrigerators are produced in 40 models in 20 plants of eight ministries; corresponding figures for washing machines are 29, 24 and seven.[22] The decade of the 1970s has witnessed repeated pleas for more specialization, along with campaigns to force plants in heavy industry to manufacture more consumer goods of some kind or other. The quality of such products is usually poor and production costs are high, as are the bills for repair. Models of appliances are obsolete (hand-wringer washing machines), and average production runs of the same model are long — 12 years for washing machines, six years for refrigerators, seven years for vacuum cleaners, for example.[23]

Possibly more important than matters relating to investment in explaining the chronic problems of quality, design, assortment and mix of consumer goods and services are factors relating to organization and incentives that are deeply imbedded in the modus operandi of centrally planned socialism. Because economic organization is hierarchical by sector, the connections among links in the production—distribution chain are administrative (bureaucratic) rather than economic in nature. That is to say, each link is oriented primarily toward satisfying its own superior in the hierarchy, rather than toward satisfying ultimate consumers. Incentives for each link — supplier, producer, shipper, distributor — always have been geared to meeting its own plan as measured by its particular set of success indicators. These indicators have been inconsistent among links in the chain, usually multiple and internally conflicting, and made more so by the failure of product pricing to reflect consumer demand. Numerous revisions (so-called "reforms") in these working arrangements over the past 15 years evidently have helped little and may even have compounded the problem by adding chronic instability in working arrangements to the features of the system (Schroeder, 1979). Finally, the vagaries of organizational and incentive arrangements have been played out in an economic evironment of increasing strain on economic resources (taut planning). None of the changes has removed a fundamental impediment to the avowed efforts to satisfy ultimate consumers, namely, that all links in the chain lack alternative suppliers, that is, there is no real competition. These systemic flaws surely have greatly reduced the payoff, in terms of consumer utility, from the resource allocations to consumption. Moreover, the consumer sector has, in fact, continued to have "second class" status in most respects (quality of resources allocated to it, prestige of jobs in it), despite many recent declarations by Soviet leaders, including Brezhnev himself, that the sector has equal status with all others.

10.5 The "Second" Economy

The chronic shortcomings of the state-directed economy in the production and distribution of consumer goods and services, along with rising incomes and unequal access to supplies, have helped to spawn a pervasive "second" or illegal economy in the consumer sector. This economy, the subject of a growing body of literature (Grossman,

1977 and 1979; Schroeder and Greenslade, 1979), takes many forms—
some of them adding to the supply of goods and services and others
merely redistributing existing supplies and raising prices. Private
producers manufacture consumer goods — knitted clothing and grave
markers are recent press examples — and render personal services that
would be legal activities in other countries. Private illegal production
of *samogon* (home brew), apparently a multibillion-ruble activity,
would be illegal elsewhere, also. Raw materials needed for such
endeavors, it seems, often are stolen from state enterprises, as are
sizeable amounts of finished consumer goods. Private activity redistributes goods and raises prices in a variety of ways; the most common
ones seem to be the "reserving" of scarce goods by retail clerks in
return for bribes, resale at higher prices of goods purchased legally,
black-market sales of stolen goods or goods from abroad somehow
acquired, paying bribes to obtain scarce goods or services, such as
housing, new cars, entrance into a university, speedy service in a clinic.
By all accounts, "second" economy activities are prevalent and are
more or less tolerated by the government, which tries to keep them
within tolerable limits through periodic campaigns against them.

What is the quantitative impact of the illegal economy on consumption as we have measured it? First of all, only those activities that add
to supply should be counted; these would be (1) private production of
goods and services and (2) consumer goods stolen from the state for
personal use or sale. If total quantities of such products and services
were known, they should be valued at established prices (prevailing
rubles, in Bergson's terminology) and added to consumption. In an
international comparison, the same must be done for other countries.
The value of these activities cannot be known with precision for any
country, for their very illegality provides strong incentives for hiding
them, most especially in the Soviet Union, with its strong penchant for
secrecy about criminal matters. As a result of much labor in this dark,
shadowy vineyard, the author is convinced that our perception of the
size and growth of real per capita consumption in the USSR relative to
other countries would not be appreciably altered by inclusion of
supply-augmenting activities of the "second" economies there and
elsewhere. Consumption probably would be raised by a small fraction
everywhere; illegal, "off the books" productive pursuits are universal
phenomena, although motivations may differ among countries.

The redistribution and repricing of goods and services through the
illegal "second" economy in the USSR may add to nominal consumption and certainly alter relative prices. They provide markets for
numerous goods and services, where prices respond to supply and
demand. They provide time and place utilities — prompt repair of a
broken window, for example, or the transporting of oranges from
Georgia to fruit-starved northern cities. The "second" economy thus
helps to compensate in part for the welfare losses to consumers
resulting from inflexible and administratively determined prices in the
legal state economy; it also makes up for some of the welfare losses due

to an erratic distribution system. In a word, consumers are better off, because the illegal economy brings the total economy nearer to equilibrium. Its political and moral impact on Soviet society is another matter.

10.6   Outlook for Consumption

The Situation in 1980

In considering how policies and performance in respect to consumption might evolve over the next two decades, we need to begin with an assessment of the present state of affairs. At the start of the 1980s, after more than a half-century of centrally planned socialism, the Soviet people have attained a level of material well-being (real per capita consumption) substantially above that in 1928 but still far below that in major capitalist countries and even below that in most of socialist Eastern Europe. Indeed, the gaps with Western Europe generally have widened since the beginning of the 1960s, when the Communist Party unveiled a grand program designed to give the Soviet people the "highest standard of living in the world" by 1980. Along with these large gaps, unflattering to socialism, the consumer sector in the USSR is qualitatively mediocre and in massive disequilibrium at the start of the decade that was to have seen the advent of Communism, with its promised abundance for all and distribution in accordance with need. This unhappy state of affairs is a clear case of "chickens coming home to roost", in my view. The government's policies relating to consumption have now, perhaps, become fetters on production.

Let us sketch the situation, even at the risk of some repetition. For three decades, Soviet government policies have accorded the population steady annual advances in the overall supply of consumer goods and services and a slow improvement in their quality. No doubt, the people expect these gains to continue. With these advances, basic needs have been satisfied for most people, so that demand is focussed increasingly on quality foods and clothing, durables of modern design and assortment, better housing, and a variety of personal services. Steadily rising money incomes have made these demands effective and also have produced an accompanying steady increase in the average savings rate. In the 1970s, the growth of incomes as well as of the supply of goods and services slowed markedly, the latter more than the former. Government price policy has kept retail prices stable for basic food products, most kinds of clothing, most public services and housing, while permitting substantial price increases to producers to cover rising costs. As a consequence, state subsidies have been rising rapidly, amounting in 1979 to 25 billion rubles for meat, milk and some other goods, and about 6 billion rubles for housing.[25] Prices on collective-farm markets have been rising rapidly and in 1979 they were approximately double those in state stores for food products traded in both markets.

The government's inability to limit the growth of incomes to the available supply of goods and services and to tailor production to demand in respect to quality, style, and assortment has produced a state of growing repressed inflation, especially since 1975, manifested in a rising marginal propensity to save (Pickersgill, 1980), widespread shortages, and queueing, notably for meat and quality foods, and evidence of spreading black markets. Moreover, rigid central planning of the consumption mix in accord with the government's preferences and priorities has perpetuated a constrained pattern of demand, based on underlying high income elasticities of demand for quality foods. As incomes have risen, people, as they are unable to obtain better housing, take more vacations, travel abroad and the like, and have chased after scarce supplies of quality foods, especially meat. Finally, the malaise in the consumer sector, according to some Soviet reports, has been eroding work effort and the efficacy of pecuniary incentives,[26] contributing to a breakdown of labor discipline, worsening social problems notably pervasive drinking on and off the job and, less tangibly, creating a popular mood of discontent and pessimism.[27]

In terms of physical assets, the USSR begins the decade with generally archaic capital plant and equipment in the food and clothing industries; with most household durables and a host of odds and ends produced as "second-class" sidelines in machinery plants; with inadequate processing, storage and distribution facilities to match agriculture's ability to produce the raw products even in an average year; with inadequate, inefficient and technologically backward facilities in the retail-trade and personal-services sectors; and, finally, with a huge housing shortage. In addition, the USSR has perpetuated a system of economic organization that is uniquely unsuited to managing the production of consumer goods and services for an increasingly affluent and sophisticated population. The working arrangements are highly centralized, rigid and deeply entrenched, whereas decentralization and flexibility (including price flexibility) would seem to be required.

Consumption and Economic Growth

The prospects for aggregate consumption will depend, of course, on the overall rate of growth of GNP and decisions about the share to be allocated to consumption. Whatever the growth of total consumption, its impact on progress in living standards will be influenced by the growth of the population. All these matters are being explored elsewhere in this volume, but it may be useful to observe here that the impact on per capita consumption of alternative assumptions about national-income allocation has been explored in Bergson (1978). From that analysis, it is clear that the key to the future fortunes of consumers lies in the rate of improvement in productivity of resource use. If no gains are made in the 1980s, as in the 1970s, if investment grows at 3.5% annually as it did in the 1970s, and if the defense share does not rise, then GNP under his model would grow at less than 2.5% annually during the decade, and per capita consumption at less than 1% annually. Productivity increases of 1% annually, retaining the other assumptions, produce annual gains of better than 2% in per capita consumption; with productivity advancing at 2% annually, the gains for consumers are over 3.5% annually. As Bergson's exercise demonstrates, at the present state of Soviet development, acceleration of the investment rate would produce less than proportionate gains in output and more than proportionate losses in consumption. An increased share for defense also would diminish the claim of consumption at a given investment rate.

Assuming continued progress in raising agricultural output, annual gains in per capita consumption of 1 to 2% at least should provide consumers with a sense of some forward motion. Whatever the quantitative gains in consumption, they will be more palpable if they are provided in highly visible areas — more meat, housing, and automobiles, for example. Unless long-run economic growth falters seriously in the West, however, increases of 1 to 2% annually in real per capita consumption will not enable Soviet consumers to catch up relatively in levels of living.

Slow economic growth, however, would make it difficult for the Soviet Union to manage the array of serious problems in the consumer and labor markets that it now faces. During the next two decades, the labor force will grow at an average annual rate of about 0.7%, half the rate that prevailed in the 1970s. Workers, therefore, are likely to be in short supply, given continued pressure for production and the poor prospects for productivity advance. This situation will make it hard to limit wage increases, a policy that will be required to accommodate to a slower increase in availabilities of goods and services and to prevent a further rise in household cash balances. But failure to do so will erode the efficacy of pecuniary incentives as stimuli to greater work effort and labor-force participation. The problem is compounded by the fact that the population has already accumulated large cash holdings; deposits in state savings banks alone amounted to over half of total disposable money incomes in 1979. In addition, the size of cash hoards is unknown. While the interpretation of these large holdings of liquid assets is controversial among Soviet economists as well as among Western observers (Katsenelinboigen, 1975; Portes, 1977; Pickersgill, 1980), the government evidently is concerned about the potential effects of the population's cash holdings on work incentives and as sources of funds for black-market activities. To reduce the monetary overhang, the government may feel compelled to undertake a currency reform of some kind, a move that would be highly unpopular.

As past experience has shown, whatever additional supplies of consumer goods become available, the government will find it difficult to make them conform to consumer demand. At present income levels, Soviet consumers display strong preferences for quality foods, stylish clothing and durables of modern design. The income elasticity of demand for meat, for example, has been estimated at 1.0, compared with .65–.75 in other countries at comparable levels of development.[28] The system's difficulties in producing meat and other quality products are well known.

Given the level of resources allocated to consumption, their payoff in terms of the population's welfare would be maximised if prices for individual goods and services were set at market-clearing levels. As already noted, many prices are heavily subsidized at present, and queues and black markets are much in evidence. Housing and meat "shortages" might disappear overnight if rents and retail prices were raised to cover production costs. Whether the Soviet government can bring itself to emulate some of the Eastern European countries in raising consumer prices remains to be seen. Although a policy of gradualism and subterfuge might reduce the political risks of serious popular unrest, a substantial price realignment probably cannot be avoided altogether.

Consumption and Economic Reform[29]

Whatever quantitative gains are achieved in the coming years, the lot of Soviet consumers would be improved if the quality and mix of output were tailored more closely to consumer preferences. One reason for poor quality and obsolescent design of products is the backward level of technology used in the production of consumer goods; diversion of investment to replace much of that capital stock with modern facilities would improve matters, no doubt. The principal causes of the problems with quality and mix, however, as well as those associated with supplying consumer goods when and where they are wanted, are rooted in the economic system itself. Whatever their other merits, central planning and pricing have proven to be unsuitable tools for managing the production of consumer goods and services in a relatively developed economy.

Over the past 15 years the Soviets have been conducting a series of so-called "reforms" in the working arrangements of the economy, a process that I have likened to being on a treadmill (Schroeder, 1979), for most of them amounted to reforming previous reforms that failed to work. The numerous revisions in chains of command, plan indicators and incentive arrangements were aimed at raising efficiency in resource use, improving product quality and inducing producers to strive to satisfy customers, rather than the plan. The latest step on the treadmill is a spate of so-called "reforms" set forth in an omnibus decree of July 29, 1979.[30] The new measures, to be carried out gradually during 1980–5, strengthen the role of the central authorities, introduce still one more round of changes in success indicators and incentive arrangements, and impose more controls. Neither the previous "reforms", nor the latest round alters any essential feature of the economic system. It remains highly centralized, with central planning of the output mix, administratively set prices, rationing of producer goods and incentives tied to meeting plans. As is evident from the dismal record of productivity growth, the continuing problems with product quality and mix of consumer goods, and the inability to significantly boost the sales of manufactures to the West, the reforms have not worked, nor will the ones now being implemented. They will not work, I believe, because they leave the system intact. In my view, only a thoroughgoing reform that actually *re*-forms, i.e. marketizes the system, holds any promise for improving matters significantly in the consumer sector. Such a reform must engage the entire production–distribution system, or virtually all of it. It would not be enough simply to marketize the consumer sector alone. The producers of consumption goods (including the farmers) must depend on the producers of raw materials, machinery and a host of other items for the timely delivery of needed inputs in the required quality and mix. A demand-oriented production–distribution system involves an intricate chain of interdependencies. The makers of final products cannot respond flexibly to consumer demand unless the producers of intermediate goods also are motivated to respond to demand. In a word, some links in the chain cannot respond effectively to consumers while other links are required to respond to planners.

Replacement of centrally planned socialism with some species of genuine market socialism in an economy in as great a disarray as the Soviet economy in 1980 would have high short-run costs, as did Lenin's NEP in 1921–3. Production would be seriously disrupted while the new modus operandi was being established, prices probably would rise sharply, and workers would lose jobs. Moreover, the long-run payoff in terms of acceleration of growth in output and efficiency are uncertain, as Bergson (1967) has argued and as the experience of Hungary with a partial market socialism has shown. Faced with certain short-run disruptions, unrelenting opposition from a huge Party and state bureaucracy, and uncertain long-run benefits, both the political leadership and the population may well prefer to muddle along with the status quo.

Consumption and Communist Ideology

Long-held and much prated-about ideological positions are likely to constrain future political decisions concerning consumer–welfare policy — about the growth and pattern of consumption, income distribution, work and leisure, and the kinds of measures that have to be taken to deal with the present disarray in the consumer-goods and labor markets. With regard to the amount and pattern of consumption, Soviet theorists have written much in the past several years about the evils of "consumerism", of excessive accumulation of material goods, of a disease labeled "thingism". Soviet ideology holds that Soviet society in the present stage of "mature socialism" and of "building communism", is (or should be) creating the "New Communist Man", who will prefer spiritual and cultural development over material acquisition and for whom work will become a deeply felt, basic need. Hence, Soviet scholars devote much attention to constructing "rational" budgets in respect to consumption and the use of time. Propaganda denounces the "frivolous" choices made by consumers in the West. These considerations suggest that the government will continue to regard with disfavor solutions involving a large degree of consumer sovereignty. As yet, there are few signs of the emergence of the "new" man, however, and the government will have to determine the extent to which to try to satisfy the "old" man, with his strongly revealed preference for things.

Ideological considerations also will constrain the range of choices open to the political leadership in seeking to deal with the present mix of problems in the consumer-goods and labor markets. The supply of food and personal services could be increased quickly and at low cost if government policy were to sanction a sizeable expansion of private activity and give it strong support by helping to supply needed inputs and by eliminating the highly discriminatory taxation of private incomes. Although policy at the moment is encouraging private agriculture, words have not yet been matched with much tangible support. To absorb excess purchasing power, the government also could sanction the supply of more private services and support small-scale cooperative production and more construction of cooperative housing. However, private-property solutions are anathema to convinced Marxists, and bureaucrats dislike spontaneous processes that they cannot control. The ideological predilection for equalizing the distribution of real incomes through price policy, along with the repeated assertion that Soviet socialism has managed to eliminate the twin evils of capitalism — unemployment and inflation — will make it difficult for the government to use profit-based incentives to eliminate redundant workers in enterprises and to use price policy to balance supply and demand in consumer-goods markets.

Unless such political-ideological constraints are relaxed, particularly the intense aversion to "spontaneity" and market forces, the Soviet government may find it impossible to satisfy even minimally the expectations of its increasingly sophisticated and more educated population. Political, social, and economic problems all may multiply as a consequence.

Addendum: Income Distribution

Socialist distribution theory proclaims two principles that hold during the period of transition to full communism — payment in accordance with individual work (differentiation) and the reduction of income differences among social groups (manual workers and white collar workers, urban and rural workers, ethnic groups). In Soviet practice, as has been pointed out (Bergson, 1944; Kirsch, 1972; Chilosi, 1980), policy makers have had to compromise between these two principles, depending on the priority for production and the state of the labor market. In the sections to follow, we shall attempt first to show how earnings differentials among various groups have developed under these policies in the postwar period, and second, to present the evidence concerning changes in the interpersonal distribution of incomes. Regrettably, the available data with which to assess these important matters leave much to be desired because of the extreme paucity of statistics on incomes published by the Soviet government in the postwar period.

Skill Differentials

The only regularly published data with which to assess the trend in skill differentials are poor indeed; they pertain to average earnings of three broad groups — workers, engineering-technical workers (ITRs), and clerical employees — in industry, state agriculture, and construction. Table 10.9 presents these data in relative form. As can be observed, a large restructuring of wage differentials has taken place in all three branches. In 1950, engineering-technical employees earned more than twice as much as production workers in state agriculture and construction and over three-fourths more than those in industry. These differentials contracted rapidly under the impact of successive increases in the minimum wage, an explicit policy of reducing some top salaries, and two major wage reforms. In 1979, ITRs earned only 29% more than workers in agriculture, less than one-fifth more than those in industry and a mere 4.3% more than the workers in construction. Differentials between earnings of ITRs and clerical employees have also narrowed steadily, although less sharply. In all three sectors, clerical employees earn substantially less than production workers, whose advantage has increased greatly over the period. The erosion of the earnings advantage of the relatively more educated groups in these branches might be expected, considering the large rise in the share of persons with a higher education in the total labor force. Nonetheless, the reduction in the status of white-collar groups relative to blue-collar groups has been steady and sharp, prompting some Soviet economists to advocate a reversal, in order to improve work incentives for the former group.

Sectoral and Industrial Differentials

Earnings differentials have also contracted among sectors of the economy, and most especially within the industrial sector. The government regularly publishes data on average monthly wages for 12 economic sectors and irregularly for 9 branches of industry. On the whole, the wage ranking of sectors has changed little in the postwar years, except for a large rise in the relative position of state agriculture and a large decline in the relative position of science. In 1950, the latter

Table 10.9   Relative Levels of Earnings of Selected Occupational Groups, USSR, 1950, 1960, 1970, 1979

	Ratio of Earnings of Engineering–Technical Workers to Earnings of Production Workers	Ratio of Earnings of Clerical Employees to Earnings of Production Workers	Ratio of Earnings of Engineering–Technical Workers to Earnings of Clerical Employees
Industry			
1950	175.8	92.6	189.9
1960	148.8	81.5	182.5
1970	136.3	85.5	159.5
1979	115.9	79.3	146.2
Construction			
1950	212.0	127.1	166.9
1960	155.8	94.1	165.5
1970	134.7	92.1	146.2
1979	104.3	72.7	143.5
State Agriculture			
1950	234.2	142.8	164.0
1960	216.9	125.3	173.1
1970	166.8	97.1	171.9
1979	128.8	84.9	151.8

Source: Trud v SSSR, 1968, pp. 140, 145. Nar.khoz. 1979, pp. 394–5.

ranked at the top and the former at the bottom; in 1979, their respective rankings were fifth and sixth or seventh (tying with public administration). The weighted coefficient of variation was .178 in 1950, .208 in 1960, .154 in 1970 and .161 in 1979. A much greater compression of average-earnings differences occurred among branches of industry, a subject investigated for the 1950s and 1960s by Chapman (1970). The coefficient of variation dropped from .288 in 1950 to .254 in 1960 and then to .151 in 1975. One should note, however, that one branch — machinery and metalworking — carried 31%, 35% and 44% of the weight in each year, respectively. Again, the hierarchy of branches has changed little over the period.

Regional Differentials

During the 1950s and 1960s, Soviet leaders repeatedly proclaimed the goal of narrowing differences in incomes (development) among union republics and nationalities. In the 1970s, this objective is no longer touted; Brezhnev has declared in late 1972 that it had been "basically" achieved. Whatever the effect of these pronouncements in practice, regional income differences have, in fact, been widening since 1960, and especially so in the 1970s. This conclusion holds, whether the measure of incomes is average wages per worker or the more inclusive concepts of personal and total incomes expressed per capita. Interrepublic differences in average wages of the state labor force are quite narrow, but they have increased somewhat. The weighted coefficients of variation are .560 in 1960, .601 in 1970, and .864 in 1978 (Schroeder, 1981). The same trend is shown by a broader measure, termed "personal incomes" by McAuley (1979), who developed with meticulous care estimates for the republics in 1960, 1965 and 1970. The author has extended these estimates to 1978 (Schroeder, 1981). The concept includes incomes from wages, money earnings received from collective farms, income in kind, transfer payments, interest on savings, and other minor incomes. The weighted coefficients of variation increased from .112 in 1960 to .124 in 1970 and to .155 in 1978, differentials that are well within the range found for other countries at similar levels of development. In general, the rankings of the republics were fairly stable during the period, with the Baltic republics consistently ranking at the top, and Central Asia and Azerbaidzhan ranking at the bottom. In 1978, per capita personal incomes in the Baltics were nearly one-fifth above the national average, while those in Central Asia were less than three-fourths and in Azerbaidzhan less than two-thirds of the national average. The latter's relative position deteriorated seriously during 1960–78, while that of Moldavia and Belorussia improved markedly. All of these findings are changed little when personal incomes are expressed per adult equivalent rather than per capita (Spechler). Nor is the picture much different, when the concept of incomes is broadened to include state expenditures on health and education services (McAuley, 1979; Schroeder, 1981).

Differentials in Agricultural and Nonagricultural Incomes

This complex subject has been attacked in various ways by Bronson and Krueger (1971); Wädekin (1975); Schroeder and Severin (1976); McAuley (1979). Calculations have been made using a variety of data sets and concepts. McAuley (1979), for example, focuses on comparisons between total and personal incomes of state employees and of collective farmers. Results differ, depending on whether the comparisons are expressed per capita, per worker, or per family. Besides farm wages, money incomes, considered often, include transfer payments and incomes of family members from work outside of agriculture. If incomes in kind are taken into account, the methods of valuation differ, and often the derivation is obscure. Rather different estimates can be obtained, depending on the approach and the data used (which often disagree). Indeed, the notable reticence of the Soviet government regarding income data, particularly peasant income, makes definitive conclusions impossible. Nonetheless, the general Western consensus, shared by Soviet writers, is that differentials between peasant and worker wages and incomes have been substantially reduced in the post-Stalin period.

Here, we shall examine two kinds of differentials — between average money wages paid by state farms and by collective farms, and between average wages of nonagricultural workers and those of state and collective farmers who work on the farms, including incomes in kind and private incomes from sale of farm products. The data are shown in Table 10.10. Between 1950 and 1976, average money wages of agricultural workers rose three times as fast as those of nonagricultural workers. Within agriculture, money wages of collective farmers rose six times as fast as those of state farmers. This spectacular reduction in money–wage differentials was the result of state policies that radically increased procurement prices for farm products, rapidly raised the share of money payments in total pay of collective farmers, and deliberately sought to bring wage rates on collective farms into conformity with those paid on state farms. These policies were part of a general process of monetizing the rural economy. As a consequence, average money earnings in agriculture rose from 11% of wages in nonagricultural sectors in 1950 to 70% in 1976. In the same period, the average pay of collective farmers increased from 13% to 75% of that of state farmers. Government policies also sanctioned a much more rapid increase in wages in state agriculture than in the state sector generally, with the result that average wages in the former tripled, whereas in the latter they doubled. These processes of reducing money differentials continued during 1977–9.

Agricultural workers receive sizable additional incomes from consumption in kind and from sale of farm products produced in the private subsidiary economy. The share of such incomes (with the in-kind portion valued at retail prices less distribution costs) in total incomes has dropped steadily. It comprised 88% of the total in 1950,

65% in 1960 and 41% in 1976. When such incomes, valued in this way, are added to farm wages, we observe that total agricultural incomes per worker thus defined increased 3.7 times during 1950–76, compared with an increase of 2.3 times in nonagricultural earnings. Thus, average agricultural earnings rose from somewhat over half of nonagricultural earnings in 1950 to nearly nine-tenths in 1976. These calculations somewhat overstate agricultural incomes per se because all income in kind is allocated to them, and because a part of the wages paid by collective farms represents pay for nonagricultural work.

If agricultural incomes in kind are valued at average prices realized by producers (farm-gate prices), rather than at retail prices, the narrowing of differentials is more pronounced. Thus, the government's proclaimed policy of reducing the differences between town and village has been translated into action in the area of primary incomes. To the same end, the government has also brought collective farmers under a unified system of social security like that for state employees, abolished discriminatory pricing arrangements that raised prices for rural consumers, and raised per capita expenditures on education and health in rural areas relative to those in urban areas. As a result of policies in the area of social welfare, payments and benefits from social-consumption funds now make up nearly the same share of total incomes of collective-farm families as they do of industrial-worker families.

Sex Differentials

The relative earnings of men and women in the USSR have been investigated in a spate of recent papers (Chapman, 1977; Swatford, 1978; Ofer and Vinokur, 1979; McAuley, 1981). Since the Soviet government does not publish data on earnings by sex, these studies, as well as those of Soviet scholars, have had to rely on a variety of indirect evidence and on sample surveys of diverse quality and representativeness. The results of these studies are remarkably similar. On average, women earn about two-thirds as much as men: this gap is similar to that found for Eastern Europe (Michael 1975), but is somewhat larger than that in Scandinavia and somewhat less than in other industrialized nations of Europe and North America (Galenson, 1973). The international comparison might be rather different if account could be taken of agricultural earnings and of differences in the extent of part-time employment. Whether or not the earnings gap has been decreasing in recent decades is an open question; the nature and quality of the data, mostly relating to the 1960s and early 1970s, do not permit a confident judgment.

The earnings gaps in the USSR are pervasive, persistent and large, as they have been elsewhere irrespective of the economic system. The explanatory variables also are similar. In the USSR, women's earnings tend to be 60 to 70 percent of those of men, whether one looks at plant or regional averages (Swatford, 1978; McAuley, 1981), or industry and

Table 10.10 Comparison of Nonagricultural and Agricultural Incomes, USSR, 1950, 1960, 1970 and 1976

	Nonagricultural Wages		Agricultural Incomes				
	Wage Bill	Employment	Wages		Income from Sales of Farm Produce[b]	Consumption in Kind[b]	Agricultural Employment
			State Farms	Collective[a] Farms			
	bill. rubles	000	bill. rubles	bill. rubles	bill. rubles	bill. rubles	000
1950	29.882	37.611	1.112	1.180	4.180	12.500	43.035
1960	55.535	55.404	4.090	4.940	5.390	11.600	39.994
1970	121.337	81.012	10.695	14.040	8.260	13.300	37.523
1976	173.258	94.265	16.116	16.620	11.140	11.600	34.320

	Average Annual Nonagricultural Wages	Average Annual Agricultural Incomes	Agricultural Incomes as Percent of Nonagricultural Incomes
	rubles	rubles	percent
1950	794	441	56
1960	1002	651	65
1970	1505	1234	82
1976	1838	1616	88

[a]Figures include payments by collective farms to members in payment for all work done, agricultural and nonagricultural.
[b]Figures include receipts from sales and income in kind earned by the entire population, agricultural and nonagricultural.

Sources: Average wages: Trud v SSSR, 1968, p. 137; Nar.khoz, 1977, p. 385. Collective farm wages (excluding wages in kind) and income from sales of farm products: Denton, 1979, p. 785. Income in kind valued at average state retail and CFM prices less distribution and processing costs: estimates were made by the author based on a wide variety of sources.
Employment: Rapawy, 1976, p. 40. Estimate for 1976 was supplied by the author.

occupational averages (Ofer and Vinokur, 1979). The most comprehensive new evidence is provided by Ofer and Vinokur in their study of earnings of a large sample of Jewish émigré families. Their data pertain to urban families and relate to the early 1970s. Overall for their sample, the female/male earnings differential was .59. By sector of the economy it ranged from .47 in art to .69 in the communal economy; the measure is average wages for the principal job. Among 35 diverse occupations, the female/male ratio ranged from 1.01 (chief doctor) to .52 (junior trade worker), the overall average being .82. Within a given occupational group, differentials tended to be smaller than those among groups and sectors. The gaps were found to be similar, whether the data were aggregated by level of education (.59 to .70), age group (.60 to .72) or years of experience (.61 to .82), where the data related to monthly wages in the main job. The picture is not much altered by using hourly wages or by including earnings from private sources. Differentials of these orders of magnitude and pervasiveness are also found in a variety of small-scale surveys conducted in the Soviet Union and summarized by Chapman (1977b) and McAuley (1981).

Diverse factors contribute to the earnings gap in the USSR and to its persistence, despite an official policy of providing equal access to occupations and education and of nondiscrimination in wage setting. The references cited treat this complex matter in a variety of ways; we can do no more than provide a summary. Although equal pay for equal work is an integral part of Soviet wage fixing, the work done by men and by women is different. Women tend to be concentrated in the consumer-goods industries and in the services; the degree of concentration has risen in the postwar period (McAuley, 1981). Moreover, sectors in which women predominate tend to be those where average wages are lowest (e.g. the light industries and food industries rank at the bottom of the industrial-wage structure, and health and trade rank near the bottom among sectors). Indeed, Soviet wage policy evidently aims to align occupational rates in the services with those in food industries and light industries (Chapman, 1977). Moreover, within industries and sectors, women tend to be concentrated in relatively less skilled and therefore lower-paying occupations. Census data demonstrate that this occupational cleavage has persisted and has even increased in recent decades (McAuley, 1981). In professional and managerial positions, the percentage of women tends to fall as the skill and responsibility level rises, even though educational attainment of women has been brought near to that of men (Dodge, 1975). Similar patterns exist in agriculture (Dodge, 1966; Stuart, 1979).

One can readily agree with Chapman that a kind of dual labor market stratified by sex has been created and maintained, largely a consequence of the Soviet government's priorities favoring heavy industry, transportation, and construction, and its use of differential wages to enforce these priorities in the labor market. Moreover, employment of women has increased much faster than that of men, and women have tended to go into the services, where pay is relatively low and where new jobs were being created most rapidly. Finally, the persistence of occupational stratification is to be explained in considerable part by women's revealed preferences, "forced" though they may be. As women bear a disproportionate share of the responsibility for housework and child care, a burden made heavier by the paucity of household appliances and the vagaries of the retail distribution system, the dual task of wage earner and home-maker is eased when jobs are physically lighter, hours shorter or more flexible, and responsibilities less.

Interpersonal Distribution of Income

The question of the degree of income inequality under Soviet socialism has long attracted the attention of scholars, for one of the proclaimed virtues of socialism is its preference for and alleged ability to achieve greater equity in income distribution than is possible under capitalism. Bergson's classic study of Soviet wages in the pre-war years (Bergson, 1944), however, showed that ideology yielded to pragmatism. Following an initial period of contraction, the differentials began to increase sharply, as the government sought to encourage and reward the acquisition of skills, so badly needed for the industrialization drive. The Soviet government's failure to publish the requisite statistics has frustrated investigation in the postwar period. Although a considerable amount of data on earnings distributions for one or another group is collected, the results have not been published officially. Increasingly, however, bits of evidence have become available in publications of individual Soviet scholars. From a variety of information for the 1950s, Yanowitch (1963) concluded that an "income revolution" favoring egalitarianism was occurring. Relying on fragmentary evidence made available in the 1960s, Wiles and Markowski (1971) attempt to evaluate the Soviet situation in international perspective; they conclude that the degree of inequality in earnings of state employees decreased sharply between 1946 and 1966 and that income distribution in the Soviet Union was less unequal than in the US and the UK, but more so than in Poland. Wiles, working over a spate of additional fragments, extended the period and groups covered and reaffirmed his earlier findings (Wiles, 1974, 1975). Wiles's conclusions are based mainly on his reconstruction of a full earnings distribution from crude diagrams and some related statistical information given by Soviet economists Rabkina and Rimashevskaia (1972). Similar reconstructions have been made by Chapman (1977a, 1979) and McAuley (1977). Although the three reconstructions differ somewhat in detail, their results are similar. All make use of additional information provided by other Soviet authors. McAuley (1977) extends the work to produce estimates of the distribution of total incomes in the USSR, including those of *kolkhozniki*; he also provides a valuable description of the statistics relating to income distribution collected by Soviet statistical agencies. Pryor (1972) and Michael (1975) have contributed a comparative perspective. Finally, Rabkina and Rimashevskaia (1978) have given some information for recent years.

When we consider how obscure data were with which they had to work, Western investigators display a large degree of agreement. To my mind, it would be fruitless to try to arbitrate their small differences, or to argue the relative merits of one or another statistical measure of income inequality. I shall refer to the decile ratio, the measure most commonly cited in the original Soviet sources. The available data indicate that income differentials are relatively small and that they have declined significantly in the postwar period. According to figures given by Rabkina and Rimashevskaia, the decile ratio for earnings of all state workers and employees declined from 7.24 in 1946 to 4.44 in 1956, and to 2.83 in 1968; however, by 1971, the ratio had increased to 3.1, and in 1976 it was 3.35.[31] Similarly, the decile ratio for earnings of industrial workers fell from 5.43 in 1946 to 2.5 in 1968 and then rose to 2.63 in 1972. According to data developed by McAuley (1977), the decile ratio for per capita earnings of nonagricultural workers fell from 4.1 in 1958 to 3.1 in 1967. According to him, the ratio pertaining to per family incomes on the collective farms (evidently including in-kind incomes) was 3.23 in 1965 and 3.15 in 1968. Combining data underlying the latter two estimates and adding an estimate of in-kind incomes of state farmers, McAuley comes up with a range of decile ratios of 3.04–3.08 for total incomes per capita in the USSR in 1966–8. He is careful to point out the crudity of the underlying data and other uncertainties, but believes that his estimate is the best available.

By way of comparison, we can cite an array of decile ratios found for other countries; these data are reported and documented in Chapman (1979) and Wiles (1974). They indicate that in the late 1960s and early 1970s the distribution of wage earnings and of incomes in the Soviet Union was less unequal, as measured by decile ratios, than that in the United States, Italy or the United Kingdom and was more or less on a par with income distributions in Eastern Europe. Following are some of the decile ratios found for other countries: for American nonagricultural, full-time wage and salary earners in 1972 — 4.48; for earnings in the socialist sector in the early 1970s in Bulgaria and Czechoslovakia—2.5, in Hungary — 2.4, in Poland — 2.95, and in Yugoslavia — 3.1. Wiles (1974) reports the following estimates of decile ratios in respect to per capita incomes for the entire population, more or less: United States in 1968 — 7.0; the United Kingdom in 1969 — 3.9; and Italy in 1969 — 5.9. These measures represent incomes gross of taxes; Wiles declares them to be comparable to values he finds of 3.0 for Hungary, 3.1 for Poland, 3.2 for Czechoslovakia, 2.73 for Bulgaria and 3.7 for the USSR, all relating to the mid-1960s. McAuley thinks that Wiles's figure for the USSR is too high. I think it is futile to argue over differences of that magnitude, given the poor quality of the underpinnings. I am willing to agree that at present official (legal) incomes are less unequally distributed in the USSR than in the West, generally. This result is to be expected, since the Soviet government has been engaged in a deliberate effort to curtail income differences through successive increases in the minimum wage, less than proportionate adjustment in middle- and upper-level wage rates, reduction in the rate ranges of skill grades, reductions in top salaries, and programs to improve the relative position of agricultural workers. Also, property incomes are almost entirely absent in the USSR.

The discussion thus far has concerned official money incomes (plus in-kind incomes from work). The extent of inequality revealed by what are essentially official data based on legal incomes might be materially altered, if illegal incomes earned and legal incomes redistributed through the so-called "second" economy could be taken into account. The effect of illegal incomes cannot be estimated even approximately with any degree of confidence. One might suppose, however, that they would tend to increase the degree of inequality by raising incomes of groups with access to scarce goods and services, relative to the mass of the population. If illegal earnings from black-market profits and from bribery could be taken into account, they might well produce the "Pareto tail", that socialist income distributions thus far have failed to display (Chapman, 1979). Working in the same direction, it would seem, are the extensive and valuable privileges enjoyed by the Soviet elite. The entrenched system of multiple "perks" that attaches to particular positions in the USSR has been well surveyed by Matthews (1978), who thinks that they add at least 50 to 100% to recipients' incomes. These benefits include: extra salary supplements that are probably not included in published wage data, the right to purchase scarce goods at reduced prices in special shops (Kremlin ration), the right to obtain better quality and more spacious living quarters, and privileged access to better-quality medical services, educational institutions, and cultural facilities. Both the special money incomes of the elite, and illegal incomes would probably make the distribution of money incomes more unequal. Perks in kind (including special privileges and access) work in the same direction in respect to real incomes. On the other hand, the distribution of real incomes is made less unequal by government pricing policies, which subsidize food and rents through low prices, and by the taxing of luxuries through high prices including large turnover taxes. The government's policy of supplying health and education services as free public goods acts in the same direction. To me, the Soviet Union presents a society where the mass of the population has been accorded a relatively low level of material well-being (real incomes) distributed rather evenly, but where elites enjoy affluent life-styles and privileges and access to higher-quality goods, all of which are effectively denied to the ordinary citizen, irrespective of income or merit.

Socialist thought supports equality in the distribution of income, and Soviet policy pronouncements continue to declare the intent to reduce income differences among various groups in society. Over the past quarter-century the Soviet population has become accustomed to relatively narrow income differences, probably approves of an egalitarian policy, and expects it to continue. However, Soviet policy makers evidently have become concerned about the adverse impact on work effort and incentives of the present relatively narrow skill and earnings differences, and scholars have begun to advocate some widening of differentials, in order to better relate effort and rewards.[32] The reform decree of July 1979 calls for an end to excessive "wage levelling" and for rewarding workers in accord with productivity. Any serious effort at an economic reform involving greater responsibility for lower-level units and profit-based bonus schemes to reward risk taking likely would widen earnings differences between white-collar and blue-collar workers, if it were to be successful. As in Hungary, such increased income differentials might generate serious opposition from unskilled and semiskilled workers. The policy itself would surely meet opposition from ideological conservatives, who would view it as a retrogressive move from the Party's long-run goal of distribution according to need.

10: Notes

1 Measured in current prices, the share has declined notably — from 64% in 1950 (Bergson, 1961, p. 85) to 54% in 1976 (Schroeder and Edwards, 1981, p. 26). In 1976 the share of household consumption in Soviet GNP (49%) was below the corresponding shares in 23 OECD countries, some of them near or below the USSR in level of development as measured by per capita GNPs. Because of rising subsidies for food, housing, and some other goods and services and the falling share of the turnover tax in product prices, the share of consumption in GNP at factor cost is now about the same as in prevailing prices, a situation much different from the 1950s, when the prevailing-price measure showed consumption to be a significantly larger share of total GNP than did the factor-cost measure (Bergson, 1961).

2 CIA, June 1979, pp. 1, 23.

3 *Pravda*, Oct. 19, 1961.

4 *Planovoe khoziaistvo*: No. 12, 1979, p. 86.

5 *Planovoe khoziaistvo*: No. 9, 1979, p. 93.

6 *Voprosy ekonomiki*: No. 7, 1978, p. 60.

7 *Ekonomicheskaia gazeta*, No. 24, June 1979, p. 2.

8 *Ekonomika i organizatsiia promyshlennogo proizvodstva*: No. 12, 1979, pp. 106–7.

9 Publication of detailed data on retail inventories ceased after 1975.

10 *Pravda*, Nov. 28, 1979.

11 R. A. Lokshin. *Planovoe khoziaistvo*: No. 9, 1979, pp. 91–2.

12 *Pravda*, Feb. 18, 1970.

13 For example, *Voprosy ekonomiki*: No. 7, 1978, p. 55.

14 *Ekonomika i organizatsiia promyshlennogo proizvodstva*: No. 3, 1978, p. 91.

15 *Ibid.*, p. 10.

16 *Ibid.*, p. 92.

17 *Ibid.*, p. 95.

18 *Ibid.*, p. 97.

19 *Oktiabr*: No. 6, 1979, p. 184.

20 *Ekonomika i organizatsiia promyshlennogo proizvodstva*: No. 3, 1978, p. 98.

21 *Oktiabr*: No. 6, 1979, p. 187.

22 *Ekonomicheskaia gazeta*: No. 24, 1979, p. 2.

23 *Ekonomika i organizatsiia promyshlennogo proizvodstva*: No. 3, 1978, p. 94.

24 A number of the points brought up in this section are treated in a somewhat different framework in Schroeder, 1980.
25 *Kommunist*: No. 8, 1980, p. 58. These subsidies were equivalent to nearly 11% of total budget expenditures.
26 *Ekonomika i organizatsiia promyshlennogo proizvodstva*: No. 3, March 1980, pp. 15–33.
27 Bushnell, 1979; *Sunday Times*, London: July 20, 1980, pp. 18–23; Feifer, 1981.
28 These rates are cited in CIA, Jan. 1979, p. 5.
29 The subject of economic reform in general is explored in detail elsewhere in this volume. We focus here on these aspects related most closely to the consumer sector.
30 *Izvestia*, July 29, 1979.
31 *Ekonomika i organizatsiia promyshlennogo proizvodstva*: No. 5, 1978, p. 20.
32 See, for example, the sources cited in footnotes 26 and 31.

10: References

Bergson, Abram, *The Structure of Soviet Wages*. Cambridge, Mass.: Harvard Univ. Press, 1944.
Bergson, Abram, *Real National Income of Soviet Russia Since 1928*. Cambridge, Mass.: Harvard Univ. Press, 1961.
Bergson, Abram, "Market Socialism Revisited. *J. Pol. Econ.* **75**, 5: 655–73, Oct. 1967.
Bergson, Abram, "The Comparative National Income of the USSR and the United States." In D. J. Daly, ed., *International Comparisons of Prices and Output*. New York: National Bureau of Economic Research, 1972.
Bergson, Abram, *Productivity and the Social System – the USSR and the West*. Cambridge, Mass.: Harvard Univ. Press, 1978a.
Bergson, Abram, "Conclusions." In *The USSR in the 1980s*. Brussels: NATO Econ. Directorate, 1978b.
Block, Herbert, "The Planetary Product." US Dept. of State, Bureau of Public Affairs, Special Report No. 58. Washington, DC, 1979.
Bornstein, Morris, "A Comparison of Soviet and United States National Product." In *Comparisons of the Soviet and United States Economies*, Part II. Papers, Joint Econ. Comm., US Congress. Washington, DC: Govt. Printing Office, 1959.
Bronson, David, and Krueger, Constance, "The Revolution in Soviet Farm Household Incomes, 1953–1967." In James Millar, ed., *The Soviet Rural Community*. Urbana: Univ. of Illinois Press, 1971.
Bushnell, John, "The New Soviet Man Turns Pessimist." *Survey* **24**, 2 (107): 1–18, Spring 1979.
Chapman, Janet G., *Real Wages in Soviet Russia Since 1928*. Cambridge, Mass.: Harvard Univ. Press, 1963a.
Chapman, Janet G., "Consumption." In Abram Bergson and S. Kuznets, eds, *Economic Trends in the Soviet Union*. Cambridge, Mass.: Harvard Univ. Press, 1963b.
Chapman, Janet G., "Wage Variations in Soviet Industry." Santa Monica, Calif.: RAND RM6076–PR, 1970.
Chapman, Janet G., "Soviet Wages Under Socialism." In Alan Abouchar, ed., *The Socialist Price Mechanism*. Durham, NC: Duke Univ. Press, 1977a.
Chapman, Janet G., "Equal Pay for Equal Work?" In Dorothy Atkinson *et al.*, eds, *Women in Russia*. Stanford, Calif.: Stanford Univ. Press, 1977b.
Chapman, Janet G., "Recent Trends in the Soviet Industrial Wage Structure." In Arcadius Kahan and B. Ruble, eds, *Industrial Labor in the USSR*. New York: Pergamon, 1979.
Chilosi, Alberto, "Income Distribution Under Soviet-type Socialism: An Interpretative Framework." *J. Comp. Econ.* **4**, 1: 1–18, March 1980.
CIA, "A Comparison of Consumption in the USSR and the US." RR ER64–1. Washington, DC, Jan. 1964.

CIA, "USSR: Long-Term Outlook for Grain Imports." ER 79–10057. Washington, DC: January 1979.

CIA, "USSR: Trends and Prospects in Educational Attainment, 1959–85." ER 79–10344. Washington, DC, June 1979.

Denton, M. Elizabeth, "Soviet Consumer Policy: Trends and Prospects." In *Soviet Economy in a Time of Change*, 1979.

Dodge, Norton T., *Women in the Soviet Economy*. Baltimore, Md.: Johns Hopkins Univ. Press, 1966.

Dodge, Norton T., "The Role of Women in the Soviet Economy." In *Economic Aspects of Life in the USSR*. Brussels: NATO Econ. Directorate, 1975.

Ernst, Maurice, "Postwar Economic Growth in Eastern Europe." In *New Directions in the Soviet Economy*, Pt. IV. Papers, Joint Econ. Comm., US Congress. Washington, DC: Govt. Printing Office, 1966.

Feifer, George, "Russian Disorders." *Harper's*: pp. 41–55, Feb. 1981.

Galenson, Marjorie, *Women at Work: An International Comparison*. Ithaca, NY: New York State School of Industrial and Labor Relations, Cornell Univ., 1973.

Goldman, Marshall, *Soviet Marketing*. Glencoe, Ill.; The Free Press, 1963.

Gross National Product of the USSR, 1950–1980. Papers, Joint Econ. Comm., US Congress. Washington, DC: Govt. Printing Office. Forthcoming.

Grossman, Gregory, "The Second Economy of the USSR." *Problems of Communism* **26**, 5: 25–40, Sept.–Oct. 1977.

Grossman, Gregory, "Notes on the Illegal Economy and Corruption." In *Soviet Economy in a Time of Change*, 1979.

Hanson, Philip, *The Consumer Sector in the Soviet Economy*. Evanston, Ill.: Northwestern Univ. Press, 1968.

Katsenelinboigen, Aron, "Disguised Inflation in the Soviet Union." In *Economic Aspects . . .* , 1975.

Kirsch, Leonard J., *Soviet Wages*. Cambridge, Mass: MIT Press, 1972.

Kravis, Irving B., Heston, Alan W., and Summers, Robert, United Nations International Comparison Project, Phase II: *International Comparisons of Real Product and Purchasing Power*. Baltimore: Johns Hopkins Press, 1978.

Kuznets, Simon S., *Modern Economic Growth*. New Haven, Conn.: Yale Univ. Press, 1966.

McAuley, Alastair, "The Distribution of Earnings and Incomes in the Soviet Union." *Soviet Studies* **29**, 2: 214–37, April 1977.

McAuley, Alastair, *Economic Welfare in the Soviet Union*. Madison, Wisc.: Univ. of Wisconsin Press, 1979.

McAuley, Alastair, *Women's Work and Wages in the Soviet Union*. London: Allen & Unwin, 1981.

Matthews, Mervyn, *Privilege in the Soviet Union*. London: Allen & Unwin, 1978.

Michael, Jan M., "An Alternative Approach to Measuring Income Inequality in Eastern Europe." In Zbigniew M. Fallenbuchl, ed., *Economic Development in the Soviet Union and Eastern Europe*, Vol. I. New York: Praeger, 1975.

Nar. khoz., see TSU.

OECD, National Accounts of OECD Countries, 1960–77. Paris, 1979.

Ofer, Gur, *The Service Sector in Soviet Economic Growth*. Cambridge, Mass.; Harvard Univ. Press, 1973.

Ofer, Gur, Vinokur, Aaron, and Barchaim Yecheil, "Family Budget Survey of Soviet Emigrants in the Soviet Union." Santa Monica, Calif.: RAND P–6015, 1979.

Ofer, Gur, and Vinokur, Aaron, "Earnings Differentials by Sex in the Soviet Union." Jerusalem: Research Report No 1120, The Hebrew University of Jerusalem, June 1979.

Pickersgill, Joyce, "Recent Evidence of Soviet Household Saving Behavior." *Rev. Econ. and Stat.* **62**, 4: 628–33, Nov. 1980.

Portes, Richard, "The Control of Inflation: Some Lessons from East European Experience." *Economica* **44**, 2: 109–30, May 1977.

Pryor, Frederic L., *Economic System and the Size Distribution of Income and Wealth*. Bloomington, Ind.: Internat. Development Research Center, 1972.

Rabkina, N. E., and Rimashevskaia, N. M., *Osnovy differentsiatsii zarabotnoi platy i dokhodov naseleniia.* Moscow: Ekonomika, 1972.

Rabkina, N. E., and Rimashevskaia, N. M., "Raspredelitel'nye otnosheniia i sotsial'noe razvitie." *Ekonomika i organizatsiia promyshlennogo proizvodstva*: pp. 17–32, no. 5, 1978.

Rapawy, Stephen, "Estimates and Projections of the Labor Force and Employment in the U.S.S.R., 1950 to 1990." Washington, DC: US Bureau of the Census, Foreign Econ. Report no. 10, 1976.

Research Project on National Income in East Central Europe. New York: IW International Financial Research, Inc. (Thad P. Alton, Director):

Czechoslovakia, Hungary and Poland: Domestic Final Uses of Gross Product, Structure and Growth, Selected Years, 1965–1978. Occ. Paper 55, 1979.

Personal Consumption in Eastern Europe, Selected Years, 1960–1978. Occ. Paper 57, 1979.

Bulgaria and East Germany: Domestic Final Uses of Gross Product Structure and Growth, Selected Years, 1965–1978. Occ. Paper 58, 1979.

Schroeder, Gertrude E., "Consumer Problems and Prospects." *Problems of Communism* **22**, 2: 1–24, March–April 1973.

Schroeder, Gertrude E., "Soviet Wages and Income Policies in Regional Perspective," *ACES Bull.* **16**, 1: 3–20, Fall 1974.

Schroeder, Gertrude E., "Consumer Goods Availability and Repressed Inflation in the Soviet Union." In *Economic Aspects* ... , 1975.

Schroeder, Gertrude E., and Severin, Barbara S., "Soviet Consumption and Income Policies in Perspective." In *Soviet Economy in a New Perspective.* Papers, Joint Econ. Comm., US Congress. Washington, DC: Govt. Printing Office, 1976.

Schroeder, Gertrude E., and Greenslade, Rush V., "On the Measurement of the 'Second Economy' in the USSR." *ACES Bull* **21**, 1: 3–22, Spring 1979.

Schroeder, Gertrude E., "The Soviet Economy on a Treadmill of 'Reforms'." In *Soviet Economy in a Time of Change*, 1979.

Schroeder, Gertrude E., "Prospects for the Consumer." In Robert Wesson, ed., *The Soviet Union: Looking to the 1980s.* Stanford, Calif.: Hoover Inst. Press, 1980.

Schroeder, Gertrude E., "Regional Living Standards." In I. S. Koropeckyj and G. E. Schroeder, eds, *The Economics of Soviet Regions.* New York: Praeger, 1981.

Schroeder, Gertrude E., and Edwards, Imogene, "Consumption in the USSR: An International Comparison." Joint Econ. Comm., US Congress. Washington, DC: Govt. Printing Office, 1981.

Soviet Economy in a Time of Change. Papers, Joint Econ. Comm., US Congress. Washington, DC: Govt. Printing Office, 1979.

Spechler, Martin C., "Regional Developments in the U.S.S.R., 1958–78." In *Soviet Economy in a Time of Change*, Vol. I, 1979.

Swatford, M., "Sex Differences in Soviet Earnings." *Amer. Sociol. Rev.* **43**, 5: 657–73, Oct. 1978.

Treml, Vladimir G., and Hardt, John P., *Soviet Economic Statistics.* Durham, NC: Duke Univ. Press, 1972.

Trud v SSSR. Moscow, 1968.

TSU, *Narodnoe khoziaistvo.* Moscow: various years.

United Nations International Comparison Project, see Kravis and assoc., 1978.

Wädekin, Karl-Eugen, "Income Distribution in Soviet Agriculture." *Soviet Studies* **28**, 1: 3–26 Jan. 1975.

Wiles, Peter, and Markowski, Stefan, "Income Distribution under Communism and Capitalism." *Soviet Studies* **22**, 3: 343–69 Jan. 1971; **22**, 4: 487–511, April 1971.

Wiles, Peter, *Distribution of Income: East and West.* Amsterdam: North Holland, 1974.

Wiles, Peter, "Recent Data on Soviet Income Distribution." In *Economic Aspects* ... , 1975.

Yanowitch, Murray, "The Soviet Income Revolution." *Slavic Rev.* **22**, 4: 683–97, Dec. 1963.

11

Planning and Management

JOSEPH S. BERLINER

Introduction

In July of 1979 the Party and Government of the USSR issued a decree announcing a variety of changes in what is now called the economic mechanism. The decree evoked a flurry of interest at the time, but in short order public attention turned to other things. There are two lessons in that incident. First, the process of modifying the system of planning and management has become routinized. The public has become used to the periodic announcement, usually in advance of the next five-year planning period, of a series of changes that had been agreed upon since the last such decree. Second, for the most part the changes are technical rather than fundamental, involving such matters as new success indicators or revised planning procedures.

The capacity of the system to review its methods of operation periodically and to seek ways of improving them must be regarded as one of its strengths. There is a view abroad, however, that the range of alternatives considered, in the public discussion at least, is too narrow to score a significant advance. If Mr Brezhnev were immortal, that restriction might continue indefinitely. But as the USSR enters the last decades of the century, there is a strong possibility that the range of discussable alternatives may widen, not only because of human mortality, but also because of the growing strains to which the economy will be subject.

The objective of this paper is to explore that wider range of alternative systems of planning and management that may be considered as the next two decades unfold. It is well to begin, however, with a review of the recent history of economic reforms.

11.1. Some Reflections on Recent History

Five cases of changes in the economic mechanism will serve as the specimens in this dissection of the past. The details are familiar to this audience and have been so well studied elsewhere (Schroeder, 1979) that they need not be recounted here. The purpose is rather to review those cases for the light they can shed on the views held by the governors of the economic system about that system. Two questions will be asked about each of the cases. First, what were the governors seeking to accomplish by that particular change? Second, what does that change reveal about their conception of how their system works? The first question is designed to identify the objectives of the leadership, and the second to understand their implicit model of their own economy. That sort of knowledge about past efforts to change the economy should provide some insight into the future course of such efforts.

The selection of the five cases examined below is somewhat arbitrary. Two of them, the Territorial Reorganization of 1957 and the Economic Reform of 1965, would appear on everybody's list of the most important efforts at system change. The others have been chosen not necessarily because of their prominence but because they deal with different facets of the planning or management system. Other analysts would select other cases, covering areas I have omitted, like agriculture. The five that have been chosen nevertheless represent, I believe, a reasonable selection of changes from which to seek some instructive generalizations.

A. *The Territorial Reorganization of 1957*

The problem to which the reform was addressed was the diversion of resources into uses different from those provided for in the plan. To some extent the issue was the deliberate violation of the plan; for example, when ministries instructed their enterprises to alter their shipping plans in favor of customers within their own ministries. In other cases the issue was not violations of the plans but restrictions on the flow of resources in ways that were contrary to the intent of the plan. A typical instance was the enterprise that possessed excess stocks of some scarce commodity while a neighboring enterprise's production plan foundered for lack of that commodity; but the redirection of that commodity from the first enterprise to the second was inhibited because they belonged to different ministries.

The source of the problem, as seen by the reformers, was captured in the slogan, *vedomstvennost'* or "departmentalism." That may be interpreted to mean that ministries tended to maximize the indicators of their own performance, which in system terms is equivalent to suboptimization by the component units at the expense of the performance of the system as a whole. The solution was thought to be a restructuring of those components by repartitioning them in such fashion that the identity of the suboptimizing units — the ministries — was obliterated. If there were no ministries there could be no suboptimization by ministries.

It is difficult to imagine, in retrospect, that the reformers did not anticipate what the consequence would be; that only the specific form of the objectionable behavior would be changed, but not that behavior in general. There had been ample evidence in the past of *mestnichestvo* (localism) in decision making by regional government and Party organizations. The outcome was indeed so predictable that a compelling case can and has been made that the whole purpose of the exercise had nothing to do with economics at all but with politics; namely, that the reform was Khrushchev's gambit for crushing the power base of the Moscow bureaucracy by transferring their power to his supporters in the provincial centers. If that was indeed the history, then we are misled in trying to draw too many lessons out of the economics of the reform. But one can recognize the political element in the reform without having to hold that there was no serious economic purpose behind it. If the reformers failed to anticipate the turn that the economy actually took after the reform, it may be because they expected either that (a) *mestnichestvo* could and would be more easily contained than the old *vedomstvennost'*, if only because none of the 110-odd provincial economic leaders could wield the power of a major industrial minister, or (b), even if that were not so, the cost of *mestnichestvo* would be less than that of *vedomstvennost'*. We know in retrospect that both of those propositions were wrong, but they could have been honestly held by reasonable men at the time.

The episode offers several insights into the thoughts of the system's governors about their system. It is clear that there was no questioning of the principle of central planning as the basis of the economic mechanism. They recognized that planning was not perfect, but that was not the issue to which this reform was addressed. The problem was that even perfect plans are not self-executing, but require persons and organizations to carry them out. The task of government was to create a management structure in which managers would make those decisions that are in closest conformity to the plan. In seeking out the villain, of the several levels of management at which the problem could have been attacked they chose the level of central management — the ministries. Presumably they saw enterprise-level management as less at fault, or perhaps as more compliant. The effective power of choice lay with the central management, and if the central management could be made to behave correctly, enterprise management could be expected to comply. In any event, even if they were not quite that starry-eyed about enterprise management, it was their judgement that the greater damage was being done where the greater overall decision-making power lay — with the central management.

Finally, the problem was seen not simply as one of incentives but of structure. If it were merely incentives, they might have sought to design new incentives — perhaps new success indicators — to induce ministers to alter their decisions. The fact that they did not take that tack indicates that they did not see that as the source of the problem. They must have felt that it was the branch structure of the management system that induced the unfortunate behavior, and no amount of fiddling with success indicators would eliminate the pressures toward maximizing the performance of the branch.

The Territorial Reorganization was introduced in 1957. It is well to recall that that was a period in which the Soviet economy was still growing very rapidly. The reform was the first major effort to eliminate some of the grosser sources of inefficiency in the rigid system of planning and management inherited from Stalin. The evidence of waste was abundant, but the system was thought to be performing quite satisfactorily at the time. The objective of the reform was to enable it to do even better. The beginnings of the decline in the growth rate date from the late 1950s. By the mid-sixties it was increasingly evident that the decline was not a short-term aberration but was perhaps something systemic. The next major reform was introduced under new conditions; the economy had seen better days and its governors wished to find a way of bringing those days back.

B. *The 1965 Economic Reform*

The problem that motivated this reform was similar to that involved in the Territorial Reorganization: enterprises were making a broad range of decisions that were contrary to the intentions of the plan. And as in the earlier reform, the source of the problem was again held to be the organs of central management; that was the meaning of the slogan, "petty tutelage." But one new source was identified this time. That was the use of poorly designed success indicators that directed enterprises into making incorrect decisions.

The petty-tutelage problem was an issue in organizational theory; the question was, what were the optimal levels at which various types of decisions should be made. One can detect in the solution the primacy of informational concerns. That is, the decision to devolve a wide range of choices from the level of central management to that of enterprise management reflected the view that those were areas in which enterprises had more precise and timely information at their disposal than the central ministries.

The success-indicator problem, in contrast, was an issue in economic theory; it was indeed the first reform in which economists rather than politicians and planners had a hand. By identifying the source of the problem as the notorious *val* (gross value of output), the reformers implicitly acknowledged that they were dealing with a process of maximization under constraints, and that in such a process it is important to get the objectives function right. That way of thinking about the economic mechanism was a giant step forward from the reasoning of the past, which held that the problem was simply to get managers to "fulfill the plan." It led eventually to the formulation that is currently in wide use: "what is best for the economy should be best for the enterprise."

The choice of sales revenue and profit as the new success indicators was a reasonable first step in the direction of designing an optimal objectives function for enterprise management. Though not usually put into the same category, the introduction of a capital charge may also be regarded as a contribution to the improvement of the success indicators. For when profit is promoted to the level of a major argument in an objectives function, it becomes more important to be sure that the relative costs of the factors of production are properly accounted for.

The change in the success indicators required a corresponding change in the incentive structure, which had formerly been linked primarily to *val*. The new system of incentive payments involved nothing new in principle, however. All the elements were there before, in the form of the Enterprise Fund, although the magnitudes of the contributions to the various incentive funds was changed.

In the course of a few years several features of the original 1965 reform were modified. Among the major modifications was the gradual increase in the number of indicators for which the enterprise had to account to the ministry. The reason for the retreat is instructive because it bears on a problem that arises in all efforts to reform the system of planning and management. The central allocative instrument is still the national plan. Gosplan must be held responsible for the consistency and optimality of the plan, and someone else must be held responsible for assuring that that plan is executed. As long as the executors are the ministries, they must be given authority equivalent to their responsibility. The Economic Reform was an attempt to permit enterprises, on informational grounds, to make a wide range of decisions that affected plan fulfillment, but to hold the ministries responsible for the results. In effect, the ministries were put in the position of being held responsible for decisions that they were forbidden to control. The impossibility of that organizational arrangement led eventually to the reassertion by the ministries of control over those kinds of enterprise decisions for which they had to account to the Party and the Council of Ministers.

In that piece of history there is an important lesson regarding the limits of decentralized decision making under central planning. A governing unit (for example, a capitalist corporation) can delegate decision-making authority to lower units on grounds of informational efficiency if it determines its own objectives function; it can decentralize purchasing while retaining control over pricing, for example. The test of that organizational arrangement is its own evaluation of whether the results are better in the light of its own profit and other objectives. But if a governing unit (like a Soviet ministry) is not an autonomous organization but is responsible to a higher organization for a very detailed plan of operations, then it cannot be limited in the kinds of controls it may exert over its operating units. Specifically, if the material balances in the national plan are carried out in physical or gross-value units, then the ministerial executors of that plan must be held accountable for the production by their operating units of the specified physical quantities or gross values. They simply cannot be denied the power to telephone their enterprises toward the end of the month to inquire how close they are to fulfilling their gross-output targets. And once the telephone calls are made, the message is fully absorbed.

To be sure, a ministry itself may delegate certain decision-making authority to its enterprises on grounds of informational efficiency. But the range of such decentralized authority is likely to be very limited, and to deal with secondary choices for which the ministry itself is not directly accountable. Thus the lesson of the Economic Reform is that genuine decentralization of authority to enterprises is strictly limited by the directive nature of a detailed national economic plan.

With respect to success indicators, the prospects are brighter. What is involved is the choices that must be made that are not dictated by the terms of the plan. The usual instances are choices among qualities not specified in the plan, or choices of output-mixes in excess of the minimal assortment-plan targets (i.e. plan overfulfillment.) Since the goal is to induce those decisions that are most consistent with the objectives of the plan, the shadow prices implicit in the plan could serve that purpose, with profits as the maximand in the objectives function. Nevertheless, if the ministry is still held to account for quantities or for gross value of output, it is those magnitudes that will prevail in enterprise decisions.

C. *The Price Reform of 1966–7*

The primary goal of the Price Reform may be judged from the kind of evidence that was presented as justification of the need for such a reform. What was thought to be the most persuasive evidence was the widely published data on the vast spread of profit rates among products and branches, ranging from highly subsidized branches like coal to highly profitable branches like machinery production. Among the reasons that such diversity of profit rates was regarded as bad, the following predominated: (1) subsidies are bad in general, because they encourage inefficiency and neglect of cost by producers who anticipate that the government will subsidize the loss; (2) high profits are generally unearned, and represent rental elements in income; they are inequitable, and they also weaken cost discipline; (3) large profit differentials between commodities bias product-mix choices by producers and input-mix choices by purchasers. The goal, therefore, was to reestablish a price structure in which most enterprises earned the normal profit rate and a few of the best and worst earned a bit more or less in proportion as their work diverged from that of the "normally operating enterprise".

What does this concern about profit differentials reveal about the leadership's analysis of the economic system? For one thing, it reveals a certain normative notion of what prices should be. The ideal presumably was one in which most enterprises earned the normal rate of profit and a few earned somewhat more or less, the excess or shortfall of profit serving both as a success indicator and as an incentive. However, the basis of pricing was to remain average branch cost plus normal profit. The objective was that prices play not an active but a neutral role in decision making. The trouble with large profit differentials is that they convert price into an active element in decision making, in the sense that managers depart from rational or socially desirable decisions because of the profit-related consequences of wide price variability. In other words, the ideal was not that price should serve as an allocative device; the plan was still the primary allocative instrument. The objective was rather a price structure in which a profit could serve as a success indicator (which requires *some* degree of variability) without at the same time serving as an allocative device by influencing production choices.

Thus the Price Reform was a reaffirmation of central planning as the allocative mechanism. Managerial decisions were to be made on the basis of plan assignments whenever those assignments were clear, and not on the basis of price and profit. The Price Reform recognized, however, that for a broad range of decisions that had to be made by management there was no clear indication of which alternative contributed most to the fulfillment of the national plan. The Economic Reform of 1965 had designated profit, along with sales, as a major criterion of performance and therefore implicitly as a proper basis of choice. By eliminating the large profit differentials of the past, the Price Reform was designed to assure that the choices made would be in closer conformity with the objectives of the plan.

There were two exceptions that are noteworthy. One was the pricing of new products. In a separate decree issued in 1965, before the Price Reform, the pricing of new products was reorganized on lines entirely separate from those of established products (Berliner, 1976, Chaps. 10–12). That decree introduced certain highly active functions for prices in the case of new technology. Profit rates were deliberately differentiated in order to induce management to choose the higher-profit alternatives. It is significant that this concession was made in order to promote technological innovation. Central planning is at its best with well-known technologies, and at its worst with technologies not yet fully developed or even yet unknown. In assigning an active function to prices and profit in this case the system's governors demonstrated a new awareness that in this major area of economic activity central planning suffers from certain limitations and that more decentralized decision making can be helpful.

The second exception was the introduction of rent-like fixed charges on commodities like petroleum and timber. The use of such charges was a victory for the marginalists and quasi-marginalists who had finally persuaded the leadership that at least in those cases in which the difference between marginal and average cost is very large, price should be used actively to discourage consumption. In this case it is not only managerial decision making that is to be influenced but also the plan itself. In deciding whether to use oil or coal in a new power plant, for example, it is the marginal cost of the two fuels that planners must take into account. Hence the purpose of this new provision is to improve the quality of central planning as well as that of managerial decision making.

D. *Production Associations*

This reform consists of the merger of groups of enterprises into new superenterprises under a single management. In one class of mergers the key feature is that a formerly independent R & D institute is a part of the new association, and sometimes the dominant member. These are the science-production associations. The other production associations follow the familiar pattern of the vertical integration of enterprises, although there are some cases of horizontal integration.

The problem that motivated the founding of the science-production associations is clear enough. It was the unsatisfactory rate of technological progress. This in fact is the first of the reforms under review in which the problem of technological progress lay at the heart of the reform, although it played a role in the others. But if technological progress were the only objective of this reform, one could not explain why the merger movement was extended to encompass virtually all of the nonagricultural economy; for most of the mergers do not involve R & D institutes. One must therefore postulate a second objective, which appears to be yet another stab at the problem of enterprise-level decision making. The specific facet of the problem in this case was that enterprises produced outputs that did not take sufficiently into account the requirements of their industrial customers. This second objective is related to the first in that it was not merely the quantities of output but also their qualities that were at issue. That is, the concern was not simply that enterprises produced types of products that did not correspond to the needs of users, but also that the quality of outputs did not correspond to the needs of users.

The selection of the production association as the device for getting at these two problems suggests a change in the analysis of the source of the problems by the system's governors. In earlier reforms it was assumed that enterprise managers were motivated to make correct choices. The problem was that they were misdirected, by the ministries in the case of the Territorial Reorganization, and by the success indicators and also the ministries in the case of the Economic Reform. In turning to production associations, it appears that the leadership has given up the view that by creating the appropriate environment (better success indicators, better prices, less misdirection by central management) enterprise management could be counted on to get things right. The production associations have virtually eliminated enterprise management, as it had operated for forty years, as a significant level of economic decision making. The former enterprise manager now occupies a position that is rather like a glorified version of what in the past was the position of shop chief. The new approach is to take responsibility out of the hands of the enterprise managers and to relocate it at a level that is very much like the central management of the past. The production associations may be regarded as micro-ministries, in the sense that they enjoy powers over the former enterprises similar to those formerly enjoyed by ministries over enterprises. They have also acquired some powers that formerly were lodged with the ministries.

With respect to the ministries, the reform is a measure of decentralization (Gorlin, 1976, pp. 180–2). But with respect to the enterprise it is a measure of recentralization. It is also a vote of confidence in the superiority of "administrative levers" over "economic levers." Before this reform, the strategy was to find ways of inducing enterprise managers to behave by creating the proper conditions for them to behave. Now they are to behave because they have a new superior authority that tells them what to do; an authority not as remote as the ministry and with a span of control not as wide as a ministry, so that it is in a much stronger position to be informed and to impose compliance.

This interpretation of the analysis that underlay the reform applies both to the general problem of enterprise decision making and to the specific problem of technological progress. With respect to the former, producer enterprise A will produce and deliver precisely the outputs required by user enterprise B because they both have the same boss whose career is on the line and who knows the capacity and needs of both enterprises. With respect to technological progress, producer enterprise A will quickly put into production a new product developed by the R & D Institute because, again, they have the same boss, who may in fact have been the former director of the Institute when it was an independent ministry organization. Nor will the Institute lose interest in the practical success of the product innovation once it has gone into production, as in the past, because the general director of the association is responsible for both units.

Thus the production-association reform is a break with the past. It reflects the continued concern with the problem that had been the major concern in the past — enterprise-level decision making. But it adds a major new concern — the promotion of technological progress. Moreover the solution chosen reflects a change in the strategy that guided past reforms. Instead of seeking ways of improving the quality of decentralized decision making, it has withdrawn decision-making authority from enterprise management and relocated it at a more central level.

E.   *The Comprehensive Planning Decree of 1979*

The reforms in the management system discussed above were widely heralded and have been deemed important enough to have acquired names of their own. It is interesting to note that while other changes in the planning system have proceeded through the post-Stalin period, history has judged none of them significant enough to have merited a name of its own. It is possible that the planning decree of 1979 (*Ekonomicheskaia gazeta*, 1979, No. 32) will pass on in anonymity like the others. I have given it a name not because I judge it to be of name-deserving proportions but because a review of the past would be incomplete without some notice of the changes in the planning system, and the most recent one is the appropriate candidate.

The decree may be regarded as a continuation and extension of a series of changes in the planning system that have been proceeding for some time, rather than as a break with the past or as the opening of a new direction. I suggest the term "comprehensive" because it roughly captures the sense of those changes. First, the planning process now comprehends a longer spread of time; the five-year plan rather than the annual plan is now officially designated as the fundamental plan, and it is to be based on a twenty-year program of scientific-technical development and on a ten-year plan that sets forth the main directions of economic and social development. Second, the planning process now comprehends both branch and regional planning; all USSR ministry plans are to be submitted to review by the republic councils of ministers, and the latter are to present to Gosplan their plans for all their enterprises. Third, the decree mandates a more comprehensive set of balances than in the past; balances are to be employed in the ten-year main-directions plan and in the five-year plan; interbranch balances are to be used for major products; and regional balances are to be used for the production and distribution of major products.[1]

Two problems can be identified as those with which the system's governors sought to deal in the planning decree. One is the promotion of technological progress. The incorporation of ten-year and twenty-year plans into the current planning process is intended to build into current planning a basis of consistency with the long lead times of technological advance; that is, to avoid current decisions that lock the economy into directions that may be inconsistent with the probable direction of future technological advance. The technique adopted is to require that current plan decisions be checked for consistency with longer-run structural choices that have already been made, and with the forecasts of future technological developments.

The second problem is, once more, enterprise-level decision making. The reforms in the management system discussed above were all directed at the problems that arise when managers have to make decisions. The necessity for managers to make decisions arises out of imperfections in the planning process; that is, with perfect planning there would be virtually no need at all for decisions to be made by enterprise managers. The system's governors must assume, however, that there will always be considerable scope for managerial discretion, either because the central plan cannot realistically provide for all possible detail, or because of errors in plans, or because of changes in plans. Accepting the inevitability of managerial discretion, the purpose of the management reforms was to improve the quality of those decisions. But the second string to that bow is the improvement of the planning system. The more comprehensive and detailed the plan, the smaller the volume of planning errors, and the less frequent the changes in the plan, the less the need to rely on managerial decision making.

The implication of this view of the relationship between planning reform and management reform is that planning is thought to be good and management bad. The less the discretion that needs to be given to management, the better. In this interpretation, the move toward increasing comprehensiveness of planning reflects the hope that eventually everything can be balanced in advance so that management can be reduced solely to carrying out pre-planned instructions. On the face of it, there can be no quarrel with the notion that in a planned economy plans should be as specific as possible. But that doesn't necessarily mean that they must be comprehensive. The alternative view is that there may be some optimal level of comprehensiveness beyond which the marginal benefit of more detailed planning diminishes and that of decentralized managerial solutions increases. It is true that as planning techniques improve the optimal level may involve greater detail. The extension of comprehensiveness does not therefore necessarily mean that the leadership is shifting the balance deliberately. But it appears to me that the push is in that direction. Better planning continues to be thought of as a way of decreasing the inefficiency associated with an obdurate management.

Some Lessons of History

I make no claim that mine is the only story that a brief review of recent economic reforms can tell. Had a different list of reforms been selected for examination, or had another analyst considered the same reforms with a different eye, the story might be different. I trust, however, that this account is a plausible one and serves as a useful prelude to an inquiry into the possible shapes of the future.

The first conclusion is that the reforms give no evidence of a disposition to doubt the efficacy of the system of central planning as the basis of the economic mechanism. On the contrary, the 1979 Planning Decree affirms the intention to strengthen the planning system by improving the quality of the national plans. In this respect the efforts of the last several decades have probably been successful. The technical equipment now available to planners, including electronic data-processing equipment and mathematical-modelling techniques for checking the consistency of plans, have no doubt been helpful. We may expect that the plan-making process will continue to improve in the future, although the growing complexity of the economy increases the size of the task from plan to plan. We may also expect that each five-year plan of the future will, like the most recent, be preceded by a decree incorporating in the forthcoming plan a series of newer techniques that have been in the process of experimentation and are ready for adoption.

The second conclusion is that the problem of management has been less tractable than that of planning, and that there have not been significant advances in improving its quality. In principle, planning and management should be expected to complement each other; planners draw up the plans and managers see to their execution. In fact, the relation appears to be viewed by the system's governors as one of tension. Planning is the friend while management is the enemy. Evidence of inefficiency is most often explained as the consequence of bungling or mismanagement. Brezhnev expressed what is probably the general view of politicians when he laid the blame for a series of excesses at the feet of people who "no matter how much you talk to them, no matter how much you appeal to their conscience and their sense of duty and responsibility, nothing helps."[2]

To see the problem as one of poorly trained or venal people is to close one's eyes to possible defects of the system itself. It obscures the fundamental problem: that central planning, which must inevitably be imperfect, makes extremely difficult demands upon management. The central managers — the ministries — are responsible for the execution of a detailed set of targets, all of which cannot be fulfilled in the normal course of events. There is no "bottom line", although gross output comes close to serving as the ultimate criterion. Their own record of performance depends on that of hundreds of enterprise (or production-association) managers, who must also constantly make a variety of decisions for which there is no clear guide in the plans. Hence alongside the tension between planners and managers, the system's governors have also to contend with the tension between ministries and enterprises. Most of the reforms have attempted to come to grips with the latter problem. In the Territorial Reorganization, it was decided to solve the problem by abolishing the ministries. In the Production-Association reform it was decided to abolish the enterprises instead. It is difficult to foresee any clear basis for a more effective distribution of authority between the two levels in the context of central planning.

Finally, the history of the recent reforms reflects the growing appreciation of the importance of technological progress. The reforms of the fifties and sixties concentrated on the coordination of management and planning and on the increase in static efficiency. But in the more recent reforms technological progress has been at the forefront of the objectives. The change in emphasis coincides with the gradual acceptance of the view that the decline in the growth rate reflects a fundamental change in economic conditions, which is reflected in the formulation of a change from "extensive" to "intensive" growth. How to adapt the system of planning and management to the new goal of promoting technological progress is likely to be the central concern of those who bear the responsibility for the economic reforms of the future.

11.2   The Conservative Model

The *status quo* rarely has passionate supporters. The passions are normally on the side of change. Support for the status quo is usually based on a lack of conviction that the untried alternatives will produce a better future than the present. That is likely to be the case if the Conservative Model is chosen as the basis of the future system of planning and management in the USSR. It is doubtful that many people, even among the system's governors, regard the present structure as having great merit in its own right. That was not the case two decades ago. At that time Soviet economists certainly, and political leaders probably, looked over the world of economic systems and pronounced their own as exceptionally good. Today the system may still command strong support, but very likely in the Churchillian vein, as a rather bad system, "except for all the others."

The Conservative Model retains all the basic structural features of the present system, but it should not be thought of as unchanging in form. Judging from the recent history of reforms, we should expect repeated efforts in the future to try new ways of dealing with old problems. Certainly the planning system will be continually changed by the incorporation of new techniques of central planning. What will remain unchanged is the commitment to central planning as the basis of the economic mechanism. Beyond that, each analyst is free to forecast efforts to change whatever is his own favorite source of inefficiency in the economy. My own guess is that many of the production associations will be dismantled after a period of time, in favor of a system containing a broader mix of large and small enterprises. The reason for this guess is that the size structure of enterprises in the USSR, even before the production associations, was strongly skewed toward large enterprises, compared to the size structure in the technologically advanced capitalist countries (Kvasha, 1967). With respect to efficiency and certainly to innovation there must be some range of activities in which there are diseconomies of scale. There are also likely to be further changes in such perennials as the success indicators of enterprise management. The indicator newly introduced in the July 1979 planning decree — normative net output — may well prove to be exceedingly costly to administer and is likely to bias decisions excessively in favor of labor-intensive choices in a period of tight labor supply. There may be some renewed flirtation with profit as a more general success indicator, but the pathological antagonism to the appropriation by enterprises of unearned economic rents will stand in the way; large profits in particular seem to constitute prima facie evidence that they were unearned, probably as a consequence of favorable price changes. New experiments in the use of contractual relations may be tried, and also new Shchekino-type efforts to reallocate labor among enterprises by various incentive devices. The recent sharp increase in the price of gasoline suggests that price policy may be called upon more often to ration scarce commodities. Price revisions every few years will continue to keep relative prices from diverging excessively from average branch costs, and there may be some further incorporation of scarcity pricing into the price structure. Extrapolating from the past, planning may become more detailed, and with the growth of electronic data-processing capacity, the number of balances is likely to increase; however, there may be a reaction at some point because of the mounting complexity of the plan-making process, and a return to more aggregated planning.

Certainly there will be new measures designed to promote techno-logical progress and the quality of production. Some would attempt to make use of "economic levers" through new forms of incentive payments. But most will consist of "administrative measures"; chang-ing the structure of authority, holding more people responsible for the completion of assigned tasks, penalties for not fulfilling quality assignments.

To accept the Conservative Model is to give up the goal of attaining the technological level of the leading industrial countries. For I take it as fairly well established that whatever the merits of the Soviet economic mechanism, the promotion of technological advance is not one of them. But that is an outcome with which the Soviet leadership ought to be able to live. There is no reason why the USSR cannot maintain a position that lags permanently behind that of the techno-logical leaders in world industry by, say, an average of about five years. There would be some loss in productivity because of delayed innovation, but that loss would be offset to some degree by savings in research and development expenditures as well as in the costs of learning-by-doing that the country pioneering in any new development must bear. It would be a reasonable strategy for the Soviets to wait until each new major breakthrough is announced elsewhere, and then to proceed to develop their own version on the basis of whatever information can be perused, purchased or purloined. For it is an axiom in the R & D community that the most valuable piece of information in technological advance is the information that a certain result has been successfully accomplished by somebody. The strategy of waiting until the results have been accomplished elsewhere is not only cost-saving but is also appealing to R&D people operating in a risk-averse bureaucratic structure. Moreover, the Soviets have shown that technological excellence can be maintained in a few priority areas where these are deemed crucial for defense or other national purposes.

Taking the foregoing as the essence of the Conservative Model, the question here is what are the outcomes that can be expected from the adoption of that model. Since the model involves no significant changes from the past, the past can serve as a guide to the economic outcomes to be expected in the future. There is little reason to expect any discontinuous increase either in static efficiency or in the rate of growth. None of the major reforms of the past has succeeded in doing what their initiators must have devoutly hoped for — attaining a quantum leap in efficiency. Indeed the term "reform" has disappeared from the public discussion and has been replaced by the expression "improving the operation of the economic mechanism."

The evaporation of the spirit of reform may reflect the view that the system of central planning and management has now reached the practical limit of its perfectability. An economic system is like a technological innovation. When first invented, a steam engine or an internal-combustion machine represents a major advance over its predecessor, but it is a very inefficient mechanism in terms of its own potential. In the course of time its efficiency increases, very rapidly at first and more slowly thereafter, with successive waves of "reforms" or "improvements." Eventually it attains a degree of efficiency that can be regarded as the effective maximum that is realistically attainable within the limits of its basic conception; there is only so much one can expect to get out of a machine the basic conception of which is a piston in a cylinder. It is rather like a Kuhnian paradigm in the development of scientific theory; not much more can be expected to happen until someone breaks out of the paradigm with a very different conception of how power may be generated.

That vision may be applied to the invention of central economic planning as an economic mechanism by the Soviet leadership of the thirties. In the course of time it became a more efficient mechanism than it was when first introduced. But like all inventions, the possibilities of improvement within the basic paradigm may have been largely exhausted by the 1960s. It should be noted that the economic mechanism was designed in a period in which the strategy of economic progress consisted of what was later described as "extensive growth." It is perhaps still a reasonably successful model for that purpose. The problem is that the conditions within which the economy operates today are not such as to generate high rates of extensive growth. Three percent per year more or less may be the most that can be expected of an economy designed according to that model. It is in that sense that the economy may be doing as well as can be expected under that economic mechanism.

It is entirely possible, of course, that this judgement may be too pessimistic. To assert that there are few opportunities for further improvement is to imply, paradoxically, that the economy is highly efficient, in the sense of operating close to its production-possibilities frontier as defined by the existing economic structure. A future government may yet find ways of extending that frontier. Some such ways have been proposed at this conference: the creation of enterprises specializing in production for export, correcting those relative prices that create perverse incentives in agriculture, providing greater autonomy for small-scale production units within the collective farm. Without abandoning the Conservative Model, its limits may be extended by adopting some of the features of the other models discussed below. While a bold package of such measures may prove that the Conservative Model contains greater potential than its recent record reveals, the history of the reforms sketched out above does not offer great encouragement. Individual changes in prices and organizational structures that make good sense in themselves have not produced the desired results because they clashed with the imperatives imposed by the dominating structures of central planning and management.

Suppose then that the Conservative Model does not in fact produce better results than those forecast on the basis of the experience of the recent past. The question is whether the leadership can continue to be satisfied with it; that is, to turn to no alternative model but simply to muddle through with only small variations on old themes. I think they can, on one condition — that the decline in the growth rate decelerate and eventually stabilize. A constant rate of growth, even if very low, would constitute a chronic condition that does not ordinarily lead to disruption. It is the acute problems, such as those encountered with continuous decline, that must ultimately lead to disruption. With a chronically low but stable growth rate, the century could end with a whimper. Otherwise it might end with a bang.

We cannot judge what the minimally sustainable growth rate is — three, or two, or one percent per capita. However, it is safe to say that it is likely to depend primarily on the consumption level. A threshold level of consumption may be defined, in political terms, as the level below which dissatisfaction would result in outbursts of disorder that would strain the authorities' instruments of political control. It would be an error for the leadership to believe, however, that there is no danger as long as consumption levels exceeded that political threshold. For there is another threshold at which the economy would begin to suffer from the erosion of incentives. If that incentives threshold, which must be higher than the political threshold, were not maintained, then it will prove to be impossible to maintain even that low level of stable growth. Output and consumption would decline reciprocally until the political threshold were reached, and then the whimper will turn into a bang. Hence, the key to the question of whether slow growth will turn from chronic to acute will depend on whether the rate of growth can be stabilized at a level sufficiently high to maintain consumption above the incentive threshold.

The Soviet leadership may possibly have some rough notion of the range within which the incentive threshold lies, but outside analysts can do little more than guess. My own guess is about the same as the judgement of Gertrude Schroeder in her contribution to this volume, that a steady increase in per capita consumption of 1–2% per year would "provide consumers with a sense of forward motion" (this volume, p. 332). Under the baseline projection of SOVMOD, GNP would grow at 3.2% and consumption per capita at 2% (Bond and Levine, this volume, Table 1.1 p. 13). With a bit of luck that outcome should keep the economy above the incentives threshold. Under the low-productivity scenario, however, (Table 1.3, p. 18) GNP grows at 2.3% and consumption per capita at only 0.7%. At that rate it is conceivable that the erosion of incentives would preclude the stabilization of the growth rate, and consumption may decline to the perilous level of the political threshold.

There is a fair chance that the economy can stabilize at the levels of the baseline projection of Bond and Levine. The long period of declining growth may presage continued decline in the future, but it need not. It may signify instead that the economy has been readjusting from the high growth rates of the past to low but stable growth rates in the future. In that case poor performance in static efficiency or in technological progress need not compel the abandonment of the Conservative Model as long as consumption does not fall below the incentive threshold.

11.3 The Reactionary Model

The political characteristics of a neo-Stalinist reaction are not difficult to portray. One thinks first of a restoration of the power of the secret police, perhaps not quite to the level of the Stalinist terror but well beyond the present level. Contacts with capitalist countries would be greatly reduced, the iron curtain reimposed, a xenophobic nationalism reinstituted, and ideological, political and social discipline generally tightened.

If one asks, however, what changes would have to be made to return to a Stalin-like economic system, the answer is not self-evident. The exercise is a reminder that, however great the changes in Soviet political life since Stalin, the essentials of the economic system have not been that greatly changed. The inclination of the leadership under the Reactionary Model is toward the restoration of discipline and order, and they will view their mission as the reassertion of strong central control. But they will find that the clock has moved so little in the system of planning and management that it hardly needs to be turned back very much.

In the organization of central planning, while the political leaders under the Reactionary Model may harbor a Stalinist contempt for theoretical economics, the practical value of "optimal planning" would overcome the aversion and it would elicit strong support. For it promises a possibility of centralization of decision making and control far beyond anything dreamed of in Stalin's time. It is, in the words of a close student of the subject, an ideal instrument for an "autocratic political mechanism" (Katsenelenboigen, 1978, p. 41). However, the possibility of introducing that form of plan making is still too remote to be of use in the near future. Short of that, it is difficult to imagine that the leaders of the Reactionary economy could contrive ways of extending the scope of central planning that are not already contained or implicit in the 1979 planning decree.

With respect to the management system, because the 1965 Economic Reform has been so greatly modified, there are few changes that will be seen as essential for the restoration of central control. No great purpose would be served by eliminating the capital charge or restoring *val* as the dominant success indicator. Those small ways in which the present-day enterprise manager is less accountable to the center than in the past are not likely to be eliminated. What might be changed is the spread of *khozraschet* (financing an organization's expenditures out of its own revenues) to the agencies of central management — ministries and chief administrations. To the extent that centralization is the desideratum, the degree of independence that *khozraschet* would provide for these units would probably be regarded as unacceptable. The inclination would more likely be to proceed with the creation of the superministries that have been discussed from time to time. Similarly, to the extent that contract-financed production has replaced planned production, for example in the financing of R&D organizations, that practice may well be ended.

Another of the post-Stalin moves toward decentralization was the establishment of the wholesale-trade program. That measure started out as the bold idea of offering an alternative to the "material-technical supply" system. The program for a large network of well-stocked stores where enterprises could purchase small quantities of whatever was needed never did materialize. What evolved instead was a system of warehouse supply, differing from the Stalinist system only in that it is managed by the hierarchy of *Gossnab* rather than by the ministries' own supply organizations. It is difficult to imagine that a neo-Stalinist leadership would find it a matter of some importance to abolish *Gossnab* and turn its functions back to the ministries. *Gossnab* may in fact be regarded as the more centralized supply system, even though its operating units are territorially based.

The production associations would very likely find favor with the Reactionary leadership, resembling as they do the vast scale of enterprise that was characteristic of Stalin's time. One of the virtues of that organizational form is that it reduces the task of central planning by "internalizing" within the superenterprise a certain number of transactions that were formerly interenterprise transactions and therefore the responsibility of the central planners. The more self-contained the producing unit, the simpler the job of the planners. There has been a growing trend toward selfcontainment in recent years that merits more attention than it has received. Many enterprises, for example, have begun to develop their own subsidiary farms to provide produce for their own workers (Rumer, 1980). That development is an extension of a very old practice by management of seeking independence of the uncertain supply system by the practice of "universalism," or the in-house production of as much of their inputs as they can manage. That practice has been criticized in the past, and the present Conservative leadership has taken a dim view of it. In the afore-mentioned speech Brezhnev was sharply critical of that he described as "a recent widespread practice for local agencies to recruit people from enterprises and to do various kinds of work — help with the harvest, work in procurement organizations, on construction jobs, on beautification projects and so forth." A Reactionary leadership, however, may be less concerned with the contraction in the division of labor and the loss of the economies of specialization that this "new feudalism" entails. It may be inclined to support large universalist enterprises that encompass a variety of activities and that relieve the burden on the central planners.

Thus planning and management will be somewhat more centralized under the Reactionary Model than under the Conservative but the difference in that respect cannot be very large. The major differences between the two models will be found not in organizational forms but in policies. High on the list would be a policy of tightening labor discipline. One might envision a return to the severe laws of the late 1930s, making it illegal to leave one's job without authorization and providing criminal penalties for such violations as lateness to work, unauthorized absence from the job, and drunkenness. There might also be a disposition to return to the high-investment growth strategy that was associated with the rapid-growth years of the post-war period, although that would require a disavowal of the intensive-growth views that have prevailed subsequently. The corollary of a high-investment strategy would be a return to a policy of slow growth of consumption, or even possibly a decline. That would very likely be a subject of dispute even among supporters of a Reactionary Model, on a variety of grounds. First, the popular hostility it would arouse would challenge even the greatly tightened political controls. Second, there would be serious doubts about the efficacy of that strategy at this time in history. Third, since agriculture is no longer the predominant sector of origin of national income, the growth-rate gains from the suppression of the consumption of the agricultural population would no longer be as great as they were thought to be in the past. However, the recent trend toward the virtual transformation of the collective farms into state farms might be accelerated rather than reversed, on the assumption that the collective farm had been an enforced compromise and the state farm is more consistent with a neo-Stalinist structure.

Since a neo-Stalinist model implies the existence of a neo-Stalin, the leadership must be presumed to possess the power to carry through the changes that it finds necessary. One is a strong drive against "speculators" and the second economy. Another is a purge of the managerial elite, both at the central and at the enterprise level. The Stalin period was characterized by rapid upward mobility of managers which, while purchased at some cost, nevertheless conveyed certain clear benefits: in weeding out dead wood, in cementing the loyalty of the new managers, in lowering their average age, and in generating an unusual level of effort (though perhaps at a cost in the form of increased risk aversion). One might guess that the long tenure enjoyed by the present managerial corps has contributed to a decline in its quality. It is interesting to note, in this context, that in present-day China the virtual lifetime tenure of the Party and management elite has come under increasing criticism, and Vice Premier Deng and his supporters seem determined to end that practice. A new and secure Soviet leadership might very likely see things the same way, though perhaps not with respect to themselves.

Finally, we are likely under this model to see a return to a policy of relative autarky, in an effort to reduce the volume of contacts with the West. Some level of import of advanced foreign technology would be maintained, but the new regime is likely to place a greater weight on the ideological costs of involvement with the West and to assign less value to its economic benefits than the Khrushchev–Brezhnev governments.

In evaluating the prospective economic performance of the USSR under the Reactionary Model, one tends to regard it as a mere romantic nostalgia for a simpler and in some ways better age that never really was and that could not be successfully restored under present-day conditions. But it would be an error to dismiss it entirely, for it might well bring some benefits of a purely economic kind.

For one thing, it might offer some short-run gains in the form of freeing up of the "hidden reserves" that are so often the object of special campaigns. A few well-publicized trials and convictions might lead to the disgorging of excess inventories and a scaling-down of the diversion of resources from public to private uses. The tempo of production is likely to be sped up and labor discipline tightened generally. It would not be surprising if the change were followed for a time by a significant rise in productivity and output.

If the economy is indeed characterized by a large degree of underemployment, in the form of excess numbers of workers whose marginal productivity is very low, as many Soviet economists claim to be case, the tightening of political controls in a time of labor shortage may make it possible to launch an effective drive to reallocate labor to more productive uses. One can imagine a campaign in which every enterprise would be obliged to deliver a quota of young workers to be relocated to the labor-short areas in the East, much as the collective farms once delivered their quotas for the staffing of new industrial enterprises. Whatever form it finally takes, the neo-Stalinist regime would very likely regard the reallocation of labor as one of its prime objectives, and that may be expected to have a favorable impact on economic performance.

In the longer run, it is possible that the recentralization of economic activity may also produce some economic gains. The view is sometimes expressed that the present-day Soviet economy is the worst of possible worlds. Change has not proceeded far enough to yield the benefits of genuine decentralized markets, yet the central-planning and management system has given up control of a variety of functions in the interest of decentralization. The system, according to this view, is neither flesh nor fowl and enjoys neither the advantages of true markets nor of full central planning. Either alternative would be better than the particular mixed economy that has evolved out of the Khrushchev–Brezhnev regimes (Zielinski, 1973, pp. 312–21).

In evaluating this point of view, one may question, as we have, whether the reforms of the post-Stalin years constitute a significant degree of decentralization. Nevertheless there may be merit in the argument that many of the forms of decentralization have brought little genuine benefit. An instructive case is the conversion of the R&D institutes from budget financing to contract financing, a change that was introduced for the purpose of increasing the client's interest in and power over the work produced by the institutes. The instrument of a contract is crucial to the operation of a market economy, and it may seem that the replacement of administrative orders by contracts in the Soviet economy is a measure of market-like decentralization. However, the contexts are so different that it is an error to associate the word "contract" with any of the real functions played by that instrument in a decentralized economy. For one thing, the client regards the payment for the services as made with "the government's money"; if it is in the enterprise plan, financing is provided for it in the plan. Secondly, the contractor's income is limited by the conditions of the incentive structure. Regardless of how profitable the innovation is, the size of the reward is stipulated in the statutory incentive schedule, and the balance of profit is simply appropriated by the Ministry of Finance as a "free remainder." It would be an exaggeration to say that there is no difference at all between a management system in which the R&D institute operates under a plan and reports to an official in the Ministry, and one in which it operates on the basis of contracts entered into with enterprises. But the nature of the dependence of a market-economy firm on its contracts, and that of a Soviet firm on its contracts, are of different orders of magnitude. In that sense this act of formal decentralization, like so many others, is more a matter of detail than of critical importance in the decision-making process.

Plan making should proceed under the Reactionary Model in much the same manner as under the Conservative Model. Nor is there any reason why, with intelligent administration, innovation should not proceed as well under a Reactionary Model as it does at present. The same material-incentive system would be employed as at present, and the prestige of science would be undiminished. Presumably the tightening of political and ideological controls would not extend to the extremes of Stalinist terror, nor to Lysenko-like constraints on science. The major loss perhaps would be that which would result from the decreased level of scientific contact with the more advanced countries, including very likely some decrease in the import of advanced technology. But if the leadership should accept realistically the policy of the permanent technological lag, the loss would not be regarded as very large. Only as long as the objective is to overtake and surpass the West in technological attainment would the decrease in scientific contact be of major significance.

The prospects for agricultural performance are probably much poorer under this model. The continued transformation of the collectives into state farms will satisfy some aspirations for ideological purity, but it is not likely to reverse what comes through the literature as the widespread demoralization of the agricultural labor force. Restrictions on private subsidiary agriculture are likely to be tightened, with a further loss in agricultural output. Agriculture may well be the sector in which the Reactionary Model will encounter its major failures.

I conclude that, with the exception of agriculture, the economy may exhibit some sharp short-run gains relative to the recent past. It is also entirely possible that in the longer run it could also outperform the Conservative Model, particularly if it is successful in tightening labor discipline and in massively reallocating labor among jobs. However, a major condition is that it avoid the excesses of Stalin, for Stalin was the worst part of Stalinism. An intelligent Reactionary leadership may well squeeze more out of the economy than the cautious and compromising leadership of the recent decades.

11.4 The Radical Model

If the Reactionary extreme is the recentralization of planning and management, the Radical extreme must entail the decentralization of planning and management. The characteristics of the model may be taken from the Hungarian experience. One may think of it simply as central planning without directive targets to enterprises. But that innocent-sounding formulation involves more than a simple modification of the centrally planned economy. For without the power to assign directive targets to enterprises, much of the fabric of central planning unravels. If enterprises cannot be required to produce according to directives, they cannot be held responsible for the delivery of specified intermediate materials and supplies, and the time-honored system of material-technical supply must be largely abandoned. In the absence of directive targets, the criteria for evaluating enterprise performance must be modified, and it is then difficult to imagine any criterion other than some suitably modified form of profit. But if profit is to serve as the dominant criterion of performance, it will become the effective objective function for management, and it is then necessary to assure that the prices and costs in terms of which decisions are made are reasonably reflective of marginal social benefits and costs. That must entail the abandonment of forty years of centralized administration of average-cost-plus-normal-profit pricing. Similar changes would have to be introduced in the management of the labor market, the financial system, and in other parts of the economy.

Party and Government control of the economy would very likely continue to be maintained in several areas. First, most investment, particularly investment in social overhead and in new plant and equipment, would continue to be a central function, and it would become the most powerful instrument for determining both the rate of investment and the direction of growth. Investment would be financed by taxation, on profits and personal income, and also on the basis of a capital charge and depreciation allowance. That is, the state would continue to own all productive assets, and would require a return on them from the collectives that hold them in trust. Incentives would be derived from some profit-sharing plan.

Second, the state would continue to maintain an interest in prices, primarily in order to prevent excessive use of market power to maintain monopoly prices. To the extent that the objective of state policy would be to trade some efficiency for equity or for some other social goal, the option of price regulation would be maintained for that purpose as well. The legitimacy of selective state price control would be based not only on state power in general but on the state ownership of the assets of enterprises. That is, the state continues not only to own the enterprise but to exercise national sovereignty.

Third, it is safe to say that the Soviet leadership will have very little interest in supporting self-management or other forms of worker control. The more delicate problem is the policy to be taken toward the possible increase in involuntary unemployment.

Fourth, income taxation (or perhaps consumption taxation, which would make more sense in an investment-conscious economy) would be relied upon to regulate income distribution. Commodity taxation could be employed for financing public expenditures, but it could not be used to regulate the powerful new entrepreneurial forces that (one would hope) would arise and would tend to widen the income distribution. For if the Radical Model succeeds in generating vigorous entrepreneurship, there will be large incomes to be earned in eliminating disequilibria in the centrally planned economy. The function of eliminating disequilibria has been one of the main economic responsibilities of the Party in the past (Grossman, 1981). The income-distribution problems will be particularly pressing during the transition period because of the large disequilibria inherited from the period of central planning that have not yet been diminished by market forces.

Turning to the question of how the Soviet economy might fare under the Radical Model, one must begin with such hard evidence as we have on that type of system operating in another country. The form of radical decentralization that the Soviets are most likely to draw upon is the New Economic Mechanism introduced in Hungary in 1968. One conclusion is clear; Hungary has produced no Economic Miracle. When the East European countries are ranked by order of their long-term growth rates, Hungary comes at about the center of the group, behind such less-developed countries as Romania and Bulgaria, as one would expect (Marer, 1977). Nor has that relative position changed, for while Hungary's growth rate increased in the years following the 1968 reform, so did that of most of the other countries that retained their central-planning systems (Portes, 1977). Per capita consumption increased during 1970–75, but that was also the case in Romania during the same period. It is true, however, that

Hungary was particularly hard hit by adverse changes in its markets abroad, and suffered from a number of costly policy errors while learning to control the new economic mechanism. Under the circumstances, Portes concludes, Hungary probably did better than it would have done under the old central-planning system.

One suspects that the statistical record may have missed something important. Most knowledgeable observers, including Hungarian economists who tend to be among the most severe critics of their own economy, report that without question there has been a considerable improvement in the quality of goods and services generally. The usual formulation is that the growth-rate performance has not been distinctive *but* the quality of goods and services has increased greatly. An alternative formulation might be that the quality of goods and services has increased greatly *but* the growth-rate performance has not been distinctive. If a significant quality change can be attributed to the system change, that is no mean claim. Perhaps the judicious conclusion is that the Hungarian economy performs generally better under the new mechanism but not by an order of magnitude. Certainly one hears no Hungarian pining for the good old days.

Hungary is no Japan. But then again the USSR is no Hungary, and one must entertain the possibility that the new economic mechanism in the USSR might perform better or worse than in Hungary. In one major respect the USSR is like Hungary. The Hungarian reform has been limited by a set of political considerations, which include a commitment to extensive job security and to strict limitations on income differentiation (Granick, 1973; Portes, 1977). Those same considerations are likely to prevail in the USSR and to limit the effectiveness of the reform in the same ways. The USSR has one potential advantage in the size of the domestic market, which could yield some of the benefits of interenterprise competition, but job-security and income-differentiation concerns could spill the wind out of the sails of competition. There is no cogent reason for expecting the USSR to perform better under this type of decentralization than Hungary.

There is one reason, however, why the USSR might be expected to perform worse. Western analysts have been struck by the vigor with which the patterns of the former centrally planned system reasserted themselves under the new Hungarian decentralized system. Hungary, however, had lived under central planning for only two decades. The managers, politicians and economists who engineered the reform of 1968 had lived the first thirty-odd years of their lives in a market economy. They found no mystery in a system in which no one tells the enterprise what it should produce and from whom it is to obtain its supplies. Many, we may also suppose, had conceived a certain fondness for aspects of that kind of economic arrangement, socialists though they are. In the USSR, by contrast, hardly a soul is now alive who remembers such a system. The notion that somehow the "right" amount of coal can be produced even though no one tells the coal mines how much to produce is not an idea that is easily grasped if one has not lived it. I can cite two pieces of evidence for this view. One is a recent study by The International Communications Agency (ICA) on Soviet perceptions of the US, based on interviews with Americans who have had close associations with Soviet officials at high levels of authority. The study reports that "Soviets who study the US have long assumed that hidden somewhere in the economic system is the key to American success, and that there must be a planning mechanism for the American private sector." Even Soviet experts on American management and industry "seem puzzled that the private sector has no apparent planning center. They know that the system works, but they are puzzled how" (Guroff, 1980). The second piece of evidence is the observation by a prominent émigré authority that most Soviet economists sincerely believe the price mechanism to be only a temporary necessity (Katsenelenboigen, 1978, p. 15). While there is a sophisticated minority who have learned to comprehend the nature of general-equilibrium decentralized systems, they are not the ones who will be managing the government and economy. The "legacies" of the centrally planned period that Neuberger once identified in the case of Yugoslavia have been found to operate in the Hungarian economy as well (Hewett, 1981; Neuberger, 1968). The legacies of a half-century of central planning must be expected to be particularly restrictive. Kenneth Boulding once remarked that the bus from capitalism to socialism runs only during the early stage of capitalism. If a nation misses the bus, capitalism is there to stay. The same may be said of the bus from central planning to socialist markets. The Hungarians caught it in time, but central planning has endured so long in the USSR that the Soviets may have missed the bus.

There are two aspects to the legacies that one structure bequeaths to another. The first may be described as the human-capital aspect. In moving from one technology to another, while new capital is being built up in the form of knowledge and experience in the operation of the new technology, old capital is being lost as knowledge and experience of the old technology disappears. That process applies to social as well as physical technology. There is a vast stock of human capital that supports the operation of a decentralized economy that is lost after a few generations of not having been learned and used.

The second feature of the legacy is the large number of points in the old system that are in disequilibrium with respect to the requirements of the new system. I refer to the structure of productive capacity relative to the structure of the demand for output under the new system, and similarly with the structure of wages and prices. Because of supply inelasticities, many of those disequilibria are likely to be large, and to endure for relatively long periods of time, making for potentially large rental incomes. It is doubtful that the market processes under the new system could readily close those disequilibria without the emergence of very large inequities. After a half-century of central planning, those disequilibria in the USSR are likely to be of massive dimensions, and therefore a source of a great deal of social tension and economic strain.

For these reasons the Radical Model established in the USSR may not secure even that modest improvement in economic performance that it secured in Hungary. And yet there could hardly fail to be some gains in the quality of goods and services, similar to that reported in Hungary. The requirement that a producing unit be obliged to decide what to produce by consulting potential purchasers rather than by instructions from the ministry — which is the heart of the model — cannot fail to discipline management to respond actively to demand, providing that demand is not in excess. To the extent that it is politically difficult in socialist countries (and increasingly in capitalist) to permit the market to determine the penalties for failure, the tightness of that discipline is attenuated, but it is likely to prevail to a greater extent than under the central planning of output. Similarly the enterprise as purchaser — now both obliged to and permitted to seek out its own sources of supply — is likely to assign a higher place to cost considerations in its calculations. These observations apply also to the quality of innovation. If the decision to introduce a new process or product is genuinely that of the enterprise, it cannot fail to be more resistant than in the past to pressures to adopt inferior work produced by the R&D centers, and more inclined to seek out and introduce genuinely superior innovations. Again, to the extent that the politics of distributional equity cuts into the rewards for risk taking, the beneficial effect of the Radical Model on innovation will be attenuated.

Perhaps that is as far as speculation should to be permitted to range. My judgement is that the USSR under the Radical Model would experience some benefit in the quality of its goods and services and in the rate and quality of technological innovation, but to a degree not quite equal to the modest gain experienced by Hungary.

11.5 The Liberal Model

I call the Radical Model by that name because it involves the total abandonment of directive target planning. From the present Soviet perspective it is difficult to get more radical than that without being downright revolutionary. This last model is properly called Liberal because it conserves the traditional planning methods for most of the economy while liberalizing the present restrictions on private initiative.

It might also be called a neo-NEP model. Like that first great reform, it would come as a response to mounting economic difficulties. In the present case those difficulties are not nearly as critical as they were at that time, but then neither is the scope of this reform as extensive as the earlier one. The heart of this reform, however, is the same as that of the other: the withdrawal of the socialized central-planning sector to the "commanding heights" of the economy. This time, however, the "commanding heights" comprise the over-whelming portion of the whole economy. Its boundaries may be demarcated by whatever limits the leadership finds politically and economically optimal. Within those boundaries the economy operates as in the past, with enterprise directive targets, material-technical supply, centralized price administration and the rest.

Outside of those boundaries, however, individuals or small groups would be encouraged to engage in any economic activity for private profit. They would be permitted to employ the labor of other people; wage rates would presumably not fall below the levels in the state sector, which remains an employer of last resort. The size of the private enterprises would be limited by law; initially the limit would be fairly small, but if the reform were successful the limit might be raised in the course of time. Enterprises would be permitted to own capital and to rent land from state agencies. They would be required to file periodic reports with the Central Statistical Agency and with the Ministry of Finance, on the basis of which taxes would be levied.

Neo-NEP enterprise would flourish in those activities in which smallness of scale has a comparative advantage. First is the consumer-service sector; food services, home-care services (clothing repair, washing and cleaning, plumbing, carpentry) and appliance repairs. Second is handicrafts and the manufacture of consumer goods in short supply (warm winter clothing) or of higher quality than is produced by state industry. Third is all manner of retailing services; small shops that purchase both state-produced and private-produced goods and com-pete with the retail services provided by government shops. Fourth is construction work by small *artels* for both private persons, coopera-tives, and private and state enterprises. Fifth is special-order and job-lot production work for industry. Sixth is the supply of specialized services to industry, like R&D and technical consulting. The supply of goods and services to industry is particularly important because it would provide the flexibility that state planning is unable to offer. It may serve the function that small-scale enterprise serves in the modern oligopolistic capitalist economy. In Japan, for example, small-scale enterprises take up the slack of the business cycle and serve as valuable supplementary sources of supply for the large corporations. In the US the small enterprise is often the vehicle for innovations that, if successful, are subsequently bought up by larger firms. It is very likely, as Dr Kvasha (1967) argued, that the absence of the small enterprise is a significant gap in Soviet organizational structure for the promotion of innovation and for industrial efficiency generally, a gap that must have widened since the Production Association reform.

Several critical decisions would have to be made on how the neo-NEP sector would transact with the state sector. The first is the conditions under which private enterprise may purchase materials and equipment from state enterprises. One possible arrangement is that the physical-output targets of state enterprises be divided into two parts, the quantity to be delivered to other state enterprises, and the quantity to be sold to private enterprise. The state deliveries would be handled by the planning agencies by use of the standard method of material balances, while the deliveries to private industry would be handled on the basis of market-demand analysis. The deliveries to private industry may thus serve as a useful balancing instrument for the central planners. Suppose for example, that in the first trial balance of wood nails, the planners find that the state industry's demand for nails exceeds the supply proposed in the draft of the enterprise-production plans. Balance could then be attained simply by reducing the quantities that the planners had originally allocated to private enterprises and increasing the quantities allocated to state enterprises. The consequence could be that in that year private industry would have to scramble for nails, develop substitutes, or reduce its output; or resort to bribery, to which we will return presently.

Second, a decision would have to be made on the prices of transactions between state and private enterprises (transactions between private enterprises and consumers need not be regulated). One approach would be to employ a purchase tax on sales by state to private enterprises. The former would receive the same price for its product regardless of whether it was sold to a state enterprise or to a private enterprise, but the private purchaser would have to pay the state tax. The purpose of the tax is partly to recapture any subsidies in the enterprise wholesale price, and partly for the political purpose of strengthening the competitive position of state industry against private enterprise. That is to say, private enterprise would have to contribute more than a marginal gain to the economy in order to justify the ideological cost of tolerating it.

Third, the private retail network would provide a higher quality and larger range of many consumer goods and services than are available in the state stores. The higher prices may kindle popular hostility if it is felt that the private stores are "crowding out" the distribution of state-supplied goods. It is therefore important that the state continue to supply the traditional array of consumer goods and services at conventional prices. They would continue to be rationed by queuing, while those whose incomes or preferences are different could purchase at the private stores.[3] Similarly, the state sector must continue to act as employer of last resort, as it in fact does now. Workers would not therefore be at the mercy of their employers as in a capitalist system, for if they are dissatisfied with the pay or working conditions in the private sector, their alternative is not unemployment.

For evidence on how the economy would perform under this model, one might go back to the experience of the original NEP. But the more relevant evidence is that of the present-day second economy. The lesson that is usually drawn from that peculiar institution is that the centrally planned economy tends to spawn corruption. The story may be told differently, however. The lesson of the second economy is that within a socialist system there is a vast store of initiative that cannot be tapped through the normal institutions of central planning. To benefit from that great productive potential, the economy must provide some institutional arrangement in which it can flourish in a socially responsible way. The introduction of a controlled domain of limited private enterprise would be such an arrangement.

Every participant in this conference can supply his own anecdotes on the kinds of initiative that burst forth even under the present inhibiting conditions. I shall mention only two that I have found particularly instructive. One is the case of the Fakel' firm. It was formed by a small group of engineers and scientists in Novosibirsk for the purpose of providing research, development and innovation services to industry on a spare-time basis. Operating out of a few dormitory rooms, they solicited contracts from enterprises, drawing upon consultants' services as needed from specialists in the area. In about four years they received 3.5 million rubles from 263 contracts, which they claim to have saved 35 million rubles for the economy, for which they received fees for themselves and their consultants. Their activities sparked an intense controversy, and they were finally forced to close down because of the objections of the State Bank and the Ministry of Finance (Löwenhardt, 1974). The second is the case of the agronomist I. Khudenko, who was given a free hand in farming a tract of unused State Farm land. Operating under the form of an "extended link," Khudenko and a few colleagues ran the operation virtually as a private farm with phenomenal success. The controversy was more bitter in this case and Khudenko was found guilty on criminal charges and died in prison in 1974 (Katsenelenboigen, 1978, p. 66). The vast store of tales like these testifies to the existence of a powerful innovative and productive potential in the nation that would flourish under the Liberal Model.

Like the Radical Model, the Liberal Model is that of a "mixed economy." There is a critical difference between the two, however. The Radical Model is a mix of central planning and markets, but all enterprises are state enterprises. What is radical about it is the abandonment of directive target-planning of enterprises, which is the heart of Soviet-type central planning. The Liberal Model retains the traditional form of central planning for most of the economy. It is a mix of state enterprises and private enterprises. I would not quarrel with the view that a mix of that kind might be regarded as more radical than the abandonment of directive planning. The main point is that the two models reflect different judgements about the pathology of the Soviet socialist economy. The Radical Model reflects the view of the major body of Western economic theory of socialism deriving from Lange and Lerner. That theory is preoccupied with issues of Pareto-efficiency and looks upon markets as a way of increasing the efficiency of socialist economies. The Liberal Model directs attention not to allocative efficiency but to something like Leibenstein's X-efficiency. It says, in effect, that the problem of centrally planned socialism is not in the central planning but in the socialism, or at least in the monopoly of socialist organizations. Concern with that issue, incidentally, can also be found in Lange (1936) in his remarks about the danger of the "bureaucratization" of economic life even in his market model of socialism.[4]

If the evidence on the Radical Model is the experience of Hungary, the relevant evidence on the Liberal Model, I have found to my surprise, is the experience of the GDR. That stern government permitted private craftsmen to operate throughout its history, and while there was some retrenchment in 1972 by the nationalization of the larger private firms, small-scale production continued to be given the "fullest support of the Socialist Unity Party and the state" (Scott, 1974, p. 196). In their judicious comparison of the performance of the two Germanys, Gregory and Leptin (1977) credit the toleration of private enterprise in handicraft, retail trade and agriculture in the GDR as one of the reasons for the success of the incentives policy of the country. The dismal state of Polish agriculture might be regarded as evidence of the failure of private enterprise in a socialist context, but the stronger argument is that the fault in that case was the gross mismanagement of agriculture policy by the national leadership. For the USSR under the Liberal Model, the prospect for agriculture is not full-scale private farming after the Polish example, but perhaps a full commitment to the "link" as the basic unit of socialized agriculture. Like the "team" in the People's Republic of China, the link can be made sufficiently small to restore one of the central elements of X-efficiency, namely, the direct association of one's income with one's effort. Along with the elevation of the link, the spirit of the Liberal Model requires that the State give full support to private subsidiary agriculture. The link and the private plot would constitute the kind of "wager on the strong" with which an earlier Russian reformer — Peter Stolypin — had sought to release the peasant's initiative from the restraints of the commune.

Two issues that would have to be faced are corruption and income distribution. The first issue is not whether the Liberal Model will produce corruption. It certainly will. The question is rather whether corruption will be larger in scope and more detrimental than that which is presently generated under central planning. The answer is not at all self-evident. The large expansion in lawful opportunities for earning private incomes will increase the gains from the illegal diversion of state property to the private market. On the other hand to the extent that the private sector succeeds in closing the disequilibrium gaps, the volume of bribes currently demanded by custodians of state-owned goods in short supply will be reduced. Moreover the Liberal Model would convert into acceptable "red markets" some of the variously colored markets that Katsenelenboigen (1978) has detailed, thus reducing the volume of corruption by defining as legal that which was formerly illegal. The principal objective of this model, however, is not simply to distribute already produced goods more efficiently but to stimulate the production of new goods and services that would not otherwise have been produced. Corruption in that kind of activity would have less undesirable social consequences than that which merely redistributes real income in favor of those who have access to goods and services in short supply. Hence it is quite possible that corruption will be less of a problem under the Liberal Model than under the present system.

More than any of the other models this one will test the limits of income inequality that the society is willing to tolerate. The period immediately following its adoption will generate the largest individual incomes because of the large disequilibria inherited from the present system. In the course of time, however, as the backlog of unrepaired TV sets is worked off and the supply of hand-knitted wool gloves expands, the initial transient windfall incomes will moderate in size. The eventual steady-state income differentiation may still be larger than the political system can tolerate. In that case it would be perfectly reasonable for the leadership to take measures to rein in the scope of the private sector. A society has the right to decide what combination of income and inequality it prefers. An informed social choice, however, requires that the price of greater equality be known. The experiment with the Liberal Model will provide both the leadership and the population with a clear measure of the price currently being paid, if there is such a price, for the prevailing degree of equality; and of the price that would have to be paid if the Liberal Model is eventually abandoned.

Finally, the Liberal Model has the virtue of administrative and political flexibility. The Radical Model would be difficult to implement in parts: to operate certain sectors without target planning while in other sectors traditional central planning prevails. As in Hungary, it is an all-or-nothing proposition. The Liberal Model, however, is infinitely divisible. Certain types of private production can be declared lawful while others remain unlawful as at present. If either the level of corruption or the degree of income differentiation should exceed the politically acceptable, the boundaries of the private sector can be constricted. The income-distribution problem can be separately controlled by tax policies that can make whatever discriminations are thought to be desirable.

The longer any model endures, the greater are the interests that become vested and the greater the resistance to reversal of policy. But that risk is slight under the conditions of present-day Soviet society. One need only to think back to the original NEP to be convinced of the difference. At that time NEP was a risk of major proportions because the state-run commanding heights didn't command a very large part of the economy. The political fears of the Left were entirely justified; the strengthening of private enterprise in trade and small-scale industry, and particularly in an agriculture that engaged some 80% of the population, could very well have eventually generated a political force to challenge the usurped power of the relatively small Communist Party. The Liberal Model poses no such threat in Soviet society today. The ideological awkwardness would be small compared to the economic gain from what may be the most effective model for the Soviet economy of the future.

11.6 Political Issues

When the choice is finally made, the economic prospects under the various models will no doubt enter into consideration. But it is politics and not economics that will dictate the choice in the end. In reviewing the array of political forces I shall first discuss the political disposition of the major social groups, and then consider the political viability of each of the four models.

For the urban working class, there are two primary concerns; job security, and the level of consumption. The evidence for the latter comes primarily from the Polish experience, and we may err in transferring the lesson directly to the Russian working class, which may be much more compliant. There is no direct evidence that Soviet workers are prepared to go to the barricades over the price of meat, but the Soviet leadership acts as if they thought that might occur. What is more certain is that a decline in real income would at some point lead to an attenuation in incentives, with possibly worse consequences for productivity and growth.

The centrality of job tenure to the workers is evident in the long-standing inability of the Soviet leadership to find a politically acceptable way of redistributing workers among jobs. The Shchekino experiment, in which part of the wages of dismissed redundant workers was added to the wage fund of the remaining workers, was the boldest move to date in that direction, but it has not had a major impact. Evidently the prospect of dividing up the wages of their dismissed comrades did not prove to be an incentive sufficient to crack labor's solidarity on this issue. Soviet analysts of innovation regard the difficulty of dismissing technologically redundant workers as a major obstacle to innovation (Berliner, 1976, Chap. 5). Nearer at hand is the evidence of the Hungarian reform, much of the potential of which had to be forgone out of a concern to avoid a clash with labor on this issue. The Yugoslav experience, on the other hand, testifies to the capability of at least one socialist government to survive extensive unemployment. But the Soviet leadership is probably correct in its own assessment that it is not an issue on which it would want to be tested.

The key to peasant sentiment is the private plot. That is the institution that is the focus of his potential political involvement, and alterations in the official status of that institution have a major impact on his material and psychic life. By contrast, the steady conversion of collective farms into state farms seems not to have aroused a ripple, suggesting that the difference between those two organizational forms has long since ceased to be salient to the peasants. One has the impression that farm life continues to be highly unattractive to young people who must be restrained from fleeing from it by social and legal pressures. The attachment to the private plot suggests that the peasants would be attracted by the possibility of greater individual autonomy over a larger piece of land. But they have had no experience with the fluctuations of farm prices and incomes that accompany that autonomy in uncontrolled markets, and it is not at all certain that they would gladly pay that price for a larger say over their own land.

The intelligentsia are likely to be the least resistant to change in the economic mechanism since the basis of their social position is least system–specific; there will be jobs for journalists and engineers under any likely economic arrangement, though the stars of some would rise while others fall. The liberal intelligentsia are likely to be disposed toward more decentralized systems that allow greater freedom for individual action. But the technical intelligentsia may well be disposed toward more conservative systems. Sharing with enterprise management the responsibility for trying to keep the trains running on time, and with no practical experience in the operation of decentralized systems, they are likely to see the solution in better planning, organization and management. Perhaps only among economists has there developed an understanding of decentralized systems and some attraction to them, but close observers regard their number to be rather small. For most economists Soviet means central planning (Katsenelenboigen, 1978).

Enterprise managers are second to none in their grumbling about the inefficiencies of the centrally planned economy within which they operate. The general view, however, is that their grumbling is of a highly conservative kind. They want the supply system to work better and the ministry to be less bureaucratic in attending to the needs of their enterprises. All the vibrations suggest that they are quite content in principle with a system in which they are told by someone else what to produce and where someone else has the responsibility for providing them with the inputs they require. It is doubtful that they would see much virtue in a system that required them to take the risks of guessing what unspecified customers would be willing to buy from them and that permitted other enterprises to steal away their customers. Doubtless they believe they merit higher incomes than they earn, but they are aware that the combination of their pay, perks, and prestige places them in the upper echelons of the society. They have achieved as a class a form of job security they never attained under Stalin, when the rapid turnover of managers was a characteristic feature of their lives. Most have held their jobs for very long periods, a state of affairs that disposes them to both managerial and political conservatism. The question of the political power that management can muster in defense of its interests has been the subject of controversy (Azrael, 1966). The most recent test of that power was the introduction of Production Associations, which threatened a substantial number of enterprise directors with the loss of their authority to the general directors of the Associations. The evidence is mixed. Many Associations were indeed formed, and although initially a controversy broke out over the status of the directors of the merged enterprises, that status was eventually largely submerged (Berliner, 1976, pp. 136–43). On the other hand, the Production Association reform appears to be proceeding very slowly, and one of the reasons is thought to be the intense opposition of managers, as well as of some ministry personnel (Gorlin, 1976). The evidence is not conclusive because this reform divided the interests of managers; those who expected to be promoted to the general directorate of the Production Associations had a great deal to gain. Hence it cannot be thought of as an issue on which management would have a unified interest. Nevertheless the rearguard action mounted by what must have been a substantial number of managerial officials was evidently successful in retarding the pace of the reform and constricting its scope, perhaps permanently.

With respect to labor relations, the demise of the Shchekino experiment suggests that management has little stomach for the job of taking on labor in a campaign to cut costs by dismissing redundant labor. Nor would they gladly share their power with worker representatives under some form of genuine self-management or democratization of the work place. The system of central planning and management thus makes for a very comfortable position for enterprise management; protecting them from workers' demands for participation that might arise under greater decentralization and relieving them of the responsibility to economize on labor in ways that would threaten workers' job security.

About the interests of the central management — the ministerial bureaucracy — there can be no doubt. They are to central planning as capitalists are to capitalism. Close to the pinnacle of power and prestige, they are as "establishment" as one can get, save perhaps the Party. The more centralized the system of planning and management, the larger the power they wield. To be sure, under most conceivable models of socialism there will still be national economic ministries, for the state will always be obliged to implement national policies and to monitor the activities of enterprises; and for that purpose national bureaucracies are necessary. But to be a ministerial official under decentralized conditions is to be a much less substantial person.

This group is likely to be the strongest defender of the system of central planning and management against efforts at substantial change. Yet their power would be limited in a conflict with a strongly supported Party policy. The classic test was Khrushchev's Territorial Reorganization, which was directed against precisely this stratum of officialdom and virtually dismembered it, with large numbers of ministry officials being sent out to the provinces to staff the new territorial economic councils. Their return to office with the restoration of the ministries after Khrushchev's departure is evidence not of their power per se but of the growing awareness that that reorganization had been a failure and needed to be reversed. More recently their power has been tested again in what is reported to be extensive ministerial opposition to the Production Associations. That reform has created a class of new association managers presiding over much larger domains than the old enterprise managers and therefore much more substantial people who are less easily intimidated by ministerial power. Here too, however, the opposition was a rearguard action and the reform has been pushed through, although the slowing of its pace may be attributed to continued ministerial as well as managerial resistance (Gorlin, 1976).

I take it as self-evident that the Party and policy *apparat* must be regarded as conservative in economic matters. The same is probably true of the military officer corps, although it ought not be surprising if the nature of their responsibilities lay them more open to alternatives. The responsibilities I have in mind are the maintenance of a fighting force equipped with the armaments required to defeat a coalition of countries all of whom are more technically advanced. No other group in Soviet society confronts foreign competition in so stark a form. I know of no evidence on the subject but it should not be surprising to learn that the military, in the vital quest for technological advance, and of necessity knowledgeable about the technological processes and products of its potential antagonists, might prove to be a force for greater autonomy at lower levels of the production system.

About the Politburo itself, three things may be said. First, in the short- or medium-term the composition of that body will change greatly. Precisely what the political-economic orientation of the new leadership will be is impossible to know, but it is a good bet that it will feel freer to entertain a wider range of alternatives than can be expected of the present leadership. Second, a younger leadership is likely to take a longer-run planning horizon and may therefore be more impelled to take action, drastic if it need be, to arrest the decline in growth and to "get the economy moving again." Third, any drastic action must be threatening to some substantial interests in the country. The new leadership will therefore have to establish a power base upon whom it can rely for support, as Khrushchev sought to rely on the provincial Party *apparat*. For these several reasons, of all the groups we have discussed in this review, the top Party leadership may be the most likely agent of change in the economic mechanism, carrying it out as a "revolution from above."

Among the national minorities, nationalist sentiments may conflict with class interests. Russified or Sovietized Party officials and managers are likely to see their interests in the same way that their Great Russian colleagues do. But where nationalist feelings run deep, centralization means Moscow which means Russian domination. A significant portion of the Party and managerial groups among the minorities are therefore likely to support decentralizing measures primarily because they will reduce the power of Moscow over their lives. The Yugoslav experience may appear to suggest the contrary; there the smaller Southern republics have promoted centralization while the larger Northern ones have pushed hard for a weakening of central government. One of the major factors in the Yugoslav case, however, is the division of the country among the less developed republics and the more developed. It is the poorer republics like Montenegro that have fought for centralization because the more powerful the central government the greater the redistribution of income and investment in their favor. For the same reason, the richer republics like Slovenia have supported increased republic power, as a means of slowing down what they regard as the draining of their resources for the support of the less productive republics to the South. The Soviet case is notably different, for at least two reasons. First, republic differences in per capita income and consumption are probably much smaller in the USSR than in Yugoslavia, although I know of no evidence on this question. Second, a number of the national minorities enjoy higher living standards than the Great Russians; particularly the Baltic nations and perhaps Georgia and Armenia as well. Nor are Central Asians notably far behind the Great Russians, if at all. Hence the special feature that operates in the Yugoslav case is not salient in the Soviet. The nationalist-minded members of the national minorities will see the issue not primarily in income-distribution terms as in Yugoslavia but in political terms. From that perspective any reform that will reduce the power of Moscow will command support.

If this review of the interests of the relevant groups conforms even roughly with political reality, it implies that the Conservative Model is most likely to prevail unless one of two conditions obtains. One condition is that the rate of growth under that model fails to stabilize at a level above what was described earlier as the incentive threshold. If it falls below that level, the erosion of work incentives would trigger off new forces that would make for continued decline. Even if the economy did not yet fall to the political threshold, but certainly if it did, a change to another model would be inevitable. The second condition is that in the succession politics after Brezhnev a new and younger leader either (a) develops a power base strong enough to force a change over the opposition of major vested interests, or (b) wins the support of a major social group, Mao-like, by forcing a change that is strongly supported by that group.

We are not charged, in this conference, to foretell the future; to forecast, in this case, whether either of these conditions will in fact obtain. The probability is large enough, however, to pursue the question of which of the other models might be adopted if the Conservative Model is abandoned.

The strongest political support, it seems to me, can be marshalled in favor of the Reactionary Model. It is the alternative that does the least violence to the interests of the groups that are most closely tied to the regime — central and enterprise management, the Party *apparat*, the military and so forth. There would be some loss to these groups from the restrictions that are likely to be placed on the second economy. But the organized system of special shops would presumably be continued.

The experience of the 1980 Polish workers' strike may lead to a reconsideration of the special shops, the abolition of which was one of the workers' demands. But political wisdom may dictate the retention of those privileges nonetheless, because it is precisely those social groups that would be most counted on to forestall such workers' action.

The Reactionary Model would also command strong ideological support from a variety of sources. There are first those Party loyalists for whom strong Party leadership and control of the economy are matters of deep conviction and are believed to be the only proper way to run a Marxist-Leninist society. Most observers hold that few people in Soviet society are motivated by Marxist–Leninist ideology today, and I do not dispute it. But the ideology I have in mind is not the grand socialist idealism associated with those revered names, but simply the set of ideas on the right way to manage the Soviet state and society that emerged from World War II. In any case, certainly much larger is that portion of the society that would support the Reactionary Model because it promises a return to a more orderly, less contentious, and perhaps simpler way of life. Though the words ring strange in Western ears, internal observers report a widespread nostalgia for the "blessed" Stalinist times, when "there was rigid discipline in the country, when there were no difficulties, for example with labor power" (Katsenelenboigen, 1978, p. 57). That this sentiment is also widely held among the elite was corroborated by the ICA survey, which found that while Soviet professionals are attracted to many features of American society, like access to information and freedom of travel, they "believe that similar access by the Soviet *narod* (people) would unbalance the society" and that "widespread freedoms would lead to chaos in society and perhaps undermine their own positions" (Guroff, 1980, p. 16).

How the *narod* would respond is harder to guess. It is likely that a strong law-and-order policy coupled with the usual combination of xenophobia, nationalism, anti-semitism and anti-intellectualism will command extensive populist support. The tightening of police controls will affect mostly intellectuals and "speculators," and while there will be some loss in consumption levels from the curtailment of the second economy, it is the producers for those markets and not the consumers who will be dispatched to the camps. If, as I have argued above, the economy will perform somewhat better under the Reactionary Model, the extent of that loss may be small.

A critical question is the response to the tightening of labor discipline, which is a major condition for the economic success of the Reactionary Model. Certainly the program would have to be presented as part of a great new national campaign, perhaps even packaged as a program to raise the consumption level of the people. Something of the sort would be necessary to sustain the compulsion that would be required to pull workers away from the "collective" in which they have worked all their lives and assign them to work in other enterprises and in other regions. In the short run there is a fair possibility that an imaginative political leadership can pull it off. In the longer run, however, it is more problematical.

The Radical Model runs counter to the interests of all the main groups that support the traditional regime. Most of the officials of the central-planning and central-management bureaucracy would be out of jobs. Enterprises would still require directors, but they are not likely to be the same persons who directed the factories in the past. As in Hungary, an effort is likely to be made to mollify the directors by assuring them of their job security under the new system (Granick, 1973). But the managers whose skills and outlook were cradled in a system of *mat-tekh snabzhenie* (centralized supply of enterprise inputs) are not likely to survive in a genuinely decentralized system; particularly if, unlike the Hungarians, they have never lived in one. They are likely to resist this model as strongly as the central managers.

The workers are likely to perceive a decentralized system, correctly, as a threat to their job security. And as in Hungary, the regime would have to give such strong assurances on that score that one of the major potential benefits of decentralization would be lost. Similar assurances had to be given in Hungary (Granick, 1973), but because of its older legacies, the cost would be greater in the USSR.

In fact, in surveying the various interest groups, the only ones that are likely to support the Radical Model are the national minorities, a small group of economists and perhaps a smattering of liberal intelligentsia who would support any weakening of the central bureaucracy as a step toward more personal freedom. Perhaps if the model included some extensive decentralization of agriculture as well, it might also command the support of the peasantry.

If this judgment about the very weak support for the Radical Model is correct, it raises the interesting question of why the USSR is different from Hungary and Czechoslovakia. In the latter case decentralization had vast support in the country, including eventually large sections of the Party. In Hungary the support was perhaps not as extensive but one has the impression that decentralization neverthe-less commanded fairly broad support. The difference, I suspect, is that in Eastern Europe the system of central planning is identified with rigid Party orthodoxy and, ultimately, with Russian domination of their countries. To smash central planning is to strike a blow at a Soviet-like Communist Party, and symbolically at the USSR. From this perspec-tive, hostility to the USSR was an important political factor in enabling the leadership to marshall support in favor of decentralization. But if a USSR is vital in promoting the Radical Model elsewhere, who will be the USSR's USSR? Perhaps China.

If the Radical Model is to be adopted in the USSR, it will come about only because the small band of liberal economists have somehow gotten the ear of the new leader and persuaded him that it is the best course for both himself and for the country. But that, as we have argued above, would be a hard case to make, for the Hungarian performance has not (yet) been so successful that its effectiveness is beyond dispute, particularly for the USSR. If the leader nevertheless did decide that the Radical Model was the best course for the USSR, he must then face the prospect of engineering a revolution from above, for he will have no support from the conventionally loyal groups. Nor is he likely to turn like Mao to an unconventional group like the students in order to create a new power base. The military might conceivably be neutral on the technical issue of whether the decentralized model will outperform the centralized, but it will hardly rally around a leader who contemplates a new revolution in favor of decentralization. A revolution from above of this magnitude would require that the new leader first concentrate in his hands the personal power of a Stalin. On the other hand, Stalins don't decentralize.

It should now be evident why the Liberal Model would command much greater support than the Radical. No one loses his job, for the centrally planned sector operates largely as it did before. The Party leader who introduces that model will, moreover, have a new basis of support in both the producers in the new private sector and the consumers who will have access to a significantly improved range of goods and services. For if the assessment presented above should prove to be correct, the population will experience a sharp improvement in the quality of life, sharp enough to leave no doubt about the success of the policy and the person who gets the credit for it.

Among the political obstacles, one thinks first of the ideological. But an imaginative leadership should have little difficulty presenting the model in a favorable light, providing that Mr Suslov has passed from the scene. It is, after all, modelled on the NEP, and what Soviet leader would not wish to be the one to pick up the baton of Lenin? Moreover the NEP is associated in the public mind with a period of hope and prosperity; I have heard even young people refer to it as the "golden age" of Soviet history. The Liberal Model could also supply the missing part of an ideological puzzle that has been created by the adoption of the notion that the USSR has entered the new historical stage of "mature socialism." It is clear that central planning was the appropriate economic model during the stage of the building of socialism, but now that socialism has entered the stage of maturity the historical process should be expected to produce a new set of production relations. The dialectician should expect a negation of the negation, producing a social formation similar to the older one but on a new and higher plane. Viewed from that perspective, central planning was the negation of private enterprise. The negation of central planning can reasonably be thought to be a new form of private enterprise, but on a higher plane in the sense that it is now socially responsible because it is embedded in a mature socialist society. Moreover since the transition to mature socialism is accompanied by the scientific-technical revolution, the historically progressive economic system is one that enables the society to reap the fullest benefits of that revolution. Central planning was an appropriate economic model in a period in which the task of socialism was to adopt the advanced technology of the time that was already known and in operation in the capitalist world. That historical task having been completed, a new economic model is required that not simply adopts known technology but also produces yet unknown technological knowledge in the age of the scientific-technical revolution. Central planning is the historically correct form for applying known technology, but planning the yet unknown is a qualitatively different task. Hence the rise of a new synthesis in which the private initiative of socialist men and women serves to promote technological innovation in the matrix of a centrally planned socialist economy.

I conclude that the prospects for change in the system of planning and management depends on the performance of the economy under the Conservative Model. If the growth rate should stabilize at a level that may be low but that nevertheless exceeds the incentive threshold, that model will be retained and the century will limp quietly to its end. Chronic cases do not normally evoke extreme measures. Only acute attacks, like depressions or rebellions, galvanize a society into such measures. If the Conservative Model cannot stabilize the growth rate even at that low level, the accumulation of social and political pressures will propel the leadership into either the Reactionary or the Liberal Model. Both are likely to improve the performance of the economy, but the greater potential lies with the latter. If the counsels of political prudence prevail, however, the lot will fall to the former.

11: Notes

1 The decree deals not only with the planning system but with the management system as well. The major new departure with respect to management is the introduction of a new success indicator — normative net value of output. The intent of the new indicator is to eliminate the benefit that enterprises derive from their assortment plans in favor of products with a large proportion of purchased inputs.

2 *Pravda*, Nov. 28, 1979. Transl. in *Current Digest of the Soviet Press* **31**, no. 48: 8, Dec. 26, 1979.

3 It may not be possible to mollify populist egalitarian hostility to the two types of stores. One of the demands of the Polish workers in the 1980 strike was the abolition of the "special shops" open only to the elite. The private-enterprise shops would be open to all purchasers, but they may kindle resentment nonetheless.

4 There is a third position, which may be taken as the Yugoslav interpretation. This interpretation shares the Radical view that markets are superior to central planning, and it shares the Liberal view that enterprises should not be state-owned. It parts company with the Liberal view, however, in holding that the best alternative to state-owned enterprise is not private enterprise but self-managed enterprise. The notion of worker self-management is so far out of the bounds of the thinkable in the USSR that I have not explored that model here.

11: References

Azrael, Jeremy R., *Managerial Power and Soviet Politics*. Cambridge, Mass: Harvard Univ. Press, 1966.

Berliner, Joseph S., *The Innovation Decision in Soviet Industry*. Cambridge, Mass.: MIT Press, 1976.

East European Economies Post-Helsinki. Papers, Joint Econ. Comm., US Congress. Washington, DC: Govt. Printing Office, 1977.

Gorlin, Alice C., "Industrial Reorganization: The Associations." In *Soviet Economy in a New Perspective*, pp. 162–88. Papers, Joint Econ. Comm., US Congress. Washington, DC: Govt. Printing Office, 1976.

Granick, David, "The Hungarian Economic Reform." *World Politics* 25, **4**: 414–429, 1973.

Gregory, Paul, and Leptin, Gert, "Similar Societies under Differing Economic Systems: The Case of the Two Germanys." *Soviet Studies* **29**: 519–42, Oct. 1977.

Grossman, Gregory, "The Party as Entrepreneur" in Gregory Guroff and Fred V. Carstensen (eds.), *Entrepreneurship in Russia and the Soviet Union*, (Princeton: Princeton University Press, forthcoming).

Guroff, Gregory, "Soviet Perceptions of the US: Results of a Surrogate Interview Project." Washington, DC: Internat. Communications Agency, June 27, 1980.

Hewett, Edward A., "The Hungarian Economy: Lessons of the 1970s and Prospects for the 1980s." In *East European Economic Assessment*. Papers, Joint Econ. Comm., US Congress. Washington, DC: Govt. Printing Office, 1981.

Katsenelenboigen, Aron, *Studies in Soviet Economic Planning*. White Plains: M. E. Sharpe, 1978.

Kvasha, Ia. "Kontsentratsiia proizvodstva i mel'kaia promyshlennost'." *Voprosy ekonomiki*, no. 5, 1967.

Lange, Oskar, "On the Economic Theory of Socialism." Repr. in B. Lippincott, ed., *On the Economic Theory of Socialism*. Minneapolis: Univ. of Minnesota Press, 1938.

Löwenhardt, John, "The Tale of the Torch — Scientists–Engineers in the Soviet Union." *Survey* **20**, 4 (93):113–21 Autumn 1974.

Marer, Paul, "Economic Performance, Strategy and Prospects in Eastern Europe." In *East European Economies* . . . , pp. 523–66, 1977.

Neuberger, Egon, "Central Planning and Its Legacies: Implications for Foreign Trade." In Alan A. Brown and E. Neuberger, eds, *International Trade and Central Planning*. Berkeley: Univ. of California Press, 1968.

Portes, Richard, "Hungary: Economic Performance, Policy and Prospects." In *East European Economies* . . . , pp. 766–815, 1977.

Rumer, Boris, "The 'Second' Agriculture in the USSR". Mimeo, Russian Research Center, Harvard University, 1980.

Schroeder, Gertrude E., "The Soviet Economy on a Treadmill of 'Reforms'." In *Soviet Economy in a Time of Change*, pp. 312–40. Papers, Joint Econ. Comm., US Congress. Washington, DC: Govt. Printing Office, 1979.

Scott, Hilda, *Does Socialism Liberate Women: Experiences from Eastern Europe*. Boston: Beacon Press, 1974.

Zielinski, Janusz G. *Economic Reforms in Polish Industry*. London: Oxford Univ. Press, 1973.

12

Politics and Priorities

SEWERYN BIALER

Introduction

It is a truism that the relationship between politics and economics in the second half of the twentieth century is very close in all societies. It is especially close in developed societies. If politics, by one standard definition, deals with who gets what, when, and how, then economics provides one of the key parameters of political actions. By the same token, and to an increasing degree, it is politics that provides the context of economic activity.

It is, of course, an exaggeration to state, as Lenin did, that politics is nothing else but condensed economics. It would be foolish to overlook the high degree of autonomy between politics and economics. Each has its own rules and *laws* independent of each other, each generates its own momentum, and each has concerns with other aspects of societal activity. Yet the autonomy of economics or politics is relative. It does not help to deny the autonomy of economics and politics, but it does not help either to overlook the relativity and the limitations of that autonomy.

Far from being an exception to this rule, the Soviet Union is the closest embodiment of this relationship. In fact, the Soviet political system was developed largely to run the economy and was shaped by a specific economic-growth strategy. But it is also impossible to understand this growth strategy and the configuration of Soviet economics — its shape and developmental tendencies — outside of the context of the political society.

This paper will deal with Soviet politics and policies in the coming decade, but from the point of view of how they will be influenced by economic developments and how they may influence economic development. In doing so, it will try briefly to answer four questions:

- First, what is the basic profile of the Soviet political system as it enters the 1980s? In other words, what are the key political characteristics of the Brezhnev period, which is now coming to an end?

- Second, what are some of the most important political developments that can be expected in the 1980s and that are generated
within the political system? In other words, what will be some of
the developments that will be indigenous to the Soviet political
sphere itself?
- Third, how may those political developments be influenced by
economic developments projected for the 1980s? What will be the
most probable political consequences of the developments generated by the Soviet economy?
- Fourth, and last, how will the interconnection of Soviet political and
economic development in the 1980s influence one crucial aspect of
the Soviet economic scene, the chance for structural reform?

12.1 Basic Profile of the Soviet Political System

What are the major characteristics of the Soviet political system as it
enters the 1980s? What impact did the Brezhnev period have on the
Soviet polity?[1]

- The Soviet leadership no longer resorts to mass terror as the means
of controlling, shaping, or changing society. Terror and police state
methods are no longer employed in controlling and shaping elite
behavior and resolving elite disputes. As it enters the 1980s, the
Soviet political system resembles very much a highly regressive,
inclusionary, authoritarian state where the forces of repression and
the enormous police machine that safeguards it are used in a more
traditional and rational way. Their actions are quite predictable to
the citizenry, are orderly and directed against the actual violators of
the established rules of behavior, and, in their punitive force,
commensurate with the weight of the offense perpetrated.
- The Brezhnev era saw the development and spread of a new
phenomenon in Soviet society, cultural and political dissent. Yet,
despite its unprecedented character under Soviet conditions, the
Soviet leadership achieved a situation where the impact of the
multifaceted dissent movement in the Soviet system remains
marginal at best. The international consequences of Soviet dissent
are incomparably stronger and more meaningful than their effects
and prospects at home.
- The Brezhnev period was a highly conservative period in Soviet
history. This conservatism was embraced both by the elites and by
the society at large. The elites displayed an overwhelming desire for
stability and security. The professional classes directed their aspirations towards material achievements and professional attainments.
The broad strata of the population displayed a high degree of apathy
with regard to political questions and remained preoccupied with
the "politics" of everyday life on the local level. Soviet youth has
basically retained its career orientation. The conservatism of Soviet

society, primarily political, also expresses itself in other spheres of Soviet life, particularly in the cultural area. The old conservative themes of law and order, national unity, and intolerance towards those who defy these norms remain the ruling principles of Soviet society.[2]

- A major dimension of the conservatism of the Soviet polity as it enters the 1980s can be discerned in the stability of the composition of the Soviet leadership and the elites. To a degree unequalled in any other period of Soviet history, the Soviet leadership and key elite groups remained stable and unchanged throughout the Brezhnev era. One index of this stability can be seen in the low turnover in the membership of the Central Committee of the Party, as the figures below demonstrate:

Survival Ratio of Members of the CC, CPSU at Consecutive Congresses (per cent)

XX	*XXII*	*XXIII*	*XXIV*	*XXV*
62.4	49.6	79.4	76.5	83.4

This stability is partly a spontaneous reaction to the experimentation and turmoil of the Khrushchev period and partly a secular trend representing the further bureaucratization of the Soviet political system, with its stress on gradualism and orderliness. Until recently, this stability represented the basic yearnings of key Soviet elite groups and the leadership responded positively. But whatever the reasons for this stability, the Soviet Union enters the 1980s with the oldest leadership and central and regional elites in its history.[3] It is a leadership and elite at the apex of the system, composed of people from the same generation. They have worked together for an extraordinarily long period of time, and were able to design a set of rules for their working relationships that were relatively benign in the light of Soviet tradition.

- The Soviet leadership was transformed from a personal dictatorship into a relatively stable oligarchy. The top leadership, which developed in the Brezhnev era, is collective; almost all the major bureaucratic interests are represented within the top leadership. No one bureaucratic group and no one personal machine dominates the leadership. Although the role of the First Party Secretary and his "loyalists" within the Politburo have clearly increased in the last few years, his role is more limited than in the past. The most important differences with the Khrushchev leadership cannot be expressed adequately by such terms as "less" or "more"; these differences are exemplified by the question of "power for what purpose." The powers of a leader are not static; their limits and scope can be evaluated only in practice. In this perspective, Brezhnev's power differs from Khrushchev's, in as much as the former uses his power differently. Khrushchev's power was expended most notably in his efforts to change institutions and policies, and its limits were tested most visibly in alternate advances and retreats in the face of the leadership's and elite's opposition. Brezhnev's power has never really been tested in those terms. It has been expended primarily in assuring the continuity of Soviet institutions and in the gradual adjustment of policies. Within the context of these aims, his position has been very strong and stable. While Khrushchev often tried to form a new consensus or to undermine an existing one within the elite, Brezhnev has been concerned primarily with maintaining consensus.[4]

- During the Brezhnev period, the Soviet elite became inundated as never before by real politics. The cult of the top leader, the centralization of the Communist Party and state, and the "planning" that supposedly permeates all aspects of Soviet life cannot hide the real interplay of the give-and-take of politics. The major actors in the Soviet political process are the major bureaucratic structures and their subsections, alliances on particular issues between various bureaucracies, and, finally, territorial interests. During the Brezhnev era, they developed a high degree of corporate existence and identity and displayed a broad range of opinions on specific issues that came up for decisions, and they were able, as never before, to resolve those issues by bargaining and compromise.[5]

- The role of one group in Soviet politics, the military, requires special consideration, not so much because of its actual importance but because of the many misconceptions concerning this group's role. Without a doubt, the role of the military *factor* in Soviet policy making is a crucial one. The question of military security is the uppermost priority in the minds of the Soviet leadership. Sometimes, however, an erroneous conclusion is drawn from the role of the military *factor* in Soviet policy, assigning an exaggerated role to the military *sector* in Soviet politics. Without a doubt the military is one of the key groups in the Soviet decision-making process of the early 1980s. Under Brezhnev, the military broadened specialized powers; in contrast to the previous period of Soviet history, it attained a higher degree of professional autonomy, a greater voice in matters concerning military questions. Yet at the same time its subordination to the political leadership remains unquestioned, and its role in influencing nonmilitary matters is quite limited. Its success in attaining so much in terms of the allocation of key resources during the Brezhnev period is not a result of its independent political weight, but rather the result of a symbiosis of the views of the military and the political leadership.[6]

- The Brezhnev period saw a very rapid growth of the size of the professional strata in Soviet society. At the same time, it saw a clear increase in the influence of professionals, experts, and especially technocrats and economists in the decision-making process. The experts, both inside and outside of the bureaucracy, increasingly provide advice and technical judgment for the policy makers to act upon. They also have a more visible role at the stage of policy implementation. It would be wrong, however, to regard the professional strata as being composed of cohesive groups. Their organization is very loose, and their corporate identity very weak and fragile; most importantly, their views and judgments concerning policy issues are very heterogeneous. In this situation, the policy makers and high-ranking bureaucrats who avail themselves of the services of the experts to an increasing degree are in most cases free to choose between their conflicting advice, according to their own judgment and interest. Thus, the dependent, service role of the experts in the Soviet political process remains undiminished. The experts provide a range of feasible choices open to the policy makers, but the selection from among those choices remains the prerogative of the policy makers themselves. However "rational" the process of designing policy options in the Soviet Union has become, the actual selection among these options remains primarily political.[7]

- The expectations of Soviet citizens have risen noticeably in the last fifteen years. What is most striking, however, especially when compared to the situation in the West, is that, first of all, these expectations in absolute terms are very modest for an industrial nation, and, secondly, they are not far removed from what is realistically possible though often unrealized under Soviet conditions. To put it differently: although material expectations are ahead of reality, I doubt whether there is a widening gap between expectations and reality. This situation, unusual in a system that for decades overindulged in utopian promises, suggests a restraint, based on past experiences, in popular expectations.[8] Visible and significant improvements in the material conditions of the population of the Soviet Union have not yet produced the phenomenon familiar to other industrial societies: a self-generating spiral of expectations that cannot be realized. The intensity of popular pressures to which the Soviet authorities are exposed is rather limited, and as long as some improvements continue to occur, the situation will probably remain stabilized in this respect. The primary pressures that produced the institutional and policy innovations in the post-Stalin era have not been the actual pressures of social groups or strata, but of the changing material conditions in the society and the changing political conditions within the elite. As examples of these pressures we cite the need to raise the standard of living of the population as a means to improve the incentives to increase productivity; the introduction of bargaining among the elite groups as a substitute for the iron rule of terror.

But however we evaluate the amorphous pressures in Soviet society today, the responsiveness of the Soviet leadership to some of these aspirations is clearly much greater now than in the past. To what kinds of pressures is the leadership responsive? In part, of course, it is responsive to changes in the distributive sector of the

Soviet economy, where the population acquired for the first time in the Soviet era a limited possibility to express its demands through selective buying. In part, this responsiveness is due to the importance that the Soviet leadership attaches to material incentives in its economic programs. But in large measure, this responsiveness can be described as an *anticipatory reaction*; not a response to the actual behavior of workers, but to the leadership's fear that if the interests of the workers are not sufficiently considered, their behavior might become disruptive and dangerous. The lessons of the dangers of workers' dissatisfaction in the East European countries — and especially in Poland — have not been lost on Soviet leaders. In a country where such a high premium is placed on stability, an organized dissent movement is active, mass terror is absent, popular expectations have long been encouraged, and the opening of Soviet society to foreigners has made material comparisons possible, the Party must pay more attention to the material satisfaction of the population, in order that it can continue to curtail cultural freedom, withhold political freedom, and preserve political stability.[9]

- In contrast to their Western counterparts, the Soviet political leadership and elite still retain a belief in the idea of progress to a very high degree. They are still committed to the goal of growth, particularly economic growth. Their belief in the inherent goodness and instrumentality of technological progress and of science remains a deeply rooted, normative commitment. This is one of the reasons why, despite widespread political cynicism and the clear decline of the instrumental effects of the Communist doctrine, they still retain a basically optimistic outlook and a belief in the solvability of the problems that face them as well as an attachment to the belief in the possibility of improving their social order. Their belief in the idea of progress remains consistent with the "comparativist" attitude about their "progression to progress". This progression is still defined by the standards established by the developed Western societies and by the Soviet desire to "catch up."

- Foreign policy and international relations in general have attained an increased emphasis in the Soviet policy-making process. More than ever before, foreign relations is the subject of attention of the Soviet leadership and major elite groups and the preoccupation of major deliberative bodies. At the same time, the connection between internal politics and external policies has become closer than ever before. This is partly a result of the decline of the Soviet economy's isolation from the world economy, and of the deliberate attempt to use foreign technological resources to stimulate Soviet economic growth as a surrogate for internal reforms. This connection is also in part a result of the decline in the isolation of the Soviet professional classes from foreign *professional* influence, which isolation, in the eyes of the Soviet leadership, had clearly proven to be an obstacle to the development of their expertise. But this connection is, for the most part, the result of new Soviet capacities and new foreign-policy resources accumulated by the Soviet Union during the Brezhnev era, which transformed it from a regional and provincial power into a global power and changed its appetites and aspirations.[10]

During the Brezhnev era, the Soviet Union faced a number of difficult problems. Its achievements were impressive, but very spotty. When the Brezhnev era started, Western analysts of Soviet affairs published long lists of trouble spots and potentially destructive problems that would confront the Brezhnev leadership. In my opinion, this leadership, on the whole, performed better than was expected of it. Most importantly, despite the fact that it did not solve or sometimes even diminish any of the major problems facing the Soviet Union, it prevented any of those problems — taken singly or in their cumulative effect — from becoming a source of systemic crisis. In the last few years, the Soviet leadership has exhibited a sense of drift and of exhaustion (particularly regarding its domestic aspects); some strata of the population have yearned for strong leadership, and members of the elites have hoped for policies that will "get the country moving again." Yet, despite this lack of vigor and these aspirations, the USSR is entering the 1980s as a basically stable state, without visible pressures for fundamental changes and without imminent threats of disintegration.

12.2   Expected Political Developments in the Eighties

The shape of Soviet politics and policies changes very slowly. One must always count on the built-in tendency of the Soviet political system to retain the above-mentioned characteristics and directions typical of the 1970s. Yet, in the 1980s, the Soviet Union will be facing issues and events that may influence incremental changes, if not — though this seems less likely — more fundamental changes in the nature of politics and the direction of policies.

Of the many political issues that the Soviet Union faces two seem especially important. The first concerns military policy, which is clearly at a crossroads. Before the Soviet Union achieved strategic parity with the United States and possessed a global military reach, its goal was clear, and not a matter of significant dispute. Now, however, the basic aims of long-term Soviet military policy, according to the evaluation of most Western observers, have been achieved, or, as some Western observers would even argue, overachieved. But it seems that the Soviet military build-up continues by the sheer force of inertia and drift. There are few signs that major disputes are taking place about the aims of Soviet military policy under the new circumstances or that an effort is being made to define more clearly what Soviet security interests are. The Soviet military build-up is, to a point, clearly beyond the range of its traditional defense needs. The change in the East–West military balance brought about a major reaction from the Western alliance, particularly from the United States. If counteracted by the Russians, the Western reaction will undoubtedly start a new, major and uncontrollable arms-race spiral. This prospect may initiate a revaluation of Soviet military-growth policy in the top echelons of the Soviet leadership and among the experts who advise them. I am not at all optimistic about the results of such a revaluation, and I have major doubts whether our own policies, with their clear denigration of arms-control measures, will have any positive influence here. Yet, it seems to me that, for a number of economic and political reasons that will be discussed below, the inertia of Soviet military policy may be broken and at least the question of its redefinition may enter the Soviet political agenda of the 1980s.

The second issue concerns the direction of Soviet foreign policy in general. What we have witnessed in recent years, in my opinion, is not a fulfillment of some master plan of expansion, but a foreign policy that exploits targets of immediate opportunity that have a relatively low cost and risk. In its ability to relate the tempting options of temporary or partial gains and strategic improvements to its other professed goals of reducing international tensions and conducting a policy of detente with the West, overall Soviet foreign policy showed a very limited coherence. Clearly, the Soviet leadership has not yet resolved the question of the proper ordering of priorities for Soviet foreign policy in the new situation. One has the impression that the leadership has not thought through, in a long-range way, what to do and how to use their newly-acquired capacity for international action.

Their policy in this respect may well continue to be incremental in responding to any possible targets of opportunity, regardless of how this policy affects the central axis of world politics, the relations between the superpowers. Yet, for various political and economic reasons, which will be described later, one may predict that the issue of the overall direction and the order of priorities of Soviet foreign policy may enter the agenda of Soviet politics in the 1980s.

But the most important stimulus for political change in the Soviet Union in the 1980s will not be the new political policy issues, but the policy-making process itself. It will originate in the impending turnover of the leaders and elites.[11] The term "succession", in its most precise meaning, describes the order in which, or the conditions under which, a person or group succeeds to political office and the effects of this process on the structure and policies of the political system of a nation-state. While the term may be applied broadly to an entire leadership group or even top elite stratum, in dealing with the Soviet Union the term is traditionally used to denote the patterns of political life and their effects on current policies during the interval between the death, ouster, or possible retirement of the top leader — usually the First or General Secretary of the Central Committee of the Communist Party — and the emergence of a new leader who consolidates his power.

There are a number of reasons why succession is such a highly important phenomenon in Soviet political development and at the same time so difficult for both participants and outside observers to evaluate and analyze. No predetermined tenure of office is ascribed to the position of the top leader. The terms of the office are not predetermined; the attributes of rights and obligations, and of power and influence are not standardized for all the occupants of the office; nor is the manner by which the incumbent of the top leadership position relinquishes his post. Most importantly, the degree of unpredictability and uncertainty in the procedures of selecting a new leader and in the process of consolidating his position is much higher than in other societies. This situation injects a more pronounced element of unpredictability and uncertainty into the entire Soviet political process than is characteristic of its operation in "normal" times.

The consequences for the political system are profound. The probabilities of deep personal and policy conflicts within the top leadership structure are increased. The possibilities for resolving these conflicts in more extreme ways are maximized. The tendency toward large-scale personnel changes within the leadership itself and among the top elites and bureaucratic hierarchies is heightened.

The period of succession offers a high potential for destroying the bureaucratic inertia of the departed leaders and for changing the inertial drift of their policies. It is a period with a high potential for ferment, for greater responsiveness to pressures, real and anticipated, for broadening political participation and for opening the political process. In sum, the succession, aside from its own intrinsic importance, acts as a catalyst for pressures and tendencies that already exist within society, but that previously had limited opportunity for expression and realization.

The approaching succession is in many respects different from those in the past. It combines a number of characteristics that make it fraught with very important political implications in the 1980s, for better or for worse from the Western point of view. The most important of these characteristics is the fact that it almost inevitably will combine the replacement of the top leader with that of the core leadership group and a large part of the central elite, and with the beginning of a generational turnover among the Soviet elites. Moreover, the age-cohort characteristics of the Soviet leadership and elites is such that the replacement will not only be massive, but will also be compressed in a relatively short time-span.

The importance of the passing of the top leader himself should not be minimized. Leonid Brezhnev has led and dominated Soviet political life for longer than all but one leader in Soviet history. Yet, if it were only a matter of the replacement of the top leader, the potential for stress and change should not be overemphasized. If one can say that the period of his leadership has represented the maturation of the Soviet system and embodied its stability, one can argue similarly that his departure could be handled at least as routinely as the post-Khrushchev succession. His very style of leadership, his very achievement and legacy, could most likely make the fact of his departure in contrast to that of his predecessors less crucial in terms of the accompanying ferment, opening for change, and political vacuum.

However, first of all, given the required combination of qualifications for the top leadership position and the extraordinary circumstances that at present severely limit the field of available candidates, the man selected for the top post, if Western evaluations are correct, will certainly be an interim leader. The most important question is: Who will *succeed* Brezhnev's immediate successor? Thus, we will in all probability see two successions to the top leadership in the 1980s.

Secondly, the coming succession will inevitably bring about a massive replacement of the top leadership stratum and will compress the turnover into a relatively short time-span. It will especially affect the inner core of the stratum, those leaders who worked together for such a long period of time. This massive replacement will occur because the most striking characteristic of this group as a whole is its advanced age; it is the oldest in Soviet history and of any preceding succession, and, incidentally, the oldest leadership group of any industrial society.

If the advanced age of this leadership group has no precedent in Soviet history, there is also no precedent for the clustering of such a high proportion of the members of this group in the highest age bracket. What is even more important from the point of view of our inquiry is the lack of a precedent for the described type of age configuration on the eve of succession.[12] The approaching succession will not consist simply of the replacement of the top leader, but also of a massive replacement and reshuffling within the highest echelons of the Soviet hierarchy during the coming years.

Thirdly, the age structure of the top leadership, far from being limited to that group, is very nearly mirrored in the case of the central elite, both with regard to its advanced age and the clustering of this age group. Its massive replacement in the 1980s is unavoidable.[13]

Fourthly, and finally, massive replacements at the levels of the top leadership and central elite, which would certainly accompany the second if not the first stage of the upcoming succession, will most probably produce political conflicts over policies and procedures, regardless of who the new leaders will be. Such a prospect is especially likely because, on the one hand, the succession will follow a period of extraordinary and long-lasting stability, during which policy differences were submerged in the name of unity, stability, and compromise, and bold initiatives, especially on the domestic scene, were lacking. On the other hand, the succession will come at a time when the Soviet Union will begin to face difficult economic choices, when the possibility of satisfying diverse interests and pressures through compromise solutions will become more difficult than in the Brezhnev period.

The massive turnover of elites, especially when compressed into a short period of time, can in itself be significant in determining the formation of the styles and behavior of the new leadership and elites. By breaking the official routine inculcated in a bureaucratic and centralized structure, by undermining the inertia of a set style of work, by disrupting the existing and fixed, informal ties, and by weakening the interests vested in long-established substantive policies, this turnover will provide a setting that will facilitate the elaboration of changed modes of political behavior. Yet the key questions still remain. Will the newcomers be favorably disposed to make use of the opportunity to be different? How much pressure will they exert and in which direction in order to change the policies and processes of the Soviet government? In short, just how different will they be from their predecessors?

The most important question, then, is whether and to what extent the succession and the subsequent replacement of large segments of the elites will coincide with the emergence of distinctive differences between the incoming group and the outgoing group, irrespective of the diverse personalities within each group. Such a coincidence will occur in the upcoming succession. A generational change within the Soviet elite will take place concurrent with the imminent replacement of the top leader and a large part of the highest leadership, because a large proportion of the new elite will have entered politics after Stalin's death.[14] Thus, the approaching succession, whatever the form and results of its initial stage, will involve the eventual replacement of the top leadership and central establishment on a scale much greater than the previous two successions and will be combined with a higher generational turnover of the Soviet political elite. This conjunction of successions in both the broad and the narrow sense has no precedent in Soviet history. It will be a political development of longterm duration and significance.

The stability and longevity of the existing pattern of leadership has been conditional on two internal structural factors: gradualism in major policy changes and gradualism, to say the least, in personnel replacement. We do not know whether the first condition will still obtain during the succession or whether, after the cycle of cautious adjustment and traditionalism of the last decade, the mood of the leadership and the elite will swing toward revitalization and major reforms, just as the frozen conditions of Stalin's Russia were replaced by the flux of the Khrushchev period. Certainly, during the succession, the nature of this tendency will depend ultimately on whether the Soviet leaders and elite will become more perceptive of the pressures and frustrations stemming from failures or dangers at home or abroad. We do know, however, that the second condition — gradualism in personnel replacement — will most probably not persist.

The effects of the pressures created by the forthcoming successions, in combination with the political issues that will become a part of the political agenda, may become significant. They may and, in all probability, will lead to the destabilization of central policy making which, in a highly centralized polity such as the Soviet Union, may have very important consequences. The destabilization will involve a breakdown of the consensus among the leadership and the elites, the intensification of factional struggles at the top and middle levels of the bureaucracy, possible realignments of existing alliances, the exploitation of policy issues for the accumulation of power by individual leaders and groups, and sharp twists and turns in central policies.

One may expect all these developments to be generated within the political system itself or to be triggered by issues that are directly political in nature.

12.3   Expected Economic Developments in the Eighties

How will the economic problems which the Soviet Union is facing influence this political situation? In the 1980s, the impact of these problems on the political system and its relation with the society will be extremely significant, probably more so than it was in the 1970s. There are important disagreements among the specialists about what the economic environment of the Soviet Union will be in the 1980s. The art of predicting the future is no more certain in the field of economics than it is in the field of politics. Moreover, the discussion among economists demonstrates that they are far from agreement about the *degree* to which the economic trends expected in the Soviet Union during the 1980s will be realized. It is precisely this question of degree that is a matter of central importance for political analysis. Yet, on the basis of a survey of Western and Soviet economic literature, and on the basis of numerous discussions with Western and Soviet economists in academia and in government, a political scientist can at least form a clear impression about the *main tendencies* of development of the Soviet economy in the 1980s and about the direction of the trends already discernible today.[15] On this basis, I can advance a few cautious, consensual propositions, which have a very high probability of being realized.

(a) In the 1980s the Soviet Union will face a secular decline in the growth rates of its economy, involving almost all sectors. Extensive development has reached such limits that retention of the high growth rates of the past is no longer possible. Even without the intervention of other negative factors, and assuming no decline in the quality of the traditional Soviet leadership of the economy, the growth of the Soviet GNP in the 1980s will be approximately 2.5% per year.

(b) The Soviet political-economic system of management, pricing, and incentives is ill-prepared to maximize the possibilities for intensive growth. The conditions for a relatively rapid change to intensive growth would require fundamental changes in the economic-political system and are unlikely to be accomplished in the foreseeable future. Among the steps already undertaken by the Soviet government to counteract the declining tendencies of growth, none will have any major impact on the Soviet economy.

(c) The Soviet Union in the 1980s is also facing unfavorable demographic trends. There will be a rapid decline in the growth of new labor resources. The situation will be further complicated by changes in the composition of the new labor force, which will be overwhelmingly non-Russian.

(d) The Soviet Union will face an energy balance unfavorable to its economic growth. This is especially true in the production of oil. It is a matter of major contention among economists as to how much this production will decline. Even if one rejects the worst-case scenarios, which predict an eight million barrel-a-day oil production, the decline will be sufficient, it seems, to impose major constraints on the Soviet economy and, under certain conditions, limit Soviet ability to utilize fully the existing economic capacities.[16]

(e) The enormous agricultural investments of the Brezhnev era have produced limited and, at best, uncertain results. Soviet agriculture in the 1980s will remain a highly volatile sector of the Soviet economy. Moreover, because of the decline in secular growth in other sectors, the unavoidable agricultural fluctuations will have a growing influence on the size of the Soviet GNP.

There can be little doubt that the Soviet Union faces a difficult economic situation in the 1980s. How difficult it will be is a matter of conjecture. According to the worst-case scenarios, it will be a period of low growth intermingled with economic stagnation. But even according to the more optimistic scenarios under which the range of Soviet growth will be about 3–3.5%, the Soviet Union will face an economic crunch far more severe than anything it encountered in the 1960s and 1970s.

The differences between the optimistic and pessimistic scenarios are, as I said before, a matter of great importance; they signify the difference between a difficult situation and a deep crisis. Moreover, the choice of the most likely scenario from among the various scenarios is not the result of a belief in more or less precise and complex computations (or, for a political scientist, the result of his faith in the skills of one or another group of economic forecasters) but a result that should include unpredictable elements, such as vagaries of nature, or, as importantly, the seriousness and the effectiveness of counteracting policies adopted by the Soviet leadership. Even assuming that the more optimistic scenario better reflects the reality of the 1980s, what will be the effects of the growing economic difficulties on the Soviet political scene? (Needless to say, those effects will be magnified many times if the worst-case scenarios become a reality.) The two most important consequences will be a sharply increased sectoral and regional competition for scarce resources.

Historically, the Soviet political system, in both its micro- and macroeconomic decision-making levels, became used to scarcities. Shortages and stringencies went hand in hand with a process of highly uneven development, concomitant with rapid overall economic growth. Moreover, during the time of extreme stringencies and particularly sharp one-sided development, the system was guarded by a mass terror apparatus introduced by Stalin and dismantled by his successors. In the post-Stalin period, the relatively high rates of growth, while still sustaining an uneven development, assured the flow of new resources to all sectors of the economy, including those totally neglected during the Stalin era.

A consideration of the changes made in the structure of the Soviet party-state over the last decade, together with a look at the policies pursued by the Brezhnev leadership and with the general political mood in the Soviet Union will support a conclusion that at first glance appears somewhat paradoxical. The establishment of the collective leadership, and the policies of this leadership in organizational, political, economic, and ideological matters led, in its first few years, to an improvement in the power position, or in the satisfaction of the group interests of almost all institutional segments of the Soviet political elite. In the years that followed, the positions of these institutional segments were not noticeably undermined. While probably no elite group welcomed all the changes or all of the policies, a rare situation has emerged. The fears of almost all elite groups have been allayed and their desires satisfied to some extent. This was the basis of the impressive stability of the elites and the elite–leadership consensus, and the basis of the social peace without terror during the Brezhnev period.

While accustomed to shortages, stringencies, and scarcities, the Soviet political system is not accustomed to dealing with prolonged periods of low overall economic growth. With regard to the question of how to stimulate higher growth rates and how to overcome critical bottlenecks, the Soviet system is ill-prepared to deal with these problems for exactly the same reason that growth has declined: the decline in the effectiveness or the exhaustion of the extensive factors of growth. Its past experience in responding to economic difficulties was based on a *mass mobilization* of *extensive* factors of growth. Its response today must be based on a *measured mobilization* of *intensive* factors of growth: a policy not of the sledgehammer but of the scalpel.

On the distributive side of the equation, the Soviet political system, on both the mass and the elite levels, will also have difficulty in dealing with prolonged low overall rates of growth. This difficulty arises from three sources: (1) the absence of a paralyzing mass terror that would make all sacrifices and demands palatable; (2) the existence of powerful organizational groups and issue-alliances in the decision-making apparatus, complicating the implementation of cutbacks and restraints; and (3) the emergence of new social constraints to such cutbacks and sacrifices.

The sharply increased sectoral competition for resources and the dilemmas that it will create are not difficult to envisage. The policy of guns, butter, and growth — the political cornerstone of the Brezhnev era — is no longer possible. To keep the rate of growth in *military spending* at the level of the last decade would necessitate a redirection of resources from other sectors. Yet in light of past Soviet behavior, growing Soviet insecurity in the face of what the USSR considers the formation of an alliance of the United States, NATO, and China, the new fear of encirclement, the growing determination of the United States to change the existing balance of military power, and the breakdown of the SALT talks, it is highly unlikely that any configuration of Soviet leaders will decide to slow down the growth in military expenditures, let alone cut actual arms spending, without a major breakthrough, both in the Sino-Soviet dispute and in the SALT negotiations, or without a major disavowal of their global ambitions. If arms spending will continue at the same pace as in the past decade, the burden of keeping the Soviet military juggernaut in shape will be felt to a much greater extent than at any time in the Brezhnev era. It will constitute one of the key internal political issues of contention.

Another issue of contention, with an even greater potential for divisiveness, concerns the whole complex of questions connected with the rate of growth and direction of Soviet nonmilitary *investment resources*. Throughout their history, the Soviets have persistently kept their share of investment in their national economy and the levels of investment growth very high. How difficult it is to maintain such high rates of investment under the present circumstances is demonstrated by their recent decline. Yet, if there ever was a period when the Soviet Union needed a very large scale of investment in their national economy, it is now. It is difficult to envisage how the Soviet leadership can lessen the difficulties brought about by the limitations of the existing pattern of extensive growth without keeping the percentage of investment in the economy, and even the growth rate of investments, at high levels.

Intensive growth, given Soviet conditions, requires a thorough modernization of the industrial plant and major investments in new technology. Without a very major, persistent, and creditable effort in this direction, there is little chance that any increased productivity of Soviet labor will overcome the downward pull of the exhaustion of the extensive factors of growth.

The energy problem facing the Soviets in the 1980s will demand mammoth and prolonged investments, which have already begun. The development of the Siberian oil and gas reserves will constitute a new, major, and increasing burden on Soviet investment resources. Yet it is a burden that the Soviets cannot avoid and can neglect only at their own peril.

The achievements of Soviet agriculture under Brezhnev — the

growth in grain production, but especially the stress on meat production — was accomplished by an extraordinarily large expenditure of capital. Yet even with those very large-scale expenditures, Soviet agricultural productivity remains uneven from year to year, and the agricultural sector continues to be highly volatile. The Soviets have not yet devised a way to assure the present inadequate levels of agricultural production without infusions of long-range massive investments. In the coming decade, when the Soviet economy slows down, the divisive pull of conflicting claims concerning investment resources will increase to a level unknown during the Brezhnev era.

One of the most significant accomplishments of the Brezhnev era was the prolonged and substantial growth of Soviet *mass consumption*. The last fifteen years saw a growth in the standard of living of the Soviet people that was rapid by any — but especially the Soviet — standard, particularly in the area of durable consumer goods. What was especially notable about this achievement is that it was accomplished simultaneously with the rapid growth of Soviet military power. In other words, the Brezhnev leadership had both a gun *and* a butter policy. The stability of the Brezhnev period in the absence of terror can be explained to a large degree by the leadership's basic ability to satisfy more fully the demand of the Soviet consumer, whether a member of the working or of the professional class. Whatever the deficiencies of the Soviet consumption system (and we all know that they still have a very long way to go to reach the level of their Western counterparts), the Soviet citizen — worker, peasant, and professional — became accustomed to an uninterrupted upward trend in his wellbeing and has become more demanding in what he expects from the government in terms of goods and services in the Brezhnev period. While we must stress, again, that there does not exist in the Soviet Union anything resembling a revolution of growing expectations, the Soviet citizen seems to expect more in terms of services and consumer goods than he expected in the past. In view of the major demands placed by other sectors on Soviet resources in a period of a declining growth rate, it will be extremely difficult for the Soviet leadership to continue its policy of consumption growth even at the lower rates of the latest Five-Year Plan.

It is probable that even without major agricultural disasters or a particularly severe energy crisis, Soviet consumption may stagnate in the 1980s. The consequences of such stagnation are difficult to assess, but they will be undeniably negative. First of all, it is difficult to see how the crucial goal of increasing Soviet productivity can be attained without an increase in remunerative incentives for the labor force. Secondly, the stagnation of the standard of living will be experienced by the working population at a time when the other basic avenue of betterment, upward mobility, also shows a downward tendency. Thirdly, and most importantly, neither the Soviet leaders nor we know how the Soviet industrial working class will react to such changing circumstances. The post-Stalin experience of a society without terror was at the same time the experience of a society with a steadily increasing standard of living.

The desire of the Soviet population for a better life never, to our knowledge, became unmanageable, never assumed the form of a revolution, or of a vicious spiral of rising expectations. In the words of one sociologist (Hollander, 1973, p. 388), "The key to the stability of the Soviet system lies in its management of expectations rather than in the power of the KGB." Yet one should not forget that it was a "management of expectations" that went hand in hand with a sometimes rapidly but certainly steadily growing rate of consumption. This growth in consumption may have been a substitute for and a damper on growing political expectations.

To what extent the existing police controls and the management of mass expectations can keep the Soviet working class docile during a prolonged stagnation of their living standards is an open question. One has the impression that the specter of "Polonization" of the Soviet working class is never far from the minds of the Soviet leadership and the elites.

Of course, not only the intersectoral competition for resources, but also the intrasectoral competition for specific priorities will be much sharper. Specific elite constituencies represent each of these priorities in the national leadership.

The sharply increased inter- and intrasectoral competition for resources will be intertwined with and complicated by a stronger, more tenacious competition for resources among the various regions of the Soviet Union. Such a competition was a normal facet of Soviet politics already in the 1970s. The budgetary squabbles and the fights concerning plans of development, between the Ukraine and Siberia, among the other republics, and among the oblasts of the RSFSR, can be documented very well.[17] They are certain to increase in the 1980s.

The difficult political decisions of how to distribute the available resources are complicated by the following underlying economic dilemma. The European part of the Soviet Union has a well-developed infrastructure, and investments there would be relatively cheap and would provide a higher return. But at the same time, the European part of the Soviet Union is on the verge of exhausting new labor resources and it is poor in natural resources; Central Asia has large labor resources, but is poor in natural resources and has a limited infrastructure, especially in the technological sector. In addition, the political claim of Central Asian elites in seeking new resources would probably be fiercely debated by the dominant Slavic elites. The regions in the RSFSR where the natural resources are located are extremely poor in labor resources and lack any infrastructure; investments will be extremely expensive and difficult to manage.

The regional struggle for resources will be conducted during a period of succession in the Soviet leadership. During such periods, the influence and the political clout of the provincial and the republican elites traditionally increases. The regional leaders assumed the role of real kingmakers during Khrushchev's rise to power.[18] The potential for playing good politics instead of good economics is quite considerable.

12.4   Internal Political Consequences of the Economic Problems

The first and foremost response of the Soviet authorities to the difficulties that they face — the economic difficulties and the volatile political situation — will be to strengthen the authoritarian character of the Soviet party-state. The stress on law and order, social discipline, unswerving loyalty, nationalism, and on punitive and restrictive measures taken against antisocial behavior may become more pronounced than they were in the 1970s. Not surprisingly, the role of the secret and not-so-secret police may increase. When the situation becomes difficult, when no prospects for rapid improvements are available, and when a tightening of the belt is in order, the natural response of the Soviet leadership — whether old or new — is to tighten the screws of political and social controls. The capacity, the potential, and the instruments for such policies already exist.

It is an open question whether such a policy will be sufficient to keep the lid on under the conditions of new and prolonged economic stringencies. In my opinion, one may expect an increase in the restlessness of the industrial labor force. It is a clear possibility that, after the Soviet population realizes that it will experience a prolonged decline in the growth of its living standard, the basic stability of the Brezhnev period and the compact between the elites and the workers may be weakened. An increase in labor unrest, work stoppages, industrial demonstrations, and growing communal dissatisfaction is a clear possibility. The degree to which this will occur may have an effect upon the allocation policies adopted by the government.

In the new situation, the nationality problems may also become aggravated. This may be the case regardless of the kind of policy adopted by the leadership vis-a-vis the non-Russian regions. The ability of the Soviet leadership in the 1970s to contain the nationality problem is partly related to the fact that the nationality areas enjoyed a quicker growth than the rest of the country, especially growth in the standard of living and in the conditions of the rural sector. If the party, under conditions of greater stringency of resources, decides to slow growth of those regions, the relative peace in Soviet relations among the nationalities will weaken.

But, in this respect, the leadership's manner of responding to the dilemma posed by the new demographic trend in the growth of Soviet labor resources will be the most important issue on the Soviet agenda concerning the nationality question in the 1980s. The need to exploit the increasing non-Slavic labor resources — particularly Central Asian — poses two options for the Soviet policy makers: first, migration of the non-Slavic labor force to the industrial areas; second, an increase in the industrial development of Central Asia. Both options carry a major destabilizing potential for nationality relations in the USSR. In my opinion, the second option is more likely to be adopted. If this is the case, aside from the major investment costs that it will involve, it may produce, in some Central Asian regions, social displacement associated with rapid industrialization. It will also involve a rapid and massive influx of Russian bureaucrats into those regions, creating dissatisfactions and tensions between the local, native elite and the newcomers. The non-Russian republics, including those of Central Asia, have only recently developed native administrative and technical cadres sufficient to administer their own affairs without Russian help. Under these conditions, local elites' awareness of their own identity may increase and provide difficulties for the central authorities.

12.5   Foreign-Policy Consequences of Political and Economic Developments

I would like also to suggest a number of consequences of the interaction of political and economic developments in the Soviet Union in the 1980s for Soviet behavior and development that seem to be directly linked to Soviet foreign policy, and that could have important international repercussions.

First, one has to mention the impact of those developments on the military policy of the Soviet Union, especially on the question of the growth of military expenditures. The pressures will be clearly contradictory. On one hand, pressures will exist to keep up the further expansion of Soviet military might at any cost. In an era of declining achievement in other fields, Soviet military might will remain a showcase of achievement and glory of the Soviet state to an even greater extent. Moreover, military power will remain the dominant foreign-policy resource of the Soviet Union for a long time to come. The inertia of the planned military build-up will maintain the importance of the likelihood of high military spending, as will the fact that in periods of succession and interim leadership the Soviet military establishment traditionally carries a greater political weight as the potential ally of many contending factions and groups.

On the other hand, pressures will develop to limit the growth of the Soviet military and to respond positively to timely and realistic proposals from the West for arms limitation and cutbacks. In a time of declining growth and increasingly scarce resources, the costs of a continuing military build-up at rates similar to those of the 1970s will impose a burden on the Soviet economy and polity much greater than at any time during the seventies. Pressures for cutting the military budget, unknown since the early 1960s, may develop among sectors of the leadership and elite groups that are competing for resources. The

ties between the military-industrial complex and the upcoming generation of Soviet elites are much weaker than they were with the elites of
the Brezhnev era. The symbiosis of the Soviet political and military
leadership, characteristic of the Brezhnev period, may break down or
weaken considerably. However, one should not have any illusions
concerning this matter. If any configuration of Soviet leadership
considers the basic security interests of the Soviet Union to be
endangered or the hard-won parity with the West put into question, it
will respond with a military build-up, regardless of the costs and
sacrifices such a build-up will entail. This is why the slogan of regaining
military superiority over the Soviet Union, so recently popular among
some politicians and analysts in the United States, seems unrealistic.
Yet what I am suggesting is that in the difficult and volatile political and
economic environment of the 1980s, the new Soviet leadership's
response to the demands of a continuous military build-up may not be
as automatic — almost a conditioned reflex — as it was in the 1970s.
Much, of course, depends upon the behavior of the American
leadership, which must steer the difficult course between the absolute
need to safeguard American strengths and interests and the need to be
sensitive to new Soviet dilemmas and to avoid belligerent actions.[19]
Second, the Soviet expansionism and international aggressiveness,
which have lately caused so much concern in the West, are rooted
almost entirely in political and strategic reasons that will almost
certainly continue to push the Soviet Union on a quest for greater
influence and power in the international arena. In terms of global
interests, the Soviet Union is, after all, still a young and expanding
power, fighting for its place in the sun. This in itself would pose an
extremely difficult challenge to the West in the 1980s. What is
disquieting, however, is that, in the 1980s, a new economic rationale
may be added to the traditional reason for Soviet expansion.

In light of Soviet economic and political difficulties, I see two main
directions for such expansionism. The first direction is the obvious one
and has to do with possible attempts to solve increasing oil problems
through adventurism and expansionism in the Persian Gulf area. I do
not at all suggest an inevitably forthcoming Soviet invasion of Iran. In
the present circumstances, such an adventure seems almost out of the
question. But circumstances do change, and in the long run a Soviet
effort to secure Iranian oil cannot be excluded. The Iranian revolution
is now only in its initial stages. The direction of and timetable for its
further development and settlement are impossible to predict. If, for
example, the irredentist pressures within Iran lead to a disintegration
of the country and of its central government, or if leftist forces
sympathetic to the Soviet Union assume an important voice in the
Iranian revolution, the temptation for a Soviet intervention into
Iranian affairs cannot be excluded, and would be maximized by
internal economic and political difficulties.[20]

Expansionism into the oil regions is not, of course, the only way in
which the Soviet Union may try to solve its energy problem by means

of foreign policy. A much more likely development may consist of overtures to friendly Arab regimes (e.g. Iraq, Libya) and the intimidation of conservative regimes (e.g. Saudi Arabia) for the purpose of buying large quantities of oil and of negotiating barter agreements. If successful (and they may well be), these agreements will be of a clearly political nature, because the *civilian* goods involved in the barter will not be competitive on the world market.

The second direction is less obvious, but it may grow in importance in the 1980s: the temptation to exercise increasing political and military pressures on Western Europe in order to secure high technology on favorable terms for the Soviet economy. The Soviet need for Western technology, know-how, and especially credits, will, in all probability, increase in the 1980s. The pattern of recent Soviet–American relations indicates that there is a rather limited likelihood that the United States will serve as a key partner of the Soviet Union in mutual economic enterprises. The economic role of Western Europe within the Soviet Union will probably increase substantially. In order to serve its political and economic interests, Soviet foreign policy in the 1980s will probably try to decouple the detente with the United States from detente with America's Western allies. The mood in Western Europe today and probably in the 1980s as well is such that, despite growing signs of Soviet expansionist ambitions, the political classes are determined to have detente with the Soviet Union at almost any price: without meaningful Soviet concessions on military matters and without a change in the direction of the military balance in Europe itself. This seems to me to be particularly true not only for France, but for the most influential European country, West Germany.[21] In its efforts to improve economic relations with Western Europe and to split further the Western alliance, the Soviet Union may adopt a tactic of taking a hard stance vis-a-vis the United States regarding strategic global military and political matters, with which the Europeans have little concern, while at the same time taking a concessionary attitude towards European questions. But the Soviet policy of a European carrot does not exclude a simultaneous policy of a European stick. The Soviet leadership cannot help noticing that the European attitude toward its increasing military power is rather conciliatory and that European resistance to Soviet political pressures is weaker than ever before. In any case, one can expect, for political and economic reasons, an increased Soviet attention to the European theater and an increased Soviet need to expand its economic relations with Western Europe.

Third, the political and economic situation of the Soviet Union may have significant and troublesome effects on its East European empire in the 1980s. Soviet problems will coincide with similar ones in some of the East European countries, particularly in the key country, Poland. The Soviet commitment to maintain control of its East European empire is unshakeable and will certainly remain so in the foreseeable future. But, due to Soviet economic difficulties and to the arsenal of tools relied upon in controlling Eastern Europe, intimidation through naked force and the threat of the use of such force assume the greatest importance. Nevertheless, the economic interdependence of Eastern Europe and the USSR is in a decline. In the 1980s, the Soviet Union will have a much more limited supply of economic muscle with which to maintain its hold on Eastern Europe. A situation will develop where although most East European countries will remain *politically* dependent on the Soviet Union, they will become increasingly *economically dependent* on the West. A crucial question here is the degree to which the Soviet Union will be forced to cut its oil deliveries to Eastern Europe, and to let the East European nations compete for available oil resources on the international market. The East European countries are ill-prepared for such competition. Their exportable resources and hard-currency reserves are very limited. The cut-off of Soviet oil deliveries, even if partial, may undercut the already precarious economic situation of many East European countries, particularly that of Poland. In Eastern Europe, serious economic difficulties have a way of being directly translatable into social and political unrest and internal destabilization, to which the Soviets are very sensitive. One cannot help but expect a strong movement for basic economic reforms that may be unacceptable to the Soviets in a country such as Poland. Until now, the Soviet Union has been quite lucky in its dealings with its East European empire. The revolts, rebellions, unrest, and reform movements in those countries were almost always isolated in one country. It may well be that in the coming decade Soviet luck will run out and that the Soviet leaders will have to concern themselves with increasingly restive elites and populations in more than one East European country at the same time.[22]

Fourth, the expansion of foreign trade, the infusion of advanced foreign technology, and the attendant questions of credits, foreign indebtedness, and corporative arrangements will acquire an importance for the Soviet leadership surpassing even that of the 1970s. The significance of this question may appreciably influence Soviet foreign policy. Is the infusion of foreign technology and economic cooperation with advanced Western nations regarded by Soviet leaders as a temporary affair or as a long-range commitment? It is unanswerable a priori. The answer depends partly on their ability to find domestic resources to arrest the decline in productive growth, which, even with major economic reforms, is very unlikely; and partly on the consistency and the cost to the Soviet Union of Western policies and cooperative arrangements.

The importance of the infusion of foreign technology for the Soviet leadership lies not only in its own intrinsic value, but also in the largely misguided belief that technological imports will diffuse throughout the economy and significantly influence Soviet domestic technological progress without major reforms. The need for foreign technology and know-how, and especially the much greater need for credit arrangements in the difficult 1980s, is not in itself a sufficient or overriding factor in determining future Soviet foreign policy. But one may presume that this need will, by means of the domestic political process, exert an additional pressure to restore detente with the United States, and to preserve and enlarge the economic relations with American and European allies, partly through intimidation and partly through concessions.

Fifth, the struggle for the top leadership position under conditions of economic stringencies and the efforts of the first victorious contender to solidify his position and to amass all the attributes that a strong leadership may create, at some points in the 1980s, a situation where foreign adventures may look attractive. The basis for the struggle for top leadership in the Soviet Union consists almost always of the building of alliances within the Politburo and among various elite groups, and of the advancement of a program in which such alliances are often transitory, temporary, and tactical in nature. From the long-term perspective the problem of getting the country moving again and of providing an attractive program for resolving its economic difficulties will be one of the two cornerstone-building alliances that will carry a contender to power. (The other cornerstone is the development and expansion of Soviet influence in the international arena.) On a short-term basis, the utilization of a timely opportunity for a foreign adventure as a rallying point for a leader, giving him the chance to show his mettle, cannot be excluded. This is especially true in a situation where the military establishment will be one of the key groups courted during the succession struggle, and at a time when the reserves available for the long-range improvement of the economic situation and for quick and flashy economic fixes will be in short supply.

Sixth, in the political-economic situation that will prevail in the Soviet Union in the 1980s, the Soviet leadership will search for methods in order to counteract the effects of the decline in the growth and possible stagnation in the population's standard of living, to counteract the frictions that will develop among the elites, to justify the greater sacrifices that will be demanded, and to mobilize the population for greater productivity. In all probability, coercive means will be used for these purposes, in a less-restrained manner than in the 1970s. An additional possibility has to be mentioned. It is highly probable that, in the political mood of the 1980s, the Soviet leadership will try to increase its persuasive, normative efforts for the purpose of mobilization and sacrifice. One such effort may be, clearly, an attempt to recreate the atmosphere of a besieged fortress, to mobilize around the theme of external enemies, and to resort increasingly to a xenophobic public mood. Détente, particularly when it concerns relations with the United States, is dead at this point. The harsh conditions and demands that will prevail in the Soviet Union in the 1980s are not conducive to the mood of détente. While I do not think that the need for an "external enemies" syndrome will constitute a crucial obstacle to the restoration of some sort of détente if countervailing pressures are present, it still seems to me that this need will be an important factor in determining Soviet international behavior, particularly in the Soviet relationship with the United States and China.

The pressures of the economic situation on Soviet politics and policies, especially on foreign policy, will often be very contradictory. Yet their main effect will be to reinforce those tendencies which have been generated within the political system itself, and which would already have been present even without the influence of these economic issues. The economic realities of the 1980s will sharply strengthen the tendency toward a markedly less benign political climate than that of the 1970s, and will contribute immensely to an environment of sharp international competition, confrontation, and discord. Without a doubt, the difficult economic issues will constitute, in my view, the most important content of the disputes, conflicts, and realignments that will accompany the Soviet successions.

12.6   Chances for Structural Change

The complex economic difficulties and the uncertain conditions of succession and strife will most likely create strong pressures for change in the Soviet system. The major dilemma of the Soviet system, as Gustafson (1921) has remarked, is how to impose effectively new priorities on old structures and processes. What are the chances that, under the pressure of necessity, a successful attempt will be made to transform those old structures and processes? If by transformation one means market socialism, or anything even close to it, as for example the Hungarian model, then the odds are overwhelmingly against it.

First of all, the vested political and economic interests against such a change are very powerful, and will remain so even when the turnover of elites and leadership will be very high and when the pressure to get the country moving again will intensify. It is not only the political and economic apparatus that is afraid of the potentially negative political repercussions of such reforms, as well as the central planners and central bureaucracies whose amassed powers would decline, but also the medium- and low-level managers and technocrats, who learned to live with the system and who are trained and experienced only in how to work within the system as it now exists. One author has aptly remarked: "After sixty years of experience with a socialist economy run by government agencies ... nearly everyone seems to have found ways to turn its shortcomings to individual advantage (Schroeder, 1979, p. 313)."

Second, as the preceding discussion suggests, the initiative and the push for such reform in the face of widespread and strong opposition at all levels will not come from a powerful coalition from below, but, to be even modestly successful, will require an energetic initiative and constant push from above, from a strong leadership, especially from the First Secretary.

An oligarchic leadership, that by its very nature has to act by means of bargaining, trade-offs, and compromises, is ill-suited for initiating and executing major reforms of structures, procedures, or even policies. Thus, the future of such reforms in the Soviet Union depends to a large degree on the inclination of the top leader, and on his ability to pursue and realize those inclinations.

One cannot expect such an initiative and push from the Brezhnev leadership during its last days in power. But can a more innovative leadership emerge during the coming succession? Even assuming that the emergent leader becomes convinced of the necessity for such far-reaching reforms — and this is a very big assumption — it will take a long time until he is strong enough to make serious efforts in this direction. If our predictions about the upcoming successions are correct, Brezhnev will be replaced by an old interim leader, probably Kirilenko, who will not have enough time to infuse the *nominal* position of First Secretary with the *real* powers required to push for a radical reform.[23] Such a leader may emerge only during the second succession; but if the past is any indication, it will take him, too, several years to amass the necessary powers. Moreover, in the process of amassing such powers it is unlikely, in the light of the powerful forces allied against radical reforms, that he could do it under the banner of radical reform.

The conditions necessary for the top leadership to implement reforms are complex and contradictory. They require a divided leadership, from which — through the process of purges — a strong leader with a loyal, personal base of support will emerge. It is unlikely that such a leader can achieve this position of power while promoting radical reforms. However, once he achieves a position of strength, he must reverse his position and wholeheartedly promote these reforms.

Third, when describing the Soviet political system under Brezhnev, we stressed the growing dependence of the leadership and the elites on the expertise and advice of professional groups. Cohen (1980) is probably quite right when he stresses that the spirit of reforms and liberalism is not dead in the USSR, but only dormant under the Brezhnev leadership. It is among the professional groups, especially among the economists, that one would probably find the greatest support for radical reforms. In light of their significant advisory capacity, it is very important that these groups unify the pro-reform advice that they provide to the leadership. (This, incidentally, was the case in Hungary, and was an important factor in explaining the implementation of their radical reforms.)

Yet in the Soviet Union, these groups are fragmented and divided in their orientation as to what kinds of reforms are needed. Moreover, they are easily manipulable by the various factions in the leadership and by the various sectoral and functional segments of the elites. If they continue to speak with a divided voice, they will neutralize their potential for influencing liberal reform. Both the proponents and opponents of reform in the leadership will be able to find or to mobilize the support of experts for their respective positions.

Fourth, one should not minimize the purely economic and technical difficulties of a thorough reform in the Soviet Union. Such a reform would most certainly involve a temporary decline in production and in productivity, would significantly increase the need for real incentives, and would entail the enormous task of reeducating the labor force and the management. The difficult transitional period from the old to the new system would require very large reserves of capital and consumer goods.

Yet, the 1980s will be a period when the Soviet economy will be stretched to its outer limits, when planning will be especially taut, with reserves dwindling. Radical reform will be extremely difficult in such conditions. Here we again have a contradiction: in order for a reform to be initiated, an enormous pressure stemming from actual failures of the economic system must be present, but in order to be successful, a reform requires a cushion of economic performance that will subsidize the transition. The political risks of attempting a thorough reform during a period of economic decline must seem very great to the leadership, probably graver than the consequences of living with the old system and its shortcomings.

Fifth, Eastern Europe very often is regarded as the funnel through which Western influence and reformist tendencies are channeled to the Soviet Union. There is undoubtedly some truth in this assertion. But more often, Eastern Europe is a thoroughly conservative influence on the *domestic* Soviet scene. The very fact of the Soviet Union's total commitment to the existence of Eastern Europe as its imperial sphere of influence and the potential instability of the East European domestic and international situation, exerts a powerful pull on Soviet domestic policy. The more restless Eastern Europe becomes, the more conservative this influence.

When attempting a thorough — or even timid — liberalizing reform in the Soviet Union, any configuration of Soviet leaders must anticipate its potential impact upon Eastern Europe. Such an impact could only encourage the forces of liberalism in Eastern Europe, the ascendency of which, in the final analysis, would endanger Soviet rule over its East European empire. In these circumstances, it would require an enormously confident — or desperate — Soviet leadership to initiate internal policies that would undermine its external holdings. The situation in Eastern Europe in the 1980s will probably be very difficult economically, explosive socially, and precarious politically, and will influence the Soviet leadership in an antireformist direction.

Sixth, the multinational and nominally federal nature of the Soviet system also exerts a conservative influence on reformist tendencies among the Russian leadership and elites. A radical liberalizing reform would undoubtedly diffuse economic authority within the Soviet Union. Such a diffusion — if the pay-offs are sufficiently high — might be tolerated by the leadership with regard to the Russian elites and subelites, but much less so with regard to the non-Russians.

The Soviet leadership during the Brezhnev period was able to achieve, through a shrewd carrot and stick policy, relatively peaceful relationships between the centrally dominant Russian elite and the non-Russians. But the balance of those relations is quite precarious, and is susceptible to destructive conflicts on both the mass and the elite levels. To institute a thorough liberalizing economic reform in the Soviet Union could — and probably would — upset the existing balance. In the minds of the Russian leadership, it may be tantamount to the acceptance of the restructuring of the relationship between the nationalities in the Soviet Union, a price that I highly doubt they are willing to pay, and a danger that they would hardly like to face.

Seventh, a thorough liberalizing economic reform in the Soviet Union would constitute an overhaul of the system that would require a basic change in the working style of the leadership, elites, and subelites, and would have — as mentioned before — a significant impact upon other spheres of Soviet life. One does not embark on such an extremely serious undertaking, to say the least, without being convinced that the old system is really played out and absolutely needs to be abandoned. This is not the case with the old leadership and the elites, and there is no compelling evidence that the emerging leadership and elites share such a conviction.

It seems that the old leaders and elites believe in the basic viability of the system in which they work, and which they directed throughout their lives. They are realistic people who see many of the system's operating shortcomings, and they are trying to improve its functioning. But they have not lost their faith in the correctness of the system, and are not ready to abandon it. Although they are no longer as naively optimistic as Khrushchev once was, their outlook on the present and the future of the entire system remains basically optimistic.

We know little about the potential of the new younger leaders and elites.[24] We know that they are much less patient with the deficiencies of the system than are the present leaders. We know that they would like to see the country moving again. We cannot exclude the possibility that there are individuals among them who are fed up with the system. But the basic impression one gets is that they do not feel that the potential of the system is exhausted. They believe, instead, that the system is not run well and that they will be able to run it much better. Such an attitude is typical of successors in all countries. Only when they themselves are running the system do they acquire the conviction that it is the system that is the problem. This, of course, may happen, but it is equally possible that by the time they assume the leadership, they will have become so involved with the day-to-day operations of the system and its innumerable emergencies that they will be incapable of devoting their attention to any overview of the system, its basic flaws, and its long-range future. What is suggested here is that it is extremely difficult for the question of the basic viability of the system to enter the political agenda in the Soviet Union. But without it, a thorough overhaul of the system is unlikely. An item of related importance is how the Soviet leaders and elites perceive the long-range outlook for the Soviet economy, its prospects beyond the 1980s. There are indications that they are conscious that the 1980s will be difficult. But the question is whether they regard it as a temporary aberration that can be corrected by the turn of the decade. Their evaluations in regard to the energy problem might be decisive here. If they consider that the energy outlook in the 1990s will be much improved over the 1980s, it will create an additional argument against attempting to revamp the system.

Eighth, a key obstacle to a successful liberal reform in the Soviet Union concerns the mechanism of the reform: i.e. the usual pattern in which reforms have developed under the conditions of post-Stalinist Soviet politics. To be effective, the introduction of far-reaching reforms must be carried out across the board without hesitation, and not in a piecemeal fashion. But until the effects of such a reform are tested and recognized as effective, the necessary determination and persistence will most likely be lacking.

As we know from past Soviet experience, the response to this contradiction tends to be largely self-defeating. From the various possibilities for reform, the leadership selects a compromise solution that will cause the least disturbance and will require the least cost and effort. Instead of introducing an across-the-board reform with determination, they try it on an experimental basis and on a limited scale. Consequently, the results of the reform are far from conclusive and even disappointing, an outcome that, in turn, fuels the arguments of opponents who prevent its further implementation. The leadership reverts to the traditional way of doing business and continues to tinker half-heartedly with the system. Instead of transforming the traditional economic system, the well-intentioned, piecemeal reforms are absorbed and changed by the system. This political mechanism explains the inherent stability of the traditional economic system and the inherent instability of reform efforts in the Soviet Union.

To sum up, I am arguing that, despite the unprecedented pressures brought about by the difficult economic situation and the very rare opportunities offered by the coming succession, the odds are against a successful, far-reaching reform that would move in the direction of market socialism. I am not arguing that reforms in this direction will not be attempted. Rather, such reforms will be hesitant, limited in scope, and ultimately absorbed by the system instead of changing it. Furthermore, other types of reforms are more likely to emerge.[25]

One of the most likely courses of development is that the Soviet leadership will continue to tinker with the economic system, intensifying its "organizational" and "mobilizational" reforms. Characteristically, such reforms try, and sometimes succeed, in improving a particular aspect of the system or in counteracting a shortcoming but do not abolish the system's basic parameters. In other words, they do not approach the "watershed" dividing this kind of reform from one that would change the system. The late Polish economist, Janusz Zielinski (1978, p. 6), suggested: "It seems that such a watershed does exist and turns on the abolition (or retention) of direct planning at plan executants' level. It is extremely important to notice that abolition of direct planning at plan executants' level means also the abolition of the *ratchet* principle — planning (and rewarding) from the achieved level — with all its far-reaching negative economic consequences, both in the sphere of plan construction (bargaining for low-high input-output plans, falsifying information in the planning process) and its implementation (keeping "reserves" for use in the next planning period, which means keeping actual enterprise productivity permanently below what its managers *know* to be possible)."

There is a further probability that another option also will be selected. It may occur at the margins of the official economy, and be directed at relieving the pressures on the consumer sector. As suggested by Berliner (1980, p. 108), this would entail "a NEP-type reform which retains the centrally planned economy largely intact, but allows for a flourishing small-scale private sector. Since it entails no retreat from central planning but, rather, the development of a new secondary economy that offers some promise of spurring new initiation and innovation, it may be entertained seriously by the proposed succession leadership."

Finally, we should consider the prospects of devolution of power in the Soviet Union and its influence on reform activities. In some areas, the stability of the Soviet system is narrowly based. It overrelies on political controls, administrative organization, and conscious manipulation and interventionism; and it is still not entirely based on socialization, tradition, and internalized controls. In the difficult conditions of the 1980s, one cannot exclude the possibility that large segments of the Soviet working class will imitate the behavior of the Polish workers and acquire a major influence on the economic policies of the Soviet government. Such an outcome, however unlikely, need not signify a turn in the Soviet leadership's policy towards basic reform of the economic system. It will certainly necessitate a change in the distributive policies in favor of the consumer, but it may go hand in hand with the retention of the traditional economic system. The experience of East European countries demonstrates that the average worker who fights for a greater share in the system is not a proponent of fundamental economic change.

In sum, we can anticipate no fundamental changes in the Soviet Union during the 1980s despite intense and divisive discussions concerning economic reforms, a number of organizational policy initiatives, experimentation with the economic structure, and significant political conflict.

Some might consider my analysis of the prospect of systemic change unduly pessimistic. The confluence of conditions necessary for such a transformation may seem too restrictive and exaggerated to those who think in terms of a historical process that *has* to transform Communist societies. It is, of course, always easier to predict continuities on the basis of past experience. The difficulty in foreseeing discontinuities lies exactly in the fact that past patterns of behavior and past experience can give little guidance to the analyst. But perhaps, as Gregory Grossman has suggested, we are still failing to appreciate fully the complicated conjuncture of favorable circumstances necessary for a successful transition of the Soviet system beyond its traditional mold.

12: Notes

1 An extensive discussion of this subject appears in Bialer, 1980.
2 For a discussion of the deep conservatism of Soviet society, see especially Cohen, 1980, pp. 11–31.
3 Consider the following data:

Age Groups, Soviet Oligarchy, 1980 (percentages)

	older than 70	60 and younger
Politburo		
Full Members	50	7.1
Alternate Members	22.2	33.3
Central Committee's Secretariat	50	20
Presidium, Council of Ministers	35.7	7.1
Presidium, Supreme Soviet	26.6	33.3
All of these	28.4	25.5

4 For a discussion of this subject, see Bialer, 1976, pp. 25–55.
5 See, for example, Hough and Fainsod, 1979, pp. 529–55.
6 For a similar point of view, see Odom, 1976. For a point of view that questions this conclusion, see Kolkowitz, 1967, pp. 11–35.
7 For the role of experts in Soviet policy making see Rennek, ed., 1977, especially the chapter by Lubrano; Holloway, 1970; and a paper by Solomon, 1971.
8 For a broader discussion of this subject, see Hollander, 1973.
9 A different type of explanation appears in Hough, 1975.
10 For a broader discussion of the changing role of foreign policy in Soviet decision making, see Bialer, ed., 1981, especially the chapter by Hodnett.
11 A detailed discussion of the succession is contained in a special issue of the *Journal of International Affairs*, devoted to this subject, especially the chapters by Bialer and Rush.

12   *Average Ages of Soviet Oligarchy in 1952, 1964 and 1980*

	1952	1964	1980
Politburo			
Full Members	55.4	61.0	70.1
Alternate Members	50.9	52.8	62.5
Central Committee's Secretariat	52.0	54.1	67.0
Presidium, Council of Ministers	54.9	55.1	68.1
All of these	54.1	56.0	66.8

13 A breakdown of the ages of leaders in the Central Government and Party Elite in 1978 goes as follows:

Average Age, 1978

Council of Ministers	65.0
Ministers	65.1
Chairman, State Committees	64.2

Central Party Secretariat
　Head of Departments　　　　　　　　　　63.6

Armed Forces
　High Command　　　　　　　　　　　　65.0
　Political Directorate　　　　　　　　　64.0

All of the Above　　　　　　　　　　　　64.7

Ministry of Foreign Affairs
　Highest-Ranking Bureaucrats　　　　　64.5

Leaders, Communication and Culture　　62.1

Trade-Union Officials　　　　　　　　　58.6

14　The post-Stalin generation is represented to only a very small degree in the central leadership and elite in 1980, comprising only 12.5% of these leaders, whereas the Great-Purge, World War II, and late-Stalin generations make up 67.5%, 10% and 10% of the members, respectively. However, on the republic and provincial levels, the post-Stalin generation already has significant representation among the leadership. Listed below are the data indicating the percentage of post-Stalin-generation representatives who occupy top positions in various institutions in 1978.

Percentage Post-Stalin-Generation Representatives in 1978 on Republic and Provincial Levels

Presidium, Council of Ministers (RSFSR)　　　　　　　　　　　　　30.7
First *OBKOM* Secretaries (RSFSR: Russian provinces)　　　　　　32.0
Second Secretaries of Republics (Russians)　　　　　　　　　　　45.4
Republic and First *OBKOM* Secretaries (Ukrainians and Belorussians)　47.6
Russian First *OBKOM* Secretaries in Non-Russian Areas of RSFSR and
Non-Slav Republics　　　　　　　　　　　　　　　　　　　　38.5
All Above-Mentioned Institutions　　　　　　　　　　　　　　36.9

75% of the leading Party and Soviet officials in Moscow and Leningrad are in this category. Among the elites of the seven non-Slav republics of Uzbekistan, Tadzhikistan, Kirgiziia, Latvia, Lithuania, Estonia, and Moldavia, the average age and representation of the Post–Stalin Generation runs as follows:

	Average age	Post-Stalin generation (%)
Republic Secretaries	55.3	27
Presidium, Council of Ministers	55.7	33.3
Central Committee, Department Heads	51.1	46.1
Members, Council of Ministers	54.2	35.2
Raykom and *Gorkom* First Secretaries	47.8	66.0
Rayispolkom and *Gorispolkom* Chairmen Including Some Chairmen of Provinces	47.2	73.2

For a more detailed discussion of this subject see Bialer, 1980, Chap. 6.

15　These tendencies and trends are well represented in *Soviet Economy in a Time of Change*. A number of papers by the CIA also provide a basis for an analysis of the Soviet outlook for the 1980s. They are Testimony of Adm Stansfield Turner, 1979, and the various CIA papers (1977–9) listed in the references. A representative nongovernmental study of the prospects for the Soviet economy in the 1980s can be found in Hunter, ed., 1978.

16　See the chapter by Bond and Levine in this volume for conditions under which the energy question will not act as a cumulative factor depressing Soviet growth and may, therefore, not limit the utilization of existing economic capacities.

17　See, for example, Dienes, 1971; Hooson, 1972; Spechler, 1979.

18　See, for example, Leonhard, 1975, pp. 237–41.

19 For a description of an American policy that will both safeguard US interests and avoid belligerence, see Legvold, 1980.
20 A scenario that envisages Soviet expansion into the Persian Gulf appears in Geiger and McMullen, 1980.
21 For a discussion of the present state of the European alliance see Stern, 1980.
22 See, for example, Connor, 1980; Kux, 1980.
23 On the difference between the nominal and real powers of the first secretary, see Hodnett, 1980.
24 An evaluation of the new upcoming elite is contained in Bialer, 1980, pp. 103–35.
25 It is not clear at all whether even a radical reform that will both change the success indicators and dismantle direct planning will largely solve Soviet problems of management flexibility and innovation as long as the full-employment constraint is present. And to move or decisively weaken this constraint in the Soviet-type economy is almost impossible, as the experience of the 1968 reform in Hungary has shown. This skepticism about the effectiveness of even radical reforms is most forcefully expressed by Granick, 1976. See especially his discussion of the Hungarian reform on p. 316.

12: References

Agnelli, Giovanni, "East-West Trade: A European View." *Foreign Affairs* **58**, 5: 1016–33, Summer 1980.
Berliner, Joseph S., "Economic Prospects." In Robert G. Wesson, ed., *The Soviet Union: Looking to the 1980s*. Stanford, Calif.: Hoover Inst. Press, 1980.
Bialer, Seweryn, "The Soviet Political Elite and Internal Developments in the USSR." In William E. Griffith, ed., *The Soviet Empire: Expansion and Detente*. Lexington, Mass.: Lexington Books, 1976.
Bialer, Seweryn, "Succession and Turnover of Soviet Elites." *J. Internat. Aff.* **32**, 2: 181–200, Fall/Winter 1978.
Bialer, Seweryn, *Stalin's Successors: Leadership, Stability and Change in the Soviet Union*. New York: Cambridge Univ. Press, 1980.
Bialer, Seweryn, ed., *The Domestic Context of Soviet Foreign Policy*. Boulder, Col.: Westview Press, 1981.
CIA, "Prospects for Soviet Oil Production." ER 77–10270. Washington, DC, April 1977.
CIA, "Soviet Economic Problems and Prospects." ER 77–10436U. Washington, DC, July 1977.
CIA, "USSR: Long Term Outlook for Grain Imports." ER 79–10057. Washington, DC, Jan. 1979.
CIA, "SOVSIM: A Model of the Soviet Economy." ER 79–10001. Washington, DC, Feb. 1979.
CIA, "Simulations of Soviet Growth Options to 1985." ER 79–10131. Washington, DC, March 1979.
Cohen, Stephen F., "The Friends and Foes of Change: Reformism and Conservatism in the Soviet Union." In Stephen F. Cohen, A. Rabinowitch, and R. Sharlet, eds, *The Soviet Union Since Stalin*. Bloomington, Ind.: Indiana Univ. Press, 1980.
Connor, Walter D., "Dissent in Eastern Europe: A New Coalition?" *Probl. of Communism* **24**, 1: 1–17, Jan/Feb. 1980.
Dienes, Leslie, "Issues in Soviet Energy Policy and Conflicts Over Fuel Costs in Regional Development." *Sov. Studies* **23**, 1: 26–58, July 1971.
Geiger, Theodore, and McMullen, Neil J., "Soviet Options in the Persian Gulf and U.S. Responses." *New Internat. Realities* **5**, 1: 7–17, July 1980.
Granick, David, *Enterprise Guidance in Eastern Europe: A Comparison of Four Socialist Economies*. Princeton, NJ: Princeton Univ. Press, 1976.
Gustafson, Thane, *Brezhnev's Reform: Political Implications of the New Soviet Agricultural Policy*. New York: Cambridge Univ. Press, 1981.
Hodnett, Grey, "Succession Contingencies in the Soviet Union." *Probl. of Communism* **24**, 2: 1–21, March/April 1975.

Hodnett, Grey, "The Pattern of Leadership Politics." In Bialer, pp. 87–118, 1981.

Hollander, Paul, *Soviet and American Society: A Comparison.* New York: Oxford Univ. Press, 1973.

Holloway, David, "Scientific Truth and Political Authority in the Soviet Union." *Government and Opposition* **5**, 3: 345–67, Summer 1970.

Hooson, David, "The Outlook for Regional Development in the Soviet Union." *Slavic Rev.* **31**, 3: 535–54, Sept. 1972.

Hough, Jerry F. "The Soviet Experience and the Measurement of Power." *J. of Politics* **37**, 3: 685–710, Aug. 1975.

Hough, Jerry F. and Fainsod, Merle, *How the Soviet Union is Governed.* Cambridge, Mass.: Harvard Univ. Press, 1979.

Hunter, Holland, ed., *The Future of the Soviet Economy 1978–1985.* Boulder, Col.: Westview Press, 1978.

Journal of International Affairs. Special Issue on Leadership Succession in Communist States. Fall/Winter 1978.

Kolkowitz, Roman, *The Soviet Military and the Communist Party.* Princeton: Princeton Univ. Press, 1967.

Kux, Ernst, "Growing Tensions in Eastern Europe." *Probl. of Communism* **24**, 2: 21–37 March/Apr. 1980.

Legvold, Robert, "Containment without Confrontation." *For. Policy* no. 40: 74–98, Fall 1980.

Leonhard, Wolfgang, *The Kremlin Since Stalin.* Tr. E. Wiskeman and M. Jackson. 2nd ed. Westport, Conn.: Greenwood Press, 1975.

Lubrano, Linda L. "Soviet Science Specialists: Professional Roles and Policy Involvement." In Rennek, ed., pp. 59–85, 1977.

Odom, William E. "A Dissenting View on the Group Approach to Soviet Politics." *World Politics* **28**, 4: 542–67, July 1976.

Rennek, Richard B., ed., *Social Scientists and Policy Making in the USSR.* New York: Praeger, 1977.

Rush, Myron, "The Problem of Succession in Communist Regimes." *J. Internat Aff.* **32**, 2: 169–79, Fall/Winter 1978.

Schroeder, Gertrude, "The Soviet Economy on a Treadmill of 'Reforms'." In *Soviet Economy in a Time of Change,* 1979.

Solomon, Peter H., Jr. "A New Soviet Administrative Ethos." Paper, prepared for Northeastern Slavic Conf. of the AAASS, Montreal, Quebec, May 1971.

Soviet Economy in a Time of Change. Vols I and II. Papers, Joint Econ. Comm., US Congress. Washington, DC: Govt. Printing Office, 1979.

Spechler, Martin C., "Regional Developments in the U.S.S.R., 1958–1978." In *Soviet Economy in a Time of Change,* Vol. I, pp. 141–63, 1979.

Stern, Fritz, "Germany in a Semi-Gaullist Europe." *For. Aff.* **58**, 4: 867–86, Spring 1980.

Turner, Adm. Stansfield, "Allocation of Resources in the Soviet Union and China." Testimony before Subcommittee on Priorities and Economy in Government, Joint Econ. Comm, US Congress, Pt. 5, pp. 2–72. Washington, DC: Govt. Printing Office, June 1979.

Zielinski, Janusz G., "On System Remodeling in Poland: A Paradigmatic Approach." *Soviet Studies* **30**, 1: 3–37, Jan. 1978.

Appraisals

In commenting on the **Bond-Levine** paper, **Michael Manove** began by noting two advantages of large, disaggregated, economy wide models. First, the explicit mathematical nature of such a model requires its developers to put down all of their procedures in black and white, for all interested analysts to examine. The modeling methodology forces internal consistency on the modelers. Model inputs, model structure, and model output must be represented precisely. The vague equivocations of the oracles of old are banished from this process. Secondly, because such models are implemented on high speed computers, an enormous volume of computations can be carried out quickly and inexpensively. This means that the economic forecasting process can utilize a wealth of detailed information. Modelers can attempt to structure their model so as to characterize real-world institutions accurately without being tightly constrained by their ability to perform complex calculations.

But large economic simulation models carry with them a substantial capacity for misuse. Perhaps most important of all is what one might call the Wizard-of-Oz effect. Remember when Dorothy and her friends were first granted an audience with the Wizard. He appeared before them as a gigantic disembodied head with a deep thundering voice. The very earth seemed to quake as he spoke. But on their second meeting, Dorothy's little dog Toto pulled aside a curtain to reveal the true Wizard-of-Oz: a little man with a small voice who controlled the frightening head that appeared above them and spoke the imposing words. Somehow, the little man inspired a lot less confidence than the magnified illusion he had created.

Unfortunately, large computerized models often have characteristics similar to those of the Wizard's gigantic head. Sometimes models merely repeat the opinions and prognostications of their very human developers, but give those opinions and prognostications an inappropriate scientific aura. I believe that SOVMOD, as it is used in the Bond-Levine paper, may inadvertently have had this effect.

Another danger of large simulation models is that the quantity of detail incorporated in the model can obscure the essential structure of the economic relationships being represented. Large models can have a secret inner life that is not understood even by the model developers. Unobserved features of the model structure, created as part of the global outcome of an extended process of model development, can drive the model in unpredictable ways and substantially determine its output. This danger can be minimized if the model is organized around a small number of principal relationships that have been explored analytically.

In long-run models it is important to capture the real-world feedback mechanisms that prevent the economy from "running wild." If a model omits important feedback mechanisms, its long-term projections may become ludicrous. Representing the feedback mechanisms of the Soviet economy is especially difficult since free-market prices, the most important feedback device in Western market economies, are not available in the USSR. As a result, Soviet feedback mechanisms are probably a lot more subtle, unpredictable, and difficult to quantify than are their Western counterparts.

In the absence of a detailed explanation of SOVMOD's structure, and the lack of very many feedbacks in its relationships, Manove expressed concern about interpreting its results. He wondered whether the growth rates of consumption and investment in model projections reflected the outcome of a complex series of computations from widely disparate structural elements of the model, or whether these growth rates were merely assumptions derived through a simple transformation of a few parameters entered by the modelers. If the latter were the case, the recorded results would merely be the opinion of the modelers with some boom and thunder behind it à la Wizard-of-Oz.

Manove wondered, therefore, if it wouldn't have been more useful to make a long-term projection for the Soviet economy using an extremely simple and easily understood model. With such a model, readers would be able to trace the derivations of the important aggregate indicators over time and decide for themselves whether the derived results seemed reasonable. Once the simple model had been formulated and analyzed, a large scale model like SOVMOD would become a useful tool for obtaining more detailed understanding of developments in individual sectors.

Judith Thornton noted that she had criticized the initial version of SOVMOD as an example of "neo-Babylonian science," referring to Stephen Toulmin's *Foresight and Understanding*. In that book, Toulmin contrasts the practice of astronomy by Aristotle and the Babylonians. Aristotle, he says, practiced theory without prediction. The Babylonians pursued prediction without theory. The Babylonians were quite successful in applying elaborate calculations to the move-ments of the planets and to lunar eclipses but far less successful in applying their methods to earthquakes and plagues of locusts. They had no theory to explain why their methodologies worked well for eclipses and badly for plagues. Their predictions represented a new and interesting set of data that needed to be explained by some adequate theory.

Similarly, the long-run version of SOVMOD before us offers a new and interesting set of data simulating what the Soviet economy might look like in the future if certain key assumptions were to hold. These key assumptions, however, especially those relating to resource-allocation policy decisions, deserve strengthening. In SOV-MOD, the behavior of economic decision makers is largely unex-plained.

The structure of SOVMOD IV pictures a Soviet economy that functions under an inflexible, inertial process whose main attribute is its internal consistency. Such structural change as does occur is imposed exogenously by the analyst. But the structure of industrial output does not respond to anything going on elsewhere in the economy. Not only in industry, but overall, SOVMOD is driven largely by scale and income effects; it is almost devoid of substitution effects. For short-run forecasting, this may be a good description of the actual behavior of Soviet planners, but in the longer run, the economic system does generate information on costs and availabilities. Policy choices are made in response, and, with some measurable lags, substitution responses occur.

Calling, as did Manove, for greater attention to feedbacks, Thornton suggested a number of potential devices for introducing more structural response into SOVMOD. Where there are already balancing equations in the model, it should be possible to use excess demand in the balance as a determinant of subsequent resource allocations or rates of growth in consuming sectors. The growth of livestock herds, for example, could depend on some measure of earlier grain balances. The choice of fuels used in electric power generation could depend on the relative size of domestic availabilities net of exports. For some variables, one could specify measures of desired demand so that comparison between desired and actual values could generate responses in the system.

Thornton observed that if, in fact, Soviet planners only operate with rules of thumb, and do not respond endogenously to the signals the system is generating, then one's expectations about their prospects for future growth and technological progress must be more pessimistic than if they are seen as having some capacity for structural adjustment to changes in their environment. If policy responsiveness exists, it should be built into SOVMOD. So far, SOVMOD has been a very successful model because it has incorporated plausible assumptions that reflect a consensus of people working in the field. If its assumptions can be grounded in tested empirical relationships, SOVMOD can shed its Babylonian origins.

Abram Bergson's analysis stimulated numerous observations throughout the conference, beginning with those of **Stanley Cohn**. He began by noting that, following Denison's approach, Bergson used differential incomes as proxies for educational attainments. However, in applying this approach to the postwar Soviet record, such an assumption may overstate the relative qualitative contribution of educated labor, since educated manpower has been inefficiently utilized. The most conspicuous example is the widespread assignment of graduate engineers to duties requiring lesser skills. Such inefficient manpower use stems from the imbalance in educational policy which has provided training for too few technicians and, apparently, excess professionals. This imbalance appears to be worsening with time. If this conclusion be accepted, the adjustment for labor quality has been overstated, which means that the upward trend for TPE and TPP is higher than as computed by Bergson.

The USSR has no doubt benefited from economies of scale in the postwar period, but Cohn noted that such economies are offset by the continued propensity of Soviet firms to integrate backward to protect themselves against supply shortages, thus negating gains from scale economies. The quantitative effect of this offset, Cohn agrees, may be minor.

As for the impact of weather on productivity improvements, Cohn suggested that the agricultural sector be separately analyzed and that the result be factored in to an economywide measurement. If the resulting adjustment were smaller, the effect would be to show lower gains in technological progress proper over the 1970–75 period.

Explanation is even harder than measurement. Why has the Soviet trend in technological progress and total factor productivity fallen so markedly compared to the experience of the West? The absence of major innovations may be involved, but this has applied to Western Europe and Japan as well as to the USSR.

Although there were declines in the growth of factor productivity in France, Germany, and Italy in the 1960s, there was a sharp rise for Japan and an increase for the US. After 1970, there were declines for all major market economies, except for the sluggish UK and US. However, nowhere was there deceleration of the magnitude experienced by the Soviet economy, after adjusting for business cycle patterns in the West. Why was there such a unique deterioration in Soviet performance?

Two reasons suggest themselves. One lies in Robert Solow's distinction between embodied and disembodied technological progress. Although the Western European and Japanese economies, like the USSR, experienced a reduction in embodied technological progress, they were cushioned in their declining growth performance by continued disembodied technological progress due partly perhaps to institutional and organizational shift. The Soviet economy does not seem to have experienced any very consequential corresponding gains in the period studied.

A second possible explanation lies in the much reduced rate of growth in capital investment, since investment is the carrier of embodied technological progress. When a capital stock grows slowly it gets older, and the aging of Soviet capital has accelerated in recent years. One notes a similar correlation for the major market economies between rates of growth of capital investment and trends in the age and productivity of both the capital stock and total factor productivity.

Looking ahead, Cohn saw forces at work which could depress the rate of TPE to even lower levels than those envisaged by Bergson. One force involves the shift in investment toward capital-intensive energy and transportation, both of which involve capital-output ratios roughly twice as high as those for other industry. Since such investments are not particularly labor saving, the impact on TPP would be clearly unfavorable. The USSR intends to replace obsolescent assets with capital that would be labor saving, especially through mechanizing previously manual auxiliary industrial processes. However, innovative replacement decisions must overcome the long-standing constraints that have made enterprise directors wary of introducing new processes and/or products. In addition, the inability of the machinery branch of heavy industry to develop and produce the high technology equipment required must be reversed. Prospects are dim for both of these imperatives.

The drastic rise in the opportunity cost of petroleum and natural gas will compel premature retirement of energy-inefficient capital equipment in the USSR, and its replacement by technologically more advanced equipment that can be more energy efficient. Even without scarcity prices, Soviet planners will be acutely aware of the cost consequences if such a policy is not followed. The accelerated pace of capital obsolescence means a rise in the incremental capital-output ratio. Its impact on technological progress is to forestall an even more drastic decline in TPP which would occur if energy constraints lead to reduced rates of utilization of energy-inefficient capital assets. At the same time, the necessity to increase the rate of investment to sustain the existing level of output will mean a further reduction in TPP.

If the USSR pays appreciable attention to fending off environmental damage and to investing in industrial health and safety measures, investment requirements would be increased, relative to the past, and unless measures of output included the social welfare gains from such investments, the effect on TPP would be negative. Given the dimension of Soviet efforts, though, the impact would be minor.

The Bergson paper generated extensive conference discussion. In speculating about Soviet prospects and limiting factors, which factors are systemic and which might yield to policy changes? **Judith Thornton**, among others, noted the importance of Bergson's point that an upward trend in resource costs would offset possible gains in the quality of Soviet labor and capital. **Gregory Grossman**, among others, stressed the operating impact of tautness, long gestation periods, uncertain supplies, etc., as factors that might be altered by sustained policy changes.

David Granick drew attention to the difficulties of interpreting the troubled period in the first five or ten years after World War II. Masses of unskilled labor were on hand, with very low productivities. He doubted the statistical significance of evidence from the 1950–60 period and suggested that attention be focused on the 1960–75 period instead.

Granick also reported some comparative analysis of Western European experience which cast doubt on the "ease" with which a relatively "backward" economy could raise labor productivity by catching up. His analysis indicates that French and West German productivity doubled between 1955 and 1977 as a percentage of American productivity during the same year, while British productivity remained unchanged as a percentage of US productivity. However, the *difference* between the French-German productivity growth rate and the American-British growth rate did not decline, as would be expected if catching up were easily carried out. Over the period of these two decades, the Gerschenkron effect does not seem to have operated on industrial productivity or on technological progress proper among these four countries. This result suggests that caution is advisable in applying the same effect to the USSR over the same period without having specific grounds to differentiate the Soviet from the West European case.

In commenting on **Murray Feshbach**'s paper, **Paul Gregory** put recent Soviet experience into a broader frame of reference by comparing it with the experience of other countries. The Soviet economy, as Feshbach shows, now confronts a serious labor adjustment problem. Within one decade, the rate of growth of the able-bodied population declined from a healthy 1.7% per year (1970–80) to a rate of .35% per year (the projection for 1980–90). One should note that a number of capitalist countries have had to adjust to declines of this magnitude in the growth rate of the able-bodied population. The US growth rate declined from 2.5% annually (1880–1900) to 1.8% (1900–30) to 1% (1930–70) and to about one-half of one percent over the last decade. The US and most other countries making the transition from a rapidly expanding able-bodied population to one that is expanding slowly have had several decades of preparation. The Soviet Union has not.

A characteristic feature of Soviet economic development is that it has speeded up the process of structural change. Structural shifts that took half a century in the West have occurred in one decade in the USSR. Witness, for example, the rapidity of the shift of labor out of agriculture, the rapid decline in the consumption share of national income, and the rapid rise of the heavy industry share in the 1930s. The same appears to be true of the demographic transition, not only in the USSR but also in Eastern Europe. The demographic transitions of the planned socialist countries of Europe began in the late 1950s and were in effect completed by the late 1960s. The direction of demographic change was by no means unusual, nor was the magnitude of the change; it is the rapidity of the change that is noteworthy.

Gregory observed also that the level of anticipated Soviet birth and death rates, and thus the expected growth rates of population and the able-bodied population for the rest of this century appear similar to what other countries have gone through. The similarity extends to regional population migration problems.

Gregory noted that Western and even planned socialist economies have been able to generate relatively high rates of output growth with labor forces that were expanding at rates of one-half of one percent per year or even less. The implication is that a flexible and adaptable Soviet economy might be able to do the same. Perhaps, however, cultural barriers and/or a lack of economic incentives for regional migration will make it harder for the Soviet economy to enjoy similar results.

Barney Schwalberg put Feschbach's labor force data into a longer term framework and subjected them to detailed analysis. Over the half-century from 1950 to 2000, the USSR displays sharp cyclical swings in the annual percentage rate of growth of the population of able-bodied ages. Superimposed on a mild, long-term downward trend are two strong cycles with peaks at 1954 and 1975 (the troughs coming around 1960 and 1986). These cycles are caused by twice-lagged effects of fertility changes (16 years to entry into, and 35–40 years to exit from, the able-bodied ages), interacting with the effects of past demographic shocks. The changes have been swift and drastic: between 1954 and 1960, the absolute increment to the able-bodied population went from plus 2.6 million to minus 150,000 people; between 1976 and 1986 the increment will drop from plus 2.7 million to 300,000.

Such sharp swings in the demographic base of the labor force would pose problems for any industrial economy. The record shows that these manpower swings have, in fact, occupied the attention of Soviet planners, and that adaptive policies have been developed in order to insulate favored sectors of the economy against the variability of manpower supply. This has been accomplished by imposing much greater variability on other branches, which have served, in effect, as buffers.

Citing a 1975 study by Yaremenko and others, Schwalberg suggested that the agricultural sector serves as a reservoir for labor in periods of rapid able-bodied population growth, releasing people in times of shortage. Construction acts as an intermediary, absorbing unskilled, largely male, labor from agriculture during periods of labor plenty, providing a couple of years of basic industrial experience, and then releasing labor to other nonagricultural branches during periods of less ample manpower supply. Agriculture and construction thus absorb the major swings in labor supply, serving somewhat as reservoirs when the working age population is growing rapidly relative to demands in other sectors. They accept sharply reduced growth rates, or absolute decreases, when aggregate labor supply tightens.

In the rest of the economy, we see different degrees of variability of employment growth, corresponding to familiar notions about Soviet priorities. For example, the trade and housing series shows more variability than do the industry or transport series. Within industry, light industry shows great variability while machine building and metal working shows almost none. Thus the burden of variability in labor supply appears to have been distributed among the sectors of nonagricultural economic activity in a systematic, purposeful manner.

Schwalberg suggested that the regime's priorities have been associated, not only with differences in wages, but with differences in both private and collective rewards of employment—housing, amenities, special services, etc. These appear to have been set, not at equilibrium levels, but at levels that create queues for positions in higher-priority branches. In periods of labor slack, queues lengthen and are concentrated in the low-skill, labor intensive jobs in high-priority branches. Constraints on labor mobility and on hiring in other branches apparently are applied to this end. When labor is scarce, these constraints are relaxed. Thus the State's monopsony power, imperfect as it is, serves to assure the "leading branches" of both adequate numbers and qualitative preference, i.e. selectivity based upon excess numbers of applicants. Despite sharp swings in aggregate manpower supply and the absence of a flexible way system, priorities are maintained with respect to labor input.

Schwalberg pointed out that during the 1970s there was very rapid growth of the able-bodied population (1.72 percent per year between 1970 and 1979), suggesting that what the USSR calls "reserves" accumulated at different places in the economy even though there was concern about labor shortage. In the 1970s the State sector as a whole was able, during a period of supposed manpower stringency, to over-fulfill employment targets by substantial margins. Even with this over-fulfillment, total employment grew much less rapidly than did the able-bodied population: employment grew by 16.4 million man-years between 1970 and 1979, while able-bodied population rose by 22.2 million persons.

If the 1970s represent a protracted period of exceptionally rapid growth in the potential labor force, leaving a legacy of "reserves", then the current sharp cyclical reduction in additions to the able-bodied population will not limit Soviet economic expansion to the extent that is often supposed. Nevertheless, drawing on these labor reserves in the 1980s is likely to pose more challenging allocative problems than those encountered in the 1960s. This time the reserves are not primarily in agriculture but already in the cities—in industrial and service jobs and in schools of various sorts. If major shifts are required as labor markets tighten, difficulties will arise. It is one thing to move young people out of agriculture and construction into better paying, higher status, urban jobs in industry and the services. It is another to move them from urban industrial and service jobs to other such jobs, often in less desirable locations. Nevertheless, Soviet manpower prospects for the 80s and 90s may not be as grim as the rapid shrinkage in increments to the able-bodied population might suggest. The economy enters this period with reserves—quantitative and qualitative—associated with adaptations to the preceding phase of the manpower cycle. Moreover there is pervasive redundancy within the State sector of the economy. Over the next 20 years, even without fundamental changes in economic organization, labor market conditions are likely to change in ways that will raise the aggregate effectiveness of the Soviet labor force.

Moshe Lewin reinforced **D. Gale Johnson's** critical analysis of Soviet agriculture with the perspective of a social historian, stressing the many ways in which the problems generated by collectivization in the

1930s remain unsolved today. Despite the achievements and improvements of the last two decades, agriculture continues to squander enormous resources without contributing its expected share to the national income and without providing an adequate, assured diet for the Soviet people. The Soviet countryside is caught in a vicious circle of low productivity, causing low income, causing low motivation, causing low productivity, and this circle is compounded by another in which rural incomes grow but shortages of consumer goods in rural areas undermine material incentives and thus inhibit productivity gains.

Lewin reviewed the many suggestions for improvement found in current Soviet discussions, noting their stress on the desirability of reduced "bureaucratization." It is difficult to be sanguine, however, about the prospects for progress. Outright pessimism remains unproven and facile optimism is of no interest. The complexities of the problem are better understood than ever before, though, and Soviet society may yet find ways to forge a new deal with the Soviet peasantry.

James Millar augmented Johnson's analysis by discussing a number of factors that may operate in the 1980s to stimulate more significant reform than Johnson anticipates. He began by noting several changes over the last quarter-century that have either contributed to, or reflected acceptance of, economic rationality in agricultural policy. These include the development of cost accounting procedures permitting unambiguous determination of the profitability or unprofitability of different agricultural products and of agricultural output as a whole; the collection and publication of statistical data; and the broad "reformation" that has allowed economists to update interpretations of Marx and Lenin, and to analyze economic performance. These changes have been essential for the reconstitution of academic economics in the USSR. Only the biological sciences suffered as severely as economics from Stalinism, and agricultural sciences, of course, suffered on both counts.

Another group of changes is illustrated by Brezhnev's first major address on agricultural policy (March 1965), which reveals an acceptance of economic rationality and a determination to accelerate favorable changes in price policy, procurement procedures, off-farm input supplies, investment allocation, and the provision of material incentives. Many improvements ensued. The Brezhnev-Kosygin regime's acceptance of substantial imports of agricultural products was even more important. Large imports of feed grains reflect an acceptance of economic rationality in achieving meat consumption targets. Khrushchev initiated the policy, but Brezhnev and Kosygin have permitted imports at levels that no analyst ever suspected would be possible in earlier years, and net imports of food products, including substantial imports of meats, vegetables, and fruits, may even expand. Tolerance of the "second economy" represents also a victory of economic rationality over revolutionary rhetoric, as does the general relaxation of constraints on private subsidiary agriculture that has continued (with intermittent interruptions).

Much economic irrationality remains in Soviet agricultural policy, and it would be unrealistic, in Millar's view, to expect doctrinal constraints to disappear altogether. The most striking example, and one that severely handicaps rational price policy today, is official adherence to stable retail prices for agricultural products. Official sanction for the enormous subsidies that many agricultural products require of the state budget today is another significant change that no one anticipated. It stems from a political commitment that no recent Soviet leader has been willing to challenge. Given the mood of the Soviet public regarding retail price increases, and the unhappy experiences of other East European countries with food-product price increases, a solution is not readily apparent.

Recognizing the intractability of Soviet agricultural problems, Millar nevertheless felt that Johnson's analysis of Soviet agricultural prospects is unduly pessimistic, that it undervalues the extent to which economic rationality has already replaced ideology, and that it underestimates the likelihood that further substantial change will accompany the rise of a new political leadership in the 1980s.

Referring to the analysis of Soviet agricultural production by **Douglas Diamond, Lee Bettis**, and **Robert Ramsson, Elizabeth Clayton** argued that their projections, based on today's Soviet situation, and many relations from past Soviet experience, are too conservative. While their approach may provide a lower-bound estimate of the future, it gives insufficient attention to more fundamental structural modifications in the Soviet food economy. Shifts are occurring on the demand side, in infrastructure, and on the supply side.

Soviet policy may, for example, find more ways to constrain the growing demand for food, especially for wheat and dairy products, than the paper by Diamond and his associates projects. An educational campaign against heart disease could significantly reduce the demand for red meat, as it has elsewhere. An effective anti-alcoholism campaign would release substantial grain and potatoes for other use. Application of Polish or US standards for meat consumption neglects the fact that a growing Moslem fraction of the Soviet population is less meat oriented. The USSR still exports grain to its allies, and Soviet policy might reduce this claim on the grain supply.

Infrastructural changes in the channels between the farmer and the consumer might contribute materially to consumer welfare. One notes, for example, the extensive distribution of meat through the employing establishment. Some employees apparently get most of their meat this way, though it is a high-cost and inefficient arrangement. Similarly, the regime has recently encouraged the raising of livestock on private plots, with the resulting products to be marketed through kolkhoz or sovkhoz channels. The effect is to reduce the expenditure of the private farmer's time in marketing and encourage it in production. With respect to the meat products distributed through enterprises, the regime may find it feasible to raise prices (also in canteens and restaurants), thus checking excess demand.

The prospects for private sector animal husbandry are subject to several imponderables. The private sector has shown large declines in the North, but it has grown in the South, especially in urban and industrial localities, where food from the plots of factories and urban households has increased not only for home consumption but for sale. Usually what is produced is not a staple but the more exotic and perishable items not found in socialized markets: garlic, sorrel, fragile berries. The scale of production is small, and the cost of production is high, but this sector in the aggregate is significant.

Also costly is the proposed diversion of northern rivers to the South and into the Volga Basin. These projects have been on the docket for many years and even if now implemented could not become operational before 1990. Potentially, however, they could open to agriculture thousands of hectares in the arid South, and though the consequences for environmental disruption may be serious, output increments might nevertheless be substantial.

Martin Weitzman's paper on industrial production elicited substantial comments from **Abraham Becker** and **Donald Green**. Becker began with a brief excursion into the past, referring to the 1952 conference that Bergson organized and Donald Hodgman's paper on industrial production in the USSR. Hodgman's projections, twenty years ago, are germane to our present discussion. He concluded that the conditions supporting growth rates of 15.7% annually over the 1928–37 period and 20.5% annually during 1946–50 would probably not be duplicated in the future. He projected a rate for the 1960s considerably below these figures, but also above the rather modest 4.7% that he estimated for 1937–40. He anticipated an average annual growth rate for industrial production during the 1960s of 8%, thus making the 1960 level somewhat more than twice as high as the 1950 level. Much more hesitantly, he ventured the guess that just possibly the economy might be able to sustain such a rate for another decade, in which case the 1970 output would be more than 4½ times greater than that of 1950.

Hodgman didn't do badly at all, as shown by the following comparison between his projection and the estimates of CIA's Office of Economic Research:

	Hodgman projection	CIA (OER) estimates
Average annual rates of growth		
1951–60	⎱8	10½
1961–70	⎰	6½
Index numbers, 1950 = 100		
1960	216	265
1970	466	501

Hodgman was certainly correct in his forecast that the rate of growth would have to drop considerably below that of the revolutionary period of Soviet industrialization and below that of the immediate postwar recovery. In the event, the USSR raised industrial output somewhat more rapidly than he expected in the 1950s, though less rapidly than he expected in the 1960s.

Becker noted that the USSR has compiled and published three different series for gross industrial production, with slightly different levels and trend, and that Weitzman spliced two of them together in a debatable manner. Interestingly, however, the error hardly seems to matter for Weitzman's result. What does matter is the continued marked contrast between the official Soviet series and a careful Western reconstruction of statistics for Soviet industrial production. According to the CIA Office of Economic Research, the 1980 level of Soviet industrial output was eight times higher than that of 1950; the counterpart official Soviet index number is 1229. Over the three decades, then, growth as measured by the official index is half again as large as the change estimated by OER. On an annual average basis this is a far smaller divergence than the one estimated by Hodgman. Nevertheless, a substantial gap still exists between the Soviet official production index and one of the best Western synthetic alternatives.

Here are the two series, showing average annual growth rates over five-year periods:

| | OER official | | Col (1) as % of col (2) |
	(1)	(2)	(3)
1951–55	10.9	13.2	83
1956–60	9.6	10.4	92
1961–65	6.8	8.6	79
1966–70	6.4	8.5	75
1971–75	6.0	7.4	81
1976–80	3.5	4.5	78

The divergence between the two series is relatively small in the last half of the 1950s and more than ordinarily large in the last half of the 1960s. The deepening of the divergence in the last half of the 1960s may have something to do with the mid-60s price reform. The official series indicates a continuous deceleration by five-year periods, except for a temporary stabilization in the last half of the 1960s. In the OER series, the rate of retardation slows down in the last half of the 1960s, but does not actually stabilize. Thus the change of regime in 1964 succeeded only temporarily in restraining the pace of retardation. The rate of growth of industrial production in the last five years is the lowest of the postwar period and is only one-third as large as that shown for the first half of the 1950s in either series.

Becker noted that the search for explanations for declining Soviet economic growth rates has generally focused on the differential between the growth of aggregate output and the growth of total (labor plus capital) inputs. He suggested that a clearer view of the patterns of change in output, input, and factor productivity, requires extension of the input analysis to include agricultural and other raw materials, along with imports, and that the analysis should be disaggregated to examine major branch groups of industry. For example, the possibly incipient peaking of Soviet oil output has been much discussed since the CIA's dramatic 1977 papers; less attention has been paid to the actual declines in the production levels of coal and ferrous metals. This and the troubles in railroad transportation probably explain some of the recent sharp drop in investment growth rates.

In Becker's judgment, the official target for industrial output growth during 1981–5 is unlikely to be met. It implies an average annual growth rate of 4.9% (mid point of targets), to be obtained with an employment increase of 0.5% per year and a 4.4% annual increase in labor productivity. That kind of growth in labor productivity was achieved in only one quinquennium since the 1950s: the first half of the 1970s. If annual labor productivity gains are no better than in the last half of the 1970s, about 2% per year, industrial output can expand by no more than 3% annually. Capital stock changes provide another constraint. According to OER estimates, the USSR expects the capital stock to grow at about 6% per year that is indicated by an estimated increase in industrial investment of about 3½% per year. But since incremental capital-output ratios increased abruptly in the 1970s, the industrial investment allocation in the plan seems quite inadequate.

Becker concluded with the observation that this view of Soviet industrial prospects underscores the economic importance of the Kremlin's apparent commitment to a steady increase in military expenditures. A decision to accelerate the military build-up, in response to a perceived increase in the external threat, or, contrarily, to relax (perhaps even freeze) the pace of the build-up, for any mix of internal or external considerations, has often been viewed as having only minor effects on the rate of growth. However, depending on the nature of the change, such reallocations could have a tangible impact on industrial investment.

Suppose that the change were to take place exclusively in the investment component of military expenditure, that is, military procurement and construction. A doubling of the rate of growth of these elements, from 4 to 8 percent per year in the first half of the 1980s, or at the other end of the spectrum, a freeze at the 1980 level, would mean a five-year increase (decrease) of about 30 billion rubles. This is equivalent to more than one-tenth of the cumulative industrial investment apparently planned for the 1981–5 period. However, it is greater than the entire increment by which 1981–5 industrial invest-ment is supposed to exceed 1976–80 industrial investment.

This is, of course, not to argue that reallocations from military to industrial investment, or vice versa, are in the cards, or that they are even being discussed. There seems at present to be little or no evidence on this subject. However, crude calculations of this sort suggest that the burden of defense may become particularly salient as the Soviet leadership confronts the task of coping with its increasingly worrisome internal and external problems in the next few years.

Donald Green first noted the desirability of extending production function analysis to recognize the productive contribution of agricultural raw materials, reserves of metals and minerals, and reserves of primary energy sources. While measuring these inputs and their contribution to final output is difficult, they can only be safely ignored when their supply functions are highly elastic (to market price or to centralized command). Both in the world economy and in the USSR, elastic supplies of energy and raw materials fostered industrial expansion until the early 1970s. Blessed with elastic supply curves for most inputs, Soviet industrial planners could focus on the structural allocation of capital investment and use Western experience to guide their introduction of new products and technologies. As long as ample reserves of raw materials and energy were available, the growth of industrial output was determined by available labor supplies, capital stock, and a long-run steady improvement in technology and organization.

By the mid-1970s, however, Soviet plus Eastern European demands for raw materials and energy pushed available supplies to the margin of declining capital effectiveness (familiar in the West as a rising marginal cost curve). These rising capital costs could not be offset by gains in Soviet technology and management, gains which often depended on technology transfer from industrial countries. Aggregate industrial growth slowed down because of the rising capital-output ratio in the extractive branches and the indirect effect of material shortages on the growth of other branches of industry.

In a competitive market economy, such a change in supply costs would shift relative prices and increase rents for owners of resources. Greater search activity would be stimulated and improvements in extractive technology and in conservation would be encouraged. In a centrally-planned economy, lacking price signals, the rising marginal cost curve is communicated through declining capital effectiveness in extractive branches and through bottlenecks in the material supply system which require adjustment by the consuming branches. Planners respond clumsily and only after appreciable delays. In the USSR, however, one notes that by 1978 a dramatic shift in Soviet investment patterns got underway. The new patterns seem likely to unfold during the 1980s. More resources are being allocated to the energy sectors (electric power, petroleum and gas, and coal) and away from industrial materials and light industry.

The shift in emphasis is showing up in research and development as well. A short-run emphasis is on redesign, to make capital plant and equipment more energy-efficient. The pressure to conserve materials and energy will fall heavily on Eastern Europe, where the GDR may take a leadership role with strong support from basic scientific research in the USSR. The USSR may delegate the task of technological adjustment to the East Europeans and continue running a large annual surplus in merchandise trade. The East European countries would then be expected to repay those debts with machinery and technology for modernizing Soviet factories in the late 1980s and early 1990s.

There appears to have been an important shift in the orientation of the USSR toward Europe as a source of advanced technology and capital, and away from relationships with the United States and Japan. Its position as a reserve for raw materials and energy allows the USSR to negotiate advantageous relationships with both Western and Eastern Europe — with Germany as a crucial partner for both camps. If Poland does not become a military and political obstacle, one can expect major West European involvement in the Soviet economy during the 1980s. Eastern Europe may become an important source of new technology for Soviet industry, playing an intermediary role between the West and the USSR.

As for prospective growth rates, Green noted that all these adjustments might hold Soviet growth rates in the early 1980s below 3%, but that with transfers of technology from Eastern Europe later in the decade, the growth rate should rise. The adjustment process could, however, be impaired if political leadership is unable to impose the authority and will necessary to commit massive resources to an uncertain and complex task. Conversely, the current sense of policy drift and the pressing economic agenda of the 1980s could help focus the political competition and help resolve the succession dilemma itself.

A further question concerns the definition of Soviet success in the 1980s. Would a 4% growth rate indicate success, and a 2½% rate, failure? Among the new generation in the Party and the technical intelligensia, the essential criterion may be a sense of purpose and mastery over the economy; if successful adaptations are well underway, even 2½% growth in the 1980s may be domestically perceived as more of a success than most Western specialists on the Soviet economy now anticipate.

Discussing **Robert Campbell**'s energy paper, **Marshall Goldman** stressed the pitfalls of projecting anything twenty years into the Soviet future, especially energy. In the early 1960s, a team of US petroleum specialists visited the West Siberian oilfields and concluded that conditions there were so different, and Soviet technology so primitive, that the USSR would never be able to develop what since has come to account for half their total annual production. More recently, in April 1977, the CIA predicted that Soviet crude oil output would fall from a 1977 level of 546 million tons (roughly 11 million barrels per day) to 400–500 million tons (8–10 MBD) by 1985. But Soviet petroleum production has continued to grow; it exceeded 12 MBD (603 million tons) in 1980. In the spring of 1981, therefore, the CIA raised its estimate for 1985 production from 8–10 MBD to 10–11 MBD (500–550 million tons). That 20% increase in the lower bound is a grudging concession to the fact that the USSR works under conditions that Westerners would not tolerate.

Though the USSR seems incapable of duplicating the high level of productivity that Western producers take for granted, Russian producers invariably seem to do better in primitive and uninviting environments than their Western counterparts. Thus there is a danger of underestimating Russian resourcefulness, patience, and survivability. Economists should not be surprised by this; it is in part a consequence of Soviet factor endowment. Given their resource abundance, the Soviets tend to be very wasteful — thus they have very low input productivities. However, given their habit of being wasteful, they will undertake difficult challenges fully prepared to waste large amounts of inputs in the process.

The propensity to waste may have another advantage: in an energy pinch, the USSR has very wide maneuvering room for increasing conservation. There is enormous waste at both the producing and the consuming ends. Yet this waste, shocking to Western observers, may not have been, and may not be today, so irrational. For some time the USSR has relied heavily on its energy resources to generate the hard currency exports necessary to pay for its hard currency imports. These imports in turn have been used to raise productivity in Soviet industry and to increase productivity in Soviet mining and drilling. Given the fact that most Soviet equipment appears 20 years out of date, imports of Western equipment should do much to increase the rate of recovery and production in the future when energy and raw materials are less abundant, and thus relatively more valuable at home and abroad. In other words, it is not economically irrational to squander resources when they are cheap in order to gain access to equipment that will increase output in the future when these resources have become more valuable.

Goldman pointed out that the USSR has already begun a number of conservation measures and that conservation efforts in the USSR and Eastern Europe may impose a restraint on economic growth. He observed, however, that given their resources, in the current international context, the USSR is not in such bad shape. The Russians will have to improve their production techniques, but among their economic and political problems over the next few years, their energy problem may be the one that best lends itself to solution.

John Hardt took a somewhat different tack. He suggested that while Soviet self-sufficiency in energy may be technically and economically feasible in the year 2000, the intervening years may be more difficult. If petroleum output is maintained and the structure of energy use shifts as planned, no major energy shortfalls need arise. However, if oil output falls to 8 million barrels per day by 1990, as now projected by the CIA, there may be serious shortfalls in energy supply. Even if petroleum output does not fall, but levels off, as planned, the officially projected increases in other energy supplies may not be attainable. During the second half of the 1980s there may be severe shortfalls in energy supply even if energy growth revives by the year 2000.

Hardt suggested that even though adequate energy supplies may be available during the 80s and 90s, many difficulties lie ahead. Energy increases may be much more capital demanding than is implied by the intention to allocate only 40% of industrial investment to energy expansion. Increasing the shares of gas, coal, nuclear and hydro in the energy balance will require a *national* electric power transmission system and a greatly expanded natural gas pipeline system. Obtaining energy from Siberian and off-shore sources entails especially high direct and indirect costs. Putting energy-intensive industry close to energy supplies involves large infrastructure costs. Replacement of energy-inefficient plant and equipment is itself costly.

Hardt observed also that Soviet leaders will not find it politically feasible to put Eastern Europe on a severe energy diet, i.e. to restrict oil and gas deliveries to the 1980 level as planned and announced. Slower East European growth may mean falling real incomes and attendant political instability. Currently, additional energy supplies and more favorable pricing may be necessary to aid Polish recovery. If Polish recovery is supported and the energy prices charged are lower than the OPEC price, will the other CMEA countries also be given benefits for performance above the Polish level? If not, other CMEA countries would be unhappy that Poland was "rewarded" for economic failure. If yes, then Soviet plans for limiting energy exports to CMEA will be exceeded.

On Soviet regional economic development **Chauncy Harris** expressed general support for the analysis by **Leslie Dienes**. Development of the Soviet periphery, along the Soviet Western frontier, in the South, and in Siberia is clearly underway. Concerning developments in Soviet Middle Asia, Harris offered an interesting insight.

During the 1970s, the proportion of the population of Soviet Middle Asia made up of Russians fell from 15.6% to 13.4%. Though the absolute number of Russians in this region increased by 11.2% (double their 5.4% increase in the RSFSR), the Central Asian peoples increased three times as fast (35.0%). One interesting question, which Dienes did not address, is the extent to which the surplus indigenous labor might find employment in existing industries within Soviet Middle Asia by displacing Russians who might return to the RSFSR to make up for labor shortages there. Investment in training an indigenous labor force for work in already-established plants could be an alternative, albeit a limited one, to capital investment in new factories.

In discussing **Edward Hewett**'s paper on Soviet foreign economic relations, **Franklyn Holzman** argued on theoretic grounds that, as long as the USSR does not have functioning exchange rates or some other device through which to evaluate its foreign trade choices, and so long as they practice taut planning, no amount of other reforms, particularly those restricted to exports, can provide them with either payments balance or rational allocation of resources in foreign trade. There will always be a tendency to import too much, and to try to expand exports beyond the optimum to finance the uneconomic level of imports. There is actually no way of determining whether a given deficit should be corrected in the short run by expanding exports via "subsidies" or by restricting imports. Thus the difficulties in making trade choices due to irrational prices are compounded by the absence of a meaningful exchange rate, and the resulting uncertainties are very large indeed.

Concurring with Edward Hewett's analysis of Soviet foreign trade developments during 1960–80, **Paul Marer** offered an evaluation of the future level and composition of Soviet exports and imports over the next two decades. Soviet requirements for imports from the West largely determine Soviet export efforts, and Soviet import requirements reflect in large part the Soviet interest in advanced Western technology. The impact of Western technology on Soviet GNP is transmitted through two channels. First, imported technology helps to accelerate the growth of output because it increases the amount of resources devoted to capital formation, especially if the machinery is purchased on credit. Second, imported technology increases output if it is more productive than the domestic technology which could be employed in its stead. These imports, however, have only made up between three and five percent of all Soviet investment in capital equipment during the 1970s, suggesting that the impact of Western technology on Soviet capital formation has been rather modest.

On the other hand, most case studies of specific Soviet high-technology imports suggest that they have a high payoff, especially where they help to break important production and transportation bottlenecks. Imported technology will continue to be very important for the USSR, though machinery imports from the West may grow at reduced rates, since the rate of growth of total investment is projected to be slow, and since Soviet imports of machinery from Eastern Europe may increase rapidly in payment for Soviet fuel and raw material exports to Eastern Europe.

In view of continued Soviet needs for substantial imports of agricultural products, principally grain, from the West, Marer concluded that there will continue to be substantial pressure on Soviet planners to obtain the foreign exchange needed to pay for high levels of grain imports. Thus the Soviet leadership will be under double pressures to continue imports from the West on a considerable scale. Marer noted that the outlook for domestic Soviet energy production, the principal source of Soviet hard-currency export earnings, has recently become somewhat more favorable. He cautioned that one of the highest economic priorities for the USSR in the 1980s will be maintaining the economic viability of the USSR's East European allies, but concluded that he was somewhat less certain than Hewett that the USSR will be unable to generate, via traditional exports, most of the convertible currency it needs to pay for essential imports.

In commenting on **Gertrude Schroeder**'s paper, **Janet Chapman** reflected further on the substantial reduction since World War II in income differentials between agricultural workers and others, and the significant reduction in earnings differentials among wage earners and salaried workers in the state sector. The policy seems to reflect both equity considerations and economic conditions. A new concern for welfare seems to have emerged in the late 1950s or early 1960s, yet economic factors were also fostering equalization. Levels of education in the Soviet labor force became less disparate, while the knowledge and skills required for low-level jobs has risen and the greater availability of capital has raised labor productivity in many lower-level jobs. Measures to raise the incomes of the agricultural population toward nonagricultural levels may be seen as steps designed to raise agricultural output, improve incentives and morale, and retain in agriculture the young people who constitute the main hope for further technological progress in agriculture.

Chapman noted that one factor affecting the meat problem from the demand side is the impact of reduced income inequality. There is some evidence that the income elasticity of demand for meat in the USSR is considerably higher at the lower income levels, explaining in part the demand pressures of recent years, while at the same time implying that a reversal of the trend toward greater income equality, which now seems possible, might serve to moderate somewhat the still-vigorous demands for meat and dairy products.

The changes in income distribution also have a bearing on the acceptability of Soviet clothing and other consumer goods. For a while, unwanted goods could be sold in the countryside, but recently the increasingly sophisticated rural resident has joined his urban cousin in demanding higher quality shoes and clothing. Low morale and the critical importance of improved labor productivity suggest that Soviet leaders will place a high priority on raising living standards and providing effective incentives through appropriate wage differentials and an improved supply of desirable goods and services. But economic constraints and competing priorities will make it more difficult than in the past to satisfy the population.

Referring to **Gertrude Schroeder**'s paper, **Gur Ofer** stressed a conviction that the ordinary Soviet citizen has now developed a shield of cynicism and disbelief reflecting very low expectations for the improvement of living standards. Coming out of the Stalin era, Soviet citizens did gradually develop higher expectations, which may even have risen when the present leadership took over in 1964. Relieved of the tyranny and hunger experienced under Stalin, they saw food supplies improve, followed by larger flows of other goods and services. With the easing of relations with the West, the Soviet consumer of the 50s and early 60s may have developed a hope that Socialism is not necessarily Stalinism and that the system might really work on the consumer's behalf. By the 70s, he may have come to realize that both the fundamental deficiencies in central planning and the low priority accorded private consumption impose a very low ceiling on the prospects for improvement.

Paradoxically, however, this lack of belief in the chances for major improvement plays—up to a point—into the hands of the leadership. As long as most citizens accept the present regime as given, and the chances for major change as very slim, they cooperate with their leaders. This may help the USSR to muddle through, even on the basis of a 1 to 1.5% increase in annual consumption per capita. The Soviet citizen will do his best to improve his own position by adjusting his on-the-job efforts in accordance with real wages and by taking advantage of the second economy. Thus Ofer found it hard to believe that the Soviet population today is over-optimistic concerning future prospects, or that the gap between expectations and reality may become a source of serious unrest on a large scale.

Abram Bergson pointed out, though, that an increase in per capita consumption of 1–1.5 percent annually in the USSR does not mean what it means in the West. That is so because of the pervasive limitations in the quality and assortment of consumers' goods and in the operation of retail trade. Such limitations are by no means new in the USSR, but, as consumption standards have risen, consumers have become increasingly sensitive to them. As a result, gains in standards that are at best only modest statistically must seem even more modest to the Soviet consumer.

In discussing **Joseph Berliner**'s paper on planning and management, **Alice Gorlin** suggested that the old powerful industrial ministries, vertically organized along product lines, are now going to have to be organized around national economic problems rather than products. There have already been suggestions for "supraministries," which would be in charge of groups of related activities, for example fuel and power, transportation, and the production and processing of agricultural products. The creation of supraministries will give an expanded role to the industrial associations that have been organized since 1973. One can imagine, for example, a group of associations subordinate to a supraministry in charge of the fuel and power sector; each association would be in charge of the production of a different type of energy resource. Through reorganization of production and reallocation of resources, the associations might achieve the same kinds of microeconomic improvements in efficiency that they have in the past. Enterprises would cease to have much significance.

Gorlin accepted Berliner's argument that the "liberal" model might be appealing to Soviet policymakers, and suggested that enterprise managers too might endorse the model because it would remove some of the hassles they must now cope with. For example, light industry enterprises could concentrate on mass production of consumer goods, leaving the specialty and very high quality items to the unplanned sector. All enterprises would benefit in being able to purchase special-order inputs and services from the unplanned sector.

Egalitarian hostility to the liberal scheme might not be serious since unplanned-sector stores will be open to all, as opposed to the present situation with special stores open only to the elite. If money, as opposed to position, has greater significance, work incentives should be strengthened—an ironic turn of events in a Marxist state!

Aron Katsenelinboigen speculated that management and planning might come to be organized on the principles of a mixed economy. Agriculture, consumers' goods and services, and a number of other branches of the economy where production can be carried out on a small scale, may be organized on the basis of a decentralized market mechanism with private institutions. Leading branches of the economy, with large-scale enterprises predominant, may be centralized under the existing hierarchical system. Large changes may occur in economic management, however, on the basis of optimal-planning theory, and the technology of modern computers.

Katsenelinboigen agreed with Berliner that references to the NEP would very likely accompany changes in a liberal direction, but noted that liberalization of the economy during the 1920s was accompanied by significant toughening in the political structure. He agreed also that whatever changes develop can readily be accounted for under official Soviet ideology. He was concerned, finally, that current domestic pessimism concerning Soviet economic prospects is so serious that, unless liberal changes produce quick economic improvements, the regime may seek to solve its difficulties through foreign adventurism and external expansion.

Discussing **Seweryn Bialer**'s paper, **Alexander Erlich** stressed the differences between the NEP in the 1920s and the current situation. Reform now would be far more difficult than it was then. Setting things right would require major organizational changes, substantial investments, and time to work through a difficult transition. Whatever might have seemed feasible, moreover, during a period of relative quiet in US–Soviet relationships, is clearly less so now that the USSR is involved in an accelerated arms race in an increasingly unsettled world.

The quantum jump in the arms race and the demise of détente not only pose grave dangers to world peace but also set the chances of a Hungarian-style reform at zero. Economic liberalization cannot be reconciled with sharply rising claims from the military sector. The *patrie-en-danger* climate does not have to be artificially manufactured; it is there, and it is bound to favor the tough conservatives over pragmatists and reformers. Whatever disagreements at the top there may have been, they are likely to subside, at least temporarily, in the face of what is perceived as a serious external threat. There may be limited reforms, especially in agriculture where they are badly needed and could be readily achieved. On the other hand, Erlich expressed skepticism about possibilities of "Polonization" of the Soviet working class.

Noting his general agreement with **Bialer**'s paper, **Gregory Grossman** offered further comments concerning the prospects for a flourishing small-scale private sector. In a sense, much of this small-scale private activity already exists in the USSR, though underground; a succession leadership might be willing to legalize it. The 1977 Constitution lays the ground for just such legalization by its open-ended description of legal individual productive activity (Article 17). Several East European countries have for some time had comparatively sizeable and rather successful legal private sectors alongside their dominant state sectors (Poland, East Germany,

Hungary). Nor would it be difficult to justify such a move in terms of the governing normative, if not necessarily Marxist, symbols: it could be presented as another step in the direction of encouraging national and popular (*narodnye*) arts and crafts.

Yet expansion of the legal private small-scale sector would bring with it, together with the legalization of some underground activity, a great deal of new illegality behind the newly legitimate facades, and by this token much new corruption of officialdom. This in turn might have an unfavorable effect on the morale of the mass of workers and employees who might suspect the "secmen" (second-economy men) of benefiting unfairly even while contributing to the greater material well-being of all. Rigid notions of distributive justice seem to be deeply ingrained in the population.

Grossman noted a number of serious economic problems facing the Soviet leadership in the 80s: an aging capital stock, especially in the transport and housing sectors; shortages of foodstuffs, consumer and producer goods; significant redistribution of private income and wealth, together with increasing corruption touching many authorities and officials; and inflation, both repressed and open, reflecting all these pressures.

The very nature of the Soviet collective leadership may aggravate the inflationary pressures. Under Soviet conditions, the process of reaching consensus at the top may be biased in favor of more optimistic and ambitious production targets, yielding a future pie that can be more easily divided among contending oligarchs. The consequence is greater pressure on resources. Thus the lack of a single dominant leader may not only hamstring significant systemic reform, but also bias the existing system toward shortages, inflationary pressures, underground economic activity and more corruption. A succession crisis would aggravate this tendency as interests are aligned and promises are made. The longer-term consequences are not easy to discern.

At different points, several participants spoke to the question of relevant comparisons. Recent Soviet economic growth has been slower than it used to be, but slower growth has characterized all economies recently, and the USSR has no monopoly on serious economic problems. Current low percentage growth rates, moreover, are generating absolute increments that match earlier increments and that yield impressive additions to national power. At a time when many countries, West and East, are troubled by inflation, unemployment, high energy costs, trade imbalances, or government deficits, the economic problems of the USSR (however unique their underlying causes) cannot seem so unfamiliar or so incurable. From a Soviet standpoint, troubles abroad may seem worse than troubles at home, and optimistic Party leaders may feel that the positive aspects of their domestic situation still warrant confidence in their comparative economic prospects.

Elaborating on this view, **Evsey Domar** noted that the papers being considered have a common theme: the Russians are facing a Sea of Troubles. As an old index-number hand, he was thinking about reducing them all to one number, that is, about constructing a Soviet Index of Troubles to aid comparisons through time and space. Of course, many difficulties about series and weights would have to be resolved, but he trusts that our expertise will be adequate for that. It would be interesting to find out whether the trend of this Index, starting from 1917, was positive or negative, and in particular how it has behaved in the last decade or so. It would be fascinating to compare the Soviet Union with other countries, including the United States!

But there is no reason why the Russians should not try their hand at this game, and in particular why they should not construct an Index of American Troubles. That Index may come out of papers to be presented at a Moscow conference appropriately entitled "The American Economy toward the Year 2000." The agenda for this conference could be very similar to ours, perhaps with some changes. On the basis of the evidence presented, our Soviet colleagues should certainly be able to construct an Index of American Troubles, with a strong upward trend and, no doubt, much larger than our Index of Their Troubles. As usual and for well-known reasons, we will not accept their handiwork and will construct our own Index of Our Troubles instead. But in truth, we will have to recognize that the latter, while not reaching the heights of the Soviet concoction, has risen sharply in the last decade or so, and now stands at or near the highest point since the Great Depression. And yet our faith in the ability of our political and economic system to survive, at least until the year 2000, will remain intact. For we know that all countries have usually been immersed in their own Seas of Troubles and yet managed to muddle through. Will the Soviet Union be an exception?

Index

References in italics are to Tables

Aganbegian, A. G.: on innovation 59; on Siberian fuels 255
Agricultural machinery 131, 146, 149–50
Agricultural rents 121–2
Agriculture: capital stock in 140; centralization 130–1; collectivization 115–23, 432; demand 143, 151–5; employment in *28*, 46, *46*, 102; fertilization 157–8, *158*, 163–6; GNP, share of *24*, 403; incomes *46*, 121, 128–9, 132–3, 140, 339–40, *341*, 442; inputs *28*, 131–2, 145–6, *146*; investment in 114, 120, 140; irrigation 241–2, 434; labor force *13*, *18*, *25*, 46, 102, 116–17, 120–1, 430; labor, hired 120–1; labor immobility 132–3; Machine Tractor Stations 135; output *13*, 14, *18*, *28*, 113–14, 144–5, *145–6*, 146–51, 151–70, *153*; output, regional 260; post-Stalin 112–13; prices 122–3, 127–30, 134, 137–8, 433; private sector 123–5, 381–2, 434; productivity 129, 145–6, *146*, 406; profitability 128, 136, 432; subsidies 114, 129, 433; weather, effect of 48, 158, 427; yields 146, *147*, 149–50, 173, 176; *see also* Crop Production; Farmland; Farms; Grain; Livestock; Meat
Alcoholism 90, 324, 433
Alkhimov, V. 280; on special export enterprises 298
Amann, Ronald: on economic indicators 52; on innovation 59
Animal products: consumption 145; milk 114, 128; output 5, *28*, 137, 169; subsidies 114, 129; *see also* Meat
Arms spending, *see* Defence expenditure
Autarky in foreign trade policy 369
Authoritarianism 392, 408

Bain, Joe S., on plant size 47
Balance of payments 278, 280
Becker, Abraham: on industrial production 434–6
Bergson, Abram: on consumption 67, 322, 331–2, 443; on production growth 17, 41; on risk-taking 60; on wages 343
Berliner, Joseph S: on innovation 56, 59–60; on private sector 419
Birthrate, *see* Population growth
Bond, Daniel L., on energy demand 8
Borrowing, foreign 290, 300

Borrowing, technological 57–8, 63, 65–6
Brezhnev, Leonid 393–4; on agricultural policy 136, 432; on demography 79, 93; on manpower 103; on universalism 367–8; succession question 398–401
Building materials: negative growth 13, *26*; regional output *234*
Bureaucracy: and new technology 59, 65; and foreign trade 302, 432
Buzdalov, I., on agricultural management 135–6

Capital investment 69; output-capital ratios *226*; and mechanization 101; and productivity 182, *183*, 247; regional comparisons *224–5*, *232*, 256; return on *38*, 39, 69
Capital replacement 63–4
Capital stock 5, *13*, *18*, 19, *25*, 74, *183*, 436; in agriculture 140
Centralization: in agriculture 130–1; in foreign economic relations 291–5, 299; *see also* Decentralization
Chapman, Janet: on income differentials 342, 343, 441–2
Chemical industry: foreign trade *277*; output growth 12, *26*, 180, 248–9; regional output 248–9
Clayton, Elizabeth: on agricultural production 433–4
Clothing, *see* Textiles and apparel
Coal: coal/gas ratio 204; domestic use *30*; exports 21, *22*, 276, 282; production 6, 11, 14, 18, *26*, *30*, 194, *196*, *206*, 207; quality 199
Cohen, Stephen F., on reform 415
Cohn, Stanley H., on productivity 41, 426–8
Collective farms, *see* Farms
Communications, *see* Transport and Communications
Communist Party: Central Committee 393, 420; First Secretary 393–4, 398–9, 415
Competition, economic 61, 65; regional 256–7, 404, 407
Conferences: All-Union Labor Conference 102; on labor resources 93–6
Conservatism 392–3
Construction costs 241, 245
Construction industry: growth 13; and GNP *24*; labor in 430

Consumer goods: choice 325; foreign
    trade *277*; growth 13, 312, 313, *320*;
    manufacturing methods 327–8;
    quality 324–5; shortages 56, 325–7
Consumption 8, 311–49, 381; elasticities
    323–4, *324*; of energy 191–2, *192*,
    198–200, *201*, *204*; and GNP 13;
    growth 12, *13*, *18*, 19, 67, *315*, 406–7;
    household 55–6, 311–12;
    international comparisons *316–17*,
    318, *319*, *321*; of meat 154–5,
    155, 163, 175, 311, 313, 433; per
    capita 17, 21, *24*, 442–3
Cooperation agreements 292; with
    CMEA countries 296
Cooperatives 124; agricultural, *see* Farms,
    collective; worker 383
Corruption 379–80
Cotton 241, 276, 282
Credits 10, 274; *see also* Debt, Foreign
Crop production *28*; output 114
Currency, convertible 278–91, 300

Debt, foreign 10–11, 280–2, *283*; debt-
    service ratio 10, 16, *25*, 282, 300;
    hard-currency *25*; *see also* Credits
Decentralization 353–5, 370, 371; in
    agriculture 125–6; New Economic
    Mechanism 372–3; *see also*
    Centralization
Decision-making, economic 19; at
    enterprise level 358–9, 425
Decision-making, political: gradualism
    401; role of military 394; of
    professional class 394–5; succession
    question 398–401
Defense expenditure 7–8, 11, 13, *13*,
    18–20, *18*, *20*, 21–3, *24*, 31, 405,
    409–10, 436; military build-up 397–8;
    research and development 55
Demography, *see* Population
Denison, Edward F., on technological
    progress 47, 56, 63
Departmentalism 351
Diamond, Douglas B., on agricultural
    labor input 115
Diminishing returns to capital 43, 186
Dissent, political 392
Domar, Evsey: on index numbers 445–6

Econometric model, *see* Models,
    economic
Economic growth, *see* Growth
Education: consumption 312, *312*, 314,
    316–17, 318, *319*, *320*; and factor
    productivity 42; imbalance 426
Elasticity of substitution 38, *38*
Electricity: demand 8, 31–2, *50*; foreign
    trade in *277*; fuel requirements 198,

202; hydro 11, *30*, *196*, 203, *206*, 208;
    nuclear 11, *30*, *50*, *53*, *196*, 202–3,
    206; production 6, 13, *26*, *30*; thermal
    8–9, *30*, 32
Employment *37*, 68–9; in agriculture *28*,
    46, *46*, 102; annual average 102;
    female 98, 100–1; in industry *46*, 102;
    in research and development *55*;
    underemployment 369
Energy 191–217, 438–40; conservation
    200, 209–12; consumption 191–2,
    192, 204; demand 8–9, 14, 21;
    domestic use 17; energy balance *30*,
    403; energy crisis 189, 405; fuel
    production 6–7; investment in 193–4,
    213, 427, 437; price policy 210–11;
    regional production 208–9;
    secondary sources 203, 208; transport
    problems 209; *see also* Fuels
Engineering 223, 233
Enterprise, individual (*predpriiatie*) 59
Exchange rate *22*, 440–1
Expansionism in foreign policy 410
Expectations, popular 114, 395, 406–7,
    442
Exports 10, *22*, *272*, *275*; agricultural
    commodities 150; commodity
    structure 276, *277*; fuels 11, 14–15,
    17, *25*, 192–3, 198, 214; incentives
    297; regional comparisons *224–5*,
    233–4; special export sector 301–2

Factor inputs *37*; agriculture 131–2, 145–
    6, *146*
Factor productivity 17, 36, *37–8*, 39, *40*,
    45, 64, 67
Farm-industry labor transfers 44–7, *45*,
    66
Farmland 39, 42, 69, 70; "corn program"
    148; fodder 159, 161, *162*, 168–9;
    "new-lands program" 149; pasture
    158, 161; private plots 123–5; rent on
    121–2; Siberia 245; sown acreage 146,
    147, 148, 151; yields 146, *147*, 149,
    150, 173, 176
Farms: collective 115–23, 125–6, 432;
    individual farmsteads (*khutors*) 259;
    scale of 115, 125–6; state 126–7, 368
Feshbach, Murray: on employment 68,
    69
Fiber, chemical *50*; synthetic *50*, *53*
Fishing 248
Fodder: production 159, 161, *162*, 168–9
Food consumption 143, 151–5, *155*, 163,
    312, 313–14, *316–17*, 318, *319*, *320*,
    322, *323*
Food industry: investment in 327; meat
    production 5, 14, *28*, 151–69, *155*;
    processing *26*, 239

Food products: foreign trade in *277*; imports 276, 432; regional output *234*, 241, 248, 260

Foreign policy 396–7, 398, 409–14; expansionism 410; relations with Eastern bloc 411–12; and with Western Europe 411

Foreign trade 10–11, 12, 18, *25*, 269–310, 440–1; commodity structure 276, *277*; foreign trade organizations 293, 297; Ministry of 292, 296; planning 293–4; price indices *22*; regional distribution 16; special export sector 301–2; total trade *272*, *275*; with capitalist countries *272–3*, 274; with OPEC countries 288; with socialist countries 274, 296; with West *25*

Forestry products 13, *26*, 276; foreign trade *277*, 282; regional output *234*, 248

Fuels 6–7, 189, *206*; consumption *316–17*, *319*; exports 11, 14–15, 17, 192–3, 198, 214, 276; extraction by region *234*, 248; foreign trade 276, *277*; fuel balance 14, *30*, *196–7*; hydrocarbons 192; pipelines 252–3; refining by region *234*; solid 192, 199; substitution 9; *see also* Coal; Gas; Oil; Petroleum products

Gardner, H. Steven: on foreign relations 294

Gas: coal/gas ratio 204; exports 21, *22*, 192–3, 241, 276, 282, 300; pipelines 252–3; production 6, 11, 14, 18, *196*, *206*, 207; use of 198–9

Gold: price *22*, 288; production 12, 286; sales 12, *281*, 284–7, *285*; stocks 286

Goldman, Marshall: on energy 438–9

Gorlin, Alice: on Ministries 443

Gosbank 293

Gosplan 39, 292, 299

Gossnab 367

Gradualism 401

Grain: balance 6, 14, *29*; corn program 148; exports 12; fertilization 157–8, *158*, 163–6; imports 12, 16, *22*, *28*, 114, 138, *147*, 150, 161, 163, 432, 441; production 5–6, *15*, *28*, 160–1; stocks 134; utilization *29*

Granberg, A. G., on Siberia 255–6

Granick, David: on labor productivity 428–9

Gray, Kenneth R., on agricultural prices 123

Green, Donald W., on production function analysis 436–8

Greenslade, Rush V., on output 36, 38, 68

Gregory, Paul: on GDR 379; on demography 429

Gross National Product 13, *13*, 17, *18*, *24*, 31, 68, 70, 402; agriculture in *24*, 403; and energy consumption 191–2, *192*; productivity growth 67

Grossman, Gregory: on private sector 444–5

Growth, economic 39, *49*, 364–5, 434; goal of leadership 396; industrial *179*; projected 21, *24–30*, *38*, 402, 403; retardation of 435

Gustafson, Thane: on structures 414

Hardt, John: on energy supply 439–40

Harris, Chauncy: on regional development 440

Health services: consumption 312, *312*, *316–17*, 318, *319–20*, 322, 326; wages 314

Hodgman, Donald: on industrial production 434

Holzman, Franklyn: on foreign trade 284, 440–1

Hours, working 36, *37*, 69, 181–2, *182*

Housing: consumption 312–13, *312*, *320*, 322, 326; investment in 327; regional comparisons 246, 250

Hungary: economic reform 303; market socialism 334, 414–18; New Economic Mechanism 372

Imports 10, 18, *22*, *25*; commodity structure 276, *277*; farm products 150–1; grain 12, 16, 22, *28*, 114, 138, *147*, 150, 161, 163, 432, 441; growth *273*, 274; machinery 16; total *272*, *275*

Incentives 34, 48; agriculture 130, 136; for exports 297; incentive threshold 365–6; managerial 60, 62, 65, 354; material 396

Income, *see* Wages

Income, national *272*, *273*; Marxian *272–3*, 275

Index-number relativity 36

Industrialization 218; decline of developed regions 223–7; of rural regions 229, 242

Industry: employment in *46*, 102; GNP share *24*; growth *26*, *179–80*; growth by region 220–1; incomes in *46*; light industry 248, 327; output 6–7, *13*, *18*, *26*, 178–89; output by region *224–5*

Inflation rate 12

Innovation 59–60, 62

Inputs, *see* Factor inputs

Inventions 56–7

Investment 254, 405; agricultural 114, 120, 140; in energy 193–4, 213, 427,

437; high-investment policy 368; industrial 5, 13, *13*, *18*, 19, *24*, *27*, 31, 64; machinery 8, 13, 201, 371; regional 229, *230–1*, 246–7; structures 13
Iur'ev V., on premia 129

Job security 373, 381

Katsenelenboigen, Aron: on planning 366, 443–4
Khruschev, Nikita 49, 393–4
Khudenko, I., 378
Kostakov, V. G., on pensioners 100
Kvasha, Ia: on enterprise scale 376

Labor *37*, 68–9; allocation of 4, 369; farm-industry transfer 44–7, *45*, 66; immobility 132–3; incentives 34, 48; labor transfers 65, 101; manpower ceilings 96; penal labor 36–8, 69; productivity 93, 182, 183, 227, 241, 247; redundant manpower 101, 381, 383; scarcity of 92, 186, 403; state committee on 93; surplus 101, 243
Labor force *4*, *18*, *25*, *99*; agricultural *13*, *18*, *25*, 46, 102, 116–17, 120–1, 430; discipline of 368, 386–7; female 98, 100–1; growth rate 21, 96, 98; industrial *13*, *25*, 102, *181*, 430; participation rate 96–8; pensioners in 100; quality of 41–2, *45*, 66, 426; "reserves" 430–1
Lewin, Moshe: on collectivization 431–2
Lewis, Robert A., on migration 242
Life expectancy 90–2
Liquidation of enterprises 61
Livestock 5, 12, 14, 138; feed 146, *147*, 149–50, *157*, 161–2, *164–5*, 166–8, *167*, 173–4; growth outlook 155–69; investment in 114–15; output 143, *153*; production mix 156; profitability 137

Machine building 12, 13, *26*, 180; employment in 102; regional output *234*, 241, 248
Machine tools *50*, *53*
Machine Tractor Stations 135
Machinery: agricultural 131, 146, 149–50, 276; exports 295; foreign trade in *277*, 278; imports of 11, 16, 63; investment in 8, 13, 241, 376
Makarov, A. A., on energy 202, 204, 208, 211
Management: departmentalism v. localism 351–3; elite 368; enterprise managers 357–8, 359, 382; incentives 60, 62, 65, 354; mismanagement 361;

production associations 357–8, 362, 367–8; self-management 372, 383
Manove, Michael: on models 424–5
Manpower, *see* Labor
Marer, Paul: on trade 441
Market socialism 68, 334, 414–18
Martens, John A., on patents 56, 61
McAuley, Alastair: on wages 342, 343, 344
Meat: consumption 154–5, *155*, 163, 175, 311, 313, 433; "meat program" 151, 153–4; output *153*; prices 114, 174–5; production 5, 14, *28*, 151–69, *155*; subsidies 129, 174–5
Mechanization 101; *see also* Technological progress
Medvedkov, Iu: on cooperation agreements 296
Mergers 357–8
Metal and metallurgy 248–9; ferrous 13, *26*, 276; foreign trade in *277*, 282; iron ore 276; metal-working 102, 180; non-ferrous 13, *26*, 276; steel *50*, *53*
Migration 80, 119, 127, 408; immigration 250; migrant workers 242, 250; outmigration 103, 132–3, 236, 242, 250
Military: arms sales 274, *281*, 287–8; military policy 397–8; role of in decision-making 394; *see also* Defence expenditure
Millar, James: on reform 432–3
Mineral resources 42–3, *45*, 67, 71, 248, 255; export of 276
Ministries 351; of Foreign Trade 292, 296
Mobility of workforce 121, 132–3, 431
Models, economic: Soviet Econometric Model 1–3; "putty-clay" model 9; livestock production model 156, 170–2; conservative 362–6; reactionary 366–71; radical 371–5, 387–8; liberal 375–81, 388; dangers of 424–6
Mortality, *see* Population growth

Nationalism 240, 384–5
Nationality problem 408
Natural resources, *see* Mineral resources
Nekrasov, A. S., on hydroelectric power 203
New Economic Mechanism 372–3
New Lands Program 42, 149
Nimitz, Nancy: on defence expenditure 55; on agricultural premia 129
Nuclear power 11, *30*, *50*, *53*, *196*, 202–3, *206*, 208

Ofer, Gur: on wages 342; on expectations 442–3

Oil: diminishing returns on 43; domestic use *30*; exports 14–15, 17, 21, *22*, 192–3; expansionism aimed at 410–11; production 6, 11–12, 21, *30*, 206–7, *206*, 403

Oligarchy 393

Output, *see* Production

Packaging 327

Paper and pulp *26*; regional output *234*

Parrott, Bruce: on research and development 57

Patenting 59; lead times 61–2

Patolichev, N., on foreign trade 298, 307–8

Penal labor 36–8, 69

Pensioners 83; in labor force 100

Petroleum products 6, 12–13, *26*, 49, *196*, 199, 203; exports 276, 282–3, 284, 300; refining 248

Planning 68; central 130–1, 133–4, 362, 419; Comprehensive Planning Decree 358–60; decentralization of 353–5, 370–1; Five-year plans 359; Ministries in 443; optimal 366; reform *45*, 48–9, 75

Plant: new construction 13; re-equipment of 13, 405; size 47, 72

Plastics and resins *50*, *53*, 259

Politburo 384; age of members 400, 420; regional members 243

Political system 392–7; future developments 397–402; oligarchy 393; stability of leadership 393, 400; succession question 398–401, 413

Population 3–4, *25*, 236; age distribution 79, 83, *87–9*; dispersion of settlements *237*; life expectancy 90–2; pensioners 83, 100; of Russian Republic 80, 83; urban *100*

Population growth 80–92, *86*, *94–5*, *104–9*, 254; birthrate 79, 83; fertility rate 79, 80, *84–5*; mortality 79, 83, 90, *92*, 312; male 90, *91*; negative trends 79, 403, 429–30; regional variations 80–2, 84–9, 236, 240, 242, 249–50, 260–2

Portes, Richard: on Hungary 373

Prices 294, 372; agricultural 114, 122–3, 127–30, 134, 137–8, 433; energy 210–11; exports 276; industrial 180; price reform 355–7, 362–3; retail 333

Primary products: exports 276, 282–4

Private enterprise 376–81, 419, 444–5; agriculture 123–5, 381–2, 434; consumer goods 328–30

Privilege 345

Production 12, 17, 35–8, *37*, 64; associations 357–8, 362, 367–8, 382–3; function 38–9, 182–4

Production, agricultural *13*, 14, *18*, 113–14, 143–77: *see also* Agriculture

Production, industrial 6–7, *13*, *18*, *26*, 178–90, 434–6; methods 34, 44; prototypes 52, *53*; *see also* Industry

Productivity: agriculture 129, 145–6, *146*, 406; compared with West 40–1; growth 12, 35–44, 67; growth, low 17–18, *18*; labor productivity 93, 182, *183*, 241, 247, 436; non-agricultural 17; total factor productivity 17, 36, *37*, 64, 67, 184–5

Professional class 394–5, 415; isolation of 396

Profitability 222, 355–6; agriculture 128, 136, 432

Progress, attitude of leadership to 396

Rabkina, N. E., on wages 343, 344

Railways 235, 251–2

Recreation services 239, *312*, 313, *316–17*, *319*, *320*, 322

Reform, economic 333–4, 418–20, 444–5; agriculture 112–13; comprehensive planning decree 358–60; market socialism 334, 414–18; of 1965 353–5; price reform 355–7; production associations 357–8, 362, 367–8; territorial reorganization 351–3; wage reform 49; working arrangements 48–9, 62

Regions, economic development of 218–67; agriculture 260; capital investment *224–5*, *232*; Central Asia 240–4, 407, 409, 440; competition 256–7, 440, 407; exports *224–5*; fuels 208–9, 228, *234*, 248, 252–3; industry *220–1*, 223–7, investment 229, *230–1*, 246–7; labor force 96; labor productivity 241, 247, nationality problem 408, 416–17, output *234*, 241, 248; pioneer regions 227–9; Politburo, attitude of 243; population growth 80–3, *84–9*, 240, 247, 249–50, 260–2; rural regions 229–44; Siberia 242–53; Transcaucasia 238–40; transport *224–5*, 228, 250–2; wage differentials 338

Rent, agricultural 121–2; comparison with other countries *316–17*, *319*

Research and development 53–7, *54*, *55*, 58, 67–8, 73, 370, 437

Retail trade 326, 377

Rubber, synthetic *51*, foreign trade *277*

Savings 332

Scale: collective farms 115, 125–6;

economies of *45*, 47–8, 66, 362, 427;
small enterprises 376
Scarcities 404; of consumer goods 325–6
Schoonover, David: on agriculture 112
Schwalberg, Barney: on labor force 430–1
"Second" economy 240, 328–30, 377–8,
432
Secrecy, commercial 59
Semifabricates: exports 276; foreign trade
277
Service industries: GNP *24*; convertible
currency earnings 288
Services, communal 314, *320*
Services, household *312*, 313
Shchenko experiment 101, 381
Siberia 243–53, 255
Sirotkin, Z., on incentives 59–60
Solow, Robert M: economic model 43; on
technological progress 427
Soviet Econometric Model (SOVMOD)
1–3, 424–6
Stagnation; economic 403; industrial 236
Standard of living: popular expectations
395, 406–7
State Committee on Labor and Social
Questions (Goskomtrud) 93
Steel industry *50*, *53*, 208
Styrikovich, M. A., on energy 202–3, 205,
208
Subsidies 355; agricultural 114, 129, 433;
consumer goods and services 330
Success indicators 353–4, 355–6, 362
Sutton, Antony C., on technology 57

Taxation 372, 377
Technological progress 34–70, 361, 427;
innovation 59; introduction of new
technology 52, *53*; research and
development 53–8, 67–8, 73, 405,
437; science-production associations
357; technological borrowing 57–8,
63, 65–6, 363, 412–13; technology
transfer 189, 438, 441
Territorial reorganization 351–3
Textiles and apparel *26*; consumption 313,
316–17, 318, *319*, 322; cotton 241,

276, 282; foreign trade *277*; regional
output 241
Thornton, Judith: on models 425–6; on
resource costs 428
Trade and distribution: GNP *24*; of meat
433; packaging 327; retail 326, 377;
wholesale 367
Trading monopoly, state 61
Transcaucasia 238–40
Transport and communications:
consumption *312*, 313, *316–17*, 318,
319–20, 322; convertible currency
earnings 288; and GNP *24*;
investment in 427; regional costs *224–
5*; and regional development 228,
250–2; shipping 288; telephones *51*;
Trans-Siberian Land Bridge 229, 288
Treml, Vladimir: on foreign trade 274

United Nations International Comparison
Project 315
Universalism 367–8
Utilities: consumption *312*, *320*

Voronin, E., on labor force 98–100, 102

Wages 8, *46*; agricultural *46*, 121, 128–9,
132–3, 140, 339–40, *341*, 442;
differentials 336–43, 372–3, 380, 441;
distribution 335–46; growth 154;
health service 314; illegal incomes
345; industrial *46*; inequalities 128–9,
132–3; perks 345; reform of 49;
women 71, 340–3
Water resources 241–2, 434
Weitzman, Martin L., on scale economies
47
Wiles, Peter: on wages 343
Women: employment of 98, 100–1; wages
71, 340–3
Worker cooperatives 383
Working arrangements 48–9, 62, 65

Yanowitch, Murray: on wages 343

Zielinski, Janusz: on planning 419